Other books sponsored by the Society include:

Individual Differences and Behavior in Organizations

Individual Differences and Behavior in Organizations

Kevin R. Murphy, Editor

Foreword by Sheldon Zedeck

Jossey-Bass Publishers • San Francisco

Substantial discounts on bulk quantities of Jossey-Bass books are available to corporations, professional associations, and other organizations. For details and discount information, contact the special sales department at Jossey-Bass Inc., Publishers. (415) 433–1740; Fax (800) 605–2665.

For sales outside the United States, please contact your local Simon & Schuster International office.

TCF Manufactured in the United States of America on Lyons Falls Pathfinder Tradebook. This paper is acid-free and 100 percent totally chlorine-free.

Library of Congress Cataloging-in-Publication Data

Individual differences and behavior in organizations / Kevin R. Murphy, editor ; foreword by Sheldon Zedeck.
    p.   cm. — (Frontiers of industrial and organizational psychology)
    "A joint publication in the Jossey-Bass business & management series and the Jossey-Bass social and behavioral science series."
    Includes bibliographical references and index.
    ISBN 0-7879-0174-1 (alk. paper)
    1. Organizational behavior.   2. Individual differences.
3. Organizational sociology.   I. Murphy, Kevin R.
II. Series.   III. Series: Jossey-Bass business & management series.
IV. Series: Jossey-Bass social and behavioral science series.
HD58.7.I529   1996
158.7—dc20   96-2586

FIRST EDITION
HB Printing   10 9 8 7 6 5 4 3 2 1

A joint publication in
The Jossey-Bass
Business & Management Series
and
The Jossey-Bass
Social and Behavioral Science Series

Frontiers of Industrial and Organizational Psychology

Contents

Part Three: Commentary

Foreword

The Society for Industrial and Organizational Psychology established the Frontiers of Industrial and Organizational Psychology Series in 1982, in part to advance the scientific status of the field. The series was specifically designed to include volumes that would deal with a single topic considered to be of major contemporary significance in the field. The volume editor, a leading contributor to the topic, would take responsibility for the development of the volume with the goal of presenting cutting-edge theory, research, and practice in chapters contributed by individuals doing pioneering work on the topic. Each volume is aimed at members of the Society for Industrial and Organizational Psychology—researchers, practitioners, and students. Volumes are to be published on a timely basis rather than on a fixed schedule, though at a projected rate of one volume per year.

The first editor of the series was Raymond Katzell, who was followed by Irwin Goldstein. I began my term as series editor in May 1993. The practice of choosing volume topics and editors that I am following is the one successfully established by my predecessors. Specifically, the choice of topics and volume editors is determined by the series editorial board; there is considerable exchange between the board and the volume editor in the planning stages of each volume. Once the volume is under contract, the series editor works with the volume editor to coordinate and oversee the activities between the board, the publisher, the volume editor, and the volume authors.

Under the excellent leadership and guidance of the first editor, Raymond Katzell, three major volumes were developed and published: *Career Development in Organizations,* edited by Douglas T. Hall (1986); *Productivity in Organizations,* edited by John P. Campbell and Richard J. Campbell (1988); and *Training and Development in Organizations,* edited by Irwin L. Goldstein (1989). Under the equally excellent stewardship of Irwin Goldstein, four additional volumes were produced: *Organizational Climate and Culture,* edited by Benjamin Schneider (1990); *Work, Families, and Organizations,* edited by Sheldon Zedeck (1992); *Personnel Selection in Organizations,* edited by Neal Schmitt and Walter C. Borman (1993), and *Team Effectiveness and Decision Making in Organizations,* edited by Richard A. Guzzo and Eduardo Salas (1995).

The success of the series is evidenced by the strong sales (over 25,000 copies have been sold), the excellent reviews written about the volumes, and the frequent citation of volumes and chapters in papers by scholars. With the completion of the seventh volume, I was chosen as series editor. Since then, the eighth volume, titled *The Changing Nature of Work,* edited by Ann Howard (1995), has been published; it is already showing signs of the same success achieved by the other volumes.

With this volume, *Individual Differences and Behavior in Organizations,* the series continues the tradition of publishing volumes that are designed to move the field forward and to present new thinking and approaches. The history of I/O psychology shows strong attention to individual differences in terms of cognitive abilities and, to a lesser extent, psychomotor abilities. Much of the literature on selection and testing has focused on the contribution and utility that cognitive abilities have on explaining performance variation. Performance in organizations is influenced by more than cognitive ability, however; people differ in terms of personality, interpersonal relations, vocational interests, values, orientations, motivations, and perceptions. Each of these individual difference variables affects behavior in organizations.

This volume provides an analysis of the role of such variables and a starting point for new research as we pursue our understanding of human behavior in organizations. The volume editor, Kevin R. Murphy, has done an excellent job in identifying the topics, selecting a diverse group of authors, and working with those authors to provide a focused volume that is sure to direct our research for many years to come. The Society owes Murphy and his chapter authors a considerable debt of gratitude for undertaking such an ambitious volume. We anticipate that this volume will serve as an important stimulus for researchers seeking to move forward and to study the role of individual differences from a broader perspective—investigating, in particular, how individual differences are linked to a wide range of outcome variables.

The production of a volume such as this one requires the cooperation and effort of many individuals. The volume editor, the volume chapter authors, and the members of the series editorial board all play an obvious and major role. They deserve our sincere appreciation and thanks for devoting their time and effort to a task undertaken for the sole purpose of contributing to our field; they received no remuneration whatsoever. Also to be thanked is Bill Hicks, senior editor of the Jossey-Bass Management Series, and his colleagues at Jossey-Bass—especially Cedric Crocker, who worked with us in the planning stages and until the manuscript went into production.

February 1996   SHELDON ZEDECK
                                             University of California, Berkeley
                                             Series Editor

Preface

Industrial and organizational (I/O) psychologists have long been interested in individual differences. The "I" side of our field has deep roots in the psychometric tradition, in which measuring individual differences and using this information to make decisions is a central concern. The "O" side of our field has long been concerned with processes in organizations in which individual differences play an important role (for example, communication, interpersonal relationships, attachment to organizations). In the last several years, the topic of individual differences has received increased attention; indeed, there has been an explosion of interest in the links between individual differences in ability, personality, values, orientation, and affective states and behavior in organizations. *Individual Differences and Behavior in Organizations* represents an effort to pull together existing research and to stimulate new research and new ways of thinking about the ways in which individual differences affect people's behaviors and experiences in organizations.

The major theme running throughout virtually all of the chapters in this book is that there is much to be gained by taking a broad view of "individual differences." For many years, I/O psychologists devoted a great deal of time and effort to studying individual differences in cognitive and (to a lesser extent) psychomotor abilities, but have paid relatively little attention to differences in personality, interests, values, or affective states. This is not unique to I/O psychology; psychologists in other areas have also paid exquisite attention to their own favorite individual difference variables (for example, *interests* for those in vocational counseling, *personality traits* for those in clinical psychology) while largely ignoring others. The chapters that follow highlight the advantages of going beyond these specific niches when thinking about how individual differences affect our experiences in organizations.

Human behavior is affected by characteristics of persons, characteristics of situations, and the interaction between the two; and a book that focuses on differences between people cannot provide a complete description of behavior in complex organizations. Nevertheless, there is considerable value in exploring the topic of individual differences in some depth. Individual differences in abilities, personality attributes, values, outlook, affective state, and so on profoundly affect our behavior, and a detailed examination of the role of individual differences provides an important starting point for understanding human behavior in organizations.

Organization of the Book

Individual Differences and Behavior in Organizations is divided into three parts. Part One (Chapters One through Four) describes and evaluates research on four individual difference domains that seem especially relevant to understanding behavior in organizations: individual differences in cognitive ability; personality attributes; values, interests, and orientation; and affective states. In Chapter One, I argue that broadening the sets of independent and dependent variables in individual difference research (for example, consideration of a wider set of individual differences related to a wider set of outcome variables) presents both opportunities and challenges for I/O psychologists, and I suggest how future research in this area might change. Leaetta M. Hough and Robert J. Schneider (Chapter Two) explore the advantages and disadvantages of the so-called Big Five as a framework for understanding personality, and they review recent advances in the treatment of personality variables in I/O research and practice. In Chapter Three, Robert Hogan and Rex J. Blake explore the topic of vocational interests and sketch the links between these interests (which have been lamentably ignored by most I/O psychologists) and broader facets of personality. Finally, Jennifer M. George (Chapter Four) reviews an extensive body of research on trait and state affect and suggests how the study of affect can enhance our understanding of a wide range of topics in I/O psychology.

Part Two includes eight chapters that examine the links between each of these four individual difference domains and a wide range of outcome variables. In Chapter Five, Stephan J. Motowidlo develops a theory of individual differences in job satisfaction that draws on a number of individual difference domains. In Chapter Six, James T. Austin and Howard J. Klein show how individual differences affect goal striving and how they are in turn linked to differences in work motivation.

John P. Campbell, Michael Blake Gasser, and Frederick L. Oswald (Chapter Seven) examine the nature and determinants of performance variability. This chapter documents the complexity of the phenomenon labeled "job performance" and suggests several avenues for further exploration into the causes and meaning of job performance variability. In Chapter Eight, John R. Hollenbeck, Jeffrey A. LePine, and Daniel R. Ilgen show how individual differences in all four areas might affect adaptation to and effectiveness in decision-making teams.

In Chapter Nine, Robert A. Baron examines the impact of individual differences on interpersonal relations in organizations and shows how differences in each of the four domains highlighted in this book might affect interactions between individuals and groups in organizations. Rodney L. Lowman (Chapter Ten) examines the relationships between work dysfunctions and mental disorders, as well as the relationship between the individual difference domains discussed in this book and psychopathology.

In Chapter Eleven, Lawrence R. James and Michael D. McIntyre draw on recent research on conditional reasoning to explain individual differences in the perception of climate. In Chapter Twelve, Joseph G. Rosse and Terry W. Noel examine the role of individual differences in ability, personality, orientation, and affective disposition in the decision to withdraw from an organization.

Part Three of this book includes two chapters that comment on the issues raised in the preceding chapters. In Chapter Thirteen, Keith Hattrup and Susan E. Jackson examine the methodological issues involved in studying individual differences and show how situational effects can (and should) be disentangled from individual effects in research on behavior in organizations. Finally, in Chapter Fourteen, Benjamin Schneider examines the history of thinking and research on the roles of individual differences in affecting behavior in organizations and shows how future research in this important area is likely to unfold.

Acknowledgments

First, I would like to express my sincere gratitude to the authors of each of the chapters that follow. Each author successfully faced the dilemma of balancing the need to cover a substantial body of research and theory with the real-world constraints of publishing—in other words, saying it all in a limited number of pages. I learned a tremendous amount by reading and commenting on the contributors' chapters, and this book stands in tribute to their collective efforts.

Second, I greatly appreciate the support of the Society for Industrial and Organizational Psychology—in particular, the Frontiers in Industrial and Organizational Psychology Series editorial board. Their input substantially shaped and improved the overall plan for the book; indeed, I have never in my career received more useful and thought-provoking feedback about a book prospectus. I owe a special debt of gratitude to Shelly Zedeck, the Frontiers in Industrial and Organizational Psychology Series editor, whose feedback to me and to the chapter authors was invaluable.

Finally, I appreciate the help and support of Jossey-Bass. If you read the prefaces of earlier entries in this series, you will see frequent reference to the quality and helpfulness of this publisher, and the praise is well deserved. I especially appreciate the encouragement I received from Bill Hicks (senior editor of the Management Series) and the help and advice I received from Cedric Crocker, Cheryl Greenway, and Byron Schneider.

February 1996　　　　　　　　　　　　　　　　KEVIN R. MURPHY
Fort Collins, Colorado

The Authors

KEVIN R. MURPHY received his Ph.D. degree (1979) in psychology from Pennsylvania State University. Currently professor of psychology at Colorado State University, he has also taught at New York University and Rice University. He serves as associate editor of *Journal of Applied Psychology* and as a member of the editorial boards of *Personnel Psychology, Human Performance,* and *International Journal of Selection and Assessment.* He is the author of over fifty articles and book chapters and is the author or editor of five books: *Psychology in Organizations: Integrating Science and Practice* (1991, with F. Saal), *Performance Appraisal: An Organizational Perspective* (1991, with J. Cleveland), *Honesty in the Workplace* (1993), *Psychological Testing: Principles and Applications* (3rd ed., 1994, with C. Davidshofer), *Understanding Performance Appraisal: Social, Organizational, and Goal-Oriented Perspectives* (1995, with J. Cleveland). In addition to performance appraisal, Murphy's areas of research include personnel selection and assessment and honesty in the workplace.

James T. Austin received his Ph.D. degree (1987) in industrial and organizational psychology from Virginia Polytechnic Institute and State University. He is now assistant professor of psychology at Ohio State University. His research interests include goal striving—particularly the effects of goal origin and the ways that individuals represent goals for others. Other areas of research interest are criterion measurement and research methodology. His research has been published in such journals as *Personnel Psychology, Journal of Applied Psychology,* and *Organizational Behavior and Human Decision Processes.*

Robert A. Baron received his Ph.D. degree (1968) in psychology from the University of Iowa. Currently professor of management and of psychology at Rensselaer Polytechnic Institute, Baron has held faculty appointments at Purdue University, the University of Minnesota, the University of Texas, the University of South Carolina, and Princeton University. In 1982, he was a visiting fellow at Oxford University. From 1979 to 1981, he served as a program director at the National Science Foundation in Washington, D.C. A fellow of the American Psychological Association since 1978, he is the author or coauthor of twenty-six books, including *Behavior in Organizations* (5th ed., 1995), *Social Psychology* (7th ed., 1994), *Human Aggression* (2nd ed., 1994), *Psychology* (3rd ed., 1994), and *Understanding Human Relations* (3rd ed., 1996). His research and consulting activities focus primarily on the following topics: the impact of the physical environment (for example, lighting, air quality, and temperature) on productivity, stress management, and management of organizational conflict.

Rex J. Blake received his Ph.D. degree (1994) in counseling psychology from the University of Minnesota. He is currently associated with MDA Consulting Group of Minneapolis. His diverse consulting activities include the design of assessment instruments, the assessment of individuals and groups, and the coaching and counseling of individual managers and executives. His research interests include personality assessment and the relationship of individual personality factors to work performance. He has presented papers at numerous scientific conferences and has authored articles and book chapters on those subjects. He maintains an active program of research on individual differences associated with job success and satisfaction.

John P. Campbell received his Ph.D. degree (1964) in psychology from the University of Minnesota. He is professor of psychology and industrial relations at the University of Minnesota, where he has been since 1967. From 1964 to 1966, he was assistant professor of psychology at the University of California, Berkeley. He served as president of the Division of I/O Psychology of the American Psychological Association in 1977–78 and served as associate editor and then editor of *Journal of Applied Psychology* from 1974 to 1982. In 1971, he authored the first *Annual Review of Psychology* chapter on training and development. He is also coauthor of *Managerial*

Behavior, Performance, and Effectiveness (1970, with M. Dunnette, E. Lawler, and K. Weick), *Measurement Theory for the Behavioral Sciences* (1978, with E. Ghiselli and S. Zedeck), *What to Study: Generating and Developing Research Questions* (1984, with R. Daft and C. Hulin), and *Productivity in Organizations* (1988, with R. Campbell). He was awarded the Society of I/O Psychology Distinguished Scientific Contribution Award in 1991. He also served as principal scientist for the comprehensive, multiyear selection and classification project known as Project A (sponsored by the Army Research Institute). Current research interests are in performance measurement, personnel selection and classification, and the modeling of personnel decision making.

Michael Blake Gasser received his Ph.D. degree (1995) in psychology from the University of Minnesota. His research interests include selection models for job assignments to foreign countries, the measurement of cultural tolerance, the measurement and calibration of self-knowledge, and the development of models of job performance. He is currently assistant professor of psychology at the University of Northern Iowa.

Jennifer M. George received her Ph.D. degree (1987) in management and organizational behavior from New York University. She is associate professor in the Department of Management at Texas A&M University. Her research on topics such as the nature, antecedents, and consequences of affect at work for both individuals and groups has been widely published in leading journals, including *Psychological Bulletin, Journal of Applied Psychology, Journal of Personality and Social Psychology,* and *Academy of Management Journal.* In 1989, she was a recipient of the Outstanding Competitive Paper Award from the Organizational Behavior Division of the Academy of Management. She is currently on the editorial boards of *Journal of Applied Psychology* and *Journal of Management* and previously served on the editorial board of *Academy of Management Journal.*

Keith Hattrup received his Ph.D. degree (1992) in psychology from Michigan State University and is now assistant professor of psychology at San Diego State University. His research interests include psychological testing, personnel assessment and selection, bias and fairness in testing, self-perception and social perception processes, and research methods. He is currently on the editorial board of *Journal of Management* and has published in *Journal of Applied Psychology* and *Personnel Psychology.*

Robert Hogan received his Ph.D. degree (1967) in psychology from the University of California, Berkeley. From 1967 to 1982, he was at Johns Hopkins University in Baltimore, where he was professor of psychology and social relations. Since 1982, he has been the McFarlin Professor of Psychology at the University of Tulsa. Formerly editor of the "personality" section of *Journal of Personality and Social Psychology,* he is the author of over one hundred articles, chapters, and books. He is interested primarily in personality theory, personality measurement, and noncognitive predictors of real-world performance.

John R. Hollenbeck received his Ph.D. degree (1984) in management and organizational behavior from New York University. He is currently professor of management at the Eli Broad Graduate School of Business Administration at Michigan State University. He serves or has served on the editorial boards of *Journal of Applied Psychology, Academy of Management Journal, Organizational Behavior and Human Decision Processes, Journal of Management,* and *Personnel Psychology.* The first recipient of the Ernest J. McCormick Award for Early Contributions to the field of industrial and organizational psychology in 1992, he also received the 1987 Teacher-Scholar Award at Michigan State University. His research focuses on self-regulation theories of work motivation, employee separation and acquisition processes, and team decision making and performance.

Leaetta M. Hough received her Ph.D. degree (1981) in psychology from the University of Minnesota. She is a founder and currently the executive vice president of Personnel Decisions Research Institutes (PDRI). She was elected a fellow of the Society for Industrial and Organization Psychology (SIOP), the American Psychological Association, and the American Psychological Society in 1993. As a member of the Project A research team, she played an important role in the current resurgence in the use of personality measures for predicting behavior in work settings. In addition to serving as a coeditor of the four-volume *Handbook of Industrial and Organiza-*

tional Psychology (2nd ed.), she has published widely in the professional literature and has been responsible for numerous technical reports, invited addresses, convention papers, and SIOP workshops. Over the years, she has directed many large and complex projects for both government and private-sector clients. She has also developed performance management systems in many settings and has been responsible for research and development efforts focusing on organizational reengineering, restructuring, competency modeling, and integrated human resource systems.

Daniel R. Ilgen received his Ph.D. degree (1969) in psychology from the University of Illinois. He is currently the John A. Hannah Professor of Psychology and Management at Michigan State University, a position he has held since 1983. Throughout most of the 1970s and early 1980s, he was on the faculty at Purdue University in the Department of Psychological Sciences. His research has focused on work motivation, performance feedback, and performance of teams that are hierarchically structured and are composed of members who have differing expertise. This research has been published in a wide variety of journals, including *Journal of Applied Psychology, American Psychologist, Organizational Behavior and Human Decision Processes, Personnel Psychology,* and *Academy of Management Journal.* He currently serves as associate editor of *Organizational Behavior and Human Decision Processes.*

Susan E. Jackson received her Ph.D. degree in psychology from the University of California, Berkeley. Now professor of psychology and management at New York University, she has previously held faculty appointments in psychology at the University of Maryland and at the University of Michigan's Graduate School of Business Administration. Her research interests include strategic human resource management, decision-making processes in top management teams, workforce diversity, and job stress and burnout. In addition to research, her other activities include serving as editor of *Academy of Management Review,* a scholarly journal published for a global audience of readers interested in organizational science, and serving on the board of governors for the Center for Creative Leadership, a nonprofit organization dedicated to improving leadership capabilities through research, education, and training.

Lawrence R. James received his Ph.D. degree (1970) in psychology from the University of Utah and now holds the Pilot Oil Chair of Excellence in Management and Industrial-Organizational Psychology at the University of Tennessee. He has also served on the faculty at the Institute of Behavior Research at Texas Christian University, Georgia Institute of Technology, and the University of Tennessee. The author of numerous articles and papers and coauthor of books on causal analysis and organizational climate, he is (or has been) a member of the editorial boards of *Journal of Applied Psychology, Organizational Behavior and Human Decision Processes, Human Performance, Human Resources Management, Journal of Management,* and *Research Methods and Analysis.* He also serves as a consultant to a number of businesses and government agencies. He has been active in studying the effects of organizational environments on individual adaptation, motivation, and productivity. His statistical contributions have been designed to make possible tests of new models in areas such as organizational climate, leadership, and personnel selection. His current efforts are devoted to the development of new measurement systems for psychology.

Howard J. Klein received his Ph.D. degree (1987) in organizational behavior and human resource management from Michigan State University. He is currently associate professor of management and human resources in the Fisher College of Business at Ohio State University. His research interests center on improving employee performance through increasing motivation, primarily through the use of goal setting and self-management. Other areas of interest include goal-directed work teams, performance management, selection, and training. His research has been published in various journals, including *Academy of Management Review, Journal of Applied Psychology,* and *Organizational Behavior and Human Decision Processes.*

Jeffrey A. LePine is a doctoral student in organizational behavior at Michigan State University. He received his M.A. degree (1993) in management from Florida State University. His primary research interests include the effects of trait, ability, and cultural differences in role assimilation, team development, and performance. His other research interests include feedback interventions and their effect on learning and motivation in team settings and individual differences in information-processing strategies.

Rodney L. Lowman received his Ph.D. degree (1979) in psychology from Michigan State University. He currently serves as director and chief psychologist of The Development Laboratories and is adjunct professor of psychology at Rice University (both in Houston). He also holds a consulting faculty appointment at Duke University Medical Center in North Carolina. Among other books, he has written *Counseling and Psychotherapy of Work Dysfunctions* (1993) and *The Clinical Practice of Career Assessment: Interests, Abilities, and Personality* (1991; a second edition is currently being completed). In addition to his professional writing, Lowman trains professionals in his career assessment and counseling methods and, through The Development Laboratories, consults with individuals and organizations on career and work issues.

Michael D. McIntyre received his Ph.D. degree in industrial and organizational psychology from the University of Tennessee, Knoxville. He is currently working for the consulting firm of Helms & Greco in Atlanta, Georgia.

Stephan J. Motowidlo received his Ph.D. degree (1976) in industrial and organizational psychology from the University of Minnesota and is now professor of management and director of the Human Resource Research Center at the University of Florida. His research interests include work attitudes, occupational stress, selection interviews, job simulations, performance appraisal, and models of the performance domain. Motowidlo serves on the editorial boards of *Human Performance* and *Journal of Applied Psychology.*

Terry W. Noel is a doctoral student in organizational management at the University of Colorado, Boulder, where he teaches management and entrepreneurship. He received his B.A. degree (1978) in economics and philosophy from Centne College. His research interests include group goal-setting behavior in organizations and employee withdrawal.

Frederick L. Oswald is a doctoral student in industrial and organizational psychology at the University of Minnesota. He received his B.A. degree (1992) in psychology from the University of Texas, Austin. Oswald is currently a National Science Foundation Graduate Research Fellow. His research interests include prediction models, personnel selection and classification, and performance measurement.

Joseph G. Rosse received his Ph.D. degree (1983) in industrial and organizational psychology from the University of Illinois and is currently associate professor of management at the University of Colorado, Boulder. His research interests include employee attitudes and adaptive behavior, workplace substance abuse, counterproductive employee behavior, and employee selection.

Benjamin Schneider received his Ph.D. degree (1967) in industrial and social psychology from the University of Maryland. Currently professor of psychology and business management at the University of Maryland, he has taught at Yale University, Michigan State University, Bar-Ilan University (Israel), Peking University, and the University of Aix-Marseilles (France). Schneider has published more than eighty articles and book chapters as well as six books, his latest being *Winning the Service Game* (1995, with D. E. Bowen). He has served as president of the Society for Industrial and Organizational Psychology as well as the Organizational Behavior Division of the Academy of Management. Schneider's research interests include organizational climate and culture, personnel selection, person-organization fit, and service quality.

Robert J. Schneider received his Ph.D. degree (1992) in industrial and organizational psychology from the University of Minnesota. He is now research associate at Personnel Decisions Research Institutes (PDRI). His research has focused on social competence, behavior change, performance management, team processes and effectiveness, and personality measurement and theory. He recently coauthored (with L. M. Hough) a chapter integrating personality and I/O psychology that appeared in the 1995 *International Review of I/O Psychology*.

Individual Differences and Behavior in Organizations

Part One

Individual Difference Domains

Chapter One

Individual Differences and Behavior in Organizations

Much More Than *g*

Kevin R. Murphy

Industrial and organizational (I/O) psychology has a long-standing tradition of concern for individual differences. Our training, research, and theory often include attention to stable individual differences. Some of the most successful applications of psychology in organizations (for example, assessment centers, vocational counseling, tools for personnel selection) rely on information about individual differences. However, until recently, most research on the roles of individual differences in organizations was very narrowly focused, with a great deal of attention given to ability-performance relationships and relatively little given to other individual differences or potential criterion variables.

Research on the roles of individual differences in understanding behavior in organizations has changed substantially in the last five to ten years. I/O psychologists are now considering a much wider range of individual difference variables and are linking them to a much wider range of potential outcomes. The purpose of this book is to review what we know (existing research), what we think it means (theory), and what we still need to know (future research directions) about the roles of individual differences in understanding and determining behavior in organizations.

Figure 1.1 illustrates the range of individual difference measures and dependent variables considered in recent work. Research

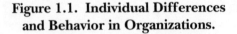

**Figure 1.1. Individual Differences
and Behavior in Organizations.**

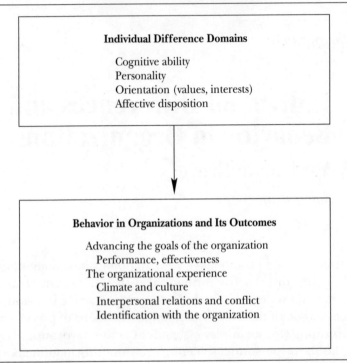

on the role of cognitive abilities continues to be an important concern of I/O psychologists, but increasing attention has been devoted to personality, orientation (for example, values, interests), and affective reactions. These individual differences have been related to variables ranging from job performance and effectiveness (and other behaviors that are related to the goals of the organization, such as organizational citizenship) to states that reflect the individual's experience of membership in an organization (for example, interpersonal relationships in the workplace, commitment to and identity with the organization).

Historical Background

Before commenting in detail about the individual difference and organizational domains considered in this book, I will briefly examine the historical background of I/O research on individual differences. The field of I/O psychology has long exhibited a nearly schizophrenic attitude toward individual differences. On the one hand, the study of individual differences has always been a central component of I/O research and training. For example, most Ph.D. programs in the field train students in psychometrics, correlation, regression, and multivariate analysis. On the other hand, I/O psychologists have purposely avoided studying or even thinking about questions that fall outside of a very narrow range of concerns. In particular, I/O psychologists have often ignored individual differences that have not seemed immediately relevant to predicting individual task performance. (For example, as is noted below, research on the role of personality in explaining job performance has only recently reemerged from a twenty-five-year hiatus.)

Individual difference research in I/O psychology from the mid 1960s to the mid 1980s can be roughly categorized as (1) research on the relationship between scores on written ability tests and job performance and (2) other research. The first category has, for the last thirty years, received the lion's share of attention (for example, even in the current edition of the *Handbook of Industrial and Organizational Psychology,* Ackerman and Humphreys's chapter on individual difference theory [1990] is concerned almost solely with cognitive ability); and systematic theory or research on the roles of other individual difference variables, or even on the influence of cognitive ability on dependent variables other than performance on the job or in training, has until recently been rare.

There are many reasons for this state of affairs, but two stand out as particularly important. First, the success of researchers in demonstrating simple and generalizable relationships between ability and performance has had the unfortunate tendency to discourage thinking and research on more complex models of peformance and has also distracted researchers interested in cognitive ability from considering the possible effects of ability on outcomes other than performance. The relevance of general cognitive ability in predicting job performance is now so firmly established in I/O psychology doctrine that it seems hard to think about ability *without* thinking about performance.

Second, early research on individual difference variables other than cognitive ability (particularly personality constructs) was of sufficiently poor quality to cast doubt on the utility and even the legitimacy of I/O psychology research and theory linking these constructs with behavior in organizations. In particular, an influential review by Guion and Gottier (1965) had the unintended consequence of virtually halting (for twenty-five years) research on the role of personality in explaining behavior in organizations.

Victims of Our Own Success

Research on the validity of measures of cognitive ability as predictors of job performance represents one of the "success stories" in I/O psychology. There is now abundant evidence that cognitive ability is highly relevant in a wide range of jobs and settings (Hough, Eaton, Dunnette, Kamp, & McCloy, 1991; Hunter, 1986; Hunter & Hunter, 1984; Ree & Earles, 1992; Schmidt, Ones, & Hunter, 1992) and that measures of general cognitive ability represent perhaps the best predictors of performance. (For dissenting views on the importance of general cognitive ability, see McClelland, 1993; Sternberg & Wagner, 1993.) Furthermore, the incremental contribution of specific abilities (defined as ability factors unrelated to g, the general factor) to the prediction of performance or training outcomes may very well be minimal (Ree & Earles, 1991a, 1992; Ree, Earles, & Teachout, 1994). The statement "Ability predicts performance" has attained the status of a truism in our field.

The apparent simplicity and generalizability of the ability-performance relationship is both a blessing and a curse. On the one hand, findings and current doctrine in this area are consistent with a long-standing goal of scientists everywhere—that is, parsimony. Twenty years ago, I/O psychologists believed that the validity of cognitive ability tests depended substantially on a number of situational variables and on the specific ability and job in question. A wide range of hypotheses about the functional relationship (if any) between ability and performance received serious attention, and there was a widespread belief in the value and necessity of new validity studies in each new testing application. It is now widely accepted that ability-performance relationships are essentially linear (Coward & Sackett, 1990) and that correlation between ability and performance is similar across jobs that differ considerably in content (Hunter & Hirsh, 1987).

The drawback of this line of thinking is that it can encourage oversimplification. First, the position that the ability-performance relationship can be adequately summarized with a single correlation coefficient (or with a relatively small range of plausible *r* values) implies that both ability and performance are unitary phenomena. There is clear evidence, however, that they are not. Current theories of job performance suggest that the performance domain is multifaceted and that it is likely to include dimensions that are not highly or even positively correlated (Borman & Motowidlo, 1993; Campbell, McCloy, Oppler, & Sager, 1992). It is unlikely that the domain of job performance can be adequately or even sensibly represented in terms of a single summary score. Second, conceptions of the domain of cognitive ability that dominate this literature are inconsistent with current research and theory on individual differences in ability (Ackerman & Humphreys, 1990; Landy, Shankster, & Kohler, 1994; Sternberg & Detterman, 1986; Sternberg & Wagner, 1993). This inconsistency is most clearly shown in a series of studies by Ree, Earles, and colleagues (for example, Ree & Earles, 1991a, 1992; Ree, Earles, & Teachout, 1994).

These studies exemplify the best and the worst of the I/O psychology tradition in the area of individual differences: they exemplify meticulous, psychometrically sophisticated research that has a clear and immediate payoff (for example, demonstrations of successful prediction on the basis of general cognitive ability measures), but they also exemplify a lack of concern with an understanding of the constructs that underlie human cognitive ability. These studies usually take the first principal component underlying the correlations among ability tests as an estimate of *g* and define specific abilities (often called "non-*g*" in these chapters) as succeeding composites that are uncorrelated with *g*. (Ree and Carretta, 1994, are an exception in that they estimate *g* as a higher-order general factor in a confirmatory factor analysis of cognitive and psychomotor tests.) A consistent finding is that composites that are orthogonal to *g* contribute little to the prediction of criteria such as job performance or training success. This method of defining *g* is not problematic; Ree and Earles (1991b) show that virtually any method of combining information from reliable paper-and-pencil tests yields similar *g* estimates. However, their treatment of abilities other than *g* is at best offhand. That is, the non-g portions of their models are simply statistical composites that are orthogonal to the first and most general principal component of the matrix. No attempt is made to understand or interpret these components or to understand the ability structure implied by the principle component model (that is, that specific abilities are mutually orthogonal and are orthogonal to general cognitive ability). In contrast to the model implicit in the papers authored by Ree, Earles, and colleagues, virtually every other structural model of human intelligence that includes a general factor also includes specific abilities that are defined in terms of their content or function and that are necessarily related to rather than orthogonal to g (Carroll, 1993; Sternberg & Detterman, 1986).

The series of papers published by Ree, Earles, and their colleagues asks the very pragmatic question of whether abilities that are unrelated to g make any incremental contribution to predicting important criteria. The answer seems to be no, meaning that a single g measure might be adequate for prediction and that other, completely distinct abilities might not contribute much new information. However, the question posed by Ree, Earles, and their colleagues could be turned around. That is, you might ask whether measures of g provide any incremental validity when added to measures of substantively important abilities (for example, verbal ability, spatial ability). Because a wide range of specific abilities are related to one another and to g, the fact that g provides accurate prediction does not mean that it contributes uniquely to understanding job performance.

I/O psychologists have shown relatively little concern for understanding exactly how cognitive ability translates into job performance. Models that have been put forth to explain ability-performance links (for example, Hunter, 1986) rarely examine the role of specific abilities but rather use ability as a generic term. This "g-ocentric view" is completely appropriate if the goal of a study is accurate and efficient prediction, but it may do little to advance our understanding of how and why cognitive ability is linked to performance (Sternberg & Wagner, 1993).

Finally, the consistent success of I/O psychologists in predicting overall job performance (or performance in job-related training) seems to have distracted them from considering the potential relevance of cognitive abilities in understanding a wide range of other behaviors in organizations. There is a scattering of research relating cognitive ability to topics such as leadership and vocational preferences (for example, F. E. Fiedler & Garcia, 1987; Lent, Brown, & Hackett, 1994), but the relative emphasis in research on the role of cognitive ability has been overwhelmingly on dependent variables such as job performance, learning, and skill acquisition. Perhaps this focus is fully justified; it is possible that these are the only meaningful correlates of ability. However, it is hard to escape the feeling that we have only scratched the surface in understanding the full relevance of individual differences in cognitive abilities to behavior in organizations.

Noncognitive Predictors: The Decline of Personality Research

Prior to 1965, research on personality—in particular, the predictive validity of personality inventories—was an active concern of I/O psychologists. Following Guion and Gottier's masterful review (1965), advocates of personality testing in employment contexts were few and far between, and research on the relationship between personality and behavior in organizations virtually dropped from sight. (One noteworthy exception is research on assessment centers, which throughout its history has often incorporated a range of personality inventories and assessments. See Thornton, 1992.) After reading Guion and Gottier's conclusions (1965), it is not hard to understand why: they conclude that "[T]here is no generalizable evidence that personality measures can be recommended as good or practical tools for employee selection. . . . [I]t is difficult to advocate, with a clear conscience, the use of personality measures in most situations as a basis for making employment decisions about people" (pp. 159–160).

Guion and Gottier's commentary certainly said as much about the haphazard nature of many of the studies they reviewed as it did about the potential for personality testing. They did note in several places that personality tests showed some potential. For example, they noted that "personality measures have predictive validity more often than can be accounted for simply by chance; . . . no blanket indictment is justified or sensible" (p. 141) and that "serious, concerted effort might yield more generalized systems of prediction using personality measures" (p. 159). Nevertheless, their

review had the apparently unintended effect of casting an immediate and long-lasting pall over personality testing in employment
contexts. Landy (1985) noted that in the twenty years following
Guion and Gottier (1965), there were "few published reports of
attempts to relate personality measures to job performance"
(p. 92). Several generations of I/O psychologists seem to have
drawn the wrong conclusion from Guion and Gottier (1965)—that
is, that the study of personality and other related individual difference variables was somehow suspect.

In recent years, research on the roles of individual difference
variables in understanding behavior in organizations has grown
dramatically. Several influential reviews (for example, Barrick &
Mount, 1991; Tett, Jackson, & Rothstein, 1991) have revived interest in the relationship between personality and performance. The
role of affect in organizations has received serious attention as well
(Isen & Baron, 1991; Judge, 1992). Testing programs that integrate
assessments of ability and vocational interests are becoming more
common (the Department of Defense's Student Testing Program,
for example, incorporates both cognitive ability measures and
interest measures to aid in selection, placement, and vocational
choice). It is time for I/O psychologists to broaden their horizons
when thinking about the roles of individual differences in understanding behavior in organizations.

Individual Differences and Their Implications in Organizations

As noted earlier, recent research has examined a wider range of
individual difference variables (and has related them to a wider
range of outcomes) than was true in the past. The sections below
describe both the predictor and criterion domains (that is, individual differences and outcomes of those differences) that have
been included in recent research and that are reviewed in this
book. Next, implications of this broadening conception of the
roles of individual differences in affecting behavior and experiences in organizations are discussed.

Individual Difference Domains

Four individual difference domains are considered in this book:
cognitive ability, personality, orientation (for example, values and

interests), and affective disposition (for example, mood, affect, and temperament). These four areas do not exhaust the set of individual differences that might have a substantial bearing on job performance or other organizationally relevant criteria (for example, differences in physical or psychomotor abilities might be very important in specific situations), but they do represent the most frequent concerns of individual difference theory and research and I/O psychology. It is useful to consider the definitions of and relationships among these four domains.

As noted earlier, the domain of cognitive ability is relatively familiar ground for I/O psychologists. Cognitive ability tests are among the most widely used and widely researched measures in personnel selection, and discussions of issues ranging from racial discrimination to utility estimation routinely cover cognitive ability. To help set the stage for later chapters dealing with cognitive ability, I will present a brief overview of some of the key issues in defining and working with ability constructs in the section that follows.

The domains of personality, orientation, and affective disposition are less familiar to many I/O psychologists. I will comment briefly in this chapter on the relationships among these domains; each of the three noncognitive domains is then discussed in detail in the chapters that follow (see Chapters Two, Three, and Four for discussions of personality, orientation and values, and affective disposition, respectively).

Cognitive Ability

Abilities are relatively stable individual differences that are related to performance on some set of tasks, problems, or other goal-oriented activities. The distinguishing characteristic of an ability is that it can be defined only in reference to some goal-directed activity. That is, every individual has the ability to do some thing or some class of things, and differences in the level of ability are manifest in terms of the success, ease, speed, and so on with which different individuals do, learn, or acquire skill in these goal-oriented activities. Cognitive abilities are involved when people are performing tasks that require the active manipulation of information. Tasks that require coordination between perception and physical action typically involve psychomotor abilities. It is possible to define more specific abilities that are restricted to a relatively narrow range of goal-directed activities (for example, music); the focus here, however, will be on the broad domain of cognitive ability, which is likely to subsume a number of specific abilities.

Before discussing the structure and content of the domain of cognitive abilities, I will consider the different meanings associated with the term ability. Typically, we think of abilities as causes of behavior. For example, if an individual does very well in school, we might explain this by noting that he or she is very intelligent (in other words, intelligence is the causal explanation for performance). The danger in this approach is that we end up treating intelligence (or mental ability) as a thing, with the assumption that the more of it you have, the better you will perform. (Gould, 1981, refers to this tendency as "reifying" intelligence.) An alternative is to treat abilities as summary statements about past performance. That is, if an individual does well in school, easily learns novel material, is able to solve complicated problems, and so on, we might say that he or she is intelligent. Furthermore, we can draw on the general principle of behavioral consistency to argue that people who have demonstrated cognitive ability in the past (that is, who have been highly successful in tasks involving information processing) will continue to do so in the future. Following this logic, we could use samples of previous behavior to (1) define a person's level of ability and (2) predict his or her future performance on cognitively demanding tasks (Wernimont & Campbell, 1968).

Neither of the approaches to defining *ability* outlined above is entirely satisfactory. Abilities are not things that people carry around inside them, and it is hard to argue seriously that abilities are causal agents. Saying that a person performs well because she has a high level of ability does not seem fundamentally different from saying that she performs well now because she performed well in the past, yet the causal link here is far from clear. On the other hand, if abilities are nothing more than summary statements about past behavior, there may be little gained by slapping a label on groups of behaviors and pretending that we have advanced our understanding. A better approach to defining and understanding abilities is through the process of construct explication.

Abilities are widely recognized as constructs (Eysenck, 1979; Humphreys, 1979), but the precise implications of this definition are not always appreciated. First, constructs are literally that: they are ideas or concepts that are constructed by researchers and/or theorists, and the locus of any construct is in the mind of the theorist, not in the body or mind of the individual who exhibits a specific level of some cognitive ability. Second, ability constructs have clear and real behavioral anchors (Jensen, 1980; Sternberg, 1977, 1984). That is, although "cognitive ability" does not exist in any physical sense, the behaviors that are linked to and define this construct are real and meaningful. The construct of cognitive ability is more than simply a label attached to a relatively narrow set of behaviors. As will be noted below, the utility of this construct stems largely from the fact that the domain of behaviors that are subsumed under the heading "cognitive ability" is broad and ubiquitous. Considered in this light, cognitive abilities can be defined as hypothetical attributes of individuals that are manifest when those individuals are performing tasks that involve the active manipulation of information. These abilities may be broad (that is, related to a wide array of tasks) or narrow (that is, related only to a specific type of task), and they may be interrelated (even though conceptually distinguishable).

The key to understanding the structure of human cognitive abilities is the fact that scores on almost any reliable measure that calls for mental processing, retrieval, or manipulation of information will be positively correlated with any other reliable measure that also involves cognitive activity. (In other words, scores on cognitively demanding tasks exhibit positive manifold. See Ackerman & Humphreys, 1990; Allinger, 1988; Carroll, 1993; Eysenck, 1979; Guttman & Levy, 1991; Humphreys, 1979; Jensen, 1980; Ree & Earles, 1991b.) Thus scores on paragraph comprehension measures will be correlated with scores on numerical problem solving, which will be correlated with scores on spatial relations tests, and so on. The existence of positive manifold virtually guarantees that the structure of human abilities will be hierarchically arranged, with virtually all specific abilities (or groups of abilities) positively correlated with ability factors that are more general. Theories of cognitive ability that give little emphasis to *g* (for example, Sternberg, 1977; Sternberg & Wagner, 1993) or that deny the utility of a general factor (for example, Guilford, 1988) do not seem to provide any convincing explanation for positive manifold.

Carroll's three-stratum model of cognitive ability (1993) (based on the results of a large number of factor-analytic studies) nicely illustrates the nature of modern hierarchical models. At the most general level, there is a *g* factor, which implies stable differences in performance on a wide range of cognitively demanding tasks. At the next level (the broad stratum), there are a number of areas of ability, implying that the rank-ordering of individuals' task performance will not be exactly the same across all cognitive tasks but rather will show some clustering. The broad abilities in Carroll's model include (1) fluid intelligence, (2) crystallized intelligence, (3) general memory ability, (4) broad visual perception, (5) broad auditory perception, (6) broad retrieval ability, and (7) broad cognitive speediness. The implication of distinguishing these broad abilities from *g* is that some people will do well on a broad range of memory tasks, and these will not be exactly the same set of people who do well on a broad range of tasks tapping cognitive speed, visual perception, and so on.

Finally, each of these broad ability areas can be characterized in terms of a number of more specific abilities (the narrow stratum) that are more homogeneous still than those at the next highest level. Examples corresponding to each of the broad spectrum abilities labeled above include (1) induction, (2) language development, (3) memory span, (4) spatial relations, (5) sound discrimination, (6) word fluency, and (7) perceptual speed. Once again, the implication of distinguishing specific narrow abilities from their broad parent abilities is that the individuals who do well on inductive reasoning tasks might not be exactly the same as those who do well on other fluid intelligence tasks (although the groups will overlap substantially; they will also overlap with those classified as high on *g*).

The importance of general versus specific ability constructs for understanding performance on cognitively demanding tasks has been a critical issue throughout much of the history of psychology. Spearman (1904, 1927) suggested that the correlations between various cognitive tests might be explained solely in terms of *g* (although he later abandoned this theory). Thurstone (1938), Vernon (1960), and others proposed models including both general and specific factors as well as conceptually distinct groups of factors, all of which might be related to *g*. Cattell (1963) proposed a distinction between fluid and crystallized intelligence and suggested that neither of these corresponded precisely to usual conceptions of *g*. As noted earlier, a number of recent studies by Ree, Earles, and colleagues have tested the proposition that we can predict performance on important tasks as well with a single *g* measure as with measures of multiple abilities.

Hierarchical models suggest that general versus specific ability constructs should be used for different purposes. If one's purpose is parsimonious prediction, *g* may be all that is needed. If one's goal is to communicate or understand the meaning of human performance, lower levels in the hierarchy are likely to be more useful. Saying that a person is high on *g* is the same as saying that he or she is likely to perform above average on some wide range of tasks. Saying that a person shows a high level of inductive reasoning ability (which implies relatively high *g*) helps to describe the content and nature of the tasks he or she performs well.

Three general conclusions can be drawn from the debate about the structure of human cognitive ability. First, as noted above, some sort of general factor is probably necessary to explain positive manifold. Theories without a *g* or some sort of hierarchical structure (which implies *g*) simply do not explain the data. Second, if many or most abilities are related to *g* (which is what all hierarchical theories imply), the question of which is more important, *g* or some specific ability or set of specific abilities, is essentially pointless. The research literature is littered with questions of this sort, despite the fact that the question is unanswerable. It is a simple reflection of the principles of multiple regression that if two variables (for example, *g* and verbal ability) are strongly related to one another and are both related to some outcome variable of interest, whichever predictor is entered first will account for the lion's share of variance. In many cases, the same data could be used to demonstrate either that a specific ability makes no contribution over and above *g* or that *g* makes no contribution over and above that specific ability. Third, no structural model of cognitive ability is so far superior to its competitors that it is likely to be accepted as a benchmark. In the area of personality, the Five-Factor Model has emerged as a dominant model (Digman, 1990; see, however, Chapter Two of this volume). In the cognitive domain, no such consensus about the "best" structural model has been achieved. It is clear that any adequate model of human cognitive ability must include some general factor (or a hierarchical structure, which implies a general factor), but it is not so clear what model should be followed.

The most obvious weakness of current structural models of cognitive ability is the fact that they leave unanswered the question of why some people are more able than others. Despite attempts to more closely link research on intelligence and cognitive ability with research on cognition, we still know relatively little about the basic cognitive processes that underlie intelligent behavior (Hunt & Pellegrin, 1985; Sternberg, 1977, 1985). Similarly, research on the biological bases of ability has not yet progressed to the point where confident conclusions can be drawn. There is clearly some biological basis for cognitive ability; like many personality attributes, cognitive abilities show moderate to high levels of heritability (Plomin & Rende, 1991; Vandenberg & Vogler, 1985). However, very little is known at this point about the neural, physiological, or biochemical roots of cognitive ability.

Noncognitive Domains

It is sometimes difficult to draw clear distinctions between personality, orientation, and affective disposition. (Guion and Gottier, 1965, for example, noted that it was difficult to distinguish interest measures from conventional personality measures.) In part, this is because there have been long-standing disagreements about how each of the three domains should be defined. The term personality is defined in many ways (Carson, 1989; Frank, 1939; Ozer & Reise, 1994; Pervin, 1985; Rorer & Widigor, 1983), and different definitions may either include or exclude values, interests, and affective reactions within the domain of personality. One way to understand the relationships among personality, orientation, and disposition is to consider the role of affect in defining each domain.

Despite its obvious importance, affect has been understudied in many areas of psychology (Forgas, 1992). Affect has an important role in social judgments of all sorts (Forgas, 1992) and may be the primary determinant of a wide range of interpersonal behaviors (Zajonc, 1980). Researchers in social and organizational psychology have demonstrated the relevance of affect for understanding behavior in organizations (Isen & Baron, 1991). Nevertheless, there is still considerable confusion about many fundamental terms in this area (for example, affect, feeling, emotion, mood; K. Fiedler & Forgas,

1988). The model shown in Figure 1.2 suggests one way of distinguishing among certain affect-relevant terms—personality, orientation, disposition—that are more and more frequently encountered in I/O research.

At the most general level of analysis is the term *personality*. Despite disagreements about exactly what constitutes personality, most researchers accept the notion that *personality* is a general term that may subsume many other individual difference variables. Current definitions tend to describe personality as the set of characteristics of a person that account for consistent patterns of response to situations (Pervin, 1980). Affective reactions are an important component of personality. These reactions are all linked to the ubiquitous general evaluative dimension that pervades social perception (Osgood, 1962). (In clinical psychology, a sadness-happiness dimension appears to be similarly ubiquitous; see Ottaviani & Beck, 1988.) Although affective reactions have a strong evaluative component, a distinction is usually drawn between affect and the general cognitive evaluation of a person, thing, or event as good or bad (Pennebaker, 1982; Zajonc, 1980; Zanna & Rempel, 1988; see, however, Forgas, 1992). Affective reactions involve feelings as well as cognitive evaluations, and some

Figure 1.2. Relationships Among Personality, Orientation, and Affective Disposition.

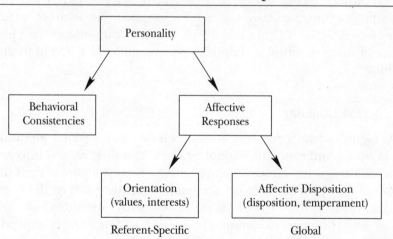

theories of affect involve separate physiological bases for the emotional or the "feeling" component of these reactions (Zajonc, 1980).

The domain of affective reactions can be usefully divided into sets of general tendencies to react positively or negatively (that is, affective disposition) and sets of affective reactions that are linked to specific referents (that is, orientation: values and interests). The relationship between overall affective tendencies and job attitudes has been a major focus of dispositional research in organizational settings; there is substantial evidence that dispositional factors play a role in shaping these attitudes (Judge, 1992; see, however, Davis-Blake & Pfeffer, 1989; Gerhart, 1987). In this research tradition, affective disposition represents a momentary or chronic tendency to exhibit specific affective states. Moods represent relatively transitory states, whereas dispositions refer to consistent tendencies to react in specific ways in a wide range of situations. Affective tendencies are often described in terms of the likelihood of generally positive or negative reactions (for example, positive versus negative affectivity); and while both mood and disposition might be affected by situational variables, dispositional reactions are usually conceived of as general rather than as linked to a specific referent.

The orientation domain, which includes values and interests, revolves around affective responses to specific people, events, and activities. For example, one classic definition of an interest is "a response of liking" (Strong, 1943, p. 6) to a particular person, thing, or event. Similarly, values refer to specific end-states that are preferred or liked (Rokeach, 1979). A value or an interest in a particular thing or end-state implies a positive affective reaction to that thing.

Criterion Domains

As Figure 1.1 suggests, recent studies have examined a wide range of criteria and outcome variables. These can be grouped into two broad categories. First, there are behaviors on the part of the individual that bear directly on accomplishing the goals of the organization (Astin, 1964). This set of behaviors includes not only individual task performance but also a wide range of nontask behaviors such as teamwork, customer service, and organizational citizenship (Borman & Motowidlo, 1993; Edwards & Morrison, 1994; Murphy, 1989; Smith, Organ, & Near, 1983) and prosocial organizational behaviors (Brief & Motowidlo, 1986). Campbell's model of soldier effectiveness (1990) includes behaviors such as volunteering, persisting, helping, and maintaining individual discipline (see also Campbell, McCloy, Oppler, & Sager, 1992). While these behaviors might not be included in an individual's job description, they are crucial to the effective function of the organization. Individual differences in ability, personality, orientation, and affective states might affect any or all of these variables.

Second, individual differences can have a profound effect on the individual's experience of life in the organization. Organizations have distinct climates and cultures; yet depending on individuals' personalities, preferences, and so on, the same organization might be experienced as congenial by one employee and as hostile by another. Individual differences color our interactions and relationships with others in the organization and can be a source of either harmony or conflict (Baron, 1989). Finally, individual differences can affect (and be affected by) an individual's orientation toward and identity with the organization (James & James, 1992; Mathieu & Zajac, 1990).

The division of the criterion domain into goal-relevant behavior and individual experience categories roughly parallels the traditional distinction between "I" and "O" psychology. That is, personnel psychologists have generally been concerned with performance and effectiveness and have usually focused on ability as the individual difference most relevant to that set of concerns. Organizational psychologists, on the other hand, have generally been more concerned with the individual's experience of working in an organization and have been somewhat more open to thinking about personality or other noncognitive variables (but have been less inclined to think about ability). It is clearly time to break down the artificial barriers between "I" and "O" psychology and to consider the role that each of the individual difference domains reviewed in this book might play in each of the criterion domains. Doing this will provide both opportunities and challenges for I/O psychologists.

Ramifications of a Broader Conceptualization of the Roles of Individual Differences

A broader conceptualization of the roles of individual differences in affecting behavior in organizations is likely to affect the types of questions that are framed in I/O research. As our research moves from a somewhat narrow focus on a small set of independent and dependent variables to consideration of a wider range of individual difference variables, as well as a wider range of effects that these variables might have, it is likely to change in a number of ways. In particular, our individual difference research traditions are likely to move from a univariate to a multivariate focus, from clear to ambiguous choices regarding dependent variables, from simple to complex models, and from the investigation of invariant to the investigation of context-bound relationships. It is not clear whether all of these changes will be beneficial, and it is likely that there will be many false starts and blind alleys in this research. Nevertheless, it seems clear that these changes will occur, and it is worth considering each of them in some detail.

Univariate Versus Multivariate Focus

As noted earlier, our experience with ability-performance research makes it is easy to fall into the habit of thinking in univariate terms when dealing with individual differences. There is so much parsimony and power in research programs that summarize the ability-performance relationship in terms of a single correlation coefficient (which may be invariant over a wide range of jobs, organizations, situations, and so on) that it might appear that similar levels of parsimony should be the goal of all individual difference research. It is unlikely, however, that such a simple structure can be obtained, or even pursued, in other areas of individual difference research.

As noted earlier, the success of "g-ocentric" prediction paradigms (that is, approaches that represent ability as a unitary phenomenon) is partially a function of a unique feature of the ability domain: positive manifold. Because all cognitive ability measures are positively correlated, it is possible to summarize a substantial portion of the domain in terms of a single general-ability score. The same is not possible in other individual difference domains;

there may be no useful general factors underlying the personality domain. A phrase such as "Personality predicts performance" would lead immediately to the question of which personality dimensions or attributes are being talked about. Even within the subdomain of affective reactions, it is difficult to identify meaningful general factors that summarize large amounts of variance.

The lack of meaningful general factors in the noncognitive domains discussed in this book implies that univariate models will survive only in areas that are so balkanized that they focus on one attribute to the exclusion of all others. That is, bodies of research examining only one attribute might still be summarized in terms of a single correlation coefficient (assuming that everyone can agree on the same dependent variable to study); but in general, it will be necessary for current and future generations of I/O individual difference researchers to consider multiple attributes, and to consider the relationships among those attributes, in constructing and testing theories and models relating individual differences to behavior.

Clear Versus Ambiguous Criteria

Although there are sometimes questions among researchers about specific ability measures, there is usually little controversy over the constructs that should be involved in validating ability measures (for example, performance, training success). Cognitive abilities might also be related to a number of other dependent variables, but both the purpose of using ability measures in organizations (for example, to select among job applicants) and the criteria of choice for validating ability measures (for example, performance measures) are usually obvious. This is not necessarily true for other individual difference measures. That is, it may not be so clear what one should do with measures of personality variables, affective disposition, interests, values, and so on, or what dependent variables should be linked with these measures.

The ease with which criterion measures are chosen in studies involving cognitive ability is symptomatic of the narrow thinking about individual differences that has characterized I/O psychology. The fact that the choice of criteria might no longer be obvious is not a problem but rather a natural outgrowth of a broader conceptualization of the roles of individual differences. Neverthe-less, the fact that different researchers are likely to study very dif-ferent sets of dependent variables makes the task of communicating and integrating research more difficult. For example, validity gen-eralization research has traditionally involved large numbers of stud-ies using comparable predictors and criteria. As the choice of both predictors and criteria in individual difference research becomes less predictable and uniform, the likelihood that studies can be meaningfully integrated via meta-analysis or other quantitative tech-niques decreases (Murphy, 1994).

A greater diversity of criteria is likely to lead to a welcome change in the way we think and talk about tests. It has long been acceptable to state that "test X is valid," in part because the phrase so clearly implies validity for predicting performance in training and/or on the job. A broader conceptualization of the roles of individual differences should lead researchers to abandon blanket statements about validity and focus instead on the more interest-ing question, "Valid for what?" This will make our communication more difficult and verbose, but statements that limit claims of valid-ity to specific criteria are also more precise and realistic.

Simple Versus Complex Relationships

In the cognitive domain, more is usually better, in the sense that cognitive ability measures typically show a linear relationship with performance (Coward & Sackett, 1990). The same is not true for other individual difference variables; individuals might have too little of, too much of, or the wrong mix of any of a number of noncognitive attributes to function effectively in particular jobs or organizational settings. For example, conscientiousness seems to be related to job performance in a number of jobs (Barrick & Mount, 1991), but an individual who is extremely high on this dimension might be so conventional and rule-bound that he or she cannot function in anything but the most bureaucratic setting.

Unlike the ability-performance relationship, where linearity is the rule, a number of individual difference variables might have nonlinear relationships with criteria of interest. Two specific types of deviations from linearity might be especially common: asymptotic relationships and inverted-U functions. Asymptotic relationships are found in a number of instances, especially where the link between the individual difference variable and the criterion variable in question takes a "deficiency-sufficiency" form. For example, an individual with no color vision might not perform well as an electrician (because wiring is so often color-coded). However, once the individual is able to reliably distinguish colors, further increases in color discrimination ability have little meaning. In other words, an individual with a highly developed sensitivity to color differences is not likely to perform better than an individual with normal color vision. Similarly, people who demonstrate no interpersonal sensitivity might function poorly in virtually all social environments, but the differences between individuals who show a normal level of sensitivity to others' feelings and reactions and those who are very finely attuned to others may be small.

Inverted-U functions occur where there is an optimal level of a particular characteristic and where either too much or too little of that same characteristic can have negative effects. For example, personality characteristics such as extraversion might show inverted-U relationships with a measures of effectiveness in interdependent teams. Introverted individuals might be uncomfortable interacting with or helping others, whereas extreme extraverts might spend most of their time and energy on interacting with other team members and little on doing their own tasks.

The possibility that nonlinear relationships will be encountered puts a premium on careful examination and interpretation of data. Unfortunately, there are good reasons to believe that researchers will not devote the time or the thought needed to choose appropriate methods of analysis or recoding in the presence of nonlinear relationships. I/O psychologists have been relatively inattentive to issues such as the proper handling of outliers (Orr, Sackett, & DuBois, 1991) and missing data (Roth, 1994), and it is reasonable to believe that the same thing will happen with regard to nonlinear relationships. The implication is that many analyses and interpretations of statistics describing relationships between individual difference variables and dependent variables of interest that incorporate strong linearity assumptions will be inaccurate.

Invariant Versus Context-Bound Relationships

The relationship between general cognitive ability and performance is essentially the same in virtually all work environments (it is, in other words, a moderately strong linear relationship), but the effect of individual differences in personality, affective disposition, or orientation might depend substantially on the context. The same attribute (for example, preference for detailed, repetitive work) might be functional in some jobs (for example, accountant) and not in others (for example, linebacker). The effects of personality, disposition, and so on might depend on the composition of the work group (a person who is conventional, for example, might be uncomfortable if other members of the work group are risk takers but might do very well in a more conventionally oriented group), and the relationship between individual differences and group processes and outcomes might change every time a group member transfers in or out. It seems unlikely that measures of personality, affective states, or orientation will show the invariant relationships with dependent variables of interest that have been shown by cognitive ability measures.

It is important to keep in mind that the stability of cognitive test validities across situations once seemed unlikely. It is possible that measures of personality, affect, and so on will show comparable levels of cross-situational stability, but there are some important differences between the body of ability-performance research and the research on other individual difference variables that make such stability less likely. First, as noted earlier, a good deal of information about cognitive ability can be sensibly summarized with a single general-ability measure. This is not true in any of the other domains studied. Most ability-performance studies examine very similar sets of abilities, but studies of personality, affect, interests, and so on are likely to involve wide-ranging sets of constructs. Second, the dependent variables in individual difference research outside of the cognitive domain are likely to vary. Finally, and most important, many of these individual differences are likely to affect interpersonal and group-oriented processes and outcomes, and the exact effects of high or low levels of any particular attribute may depend on the norms, composition, and tasks of the group.

Summary

It seems likely that future research on the roles individual differences play in understanding behavior in organizations will take a radically different direction in the next fifteen to twenty years than it has in the last fifteen to twenty years. Since the late 1970s, the underlying theme in individual difference research has been the pursuit of simplicity, parsimony, and predictive efficiency. Validity generalization research exemplifies the successful pursuit of simplicity and parsimony. This research has produced compelling evidence that ability tests are valid and useful in a wide range of situations and that variables once thought to substantially affect validity (for example, the specific content of the job) may have only minor effects. Studies by Ree, Earles, and colleagues exemplify the successful pursuit of predictive efficiency. These studies show that a simple measure of *g* is often so useful for predicting performance that there is not much meaningful room for improving prediction by adding more cognitive tests.

The goals of simplicity, parsimony, and predictive efficiency might no longer be appropriate as the range of individual differences studied by I/O psychologists expands. Predictive efficiency will not always be relevant, in part because a broader conceptualization of the roles of individual differences implies some ambiguity about exactly what to predict. Simplicity and parsimony might not be easily attained, and efforts to attain them (for example, an attempt to make a blanket statement about the validity of personality tests) will only lead researchers to collapse variables that are conceptually and empirically distinct into relatively meaningless composites. While it might be possible to treat *ability* as a generic term and to use a measure of general cognitive ability as a description of ability levels, it is unlikely that any meaningful general measure of personality, affective disposition, interests, and so on can be developed; and whenever individual differences in these realms are cited as possible causes or outcomes of behavior in organizations, it will be necessary to specify the particular dimensions, contexts, and settings involved.

Individual difference research that goes beyond the traditional ability-performance bounds is likely to be a messy, confusing affair.

Nevertheless, the study of a wider range of individual difference variables and effects holds great promise, and it is likely to significantly advance our thinking, research, and practice in several areas of I/O psychology.

References

Ackerman, P. L., & Humphreys, L. G. (1990). Individual differences theory in industrial and organizational psychology. In M. D. Dunnette & L. M. Hough (Eds.), *Handbook of industrial and organizational psychology* (2nd ed.; Vol. 1, pp. 223–282). Palo Alto, CA: Consulting Psychologists Press.

Allinger, G. M. (1988). Do zero correlations really exist among measures of different cognitive abilities? *Educational and Psychological Measurement, 48*, 275–280.

Astin, A. (1964). Criterion-centered research. *Educational and Psychological Measurement, 24*, 807–822.

Baron, R. A. (1989). Personality and organizational conflict: The Type A behavior pattern and self-monitoring. *Organizational Behavior and Human Decision Processes, 44*, 281–297.

Barrick, M. R., & Mount, M. K. (1991). The Big Five personality dimensions and job performance: A meta-analysis. *Personnel Psychology, 44*, 1–26.

Borman, W. C., & Motowidlo, S. J. (1993). Expanding the criterion domain to include elements of contextual performance. In N. Schmitt, W. Borman, & Associates, *Personnel selection in organizations* (pp. 71–98). San Francisco: Jossey-Bass.

Brief, A. P., & Motowidlo, S. J. (1986). Prosocial organizational behaviors. *Academy of Management Review, 11*, 710–725.

Campbell, J. P. (1990). An overview of the army selection and classification project (Project A). *Personnel Psychology, 43*, 231–239.

Campbell, J. P., McCloy, R. A., Oppler, S. H., & Sager, C. E. (1992). A theory of performance. In N. Schmitt, W. Borman, & Associates, *Personnel selection in organizations* (pp. 35–70). San Francisco: Jossey-Bass.

Carroll, J. B. (1993). *Human cognitive abilities: A survey of factor-analytic studies.* Cambridge, UK: Cambridge University Press.

Carson, R. C. (1989). Personality. *Annual Review of Psychology, 40*, 227–248.

Cattell, R. B. (1963). Theory of fluid and crystallized intelligence: A critical experiment. *Journal of Experimental Education, 54*, 1–22.

Coward, W. M., & Sackett, P. R. (1990). Linearity of ability-performance relationships: A reconfirmation. *Journal of Applied Psychology, 75*, 297–300.

Davis-Blake, A., & Pfeffer, J. (1989). Just a mirage: The search for dispositional effects in organizational research. *Academy of Management Review, 14,* 385–400.

Digman, J. M. (1990). Personality structure: Emergence of the Five-Factor Model. *Annual Review of Psychology, 41,* 417–440.

Edwards, J. E., and Morrison, R. F. (1994). Selecting and classifying future naval officers: The paradox of greater specialization in broader arenas. In M. Rumsey, C. Walker, & J. Harris (Eds.), *Personnel selection and classification* (pp. 69–84). Newbury Park, CA: Sage.

Eysenck, H. J. (1979). *The structure and measurement of intelligence.* Baltimore, MD: University Park Press.

Fiedler, F. E., & Garcia, J. E. (1987). *New approaches to effective leadership: Cognitive resources and organizational performance.* New York: Wiley.

Fiedler, K., & Forgas, J. P. (1988). *Affect, cognition, and social behavior.* Toronto: Hogrefe International.

Forgas, J. P. (1992). Affect in social judgments and decisions: A multiprocess model. In M. Zanna (Ed.), *Advances in experimental social psychology* (Vol. 25, pp. 227–275). San Diego, CA: Academic Press.

Frank, L. K. (1939). Projective methods for the study of personality. *Journal of Psychology, 8,* 389–409.

Gerhart, B. (1987). How important are dispositional factors as determinants of job satisfaction? Implications for job design and other personnel programs. *Journal of Applied Psychology, 72,* 366–373.

Gould, S. J. (1981). *The mismeasure of man.* New York: W. W. Norton.

Guilford, J. P. (1988). Some changes in the structure-of-intellect model. *Educational and Psychological Measurement, 48,* 1–4.

Guion, R. M., & Gottier, R. F. (1965). Validity of personality measures in personnel selection. *Personnel Psychology, 18,* 135–164.

Guttman, L., & Levy, S. (1991). Two structural laws for intelligence tests. *Intelligence, 15,* 79–103.

Hough, L. M., Eaton, N. K., Dunnette, M. D., Kamp, J. D., & McCloy, R. A. (1991). Criterion-related validities of personality constructs and the effects of response distortion on those validities. *Journal of Applied Psychology, 75,* 581–595.

Humphreys, L. G. (1979). The construct of general intelligence. *Intelligence, 3,* 105–120.

Hunt, E. B., & Pellegrin, J. W. (1985). Using interactive computing to expand intelligence testing. *Intelligence, 9,* 206–236.

Hunter, J. E. (1986). Cognitive ability, cognitive aptitudes, job knowledge, and job performance. *Journal of Vocational Behavior, 29,* 340–362.

Hunter, J. E., & Hirsh, H. R. (1987). Applications of meta-analysis. In C. L.

Cooper & I. T. Robertson (Eds.), *International review of industrial and organizational psychology* (pp. 321–357). New York: Wiley.

Hunter, J. E., & Hunter, R. F. (1984). Validity and utility of alternate predictors of job performance. *Psychological Bulletin, 96,* 72–98.

Isen, A. M., & Baron, R. A. (1991). Positive affect as a factor in organizational behavior. In B. M. Staw & L. L. Cummings (Eds.), *Research in organizational behavior* (Vol. 13, pp. 1–53). Greenwich, CT: JAI Press.

James, L. R., & James, L. A. (1992). Psychological climate and affect: Test of a hierarchical dynamic model. In C. J. Cranny, P. C. Smith, & E. F. Stone (Eds.), *Job satisfaction: How people feel about their jobs and how it affects their performance* (pp. 89–117). New York: Lexington Books.

Jensen, A. R. (1980). *Bias in mental testing.* New York: Free Press.

Judge, T. A. (1992). The dispositional perspective in human resources research. In G. Ferris & K. Rowland (Eds.), *Research in personnel and human resource management* (Vol. 10, pp. 31–72). Greenwich, CT: JAI Press.

Landy, F. J. (1985). *Psychology of work behavior* (3rd ed.). Belmont, CA: Dorsey Press.

Landy, F. J., Shankster, L. J., & Kohler, S. S. (1994). Personnel selection and placement. *Annual Review of Psychology,* 45, 261–296.

Lent, R. W., Brown, S. D., & Hackett, G. (1994). Toward a unifying social cognitive theory of career and academic interest, choice, and performance. *Journal of Vocational Behavior, 45,* 79–122.

Mathieu, J. E., & Zajac, D. M. (1990). A review and meta-analysis of the antecedents, correlates, and consequences of organizational commitment. *Psychological Bulletin, 108,* 171–194.

McClelland, D. C. (1993). Intelligence is not the best predictor of job performance. *Current Directions in Psychological Science, 2,* 5–6.

Murphy, K. R. (1989). Dimensions of job performance. In R. Dillon & J. Pelligrino (Eds.), *Testing: Applied and theoretical perspectives* (pp. 218–247). New York: Praeger.

Murphy, K. R. (1994). Advances in meta-analysis and validity generalization. In N. Anderson & P. Herriot (Eds.), *Handbook of selection and appraisal: First update and supplement,* 1994 (pp. 57–76). Chichester, UK: Wiley.

Orr, J. M., Sackett, P. R., & DuBois, C.L.Z. (1991). Outlier detection and treatment in I/O psychology: A survey of researcher beliefs and an empirical illustration. *Personnel Psychology, 44,* 473–486.

Osgood, C. E. (1962). Studies on the generality of affective meaning systems. *American Psychologist, 17,* 10–28.

Ottaviani, R., & Beck, A. T. (1988). Cognitive theory of depression. In K. Fiedler & J. P. Forgas (Eds.), *Affect, cognition, and social behavior* (pp. 209–218). Toronto: Hogrefe International.

Ozer, D. J., & Reise, S. P. (1994). Personality assessment. *Annual Review of Psychology, 45,* 357–388.

Pennebaker, J. W. (1982). *The psychology of physical symptoms.* New York: Springer-Verlag.

Pervin, L. A. (1980). *Personality theory and assessment.* New York: Wiley.

Pervin, L. A. (1985). Personality: Current controversies, issues, and directions. *Annual Review of Psychology, 36,* 83–114.

Plomin, R., & Rende, R. (1991). Human behavioral genetics. *Annual Review of Psychology, 84,* 782–799.

Ree, M. J., & Carretta, T. R. (1994). The correlation of general cognitive ability and psychomotor tracking tests. *International Journal of Selection and Assessment, 2,* 209–216.

Ree, M. J., & Earles, J. A. (1991a). Predicting training success: Not much more than g. *Personnel Psychology, 44,* 321–332.

Ree, M. J., & Earles, J. A. (1991b). The stability of g across different methods of estimation. *Intelligence, 15,* 271–278.

Ree, M. J., & Earles, J. A. (1992). Intelligence is the best predictor of job performance. *Current Directions in Psychological Science, 1,* 86–89.

Ree, M. J., Earles, J. A., & Teachout, M. S. (1994). Predicting job performance: Not much more than g. *Journal of Applied Psychology, 79,* 518–524.

Rokeach, M. (1979). *Understanding human values: Individual and social.* New York: Free Press.

Rorer, L. G., & Widigor, T. A. (1983). Personality structure and assessment. *Annual Review of Psychology, 34,* 431–463.

Roth, P. L. (1994). Missing data: A conceptual review for applied psychologists. *Personnel Psychology, 47,* 537–560.

Schmidt, F. L., Ones, D. O., & Hunter, J. E. (1992). Personnel selection. *Annual Review of Psychology, 43,* 627–670.

Smith, C. A., Organ, D. W., & Near, J. P. (1983). Organizational citizenship behavior: Its nature and antecedents. *Journal of Applied Psychology, 68,* 653–663.

Spearman, C. (1904). The proof and measurement of association between two things. *American Journal of Psychology, 15,* 72–101.

Spearman, C. (1927). *The abilities of man.* New York: Macmillan.

Sternberg, R. J. (1977). *Intelligence, information processing, and analogical reasoning: The componential analysis of human abilities.* Hillsdale, NJ: Erlbaum.

Sternberg, R. J. (1984). What should intelligence tests test? Implications of a triarchic theory of intelligence for intelligence testing. *Educational Research, 13,* 5–15.

Sternberg, R. J. (1985). *Beyond IQ: A triarchic theory of human intelligence.* New York: Cambridge University Press.

Sternberg, R. J., & Detterman, D. K. (1986). *What is intelligence?* Norwood, NJ: ABLEX.

Sternberg, R. J., & Wagner, R. K. (1993). The g-ocentric view of intelligence and performance is wrong. *Current Directions in Psychological Science, 2,* 1–5.

Strong, E. K. (1943). *Vocational interests of men and women.* Stanford, CA: Stanford University Press.

Tett, R. P., Jackson, D. N., & Rothstein, M. (1991). Personality measures as predictors of job performance: A meta-analytic review. *Personnel Psychology, 44,* 703–742.

Thornton, G. C. (1992). *Assessment centers in human resource management.* Reading, MA: Addison-Wesley.

Thurstone, L. L. (1938). *Primary mental abilities* (Psychometric Monographs No. 1). Chicago: University of Chicago Press.

Vandenberg, S. G., & Vogler, G. P. (1985). Genetic determinants of intelligence. In B. Wolman (Ed.), *Handbook of intelligence* (pp. 3–57). New York: Wiley.

Vernon, P. E. (1960). *The structure of human abilities* (rev. ed.). London: Methuen.

Wernimont, P. F., & Campbell, J. P. (1968). Signs, samples, and criteria. *Journal of Applied Psychology, 52,* 372–376.

Zajonc, R. B. (1980). Feeling and thinking: Preferences need no inferences. *American Psychologist, 25,* 151–175.

Zanna, M. P., & Rempel, J. K. (1988). Attitudes: A new look at an old concept. In D. Bar-Tal & A. Kruglanski (Eds.), *The social psychology of knowledge* (pp. 314–334). New York: Cambridge University Press.

Chapter Two

Personality Traits, Taxonomies, and Applications in Organizations

Leaetta M. Hough
Robert J. Schneider

Personality has had a phoenixlike existence in industrial and organizational (I/O) psychology in the United States. Currently, it is enjoying a rebirth. From the mid 1960s to the early 1990s, many psychologists—particularly those in academe—thought that personality variables were unimportant individual difference characteristics. In spite of the less than respectable position that personality variables held in academic I/O psychology during that time, however, many I/O practitioners advocated the use of, used, and investigated the usefulness of personality variables in work settings. This is an area in which I/O practitioners led our field.

Background: A Short History

Theoretical, empirical, and practical issues converged in the 1960s to discredit personality variables and their use in work settings. A

Note: We gratefully acknowledge Jack Block, Marvin Dunnette, Lewis Goldberg, Robert Hogan, Oliver John, Robert McCrae, Kevin Murphy, Deniz Ones, Richard Robins, and Sheldon Zedeck for their helpful comments on an earlier draft of this chapter.

rebirth occurred as a result of programmatic research that demonstrated the usefulness of personality variables for describing, explaining, and predicting behavior.

Demise of Personality Variables

Mischel published a highly influential book in 1968 that precipitated an intense examination of and debate over trait conceptions. He argued that traits are an illusion, that behavior is explained more by differences in situations than differences in people. Guion (1965) and Guion and Gottier (1965) reviewed criterion-related validities of personality variables and concluded that the empirical evidence suggested that personality variables have little or no systematic relationship to the criterion variables relevant to I/O psychologists. About the same time, Ghiselli (1966) published a book entitled *The Validity of Occupational Aptitude Tests*. In it, he summarized criterion-related validities of various types of predictors, including personality variables. He summarized the validities according to type of job and included only those variables for which the "trait seemed pertinent to the job in question" (p. 21). The median uncorrected validity for personality variables across the different job types was a respectable .24. (See Ghiselli, 1966, Tables 3.1 to 3.8.) Unfortunately, Ghiselli neglected to indicate how he determined which traits were pertinent to the job in question. His review of the criterion-related validities of personality variables was largely ignored.

While psychologists worried about theoretical and empirical issues, the American public was concerned about invasion of privacy. Some, though not all, personality scales asked questions about bodily functions and religious intensity—questions that many people considered offensive. People resented being asked to respond to such survey items. In addition, many psychologists were concerned that personality scales might be viewed as inappropriate or unfair for people protected under the federal Civil Rights Act of 1964. Furthermore, all groups—academic psychologists, I/O practitioners, and their clients—were concerned about intentional distortion of self-descriptions in an applicant/evaluative setting.

These forces, in combination, conspired against personality variables and caused their virtual demise in I/O psychology. Nevertheless, during the dark period between the 1960s and 1990s, many practitioners continued to use and research personality variables. Among the significant programmatic efforts were those by Bray (Bray & Howard, 1983) and Bentz (1984). Many management consultants also understood the importance of personality variables for their clients and continued to measure personality characteristics as a part of their multifaceted, whole-person assessment of job candidates.

Rebirth

By the late 1980s, the person-versus-situation debate was largely over. The zeitgeist of situationism that followed the publication of Mischel's book (1968) had shifted. Summarizing the large amount of research addressing the person-versus-situation issue, Kenrick and Funder (1988) concluded that evidence supports the following statements: (1) traits are not merely illusions; (2) traits are not merely in the eye of the beholder; (3) traits are not merely artifacts of base-rate accuracy; (4) traits are not merely artifacts of shared stereotypes; (5) traits are not simply by-products of situational consistencies; and (6) the magnitude of the relationships between traits and behavior is not inconsequential. They point out, however, that the new zeitgeist is not a "pure trait" position. They state that "systematic sources of judgmental bias, systematic effects of situations, and systematic interactions between persons and situations must be explicitly dealt with before we can predict from trait measures" (p. 31).

The situation-trait debate produced some important tips for predicting behavior from traits. One of the most important lessons (which was well understood by Ghiselli) is that the trait under investigation needs to be relevant to the criterion measure. For I/O psychologists, this means that both predictor and criterion measures need to be conceptualized as constructs and that both the predictor and the criterion (job performance) space need to be conceptualized as multidimensional.

Within this more trait-friendly environment, I/O personality researchers began to gather evidence to bolster the acceptance of personality traits. Meta-analytic studies of the criterion-related validities of personality variables clearly demonstrated the usefulness of personality variables for predicting important work criteria (for example, Barrick & Mount, 1991; Hough, 1989, 1992; Kamp & Hough, 1986; McDaniel & Frei, 1994; Ones, Viswesvaran, & Schmidt, 1993). Research also demonstrated that distortion in self-descriptions may not adversely affect criterion-related validities (Hough, Eaton, Dunnette, Kamp, & McCloy, 1990). Moreover, meta-analytic evidence suggested that most personality variables have significantly less adverse impact against protected classes than cognitive ability variables do (Feingold, 1994; Hough, 1996; Ones et al., 1993; Sackett, Burris, & Callahan, 1989).

A critically important difference between the earlier Guion (1965) and Guion and Gottier (1965) reviews and the more recent reviews is the new strategy of clustering personality scales into groups that measure reasonably similar personality characteristics. Both Barrick and Mount (1991) and Hough and her colleagues (Hough, 1989, 1992; Hough et al., 1990; Kamp & Hough, 1986) used personality taxonomies to guide their classification of personality scales. Although these researchers used different taxonomies, their exploration of personality-performance relationships within, rather than across, personality constructs revealed statistically and practically significant relationships where they had not been revealed before.

New multidimensional conceptualizations of job performance have also been critically important in highlighting the relevance of personality variables for predicting job performance. J. P. Campbell's model of job performance (1990; see also J. P. Campbell, McCloy, Oppler, & Sager, 1993) and Borman and Motowidlo's distinction between task and contextual performance (1993) are both important contributions to this largely overlooked domain of study. It is now clear that personality variables correlate differently with different job performance constructs (Day & Silverman, 1989; Gellatly, Paunonen, Meyer, Jackson, & Goffin, 1991; Hough, 1989, 1992; Hough et al., 1990; Kamp & Hough, 1986; McHenry, Hough, Toquam, Hanson, & Ashworth, 1990). Failure to take into account the multidimensionality of job performance undoubtedly led to underestimates of the predictiveness of personality variables in work settings.

The U.S. economy in the late twentieth century was also a factor in the rebirth of personality variables in I/O psychology. Today significantly more than half of the U.S. economy is considered a service economy (Albrecht & Zemke, 1985). This growth in the service sector has affected how I/O psychologists define and measure job performance. For many jobs, customer service is now an important, if not the most important, performance criterion. The evidence that personality variables predict customer service on the job (McDaniel & Frei, 1994) has further enhanced the recognition that personality variables are important to I/O psychologists.

Focus of This Chapter

Now that personality has found new life in I/O psychology, the nature of I/O personality research has changed. The most pressing research question is no longer simply whether personality predicts job performance. Researchers now address more subtle research issues, such as the merits of different taxonomies, the predictability and construct validity of compound personality variables (measures that are combinations of basic personality variables—see discussion below), and factors that affect the personality-performance relationship.

This chapter focuses initially on taxonomic issues. We present a very brief history of the Five-Factor Model (FFM), a set of criteria against which to evaluate a taxonomy of basic personality variables, and an evaluation of the FFM using those criteria. We then turn to applied issues. We review criterion-related validities of compound personality variables such as integrity and customer service orientation. Then we analyze factors that affect criterion-related validity (that is, moderator variables). We describe research on type of job, criterion construct, criterion measurement method, validation strategy, type of situation, and rater perspective and conclude that they are nonmythical moderator variables (that is, they moderate criterion-related validities of personality variables). We describe research on social desirability and administration mode (paper and pencil versus computer) and conclude they are mythical moderator variables (that is, they do not moderate criterion-related validities of personality variables).

Taxonomic Issues: The Structure of Personality

Taxonomies are critically important to the advancement of science. By classifying scientific phenomena into taxons using an appropriate similarity measure, taxonomies facilitate the organization and accumulation of knowledge, hypothesis generation, efficient communication among scientists, and retrieval of information (Fleishman & Quaintance, 1984). Moreover, the description of scientific phenomena afforded by taxonomies usually precedes (and facilitates) their explanation. In this sense, the development of an adequate taxonomy is an important milestone in the maturing of a science.

It is personality taxonomies that have provided the organizing principles that have enabled personality researchers to establish relationships between personality constructs (taxons) and important life- and job-related criteria—relationships that had been obscured previously because correlation coefficients were summarized across taxons (that is, personality constructs). Yet I/O personality researchers have used different taxonomies to organize and summarize their data, and different conclusions have resulted (compare Barrick & Mount, 1991; Hough, 1992; Hough et al., 1990). Thus, while having a taxonomy is important, the nature of the taxonomy is also important.

Many respected personality psychologists appear to assume that the FFM—described below—is an adequate taxonomy for I/O psychology (for example, Costa & McCrae, 1995a; Digman, 1990; Goldberg, 1990, 1993a; Goldberg & Saucier, 1995; John, 1990; McCrae & John, 1992; McCrae & Costa, 1987, in press). Certainly, the FFM has been shown to be useful as an organizing taxonomy for I/O personality research (Barrick & Mount, 1991; Ones, Schmidt, & Viswesvaran, 1994). And yet a number of researchers have expressed skepticism regarding the adequacy of the FFM (Block, 1995; H. J. Eysenck, 1991; Hough, 1992; Pervin, 1994; Schneider & Hough, 1995; Tellegen, 1993; Waller & Ben-Porath, 1987).

The taxonomy that I/O psychologists use makes a difference. Indeed, conclusions about the usefulness of personality and the nature of the personality-performance relationship depend upon the taxonomy used. We therefore devote considerable time to taxonomic issues in this chapter. In this section, we briefly review the history of the FFM, articulate criteria for a basic personality taxonomy, and then evaluate the FFM against those criteria. (For detailed reviews of the history of the FFM, interested readers are referred to Block, 1995; John, 1990; and John, Angleitner, and Ostendorf, 1988.)

History of the Five-Factor Model

The birth of the FFM can be traced to Sir Francis Galton's idea (1884) that the task of scientifically describing personality should begin with the identification of the words in dictionaries that people use to describe one another. This methodology is typically referred to as the "lexical" approach. Allport and Odbert (1936) ultimately identified 17,953 such words, to which Cattell (1943, 1945) applied then state-of-the-art data reduction techniques. Ultimately, Cattell reduced Allport and Odbert's list of personality descriptors to thirty-five.

Several researchers sought to derive a theoretically meaningful structure from data sets based on Cattell's thirty-five variables. Tupes and Christal (1961/1992) are credited with discovery of the FFM as we now know it. They labeled their five factors Surgency, Agreeableness, Dependability, Emotional Stability, and Culture. Subsequent replications of Tupes and Christal's findings were reported by Norman (1963) and Digman and Takemoto-Chock (1981). Other researchers have used a variety of labels for these five factors. For example, Surgency is often referred to as Extraversion; Dependability is often referred to as Conscientiousness; Emotional Stability as adjustment or Neuroticism; Culture as Openness to Experience, Intellect, or Intellectance.

Goldberg (1990) made a major contribution by rediscovering the FFM from a data set not based on Cattell's set of thirty-five trait-descriptors; and Costa and McCrae's development of the NEO-Personality Inventory (NEO-PI; Costa & McCrae, 1985, 1992) brought the FFM into the realm of questionnaires. Costa and McCrae systematically related the NEO-PI to most of the major measures of personality and showed that the FFM could indeed account for much of the variance in these other respected measures. Whether it satisfactorily accounted for virtually all of that variance has been a matter of debate (for example, Block, 1995; Goldberg & Saucier, 1995; McCrae & Costa, 1994, in press; R. J. Schneider & Hough, 1995; Tellegen, 1993).

Recently, thoughtful discussions of the limitations of the FFM have been appearing (for example, Block, 1995; McAdams, 1992; Pervin, 1994). Meanwhile, research on the FFM has continued in a number of areas, including the cross-cultural replicability of the five factors (for example, Bond, 1994), the identification of lower-order facets of the factors (Costa, McCrae, & Dye, 1991; Costa & McCrae, 1995b), external correlates of the factors (for example, Barrick & Mount, 1991; Freidman et al., 1993; Tett, Jackson, & Rothstein, 1991), and the heritability of the FFM factors (Bergeman et al., 1993; Gilbert & Ones, 1995a, 1995b; Loehlin, 1992).

Given the extensive history and research base of the FFM, should I/O psychology embrace it as its basic personality taxonomy? Careful consideration of this issue requires that we first consider appropriate criteria for a basic personality taxonomy.

Criteria for a Taxonomy of Basic Personality Constructs

Largely on the basis of work by H. J. Eysenck (1991), we suggest that, at a minimum, a basic personality taxonomy should (1) consist of traits that have been replicated, (2) be comprehensive, (3) consist of traits that have external correlates, (4) consist of source traits, and (5) consist of multiple levels of traits. Any basic personality taxonomy that is a contender for use by a specialty area should be evaluated on at least these five criteria.

Replicability of Taxons

Replication is a staple of the scientific method. Ideally, an acceptable personality taxonomy should consist of a set of traits that have been replicated across samples, subgroups, time, cultures, languages, measurement strategies (for example, self-report versus peer report), and data-analytic methods. Some replication failures are, of course, more serious than others. For example, failure to replicate a set of traits across a period of two weeks calls into question whether the taxonomy consists of personality traits. Similarly, failure to replicate the traits in a taxonomy across data-analytic strategies is strong evidence against the adequacy of a taxonomy. On the other hand, failure to replicate cross-culturally, though unfortunate, merely limits the generalizability of one or more traits in a taxonomy. (It is, of course, conceivable that some traits are culture-specific while others are universal.)

Comprehensiveness of Taxonomy

A personality taxonomy should provide for the classification of all known personality traits. This is not the same thing as saying that the taxonomy should include all personality traits. Even the Periodic Table of Elements is not comprehensive in that way; new elements may be discovered at any time. The point of this criterion is that, other things being equal, if taxonomy A includes known personality traits that taxonomy B does not, taxonomy A is preferable to taxonomy B.

Existence of External Correlates

It is imperative that each of the personality variables embedded in a personality taxonomy relate to important real-world outcomes. What Lubinski and Dawis (1992) said in the context of cognitive abilities is equally true of personality constructs: "For a psychological construct to be scientifically significant, measures of the construct must not only display a respectable degree of internal consistency and replicability, but they must also relate to an array of meaningful psychological criteria. That is, they must display relationships with external criteria that we are interested in predicting and understanding" (p. 5). Indeed, the quality of a trait can be determined in part on the basis of its ability to generate accurate behavioral predictions—particularly predictions of behaviors for which the personality correlates have not been previously established. We can evaluate alternative trait concepts by comparing them in terms of the number of behavioral criteria they can explain and predict. If a given trait can explain all of the behavioral phenomena that other, alternative traits can explain, in addition to some others that they cannot, then that trait can be considered superior (Lakatos, 1970). The alternative traits are deemed falsified even though they are not literally "false" (Meehl, 1990).

Conceptualization of Taxons as Source Traits

Drawing on the work of Cattell (1946), Meehl (1986) distinguished between traits that are comprised of (1) sets of responses that are similar in content and (2) sets of responses that may be dissimilar in content but nevertheless covary because of the presence of an inferred internal entity. The former are surface traits; the latter are source traits. Surface traits are purely descriptive, whereas source traits, by definition, invoke an explanatory mechanism that can be used to predict novel phenomena. Source traits therefore are more likely to advance our science, since they facilitate theory formulation as well as description.

A personality taxonomy that consists of source traits will benefit practice as well as theory. Movement from description, based on phenotypic personality traits, to explanation, based on genotypic personality traits, will lead to greater predictive power (Fleishman & Quaintance, 1984). The more we know about a trait, the greater our ability to determine how and when it will manifest itself. If a taxonomy consists of surface traits, one knows only that the traits "predict" the phenotypic indicators of which their measures are comprised. By positing an explanatory mechanism, psychologists are in a position to make informed guesses regarding the relationships between a trait and many behaviors not directly included in the current operationalization of the trait. The accuracy of those guesses will improve as the nomological net in which the trait is embedded, which articulates the essence of the construct (Cronbach & Meehl, 1955), is elaborated.

Inclusion of Multiple Levels of Specificity

Personality traits differ in their level of specificity (see, for example, Costa & McCrae, 1995b; Goldberg, 1993b; Hampson, John, & Goldberg, 1986; R. Hogan & J. Hogan, 1992). An adequate personality taxonomy should reflect this fact. This is not to say that a personality taxonomy should be strictly hierarchical; in fact, data discussed below suggest that the structure of personality traits is not strictly hierarchical. A latticelike structure—one in which lower-order facets are multiply determined by more than one higher-order trait—appears to provide a more accurate description of personality. Regardless of what the true structure turns out to be, it is clear that a personality taxonomy at only one level of specificity is unnecessarily truncated. Consensus will be harder to achieve at lower (more specific) levels of personality description than at the highest level, but such consensus is extremely important to the advancement of personality theory and research.

Evaluating the Five-Factor Model

In this section, we evaluate the FFM against each of the taxonomic criteria set forth in the previous section.

Replicability of Taxons

The replicability of the FFM has been touted as one of its biggest selling points, and indeed the FFM has been replicated many times across several decades and numerous samples. In addition, the FFM has emerged from both self-report and peer-report data, across various factor extraction and rotation methods (Goldberg, 1990), and in both adjective rating and questionnaire data. The fifth factor is problematic in that it differs in the adjective and questionnaire data, but this difference appears simply to be a function of the fact that the FFM questionnaire research used a slightly different pool of items, leading to the "discovery" of an Openness to Experience factor rather than an Intellect (or Intellectance) factor. Finally, some data indicate that the FFM emerges in different cultures. Bond (1994), for example, argues that factor analysis of ratings of translated FFM descriptors shows that at least four factors in the FFM (Openness to Experience is the exception) are replicable in various Oriental languages (for example, Mandarin Chinese, Japanese, and Hong Kong Chinese).

We acknowledge that the FFM has been shown to be highly replicable in many contexts. We feel that it is important, however, to add some cautionary notes. First, as Block (1995) has observed, the FFM was derived from factor-analytic research. Replication across different scientific methods would be desirable. Replication across different factor-analytic extraction and rotation methods does not constitute strong replication, because factor indeterminacy and dependence on the correlation coefficient as a structuring statistic are common to all extraction and rotation methods. Furthermore, as Cudeck (1989) pointed out, factor analysis assumes linear regressions. Such an assumption may not fit personality data as well as, say, ability data. The use of other multivariate methods, such as multidimensional scaling or cluster analysis, would be informative, as would the use of experimental methods that attempt to unconfound, refine, and/or expand the FFM by investigating the cognitive and physiological underpinnings of personality. The use of these additional methodologies should, of course, be supplemented with careful and informed theoretical reflection.

In addition, it has yet to be established that the FFM factors are cross-culturally replicable when indigenous lexical terms are used to generate personality data (a so-called emic strategy). For example, Ostendorf and Angleitner (1993) did a lexical study using trait-descriptive adjectives culled from a German dictionary and found more than five personality dimensions. Yang and Bond (1990) investigated the structure of personality trait–descriptors in Chinese. While they found five factors, the overlap of those factors with the U.S. FFM was only moderate (and in the case of one of the Chinese factors, there was very little overlap). De Raad and Szirmák (1994) did a lexical study using Hungarian trait-descriptors. They found reasonably good replications of Extraversion, Agreeableness, Conscientiousness, and Emotional Stability. They were not able, however, to replicate Openness to Experience (Intellectance); and in a five-component solution, they found a dimension not included in the U.S. FFM, which they labeled Integrity.

In sum, the FFM has shown impressive replicability in some areas, but it needs further replication in others. The five factors have been replicated across time and samples, across self and peer data, and across adjective and questionnaire data. However, they need to be replicated using scientific methods other than factor analysis. In addition, the FFM has shown evidence of cross-cultural replicability, but the status of the five factors as cross-cultural universals has by no means been established.

Comprehensiveness of Taxonomy

The comprehensiveness of the FFM has been vigorously challenged. Its challenges can be classified into two types: one type argues that some of the FFM factors are too broad to be cohesive and thereby confound two or more highest-order personality traits; the second type argues that additional traits that fall outside the scope of the current FFM are necessary to describe personality.

R. Hogan (1982) argues that extraversion, as assessed by the FFM, confounds sociability and ambition. He notes that sociability and ambition are conceptually distinct, are associated with different goals, and intercorrelate only about .30. Similarly, Hough and her colleagues (Hough, 1989, 1992; Hough et al., 1990; Kamp & Hough, 1986) argue that extraversion confounds affiliation and potency/surgency. In their effort to classify personality scales, they obtained 157 correlations between affiliation and potency/surgency scales; the mean correlation between scales operationalizing the two constructs was .09, suggesting that affiliation scales are independent of potency/surgency scales.

Hough (1992) also argues that the FFM confounds achievement with both extraversion and conscientiousness. Different conceptualizations of the FFM include achievement in different factors. In Tupes and Christal's (1961/1992) original FFM, achievement is confounded with surgency. In later conceptualizations (Digman & Inouye, 1986; Goldberg, 1990; McCrae, Costa, & Busch, 1986), achievement is confounded with conscientiousness. Indeed, Digman and Inouye (1986) label their conscientiousness factor Will to Achieve.

Past associations between achievement and extraversion are probably due to the fact that FFM Extraversion is so broad that it encompasses constructs such as dominance, ambition, and ascendance—constructs to which achievement is highly related. The degree of association between achievement and extraversion, however, is actually quite low. Tellegen and Waller (in press), for example, reported a correlation of .07 between the Multidimensional Personality Questionnaire (MPQ; Tellegen, 1982) Achievement scale and the Extraversion scale in their "Big Seven" questionnaire.

Achievement has as little (or as much) in common with conscientiousness as it does with extraversion. In Costa and McCrae's NEO-PI-R, the Conscientiousness factor includes Achievement Striving and Competence as facet scales. These facets, both of which relate to R. W. White's concept of effectance (1959), are quite dissimilar from the other NEO-PI-R Conscientiousness facets: Dutifulness, Order, Self-discipline, and Deliberation. Achievement Striving and Competence involve self-expansive striving, whereas the other facets of Conscientiousness involve self-restrictive caution and conventionality. Achievement striving and competence involve setting one's own goals to further master one's environment (see also Dweck's construct of mastery orientation, 1986), whereas the other facets of Conscientiousness involve adapting to goals set by others. Work by Tellegen (1985), discussed in more detail below, suggests that Achievement/Competence and the set of other facets of NEO-PI-R Conscientiousness may actually be subserved by entirely different psychobiological substrates—one involving sensitivity to reward and the other involving sensitivity to unconditioned aversive stimuli.

Hough and her colleagues (Hough, 1989, 1992; Hough et al., 1990; Kamp & Hough, 1986) argue that more than five basic personality traits are necessary if prediction is the goal. They argue that the FFM not only confounds basic traits (see above) but also fails to include additional basic traits. Their nine-factor taxonomy evolved using first theory and then data to modify and refine it. Hough and her colleagues began by attempting to classify existing personality scales into the FFM factors. Quickly, however, they switched to R. Hogan's six-factor taxonomy (1982) as their provisional taxonomy because, in their experience, sociability and ambition correlated differently with job performance criteria. When it became clear that a number of scales did not fit within any of Hogan's six constructs, Hough and her colleagues created a miscellaneous category. They summarized criterion-related validities within each taxon and found that the highest validities appeared in the miscellaneous category. Examination and classification of personality scales in the miscellaneous category revealed the presence of additional constructs: rugged individualism (masculinity/ femininity) and achievement. Hough (1992) has shown that all their constructs correlate differently and meaningfully with various criteria. In sum, their data indicate that, for predicting criteria important to I/O psychologists, the personality taxonomy should include rugged individualism, and the constructs of extraversion and conscientiousness should be divided into dependability, affiliation, achievement, and potency/surgency.

Work by Costa and McCrae also suggests the existence of additional factors not included in the FFM. Costa and McCrae (1988) explored the structure of the Personality Research Form (PRF; Jackson, 1984), a measure of Murray's catalog of needs (1938). They did a joint principal components analysis of the PRF and their own NEO-PI (Costa & McCrae, 1985), a prominent measure of the FFM. Though they presented only a five-component solution, they noted that a seven-component solution was also justifiable. One of the additional components contrasted autonomy with succorance and social recognition. Costa and McCrae argued that this component was a facet of FFM Neuroticism (also called Emotional Stability). Another possibility, however, is that it is part of a broader masculinity/femininity construct.

FFM advocates argue that masculinity/femininity can be adequately represented within the factor space of the FFM—primarily by Agreeableness and Neuroticism (Goldberg, personal communication, Nov. 2, 1994; McCrae & John, 1992; McCrae, Costa, & Piedmont, 1993). Yet when Hofstee, de Raad, & Goldberg (1992) used principal components analysis to place the adjectives *masculine* and *feminine* in the FFM factor space, the five factors accounted for only 15 percent and 13 percent of the variance, respectively (Goldberg, personal communication, Mar. 21, 1995). Based on this, we suggest that masculinity/femininity is not adequately accounted for in the FFM.

It is also yet to be established that the FFM can account for all of the personality disorders. Soldz, Budman, Demby, and Merry (1993) regressed measures of the personality disorders on a measure of the FFM using a sample of 102 patients with chronic personality difficulties. Their analyses indicate that the FFM accounts for a moderate amount of the variance in several of the personality disorder measures. The FFM accounts for little variance, however, in the case of the paranoid, antisocial, dependent, obsessive compulsive, and sadistic personality disorders.

It is likely that at least some of these personality disorders are compounds of several personality variables (R. Hogan, personal communication, Apr. 15, 1995). If so, the implication is that as yet unspecified personality dimensions are needed to adequately account for those disorders. We suggest that these yet-to-be-specified dimensions are the "dark matter" of the personality universe and wonder if they constitute as large a percentage of the personality universe as the dark matter studied by astrophysicists does of the astronomical universe (Lemonick & Nash, 1995).

Personality dimensions beyond the FFM factors have also emerged in analyses of the California Q-Set (CAQ; Block, 1961). The CAQ was developed from the descriptive language of contemporary psychological clinicians—the language of experts—whereas the FFM was derived from the language of laypeople. Lanning (1994) performed a principal components analysis of ratings of 940 individuals who had been rated on the CAQ by five to eight judges. He used several different methods to suggest an appropriate number of components to retain. These criteria suggested solutions that ranged from five to fifteen dimensions. The eight-component solution consisted of five components that corresponded fairly well to the FFM factors. The remaining three were labeled Attractiveness, Insight, and Ambition. Attractiveness was defined by variables such as "physically attractive" and "heterosexual interest." Insight was defined by variables such as "assesses others' motives," "socially perceptive," "aware of own motives," and "aware of impression made." Ambition was defined by variables such as "aspiration level," "values own autonomy," and "productive." These three additional dimensions were also found in another factor analysis of the CAQ reported by McCrae, Costa, and Busch (1986).

Attractiveness does not appear to be a personality trait. Ambition, however, appears similar to Hogan's ambition and Hough's achievement. Insight, which appears to be more accurately labeled "social insight," is a more problematic case. It may well be worth considering as an additional personality variable, despite its partial overlap with cognitive ability (Gough, 1965; Riggio, Messamer, & Throckmorton, 1991; see Schneider, 1992, for a summary of relevant research). Indeed, the FFM's Openness to Experience (or Intellectance) factor also overlaps with cognitive ability. On the other hand, it is also possible that social insight is a compound consisting of cognitive ability and several personality variables already included in the FFM. Further research is needed to determine whether social insight merits consideration as an additional major personality dimension.

It is also important to examine relationships between the FFM and constructs such as Loevinger's ego development (Loevinger, 1966, 1976). That construct is measured on an ordinal scale consisting of stages (for example, impulsive, opportunistic, conformist, conscientious, autonomous, and integrated), where each stage "builds on, incorporates, and transmutes the previous one" (Loevinger, 1966, p. 264). Development moves from a self-orientation and barren inner life to increasingly rich and differentiated (1) thoughts about self and others, (2) interpersonal relationships, (3) acceptance and tolerance for paradox and contradiction, and (4) sense of identity. Ego development is not a continuous trait variable in the way the FFM factors are; thus it may not be reasonable to fault the FFM for failure to encompass it. Nevertheless, a comprehensive taxonomy of personality variables cannot ignore ego development and other important personality variables simply because they are not continuous.

In sum, the FFM confounds some personality variables and excludes other potentially viable personality variables. Those who believe that the FFM is comprehensive, and conduct their research accordingly, risk foreclosing discovery of additional traits necessary to provide an adequate description of personality and prediction of behavior.

Existence of External Correlates

In summarizing evidence linking the FFM constructs to several outcomes, Costa and McCrae (1985) reported an interesting link between openness to experience and midlife career changes. Robins, John, and Caspi (1994), also examining the relationships of the FFM factors, reported a significant correlation between openness to experience and school performance. A particularly striking finding was reported by Freidman and colleagues (Freidman et al., 1993), who found that conscientiousness, measured during childhood, is associated with human longevity. People at the 75th percentile on conscientiousness were less likely (77 percent as likely) to die by age seventy as people at the 25th percentile. Taking into account curvilinearity, Freidman and his colleagues observed that the magnitude of the longevity effect for conscientiousness is comparable to those of other known risk factors for mortality, including systolic blood pressure and serum cholesterol (although Freidman's study does not demonstrate a causal relationship between conscientiousness and longevity). Conscientiousness also correlates significantly (negatively) with another important criterion, delinquency (Hough, 1992; Robins et al., 1994).

Barrick and Mount's research (1991) on the relationship between FFM constructs and job performance focused the attention of I/O psychologists on conscientiousness. In their meta-analysis, they found that, among the FFM constructs, only Conscientiousness was predictive across occupations (professionals, police officers, managers, people in sales, and those in skilled or semiskilled occupations) and criteria (job proficiency, training proficiency, and personnel data). The estimated true validity of conscientiousness equaled .22; the mean observed validity equaled .13. Also of note was the fact that extraversion and openness to experience correlated with training proficiency. The estimated true validities, respectively, were .26 (observed $r = .15$) and .25 (observed $r = .14$).

A meta-analysis by Tett, Jackson, and Rothstein (1991) yielded results different from those of Barrick and Mount (1991). The paper by Tett and colleagues (1991) contained apparent evidence that the FFM constructs of Agreeableness, Openness to Experience, and Neuroticism all had substantial correlations with job performance. Estimated true correlations were .33, .27, and −.22, respectively. (Observed mean r's = .22, .18, and −.15.) Conscientiousness was shown to have an estimated true correlation of .18. (Observed mean r = .12.)

There is some controversy over the differences in these two meta-analyses (Ones, Mount, Barrick, & Hunter, 1994; Tett, Jackson, Rothstein, & Reddon, 1994), but there is support for the finding that factors other than Conscientiousness are important predictors of job performance. Contrary to Barrick and Mount's findings (1991), Hough (1989, 1992) found that conscientiousness was not the best predictor of performance. Using a different basic personality taxonomy, Hough (1992) found that achievement, a variable confounded with other variables in the FFM, was a better predictor of important criteria than was conscientiousness. An examination of correlations with meaningful levels of validity indicated that, in comparison with conscientiousness, achievement was a better predictor of overall job performance, job proficiency, training success, educational success, commendable behavior, sales effectiveness, creativity, effort, and even combat effectiveness (Hough, 1992). The only criteria that conscientiousness scales predicted better than achievement scales were counterproductive/ irresponsible behavior, law abiding behavior, and teamwork (Hough, 1992).

Also in contrast to Barrick and Mount (1991), Hough's data (Hough, 1989, 1992; Hough et al., 1990) suggest that all of the basic personality constructs she examined (including personality constructs not included in the FFM) correlate at meaningful levels with external outcomes when the multidimensional nature of job performance is considered. Moreover, her data suggest that achievement needs to be disentangled from conscientiousness and extraversion and that affiliation needs to be disentangled from extraversion to highlight relationships with external criteria.

In sum, the FFM constructs clearly have external validity. In particular, conscientiousness is a useful predictor of a variety of important criteria in both work and nonwork environments. Nonetheless, other basic personality traits (both traits not included and traits included but not well differentiated in the FFM) also have substantial criterion-related validity—validity that is often higher than that of the FFM factors.

Conceptualization of Taxons as Source Traits

There is disagreement among FFM advocates as to whether the FFM factors are source traits. Goldberg and Saucier (1995; see also Saucier & Goldberg, in press) regard the factors as surface traits. They argue that people can perceive only phenotypic attributes and that, since the FFM factors were discovered via ratings based on perceptions of others, they are appropriately regarded as inductive summaries of those attributes. Goldberg and Saucier (1995) see the FFM factors as concepts to be explained but do not assume that they are source traits. Still, they do allow for the possibility that phenotypic personality attributes are caused by a combination of genetic and environmental influences. In contrast, McCrae and Costa (1994, in press) view the FFM factors as source traits. They propose that the "Big Five" (as the five FFM factors are often called) are biologically based and manifest themselves through "characteristic adaptations" that are in turn manifested through behavior. Characteristic adaptations include social skills, schemas and strategies, attitudes, beliefs, and goals.

Behavior genetics research indicates that all of the FFM factors are heritable and thus are source traits. H. J. Eysenck (1990), for example, reviewed results from six major recent behavior genetics studies involving twins and concluded that personality variables (including his extraversion, neuroticism, and psychoticism constructs) are approximately 50 percent heritable. He suggested that taking the reliability of the measuring instruments into account leads to the conclusion that these personality traits are approximately 60 percent heritable. Loehlin (1992) summarized research on heritability by FFM construct and found that all of the FFM factors have sizable heritability coefficients. Gilbert and Ones (1995a, 1995b) recently completed large-scale meta-analyses that further demonstrate the heritability of FFM Agreeableness and Conscientiousness.

Genetic causation of personality traits should manifest itself as differences in psychophysiology and cognitive processes (Buss, 1990; Revelle, 1995), and researchers have begun the task of linking the FFM factors (and their variants) to such constructs. Tellegen (1985), for example, suggested that the three higher-order factors of the MPQ—Positive Emotionality (which is related to FFM Extraversion), Negative Emotionality (which is related to FFM Neuroticism), and Constraint (which is related to FFM Conscientiousness)—correspond, respectively, to Gray's Behavioral Activation System, Behavioral Inhibition System, and Fight/Flight System (FFS) (1994). Though the linkage between Constraint and Gray's FFS seems unlikely, FFS may be related to H. J. Eysenck's Psychoticism scale (Revelle, 1995). Linkages between physiological constructs and higher-order personality traits are worth pursuing.

H. J. Eysenck has also investigated the physiological correlates of personality traits. His best-known work concerns extraversion. In brief, his theory states that introverts are more cortically aroused than extraverts. As noted in H. J. Eysenck and M. W. Eysenck (1985), there are really two hypotheses: (1) extraverts differ from introverts in their typical (tonic) level of arousal, and (2) extraverts differ from introverts in their level of arousal after experiencing a stimulus (that is, their phasic response). After reviewing the evidence, Stelmack (1990) concluded that the data support extraversion-related differences in people's phasic response to stimuli but not in their tonic level of arousal.

In sum, there is theory and evidence suggesting that FFM factors are source traits. They are all heritable, and some work has been done linking FFM variables with psychophysiological structures. A great deal more research, however, is needed to more definitively and elaborately link the FFM with underlying structures and processes.

Inclusion of Multiple Levels of Specificity

There appears to be a consensus that embedding the FFM in a multilevel personality structure is inevitable and will have utility. H. J. Eysenck (1991), for example, indicates that a personality trait taxonomy must be hierarchical if it is to "fit the facts" and has developed four-level hierarchical models of his extraversion, neuroticism, and psychoticism constructs. The lowest level in Eysenck's hierarchical representations of personality traits consists of single acts (behaviors). The next level up consists of habits (often-repeated behaviors). The next level up consists of traits, or correlated clusters of habits (for example, sociability). The highest level consists of what Eysenck calls types, or correlated clusters of traits (for example, extraversion).

R. Hogan and J. Hogan (1992) report that the construction of the Hogan Personality Inventory (HPI) led to the discovery of "subthemes" related to the six broad personality dimensions originally measured by that instrument (which are related to the FFM factors). They subsequently operationalized these subthemes (which they refer to as "homogeneous item composites," or HICs) and empirically refined them based on a criterion of internal consistency. Factor analysis of the HICs has shown that most load saliently on only one of the scales measured by the HPI, thereby supporting a hierarchical structuring of the Hogan factors.

Costa and McCrae (1995b; Costa, McCrae, & Dye, 1991) have also assumed that personality structure is hierarchical and have identified facets of the FFM. They examined the literature and associated six facets, at roughly comparable levels of breadth, with each of their FFM dimensions. Costa and McCrae (1995b) report that each FFM facet loads saliently on its associated FFM dimension, although factorial complexity does exist. Additionally, they note that each facet possesses substantial uniqueness (in the factor-analytic sense), indicating that the facet carries meaningful variance of its own, beyond the common variance shared with its associated FFM dimension. This, they argue, supports the reasonableness of a multilevel personality structure.

The recurrent finding that FFM facets load saliently on more than one FFM dimension has led some researchers to represent them in the form of circumplexes rather than hierarchies. A circumplex is a two-dimensional circular structure. A trait's position on a personality circumplex depends on its loadings on the two personality dimensions that define the plane of the circumplex and its communality in the two-factor space. The best-known circumplex in personality psychology is the interpersonal circle (Kiesler, 1983; Leary, 1957; Wiggins, 1979; Wiggins, Trapnell, & Phillips, 1988), which has been used to represent the structure of interpersonal traits. McCrae and Costa (1989a) have shown that the two interpersonal circle dimensions correspond to FFM Extraversion and

Agreeableness (which are a forty-five-degree rotation away from the Dominance and Love labels preferred by interpersonal circle theorists). Hofstee, de Raad, and Goldberg (1992) extended the thinking of interpersonal circle theorists by placing 540 trait-descriptive adjectives on ten circumplexes representing each possible pairing of the FFM dimensions.

Goldberg (1993b) suggests that personality traits can be depicted by either hierarchical or circumplex representations. He correctly observes, however, that forcing a hierarchical representation on the data will result in some loss of information. He therefore suggests that circumplex representations be used for basic research on the structure of personality traits. Note that a circumplex can be transformed into a multilevel, latticelike structure, making more explicit the observed multiple causation of facets by higher-order traits. Such a structure, encompassing facets of FFM Extraversion and Agreeableness, is shown in Figure 2.1.

Some researchers believe that some of the FFM factors can be embedded hierarchically within factors that are of an even higher order. For example, H. J. Eysenck (1991) argues that the constructs of agreeableness and conscientiousness are lower-order facets of psychoticism. Goldberg and Rosolack (1994), however, provide evidence that Eysenck's psychoticism construct is probably too broad to be considered a cohesive basic personality construct.

Summary of the Evaluation of the FFM Against Taxonomic Criteria

The FFM has done moderately well against our taxonomic criteria. There is evidence that the model is replicable across time, samples, perspectives, adjective-versus-questionnaire data, and to some extent cultures. The universality of the FFM, however, has not been established. Moreover, the FFM needs to be replicated using methods other than factor analysis.

The model is not comprehensive, but the evidence indicates that the FFM does indeed cover much of the terrain of personality description. Other variables that merit attention as basic personality variables are achievement, social insight, affiliation, masculinity/ femininity (rugged individualism), and certain personality disorders (or yet-to-be-specified dimensions necessary to account for those personality disorders). When the criterion construct is considered, the FFM variables all relate to a variety of important

Figure 2.1. Multilevel Structure for Displaying Relationships Between Trait Terms at Different Levels of Specificity.

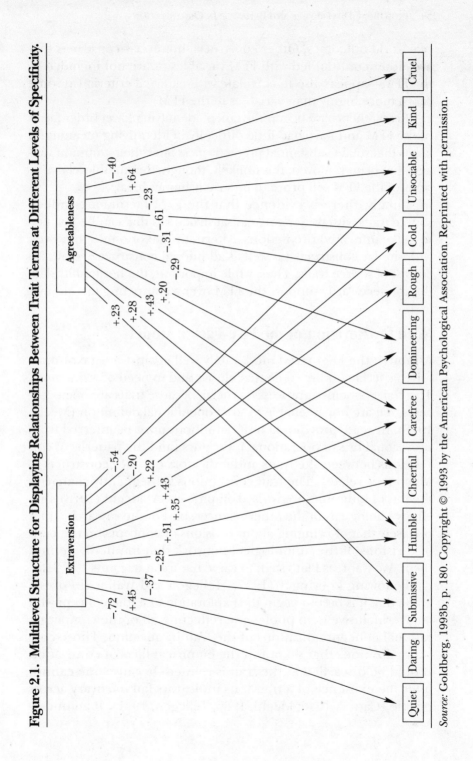

Source: Goldberg, 1993b, p. 180. Copyright © 1993 by the American Psychological Association. Reprinted with permission.

real-world outcomes. Other constructs, however—constructs that are either confounded with FFM variables or are not included in the FFM—appear also to correlate with external criteria (in some cases, more highly than variables in the FFM).

Researchers have begun the task of identifying lower-order facets of the FFM and have had little difficulty in identifying meaningful facets that retain substantial predictiveness after their common variance has been removed. It is unlikely, though, that multilevel extensions of the FFM will prove to be strictly hierarchical.

Finally, there is evidence that the FFM factors are indeed source traits with underlying causal structures that can be invoked to make informed predictions. Alternative taxonomies, however, with similar constructs (as well as additional constructs), may also consist of source traits. Thus, while important, the heritability data do not necessarily support the FFM over a competing taxonomy.

Need for Revision of the Five-Factor Model

Although the FFM fared moderately well against our taxonomic criteria, its factors are somewhat elusive and in need of refinement. This trait refinement process is crucial, because traits are open concepts that are not amenable to strict operational definition (Meehl, 1978). Instead, provisional trait definitions must be inferred from provisional lists of operational indicators (and the patterns of correlations between the traits and indicators of other constructs to which they relate). The trait conceptions subsequently change as the lists of indicators are revised empirically. As Meehl (1978) said, "In psychology, as in the other sciences, part of the research aim is precisely that of bringing about revisions of concepts on the basis of revisions of the nomological network that implicitly defines them. We want, as Plato said, to carve nature at its joints" (p. 816).

Following Loevinger (1957), Tellegen and Waller (in press) argue that it is best to begin the exploration of a trait concept with an overinclusive item pool—one reflecting all of the competing rational conceptualizations of the trait in question. Those conceptualizations that do not fit the empirical facts of covariation should be discarded as the trait is refined, because one cannot infer the existence of a trait if its indicators fail to covary across people (Cattell, 1946; Meehl, 1986; Tellegen, 1991). If an under-inclusive item pool is used, a trait construct may need to be expanded based on examination of convergent and discriminant correlations and theoretical reflection. Failure to expand and/or refine a trait construct should result in a trait measure with less potential for predictive utility and scientific illumination.

Have the FFM constructs been developed in such a way as to make them likely to carve nature at its joints? Has their inherent openness been acknowledged? Despite the large number of trait-descriptive adjectives that form the basis for the FFM (Allport & Odbert, 1936; Norman, 1967), the Goldberg and the Costa and McCrae versions of the FFM were probably based on an under-inclusive item pool. The exclusion of evaluative (including self-evaluative) and emotional terms, the exclusion by Norman of trait-descriptors that college undergraduates could not understand, and the inadequacies of the lexical approach to describing personality scientifically (Block, 1995; Tellegen, 1993; but see Saucier & Goldberg, in press) all contributed to this underinclusiveness. In addition, the faceting of the NEO-PI (Costa & McCrae, 1985) and its successor inventory, the NEO-PI-R (Costa & McCrae, 1992), was done in a manner—more confirmatory than exploratory—that may have resulted in nonoptimal facet constructs (and therefore nonoptimal conceptualizations of the FFM constructs themselves).

More specifically, each of the NEO-PI FFM constructs is defined by six facets—a number selected based not on empirical but on pragmatic considerations. After the facets were selected, items were written to measure each facet. To determine which items would ultimately be included in the NEO-PI, McCrae and Costa factor-analyzed the items within each of the five trait domains. They applied procrustes rotation, based on their rational assignment of items to facets, to the factors they extracted. They then selected items based on that rotation. In our view, this approach was flawed in that it did not allow the data to help shape conceptualization of the FFM facets (and therefore the FFM).

The construct definitions of the NEO-PI FFM could have been adjusted at least somewhat during the course of the programmatic, integrative research in which McCrae, Costa, and their colleagues tried to assimilate many of the major existing personality instruments into the NEO-PI. During the course of this research, the NEO-PI factors were related to the California Psychological Inventory (McCrae,

Costa, & Piedmont, 1993), the Eysenck Personality Questionnaire (McCrae & Costa, 1985), the Revised Interpersonal Adjective Scales (McCrae & Costa, 1989a), the Myers-Briggs Type Indicator (McCrae & Costa, 1989b), the Personality Research Form (Costa & McCrae, 1988), and the California Q-Set (Lanning, 1994; McCrae, Costa, & Busch, 1986), among other inventories. McCrae and Costa (in press) state that "the continuing value of studies relating the FFM to other systems is in deepening conceptualization of the five factors and in reconceptualizing other systems." Part of this "deepening," however, should include deliberate conceptual adjustment of McCrae and Costa's own FFM. This sort of conceptual adjustment should not be frequent or willy-nilly, certainly; but it must occur. Accuracy of prediction depends on the quality of the predictor taxonomy (as well as the criterion taxonomy).

Incrementing Criterion-Related Validity

Historically, a major concern over the use of personality constructs for predicting behavior has been their relatively low level of validity. In addition to having a better taxonomy of personality constructs, there are at least two other ways to increment the criterion-related validity of personality variables for predicting behavior. One way is to combine basic personality traits into compound traits that are designed to predict particular criteria. The other way is to identify and take into account moderator variables. In this section, we define and distinguish basic and compound traits and describe four compound personality measures (integrity, customer service, management potential, and sales potential) and the validities associated with them. In addition, we identify variables that moderate criterion-related validity and dispel some myths about variables thought to moderate criterion-related validity.

Compound Personality Variables

We distinguish two kinds of personality traits: basic personality traits and compound traits (sometimes called "emergent" traits). For purposes of this discussion, we define a basic personality trait as a personality variable that meets the standard tests of internal consistency, temporal stability, and conceptual coherence. Compound personality traits are comprised of basic personality traits that do not all covary. In I/O psychology, compound traits arise when researchers seek to synthesize a personality construct by first identifying the criterion constructs they want to predict and then identifying basic personality variables that will maximally predict those criteria. Because this process involves customized combinations of basic personality traits specifically targeted to certain criterion constructs, the criterion-related validity of compound traits should exceed that of basic personality traits. In the following sections, we discuss several promising compound traits.

Integrity Measures and Their Validity

Integrity tests are designed to assess employee theft and other counterproductive behaviors. Sackett, Burris, and Callahan (1989) classified integrity tests into *overt tests,* which directly assess attitudes toward theft and dishonest and illegal acts, and *personality-based tests,* which are designed to predict a broad range of counterproductive behaviors. The use of integrity tests has increased substantially over the past decade, partly because use of the polygraph is now illegal for employment screening in many jobs (Camara & D. L. Schneider, 1994). Indeed, the use of integrity tests is so common that the American Psychological Association empaneled a task force to assess the usefulness of commercially available tests for predicting untrustworthiness (Goldberg, Grenier, Guion, Sechrest, & Wing, 1991).

Ones, Viswesvaran, and Schmidt (1993) conducted a large-scale meta-analysis of integrity test validities. The results showed that integrity tests possess impressive criterion-related validity. For example, both overt and personality-based integrity tests correlated with measures of broad counterproductive behaviors such as violence on the job, tardiness, and absenteeism. The researchers reported a mean estimated true validity of .29 (observed mean $r = .20$; total $n = 93,092$) between personality-based integrity tests and external measures of broad counterproductive behavior criteria (with applicant samples and predictive validity designs) and a mean estimated true validity of .39 (observed mean $r = .27$; total $n = 5,598$) between overt integrity tests and counterproductive behaviors (with applicant samples and predictive validity designs). With supervisory ratings of overall job performance as the criterion, the mean estimated true validity of integrity tests across overt and personality-based measures in applicant settings with a predictive validity design was .41 (observed mean $r = .25$; total $n = 7,550$).

Ones, Schmidt, and Viswesvaran (1994) addressed the construct validity of integrity measures. Integrity tests have typically been linked primarily to FFM Conscientiousness (Collins & Schmidt, 1993; Ones et al., 1993), although Kanfer, Ackerman, Murtha, and Goff (1995) also noted a link to Emotional Stability. Ones, Schmidt, and Viswesvaran (1994), however, argue that integrity tests derive their predictive power by tapping into a higher-order personality factor consisting of three of the FFM factors: Conscientiousness, Agreeableness, and Emotional Stability. Their meta-analysis, based on thousands of cases, indicates that the estimated true intercorrelations of Conscientiousness, Agreeableness, and Emotional Stability range from .25 to .27 (Ones, Schmidt, et al., 1994). Moreover, integrity correlated .42 with Conscientiousness, .40 with Agreeableness, and .33 with Emotional Stability. Correlations between integrity and the other two FFM dimensions, Extraversion and Openness to Experience, were considerably lower.

Hough's data (1992) also bear on the construct validity of integrity. Included in her meta-analysis of the validities of nine basic personality traits was a counterproductivity criterion which she labeled "irresponsible behavior." She defined that criterion as "poor attendance, counterproductive behavior, number of disciplinary actions, not following directions, being absent without authorization, use of drugs (including alcohol) on the job" (p. 151). She found observed mean correlations of $-.19$, $-.24$, $-.15$, and $-.08$ for achievement, dependability, adjustment, and agreeableness, respectively, in sample sizes of 19,476, 98,676, 21,431, and 24,259, respectively. (Hough, in her meta-analytic work, codes the sign of a validity coefficient to indicate the direction of the relationship with the definition of the criterion construct. For example, achievement, dependability, adjustment, and agreeableness all correlate negatively with poor attendance, counterproductive behavior, number of disciplinary actions, and so on. Thus a $-.20$ in Hough's data is the same as a $+.20$ in data found in Ones et al., 1993.) Hough's data suggest that agreeableness correlates only modestly with counterproductive behavior but that three basic personality characteristics—achievement, dependability, and adjustment— could be combined to predict counterproductive behavior quite well.

Ones, Schmidt, et al. (1994) suggest that integrity functions in the personality domain much as g does in the cognitive ability domain. Some performance criteria, however, are either unrelated to or are negatively related to the basic personality characteristics that Ones, Schmidt, et al. (1994) suggest comprise integrity (conscientiousness, agreeableness, and adjustment). For example, in Hough's meta-analysis (1992), creativity, an important criterion for many endeavors, is negatively correlated with all three of the basic personality traits that appear to comprise integrity. That is, dependability, agreeableness, and adjustment correlate with creativity –.07, –.29, and –.05 (uncorrected), respectively (Hough, 1992). Executive performance is another important criterion that personality characteristics other than integrity appear to predict. Bray and Howard (1983) report that need for advancement and inner work standards are important determinants of managerial/executive performance. Bentz (1984) reports that sociability, social ascendancy, and self-confidence are important predictors of executive performance. Hough (1992), in her meta-analysis, found that potency and achievement both correlate .18 (uncorrected) with overall managerial/executive performance, whereas dependability, adjustment, and agreeableness correlate, respectively, –.03, .11, .07 (uncorrected) with overall managerial/executive performance.

Integrity measures clearly predict important criteria, and the number of correlations and sample sizes in the Ones et al. (1993) meta-analysis are very impressive. Nevertheless, we believe that it is premature to suggest that integrity functions in the personality domain as g does in the cognitive ability domain. While relatively fewer people may occupy jobs that require creativity or executive talent, those positions are clearly important to the world of work. Indeed, if one compares the validity coefficients for personality traits for different job families (for example, service jobs versus managerial jobs) and different job performance constructs (for example, creativity versus counterproductive behavior), traits besides integrity are likely to be important.

Customer Service Measures and Their Validity

After integrity, the job requirements–based personality construct that seems to be receiving the most attention is customer service orientation. Given that our economy is substantially more than half service-oriented, it is hardly surprising that the prediction of service-oriented behavior has become increasingly important.

The available evidence indicates that the criterion-related valid-ity of customer service orientation measures is impressive. McDaniel and Frei (1994) performed a meta-analysis of customer service mea-sures and reported a mean estimated true validity of .50 between customer service and job performance (total n = 6,945). They found that the validity of customer service measures did not differ depending on whether job performance was assessed globally or by measures that targeted customer service behaviors. A possible expla-nation for this finding is that jobs included in the studies may have been customer service jobs for which the overall job performance criterion was customer service.

Costa and McCrae (1995b) provide useful information regard-ing the construct validity of the customer service construct by cor-relating their FFM facet scales with J. Hogan and R. Hogan's Service Orientation scale (1986). These data indicate that service orienta-tion is primarily associated with the Emotional Stability (Neuroti-cism), Agreeableness, and Conscientiousness domains—the same three constructs that Ones, Schmidt, et al. (1994) suggest comprise integrity. Within the Emotional Stability (Neuroticism) domain, the facet scale Angry Hostility correlates most highly with Service Ori-entation ($r = -.62$, $p < .001$), and the facet scale Vulnerability cor-relates least highly ($r = -.22$, $p < .05$). Within the Agreeableness domain, Compliance correlates most highly with Service Orien-tation ($r = .52$, $p < .00$), and Trust correlates least highly ($r = .21$, $p < .05$). Finally, within the Conscientiousness domain, the facet scales Dutifulness and Deliberation correlate most highly with Ser-vice Orientation (r's = .35 and .30, respectively; both $p < .001$), whereas Achievement Striving is uncorrelated with Service Orien-tation ($r = -.01$, ns).

Construct validity data provided by McDaniel and Frei (1994) provide a somewhat different picture of customer service orienta-tion. Their data indicate that customer service orientation relates primarily to FFM Agreeableness, Emotional Stability, and Extra-version. Their data also indicate that customer service orientation appears to be largely independent of cognitive ability and is only moderately related to social interests. Examination of the highest

correlations between customer service and other variables suggests that an individual who is customer service–oriented can be
characterized as resilient and coolheaded; cautious, planful, and
thoughtful; willing to cooperate and defer to others; willing to
adhere to strict standards of conduct; and interested in helping
others and providing them service (Costa & McCrae, 1985; Costa,
McCrae, & Dye, 1991; R. Hogan & J. Hogan, 1992).

Management Potential Measures and Their Validity

Identification of the characteristics of a good manager has been
an abiding interest of I/O psychologists; fortunately, the prediction of management success has attracted the attention of personality researchers as well. For example, Gough (1984) developed a
Managerial Potential scale using an empirical keying strategy. Both
managerial interests and managerial competence were used as criteria to select items from a large pool of California Psychological
Inventory (CPI) items (Gough, 1987). J. Hogan and R. Hogan
(1986) also developed a Managerial Potential scale. They developed their scale by correlating homogeneous item composites
(HICs) from the HPI with organizational level attained by employees in a trucking firm. The HICs that correlated most highly with
this organizational-level variable were retained. Together, they
formed a fifty-seven-item scale.

Gough (1984) reported a cross-validated correlation of .20
between the CPI Managerial Potential scale and job performance
in a sample of 143 male military officers. J. Hogan and R. Hogan
(1986) reported that their Managerial Potential scale correlated
.30, .29, and .26 with supervisory ratings of interpersonal relations,
organizational skills, and overall job performance, respectively, in
a sample of 108 insurance underwriters and claims analysts. They
also reported an uncorrected correlation of .28 between their Managerial Potential scale and ratings of 103 public school principals
by school superintendents.

Costa and McCrae (1995b) correlated their FFM facet scales
with both the Gough (1984) and the J. Hogan and R. Hogan
(1986) Managerial Potential scales. Interestingly, the general pattern of correlations is the same for both scales, but the magnitude
of the correlations tends to be much larger for the J. Hogan and
R. Hogan Managerial Potential scale. (This is perhaps not a

surprising finding, since the HPI is an FFM derivative.) Based on Costa and McCrae's data (1995b), one can conclude that managerial potential is most strongly associated with FFM Conscientiousness, Emotional Stability, and Extraversion. For the J. Hogan and R. Hogan scale, there is also a moderate association with several Openness to Experience facets. The Gough scale is more highly related to facets of Agreeableness than is the J. Hogan and R. Hogan Managerial Potential scale.

Do the basic personality variables that have been linked to managerial potential predict managerial performance? Hough's meta-analysis (1992) indicates that potency (FFM Extraversion without the affiliation component) and adjustment do indeed correlate with managerial performance. Potency correlated .18 (uncorrected) with managerial job proficiency, and adjustment correlated .11 (uncorrected) with managerial job proficiency. On the other hand, dependability correlated $-.03$ (uncorrected) with managerial job proficiency, whereas achievement correlated .18 (uncorrected) with managerial job proficiency.

Sales Potential Measures and Their Validity

J. Hogan and R. Hogan (1986) also developed a Sales Potential scale. They used a deductive scale development strategy to assemble a twenty-four-item scale. They then administered the HPI to 127 (primarily male) sales representatives in a large trucking firm. Sales representatives' Sales Potential scale scores correlated between .22 and .57 (all $p < .09$) with (1) sales manager nominations of sales representatives they would take with them if asked to open a new regional sales office, (2) ratings by the vice president of sales, and (3) sales revenue produced.

Costa and McCrae (1995b) found that the J. Hogan and R. Hogan (1986) Sales Potential scale correlated most highly with facets of Extraversion (although not with the Gregariousness or Excitement Seeking facet scales), Openness to Experience (with the exception of the Values facet scale, which reflects a tolerant, broad-minded, nonconforming attitude toward life), and Agreeableness. It is interesting to note that the Sales Potential scale correlated negatively with several facets of Agreeableness: Straightforwardness ($r = -.36$, $p < .001$), Compliance ($r = -.32$, $p < .001$), and Modesty ($r = -.48$, $p < .001$). Taken together, these data suggest that the effective salesperson is not direct and frank with others; is not meek, mild, and cooperative; and is not humble (Costa, McCrae, & Dye, 1991).

Do the basic personality variables that have been linked to sales potential predict a sales effectiveness criterion? Hough (1992), who included sales effectiveness as one job performance construct in her meta-analysis, found that potency (FFM Extraversion without the affiliation component), affiliation, and Intellectance (Openness to Experience) do indeed correlate with sales effectiveness. She reported uncorrected mean correlations of .25, .19, and .15, respectively, with sales effectiveness. In addition, other basic personality variables—variables apparently not included in the J. Hogan and R. Hogan Sales Potential measure—correlate with sales effectiveness. For example, Bluen, Barling, and Burns (1990) found that achievement striving correlated .18 (uncorrected) with insurance policies sold. Similarly, Hough (1992) found that achievement correlated .27 (uncorrected) with sales effectiveness. (Dependability, on the other hand, correlated only .06 with sales effectiveness.) Hough also found that locus of control correlated .19 (uncorrected) with sales effectiveness. These data suggest that, in addition to Extraversion, Openness to Experience, and Agreeableness, other basic personality variables should be included in a sales potential measure.

Summary of Validity of Compound Personality Variables

Several compound personality traits have been identified by various researchers. Some of these traits have been shown to possess high criterion-related validities. Meta-analyses of integrity and customer service orientation measures indicate that the criterion-related validities associated with those measures far surpass Mischel's $r = .30$ prediction barrier (1968). These compound variables are combinations of personality traits and, when properly constructed, should outpredict basic personality traits. Thus development of management potential and sales potential measures should benefit from meta-analyses of validities of basic personality scales with appropriate criteria (such as managerial and sales effectiveness).

Nonmythical Moderator Variables

Both basic personality traits and compound personality traits predict job performance criteria. Creating compound variables can and does increment the personality-performance relationship. Taking into account moderators of the relationship between personality and job performance can further increment, as well as illuminate, criterion-related validities. Indeed, some personality variables that appear to be essentially uncorrelated with performance criteria correlate substantially with job performance when various moderators of the personality-performance relationship are considered. Type of job, criterion construct, criterion measurement method, validation strategy, type of situation, and rater perspective are all examples of variables that appear to moderate personality-performance relationships.

Type of Job

Common sense suggests that certain personality traits will be predictive of job performance only for certain types of jobs, and the available evidence supports this assertion. In Barrick and Mount's meta-analysis (1991), for example, FFM Extraversion was a stronger (though still weak) correlate of job performance in managerial and sales jobs than in professional, police, and skilled/semiskilled jobs. Similarly, in Hough's meta-analysis (1992), substantially different criterion-related validities were observed for managers and executives than for health care workers. For example, measures of dependability and agreeableness correlated more highly with job proficiency for health care workers (mean uncorrected r's = .24 and .19, respectively) than for managers and executives (mean uncorrected r's = −.03 and .07, respectively). Potency, however, was more highly correlated with job proficiency for managers and executives than it was for health care workers (mean uncorrected r's = .18 and .05, respectively). Ghiselli's research (1966) also suggests that type of job moderates the criterion-related validity of personality variables.

Criterion Construct

There is now a substantial amount of evidence that the predictiveness of most personality variables depends upon the criteria being predicted. For example, Hough (1992) coded the criterion variables used in the studies included in her meta-analysis into categories including (1) overall job performance, (2) training success, (3) educational success, (4) technical proficiency, (5) counterproductive/

irresponsible behavior, (6) law-abiding behavior, (7) sales effectiveness, (8) creativity, (9) effort, and (10) combat effectiveness. Each personality variable correlated differently with this set of criteria, and each of the constructs in Hough's taxonomy correlated substantially with at least one criterion.

Results of Project A, a significant validation study funded by the Army Research Institute during much of the 1980s, also provides evidence that personality scales correlate differently with different criteria. In that project, five broad performance constructs—technical proficiency, general soldiering proficiency, effort and leadership, personal discipline, and physical fitness and military bearing—were developed. A variety of measures were used to obtain criterion scores for soldiers on these five constructs, including supervisory ratings, job-knowledge tests, work samples, and personnel records. (See J. P. Campbell, McHenry, & Wise, 1990, and C. H. Campbell et al., 1990, for a complete description of these criterion variables.) The predictor measures included cognitive ability, perceptual/psychomotor ability, personality, and interest scales. (See Peterson et al., 1990, or various chapters in a book edited by J. P. Campbell, 1996, for a complete description of the predictor measures.) In a sample of 4,039 soldiers in nine military occupational specialties, the cognitive and perceptual/psychomotor ability tests provided the best prediction of job-specific and general task proficiency, while the personality composite provided the best prediction of expending extra effort, supporting peers, and exhibiting personal discipline (Hough et al., 1990; McHenry, Hough, Toquam, Hanson, and Ashworth, 1990).

Moreover, the personality scales differentially predicted effort and leadership and personal discipline (Hough et al., 1990). That is, the dependability scales, which were developed to predict the personal discipline criterion, did, in fact, predict the personal discipline criterion better than any of the other predictors. Similarly, the surgency and achievement personality scales, which were developed to predict the effort and leadership criterion, did, in fact, predict the effort and leadership criterion better than any of the other predictors. Uncorrected validities were in the mid twenties for personality scales and their targeted criterion. (Sample size ranged from 7,666 to 8,477.)

Motowidlo and Van Scotter (1994) also provided evidence that personality variables predict criterion constructs differentially. They correlated the personality scales of the Assessment of Background and Life Experiences (ABLE; Hough, Barge, & Kamp, 1996) with supervisory ratings of the task performance and contextual performance of 715 Air Force mechanics. *Task performance* is defined as activities that (1) contribute directly to the transformation of raw materials into finished products and (2) support core technical activities; whereas *contextual performance* refers to activities that support the social and psychological environments of organizations (Borman & Motowidlo, 1993). According to Borman and Motowidlo (1993), contextual activities include the following:

- Volunteering for tasks that are not formally part of the job
- Persisting with extra enthusiasm or effort when necessary to complete one's own task activities successfully
- Helping, cooperating with, and assisting co-workers
- Following organizational rules and procedures even when it is personally inconvenient
- Supporting organizational goals

Motowidlo and Van Scotter (1994) showed, through hierarchical regression, that the ratings of task and contextual performance were largely independent. Each contributed significantly and substantially to ratings of overall performance after the other had already been entered as an independent variable into a regression equation. They also showed that four out of the six ABLE content scales correlated significantly more highly with contextual performance than with task performance. Moreover, each of the six ABLE content scales correlated significantly and positively with contextual performance (correlations ranged from .11 for Dominance to .36 for Work Orientation); only two of the six scales (Work Orientation and Dependability) correlated significantly with task performance.

Gellatly, Paunonen, Meyer, Jackson, and Goffin (1991) investigated the relationships between various individual difference variables and six job performance dimensions in a sample of 114 managers employed in a large food-service organization. The six dimensions, derived from a job analysis, were public relations, administration, communication (written and oral), management, policy (following operational policies and procedures), and routine (conducting routine job tasks). Among the individual difference variables included in this study were six personality dimensions derived from a principal components analysis of the Personality Research Form-E (PRF; Jackson, 1984). Gellatly and his colleagues found that three of the six PRF components correlated significantly with at least one of the six criteria, and each correlated significantly with different criteria.

Criterion Measurement Method

The usefulness of distinguishing between different criterion measurement methods was demonstrated in Barrick and Mount's meta-analysis (1991). In one analysis, criteria were categorized into objective and subjective criteria. Only the FFM Conscientiousness construct had meaningful levels of validity for both subjective and objective criteria. It correlated .14 (estimated true correlation) with objective criteria and .26 (estimated true correlation) with subjective ratings. Ones, Viswesvaran, and Schmidt (1993) compared the validity of integrity tests for predicting overall job performance using supervisory ratings and production records criteria. They found that integrity tests correlated .35 (estimated true correlation) with supervisory ratings of overall job performance (subjective criteria) and .28 (estimated true correlation) with production records (objective criteria). In addition, Ones et al. (1993) compared the validities of integrity tests for predicting counterproductive criteria using admissions versus external measures of counterproductive criteria. They found that integrity tests correlated .58 (estimated true correlation) with admissions of counterproductivity and .32 (estimated true correlation) with externally measured counterproductivity. These findings suggest that the method of criterion measurement moderates validity.

Type of Situation

Both theory and data indicate that the situation affects personality-performance relationships. One way to conceptualize situations is in terms of their strength. Situational strength is the extent to which a situation provides clearly communicated incentives and expectations that induce people to behave similarly (Mischel, 1977). Behavior in "strong" situations is thus similar regardless of the individual differences of the people. Funerals and weddings are strong situations; being alone in one's bedroom is not.

Barrick and Mount (1993), in their study of U.S. Army civilian managers, tested the hypothesis that personality would predict better in jobs characterized by low situational strength than in jobs characterized by high situational strength. They contended that high-autonomy jobs tend to be low in situational strength and low-autonomy jobs tend to be high in situational strength. They tested their hypothesis using a moderated multiple regression strategy. They regressed supervisory performance ratings on each of the FFM factors, a measure of job autonomy, and the cross-product of personality and autonomy to test for the hypothesized interactions. They entered managerial grade level and type of supervision (military versus civilian) first, to control for possible effects of those factors on the personality-performance relationship. Barrick and Mount found significant personality-by-autonomy interactions for FFM Conscientiousness, Extraversion, and Agreeableness.

If autonomy is an indicator of complexity, the Barrick and Mount (1993) results are similar to, but also intriguingly different from, the meta-analyses of Ones, Viswesvaran, and Schmidt (1993) and Ones, Schmidt, and Viswesvaran (1994), which addressed the criterion-related and construct validity of integrity measures. Ones, Viswesvaran, and Schmidt (1993) found that job complexity moderates the criterion-related validity of integrity tests. Ones, Schmidt, and Viswesvaran (1994) found that integrity consists of the FFM factors of Conscientiousness, Agreeableness, and Emotional Stability. In the Barrick and Mount study, Agreeableness was negatively related to job performance in managerial jobs high in complexity. In the Ones, Viswesvaran, and Schmidt (1993) meta-analysis, integrity, of which Agreeableness is a part, was positively related to job performance in jobs high in complexity. This anomaly highlights the importance of the personality taxonomy that I/O researchers use, as well as the importance of understanding the nomological net of each construct.

I/O psychology would benefit from additional programmatic research on situational strength. R. J. Schneider and Hough (1995), for example, suggested that norms and roles are sources of situational strength in organizations, because both generate expected sets of behaviors. Behavioral norms serve to integrate organizational behavior in that they constrain everyone's behavior, whereas roles serve to differentiate organizational behavior by constraining the behavior of role occupants only (Katz & Kahn, 1978).

Another potential source of situational strength may, paradoxically, be people. People are, after all, situations from the perspective of those with whom they interact. It is possible, for example, that individuals who are high on dominance are stronger "situations" than individuals who are low on that trait. Certainly, good leadership involves creating a situational press that fosters the expression of desired personality characteristics and inhibits the expression of undesired characteristics.

Rater Perspective

Mount, Barrick, and Strauss (1994) provided evidence that rater perspective affects the correlation between ratings of personality characteristics and ratings of job performance. They obtained self-ratings of basic personality traits from 105 sales representatives employed in a large appliance manufacturing organization. In addition, they obtained observer (that is, supervisor, co-worker, and customer) ratings of the personality characteristics of the sales representatives. They correlated the personality ratings with supervisor and co-worker ratings of the sales representatives' job performance. Job performance ratings were based on job knowledge, quality of work, quantity of work, initiative, customer communication, account management, interpersonal skills, commitment to the job, and job attitude. Mount et al. (1994) found that self-ratings of personality traits typically had lower correlations with performance ratings than did observer ratings. For example, customer ratings of the sales representatives' personality characteristics of extraversion, agreeableness, and conscientiousness correlated substantially higher with both supervisor and co-worker ratings of the sales representatives' job performance than did self-ratings of those personality characteristics. In the case of Extraversion and Agreeableness, the correlation between self-ratings and the performance criteria did not even reach statistical significance.

Similarly, Nilsen (1995) had a group of 131 executives respond to personality and performance measures; managers, peers, and subordinates who had close working relationships with the executives were also asked to respond. Her findings are similar to those reported by Mount et al. (1994): concurrent validities of personality scales against performance measures were higher for personality descriptions made by others than for the executives' self-descriptions. Nilsen's results are likely to be more robust than the similar finding by Mount and colleagues, however, because the personality inventory and the performance measures were not completed by the same others. Instead, Nilsen randomly assigned the knowledgeable others to two groups—one to complete the personality inventory and the other to complete the performance description scales.

One must be cautious, however, in interpreting these results. Validities of supervisor, co-worker, and customer ratings of personality are likely to be inflated to an unknown degree by common method variance. That is, the predictor and criterion measures (in this case) share an "other" perspective. As pointed out by Mount and colleagues (1994), however, inflated correlations may also be accounted for by the fact that personality ratings provided by supervisors, co-workers, and customers are based on manifestations of personality in work situations, whereas self-ratings of personality are likely to be based on self-observations across both work and nonwork situations. People may display different personality-related behaviors in work environments than they do in other environments.

Validation Strategy

Validation strategy—concurrent versus predictive—appears to moderate many personality-performance relationships. Whether it moderates all personality-performance relationships, however, is unclear.

Hough (1996) conducted a meta-analysis of criterion-related validity coefficients of personality constructs for various performance constructs separately for concurrent and predictive validity strategies. A comparison of the observed concurrent and predictive validity coefficients indicated that predictive coefficients were on average .07 points lower than the concurrent validity coefficients. Furthermore, the size of the difference in validity coefficients depended on the criterion construct. The largest differences between observed concurrent and predictive validities were for the criterion counterproductive behavior. Observed validity coefficients (across personality variables) for that criterion for predictive validity studies were, on average, 115 points lower than the observed coefficients for concurrent validity studies.

Ones et al. (1993) examined the validity of integrity tests separately by type of validation strategy. They found that for concurrent validation strategies, integrity tests correlated .56 (estimated true correlation) with counterproductive behaviors; whereas for predictive validation strategies, integrity tests correlated .36 (estimated true correlation) with counterproductive behaviors. They state that "these results suggest that concurrent validities might overestimate predictive validities" (p. 690). However, when they examined only personality-based integrity tests and the criteria were broad external measures of counterproductive behavior (rather than theft and personal admissions), the correlation for the concurrent validation strategy (using employees) was .29 (estimated true correlation). They found the same level of validity (.29) for the predictive validation strategy (using applicants). Thus conclusions derived from Ones et al.'s fully hierarchical moderator analysis (which is more relevant to understanding the validity of personality variables than analyses that include overt measures of integrity) suggest that validation strategy does not moderate validity of personality-based integrity measures.

Additional research is needed to determine whether validation strategy moderates the relationship between integrity measures and counterproductive behavior. Nonetheless, validation strategy does appear to moderate many personality-performance relationships.

Mythical Moderators

In this section, we describe evidence that suggests that social desirability, validation strategy, and mode of administration (computer versus paper-and-pencil administration)—variables thought to be promising as moderators—do not appear to affect validities of personality measures.

Social Desirability

Concern about the effect of the social desirability of self-report items on response-option endorsement has a long history in personality psychology. Many psychologists believe that intentional response distortion (or "impression management") in self-report measures attenuates the validity of self-reports for personnel decisions. For example, Kluger, Reilly, and Russell (1991) state that "response distortion . . . should in turn lead to lowered validity" (p. 896). Indeed, the possibility of response distortion is often cited as one of the main arguments against using personality measures to aid in selection, placement, and other staffing decisions.

The evidence is clear. People can, when instructed to do so, distort their responses in the desired direction (for example, Borislow, 1958; Dunnett, Koun, & Barber, 1981; Dunnette, McCartney, Carlson, & Kirchner, 1962; Hough et al., 1990; Schwab, 1971; Thornton & Gierasch, 1980). However, the extent of distortion in real-life applicant settings is not as great as the distortion that results when participants are instructed to slant their responses (Dunnette et al., 1962; Hough et al., 1990; Michaelis & H. J. Eysenck, 1971; Ryan & Sackett, 1987).

Research examining the impact of intentional distortion on criterion-related validity favors the conclusion that such distortion does not attenuate the criterion-related validity of personality scales. Evidence that intentional distortion that occurs in real-life applicant settings lowers criterion-related validity comes from research by Dunnette et al. (1962) and some analyses by Ones et al. (1993) comparing concurrent and predictive validities. Evidence that intentional distortion in real-life applicant settings does not affect criterion-related validity comes from (1) in-depth analyses by Ones and colleagues comparing predictive and concurrent validities of personality-based versus overt integrity measures; (2) studies by Paajanen (1988) examining differences in criterion-related validity between applicants who had slanted their responses and those who had been frank; (3) a study by Hough et al. (1990) that specifically examined the effect of overly desirable responding and its affect on validity; (4) a study by Christiansen, Goffin, Johnston, and Rothstein (1994) examining the criterion-related validities of uncorrected Sixteen Personality Factor Questionnaire (16PF; Cattell, Eber, & Tatsuoka, 1970) personality scale scores and scale scores that were corrected for intentional distortion; and (5) an analysis in a series of studies by Cunningham, Wong, and Barbee (1994) involving partialing social desirability out of the correlation between an integrity measure and a criterion measure. These five groups of studies involve thousands of cases, whereas the Dunnette study involved validities from only two samples—one with a sample size of 45, and the other, a sample size of 159. In summary, intentional distortion does not appear to affect criterion-related validity negatively, as is often assumed.

Administration Mode

Individual difference measures are increasingly administered via computers. With this increase has come concern that computer-administered tests result in different mean scores than paper-and-pencil tests. For self-report inventories, some people have hypothesized that computer administration reduces the tendency to describe oneself in a socially desirable manner (Booth-Kewley, Edwards, & Rosenfeld, 1992). In other words, these people expect scale scores to be lower when questions are computer-administered.

Research comparing computerized versus paper-and-pencil attitude and personality questionnaires suggests that mode of administration has little or no effect on the level of socially desirable responding, however. Several studies have found that the two types of administration yield very similar results (Booth-Kewley et al., 1992; Kantor, 1991; Katz & Dalby, 1981; Lukin, Dowd, Plake, & Kraft, 1985; Millstein, 1987; Rosenfeld, Doherty, Vicino, Kantor, & Greaves 1989; Rozensky, Honor, Rasinski, Tovian, & Herz, 1986; Skinner & Allen, 1983; D. M. White, Clements, & Fowler, 1985; Wilson, Genco, & Yager, 1985). A few studies have found greater socially desirable responding with computerized administration (for example, Davis & Cowles, 1989; Lautenschlager & Flaherty, 1990; and Schuldberg, 1988), and a few studies have found that computer administration results in less socially desirable responding (for example, Evan & Miller, 1969; Kiesler & Sproull, 1986). On balance, however, mode of administration does not appear to affect the level of socially desirable responding (and hence mean scores). This being the case, it would also seem unlikely that mode of administration acts as a moderator of the personality-performance relationship.

Summary of Moderator Variable Research

The literature reviewed suggests that type of job, criterion construct, criterion measurement method (objective versus subjective), validation strategy (for several variables), and type of situation affect personality-performance relationships, while social desirability and administration mode do not. Research is less clear about the effects of rater perspective. Preliminary evidence suggests that rater perspective might affect the validity of personality variables.

Summary

Personality taxonomies have provided the organizing principles that have enabled personality researchers to establish relationships between personality constructs (taxons) and important life- and job-related criteria—relationships that had been obscured previously because correlation coefficients were summarized across personality constructs (or taxons). I/O personality researchers have used different taxonomies to organize and summarize their data, and different conclusions have resulted. Thus, while having a taxonomy is important, the nature of the taxonomy is also important.

Any basic personality taxonomy that is a contender for use by I/O psychologists should (1) consist of traits that have been replicated, (2) be comprehensive, (3) have external correlates, (4) consist of source traits, and (5) consist of multiple levels of traits. The Five-Factor Model of personality (consisting of Extraversion, Agreeableness, Conscientiousness, Emotional Stability, and Openness to Experience) did moderately well against our criteria:

1. The FFM factors have shown impressive replicability in some areas but need further replication in others. They have been replicated across time and samples, across self and peer data, and across adjective and questionnaire measures. However, they need to be replicated using a scientific method other than factor analysis. The FFM factors have shown evidence of cross-cultural replicability as well, but their status as cross-cultural universals has by no means been established.
2. The FFM is not comprehensive, though the evidence indicates that it does indeed cover much of the terrain of personality description. Additional variables that merit attention as possible basic personality variables are achievement, social insight, affiliation, masculinity/femininity (rugged individualism), and various personality disorders (or yet-to-be-discovered personality variables necessary to account for those disorders).

3. All of the FFM factors have external validity if the multi-dimensional nature of the job performance domain is taken into account. Other constructs, however—constructs that are either confounded or are not well conceptualized by the FFM—appear to correlate more highly with external criteria than FFM variables.

4. There is evidence that the FFM factors are indeed source traits with underlying causal structures that can be invoked to make informed predictions.

5. Researchers who have begun the task of identifying lower-order facets of the FFM have had little difficulty identifying meaningful facets that retain substantial predictiveness after their common variance has been removed. It is doubtful, though, that the model is (or should be) strictly hierarchical.

Despite the fact that the FFM fared reasonably well against our taxonomic criteria, the FFM traits are somewhat elusive and in need of refinement. The FFM factors were derived in such a way as to make them unlikely to carve nature at its joints. The exclusion by Norman (1967) of trait-descriptors that college undergraduates could not understand and the inadequacies of the lexical approach to describing personality contributed to the underinclusiveness of the item pool from which the FFM was derived. In addition, the faceting of the FFM has been done in a confirmatory rather than an exploratory way. This has likely resulted in nonoptimal facet constructs and, as a consequence, nonoptimal conceptualizations of the FFM constructs themselves.

In this chapter, we distinguished between two kinds of personality traits: basic personality traits and compound traits. Compound personality traits are customized combinations of basic personality traits specifically targeted to certain criterion constructs. Meta-analyses of compound traits such as integrity and customer service orientation indicate that the criterion-related validities associated with measures of those traits surpass Mischel's $r = .30$ prediction barrier (1968).

Both basic personality traits and compound personality traits predict job performance criteria. For example, conscientiousness, achievement, integrity, and service orientation predict performance across many occupations. Several other personality traits, however, correlate substantially with job performance when other factors are considered. Type of job, criterion construct, criterion measurement method (objective versus subjective), validation strategy (for several variables), and type of situation affect personality-performance relationships. Social desirability and mode of administration (computer versus paper-and-pencil administration) do not appear to affect criterion-related validity, however. Research is less clear about the effects of rater perspective. What evidence there is suggests that rater perspective affects the validity of personality variables.

Conclusion

Our conclusion can be simply stated. Careful consideration of taxonomic issues is important to applied psychologists; taxonomic issues are not simply the province of theoreticians who are largely disconnected from the real world. Increasing consensus on what is an appropriate personality taxonomy will facilitate the accumulation of practical knowledge and will result in higher validity coefficients. The identification of compound variables and moderator variables—two vitally important and underexploited methods for incrementing our validity coefficients and enhancing our understanding—is inextricably tied to the formulation and general acceptance of an adequate personality taxonomy.

The mythical bird of personality is alive, its influence ascending. As we approach the new millennium, the relevance of personality to I/O psychology is no myth; it is an undeniable and scientifically exciting reality.

References

Albrecht, K., & Zemke, R. (1985). *Service America.* Homewood, IL: Dow Jones–Irwin.

Allport, G. W., & Odbert, H. S. (1936). Trait-names: A psycho-lexical study. *Psychological Monographs, 47* (serial No. 211).

Barrick, M. R., & Mount, M. K. (1991). The Big Five personality dimensions and job performance: A meta-analysis. *Personnel Psychology, 44,* 1–26.

Barrick, M. R., & Mount, M. K. (1993). Autonomy as a moderator of the relationships between the Big Five personality dimensions and job performance. *Journal of Applied Psychology, 78,* 111–118.

Bentz, V. J. (1984, Aug.). *Explorations in executive behavior.* Invited address presented at the 92nd annual meeting of the American Psychological Association, Toronto.

Bergeman, C. S., Chipuer, H. M., Plomin, R., Pedersen, N. L., McClearn, G. E., Nesselroade, J. R., Costa, P. T., & McCrae, R. R. (1993). Genetic and environmental effects on Openness to Experience, Agreeableness, and Conscientiousness: An adoption/twin study. *Journal of Personality, 61,* 159–179.

Block, J. (1961). The Q-sort method in personality assessment and psychological research. Springfield, IL: Thomas.

Block, J. (1995). A contrarian view of the five-factor approach to personality description. *Psychological Bulletin, 117,* 187–215.

Bluen, S. D., Barling, J., & Burns, W. (1990). Predicting sales performance, job satisfaction, and depression by using Achievement Strivings and Impatience-Irritability dimensions of Type A behavior. *Journal of Applied Psychology, 75,* 212–216.

Bond, M. H. (1994). Trait theory and cross-cultural studies of person perception. *Psychological Inquiry, 5,* 114–117.

Booth-Kewley, S., Edwards, J. E., & Rosenfeld, P. (1992). Impression management, social desirability, and computer administration of attitude questionnaires: Does the computer make a difference? *Journal of Applied Psychology, 77,* 562–566.

Borislow, B. (1958). The Edwards Personal Preference Schedule and fakeability. *Journal of Applied Psychology, 42,* 22–27.

Borman, W. C., & Motowidlo, S. J. (1993). Expanding the criterion space to include elements of contextual performance. In N. Schmitt, W. C. Borman, and Associates, *Personnel selection in organizations* (pp. 71–98). San Francisco: Jossey-Bass.

Bray, D. W., & Howard, A. (1983). Personality and the assessment center method. In C. D. Spielberger & J. N. Butcher (Eds.), *Advances in personality assessment* (Vol. 3, pp. 1–34). Hillsdale, NJ: Erlbaum.

Buss, D. M. (1990). Toward a biologically informed psychology of personality. *Journal of Personality, 58,* 1–16.

Camara, W. J., & Schneider, D. L. (1994). Integrity tests: Facts and unresolved issues. *American Psychologist, 49,* 112–119.

Campbell, C. H., Ford, P., Rumsey, M. G., Pulakos, E. D., Borman, W. C., Felker, D. B., deVera, M. V., & Riegelhaupt, B. J. (1990). Development of multiple job performance measures in a representative sample of jobs. *Personnel Psychology, 43,* 277–300.

Campbell, J. P. (1990). Modeling the performance prediction problem in industrial and organizational psychology. In M. D. Dunnette & L. M. Hough (Eds.), *Handbook of industrial and organizational psychology*

(2nd ed.; Vol. 1, pp. 687–732). Palo Alto, CA: Consulting Psychologists Press.

Campbell, J. P. (Ed.). (1996). *Exploring the limits: Performance improvement through personnel selection and differential job assignments.* Hillsdale, NJ: Erlbaum.

Campbell, J. P., McCloy, R. A., Oppler, S. H., & Sager, C. E. (1993). A theory of performance. In N. Schmitt, W. C. Borman, and Associates, *Personnel selection in organizations* (pp. 35–70). San Francisco: Jossey-Bass.

Campbell, J. P., McHenry, J. J., & Wise, L. L (1990). Modeling job performance in a population of jobs. *Personnel Psychology, 43,* 313–333.

Cattell, R. B. (1943). The description of personality: Basic traits resolved into clusters. *Journal of Abnormal and Social Psychology, 38,* 476–506.

Cattell, R. B. (1945). The description of personality: Principles and findings in a factor analysis. *American Journal of Psychology, 58,* 69–90.

Cattell, R. B. (1946). *Description and measurement of personality.* Yonkers-on-Hudson, NY: World.

Cattell, R. B., Eber, H. W., & Tatsuoka, M. M. (1970). *Handbook of the Sixteen Personality Factor Questionnaire* (16PF). Champaign, IL: Institute for Personality Testing.

Christiansen, N. D., Goffin, R. D., Johnston, N. G., & Rothstein, M. G. (1994). Correcting the 16PF for faking: Effects on criterion-related validity and individual hiring decisions. *Personnel Psychology, 47,* 847–860.

Collins, J. M., & Schmidt, F. L. (1993). Personality, integrity, and white-collar crime: A construct validity study. *Personnel Psychology, 46,* 295–311.

Costa, P. T., & McCrae, R. R. (1985). *The NEO Personality Inventory manual.* Odessa, FL: Psychological Assessment Resources.

Costa, P. T., & McCrae, R. R. (1988). From catalogue to classification: Murray's needs and the Five-Factor Model. *Journal of Personality and Social Psychology, 55,* 258–265.

Costa, P. T., & McCrae, R. R. (1992). *Revised NEO Personality Inventory (NEO-PI-R) and NEO Five-Factor Inventory (NEO-FFI) professional manual.* Odessa, FL: Psychological Assessment Resources.

Costa, P. T., & McCrae, R. R. (1995a). Solid ground in the wetlands of personality: A reply to Block. *Psychological Bulletin, 117,* 216–220.

Costa, P. T., & McCrae, R. R. (1995b). Domains and facets: Hierarchical personality assessment using the Revised NEO Personality Inventory. *Journal of Personality Assessment, 64,* 21–50.

Costa, P. T., McCrae, R. R., & Dye, D. A. (1991). Facet scales for Agreeableness and Conscientiousness: A revision of the NEO Personality Inventory. *Personality and Individual Differences, 12,* 887–898.

Cronbach, L. J., & Meehl, P. E. (1955). Construct validity in psychological tests. *Psychological Bulletin, 52,* 281–302.

Cudeck, R. (1989). Simple solutions and complex problems. In R. Kanfer, P. L. Ackerman, & R. Cudeck (Eds.), *Abilities, motivation, and methodology: The Minnesota Symposium on Learning and Individual Differences* (pp. 165–172). Hillsdale, NJ: Erlbaum.

Cunningham, M. R., Wong, D. T., & Barbee, A. P. (1994). Self-presentation dynamics on overt integrity tests: Experimental studies of the Reid Report. *Journal of Applied Psychology, 79,* 643–658.

Davis, C., & Cowles, M. (1989). Automated psychological testing: Method of administration, need for approval, and measures of anxiety. *Educational and Psychological Testing, 49,* 311–320.

Day, D. V., & Silverman, S. B. (1989). Personality and job performance: Evidence of incremental validity. *Personnel Psychology, 42,* 25–36.

de Raad, B., & Szirmák, Z. (1994). The search for the Big Five in a non-Indo-European language: The Hungarian trait structure and its relationship to the EPQ and the PTS. *European Review of Applied Psychology, 44,* 17–24.

Digman, J. M. (1990). Personality structure: Emergence of the Five-Factor Model. *Annual Review of Psychology, 41,* 417–440. Palo Alto, CA: Annual Reviews.

Digman, J. M., & Inouye, J. (1986). Further specification of the five robust factors of personality. *Journal of Personality and Social Psychology, 50,* 116–123.

Digman, J. M., & Takemoto-Chock, N. K. (1981). Factors in the natural language of personality: Re-analysis, comparison, and interpretation of six major studies. *Multivariate Behavioral Research, 16,* 149–170.

Dunnett, S., Koun, S., & Barber, P. (1981). Social desirability in the Eysenck Personality Inventory. *British Journal of Psychology, 72,* 19–26.

Dunnette, M. D., McCartney, J., Carlson, H. E., & Kirchner, W. K. (1962). A study of faking behavior on a forced-choice self-description checklist. *Personnel Psychology, 15,* 13–24.

Dweck, C. (1986). Motivational processes affecting learning. *American Psychologist, 41,* 1040–1048.

Evan, W. M., & Miller, J. R. (1969). Differential effects on response bias of computer vs. conventional administration of a social science questionnaire: An exploratory methodological experiment. *Behavioral Science, 14,* 216–227.

Eysenck, H. J. (1990). Genetic and environmental contributions to individual differences: The three major dimensions of personality. *Journal of Personality, 58,* 245–261.

Eysenck, H. J. (1991). Dimensions of personality: 16, 5, or 3?—Criteria for a taxonomic paradigm. *Personality and Individual Differences, 12,* 773–790.

Eysenck, H. J., & Eysenck, M. W. (1985). *Personality and individual differences: A natural science approach.* New York: Plenum.

Feingold, A. (1994). Gender differences in personality: A meta-analysis. *Psychological Bulletin, 116,* 429–456.

Fleishman, E. A., & Quaintance, M. K. (1984). *Taxonomies of human performance.* San Diego, CA: Academic Press.

Freidman, H. S., Tucker, J. S., Tomlinson-Keasey, C., Schwartz, J. E., Wingard, D. L., & Criqui, M. H. (1993). Does childhood personality predict longevity? *Journal of Personality and Social Psychology, 65,* 176–185.

Galton, F. (1884). Measurement of character. *Fortnightly Review, 36,* 179–185.

Gellatly, I. R., Paunonen, S. V., Meyer, J. P., Jackson, D. N., & Goffin, R. D. (1991). Personality, vocational interest, and cognitive predictors of managerial job performance and satisfaction. *Personality and Individual Differences, 12,* 221–231.

Ghiselli, E. E. (1966). *The validity of occupational aptitude tests.* New York: Wiley.

Gilbert, J. A., & Ones, D. S. (1995a). *Are cooperative work group members born or made? A meta-analysis of cooperativeness heritabilities.* Unpublished manuscript, Department of Management, University of Houston.

Gilbert, J. A., & Ones, D. S. (1995b, May). *How heritable is conscientiousness: Implications for personnel selection, employee training, and job performance.* Paper presented at the 10th annual meeting of the Society for Industrial and Organizational Psychology, Orlando, FL.

Goldberg, L. R. (1990). An alternative "description of personality": The Big Five factor structure. *Journal of Personality and Social Psychology, 59,* 1216–1229.

Goldberg, L. R. (1993a). The structure of phenotypic personality traits. *American Psychologist, 48,* 26–34.

Goldberg, L. R. (1993b). The structure of phenotypic personality traits: Vertical and horizontal aspects. In D. C. Funder, R. P. Parke, C. Tomlinson-Keasey, & K. Widaman (Eds.), *Studying lives through time: Personality and development* (pp. 169–188). Washington, DC: American Psychological Association.

Goldberg, L. R., Grenier, J. R., Guion, R. M., Sechrest, L. B., & Wing, H. (1991). *Questionnaires used in the prediction of trustworthiness in preemployment selection decisions.* Washington, DC: American Psychological Association.

Goldberg, L. R., & Rosolack, T. K. (1994). The Big Five factor structure as an integrative framework: An empirical comparison with Eysenck's P-E-N model. In C. F. Halverson, G. A. Kohnstamm, & R. P. Martin (Eds.), *The developing structure of temperament and personality from infancy to adulthood* (pp. 7–35). Hillsdale, NJ: Erlbaum.

Goldberg, L. R., & Saucier, G. (1995). So what do you propose we use instead? A reply to Block. *Psychological Bulletin, 117,* 221–225.

Gough, H. G. (1965). A validational study of the Chapin Social Insight Test. *Psychological Reports, 17,* 355–368.

Gough, H. G. (1984). A managerial potential scale for the California Psychological Inventory. *Journal of Applied Psychology, 69,* 233–240.

Gough, H. G. (1987). *Manual: The California Psychological Inventory.* Palo Alto, CA: Consulting Psychologists Press.

Gray, J. A. (1994). Framework for a taxonomy of psychiatric disorder. In S.H.M. van Goozen, N. E. Van de Poll, & J. A. Sergeant (Eds), *Emotions: Essays on emotion theory.* Hillsdale, NJ: Erlbaum.

Guion, R. M. (1965). *Personnel testing.* New York: McGraw-Hill.

Guion, R. M., & Gottier, R. F. (1965). Validity of personality measures in personnel selection. *Personnel Psychology, 18,* 135–164.

Hampson, S. E., John, O. P., & Goldberg, L. R. (1986). Category breadth and hierarchical structure in personality: Studies of asymmetries in judgments of trait implications. *Journal of Personality and Social Psychology, 51,* 37–54.

Hofstee, W.K.B., de Raad, B., & Goldberg, L. R. (1992). Integration of the Big Five and circumplex approaches to trait structure. *Journal of Personality and Social Psychology, 63,* 146–163.

Hogan, J., & Hogan, R. (1986). *Hogan Personnel Selection Series manual.* Minneapolis, MN: National Computer Systems.

Hogan, R. (1982). Socioanalytic theory of personality. In M. M. Page (Ed.), *1982 Nebraska Symposium on Motivation: Personality—current theory and research* (pp. 55–89). Lincoln: University of Nebraska Press.

Hogan, R., & Hogan, J. (1992). *Hogan Personality Inventory manual.* Tulsa: Hogan Assessment Systems.

Hough, L. M. (1989). Development of personality measures to supplement selection decisions. In B. J. Fallon, H. P. Pfister, & J. Brebner (Eds.), *Advances in industrial organizational psychology* (pp. 365–375). Holland: Elsevier Science.

Hough, L. M. (1992). The "Big Five" personality variables—construct confusion: Description versus prediction. *Human Performance, 5,* 139–155.

Hough, L. M. (1996). Personality at work: Issues and evidence. In M. D. Hakel (Ed.), *Beyond multiple choice: Evaluating alternatives to traditional testing for selection.* Hillsdale, NJ: Erlbaum.

Hough, L. M., Barge, B. N., & Kamp, J. D. (1996). Assessment of personality, temperament, interest, and motivational dispositions. In J. P. Campbell (Ed.), *Exploring the limits: Performance improvement through personnel selection and differential job assignments.* Hillsdale, NJ: Erlbaum.

Hough, L. M., Eaton, N. K., Dunnette, M. D., Kamp, J. D., & McCloy, R. A. (1990). Criterion-related validities of personality constructs and the effect of response distortion on those validities [Monograph]. *Journal of Applied Psychology, 75,* 581–595.

Jackson, D. N. (1984). *Personality Research Form manual* (3rd ed.). Port Huron, MI: Research Psychologists Press.

John, O. P. (1990). The "Big Five" factor taxonomy: Dimensions of personality in the natural language and in questionnaires. In L. A. Pervin (Ed.), *Handbook of personality: Theory and research* (pp. 66–100). New York: Guilford.

John, O. P., Angleitner, A., & Ostendorf, F. (1988). The lexical approach to personality: A historical review of trait taxonomic research. *European Journal of Personality, 2,* 171–203.

Kamp, J. D., & Hough, L. M. (1986). Utility of personality assessment: A review and integration of the literature. In L. M. Hough (Ed.), *Utility of temperament, biodata, and interest assessment for predicting job performance: A review and integration of the literature* (ARI Research Note No. 88–02, pp. 1–90). Alexandria, VA: U.S. Army Research Institute for the Behavioral and Social Sciences.

Kanfer, R., Ackerman, P. L., Murtha, T., & Goff, M. (1995). Personality and intelligence in industrial and organizational psychology. In D. H. Saklofske & M. Zeidner (Eds.), *International handbook of personality and intelligence.* New York: Plenum.

Kantor, J., (1991). The effects of computer administration and identification on the Job Descriptive Index (JDI). *Journal of Business and Psychology, 5,* 309–323.

Katz, D., & Kahn, R. L. (1978). *The social psychology of organizations* (2nd ed.). New York: Wiley.

Katz, L., & Dalby, J. T. (1981). Computer and manual administration of the Eysenck Personality Inventory. *Journal of Clinical Psychology, 37,* 586–588.

Kenrick, D. T., & Funder, D. C. (1988). Profiting from controversy: Lessons from the person-situation debate. *American Psychologist, 43,* 23–34.

Kiesler, D. J. (1983). The 1982 interpersonal circle: A taxonomy for complementarity in human transactions. *Psychological Review, 90,* 185–214.

Kiesler, S., & Sproull, L. (1986). Response effects in the electronic survey. *Public Opinion Quarterly, 50,* 402–413.

Kluger, A. N., Reilly, R. R., & Russell, C. J. (1991). Faking biodata tests: Are option-keyed instruments more resistant? *Journal of Applied Psychology, 76,* 889–896.

Lakatos, I. (1970). Falsification and the methodology of scientific research programmes. In I. Lakatos & A. Musgrave (Eds.), *Criticism and the growth of knowledge* (pp. 91–195). Cambridge, UK: Cambridge University Press.

Lanning, K. (1994). Dimensionality of observer ratings in the California Adult Q-Set. *Journal of Personality and Social Psychology, 67,* 151–160.

Lautenschlager, G. J., & Flaherty, V. L. (1990). Computer administration of questions: More desirable or more social desirability? *Journal of Applied Psychology, 75,* 310–314.

Leary, T. (1957). *Interpersonal diagnosis of personality.* New York: Ronald Press.

Lemonick, M. D., & Nash, J. M. (1995, Mar. 6). Unraveling the universe. *Time,* pp. 76–84.

Loehlin, J. C. (1992). *Genes and environment in personality.* Newbury Park, CA: Sage.

Loevinger, J. (1957). Objective tests as instruments of psychological theory. *Psychological Reports, 3,* 635–694.

Loevinger, J. (1966). The meaning and measurement of ego development. *American Psychologist, 21,* 195–206.

Loevinger, J. (1976). *Ego development: Conceptions and theories.* San Francisco: Jossey-Bass.

Lubinski, D., & Dawis, R. V. (1992). Aptitudes, skills, and proficiencies. In M. D. Dunnette & L. M. Hough (Eds.), *Handbook of industrial and organizational psychology* (2nd ed.; Vol. 3, pp. 1–59). Palo Alto, CA: Consulting Psychologists Press.

Lukin, M. E., Dowd, E. T., Plake, B. S., & Kraft, R. G. (1985). Comparing computerized versus traditional psychological assessment. *Computers in Human Behavior, 1,* 49–58.

McAdams, D. P. (1992). The Five-Factor Model in personality: A critical appraisal. *Journal of Personality, 60,* 329–361.

McCrae, R. R., & Costa, P. T. (1985). Comparison of EPI and psychoticism scales with measures of the Five-Factor Model of personality. *Personality and Individual Differences, 6,* 587–597.

McCrae, R. R., & Costa, P. T. (1987). Validation of the Five-Factor Model across instruments and observers. *Journal of Personality and Social Psychology, 52,* 81–90.

McCrae, R. R., & Costa, P. T. (1989a). The structure of interpersonal traits: Wiggins' circumplex and the Five-Factor Model. *Journal of Personality and Social Psychology, 56,* 586–595.

McCrae, R. R., & Costa, P. T. (1989b). Reinterpreting the Myers-Briggs Type Indicator from the perspective of the Five-Factor Model of personality. *Journal of Personality, 57,* 17–40.

McCrae, R. R., & Costa, P. T. (1994). *Trait explanations in personality psychology.* Unpublished manuscript, Gerontology Research Center, National Institute on Aging, NIH, Baltimore.

McCrae, R. R., & Costa, P. T. (in press). Toward a new generation of personality theories: Theoretical contexts for the Five-Factor Model. In J. S. Wiggins (Ed.), *The Five-Factor Model of personality: Theoretical perspectives.* New York: Guilford.

McCrae, R. R., Costa, P. T., & Busch, C. M. (1986). Evaluating comprehensiveness in personality systems: The California Q-Set and the Five-Factor Model. *Journal of Personality, 54,* 430–446.

McCrae, R. R., Costa, P. T., & Piedmont, R. L. (1993). Folk concepts, natural language, and psychological constructs: The California Psychological Inventory and the Five-Factor Model. *Journal of Personality, 61,* 1–26.

McCrae, R. R., & John, O. P. (1992). An introduction to the Five-Factor Model and its applications. *Journal of Personality, 60,* 175–215.

McDaniel, M. A., & Frei, R. L. (1994). *Validity of customer service measures in personnel selection: A meta-analysis.* Unpublished manuscript, University of Akron.

McHenry, J. J., Hough, L. M., Toquam, J. L., Hanson, M. A., & Ashworth, S. (1990). Project A validity results: The relationship between predictor and criterion domains. *Personnel Psychology, 43,* 335–353.

Meehl, P. E. (1978). Theoretical risks and tabular asterisks: Sir Karl, Sir Ronald, and the slow progress of soft psychology. *Journal of Consulting and Clinical Psychology, 46,* 806–834.

Meehl, P. E. (1986). Trait language and behaviorese. In T. Thompson & M. D. Zeiler (Eds.), *Analysis and integration of behavioral units* (pp. 315–334). Hillsdale, NJ: Erlbaum.

Meehl, P. E. (1990). Appraising and amending theories: The strategy of Lakatosian defense and two principles that warrant it. *Psychological Inquiry, 1,* 108–141.

Michaelis, W., & Eysenck, H. J. (1971). The determination of personality inventory factor pattern and intercorrelations by changes in real-life motivation. *Journal of Genetic Psychology, 118,* 223–234.

Millstein, S. G. (1987). Acceptability and reliability of sensitive information collected via computer interview. *Educational and Psychological Measurement, 47,* 523–533.

Mischel, W. (1968). *Personality and assessment.* New York: Wiley.

Mischel, W. (1977). The interaction of person and situation. In D. Magnusson & N. S. Endler (Eds.), *Personality at the crossroads: Current issues in interactional psychology* (pp. 333–352). Hillsdale, NJ: Erlbaum.

Motowidlo, S. J., & Van Scotter, J. R. (1994). Evidence that task performance should be distinguished from contextual performance. *Journal of Applied Psychology, 79,* 475–480.

Mount, M. K., Barrick, M. R., & Strauss, J. P. (1994). Validity of observer ratings of the Big Five personality factors. *Journal of Applied Psychology, 79,* 272–280.

Murray, H. A. (1938). *Explorations in personality.* New York: Oxford.

Nilsen, D. (1995). *Investigation of the relationship between personality and leadership performance.* Unpublished doctoral dissertation, University of Minnesota.

Norman, W. T. (1963). Toward an adequate taxonomy of personality attributes: Replicated factor structure in peer nomination personality ratings. *Journal of Abnormal and Social Psychology, 66,* 574–583.

Norman, W. T. (1967). *Two thousand eight hundred personality trait descriptors: Normative operating characteristics for a university population.* Ann Arbor: Department of Psychology, University of Michigan.

Ones, D. S., Mount, M. K., Barrick, M. R., & Hunter, J. E. (1994). Personality and job performance: A critique of the Tett, Jackson, and Rothstein (1991) meta-analysis. *Personnel Psychology, 47,* 147–172.

Ones, D. S., Schmidt, F. L., & Viswesvaran, C. (1994, Apr.). Do broader personality variables predict job performance with higher validity? In R. Page (Chair), *Personality and job performance: Big Five versus specific traits.* Symposium conducted at the 9th annual meeting of the Society for Industrial and Organizational Psychology, Nashville, TN.

Ones, D. S., Viswesvaran, C., & Schmidt, F. L. (1993). Comprehensive meta-analysis of integrity test validities: Findings and implications for personnel selection and theories of job performance [Monograph]. *Journal of Applied Psychology, 78,* 679–703.

Ostendorf, F., & Angleitner, A. (1993, July). A German replication study of the Five-Factor Model based on a comprehensive taxonomy of personality descriptive adjectives. In P. T. Costa (Chair), *The Five-Factor Model in Europe: Recent developments.* Symposium conducted at the 4th annual meeting of the International Society for the Study of Individual Differences, Baltimore.

Paajanen, G. E. (1988). *The prediction of counterproductive behavior by individual and organizational variables.* Unpublished doctoral dissertation, University of Minnesota.

Pervin, L. A. (1994). A critical analysis of current trait theory. *Psychological Inquiry, 5,* 103–113.

Peterson, N. G., Hough, L. M., Dunnette, M. D., Rosse, R. L., Houston, J. S.,

Toquam, J. L., & Wing, H. (1990). Project A: Specification of the predictor domain and development of new selection/classification tests. *Personnel Psychology, 43,* 247–276.

Revelle, W. (1995). Personality processes. *Annual Review of Psychology, 46,* 295–328.

Riggio, R. E., Messamer, J., & Throckmorton, B. (1991). Social and academic intelligence: Conceptually distinct but overlapping constructs. *Personality and Individual Differences, 12,* 695–702.

Robins, R. W., John, O. P., & Caspi, A. (1994). Major dimensions of personality in early adolescence. In C. F. Halverson, G. A. Kohnstamm, & R. P. Martin (Eds.), *The developing structure of temperament and personality from infancy to adulthood* (pp. 267–291). Hillsdale, NJ: Erlbaum.

Rosenfeld, P., Doherty, L. M., Vicino, S. M., Kantor, J., & Greaves, J. (1989). Attitude assessment in organizations: Testing three microcomputer-based survey systems. *Journal of General Psychology, 116,* 145–154.

Rozensky, R. H., Honor, L. F., Rasinski, K., Tovian, S. M., & Herz, G. I. (1986). Paper-and-pencil versus computer-administered MMPIs: A comparison of patients' attitudes. *Computers in Human Behavior, 2,* 111–116.

Ryan, A. M., & Sackett, P. R. (1987). Pre-employment honesty testing: Fakability, reactions of test takes, and company image. *Journal of Business and Psychology, 1,* 248–256.

Sackett, P. R., Burris, L. R., & Callahan, C. (1989). Integrity testing for personnel selection: An update. *Personnel Psychology, 42,* 491–529.

Saucier, G., & Goldberg, L. R. (in press). The language of personality: Lexical perspectives on the Five-Factor Model. In J. S. Wiggins (Ed.), *Theoretical perspectives for the Five-Factor Model.* New York: Guilford.

Schneider, R. J. (1992). *An individual-differences approach to understanding and predicting social competence.* Unpublished doctoral dissertation, University of Minnesota.

Schneider, R. J., & Hough, L. M. (1995). Personality and industrial/organizational psychology. In C. L. Cooper & I. T. Robertson (Eds.), *International review of industrial and organizational psychology* (pp. 75–129). Chichester, UK: Wiley.

Schuldberg, D. (1988). The MMPI is less sensitive to the automated testing format than it is to repeated testing: Item and scale effects. *Computers in Human Behavior, 4,* 285–298.

Schwab, D. P. (1971). Issues in response distortion studies of personality inventories: A critique and replicated study. *Personnel Psychology, 24,* 637–647.

Skinner, H. A., & Allen, B. A. (1983). Does the computer make a difference? Computerized versus face-to-face versus self-report assessment of alcohol, drug, and tobacco use. *Journal of Consulting and Clinical Psychology, 51,* 267–275.

Soldz, S., Budman, S., Demby, A., & Merry, J. (1993). Representation of personality disorders in circumplex and five-factor space: Explorations with a clinical sample. *Psychological Assessment, 5,* 41–52.

Stelmack, R. M. (1990). Biological bases of extraversion: Psychophysiological evidence. *Journal of Personality, 59,* 293–311.

Tellegen, A. (1982). *Brief manual for the Multidimensional Personality Questionnaire.* Unpublished manuscript, Department of Psychology, University of Minnesota.

Tellegen, A. (1985). Structures of mood and personality and their relevance to assessing anxiety with an emphasis on self-report. In A. Tuma & J. Maser (Eds.), *Anxiety and the anxiety disorders* (pp. 681–706). Hillsdale, NJ: Erlbaum.

Tellegen, A. (1991). Personality traits: Issues of definition, evidence, and assessment. In D. Cicchetti & W. Grove (Eds.), *Thinking clearly about psychology: Essays in honor of Paul Everett Meehl* (Vol. 1, pp. 10–35). Minneapolis: University of Minnesota Press.

Tellegen, A. (1993). Folk concepts and psychological concepts of personality and personality disorder. *Psychological Inquiry, 4,* 122–130.

Tellegen, A., & Waller, N. G. (in press). Exploring personality through test construction: Development of the Multidimensional Personality Questionnaire. In S. R. Briggs & J. M. Cheek (Eds.), *Personality measures: Development and evaluation* (Vol. 1). Greenwich, CT: JAI Press.

Tett, R. P., Jackson, D. N., & Rothstein, M. (1991). Personality measures as predictors of job performance: A meta-analytic review. *Personnel Psychology, 44,* 703–742.

Tett, R. P., Jackson, D. N., Rothstein, M., & Reddon, J. R. (1994). Meta-analysis of personality–job performance relations: A reply to Ones, Mount, Barrick, and Hunter (1994). *Personnel Psychology, 47,* 157–172.

Thornton, G. C., & Gierasch, P. F. (1980). Fakability of an empirically derived selection instrument. *Journal of Personality Assessment, 44,* 48–51.

Tupes, E. C., & Christal, R. E. (1992). Recurrent personality factors based on trait ratings. *Journal of Personality, 60,* 225–251. (Originally released 1961.)

Waller, N. G., & Ben-Porath, Y. S. (1987). Is it time for clinical psychology to embrace the Five-Factor Model of personality? *American Psychologist, 42,* 887–889.

White, D. M., Clements, C. B., & Fowler, R. D. (1985). A comparison of computer administration with standard administration of the MMPI. *Computers in Human Behavior, 1*, 153–162.

White, R. W. (1959). Motivation reconsidered: The concept of competence. *Psychological Review, 66*, 297–333.

Wiggins, J. S. (1979). A psychological taxonomy of trait-descriptive terms: The interpersonal domain. *Journal of Personality and Social Psychology, 37*, 395–412.

Wiggins, J. S., Trapnell, P., & Phillips, N. (1988). Psychometric and geometric characteristics of the Revised Interpersonal Adjective Scales (IAS-R). *Multivariate Behavioral Research, 23*, 517–530.

Wilson, F. R., Genco, K. T., & Yager, G. G. (1985). Assessing the equivalence of paper-and-pencil vs. computerized tests: Demonstration of a promising methodology. *Computers in Human Behavior, 1*, 265–275.

Yang, K., & Bond, M. H. (1990). Exploring implicit personality theories with indigenous or imported constructs: The Chinese case. *Journal of Personality and Social Psychology, 58*, 1087–1095.

Chapter Three

Vocational Interests

Matching Self-Concept with the Work Environment

Robert Hogan
Rex J. Blake

This chapter reviews the implications of individual differences in interests and values for how people behave at work and how they are regarded by their co-workers. Let us begin with some definitions.

Introduction and Definitions

Peters (1958), in an important analysis of the concept of motivation, distinguishes between *causes* and *reasons* as explanations for social behavior. Causes as explanations are processes (biological or physiological) inside people that somehow propel them into action. Reasons as explanations, on the other hand, refer to people's intentions, goals, and agendas; reasons are mental or intrapsychic constructs that provide direction and focus for people's actions. Peters goes on to argue that, for most everyday purposes, we explain a person's actions in terms of what he or she intends or wishes to achieve by a course of action. Thus *intentions, goals,* and *agendas* have a unique role to play in the explanation of social action.

Needs, drives, values, and *interests* are closely related concepts; they are motivational terms that refer to the intentions or goals of a person's actions. Needs are typically seen as the most fundamental of these constructs, and many people regard needs or drives as having a physiological basis. Peters (1958) takes exception to this popular notion. The concept of need or drive, Peters notes, postulates a mysterious end-state of quiescence, satisfaction, or tension reduction that is never measured or observed: "Psychology's advance, at any rate toward conceptual clarity, would surely be more rapid still if it were admitted that it is only the directedness of behavior that is entailed by saying that it is motivated, not any specific causal conditions of 'drive' or anything else" (p. 42).

To distinguish among needs, values, and interests may be as much a matter of semantics and personal choice as anything else because the terms have been used interchangeably in much of psychology. Values generally have been the most inclusive construct; Dawis (1980) notes that various authors regard values as equivalent to beliefs (Allport, 1961; Rokeach, 1973), attitudes (D. T. Campbell, 1963), needs (Maslow, 1954), interests (Allport, 1961; Perry, 1954), and preferences (Katzell, 1964; Rokeach, 1973).

Needs, values, and interests are constructs inferred from the patterns of an individual's activities or stated intentions. They differ primarily in their breadth and level of abstraction. Super (1973) puts needs at the top of the hierarchy of abstraction. He sees both values and interests as lower-order constructs derived from needs. Values are conceptualized as objectives sought to satisfy needs. Interests comprise the specific activities and objects through which an individual attains values and satisfies his or her needs. Interests, then, are the least abstract constructs in Super's hierarchical representation of motivational terms. Dawis (1980) suggests that interests, along with attitudes, needs, values, and preferences, are a set of constructs that represent "an affective orientation toward stimulus objects" (p. 77). Like Super, he suggests a hierarchical arrangement of the constructs: "*Attitudes* appear to be the most general construct and refer to a favorable-unfavorable (accept-reject) orientation toward attitude objects. *Needs* and *values* refer to the importance-unimportance to the subject of the stimulus object. By contrast, *preferences* and *interests* refer to the dimension of liking-disliking for the stimulus object" (p. 77). Although there are some differences between Dawis's and Super's hierarchies, both people regard interests as the most specific and least abstract construct in a hierarchy of motivational terms.

Constructs at the more abstract levels of the hierarchy have been linked to lower-order variables by means of measures of those constructs. To assess individual differences in the higher-order constructs requires translating them into more specific exemplars. For that reason, constructing a measure of a particular need (for example, the need for achievement) requires identifying the values, preferences, and interests that characterize that need (for example, valuing success and accomplishment, preferring recognition over anonymity, and expressing interest in competitive activities).

The availability of instruments to assess for constructs at the lowest level of the hierarchy has not automatically forged links to other motivational constructs. In particular, the measurement of particular interests does not require inferences about relationships to higher-order constructs. Interpreting a respondent's endorsement of the item "I like tennis" requires no assumptions about the motive(s) or goal(s) that explain his or her expressed attraction to the sport; that preference could be based on any of a number of underlying motives. Klinger's distinction (1977) between *needs* and *current concerns* seems relevant. According to Klinger, "A need or motive such as 'achievement' or 'affiliation' can subsume a wide range of possible concrete goals, any one of which may be the focus of a current concern. Thus, someone with a high 'need to achieve' may have separate current concerns about setting a new sales record, beating his or her tennis partner, and patenting a new design for a mousetrap. On the other hand, someone interested in setting a new sales record may be doing it for the money, not because of a need to achieve" (p. 350).

Thus, connecting interests with the constructs from other motivational domains may be a rather complex process; an interest in a particular activity could conceivably represent any of a number of underlying motives. Moreover, interests can have predictive utility (in that an individual's future choices of and reported satisfaction with particular activities, occupations, and types of people often reflect those that the individual found satisfying in the past) without requiring the identification of a higher-order construct as the source of the covariation. That is indeed how vocational interest measurement developed. Researchers have generated a considerable empirical literature demonstrating significant predictive utility for measured vocational interests. Thus far, however, there has been little progress in connecting interests to constructs in other domains (Dawis, 1980; Holland, 1976). Holland (1976) notes the separation of interest measurement from the rest of psychology with marked dissatisfaction: "The interest literature still remains largely outside the mainstream of psychology and sociology. The sheer empirical success of these inventories may have relieved interest enthusiasts of the need to cultivate other parts of psychology. Subsequently, neither group—interest types and the other types in psychology—have developed useful dependencies upon one another. Consequently, the interest literature remains a rambling, formless literature integrated only by a few popular inventories and unable to draw on the strengths of personality and learning theory and vice versa" (p. 523).

The foregoing discussion can be summarized in terms of three points. First, terms such as *needs, values,* and *interests* overlap substantially in their meaning. Second, these terms can be placed in a hierarchy of abstraction, with interests as the least and values as the most abstract. Third, although philosophers regard these terms as crucial for explaining social action, psychologists have been largely uninterested in the conceptual relations among them.

The Meaning of Interests

For most of the history of interest measurement, researchers have been concerned with demonstrating the utility of the measures and have focused on operational rather than conceptual definitions. The need to demonstrate the practical utility of interest measurement may have been driven by early questions regarding the point of studying interests. Interest measurement was clearly seen as a somewhat questionable enterprise in its infancy. Strong (1943) observed that "some people in various walks of life, including psychologists, have considered the study of interests as of 'no scientific value,' 'extremely silly and pernicious stuff,' 'a sheer waste of time,' 'useless and inane'" (p. x). Perhaps in response to such criticisms, interest measurement assumed from the outset a distinctly pragmatic character and emphasized its ability to predict meaningful outcomes—work satisfaction, occupational tenure, vocational choice, and so on. Researchers have also investigated the stability of vocational interests as well as the covariance structures underlying the items and scales of various self-report interest inventories. Theory—about what interests are—has generally taken a back seat to those other endeavors. Strong was content to define interests solely in terms of the responses to the interest test items. According to Strong (1960), interests are "activities that are liked or disliked. Each person engages in thousands of activities, or habits, if you prefer that term, and attached to each is a liking-disliking affective tone. They remind me of tropisms. We go toward liked activities, go away from disliked activities" (p. 12). Not surprisingly, many writers regard the interest literature as conceptually barren.

Nevertheless, Strong's statement contains an implicit assumption about the motivational nature of interests; he regards them as having "directional" properties. Yet another statement by Strong (1955) acknowledges both the practical concerns that drove the construction of interest inventories (that is, career guidance and placement) and their conceptual/theoretical connection to other theories of human motivation: "Interest scores measure a complex of liked and disliked activities selected so as to differentiate members of an occupation from non-members. Such a complex is equivalent to a 'condition which supplies stimulation for a particular type of behavior,' i.e., toward or away from participation in the activities characteristic of a given occupation. Interest scores are consequently measures of drives" (p. 142).

Personality and Interests

We noted above that interests can be thought of as representing the lower level of a hierarchical arrangement of motivational constructs—a personality hierarchy of increasing abstractness and decreasing specificity as one ascends to successively higher levels. We would like to examine a bit more closely here the links between personality and interests. The notion that personality and interests are related, even equivalent, constructs has always appealed to vocational psychologists. Hansen (1984) characterizes that notion as "one of the most enduring hypotheses within interest measurement" (p. 116). If one probes beyond operational definitions of interests, virtually *all* the major players have, at one time or another, suggested that inventoried interests are manifestations of a more basic set of personality characteristics. Darley and Hagenah (1955), for example, regarded vocational interest measurement as "a special case in personality theory" and proposed that "interests reflect, in the vocabulary of the world of work, the value systems, the needs, and the motivations of individuals" (p. 191). Layton (1958) considered interests to be "one aspect of what is broadly considered as the motivation of an individual . . . a part of the person's personality structure or organization" (pp. 3–4). Bordin (1943) regarded interest inventory scores as measures of "self-concept." Strong (1955) spoke of interest scores as measures of "drives" (p. 142). Super and Crites (1962) suggested a biological basis, arguing that interests are "the product of interaction between inherited neural and endocrine factors, on the one hand, and opportunity and social evaluation on the other" (p. 410). Roe (1957; Roe and Siegelman, 1964) regarded interests primarily as a reflection of one's social orientation; she suggested that parental relations during early childhood produced an orientation toward either "persons" or "nonpersons"—an orientation that in turn affected the development of an individual's pattern of interests.

Holland made what is easily the strongest statement regarding the relationships between interests and personality: "If vocational interests are construed as an expression of personality, then they represent the expression of personality in work, school subjects, hobbies, recreational activities, and preferences. In short, what we have called 'vocational interests' are simply another aspect of personality. . . . If vocational interests are an expression of personality, then it follows that interest inventories are personality inventories" (1973, p. 7).

On the face of it, however, the content of the two types of inventories suggests that something quite different is being sampled in each. Hofstee (1990) suggests that the prototypical structure of the items comprising personality questionnaires is a "conditional" trait—that is, "an expressed predisposition to behave in a certain way in a particular situation" (p. 79). He also notes that the items comprising personality inventories typically consist of "a hodge-podge of descriptions of overt and covert reactions, trait attributions, wishes and interests, biographical facts, attitudes and beliefs, descriptions of others' reactions to the subject, and more or less bizarre opinions (e.g., 'Somebody is trying to poison me')" (p. 79). Latent characteristics of the respondent are inferred from the responses of those items. Rounds (in press) summarizes the content of interest items and scales as follows:

Broadly speaking, interest items and scales involve preferences for behaviors (response and activity families), situations (the context in which the preferred behaviors occur, usually occupations or physical settings), and reinforcer systems (outcomes or reinforcers associated with the behavior in the situation). On the response side, vocational interests are usually characterized by a shared property of the activities (Selling, Technical Writing, Teaching), and are often implied in the objects of interest (Mathematics, Physical Science, Religion) or inferred as a latent entity (Enterprising, Inquiring, Leading- Influencing); on the stimulus side a shared property of the context (Outdoor Work, Office Work, Industrial) is invoked to explain interest covariation [p. 11].

Our view is closest to Bordin's argument (1943)—that is, equating interests with self-concept. R. Hogan (1983, 1995) points out that our evolutionary history as a group-living animal suggests that, at a deep level, people need attention and approval; at the same time, they need power, status, and control of resources, because persons who enjoy social acceptance and status have preferential opportunities for reproductive success.

Status and acceptance are exchanged during social interaction; thus most people spend their lives moving from one interaction sequence to another, seeking to gain, or not to lose, acceptance and status. During adolescence, people develop identities, idealized self-concepts—for example, scholar, athlete, fun-loving partygoer—and they use their identities to structure interactions.

When people respond to items on psychological inventories, the process is formally identical to what goes on during other forms of social interaction. People use their responses to tell an anonymous interlocutor about their idealized self-concepts—about how they would like to be regarded by the other person. Here, however, we come to a crucial difference between personality and interest inventories. Personality measures ask about typical responses in various situations, but interest measures ask about preferred activities, roles, and types of people. In doing so, they allow people to describe the preferred roles that constitute their ideal self-images. Thus interest inventories get much closer to the actual content of a person's self-concept and more directly reflect the image that he or she would like to be credited with.

Interest inventories may also allow self-description to proceed in a manner much more consistent with that found in social interactions between near strangers. Consider a typical conversation between people who have only just met in an informal, unstructured social situation. In response to the inquiry "Tell me about yourself," we are much more likely to hear "I like tennis" than "In most situations, I am highly competitive." People are accustomed to talking to others about themselves in terms of interests; interests are at the core of the language of social self-description.

The conventional wisdom of industrial and organizational (I/O) psychology is that interests and values reflect affective responses to specific people, events, and activities. Thus interests and values are stimulus-linked, in the sense that they are tied to specific references. In contrast with this view, we believe that interests reflect identities or idealized self-concepts; when people tell us about their interests, they are telling us about themselves and how they want or hope to be regarded.

The Structure of Interests

The structures that have emerged from analyses of the item and scale covariations in the personality and interest domains appear to be quite different. As recently as 1977, Kuder observed that "a definitive structure of interests has not been established" (p. 170). Like personality assessment, interest measurement has progressed toward a consensus regarding the structural properties of its domain, but the process has been influenced by the pragmatic orientation of the vocational interest field. As noted earlier, the field of interest assessment has had a markedly atheoretical quality. Whereas factor analysis has been only one route to theory development in personality assessment, Rounds (in press) suggests that "our current understanding of the interest domain, our approach to describing vocational interests, and the emergence of theoretical models have been largely the result of factor analytic research" (p. 3).

According to Rounds (in press), the application of factor analysis to the interest domain has suggested a roughly hierarchical structure within the domain, with approximately three levels of generality. At the lowest level are "occupational interest factors"; each represents a heterogeneous set of work activities that are characteristic of a particular work setting or occupation. Rounds offers "elementary education" and "library science" as examples of occupational interest factors. At a somewhat more general level are what Rounds calls "basic interest dimensions"; these "comprise work activities that transcend particular situations (occupations)" (p. 11). These are the dimensions that seem to emerge most reliably in item-level factor analyses of vocational interest inventories. They include such factors as "mechanical activities," "mathematics," or "outdoor activities." The activities defining each of these factors seem intuitively similar, and Rounds notes that "most people describe their vocational interests using the language of basic interests" (p. 12). Finally, at the highest level are what have been called "general interest factors." These typically emerge from higher-order analysis of the covariance structures of the basic interest dimensions. At this level, "the elements of the activity family (or occupational family) are dissimilar and an internal entity is postulated to explain their covariation" (Rounds, in press, p. 11). Rounds suggests that, for the interest domain, the distinction between basic interest dimensions and the general interest themes corresponds to that between Meehl's "surface" and "source" traits (1986). Scales designed to measure the higher-order, general interest themes have only recently become a regular feature of interest inventories. The increased attention to higher-level constructs is reflected in successive revisions to our longest-lived interest measurement tool, the Strong Interest Inventory (SII). This inventory began as a series of empirically keyed occupational scales. The number of occupational scales and the addition of both basic interest and general interest themes means that the current form of the SII contains scales corresponding to all three of the levels proposed by Rounds.

Although Strong (1943), Roe (1956), Holland (1973), and Jackson (1977) have proposed general interest schemes, Holland's system is the most widely accepted and popular in the United States. Building on Roe's work and on factor analyses reported by Guilford, Christensen, Bond, and Sutton (1954), Holland (1973) proposed a sixfold taxonomy for organizing individuals and occupations and described six occupational "personality types" (1985). (See Table 3.1.)

Realistic (R) types are practical, hands-on, real-world people who are action-oriented; *Investigative* (I) types are abstract, analytical,

Table 3.1. Holland's Adjectival Descriptions of Six Personality Types.

Realistic	Asocial, conforming, frank, genuine, hard-headed, materialistic, natural, normal, persistent, practical, self-effacing, inflexible, thrifty, uninsightful, uninvolved
Investigative	Analytical, cautious, critical, complex, curious, independent, intellectual, introspective, pessimistic, precise, rational, reserved, retiring, unassuming, unpopular
Artistic	Complicated, disorderly, emotional, expressive, idealistic, imaginative, impractical, impulsive, independent, introspective, intuitive, nonconforming, original, sensitive, open
Social	Ascendant, cooperative, patient, friendly, generous, helpful, idealistic, empathic, kind, persuasive, responsible, sociable, tactful, understanding, warm
Enterprising	Acquisitive, adventurous, agreeable, ambitious, domineering, energetic, exhibitionistic, excitement-seeking, extroverted, flirtatious, optimistic, self-confident, sociable, talkative
Conventional	Careful, conforming, conscientious, defensive, efficient, inflexible, inhibited, methodical, obedient, orderly, persistent, practical, prudish, thrifty, unimaginative

and theory-oriented; *Artistic* (A) types are imaginative and imprac-tical and try to entertain, amuse, and fascinate others; *Social* (S) types enjoy helping, serving, and assisting others; *Enterprising* (E) types try to manipulate, persuade, and outperform others; and *Con-ventional* (C) types count, regulate, and organize people or things.

These types are portrayed in a hexagonal configuration in Fig-ure 3.1. Their physical proximity indexes their relative similarity; adjacent types are more similar to one another than are types located at opposite sides of the hexagon. Although multidimensional analy-ses of scales designed to measure Holland's types rarely, if ever, reproduce a perfectly shaped hexagon, they generally replicate a cir-cumplical ordering of the types (that is, RIASEC), suggesting that the internal relations among the types match Holland's model

Figure 3.1 Personality Dimensions Underlying the Hexagonal Representation of Holland's Vocational Typology.

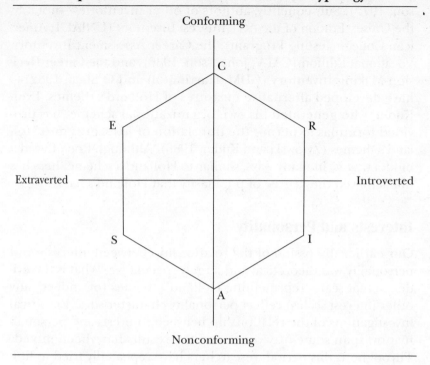

(Rounds, Davison, & Dawis, 1979; Rounds & Zevon, 1983). Alternative structural models summarizing the relations among the types have been offered (for example, Gati, 1991), but the evidence consistently supports Holland's hexagonal model as the most adequate representation of the structure of interests (Tracey & Rounds, 1992).

In the domain of interest measurement, Holland's model has attained about the same status as the Five-Factor Model (FFM) in personality assessment. The *Journal of Vocational Behavior,* vocational psychology's flagship publication, recently devoted an entire issue to Holland's taxonomic scheme. Holland's model has clearly had a major impact on the construction of interest inventories, his own—the Vocational Preference Inventory (VPI; Holland, 1965) and the Self-Directed Search (SD; Holland, 1973)—as well as those of others. In the early seventies, Holland's scales were incorporated into the

Strong-Campbell Interest Inventory (now Strong Interest Inventory, SII; D. P. Campbell and Holland, 1972; Hansen and Johansson, 1972). Subsequently, authors of other inventories—notably, the Unisex Edition of the ACT Interest Inventory (UNIACT; American College Testing Program), the Career Assessment Inventory, Vocational Edition (CAI-V; Johansson, 1986), and the Career Decision-Making Inventory (CDM; Harrington and O'Shea, 1982)—have developed alternative measures of Holland's themes. Even Kuder, who generated his own organizational scheme, has provided formulas to permit the translation of his scores into Holland's themes (Zytowski and Kuder, 1986). Although Roe offered a model that is, in many ways, similar to Holland's scheme, hers has not achieved the degree of popularity that Holland's has.

Interests and Personality

Our earlier discussion of the relationship between interests and personality was theoretical and largely speculative. What is the evidence that scales representing Holland's themes (or, indeed, any other interest scales) reflect personality characteristics? Empirical investigations of the relationship between interests and personality now span some fifty years, and the results have been mixed. Throughout this period, researchers have repeatedly tried to link measures of vocational interest to the scales of more prototypical "personality" measures (for example, Athansou, O'Gorman, & Meyer, 1986; Berdie, 1943; Blake & Sackett, 1994; Bolton, 1985; Costa, Fozard, & McCrae, 1977; Costa, McCrae, & Holland, 1984; Cottle, 1950; Dunnette, Kirchner, & DeGidio, 1958; Gottfredson, Jones, & Holland, 1993; Hansen & Johansson, 1974; R. Hogan & J. Hogan, 1995; R. W. Johnson, Flammer, & Nelson, 1975; Naylor & Thorneycroft, 1986; Peraino & Willerman, 1983; Pryor, 1986; Siess & Jackson, 1970; Stewart, 1971; Turner & Horn, 1975, 1977; Wakefield & Cunningham, 1975; Ward, Cunningham, & Wakefield, 1976). The results of such correlational studies are remarkably consistent: small to moderate correlations between interest and personality scales that Hansen (1984) regards as "extremely disappointing" (p. 117). Hansen and others also acknowledge that the correlations nevertheless appear to be meaningfully patterned and systematic. Holland, who admits that "studies rarely result in substantial correlations between interest and personality variables"

(1976, p. 532), nevertheless interprets the results as generally supporting his theory: "[T]he low-to-moderate significant correlations are largely expected ones: people with social interests have high scores on sociability scales, people with scientific interests appear less social, accounting interests go with being orderly, etc." (p. 532).

In the earliest studies, the lack of an accepted model of the structure of either domain hampered researchers' efforts to generalize their results beyond the scales of particular inventories. The study by Dunnette et al. (1958) is a case in point. Based on correlations between the basic scales of the Edwards Personal Preference Schedule (EPPS; Edwards, 1959), the California Psychological Inventory (CPI; Gough, 1957, 1987), and the occupational scales of the Strong Vocational Interest Blank (SVIB), the authors could conclude only that "the direction of the association among the various variables makes good 'clinical sense'" (p. 179). The authors appear to have had as much difficulty discerning meaningful relationships between the personality inventories as they did between either of the personality inventories and the occupational interest scales. By the time of R. W. Johnson et al.'s study (1975), the introduction of Holland's taxonomy afforded a "higher-order" view of the interest domain that could guide their interpretation of the correlations between the CPI and the occupational scales of the SVIB and illuminate potentially meaningful patterns within the tabulated correlations. Hansen (1984) cites the study by R. W. Johnson et al. as an example of empirical research that begins to converge on at least two broad dimensions of personality—social orientation and independent thought—which appear to account for most of the significant correlations between interest and personality scales. R. Hogan (1983) likewise proposes two broad personality factors as dimensions underlying Holland's hexagonal typology. Specifically, Hogan suggests that two orthogonal dimensions—Sociability and Conformity—define the plane occupied by the hexagon/circumplex. The proposed relationship of these dimensions to the hexagon is depicted in Figure 3.1. Hogan aligned the Conformity dimension (labeled Conforming/Nonconforming) with the hexagon such that Holland's Artistic and Conventional types respectively represent its low and high poles. The Sociability dimension (labeled Extraverted/Introverted) bisects the angle between the Enterprising and Social types on one side of the hexagon and between the Realistic and Investigative types on the other; Social and Enterprising persons are thus "extraverted types" and Realistic and Investigative persons are "introverted types." Blake and Sackett's multidimensional scaling analysis of interest and personality scales (1994) indicates that two broad factors derived from self-report personality inventories and corresponding approximately to Hogan's Sociability and Conformity differentiate among the Holland themes in a manner fully consistent with that proposed by Hogan.

In the last few years, there has been marked progress in developing an "adequate" taxonomy for the organization of major personality constructs; consensus is building around a set of three to seven broad dimensions that have been identified in factor analyses of natural language trait-descriptors and that also seem to be well represented in a number of self-report personality inventories. The same limited set of robust personality factors or themes can also be reliably recovered from analyses of adjective-based interpersonal ratings, self-descriptions, and standardized questionnaires (John, 1990; McCrae & Costa, 1985). The strongest proponents of what has come to be known as the Five-Factor Model assert that these themes "are both necessary and reasonably sufficient for describing at a global level the major features of personality" (McCrae & Costa, 1986, p. 1001). The so-called Big Five—Extraversion, Emotional Stability (or Neuroticism), Conscientiousness, Agreeableness, and Intellect (or Openness to Experience)—offer a framework for organizing and summarizing some of the existing research regarding the relationship of personality and interest domains (for example, Gottfredson et al., 1993) and validating scales intended to represent Holland's types (for example, Blake and Sackett, 1993). Research indicates that four broad dimensions of personality (Extraversion, Conscientiousness, Intellect, and Agreeableness) are consistently and significantly related to interests, while one (Emotional Stability) is not. Table 3.2 presents correlations between scales intended to measure a respondent's similarity to the Holland types and scales from various personality inventories identified as markers for the dimensions of the Five-Factor Model. It is easy to discern a distinctive pattern of correlations between each of the higher-order personality factors and the Holland types. Although the results support a fundamental connection between the two domains, the magnitude of the correlations suggests limited overlap. Interest inventories thus appear to provide unique information about respondents.

Table 3.2. Correlations Between Personality Factors and Holland's Occupational Personality Types.

Personality Scales	Holland Type Scales					
	R	I	A	S	E	C
Extraversion						
Sociability (CPI)	.06	.19	.14	**.26**	**.27**	.11
Social Presence (CPI)	.05	.04	.06	.08	.16	−.01
Person Orientation (CPI)	−.04	−.12	−.12	**−.27**	**−.34**	−.18
Social Activity (GZTS)	−.08	−.02	.13	**.20**	**.48**	.11
Sociability (HPI)	.03	−.01	**.21**	**.27**	**.36**	−.02
Ambition (HPI)	.04	.11	.01	**.31**	**.43**	.14
Extraversion-Introversion (MBTI) (−)	−.01	.00	−.02	.19	**.20**	.03
Social Potency (MPQ)	−.06	.04	.15	**.20**	**.32**	−.05
Social Closeness (MPQ)	−.16	−.06	.16	**.24**	**.22**	.01
Positive Emotionality (MPQ)	.02	.10	.16	**.24**	**.22**	.01
Extraversion (NEO-PI)	.04	.12	.01	**.26**	**.38**	.12
Self-Sufficiency (16PF) (−)	−.15*	−.05	−.03	**.21**	**.20**	.12
Conscientiousness						
Flexibility (CPI) (−)	.00	−.02	**−.22**	−.08	−.04	.08
Value Orientation (CPI)	.10	.18	−.09	.14	.05	.17
Restraint (GZTS)	−.13	.05	−.09	−.03	−.09	**.29**
Prudence (HPI)	−.07	.04	−.13	.00	−.03	**.21**
Judging-Perceiving Orientation (MBTI) (−)	−.03	−.01	−.14	.01	.03	.18
Control (MPQ)	−.03	.00	−.16	−.01	−.09	**.22**
Constraint (MPQ)	−.07	−.12	**−.29**	.00	−.02	**.24**
Conscientiousness (NEO-PI)	.03	.03	−.02	.11	.24	**.34**
Self-Discipline (16PF)	.05	.00	−.16	−.01	.06	.16
Superego Strength (16PF)	.17	.14	−.05	.09	.13	**.26**
Agreeableness						
Likability (HPI)	−.07	−.07	.09	**.47**	**.22**	.05
Thinking-Feeling Orientation (MBTI)	−.18	−.04	.17	**.26**	−.09	−.15
Aggression (MPQ) (−)	−.05	−.03	−.08	.13	−.10	−.03
Agreeableness (NEO-PI)	**−.29**	−.12	.10	**.23**	−.04	.05
Tendermindedness (16PF)	**−.32**	.03	**.40**	**.31**	.01	−.06
Warmth (16PF)	**−.36**	**−.26**	−.03	**.35**	**.24**	.09
Suspiciousness (16PF) (−)	.09	.14	.12	.16	−.04	−.03

Table 3.2. Correlations Between Personality Factors and Holland's Occupational Personality Types, Cont'd.

Personality Scales	Holland Type Scales					
	R	I	A	S	E	C
Openness to Experience						
Achievement via Independence (CPI)	.03	.12	**.27**	.15	.02	−.02
Thoughtfulness (GZTS)	.02	.09	.10	.19	−.07	.18
Absorption (MPQ)	.07	.10	**.37**	.09	−.01	−.09
Sensing-Intuition (MBTI)	.08	**.34**	**.39**	.08	.01	−.07
Openness (NEO-PI)	**.24**	**.36**	**.52**	**.24**	.09	**−.26**
Intellectance (HPI)	**.35**	**.36**	**.49**	.15	.19	−.03
Imagination (16PF)	.06	.18	**.28**	.12	.12	−.02
Adjustment						
Well-Being (CPI)	.12	.15	.07	.14	.10	.05
Objectivity (GZTS)	**.20**	−.09	.09	−.05	−.06	.01
Adjustment (HPI)	−.03	.09	−.01	.06	.05	.02
Stress Reaction (MPQ) (−)	−.02	.00	−.04	.06	.06	.00
Neuroticism (NEO-PI) (−)	.01	.14	.01	−.03	.07	−.02
Emotional Stability (16PF)	.03	.00	−.06	.06	.02	−.04
Apprehensiveness (16PF) (−)	.12	.03	−.05	.06	.11	.05

Note: Values of .20 and greater are shown in bold.

Key: R = Realistic; I = Investigative; A = Artistic; S = Social; E = Enterprising; C = Conventional.

Source: MPQ (Multidimensional Personality Questionnaire) correlations with Strong Interest Inventory reported by Blake and Sackett (1993); CPI (California Psychological Inventory) correlations with Strong-Campbell Interest Inventory reported by Blake and Sackett (1993); GZTS (Guilford-Zimmerman Temperament Survey) correlations with Vocational Preference Inventory reported by Holland (1978); HPI (Hogan Personality Inventory) correlations with Vocational Preference Inventory reported by R. Hogan and J. Hogan (1992); MBTI (Myers-Briggs Type Indicator) correlations with Strong-Campbell Interest Inventory reported by Blake and Sackett (1993); NEO-PI (NEO Personality Inventory) correlations with Self-Directed Search reported by Holland, Johnson, Asama, and Polys (1993); 16PF (Sixteen Personality Factors Questionnaire) correlations with Strong-Campbell Interest Inventory from Blake (unpublished data).

Interests and Occupational Criteria

Strong (1943) noted that he could think of "no better criterion for a vocational interest test than that of satisfaction enduring over a period of time" (p. 385). Although job satisfaction has been studied directly, much research with interest measures has assumed that occupational membership implies satisfaction, and occupational membership has been the most popular dependent variable in the study of interests. This research has yielded relatively consistent results; members of different occupations respond differently to interest items, and many occupational groups can be distinguished on the basis of their interests. Furthermore, later occupational membership can be reliably predicted from interests measured at an earlier age. Strong (1935, 1943) reported long-term follow-up studies with the SVIB yielding impressive "hit rates" (as high as 78 percent) in the prediction of occupational membership based on interest scale scores obtained five to eighteen years earlier. Strong's findings have been replicated by many investigators using a variety of samples and methods (for example, Bartling & Hood, 1981; Brandt & Hood, 1968; Cairo, 1982; D. P. Campbell, 1966; Dolliver, Irvin, & Bigley, 1972; Dolliver & Will, 1977; Gade & Soliah, 1975; Hansen, 1986; Hansen & Swansen, 1983; Lau & Abrahams, 1971; Worthington & Dolliver, 1977; Zytowski, 1976). This body of work provides solid evidence that measured interests are valid predictors of occupational membership criteria.

Although these results are impressive, they nonetheless raise a question about more basic processes involved in occupational choice and tenure: What are the factors that contribute to a person's tenure in a particular organization or occupation? Dawis and Lofquist (1984) propose that two relatively distinct appraisal processes affect tenure in a particular occupation. One is the degree to which a person is satisfied with the environment—the nature of the work, the working conditions, the compensation, the quality of relationships with co-workers and supervisors. The other is the degree to which the environment (that is, the employer) is satisfied with the employee. The implications of each of these appraisals for tenure is relatively straightforward. A dissatisfied employee will be more likely to leave an occupation or organization; an unsatisfactory employee will be more likely to be expelled. A more fine-grained analysis of the relationship between interests and occupational success requires that the validity of measured interests for each of these criteria be considered separately.

Satisfaction

As noted above, Strong (1943) believed that the most appropriate criterion for assessing the validity of interests is satisfaction. Research on this topic, however, has produced mixed results. A number of studies have failed to find a significant relationship between interests and job satisfaction (for example, Bartling & Hood, 1981; Butler, Crinnion, & Martin, 1972; Cairo, 1982; Dolliver, Irvin, & Bigley, 1972; McArthur, 1954; Schletzer, 1966; Trimble, 1965; Zytowski, 1976). Others, however, have reported significant relations between job satisfaction and group differences in vocational interests (for example, Barak & Meir, 1974; DiMichael & Dabelstein, 1947; Hahn & Williams, 1945; Herzberg & Russell, 1953; Klein & Weiner, 1977; McRae, 1959; North, 1958; Trimble, 1965; Worthington & Dolliver, 1977). In the positive studies, the correlations have generally been low to moderate. Barge and Hough (1988) cite eighteen studies with a median correlation of .31 between interests and job satisfaction.

D. P. Campbell (1971) suggests that the modest relationships between interests and job satisfaction reported in the literature reflect a restriction in the range of the criterion variable. Depending on how the question is asked, most incumbents express satisfaction with their work. In a study of U.S. workers, for example, Weaver (1980) reports that more than 80 percent said that they were either somewhat or very satisfied with their jobs. It is also becoming clear that a variety of factors influence workers' judgments about whether a job is "satisfying." It is not clear that having "interesting" work, for example, is a major concern for all employees. Moreover, many features of the work environment—pay, security, and supervision, among others—that have little to do with the content of the work also influence satisfaction. Furthermore, there are marked individual differences in the degree to which any of these factors influence workers' feelings of satisfaction with a job (Dawis & Lofquist, 1984). Finally, there is increasing evidence for individual differences in the degree to which workers express satisfaction with *any* job. Although some researchers disagree, individual differences in the disposition to experience positive and negative affective states appear to have significant implications for the use of self-reported job satisfaction as a dependent variable (for example, Burke, Brief, & George, 1993; Costa & McCrae, 1980; Levin & Stokes, 1989).

Satisfactoriness

There is little systematic research on the link between interests and the degree to which an employee is regarded by others as satisfactory. Nonetheless, surveys of existing studies typically yield reasonable validity coefficients. Most studies use performance ratings as criteria. Such studies involve a variety of occupational groups, including Navy enlisted personnel (Borman, Toquam, & Rosse, 1979; Dann & Abrahams, 1977; Lau & Abrahams, 1970), Naval Academy cadets (Abrahams & Neumann, 1973), forest rangers (Miner, 1960), supervisors (Strong, 1943), foremen and assistant foremen (Schultz & Barnabas, 1945), managers (J. C. Johnson & Dunnette, 1968; Nash, 1966), engineers (Dunnette & Aylward, 1956), and counselors (Wiggins & Weslander, 1979). Barge and Hough (1988) reviewed the results of eleven studies using performance ratings as the dependent variable and report correlations ranging from .01 to .40 (median $r = .20$). There is variability even within a single study: Lau and Abrahams (1970), for example, in a study of Navy enlisted recruits, report correlations between interest scores and performance ratings ranging from .15 to .38 (median $r = .25$). Although there are occasional negative findings (for example, Dunnette & Aylward, 1956), the validity coefficients compare favorably with those obtained with personality inventories and are occasionally quite large. Wiggins and Weslander (1979) report correlations of −.60 and .56 between the Realistic and Social scales of the VPI and the rated performance of counselors.

Although these results are intriguing, they are nonetheless tentative, because researchers have only a rudimentary understanding of the reasons for a relationship between interests and job performance. At present, there seem to be two lines of thought regarding the interest-performance relationship. These perspectives might be described as the *task motivational* and *social evaluation* models.

The task motivational model reflects the traditional view of task performances as an interaction between ability and motivation—P = f(A × M)—where task-relevant interests are the motivational variable. This is a conditional model of task performance; in order to be successful at a task, an individual must be both able and willing to do it. In the absence of either sufficient ability or interest, successful task performance is unlikely. Interest alone is insufficient to guarantee performance; ability alone *may* be a sufficient condition for task accomplishment, but the likelihood of effective performance should increase with greater interest in the task. At lower levels of interest, a person will be less willing to engage the task and less likely to persist on a difficult task even if he or she begins it. At even lower levels of interest, disinterest becomes dislike and a person's antipathy toward a task leads to avoidance, making performance impossible—even for someone with adequate ability.

A handful of studies have found positive relations between interests and objective indices of worker productivity. Three of the studies cited by Barge and Hough (1988) used archival production records as dependent variables, and those studies found a median correlation between interests and performance of .33 (ranging from .24 to .53). Strong (1943) reported a correlation of .40 between interest scores and the productivity of insurance agents. Knauft (1951) reported a cross-validated correlation of .53 between a specially developed key and an objective criterion of performance (cost/sales ratio) for bakery shop managers. Clark (1961) concluded that work performance is an interaction between ability and interests; Clark's data indicate that interest scores predict job performance better at some ability levels than at others.

The ability of the task motivational model to account for the observed relations between interests, occupational membership, satisfaction, and employee satisfactoriness has some empirical problems. If interests predict occupational criteria primarily because they reflect task-relevant motivation, then the interests that characterize tenured workers in a particular occupation should parallel the activities required as part of the job. However, occupational groups often show distinctive patterns of interests that are not easily explainable on the basis of their "job-relatedness."

D. P. Campbell (1987), for example, compares personality and interest data from a sample of generals in the U.S. Army with samples of managers and executives from civilian organizations. Not surprisingly, the generals scored much higher than the members of the other two groups on a scale reflecting interest in "military activities." It is easy to understand why the military group had distinctive scores on "military" items; it seems unlikely, after all, that a person would have a career in the military if he or she disliked "drilling soldiers," "military people," and so on. It is harder to explain why the Army officers received low scores on measures of "artistic" interests. Actually, although the generals received the lowest scores in this area, all three groups scored well below the mean for the general population on "artistic" interests. The three groups resembled one another on a variety of dimensions, but they were distinguished from other occupational groups on a dimension that seems to have no direct bearing on their occupational activities. It is difficult to explain why these groups received low scores for artistic interests if we look only at job-relevant task motivation. Nor does this outcome seem to be a matter of the psychometric properties of the interest inventory. The Strong-Campbell Interest Inventory, which was used in the study, is not a forced-choice inventory. That is, respondents do not have to choose between military and artistic items; they can endorse both (but in the Campbell study generally chose not to). Nor are Campbell's data unique. Borgen (1986) notes that most of the empirical evidence regarding the occupational relevance of measured interests amounts to statements that have the form of "real estate salespeople like sales activities and dislike science." Interest in sales makes sense based on what real estate agents do; lack of interest in science is more difficult to explain. Borgen suggests that the blind empiricism that characterizes vocational interest research leaves many questions unanswered—for example, "Is it necessary to dislike science in order to be a successful realtor?" (p. 106).

The social evaluation model of the interest-performance relationship may contain the answers to these questions. For at least thirty years, I/O psychology has used performance ratings as an indirect method of sampling job performance, based on the hope that raters can evaluate the performance of ratees accurately with respect to job-relevant tasks and behaviors. An emerging perspective—the social evaluation model—regards performance ratings as evaluative phenomena that may not be directly related to work performance. Stockford and Bissell (1976), for example, suggest that ratings reflect "primarily the personal-social relationships between supervisor and subordinate rather than the output of the subordinate in question." Borman (1983) notes that performance ratings depend on the same principles that characterize social perception and evaluation in general.

Subsequent studies by Borman (1974, 1987), Werner (1994), and others suggest that raters normally take a broader view of job performance than is indicated by the role prescriptions that come from a typical job analysis. It is increasingly clear that task performance typically accounts for only a part—and not always the major part—of a rater's evaluation of his or her co-workers' performance. In addition to the specific tasks required by a job, workers are usually expected to fulfill other role demands that are implicit in the interdependent social nature of most work settings.

When evaluating another member of a work group, raters consider, in addition to that co-worker's actual task performance, the degree to which that person goes along with rules, does what he or she is supposed to do, and maintains pleasant relations with supervisors and peers. Consequently, Dawis (1991) suggests that the term *worker satisfactoriness* be substituted for *job performance*. The former term more accurately describes the fact that criterion ratings usually consist of a rater's reported satisfaction with the ratee. These considerations suggest that performance ratings can be seen as *social evaluations* that reflect raters' reactions to ratees rather than veridical reports of specific ratee behavior. This leads in turn to questions about the factors that influence such ratings, and these certainly include the values and characteristics of the raters. J. P. Campbell, Dunnette, Lawler, and Weick (1970) suggest that what observers "define as effective in others' job behavior depends importantly on their own characteristics" (p. 201); nonetheless, this view has not been well developed in I/O psychology.

The social psychological literature on interpersonal attraction also seems relevant to this discussion. That literature shows that *similarity* (of attitudes, values, interests, and backgrounds) is an important determinant of interpersonal attraction (Berscheid, 1985; Byrne, 1971; Levine & Moreland, 1990; Lott & Lott, 1965). A few studies have examined the effects of perceived similarity on hiring and selection decisions (Baskett, 1973; Wexley & Nemeroff, 1974;

Rand & Wexley, 1975; Latham, Wexley, & Pursell, 1975) and performance evaluations (Miles, 1964; Pulakos & Wexley, 1983; Senger, 1971; Weiss, 1977; Wexley, Alexander, Greenawalt, & Couch, 1980). Their findings have generally been positive—that is, persons who are more similar to the raters get higher ratings.

Holland (1973, 1985) and Schneider (1987) suggest that, in order to understand organizational behavior, we need to understand the values, interests, and personalities of an organization's members. Holland has long maintained that "the character of an environment reflects the typical characteristics of its members. If we know what kind of people make up a group, we can infer the climate the group creates" (1985, p. 35). Schneider (1987) also argues that particular organizations attract, select, and retain particular kinds of people and that the behavior of an organization is a function of the kind of people it retains. Pfeffer's "organizational demography model" (1983) is similar, but it focuses on the shared biographical characteristics of incumbents. In each of these schemes, interpersonal compatibility determines an individual's "fit" with an organization. Consistent with the social psychological literature, interpersonal compatibility is associated with perceived similarity, and this in turn creates a tendency toward relative homogeneity of values, interests, and personality within organizations. Both Holland and Schneider define the environment of an organization in terms of the members' characteristics rather than their requisite tasks. They also suggest that taxonomies of work environments based on characteristic tasks may not predict particular work outcomes as well as taxonomies based on worker characteristics; in other words, person analysis may be more important than task analysis.

There is substantial empirical support for these ideas in the vocational interest literature. The notion that interpersonal similarity is psychologically important and that "birds of a feather flock together" is a cornerstone of vocational psychology (Darley & Hagenah, 1955, p. 19). Although the view has been criticized as unsophisticated and simplistic (for example, Crites, 1969), it has nevertheless generated an extensive empirical literature showing that the fit between workers in a particular occupation predicts work outcomes. Beginning with Strong's research, much vocational interest measurement has focused on identifying the distinctive interest patterns of work environments. As noted earlier, occupational choice, membership, and job tenure are all related to the similarity of an individual's interests with those of a target occupation. It is also possible that interests may be related to performance ratings, because they moderate the relationship between ability and task performance and because interests influence raters' evaluations of others—both as co-workers and as friends.

As noted earlier, Holland's taxonomy (1976) defines occupational environments in terms of members' personality characteristics. The model also predicts how compatible individuals will be with others in particular occupational or organizational settings—and this in turn predicts how others in the work environment will react to that individual. To the extent that individual success depends on others' reactions to—and subjective evaluations of—an incumbent, interest inventories are likely to be useful in a selection context.

Although vocational interest measures can forecast occupational success, they have a potential limitation as a personnel selection tool: because their items are transparent, they can easily be faked. D. P. Campbell (1971) reviewed forty years of research on the question of faking on the SVIB and concluded that scores on the inventory could be distorted by respondents but that the degree of distortion varied according to occupational scale and the transparency of the items. In most of the early studies reviewed by Campbell, the research consisted of asking examinees to complete the inventory with a normal set of instructions and then, after a delay, to fake their responses to resemble those of members of particular occupations. This research design was assumed to be analogous to a selection context in which applicants might try to distort their responses.

It is not clear, however, that people necessarily dissimulate when completing an interest inventory under those conditions. Gray (1959) provides more direct information on respondents' performance in selection contexts. He compared the scores for a group of college students who completed an interest inventory first when seeing a counselor and then again several months later when applying for medical school: "Forty-seven percent of the medical applicant group did not or could not raise their physician score between testing for counseling and testing for admission to medical school. Twenty-four percent raised their physician score enough to have a serious effect on its interpretation by an admissions officer; twenty-nine percent raised their score by a less important amount" (p. 296).

Abrahams, Neumann, and Githens (1971), comparing scores obtained from Navy ROTC applicants with scores obtained from those same applicants under earlier circumstances, reinforce Gray's conclusions. They report a 97 percent overlap in the distribution of scores obtained under the two conditions and conclude that "there is neither a consistent nor significant tendency for applicants to increase their selection scores" (p. 11).

Conscientiousness and Work Outcomes: Implications of Holland's Typology of Persons and Environments

We have made two major points thus far. First, motivational constructs can be organized in a roughly hierarchical structure. Abstract dispositional concepts (values) occupy the highest level of the hierarchy, and the concrete manifestations of those dispositions (interests) occupy the lowest level. Second, the pattern of an individual's preferences as seen in his or her responses to an inventory of those preferences has important real-world consequences. Patterns of interests are demonstrably associated with vocational success and satisfaction. We have so far discussed these notions only in general terms. At this point, we would like to be more specific about the relevance of individual differences for outcomes in particular work environments. In particular, we would like to focus on the implications of research on Holland's typology for the role of conscientiousness in worker success.

Much of the current literature concerning the relationship between personality and job performance assumes that conscientiousness is a universally valued personal characteristic—at least insofar as work behaviors are concerned. That assumption is reflected in Peabody and Goldberg's suggestion (1989) of Work as an alternative label for the dimension known variously as Conscientiousness, Constraint, Dependability, Will to Achieve, Prudence, Self-Control, or Normative Orientation. Barrick and Mount (1991) explicitly state that "Conscientiousness is expected to be related to job performance because it assesses personal characteristics such as persistent, planful, careful, responsible, and hardworking, which are important attributes for accomplishing work tasks in all jobs. . . . Thus, we expect that the validity of this dimension will generalize across all occupational groups and criterion categories" (p. 5).

Although Barrick and Mount find it "difficult to conceive of a job in which the traits associated with the Conscientiousness dimension would not contribute to job success" (p. 22), the evidence suggests rather wide variability in the relationship of conscientiousness to performance ratings across types and levels of occupations (for example, J. Hogan & R. Hogan, 1993; Hough, 1992). Hough (1992) surveys the results of a large-scale literature review of the relationship between higher-order personality dimensions and occupational criteria and concludes that conscientiousness (labeled Dependability in Hough's scheme) predicts law-abiding behavior (mean $r = .58$) better than job proficiency (mean $r = .08$). Its effectiveness as a predictor of job performance also varies across occupational types. Hough reports, for example, a mean correlation of .24 between Dependability and job proficiency for samples of health care workers but a mean correlation of $-.03$ between Dependability and job proficiency for samples of managers and executives.

Before discussing the reasons for this variability, let us reflect on the nature of the conscientiousness construct. A broad, multifaceted construct evident in the natural language, it is marked by such adjectives as *organized, responsible, practical, thorough, hardworking,* and *thrifty* (Goldberg, 1992). It also appears in most comprehensive personality inventories, either at the level of higher-order factors or as a single scale. In omnibus personality inventories, it involves such attributes as orderliness, impulse control, group conformity, and social conservatism. Normative Orientation (Gough, 1987), (low) Impulsivity (Buss & Plomin, 1975), Constraint (Tellegen, 1985), Superego Strength (Cattell, Eber, & Tatsuoka, 1970), Prudence (R. Hogan, 1986), and Orderliness and Social Conformity (Comrey, 1970) are all labels for this factor. As operationalized in most questionnaires, conscientiousness is not unidimensional. The various measures are typically complex, containing themes of independent thought, individuality, autonomy, spontaneity, and impulsivity, along with self-control, rule adherence, and rigidity. Consider Tellegen's higher-order factor Constraint, which includes impulse control or restraint in both the task domain (that is, the lexical factor Conscientiousness) and the ideational or affective domain (that is, Openness to Experience). Tellegen's Constraint emerges as a higher-order dimension from factor analyses of his Multidimensional Personality Questionnaire (MPQ; Tellegen, 1982; Tellegen and Waller, in press). According to Tellegen (1982), the MPQ "evolved out of attempts to clarify both the structure and content of the self-view domain" (p. 1). Through an iterative process consisting of assembling, administering, analyzing, and revising successive research questionnaires, researchers identified eleven primary and three higher-order dimensions. Because Tellegen's object "was not to explore wholly unknown territory, but to arrive at a more instructive and useful map" (p. 2) of the self-view domain, there are clear linkages between both primary and higher-order MPQ scales and scales on other inventories. The higher-order MPQ factor Positive Emotionality is defined by the MPQ primary scales Well-Being, Social Potency, Achievement, and Social Closeness (Tellegen, 1982; Tellegen and Waller, in press). Negative Emotionality (the MPQ's second higher-order dimension), which is marked by Stress Reaction, Alienation, and Aggression scales, defines a broad adjustment or emotional stability dimension. The MPQ's third higher-order dimension, Constraint, is marked by three distinct primary scales: Control, Harm Avoidance, and Traditionalism. Tellegen (1982) describes high scorers on Control (versus Impulsivity) as reflective, cautious, careful, plodding, rational, sensible, level-headed, and habitually planful. Low scorers are impulsive and spontaneous, can be reckless or careless, and make no detailed plans, preferring instead to "play things by ear." High scorers on the MPQ Harm Avoidance scale prefer "safer activities and experiences, even if they are tedious or aggravating" (p. 7). According to Tellegen, the item content of the MPQ Traditionalism scale reflects high moral standards, religious values and institutions, and strict childrearing practices. High scorers express positive regard for parents, value conventional propriety and a good reputation, oppose rebelliousness and unrestricted freedom of expression, and condemn selfish disregard of others. The three scales are relatively independent of one another, with intercorrelations ranging from $r = .17$ for Harm Avoidance and Traditionalism to $r = .27$ for Harm Avoidance and Control. Based on

Tellegen's description of Constraint (1982), John (1990) suggests that the factor shares a number of central features with the Conscientiousness dimension of the Five-Factor Model, "including caution, attention to detail, and appropriate impulse control, as contrasted with impulsiveness and distractability" (p. 87).

The Prudence scale of the Hogan Personality Inventory (HPI) resembles the MPQ Constraint factor and is composed of seven clusters of highly correlated items called homogeneous item composites (HICs; Zonderman, 1980). They are identified as Moralistic (showing strict adherence to conventional values), Mastery (hardworking), Virtuous (pursuing perfectionism), Not Autonomous (showing concern for others' opinions), Not Spontaneous (preferring predictability), Impulse Control, and Avoids Trouble (professing probity). Factor analyses used to develop the HPI scales suggest two distinct clusters among these HICs. One reflects conformity, self-control, and responsiveness to authority. The second is defined by a concern for traditional values, social appropriateness, and a degree of self-righteousness. The parallel between these two underlying themes and those reflected in the Control and Traditionalism scales of the MPQ is unmistakable.

These two aspects of the broad concept of conscientiousness reflect two recurring themes in discussions of values and value orientations. They correspond to the notions of "work ethic" and "attitude toward authority"—notions that in the popular mind are particularly relevant to occupational performance and organizational citizenship.

Work Ethic

Certain people are believed to work hard because of their work ethic. We might say, for example, "They have a good work ethic in Oklahoma." The concept of work ethic is usually attributed to the German historian Max Weber (1904), who argued in his classic *The Protestant Ethic and the Spirit of Capitalism* that (1) the economies of Protestant countries after the Reformation grew more rapidly than the economies of Catholic countries and (2) this was a function of the value system of the Protestant cultures. Specifically, the core of the Protestant ethic was the belief that salvation would come not through adherence to church teachings but rather through divine grace; only some people would be saved, and no one could know for sure who that would be. But there were clues: each person, Weber thought, had a "calling"; and in order to be chosen, one had to perform assiduously the duties associated with one's calling. If one were a worker, one had to work very hard indeed; if one were an entrepreneur, one had to make a lot of money—which was not to be spent on worldly display but rather to be put back into the business.

McClelland's research on Achievement Motivation (1961) was essentially designed to test the hypothesis implicit in Weber's thesis—that is, that hardworking people are characterized by a particular set of values. In perhaps his most imaginative demonstration of the link between Protestant values and worldly achievement, McClelland compared the economic development of all countries in the temperate zones in 1950, defined in terms of electricity consumption; the average value for twelve Protestant countries (including Norway, Canada, and South Africa) was 1,983 kilowatt hours per capita; the average value for thirteen Catholic countries (including Austria, Chile, and Belgium) was 474 kilowatt hours per capita.

McClelland also developed a methodology for scoring Achievement Motivation from "fantasy" material. Using that methodology, he showed that a certain set of childrearing tactics could produce children with higher levels of Achievement Motivation. The overall effort is an interesting and impressive accomplishment; in our judgment, however, the bottom line for the purposes of this chapter is that Weber's original definition of the Protestant ethic— working hard and being successful—and McClelland's measure of the concept—Achievement Motivation—confound two distinct "values": hard work and financial or worldly success. Many hardworking people do not crave success, and many people who crave success are not hardworking.

Bray and Howard (1983) support the distinction between these themes. In a summary of the Management Progress Study at AT&T, they note that two motivational themes predicted managerial performance in that company. The first, called Need for Advancement, refers to the degree to which a person wants successively more demanding responsibilities. The second, called Work Standards, refers to the degree to which a person maintains high standards for his or her performance. Need for Advancement roughly corresponds to the worldly success component of the Protestant ethic; Work Standards roughly corresponds to the hardworking component. Composite ratings for these two motive patterns are essentially uncorrelated. Ratings on these two variables have also been correlated with scales from various personality inventories. The highest correlation for the Need for Advancement ratings was $r = .39$ with the Ascendance scale of the Guilford-Martin Inventory of Factors (Martin, 1945) and $r = .33$ with the Dominance scale of the Edwards Personal Preference Schedule (EPPS; Edwards, 1959). The highest correlation with the Work Standards criterion was obtained with the Achievement scale of the EPPS.

Despite its label, "work ethic" includes somewhat different themes from those typically subsumed under the rubric of conscientiousness or emphasized in either the MPQ's Constraint or the HPI's Prudence scales. In each of those inventories, other scales appear more closely aligned with the folk notion of hard work. On the MPQ, the Achievement scale seems to approximate the central concepts of the work ethic. According to Tellegen (1982), the MPQ Achievement scale measures the degree to which a person works hard, welcomes difficult and demanding tasks, persists where others give up, puts work and accomplishment before many other things, and sets high standards. Achievement is most strongly related to Well-Being ($r = .33$ males; $r = .24$ females) and Social Potency ($r = .29$ males and females) on the MPQ. Interestingly, it is slightly more highly correlated with the Control scale than are the other two scales that constitute the MPQ Constraint factor ($r = .30$ males; $r = .20$ females). The corresponding scale on the HPI is Ambition. That scale is composed of themes of competitiveness, energy, and achievement orientation, along with social assertiveness and self-assurance. It is more highly correlated with all of the other HPI scales than it is with Prudence ($r = .28$). Its highest correlation is with Adjustment ($r = .51$).

Gough's effort to derive a measure of the Protestant ethic reinforces the notion that this folk concept is multidimensional and somewhat distinct from conscientiousness. Gough (1985) asked three experts to describe the Protestant ethic using his 300-item adjective checklist. The items that defined the Protestant ethic in the positive direction were *capable, conscientious, dependable, efficient, industrious, loyal, patient, persevering, reasonable, responsible, sincere, stable, steady,* and *thrifty.* Based solely on that sample of adjectives, the construct appears to overlap with conscientiousness, because a number of those adjectives also appear on Goldberg's list (1992) of adjectives defining conscientiousness. However, Gough did not stop with a list of adjectives. He assigned a sample of men and women scores on the basis of their resemblance to the adjectival profile of the Protestant ethic. He then compared their CPI item responses with Protestant ethic scores. Additionally, he compared the CPI responses of a large sample of correctional officers with their job performance ratings. Finally, Gough composed a Work Orientation scale using items that were significant in both samples. The most interesting part of Gough's analysis, in our view, is that scores on Work Orientation correlate more highly with measures of adjustment than with measures of conscientiousness. The highest correlations reported by Gough are with the Well-Being scale of the CPI ($r = .84$ for men; $r = .85$ for women), Emotional Stability on the Guilford-Zimmerman Temperament Survey ($r = .78$), and (low) Anxiety Level on the Omnibus Personality Inventory ($r = .78$). Work Orientation apparently includes themes of stability, responsibility, impulse control, conservative values, friendliness in dealing with others, and achievement orientation. This suggests, once again, that the folk notion of a work ethic confounds a number of individual attributes, most of which are relatively distinct from the core characteristics of the lexical dimension of conscientiousness.

These data suggest that the term "good work ethic" can be used to describe the attitude of people who work hard, do not complain, and seek out challenging assignments. Thus conscientiousness, in the sense of self-control and behavioral inhibition, is only part of one's work ethic; in other words, persons with a good work ethic not only mind their manners but also persevere at difficult tasks and refrain from complaining about problems and reversals.

These data are relatively consistent with the hierarchy of motivational constructs discussed in the opening sections. Characteristics such as achievement orientation, adjustment, extraversion, ambition, and conscientiousness are at the highest level of the hierarchy. At lower levels, those qualities, individually or in combination, are labeled according to their impact and perceived value in the social group. Thus the work ethic is a configuration of characteristics representing a prototype of the effective worker. It is the set of qualities that make up the ideal employee or co-worker in the popular mind.

These studies argue against the notion that conscientiousness is a universally valued work orientation. Instead, the data indicate that, while conscientiousness is a part of that orientation, ambition, energy, and a positive outlook account for a greater part of the variance in folk notions of worker effectiveness.

Attitudes Toward Authority

Attitudes toward authority are also part of what psychologists have labeled *conscientiousness*. As noted above, the HPI Prudence and MPQ Constraint scales each contain items concerning attitudes toward external rules and formal authority that are different from items reflecting caution, planfulness, and impulse control.

According to Tellegen and Waller (in press), the MPQ Traditionalism scale was developed to understand the relationship between the trio of conformity, conventionality, and authoritarian attitudes and other psychological constructs. Tellegen and Waller were influenced in the development of that scale by Sells, Demaree, and Will's analysis (1968) of some 600 items provided by Guilford and Cattell. From those 600 items, Sells et al. had identified a Conscientiousness factor marked by statements expressing "conforming, conventional, and moralistic attitudes." Tellegen and Waller noted that some of the Conscientiousness items concerned such authoritarian themes as respecting parental authority and advocating strict discipline and childrearing practices. Tellegen and Waller then adapted some of those items—along with others drawn from the F scale, as revised by Lee and Warr (1969), the Dogmatism scale (Rokeach, 1960), and Ernhart and Loevinger's measure of Authoritarian Family Ideology (Ernhart & Loevinger, 1969)—to form an initial item pool. Subsequent analyses confirmed that the items defined a distinct and replicable factor. The initial item pool evolved into the current MPQ Traditionalism scale.

Although Hogan did not set out to assess authoritarianism with the HPI, his efforts to sample the conscientiousness domain produced a similar subset of items. As noted earlier, the HPI Prudence scale can be decomposed into two subscales; one is an index of self-control, and the other reflects concern for traditional values and social appropriateness.

Attitudes toward authority may be an important future area of research for I/O psychology. As noted earlier, researchers have begun to study how raters evaluate their subordinates and co-workers. This represents a shift from thinking about performance appraisals as *reports* of ratees' behaviors to thinking about performance appraisals as reactions or *responses* to ratees' behavior. Terms such as "performance schemata" (Borman, 1987), "prototypes" (Foti & Lord, 1987), "cognitive categorization" (Mount & Thompson, 1987; Phillips, 1984), and "schematic information processing" (Phillips & Lord, 1982) are now used to describe the cognitive structures that raters use to make performance judgments. Studies by Borman (1974, 1987) and Werner (1994) are part of a growing literature examining the content of those cognitive structures. A consistent finding is that workers' attitudes toward rules and formal authority contribute a distinct dimension of evaluation.

Raters seem to recognize the interdependent nature of work and to value "cooperation, helpfulness, suggestions, gestures of goodwill, altruism, and other instances of what we might call citizenship behavior" (Smith, Organ, & Near, 1983, p. 653). Smith et al. (1983) interviewed a number of managers and asked them to "identify instances of helpful, but not absolutely required, job behavior" (p. 656). The instances were translated into sixteen items that were combined into a questionnaire. A second group of managers rated employees on those items according to how characteristic each statement was of the employee. Two factors emerged. The first, labeled Altruism, consisted of efforts to assist other people (as reflected in items such as "helps others who have been absent," "volunteers for things that are not required," "helps others who have heavy work loads"). The second factor concerned "a more impersonal form of conscientiousness that does not provide aid to any one person, but rather is indirectly helpful to others involved in the system. . . . The behavior . . . seems to represent something akin to compliance with internalized norms defining what a 'good employee ought to do'" (p. 657). The second factor, defined by such items as "punctuality," "attendance at work is above the norm," and "does not take unnecessary time off work," the authors labeled Generalized Compliance. Organ (1988) later refers to this dimension as Conscientiousness. Although there is still some debate regarding the dimensionality of these "citizenship behaviors" (for example, MacKenzie, Podsakoff, & Fetter, 1991; Moorman & Blakely, 1992; Organ, 1988; Williams & Anderson, 1991), these two factors are relatively discrete and recurring themes that reflect attitudes toward co-workers and attitudes toward rules and authority.

Research on the outcome of vocational rehabilitation services also distinguishes between working hard and complying with rules and authority. The Minnesota Satisfactoriness Scales (MSS; Gibson, Weiss, Dawis, and Lofquist, 1970) are designed to assess the degree to which an employer is satisfied with a worker. A worker's supervisors or peers compare the quality of that worker's performance on a series of dimensions with other members of his or her work group ("not as well," "about the same," or "better") or rate the frequency of certain behaviors relative to others ("less," "about the same," or "more"). Other items ask whether the rater would give the employee a pay raise or promote him or her to a position of greater responsibility. The final item asks for an overall appraisal of the employee's performance, in comparison to others doing the same work; the rater is asked to indicate in which quarter of the overall distribution the employee would fall. The content of the scales anticipates the current interest in "citizenship" or "extra-role" behaviors in the workplace (for example, Organ, 1988; Werner, 1994). In addition to items rating quality and quantity of task performance, the form includes ratings of absenteeism, lateness, adherence to rules and regulations, and the quality of the worker's relationship with both supervisors and co-workers. Gibson et al. (1970) conclude that the instrument assesses four factors: Performance (task performance, suitability for positions of greater responsibility, and an overall high rating relative to the worker's peers), Conformance (adherence to standard work rules and procedures and acceptance of the supervisor's authority), Dependability (the absence of discipline-invoking actions, lateness, or absenteeism), and Personal Adjustment (negative emotionality, fatigue, and unusual or bizarre behavior at work). Thus employee satisfactoriness is multidimensional; ratings on various aspects of work-related behavior are clearly distinguishable from ratings on the performance of specific tasks as well as overall appraisals of worker satisfactoriness.

Of these various facets of employee satisfactoriness, the Conformance and Dependability factors are most clearly related to conscientiousness. Measures of conscientiousness consistently predict a wide variety of negative work outcomes: absenteeism, alcohol and drug use, rule breaking, disciplinary actions, and other delinquency criteria (compare J. Hogan & Ones, in press; Hough, Eaton, Dunnette, Kamp, & McCloy, 1990; Kamp & Hough, 1988; McHenry, Hough, Toquam, Hanson, and Ashworth, 1990; Potter & Blake, 1994). The ability of conscientiousness measures to predict objective indices of worker performance or productivity or to assess supervisors' or co-workers' judgments of employee satisfactoriness is less clear (compare Hough, 1992). To begin to understand the possible reasons for the inconsistency of results in these areas, we need to consider an earlier body of work.

Social scientists have been interested in attitudes toward authority since the late nineteenth century; virtually every major social theorist (for example, Durkheim, Piaget, G. H. Mead, Freud) has noted that the most important psychological transformation during human development takes place when children accommodate to adult authority. Subsequent transformations of other sorts are possible and necessary, but each child must first learn a sense of duty and obligation to the laws, norms, and precepts of his or her society, all of which are reflected in the rules, values, and standards of his or her family.

Freud devoted more attention to this issue than the others—the problem of authority is the fundamental issue in psychoanalysis. In psychoanalytic theory, persons with well-developed superegos have positive attitudes toward authority; indeed, as adults (and prior to undergoing analysis), their attitudes toward authority are *too* positive. As a result, such persons are often guilt-ridden, rigid, and self-critical, and (although they are utterly dependable organizational citizens) their obsessive self-recriminations leave them joyless and exhausted.

Much of the subsequent research concerning attitudes toward authority has acknowledged its positive and negative aspects (Adorno, Frenkel-Brunswik, Levinson, & Sanford, 1950). Modern research on conscientiousness also suggests two well-established points: first, valid measures of conscientiousness index attitudes toward authority; second, these measures predict a wide variety of work outcomes associated with rule adherence and self-control. We in the field of I/O psychology have tended, however, to assume that dependability is important regardless of the occupational setting, and we ignore the negative aspects of conformity. Although there are environments in which conscientiousness is valued, there are other environments in which it is not. Conscientiousness is negatively correlated with creativity (Barron, 1965), for example, so that high conscientiousness may be counterproductive in art, music, poetry, dance, or architecture—in short, in any job that requires flexibility, spontaneity, and a willingness to depart from established and approved ways of doing things. Nor is the impact of conscientiousness relevant solely to individual creativity. In the context of small work teams, Morrison (1993) found that when a task requires solving open-ended problems, teams that lack a member with low conscientiousness scores are unable to provide any adequate solutions.

Holland's Environmental Taxonomy

Parsons (1909) developed the conceptual model that has guided most vocational psychologists during this century. He described a three-step process for choosing a vocation. In order to make an effective decision regarding a career, an individual needs the following: "(1) a clear understanding of himself, his aptitudes, abilities, interests, ambitions, resources, limitations, and their causes; (2) knowledge of the requirements and conditions of success, advantages and disadvantages, compensation, opportunities, and prospects in different lines of work; and (3) true reasoning on the relations of these two groups of facts" (p. 5). In short, Parsons proposed that vocational adjustment depends on the characteristics of both the individual and his or her environment. Holland appreciates this perspective and understands that, in attempts to facilitate vocational adjustment, information about personality must be supplemented by information on the kinds of environments in which each personality type will flourish. Therefore, in addition to describing six personality prototypes, Holland (1985) provides a corresponding classification system designed to predict "the outcome of pairing people and environments" (p. 34). His typology of work environments parallels his typology of persons. According to Holland (1985), "[W]e can predict what will happen when a particular person is put into a particular environment by characterizing the person and his or her environment in terms of the types and models and reviewing the appropriate formulations in order to discover the congruities and incongruities the models suggest. For example, the interaction of a Conventional type and a Conventional environment should produce a number of desirable outcomes, such as work satisfaction, achievement, and vocational stability" (pp. 34–35).

We earlier noted that conscientiousness distinguishes Artistic and Conventional people in Holland's scheme. As was seen in the earlier list, Holland (1985) describes Artistic persons as "complicated, disorderly, emotional, expressive, idealistic, imaginative, impractical, impulsive, independent, introspective, intuitive, nonconforming, original, sensitive, open" (p. 21). In contrast, Conventional persons are likely to be "careful, conforming, conscientious, defensive, efficient, inflexible, inhibited, methodical, obedient, orderly, persistent, practical, prudish, thrifty, unimaginative" (p. 23). Based on Holland's classification of work environments, therefore, highly conscientious individuals will select Conventional work environments, because such environments demand, support, and/or reward the qualities associated with that trait. According to Holland (1985), the Conventional environment "encourages people to see themselves as conforming, orderly, nonartistic" and to "see the world in conventional, stereotyped, constricted, simple, dependent ways." Holland also suggests that Conventional environments "reward people for the display of conventional values: money, dependability, and conformity" (p. 40). Conversely, according to Holland, low-conscientiousness people tend to select an Artistic work environment that "encourages people to see themselves as expressive, original, intuitive, nonconforming, independent" and to "see the world in complex, independent, unconventional, and flexible ways" (p. 38).

Scores on conscientiousness measures obtained from samples of persons in various occupations classified according to Holland's scheme are consistent with his predictions. J. Hogan and R. Hogan (1993) examined the mean scores on the HPI Prudence scale for six occupational samples. Using Gottfredson, Holland, and Ogawa's classification system (1982), they identified archival samples that represented each type. The occupations were as follows:

steel-mill workers (R), physicians (I), musicians (A), food-service directors (S), sales representatives (E), and accounting clerks (C). Table 3.3 presents mean scale scores, standard deviations, and percentiles for the HPI Prudence scale by occupational group. Accounting clerks received the highest mean score (80th percentile), and musicians received the lowest (25th percentile). For the other occupational groups, mean Prudence scores decreased along the axis from Conventional to Artistic across the hexagon. Differences among the groups were statistically significant. Similar findings occur when mean scores on other conscientiousness measures are compared for occupational samples (compare Gough, 1987; Myers & McCaulley, 1985); members of occupations classified as Conventional and Enterprising by Holland consistently produce relatively higher mean scores on conscientiousness measures than do members of occupations classified as Artistic, Investigative, or Social.

Gottfredson et al.'s (1982) classification of jobs from the *Dictionary of Occupational Titles* (DOT; U.S. Department of Labor, 1979) into the Holland taxonomy reveals large differences in the frequency with which the six types occur in the U.S. economy. Of the 12,099 occupational titles classified by Gottfredson et al., the greatest number were classified as Realistic (66.7 percent). The next most frequently assigned categories were Conventional (13.4 percent) and Enterprising (11.1 percent). Artistic environments were rare, accounting for only 1.2 percent of the occupations classified. When high-conscientiousness people choose Artistic environments or low-conscientiousness people choose Conventional work environments, the outcome is usually negative. Because there are more Conventional than Artistic occupations, the latter situation will occur much more often.

This breakdown of the frequency of the various occupational types suggests that most I/O research involves persons in Realistic, Enterprising, or Conventional environments—and with predictable results: most of those studies find correlations between low scores in the area of conscientiousness and ineffective job performance. J. Hogan and R. Hogan (1995) studied attrition in the Navy's rigorous training school for Explosive Ordnance Disposal (EOD) divers. These divers dismantle live bombs and warheads underwater. It is an unusually dangerous job, and the attrition rate at the

Table 3.3. Mean Scores, Standard Deviations, and Percentiles for Six Occupational Groups on the HPI Prudence Scale.

Occupational Title/ Holland Code	HPI Prudence Scale Mean SD Percentile
Steel-Mill Laborers/REI (*n* = 66)	21.88 4.02 64 percent
Physicians/ISR (*n* = 19)	20.10 2.96 47 percent
Musicians/ASI (*n* = 40)	16.90 4.71 25 percent
Food-Service Directors/SEC (*n* = 422)	20.03 4.07 47 percent
Sales Representatives/ESR (*n* = 55)	20.14 4.14 47 percent
Accounting Clerks/CSE (*n* = 45)	24.31 3.37 80 percent

EOD school at the time of the study was about 50 percent. The study revealed that the attrition was largely accounted for by persons with Artistic interests. Dismantling bombs and other ammunition requires following a set of procedures exactly; there is little opportunity for creative self-expression. Similarly, in a study of police officers, J. A. Johnson and R. Hogan (1981) showed that Artistic types are overrepresented among officers who are disliked by their superiors and the public they are supposed to serve—again, it would seem, because the job requires close adherence to a set of prescribed procedures. We likewise suspect that many cases of stress and burnout among air traffic controllers and nuclear power plant operators reflect similar dynamics: Artistic types, needing work but faced with a job market that contains primarily Realistic, Conventional, and Enterprising work environments, take jobs that are composed largely of vigilance tasks. These Artistic types may have pursued jobs that seemed to promise autonomy, variety, and stimulation only to find themselves performing structured and highly routinized tasks. The mismatch between their needs, values, and capabilities and the demands of inflexible jobs often leads to personal dissatisfaction and unsatisfactory performance.

J. Hogan and R. Hogan (1993) note that they know of "no studies that evaluate the relationship between conscientiousness and effective performance in Artistic or Investigative jobs" (p. 15). They report data obtained from a sample of orchestral musicians: correlations between the Prudence scale of the HPI and peer ratings of musical talent ranged from −.25 to −.40; lower Prudence scores were consistently associated with higher peer evaluations of musical talent. Hogan and Hogan conclude that the importance of conscientiousness depends on the requirements of each occupational context. They suggest that the attributes characterizing individuals high on conscientiousness (for example, "rule compliance, orderliness, carefulness, and attention to detail") are assets in Conventional environments but may "inhibit the innovation, flexibility, ideational fluency, and originality" required in Artistic environments (pp. 16–17).

As noted above, however, both Schneider and Holland suggest that differences in organizational (or occupational) climate reflect the differences in the people who work in the organizations. Schneider's thesis is that organizations attract, select, and retain particular kinds of individuals and that the climate of the organization is a function of the kind of people it has retained. The ratings observed in Hogan and Hogan's Artistic environment may therefore reflect peculiarities of that population as much as the nature of the particular work tasks being rated. It is conceivable that low-conscientiousness raters use different criteria to judge the satisfactoriness of their colleagues. Thus low-conscientiousness people may not be better musicians; rather, they may merely be regarded more favorably by others who are themselves low on conscientiousness.

At one of the nation's military academies, Blake (1994) tested the hypothesis that high- and low-conscientiousness raters have different views of what an "ideal" co-worker or subordinate is and therefore use different criteria to evaluate overall satisfactoriness. The military academy features a peer rating system that includes (1) a number of individuals performing essentially the same work tasks and subject to the same job requirements, (2) personality information for both raters and ratees, and (3) multiple raters, thereby allowing direct comparison of interrater differences in the evaluation of the same individual(s). Further, the military academy is a highly structured environment with complex and extensive systems of rules and carefully defined lines of authority. Because the system of regulations is so heavily emphasized, it may be inferred that rule-adhering behavior *should* be highly valued; it is likewise easy to show that military academies are Conventional environments in Holland's taxonomic scheme.

Ratings on six satisfactoriness dimensions (Conformance, Dependability, Altruism, General Adjustment, Emotional Stability, and Task Performance) taken from a modified form of the Minnesota Satisfactoriness Scales (Gibson et al., 1970), along with an overall satisfactoriness rating, were collected from students' peers. Two sets of average satisfactoriness facet ratings and overall satisfactoriness ratings were calculated for each ratee—one based on his or her high-conscientiousness peers and the other based on low-conscientiousness peers. Blake found distinctly different rating policies in the two groups. The raters within each group, however, held similar views of their peers; their ratings on each of the satisfactoriness dimensions were highly similar. For example, the average ratings on Conformance and Dependability for the two groups correlated $r = .87$ and .83, respectively. However, the groups differed significantly on the degree to which ratings on those dimensions were associated with an overall appraisal of their peers. For the high-conscientiousness raters, ratings on the Conformance and Dependability dimensions were highly correlated with overall performance ratings ($r = .80$ and .70, respectively). For the low-conscientiousness raters, the correlations of those dimensions with the ratees' overall rank fell to $r = .37$ for Conformance and $r = .19$ for Dependability. Even in the highly structured and regimented environment of a military academy, raters differed significantly in the degree to which they valued conformance to authority and adherence to rules and standard procedures. Nor were the differences random. Instead, "they appear to reflect systematic differences in the value systems of raters—differences that covary with the raters' own standing on the conscientiousness dimension" (Blake, 1994, p. 16).

The implications of these data are significant. If one wants to predict counterproductive work behavior (for example, absenteeism, tardiness, and discipline-invoking actions), then conscientiousness is important. If, however, one wishes to predict a broader range of outcomes, including how an individual is likely to be evaluated by his or her co-workers, then we need to know something about those co-workers.

Final Comments

We have thus come full circle, returning to the perspective that has guided most vocational interest research. The field of vocational interest measurement reflects a perspective on the individual in the world of work that is quite different from that in I/O psychology. Vocational psychologists are generally concerned with providing services to individuals; they help individuals move into compatible work environments. That involves helping a single individual choose from among an array of employment options and matching individual differences to characteristics of occupations.

The nature of vocational counseling has necessitated comparing and classifying work environments. Holland's taxonomy is one example of how vocational psychologists have developed psychologically meaningful taxonomies of work environments (compare Borgen, Weiss, Tinsley, Dawis, & Lofquist, 1968; Dawis, Dohm, Lofquist, Chartrand, & Due, 1987; Rosen, Weiss, Hendel, Dawis, & Lofquist, 1972). Industrial/organizational psychology has yet to avail itself of much of this work. Nevertheless, the advantages of these taxonomic schemes for researchers undertaking meta-analyses in order to uncover important relationships between individual differences and important work outcomes should be obvious.

References

Abrahams, N. M., & Neumann, I. (1973). Predicting the unpredictable: A validation of the Strong Vocational Interest Blank for predicting military aptitude ratings of Naval Academy midshipmen. *Proceedings of the 81st annual convention of the American Psychological Association,* 8(2), 747–748.

Abrahams, N. M., Neumann, I., & Githens, W. H. (1971). Faking vocational interests: Simulated versus real-life motivation. *Personnel Psychology, 24,* 5–12.

Adorno, T. W., Frenkel-Brunswik, E., Levinson, D. J., & Sanford, N. (1950). *The authoritarian personality.* New York: HarperCollins.

Allport, G. W. (1961). *Pattern and growth in personality.* Troy, MO: Holt, Rinehart & Winston.

Athansou, J. A., O'Gorman, J. G., & Meyer, E. (1986). Two comparisons of the Holland and Eysenck personality typologies among Australian high school students. In J. Lokan & K. F. Taylor (Eds.), *Holland in Australia* (pp. 52–60). Melbourne: Australian Council for Educational Research.

Barak, A., & Meir, E. I. (1974). The predictive validity of a vocational interest inventory—"RAMAK": Seven-year follow-up. *Journal of Vocational Behavior, 4,* 377–387.

Barge, B. N., & Hough, L. M. (1988). Utility of interest assessment for predicting job performance. In L. M. Hough, *Utility of temperament, biodata, and interest assessment for predicting job performance: A review and integration of the literature* (ARI Research Note 88–02). Alexandria, VA: U.S. Army Research Institute for the Behavioral and Social Sciences.

Barrick, M. R., & Mount, M. K. (1991). The Big Five personality dimensions and job performance: A meta-analysis. *Personnel Psychology, 44,* 1–26.

Barron, F. X. (1965). The psychology of creativity. In D. Cartwright (Ed.), *New Directions in Psychology* (Vol. 2, pp. 1–134). Troy, MO: Holt, Rinehart & Winston.

Bartling, H. C., & Hood, A. B. (1981). An 11-year follow-up of measured interest and vocational choice. *Journal of Counseling Psychology, 28,* 27–35.

Baskett, G. D. (1973). Interview decisions as determined by competency and attitude similarity. *Journal of Applied Psychology, 57,* 343–345.

Berdie, R. F. (1943). Factors associated with vocational interests. *Journal of Educational Psychology, 34,* 257–277.

Berscheid, E. (1985). Interpersonal attraction. In G. Lindzey & E. Aronson (Eds.), *The handbook of social psychology* (Vol. 2, pp. 413–484). New York: Random House.

Blake, R. J. (1994, Aug.). In the eye of the beholder: The relevance of conscientiousness to appraisals of overall satisfactoriness. In E. H. Potter (Chair), *The relevance of conscientiousness to occupational criteria.*

Symposium conducted at the 102nd annual meeting of the American Psychological Association, Los Angeles.

Blake, R. J., & Sackett, S. A. (1993, Aug.). *Holland's typology and the Five-Factor Model: A rational-empirical analysis.* Paper presented at the 101st annual meeting of the American Psychological Association, Toronto.

Blake, R. J., & Sackett, S. A. (1994, Aug.). *Multidimensional scaling analysis of relations between Holland's hexagon and major dimensions of personality.* Paper presented at the 102nd annual meeting of the American Psychological Association, Los Angeles.

Bolton, B. (1985). Discriminant analysis of Holland's occupational types using the Sixteen Personality Factors Questionnaire. *Journal of Vocational Behavior, 27,* 210–217.

Bordin, E. S. (1943). A theory of vocational interests as dynamic phenomena. *Educational and Psychological Measurement, 3,* 49–65.

Borgen, F. H. (1986). New approaches to the assessment of interests. In W. B. Walsh & S. H. Osipow (Eds.), *Advances in vocational psychology: Vol. 1. The assessment of interest* (pp. 83–126). Hillsdale, NJ: Erlbaum.

Borgen, F. H., Weiss, D. J., Tinsley, H.E.A., Dawis, R. V., & Lofquist, L. H. (1968). *Occupational reinforcer patterns* (Minnesota Studies in Vocational Rehabilitation XXIV). Minneapolis: Industrial Relations Center, University of Minnesota.

Borman, W. C. (1974). The rating of individuals in organizations: An alternate approach. *Organizational Behavior and Human Performance, 12,* 105–124.

Borman, W. C. (1983). Implications of personality theory and research for the rating of work performance in organizations. In F. Landy, S. Zedeck, and J. Cleveland (Eds.), *Performance measurement and theory* (pp. 127–165). Hillsdale, NJ: Erlbaum.

Borman, W. C. (1987). Personal constructs, performance schemata, and "folk theories" of subordinate effectiveness: Explorations in an army officer sample. *Organizational Behavior and Human Decision Processes, 40,* 307–322.

Borman, W. C., Toquam, J. L., & Rosse, R. L. (1979). *Development and validation of an inventory battery to predict Navy and Marine Corps recruiter performance* (Technical Report No. 22). Minneapolis, MN: Personnel Decisions Research Institute.

Brandt, J. E., & Hood, A. B. (1968). Effect of personality adjustment on the predictive validity of the Strong Vocational Interest Blank. *Journal of Counseling Psychology, 15,* 547–551.

Bray, D. W., & Howard, A. (1983). The AT&T longitudinal study of managers. In K. W. Schaie (Ed.), *Longitudinal studies of adult psychological development* (pp. 112–146). New York: Guilford.

Brayfield, A. H., & Marsh, M. M. (1957). Aptitudes, interests, and personality characteristics of farmers. *Journal of Applied Psychology, 41,* 98–103.

Burke, M. J., Brief, A. P., & George, J. M. (1993). The role of negative affectivity in understanding relations between self-reports of stressors and strains: A comment on the applied psychology literature. *Journal of Applied Psychology, 78,* 402–412.

Buss, A. H., & Plomin, R. (1975). *A temperament theory of personality development.* New York: Wiley.

Butler, F. J., Crinnion, J., & Martin, J. (1972). The Kuder Preference Record in adult vocational guidance. *Occupational Psychology, 46,* 99–104.

Byrne, D. (1971). *The attraction paradigm.* San Diego, CA: Academic Press.

Cairo, P. C. (1982). Measured interests versus expressed interests as predictors of long-term occupational membership. *Journal of Vocational Behavior, 20,* 343–353.

Campbell, D. P. (1966). Occupations ten years later of high school seniors with high scores on the SVIB Life Insurance Salesman scale. *Journal of Applied Psychology, 50,* 51–56.

Campbell, D. P. (1971). *Handbook for the Strong Vocational Interest Blank.* Stanford, CA: Stanford University Press.

Campbell, D. P. (1987). *Psychological test profiles of brigadier generals: Warmongers or decisive warriors?* Paper presented at the annual meeting of Division 14 of the American Psychological Association, New York.

Campbell, D. P., & Holland, J. L. (1972). Applying Holland's theory to Strong's data. *Journal of Vocational Behavior, 2,* 353–376.

Campbell, D. T. (1963). Social attitudes and other acquired behavioral dispositions. In S. Koch (Ed.), *Psychology: A study of a science.* New York: McGraw-Hill.

Campbell, J. P., Dunnette, M. D., Lawler, E. E., & Weick, K. E. (1970). *Managerial behavior, performance, and effectiveness.* New York: McGraw-Hill.

Cattell, R. B., Eber, H. W., & Tatsuoka, M. M. (1970). *Handbook for the 16 PF.* Champaign, IL: Institute for Personality Assessment and Testing.

Clark, K. E. (1961). *Vocational interests of non-professional men.* Minneapolis: University of Minnesota Press.

Comrey, A. L. (1970). *Manual for the Comrey Personality Scales.* San Diego, CA: Educational and Industrial Testing Service.

Costa, P. T., Fozard, J. L., & McCrae, R. R. (1977). Personological interpretation of factors from the Strong Vocational Interest Blank scales. *Journal of Vocational Behavior, 10,* 231–243.

Costa, P. T., & McCrae, R. R. (1980). Influence of extraversion and neuroticism on subjective well-being: Happy and unhappy people. *Journal of Personality and Social Psychology, 38,* 668–678.

Costa, P. T., & McCrae, R. R. (1985). *The NEO Personality Inventory: Manual Form S and Form R.* Odessa, FL: Psychological Assessment Resources.

Costa, P. T., McCrae, R. R., & Holland, J. L. (1984). Personality and vocational interests in an adult sample. *Journal of Applied Psychology, 69,* 390–400.

Cottle, W. C. (1950, Feb.). Relationship among selected personality and interest inventories. *Occupations: The Vocational Guidance Journal,* pp. 306–310.

Crites, J. O. (1969). *Vocational psychology: The study of vocational behavior and development.* New York: McGraw-Hill.

Dann, J. E., & Abrahams, N. M. (1977). *Occupational scales of the Navy Vocational Interest Inventory: III. Relationship to job satisfaction, "A" school grades, and job performance* (Technical Report No. 78–3). San Diego, CA: Navy Personnel Research and Development Center.

Darley, J. B., & Hagenah, T. (1955). *Vocational interest measurement: Theory and practice.* Minneapolis: University of Minnesota Press.

Dawis, R. V. (1980). Measuring interests. *New Directions in Testing and Measurement, 7,* 77–91.

Dawis, R. V. (1991). Vocational interests, values, and preferences. In M. D. Dunnette & L. M. Hough (Eds.), *Handbook of industrial and organizational psychology* (2nd ed.; Vol. 2, pp. 833–871). Palo Alto, CA: Consulting Psychologists Press.

Dawis, R. V., Dohm, T. E., Lofquist, L. H., Chartrand, J. M., & Due, A. M. (1987). *Minnesota Occupational Classification System III.* Minneapolis: Vocational Psychology Research, Department of Psychology, University of Minnesota.

Dawis, R. V., & Lofquist, L. H. (1984). *A psychological theory of work adjustment.* Minneapolis: University of Minnesota Press.

DiMichael, S. G., & Dabelstein, D. H. (1947). Work satisfaction and work efficiency of vocational rehabilitation counselors as related to measured interests (Abstract). *American Psychologist, 2,* 342–343.

Dolliver, R. H., Irvin, J. A., & Bigley, S. S. (1972). Twelve-year follow-up of the Strong Vocational Interest Blank. *Journal of Counseling Psychology, 19,* 212–217.

Dolliver, R. H., & Will, J. A. (1977). Ten-year follow-up of the Tyler Vocational Card Sort and the Strong Vocational Interest Blank. *Journal of Counseling Psychology, 24,* 48–54.

Dunnette, M. D., & Aylward, M. S. (1956). Validity information exchange, No. 9–21. *Personnel Psychology, 9,* 245–247.

Dunnette, M. D., Kirchner, W. K., & DeGidio, J. (1958). Relations among scores on Edwards Personal Preference Schedule, California Psychological Inventory, and Strong Vocational Interest Blank for an industrial sample. *Journal of Applied Psychology, 42,* 178–181.

Edwards, A. L. (1959). *Edwards Personal Preference Schedule manual.* New York: Psychological Corporation.

Ernhart, C. B., & Loevinger, J. (1969). Authoritarian family ideology: A measure, its correlates, and its robustness. *Multivariate Behavioral Research Monographs,* 69–1.

Foti, R. J., & Lord, R. G. (1987). Prototypes and scripts: The effect of alternative methods of processing information on rating accuracy. *Organizational Behavior and Human Decision Processes, 39,* 318–340.

Gade, E. M., & Soliah, D. (1975). Vocational preference inventory high point codes versus expressed choices as predictors of college major and career entry. *Journal of Counseling Psychology, 22,* 117–121.

Gati, I. (1991). The structure of vocational interests. *Psychological Bulletin, 109,* 309–324.

Gibson, D. L., Weiss, D. J., Dawis, R. V., & Lofquist, L. H. (1970). *Manual for the Minnesota Satisfactoriness Scales* (Minnesota Studies in Vocational Rehabilitation Monograph No. 27). Minneapolis: Industrial Relations Center, University of Minnesota.

Goldberg, L. R. (1992). The development of markers for the Big Five factor structure. *Psychological Assessment, 4,* 26–42.

Gottfredson, G. D. (1988). *Development of the Civilian-Military Interest Survey (C-MIS)* (NPRDC TN 88–20). San Diego, CA: Navy Personnel Research and Development Center.

Gottfredson, G. D., Holland, J. L., and Ogawa, D. K. (1982). *Dictionary of Holland Occupational Codes.* Palo Alto, CA: Consulting Psychologists Press.

Gottfredson, G. D., Jones, E. M., & Holland, J. L. (1993). Personality and vocational interests: The relation of Holland's six interest dimensions to five robust dimensions of personality. *Journal of Counseling Psychology, 40,* 518–524.

Gough, H. G. (1957). *Manual for the California Psychological Inventory.* Palo Alto, CA: Consulting Psychologists Press.

Gough, H. G. (1985). A work orientation scale for the California Psychological Inventory. *Journal of Applied Psychology, 70,* 505–513.

Gough, H. G. (1987). *California Psychological Inventory administrator's guide.* Palo Alto, CA: Consulting Psychologists Press.

Gray, C. W. (1959). *Detection of faking in vocational interest measurement.* Unpublished doctoral dissertation, University of Minnesota.

Guilford, J. P., Christensen, P. R., Bond, N. A., & Sutton, M. A. (1954). A factor analysis study of human interest. *Psychological Monographs, 68* (entire No. 375).

Hahn, M. E., & Williams, C. T. (1945). The measured interest of Marine Corps women reservists. *Journal of Applied Psychology, 29,* 198–211.

Hansen, J. C. (1984). The measurement of vocational interests: Issues and future directions. In S. D. Brown & R. W. Lent (Eds.), *Handbook of Counseling Psychology* (pp. 99–136). New York: Wiley.

Hansen, J. C. (1986, Aug.). *12-year longitudinal study of the predictive validity of the SVIB-SCII.* Paper presented at the 94th annual meeting of the American Psychological Association, Washington, DC.

Hansen, J. C., & Campbell, D. P. (1985). *Manual for the SVIB-SCII* (4th ed.). Palo Alto, CA: Consulting Psychologists Press.

Hansen, J. C., & Johansson, C. B. (1972). The application of Holland's vocational model to the Strong Vocational Interest Blank for Women. *Journal of Vocational Behavior, 2,* 479–493.

Hansen, J. C., & Johansson, C. B. (1974). Strong Vocational Interest Blank and dogmatism. *Journal of Counseling Psychology, 21,* 196–201.

Hansen, J. C., & Swansen, J. L. (1983). Stability of vocational interests of adolescents and young adults. *Measurement and Evaluation in Guidance, 13,* 173–178.

Harrington, T. F., & O'Shea, A. J. (1982). *The Harrington-O'Shea Career Decision-Making System manual.* Circle Pines, MN: American Guidance Service.

Herzberg, F., & Russell, D. (1953). The effects of experience and change of job interest on the Kuder Preference Record. *Journal of Applied Psychology, 37,* 478–481.

Hofstee, W.K.B. (1990). The use of everyday personality language for scientific purposes. *European Journal of Personality, 4,* 77–88.

Hogan, J., & Hogan, R. (1989). Noncognitive predictors of performance during explosive ordnance disposal training. *Military Psychology, 3,* 117–133.

Hogan, J., & Hogan, R. (1993, May). The ambiguity of conscientiousness. In F. L. Schmidt (Chair), *The construct of "conscientiousness" in personnel selection.* Symposium presented at the Conference of the Society for Industrial and Organizational Psychology, San Francisco.

Hogan, J., & Ones, D. (in press). Conscientiousness and integrity at work. In R. Hogan, J. A. Johnson, & S. R. Briggs (Eds.), *Handbook of personality psychology.* San Diego, CA: Academic Press.

Hogan, R. (1983). Socioanalytic theory of personality. In M. M. Page (Ed.), *1982 Nebraska Symposium on Motivation: Personality—current theory and research* (pp. 55–89). Lincoln: University of Nebraska Press.

Hogan, R. (1986). What every student should know about personality psychology. In V. P. Makosky (Ed.), *The G. Stanley Hall Lecture Series* (Vol. 6). Washington, DC: American Psychological Association.

Hogan, R. (1995). A socioanalytic perspective on the Five-Factor Model. In J. S. Wiggins (Ed.), *Theories of the Five-Factor Model.* New York: Guilford.

Hogan, R., & Hogan, J. (1995). *Hogan Personality Inventory manual.* Tulsa, OK: Hogan Assessment Systems.

Holland, J. L. (1965). *Manual: Vocational Preference Inventory.* Palo Alto, CA: Consulting Psychologists Press.

Holland, J. L. (1973). *Making vocational choices: A theory of careers.* Englewood Cliffs, NJ: Prentice-Hall.

Holland, J. L. (1978). *Manual for the Vocational Preference Inventory.* Palo Alto, CA: Consulting Psychologists Press.

Holland, J. L. (1985). *Making vocational choices: A theory of vocational personalities and work environments* (2nd ed.). Englewood Cliffs, NJ: Prentice-Hall.

Holland, J. L., & Hough, L. M. (1976). Vocational preferences. In M. D. Dunnette (Ed.), *Handbook of industrial and organizational psychology* (pp. 521–570). Skokie, IL: Rand McNally.

Holland, J. L., Johnson, J. L., Asama, N. F., & Polys, S. M. (1993). Validating and using the Career Beliefs Inventory. *Journal of Career Development, 19,* 233–244.

Hough, L. M. (1992). The "Big Five" personality variables—construct confusion: Description versus prediction. *Human Performance, 5,* 139–155.

Jackson, D. N. (1977). *Jackson Vocational Interest Survey manual.* Port Huron, MI: Research Psychologists Press.

Johansson, C. B. (1986). *Manual for the Career Assessment Inventory* (2nd ed.). Minneapolis, MN: National Computer Systems.

John, O. P. (1990). The "Big Five" factor taxonomy: Dimensions of personality in the natural language and in questionnaires. In L. Pervin (Ed.), *Handbook of personality theory and research* (pp. 66–100). New York: Guilford.

Johnson, J. A., & Hogan, R. (1981). Vocational interests, personality, and effective police performance. *Personnel Psychology, 34,* 49–53.

Johnson, J. C., & Dunnette, M. D. (1968). Validity and test-retest stability of the Nash managerial effectiveness scale on the revised form of the Strong Vocational Interest Blank. *Personnel Psychology, 21,* 283–294.

Johnson, R. W., Flammer, D. P., & Nelson, J. G. (1975). Multiple correlations between personality factors and SVIB occupational scales. *Journal of Counseling Psychology, 22,* 217–223.

Kamp, J. D., & Hough, L. M. (1988). Utility of personality assessment: A review and integration of the literature. In L. M. Hough (Ed.),

Utility of temperament, biodata, and interest assessment for predicting job performance: A review and integration of the literature (ARI Research Note No. 88–02, pp. 1–90). Alexandria, VA: U.S. Army Research Institute for the Behavioral and Social Sciences.

Katzell, R. A. (1964). Personal values, job satisfaction, and job behavior. In H. Borow (Ed.), *Man in a world of work.* Boston: Houghton Mifflin.

Klein, K. L., & Weiner, Y. (1977). Interest congruency as a moderator of the relationships between job tenure and job satisfaction and mental health. *Journal of Vocational Behavior, 10,* 92–98.

Klinger, E. (1977). *Meaning and void: Inner experiences and the incentives in people's lives.* Minneapolis: University of Minnesota Press.

Knauft, E. B. (1951). Vocational interests and managerial success. *Journal of Applied Psychology, 35,* 160–163.

Kuder, G. F. (1977). *Activity interests and occupational choice.* Chicago: Science Research Associates.

Latham, G. P., Wexley, K. N., & Pursell, E. D. (1975). Training managers to minimize rating errors in the observation of behavior. *Journal of Applied Psychology, 60,* 550–555.

Lau, A. W., & Abrahams, N. M. (1970). *The Navy Vocational Interest Inventory as a predictor of job performance* (Research Report SSR 70–28). San Diego, CA: Navy Personnel and Training Research Laboratory.

Lau, A. W., & Abrahams, N. M. (1971). *Reliability and predictive validity of the Navy Vocational Interest Inventory* (Research Report SSR 71–16). San Diego, CA: Navy Personnel and Training Research Laboratory.

Layton, W. L. (1958). *Counseling use of the Strong Vocational Interest Blank* (Minnesota Studies in Student Personnel Work, No. 8). Minneapolis: University of Minnesota Press.

Lee, R. E., & Warr, P. B. (1969). The development and standardization of a balanced F scale. *Journal of General Psychology, 81,* 109–129.

Levin, I., & Stokes, J. P. (1989). Dispositional approach to job satisfaction: Role of negative affectivity. *Journal of Applied Psychology, 74,* 752–758.

Levine, J. M., & Moreland, R. L. (1990). Progress in small group research. *Annual Review of Psychology, 41,* 585–634.

Lott, A. J., & Lott, B. E. (1965). Group cohesiveness and interpersonal attraction: A review of relationships with antecedent and consequent variables. *Psychological Bulletin, 4,* 259–302.

MacKenzie, S. B., Podsakoff, P. M., & Fetter, R. (1991). Organizational citizenship and objective productivity as determinants of managerial evaluations of salespersons' performance. *Organizational Behavior and Human Decision Processes, 50,* 123–150.

Martin, H. G. (1945). The construction of the Guilford-Martin Inventory of Factors G-A-M-I-N. *Journal of Applied Psychology, 29,* 298–300.

Maslow, A. H. (1954). *Motivation and personality.* New York: HarperCollins.

McArthur, C. (1954). Long-term validity of the Strong Interest Test in two subcultures. *Journal of Applied Psychology, 38,* 184–189.

McClelland, D. C. (1961). *The achieving society.* New York: Van Nostrand.

McCrae, R. R., & Costa, P. T. (1985). Updating Norman's "adequate taxonomy": Intelligence and personality dimensions in natural language and in questionnaires. *Journal of Personality and Social Psychology, 49,* 710–721.

McCrae, R. R., & Costa, P. T. (1986). Clinical assessment can benefit from recent advances in personality psychology. *American Psychologist, 41,* 1001–1003.

McHenry, J. J., Hough, L. M., Toquam, J. L., Hanson, M. A., & Ashworth, S. (1990). Project A validity results: The relationship between predictor and criterion domains. *Personnel Psychology, 43,* 335–354.

McRae, G. G. (1959). *The relationship of job satisfaction and earlier measured interests.* Unpublished doctoral dissertation, University of Florida.

Meehl, P. E. (1986). Trait language and behaviorese. In T. Thompson & M. D. Zeiler (Eds.), *Analysis and integration of behavioral units* (pp. 315–334). Hillsdale, NJ: Erlbaum.

Miles, R. E. (1964). Attitudes toward management theory as a factor in managers' relationships with their superiors. *Academy of Management Journal, 7,* 303–313.

Miner, J. B. (1960). The Kuder Preference Record in managerial appraisal. *Personnel Psychology, 13,* 187–196.

Moorman, R. H., & Blakely, G. L. (1992). A preliminary report on a new measure of organizational citizenship behavior. In M. Schnake (Ed.), *Proceedings* (pp. 185–187). New Orleans: Southern Management Association.

Morrison, J. (1993). *Group composition and creative performance.* Unpublished doctoral dissertation, University of Tulsa.

Mount, M. K., & Thompson, D. E. (1987). Cognitive categorization and quality of performance ratings. *Journal of Applied Psychology, 72,* 240–246.

Myers, I. B., & McCaulley, M. H. (1985). *Manual: A guide to the development and use of the Myers-Briggs Type Indicator.* Palo Alto, CA: Consulting Psychologists Press.

Nash, A. N. (1966). Development of an SVIB key for selecting managers. *Journal of Applied Psychology, 50,* 250–254.

Naylor, F. D., & Thorneycroft, P. W. (1986). The relations between Holland's and Eysenck's types: A further perspective. In J. Lokan & K. F. Taylor (Eds.), *Holland in Australia* (pp. 61–67). Melbourne: Australian Council for Educational Research.

North, R. D. (1958). Tests for the accounting profession. *Educational and Psychological Measurement, 18,* 691–713.

O'Neill, W. M., & Levinson, D. J. (1954). A factorial exploration of authoritarianism and some of its ideological concomitants. *Journal of Personality, 22,* 449–463.

Organ, D. W. (1988). *Organizational citizenship behavior: The good soldier syndrome.* New York: Lexington Books.

Parsons, F. (1909). *Choosing a vocation.* Boston: Houghton Mifflin.

Peabody, D., & Goldberg, L. R. (1989). Some determinants of factor structures from personality-trait descriptors. *Journal of Personality and Social Psychology, 57,* 552–567.

Peraino, J. M., & Willerman, L. (1983). Personality correlates of occupational status according to Holland types. *Journal of Vocational Behavior, 22,* 268–277.

Perry, R. B. (1954). *Realms of value: A critique of human civilization.* Cambridge, MA: Harvard University Press.

Peters, R. S. (1958). *The concept of motivation.* London: Blackwell.

Pfeffer, J. (1983). Organizational demography. In L. L. Cummings & B. M. Staw (Eds.), *Research in organizational behavior* (Vol. 5, pp. 299–357). Greenwich, CT: JAI Press.

Phillips, J. S. (1984). The accuracy of leadership ratings: A cognitive categorization perspective. *Organizational Behavior and Human Performance, 33,* 125–138.

Phillips, J. S., & Lord, R. G. (1982). Schematic information processing and perceptions of leadership in problem-solving groups. *Journal of Applied Psychology, 67,* 486–492.

Porter, A. (1962). Effect of organizational size on the validity of masculinity-femininity score. *Journal of Applied Psychology, 46,* 228–229.

Potter, E. H., & Blake, R. J. (1994, Aug.). The relationship of conscientiousness to rule-keeping behavior: It depends on who's keeping track. In E. H. Potter (Chair), *The relevance of conscientiousness to occupational criteria.* Symposium conducted at the 102nd annual meeting of the American Psychological Association, Los Angeles.

Pryor, R.G.L. (1986). The integration and interpretation of vocational preferences, personality traits, and work aspect preferences. In J. Lokan & K. F. Taylor (Eds.), *Holland in Australia* (pp. 29–37). Melbourne: Australian Council for Educational Research.

Pulakos, E. D., & Wexley, K. N. (1983). The relationship among perceptual similarity, sex, and performance ratings in manager-subordinate dyads. *Academy of Management Journal, 26,* 129–139.

Rand, T. M., & Wexley, K. N. (1975). Demonstration of the effect, "similar to me," in simulated employment interviews. *Psychological Reports, 36,* 535–544.

Roe, A. (1956). *The psychology of occupations.* New York: Wiley.

Roe, A. (1957). Early determinants of vocational choice. *Journal of Counseling Psychology, 4,* 212–217.

Roe, A., & Siegelman, M. (1964). *Origin of interests* (APGA Inquiry Studies No. 1). Washington, DC: American Personnel and Guidance Association.

Rokeach, M. (1954). The nature and meaning of dogmatism. *Psychological Review, 61,* 194–204.

Rokeach, M. (1960). *The open and closed mind.* New York: Basic Books.

Rokeach, M. (1973). *The nature of human values.* New York: Free Press.

Rosen, S. D., Weiss, D. J., Hendel, D. D., Dawis, R. V., & Lofquist, L. H. (1972). *Occupational reinforcer patterns* (Vol. 2) (Minnesota Studies in Vocational Rehabilitation Monograph No. 29). Minneapolis: Industrial Relations Center, University of Minnesota.

Rounds, J. B. (in press). Vocational interests: Evaluating structural hypotheses. In R. V. Dawis & D. Lubinski (Eds.), *Assessing individual differences in human behavior: New concepts, methods, and findings.* Minneapolis: University of Minnesota Press.

Rounds, J. B., Davison, M. L., & Dawis, R. V. (1979). The fit between Strong-Campbell Interest Inventory General Occupational Themes and Holland's hexagonal model. *Journal of Vocational Behavior, 15,* 303–315.

Rounds, J. B., & Dawis, R. V. (1979). Factor analysis of Strong Vocational Interest Blank items. *Journal of Applied Psychology, 64,* 132–143.

Rounds, J. B., & Zevon, M. A. (1983). Multidimensional scaling research in vocational psychology. *Applied Psychological Measurement, 7,* 491–510.

Schletzer, V. A. (1966). SVIB as a predictor of job satisfaction. *Journal of Applied Psychology, 50,* 5–8.

Schneider, B. (1987). The people make the place. *Personnel Psychology, 40,* 437–453.

Schultz, I. T., & Barnabas, B. (1945). Testing for leadership in industry. *Transactions of the Kansas Academy of Science, 4,* 160–164.

Sells, S. B., Demaree, R. G., & Will, D. P. (1968). *A taxonomic investigation of personality: Conjoint factor structure of Guilford and Cattell trait markers* (Technical Report). Washington, DC: U.S. Office of Education, Department of Health, Education, and Welfare.

Senger, J. (1971). Managers' perceptions of subordinates' competence as a function of personal value orientations. *Academy of Management Journal, 14,* 415–423.

Siess, T. F., & Jackson, D. N. (1970). Vocational interests and personality: An empirical integration. *Journal of Counseling Psychology, 17,* 27–35.

Smith, C. A., Organ, D. W., & Near, J. P. (1983). Organizational citizenship behavior: its nature and antecedents. *Journal of Applied Psychology*, *68*, 653–663.

Stewart, L. H. (1971). Relationships between interests and personality scores of occupation-oriented students. *Journal of Counseling Psychology*, *18*, 31–38.

Stockford, L., & Bissell, H. W. (1976). Establishing a graphic rating scale. In W. E. Fleishman (Ed.), *Studies in personnel and industrial psychology*. Belmont, CA: Dorsey Press.

Strong, E. K. (1935). Predictive value of the Vocational Interest Test. *Journal of Educational Psychology*, *26*, 332.

Strong, E. K. (1943). *Vocational interests of men and women*. Stanford, CA: Stanford University Press.

Strong, E. K. (1955). *Vocational interests 18 years after college*. Minneapolis: University of Minnesota Press.

Strong, E. K. (1960). An 18-year longitudinal report on interests. In W. L. Layton (Ed.), *The Strong Vocational Interest Blank: Research and uses*. Minneapolis: University of Minnesota Press.

Super, D. E. (1973). The Work Values Inventory. In D. G. Zytowski (Ed.), *Contemporary approaches to interest measurement*. Minneapolis: University of Minnesota Press.

Super, D. E., & Crites, J. O. (1962). *Appraising vocational fitness*. New York: HarperCollins.

Sweet, R. (1986). Work values and Holland's typology: Some side excursions. In J. Lokan & K. F. Taylor (Eds.), *Holland in Australia* (pp. 38–51). Melbourne: Australian Council for Educational Research.

Tellegen, A. (1982). *Brief manual for the Differential Personality Questionnaire*. Unpublished manuscript, University of Minnesota.

Tellegen, A. (1985). Structures of mood and personality and their relevance to assessing anxiety, with an emphasis on self-report. In A. H. Tuma & J. D. Maser (Eds.), *Anxiety and the anxiety disorders* (pp. 681–716). Hillsdale, NJ: Erlbaum.

Tellegen, A., Lykken, D. T., Bouchard, T. J., Wilcox, K. J., Segal, N. L., & Rich, S. (1988). Personality similarity in twins reared apart and together. *Journal of Personality and Social Psychology*, *54*, 1031–1039.

Tellegen, A., & Waller, N. G. (in press). Exploring personality through test construction: Development of the Multidimensional Personality Questionnaire. In S. R. Briggs & J. M. Cheek (Eds.), *Personality measures: Development and evaluation* (Vol. 1). Greenwich, CT: JAI Press.

Tracey, T. J., & Rounds, J. (1992, Aug.). *Evaluating Holland's and Gati's vocational interest models: A structural meta-analysis*. Paper presented at the 100th annual meeting of the American Psychological Association, Washington, DC.

Trimble, J. T. (1965). *Ten-year longitudinal follow-up study of inventoried interests of selected high school students.* Unpublished doctoral dissertation, University of Missouri.

Turner, R. G., & Horn, J. M. (1975). Personality correlates of Holland's occupational types: A cross-cultural study. *Journal of Vocational Behavior, 6,* 379–389.

Turner, R. G., & Horn, J. M. (1977). Personality, husband-wife similarity, and Holland's occupational types. *Journal of Vocational Behavior, 10,* 111–120.

U.S. Department of Labor (1979). *Dictionary of occupational titles* (4th ed.). Washington, DC: U.S. Government Printing Office.

Wakefield, J. A., & Cunningham, C. H. (1975). Relationships between the Vocational Preference Inventory and the Edwards Personal Preference Schedule. *Journal of Vocational Behavior, 6,* 373–377.

Waller, N. G., Lykken, D. J., & Tellegen, A. (in press). Occupational interests, leisure time interests, and personality: Three domains or one? In R. V. Dawis & D. Lubinski (Eds.), *Assessing individual differences in human behavior: New concepts, methods, and findings.* Minneapolis: University of Minnesota Press.

Ward, G. R., Cunningham, C. H., & Wakefield, J. A. (1976). Relationships between Holland's VPI and Cattell's 16PF. *Journal of Vocational Behavior, 8,* 307–312.

Weaver, C. N. (1980). Job satisfaction in the United States in the 1970s. *Journal of Applied Psychology, 65,* 364–367.

Weber, M. (1904). *The Protestant ethic and the rise of the spirit of capitalism.* London: Oxford University Press.

Weiss, H. M. (1977). Subordinate imitation of supervisor behavior: The role of modeling in organizational socialization. *Organizational Behavior and Human Performance, 19,* 89–105.

Werner, J. M. (1994). Dimensions that make a difference: Examining the impact of in-role and extrarole behaviors on supervisory ratings. *Journal of Applied Psychology, 79,* 98–107.

Wexley, K. N., Alexander, R. A., Greenawalt, J. P., & Couch, M. A. (1980). Attitudinal congruence and similarity as related to interpersonal evaluations in manager-subordinate dyads. *Academy of Management Journal, 23,* 320–330.

Wexley, K. N., & Nemeroff, W. F. (1974). The effects of racial prejudice, race of applicant, and biographical similarity on interviewer evaluations of job applicants. *Journal of Social and Behavioral Science, 20,* 66–78.

Wiggins, J. D., & Weslander, D. L. (1979). Personality characteristics of counselors rated as effective or ineffective. *Journal of Vocational Behavior, 15,* 175–185.

Williams, L. J., & Anderson, S. E. (1991). Job satisfaction and organizational commitment as predictors of organizational citizenship and in-role behaviors. *Journal of Management, 17,* 601–617.

Worthington, E. L., & Dolliver, R. H. (1977). Validity studies of the Strong Vocational Interest Inventories. *Journal of Counseling Psychology, 24,* 208–216.

Zonderman, A. B. (1980). *Inventory construction by the method of homogeneous item composites.* Unpublished manuscript, Johns Hopkins University.

Zytowski, D. G. (1976). Predictive validity of the Kuder Occupational Interest Survey: A 12- to 19-year follow-up. *Journal of Counseling Psychology, 23,* 221–233.

Zytowski, D. G., & Kuder, F. (1986). Advances in the Kuder Occupational Interest Survey. In W. B. Walsh & S. H. Osipow (Eds.), *Advances in vocational psychology: Volume 1. The assessment of interest* (pp. 31–54). Hillsdale, NJ: Erlbaum.

Chapter Four

Trait and State Affect

Jennifer M. George

Increasing attention is being paid in the organizational psychology literature to the role of affect in organizations. *Affect* is a broad, generic term that covers both the intense feelings and reactions people have, which are commonly referred to as emotions, and the less intense, but no less important, feelings often called *moods*. While the cognitive revolution in psychology and related fields in the 1970s and 1980s shifted attention away from affect, researchers have rediscovered the importance of affect for understanding how people think and process information, respond to situations and events, and behave in organizations.

In this chapter, I provide a basic overview of the literature on affect and its implications for understanding organizational behavior. While terms such as *mood* and *emotion* conjure up relatively short-term or fluctuating affective states, people are predisposed to experience different kinds and levels of affect based upon their personalities or dispositions. Thus I first discuss the dispositional underpinnings of affect—namely, the personality traits of positive affectivity and negative affectivity, their genetic origins, and their implications for behavior in organizations. Next, I discuss affective states, their determinants, and their consequences for understanding organizational behavior. The literature on affect (as both a trait and a state) is voluminous, and it is not my intention to overwhelm the reader with an exhaustive review of the many issues and controversies involved. Rather, I aim to impart a good understanding of the meaning of these constructs and their implications for understanding organizational behavior based upon past and current theorizing and research.

Affective Disposition: Positive and Negative Affectivity

Hundreds of personality traits have been identified and studied throughout the years, many of which would appear to predispose people to feel certain ways or experience different kinds of affect over time and across situations. However, personality is not just a random collection of traits; rather, it is hierarchically structured, with a few very broad, general traits at the top of the hierarchy and more specific traits at lower levels.

While researchers are in agreement about this hierarchical structure, there is some controversy over the precise number and type of traits at the top of the hierarchy. The dominant view, called the Five-Factor Model (or the Big Five), suggests that there are five broad-based traits at the top of the trait hierarchy: Extraversion (or positive affectivity), Neuroticism (or negative affectivity; this trait is sometimes referred to more broadly as Emotional Stability), Agreeableness, Conscientiousness, and Openness to Experience (Church & Burke, 1994; Digman, 1990; McCrae, 1989; Norman, 1963). While considerable theorizing and research supports the Big Five model, some researchers have proposed a somewhat different structure of traits at the top of the hierarchy. For example, Tellegen (1982, 1985) proposed that there are three broad-based, general personality traits: he labeled them Positive Affectivity, Negative Affectivity, and Constraint. However, as in Tellegen's model, the traits of positive affectivity (or Extraversion) and negative affectivity (or Neuroticism) are present in most alternatives to the Big Five. Hence, while researchers may disagree over whether there are three, four, five, or six traits at the top of the hierarchy, they do tend to agree that positive affectivity and negative affectivity should be among these traits, as they are in the robust Big Five model (for example, Zuckerman, Kuhlman, Joireman, Teta, & Kraft, 1993).

Positive Affectivity

Positive affectivity (PA) is the disposition to experience positive emotions and moods. People who are high on positive affectivity tend to have an overall sense of well-being and to be positively engaged in the world around them, in terms of both achievement and interpersonal relations (Tellegen, 1982, 1985). People high on PA tend to feel self-efficacious, experience positive moods and emotions, and feel good about the activities they are engaged in (Tellegen et al., 1988; Watson & Pennebaker, 1989). High-PA individuals also tend to perceive stimuli (including other people), think, and behave in a way that will support and maintain their positive feelings. Due to their positive outlook, individuals high on PA tend to enjoy and seek out social interaction.

Individuals who are low on PA tend to be disengaged from activities and the world around them in a nonpleasurable manner or style (Tellegen, 1985). They do not think and behave in ways that will promote positive moods and emotions and do not have a strong sense of overall well-being. They are less likely to experience positive moods and emotions than their high-PA counterparts and may have somewhat of a depressive outlook or orientation (George, 1992; Tellegen, 1985). Individuals who are low on PA are not necessarily "unhappy" people; rather, they lack some of the enthusiasm and positiveness of those high on PA.

Negative Affectivity

Negative affectivity (NA) is the disposition to experience negative emotions and moods. People who are high on NA tend to have negative feelings, be nonpleasurably engaged, and be distressed by their own thoughts and behaviors and the thoughts and behaviors of others (Tellegen, 1982, 1985; Watson & L. A. Clark, 1984; Watson & Pennebaker, 1989). High NAs tend to think and act in ways that result in negative affective experiences and have an overall negative orientation toward themselves and the world around them. Thus they are prone to experiencing distress over time and across situations.

Individuals who are low on NA are not prone to being distressed and experiencing negative moods and emotions. They do not tend to view conditions and events from a negative point of view and are less likely to think and behave in ways that promote negative affective experiences.

It is important to note that PA and NA are independent dimensions of personality (Meyer & Shack, 1989; Tellegen, 1982, 1985; Tellegen et al., 1988; Watson & L. A. Clark, 1984; Watson & Pennebaker, 1989). For example, a person could be high on both, low on both, or high on one and low on the other. If a person is prone to experience negative moods (because he or she is high on NA), this does not preclude the person from also experiencing positive moods (and vice versa). As I will discuss later, positive and negative affective states tend to be relatively independent of one another, consistent with the independence of the traits PA and NA (for example, Watson & Tellegen, 1985).

Genetic and Biological Determinants of PA and NA

PA and NA are enduring dimensions of personality. In fact, research suggests that there are genetic and biological bases for these traits. For example, in a study of identical and fraternal twins raised together and apart, Tellegen et al. (1988) found approximately 40 percent of the variance in PA and 55 percent of the variance in NA to be due to genetic factors. These heritabilities for PA and NA are similar in magnitude to the heritabilities found for other personality traits (for a brief review, see Arvey & Bouchard, 1994).

Viken, Rose, Kaprio, and Koskenvuo (1994) investigated the genetic origins of PA and NA in a twin study that measured PA and NA levels in the same respondents at two points in time (six years apart) and also at varying ages ranging from eighteen to fifty-nine. While heritabilities tended to drop by small amounts depending upon the ages of the respondents, there was strong evidence of a genetic basis for PA and NA at all ages, and heritabilities in this study were similar to those found by Tellegen et al. (1988).

Consistent with a genetic origin of PA and NA, some research has focused on determining the biological basis for these traits. For example, it has been suggested that PA may be related to differences in brain dopamine activity (Depue, Luciana, Arbisi, Collins, & Leon, 1994).

The logical conclusion to be drawn from the recognition that a person's levels of PA and NA are partially rooted in his or her genetic makeup is that these are enduring traits that are not likely to change significantly in the short or long run. Consistent with this conclusion, Costa and McCrae (1988) found that measures of PA and NA had six-year test-retest correlations of .82 and .83. This does not mean that PA and NA are invariant over the life course but rather that they tend to be stable traits.

Consequences of Affective Disposition for Organizations and Their Members

What are the implications of affective disposition for understanding behavior in organizations? While perhaps ten to fifteen years ago this question might not even have been asked, a growing body of evidence suggests that PA and NA do affect how people feel, think, and behave in organizations. Here I will sample some of this research as it pertains to job behaviors and performance, work-related strain, and work attitudes and affective reactions.

Job Behaviors and Performance

Traditionally, personality traits have not been seen as significant determinants of job behaviors and performance (for example, Ghiselli, 1973; Guion & Gottier, 1965). Recent research, however, is more optimistic about the role of disposition in understanding behavior and performance in organizations (for example, Baehr & Orban, 1989; Day & Silverman, 1989; Hough, Eaton, Dunnette, Kamp, & McCloy, 1990; Pulakos, Borman, & Hough, 1988). One overall conclusion that can be drawn from these and other studies is that there are several important preconditions that should be met before we can expect personality traits to be related to work behaviors and performance. First, there must be a theoretical link between the personality traits and behaviors investigated. Second, the traits and behaviors must be at the same level of specificity/ generality. And third, job holders must have some freedom or discretion in terms of the behaviors under consideration. That is, the situation must not be so "strong" (Bem & Allen, 1974; Bem & Funder, 1978; Monson, Hesley, & Chernick, 1982) as to wipe out most sources of individual variation in behavior.

PA, and to a lesser extent NA, have been linked to job behaviors and performance. Tett, Jackson, and Rothstein (1991) and Barrick and Mount (1991) have each conducted meta-analyses to determine the relationships between the Big Five personality traits and overall job performance. While their results differ somewhat, the two teams do paint a consistent picture of PA and NA playing a role in job performance. Tett et al. (1991) provide only data pertaining to PA and NA collapsing across occupations; they report a corrected mean correlation of .16 between PA and job performance and −.22 between NA and job performance.

Barrick and Mount hypothesized specific relationships between PA and NA and various dimensions of job performance for different occupational groups. Collapsing across job performance dimensions, the estimated true correlations between PA and job performance found in their meta-analyses are as follows: −.09 (professionals), .09 (police), .18 (managers), .15 (sales), and .01 (skilled/ semiskilled). These results are theoretically meaningful, and they are consistent with Barrick and Mount's expectations. That is, PA shows the strongest relationship with performance in occupations requiring social interactions with others—management and sales— consistent with high-PA individuals' proclivity toward and enjoyment of social interaction. Congruent with these results, Mount, Barrick, & Strauss (1994) also found PA (assessed by supervisors, co-workers, and customers) to be related to sales performance. However, PA was not found to be related to performance in another recent study conducted by these authors (Barrick, Mount, & Strauss, 1993).

While Barrick and Mount expected NA to be related to job performance across occupational groups, meta-analyses failed to confirm their expectations. NA was only very weakly related to performance. Given that the specific findings of Tett et al. and Barrick and Mount differ, both sets of authors have attempted to uncover and explain some potential reasons for these conflicting findings (Ones, Mount, Barrick, & Hunter, 1994; Tett, Jackson, Rothstein, & Reddon, 1994).

Cortina, Doherty, Schmitt, Kaufman, and Smith (1992) explored relationships between PA and NA and police performance. Both PA and NA had some significant relationships with various performance indices, although sometimes the directions of these relationships were counterintuitive. Finally, Staw and Barsade (1993) found that PA was positively associated with both effective decision making and interpersonal behavior.

Taken together, these research results suggest that PA and NA are likely to be related to job behaviors and performance, at least under certain conditions. In order to gain a better understanding of how and when these dispositions influence performance, researchers need to move beyond simply correlating measures of PA and NA with various performance indices and construct theoretical models of when and why PA and NA should have significant effects. For example, Barrick and Mount (1993) hypothesized and found that PA was more strongly related to managerial performance when managers had high levels of autonomy. Building off these findings, more generally it is likely that personality will have greater effects on organizational outcomes when workers are free to vary their behavior at least within a certain range of acceptability.

Work-Related Strain

Considerable evidence suggests that individuals high on NA are more likely to report that they are exposed to stressful conditions at work and also that they experience work-related strain than individuals low on NA (for example, Brief, Burke, George, Robinson, & Webster, 1988; Burke, Brief, & George, 1993). This, along with other research, suggests that correlating self-reports of stressors and strains to understand the linkage between actual stressors and strains can be problematic: observed relationships are likely to be partially a result of the spurious influence of NA. That is, individuals who are high on NA are more likely to report being exposed to stressors and experiencing strain than individuals low on NA.

NA has been frequently called a "nuisance" variable in stress research because of its influence on such self-reports. Nonetheless, it is likely that the higher levels of strain self-reported by individuals high on NA are indeed very "real" to them—just as real as strain reported by individuals who are not dispositionally prone to experiencing distress (that is, those low on NA). It is important to ask why NA appears to have these effects.

There are at least two ways in which NA may impact the levels of strain experienced by workers (McCrae & Costa, 1991). First, NA may impact levels of susceptibility to work stressors (Larsen & Katelaar, 1991). Individuals high on NA may react more strongly to potential stressors than individuals low on NA, given their tendencies to react in a negative manner to stimuli that are ambiguous or potentially stressful. Gray's work (1971, 1981, 1987) suggests that this increased susceptibility may be due to the operation of a neurological system known as the behavioral inhibition system (BIS). The BIS is thought of as regulating responses when individuals are in the presence of negative stimuli (those indicative of punishment) (Larsen & Katelaar, 1991). The work of Gray and others suggests that individuals high on NA have a particularly sensitive BIS, which causes them to react more intensively to negative stimuli.

A second path through which NA might impact levels of strain is more indirect, but potentially no less important: individuals high on NA may inadvertently create stressful situations and life events for themselves, which in turn result in increased strain. For example, because of their negative orientation and outlook, individuals high on NA may have more interpersonal problems at work; these interpersonal problems may result in more strain being experienced by these workers. Consistent with this reasoning, Magnus, Diener, Fujita, and Pavot (1993) found that individuals high on NA tended to experience more objective negative life events (for example, failure to get into graduate school, divorces/separations, nonviolent crimes, job dismissals/layoffs, and overdue projects or assignments), while individuals high on PA tended to experience more objective positive life events (for example, admission into graduate school, promotions/raises, awards or other public recognition, car purchases, and acceptance into clubs or groups).

In order to further understand the role that NA plays in work-related stress, future research should focus on (1) uncovering the causal mechanisms through which NA has its effects on strain in the workplace and (2) discovering how strain is experienced, in a phenomenological sense, by individuals who are high and low on NA. Having established that NA is related to strain, it is time to move beyond simply exploring relations between self-reports of stressors and strains and NA to some of the underlying (and potentially more interesting and important) issues involved.

Work Attitudes and Affective Reactions

Given the positive outlook and negative outlook of individuals high on PA and NA respectively, it is not surprising that these dispositions are related to work attitudes and affective reactions. Because the second part of this chapter deals specifically with affect as a state, in this section I will focus on the impact of affective dispositions on work attitudes, particularly job satisfaction.

Research has found, as would be expected, that PA is positively related and NA is negatively related to job satisfaction (for example, Brief, Butcher, & Roberson, 1995; Cropanzano, James, & Konovksy, 1993; George, 1991a; Necowitz & Roznowski, 1994). Watson and Slack (1993) found this to be the case even when job satisfaction was measured approximately two years after the measurement of affective disposition (that is, PA and NA). These findings do not suggest that individuals high on PA are always going to be satisfied or that individuals high on NA are always going to be dissatisfied, of course. Rather, they suggest that disposition plays a role in influencing job attitudes, as do situational factors such as the nature of the work itself.

Summary

The issues and research discussed above, while by no means definitive, certainly suggest that PA and NA play important roles in at least certain outcomes relevant to both individuals and organizations (for example, stress and job behaviors). The field is ripe for additional research aimed at understanding the nature of these effects. Theory-driven research that focuses on the dynamics and causal mechanisms involved is likely to have the biggest payoff in terms of increased understanding.

Aside from the main and interactive effects of affective disposition on outcomes, PA and NA play perhaps an even more important role vis-à-vis their impact on affective states at work, the focus of the next part of this chapter.

Affective States and Moods at Work

Unlike affective *dispositions* (PA and NA), which are enduring over time, affective *states* fluctuate and change, capturing how people feel from moment to moment, hour to hour, and day to day. At the most general level, there are two types of affective states: emotions and moods. Emotions are intense feelings that demand attention, interrupt ongoing cognitive processes and behaviors, and are tied to or associated with specific events or circumstances (Simon, 1982).

Moods, which are less intense than emotions, encompass more of the day-to-day feelings people experience—feelings that, while not interrupting cognitive processes and behaviors, affect them in more subtle but also important ways (M. S. Clark & Isen, 1982; Thayer, 1989). Moods are generalized affective states that are not necessarily linked to specific events or circumstances (Brady, 1970; Nowlis, 1970; Ryle, 1950). While an event may initiate a mood state, the mood, once initiated, provides the affective context for ongoing thought processes and behaviors unrelated to the mood-inducing event. Moods are pervasive and nonspecific and have the potential to have wide-ranging effects on thought processes and behaviors (Morris & Reilly, 1987).

A considerable body of literature suggests that affective states (like affective traits) are best described by two major and independent dimensions, positive affect and negative affect, rather than a single dimension (ranging from positive to negative) (Costa & McCrae, 1980; Meyer & Shack, 1989; Watson & Pennebaker, 1989; Watson & Tellegen, 1985). Positive and negative affective states have different antecedents, correlates, consequences, and relationships with life events (Costa & McCrae, 1980; Watson & L. A. Clark, 1984; Zautra, 1983). Indeed, they have been found to be largely independent of each other even over short periods of time (Watson, 1988; Watson, L. A. Clark, & Tellegen, 1988); however, at intense levels (for example, as emotions), positive and negative affective states have not been found to be experienced simultaneously (Diener & Iran-Nejad, 1986).

These two dimensions of affect describe how a person is engaged: how the person feels, the person's cognitive style, and the person's relationship with his or her surroundings (Tellegen, 1985). Positive affective states signal positive or pleasurable engagement, while negative affective states signal negative or nonpleasurable engagement. A high positive affective state is described by terms such as *enthusiastic, active, elated, peppy, strong,* and *excited,* while a low positive affective state is described by terms such as *drowsy, dull, sluggish,* and *sleepy.* A high negative affective state is characterized by terms such as *distressed, hostile, nervous, jittery, scornful,* and *fearful,* while a low negative affective state indicates feeling *placid, relaxed, calm,* and *at rest* (Tellegen, 1985; Watson et al., 1988; Watson & Tellegen, 1985).

These descriptions of positive and negative affective states apply to both emotions and moods. Again, it is the intensity of the affective state that distinguishes between emotions and moods. Strong affective states (in the form of emotions) interrupt ongoing cognition and behavior and demand attention, while less intense affective states (in the form of moods) impact ongoing cognition and behavior without necessarily interrupting them or causing a change in a person's focus of attention. Emotions can often feed into moods; once an individual has "dealt with" or habituated to a positive or negative emotion (Frijda, 1988), that emotion might continue to affect the individual's functioning by promoting an analogous type of mood. Positive emotions prompted by the news that you are going to receive a substantial raise, for example, may lead to a positive mood for the remainder of the day. Similarly, negative emotions resulting from learning that your best friend and co-worker has been laid off may lead to a negative mood that persists even once you have gotten over the initial shock.

Because emotions are specific to events or circumstances, how people respond to them and their consequences for organizational behavior depend upon the particular factor that caused the emotion. Moods, on the other hand, are nonspecific and affect behavior irrespective of their cause or origin. In the remainder of the chapter, therefore, I focus on moods. At this point, I would also like to note that since work moods have been the focus of scholarly theorizing and research only in the last several years, much of what I discuss is tentative and in need of further research.

Determinants of Work Moods

Recently, George and Brief (1992) reviewed some of the determinants of positive moods at work. Building off their model, I discuss below potential determinants of positive and negative moods at work that are found at three levels of analysis: individual, group, and organizational.

Individual-Level Determinants of Work Moods

There are two basic categories of determinants at the individual level: affective disposition and life events. Affective disposition refers to people's tendencies to experience positive and negative moods, while life events capture the impact of an individual's life circumstances on his or her work moods.

Active Disposition

Based upon my earlier descriptions of the personality traits PA and NA, it should come as no surprise that individuals who are high on PA are more likely to experience positive moods than those low on this trait. Likewise, individuals who are high on NA are more likely to experience negative moods than those low on this trait (for example, Tellegen, 1985; Watson & Pennebaker, 1989).

Research has confirmed that these relationships between affective disposition and mood in general also apply to moods experienced at work. For example, Brief, Burke, George, Robinson, & Webster (1988) found NA to be significantly associated with negative mood at work among a sample of professional and managerial personnel of an insurance company; George (1989) found measures of PA and NA to be significantly associated with positive and negative mood at work, respectively, in a sample of salespeople; and George (1995) found a measure of PA to be significantly associated with positive mood at work among a sample of managers.

Life Events

The term *life events* refers to the different things that happen to people in their daily lives, both at work and in other domains (such as home and family). Life events can be major (for example, a promotion) or minor (for example, going out to lunch with co-workers) and positive (as in the former two examples) or negative (for example, an argument with one's boss). All of these different kinds of life events have the potential to influence workers' moods both on and off the job.

Research has found that positive life events are more likely to influence positive moods than negative moods, while negative life events are more likely to influence negative moods than positive moods (Zautra, 1983; Zautra & Reich, 1983; Zautra & Simons, 1979). Negative events do not necessarily decrease positive moods over time, and positive events do not necessarily decrease negative moods over time (Emmons, 1986).

Group-Level Determinants of Work Moods

There are a variety of potential group-level determinants of work moods, and research has just begun to explore these factors. Evidence to date suggests that several types of group factors are especially likely to impact mood at work, and these can be grouped into two main categories: group affective tone and group characteristics.

Group Affective Tone

George (1990) hypothesized and found that work groups often have group affective tones or characteristic feelings that are experienced consistently by group members. Some groups may be enthusiastic and energetic (those with a high positive affective tone), and other groups may be troubled and distraught (those with a high negative affective tone). To the extent that a group has an affective tone, that tone is likely to influence individual members' positive and negative moods at work. (For information on the measurement of group affective tone, see, for example, George, 1990; George & Brief, 1992; and George & James, 1993.)

Group Characteristics

Group characteristics such as group size, the proximity of group members, group norms, and leader mood also are likely to influence moods at work. Let us look at each of these characteristics in turn.

First, research has found that as group size increases, members of a group interact less frequently with each other, feel less close to each other, are less attracted to the group, and are more likely to have conflicts and disagreements with one another (for example, Bass & Norton, 1951; Berger & Cummings, 1979; Hare, 1952; Katz, 1949; Schull, Delbecq, & Cummings, 1970; Shaw, 1981). These findings suggest that work moods are likely to be more favorable when work-group size is kept relatively small.

The term *proximity* has traditionally been used to describe the physical distance between group members. However, with advances in information and communication technology, physical distance may not necessarily be a good indicator of "experienced" proximity. Group members who are separated by thousands of miles but communicate daily with each other via video conferences may be more proximate than group members who share a building but rarely interact. Given new technological developments, perhaps it is more appropriate to view proximity in terms of the extent to which group members have access to and communicate with each other. Viewed in these terms, proximity is likely to foster more favorable work moods because it results in social interaction, which has been related to positive moods (for example, Bradburn, 1969; Bradburn & Caplovitz, 1965; Harding, 1982; Headey, Holstrom, & Wearing, 1985; Phillips, 1967; Zautra, 1983). Proximity may also help to reduce the incidence of negative moods to the extent that group members are sources of social support.

Group norms and leader moods also are likely to influence individual members' moods at work. Norms that stress the importance of helping each other out, being friendly and cooperative, and having "fun" at work, for example, are likely to promote favorable moods. Leaders who experience positive moods themselves may have a favorable effect on their subordinates' moods. Likewise, leaders who experience negative moods may find themselves with subordinates who are similarly distressed.

Organizational-Level Determinants of Work Moods

A wide variety of contextual and environmental factors also are likely to influence work moods (L. A. Clark & Watson, 1988; M. S. Clark & Isen, 1982). These factors include the physical design of the workplace, the attractiveness of office furnishings and fixtures, the extent to which the organizational layout promotes or inhibits social interaction, placement of windows, and so forth. Moods can be significantly impacted by these relatively commonplace and taken-for-granted aspects of the workplace.

Summary

Work moods are ultimately determined by the interaction of personality or disposition (in the form of positive and negative affectivity) and situational factors (at the individual, group, and organizational levels). Just as looking solely at disposition will lead to an incomplete understanding of why workers experience the moods they do, so too will an examination of situational determinants in isolation from disposition yield an incomplete picture of the etiology of work moods.

Consequences of Work Moods

Research on the consequences of work moods is in its infancy. However, the growing body of research points to some of the ways in which workers' feelings may influence their behaviors in organizations. I consider here four potential areas in which work moods may play a role: job behaviors and performance, organizational spontaneity, withdrawal behaviors, and leader effectiveness.

Job Behaviors and Performance

George and Brief (1996) have recently proposed a model of work motivation in which moods—particularly positive moods—play a pivotal role. In their model, positive moods are proposed to influence distal motivation (for example, choice of behaviors or effort levels) by causing workers to have higher expectancies, instrumentalities, and valences due to the effects that positive moods are likely to have on the cognitive processes underlying these judgments (through the mechanisms of mood-congruent judgment, mood-congruent recall, and mood effects on attributions). Positive moods are also proposed to influence proximal motivation (for example, ongoing behavior when actually engaged on a task) by causing workers to maintain higher standards (or "reference criteria," in control theory terms; Hyland, 1988) for themselves. While negative moods are also likely to influence work motivation, their potential effects are more difficult to tease out.

The results from some initial research are consistent with George and Brief's reasoning (1994). For example, Staw, Sutton, and Pelled (1994) found, in a sample of workers from a hospital and two manufacturing plants, that positive moods predicted performance as rated by supervisors eighteen months later. As another example, George (1991b) found that the positive moods experienced by salespeople at work were significantly and positively associated with the performance of customer service behaviors as rated by their supervisors. However, contrary to these finding, T. A. Wright and Staw (1994) found that moods (both positive and negative) were not significantly related to job performance, while affective disposition was. (It should be noted that their sample size was small, which may have resulted in some statistical power issues.)

Organizational Spontaneity

Increasing attention is being paid in the organizational psychology literature to extra-role behaviors—behaviors that are not required of organizational members yet contribute to and are necessary for organizational survival and effectiveness. Various labels for these behaviors have been proposed, such as prosocial organizational behavior (Brief & Motowidlo, 1986) and organizational citizenship behavior (Organ, 1988), and their defining characteristics and types have been the subject of some debate. George and Brief (1992) expanded on and further developed Katz's original treatment of such behaviors (1964), which (based on Katz's formulations) they subsume under the concept of *organizational spontaneity.*

Organizational spontaneity refers to behaviors that are extra-role, are performed voluntarily, and contribute to organizational effectiveness. The five forms of organizational spontaneity (as outlined by George and Brief, 1992) are helping co-workers, protecting the organization, making constructive suggestions, developing oneself, and spreading goodwill. George and Brief (1992) developed a theoretical rationale for their expectation that positive moods at work would foster or facilitate each of these five forms of organizational spontaneity—a rationale that is briefly recapped as follows:

1.   Positive moods are expected to foster helping co-workers based on extensive literature in psychology supporting the finding that people who are in positive moods are more likely to be helpful to others or engage in prosocial behavior (for example, Aderman, 1972; Cunningham, Steinberg, & Grev, 1980; Isen, M. S. Clark, & Schwartz, 1976; Isen & Levin, 1972; Levin & Isen, 1975; Rosenhan, Salovey, & Hargis, 1981). Carlson, Charlin, and Miller (1988) reviewed complementary theoretical underpinnings for these findings based on processes such as priming, attraction, and positive mood maintenance.

Consistent with this literature, George (1991b) found that the positive moods of salespeople were significantly and positively associated with helping co-workers as well as with helpful behaviors directed at customers. While Organ and Konovsky (1989) did not find mood to be predictive of helping co-workers in their study, George (1991b) has suggested that they may have inadvertently measured positive mood as a *trait* (that is, positive affectivity) rather than a *state,* consistent with the work of Watson, L. A. Clark, and Tellegen (1988).

2.   Positive moods are expected to encourage protecting the organization based on the idea that people who are in positive moods often take steps to maintain their good feelings (Carlson et al., 1988). If workers experience positive moods at work, they may see it as in their best interest to protect the organization from harm so as to maintain their own good feelings on the job.

3.   Positive moods are expected to result in workers' making constructive suggestions in organizations. This expectation is based on the work of Isen and her colleagues, who hypothesized and found that positive moods foster creativity via their effects on cognitive processes (Carnevale & Isen, 1986; Isen & Daubman, 1984; Isen, Daubman, & Nowicki, 1987; Isen, Johnson, Mertz, & Robinson, 1985).

4.   Positive moods are expected to facilitate self-development efforts based on work suggesting that people who are in positive moods (a) think that they are more likely to be successful at different activities and (b) are indeed more successful, which can lead to greater persistence (for example, Brown, 1984; Bower & Cohen, 1982; Taylor & Brown, 1988; J. S. Wright & Mischel, 1982).

5.   It is hypothesized that workers who are in positive moods are more likely to spread goodwill based on their increased likelihood of having positive cognitions about their organizations and their tendency toward increased social interaction with others (A. S. Rossi & P. E. Rossi, 1977; Watson, 1988).

Withdrawal Behaviors

Work moods, with their origins in person-situation interactions, have the potential to influence withdrawal behaviors such as absenteeism and turnover. In terms of absenteeism, George (1989) reasoned that the characteristic moods people experience at work (as a result of the interaction of their personality with the situation) may influence their attendance patterns. Workers who tend to experience positive moods at work may be more inclined to come to work (or less inclined to be absent), because doing so maintains their good feelings. Conversely, workers who experience negative moods at work may use absence to control or change their bad feelings. Consistent with this reasoning, George (1989) found that positive mood at work was significantly and negatively associated with absence. However, negative mood was not significantly associated with absence, contrary to George's expectations.

Turnover, as a permanent form of withdrawal, may also be impacted by work moods. To the extent that workers consistently experience negative moods at work, this may prompt them to seek out alternative opportunities and eventually quit their jobs. Conversely, workers who consistently experience positive moods at work may be motivated to keep their present jobs to prolong these good day-to-day feelings. However, given the fact that positive and negative moods have not been found to have symmetrical effects on absence (George, 1989), it may be that relations with turnover are also more complex.

It is obviously too soon to tell if, when, and how mood states affect withdrawal behaviors such as absence and turnover. However, based on an initial study (George, 1989), as well as on potential theoretical links between moods at work and withdrawal behaviors, future research certainly seems warranted.

Leader Effectiveness

George and Bettenhausen (1990) reasoned that the extent to which leaders experience positive moods at work may contribute to their effectiveness. When leaders feel excited, enthusiastic, and active (Watson & Tellegen, 1985), they may be more likely to energize their subordinates and convey a sense of efficacy, competence, optimism, and enjoyment. Leaders in positive moods may also be more likely to positively reinforce their subordinates and be a positive interpersonal force. Consistent with this reasoning, George and Bettenhausen found that store managers who experienced positive moods at work had higher-performing subordinates who also were less subject to turnover. In another sample (building off these findings), George (1995) also found positive leader mood to be related to indicators of leader effectiveness.

Additional research is needed to understand the mechanisms through which leader mood (both positive and negative) influences leader effectiveness, subordinate behavior and performance, and other outcomes. For example, leader mood may impact subordinate self-efficacy and motivation and may result in more open and effective communication between a leader and his or her subordinates.

Summary

The ideas and proposed relationships between work moods and the outcomes considered in this section are reasonable, based on current theorizing and research; but they are also very tentative, given the lack of a body of literature that directly addresses them. What is clear, however, is that work moods do have the potential to impact a wide variety of important organizational behaviors. Thus the field is ripe for theoretically based investigations into the consequences of work moods.

My treatment of work moods in this section has tended to be skewed toward the consideration of positive work moods; the consequences of negative moods have, in a sense, gotten short-changed. This imbalance is due to the fact that many of the relevant findings and relations are more clear-cut in the case of positive moods and more equivocal in the case of negative moods. For example, while positive moods have been found to foster helping behaviors, negative moods sometimes result in more helping behaviors but other times do not (Carlson & Miller, 1987). Although negative work moods are likely to have just as important implications for understanding organizational behavior as positive work moods, negative moods may present researchers with more of a challenge in terms of theoretically and empirically ascertaining their effects on organizationally relevant outcomes. In this regard, researchers need to keep in mind that while intuitively we may expect positive and negative moods to have symmetrical effects on cognitions and behaviors, this is often not the case.

Conclusion

By now it should be clear that affect, as both a trait and a state, has important implications for understanding work behavior. Workers' feelings, or their moods, can have powerful effects on their thought processes and behaviors in organizations. While in the past, attention has been focused on cognition more than affect (as it relates to such topics as work motivation or withdrawal), both cognition and affect are clearly integral aspects of the human and work experience.

Affective dispositions (positive affectivity and negative affectivity) represent the affective tendencies workers bring with them to the workplace, and thus have the potential to impact organizational behavior. These tendencies interact with situational factors emanating both within and outside the workplace to determine affective states such as moods.

The diverse studies and perspectives covered in this chapter lead to one overarching conclusion: a rich understanding of behavior in organizations requires a consideration of affective traits and states. The time is ripe for theoretically driven empirical studies to uncover when, how, and why affective traits and states impact organizational behavior.

References

Aderman, D. (1972). Elation, depression, and helping behavior. *Journal of Personality and Social Psychology, 24,* 91–101.

Arvey, R. D., & Bouchard, T. J. (1994). Genetics, twins, and organizational behavior. In B. M. Staw & L. L. Cummings (Eds.), *Research in organizational behavior.* Greenwich, CT: JAI Press.

Baehr, M. E., & Orban, J. A. (1989). The role of intellectual abilities and personality characteristics in determining success in higher-level positions. *Journal of Vocational Behavior, 35,* 270–287.

Barrick, M. R., & Mount, M. K. (1991). The Big Five personality dimensions and job performance: A meta-analysis. *Personnel Psychology, 44,* 1–26.

Barrick, M. R., & Mount, M. K. (1993). Autonomy as a moderator of the relationships between the Big Five personality dimensions and job performance. *Journal of Applied Psychology, 78,* 111–118.

Barrick, M. R., Mount, M. K., & Strauss, J. P. (1993). Conscientiousness and performance of sales representatives: Test of the mediating effects of goal setting. *Journal of Applied Psychology, 78,* 715–722.

Bass, B. M., & Norton, M. (1951). Group size and leaderless discussion. *Journal of Applied Psychology, 35,* 397–400.

Bem, D. J., & Allen, A. (1974). On predicting some of the people some of the time: The search for cross-situational consistencies in behavior. *Psychological Review, 81,* 506–520.

Bem, D. J., & Funder, D. C. (1978). Predicting more of the people more of the time: Assessing the personality of situations. *Psychological Review, 85,* 485–501.

Berger, C., & Cummings, L. (1979). Organizational structure, attitudes, and behaviors. In B. M. Staw & L. L. Cummings (Eds.), *Research in organizational behavior* (pp. 169–208). Greenwich, CT: JAI Press.

Bower, G. H., & Cohen, P. R. (1982). Emotional influences in memory and thinking: Data and theory. In M. S. Clark & S. T. Fiske (Eds.),

Affect and cognition: The seventeenth annual Carnegie Symposium on Cognition (pp. 229–231). Hillsdale, NJ: Erlbaum.

Bradburn, N. M. (1969). *The structure of psychological well-being.* Hawthorne, NY: Aldine.

Bradburn, N. M., & Caplovitz, D. (1965). *Reports on happiness.* Hawthorne, NY: Aldine.

Brady, J. V. (1970). Emotion: Some conceptual problems and psychophysiological experiments. In M. B. Arnold (Ed.), *Feelings and emotions: The Loyola Symposium* (pp. 69–100). San Diego, CA: Academic Press.

Brief, A. P., Burke, M. J., George, J. M., Robinson, B., & Webster, J. (1988). Should negative affectivity remain an unmeasured variable in the study of job stress? *Journal of Applied Psychology, 73,* 193–198.

Brief, A. P., Butcher, A. H., & Roberson, L. (1995). Cookies, disposition, and job attitudes: The effects of positive mood inducing events and negative affectivity on job satisfaction in a field experiment. *Organizational Behavior and Human Decision Processes, 62,* 55–62.

Brief, A. P., & Motowidlo, S. J. (1986). Prosocial organizational behaviors. *Academy of Management Review, 11,* 710–725.

Brown, J. D. (1984). Effects of induced mood on causal attributions for success and failure. *Motivation and Emotion, 8,* 343–353.

Burke, M. J., Brief, A. P., & George, J. M. (1993). The role of negative affectivity in understanding relations between self-reports of stressors and strains: A comment on the applied psychology literature. *Journal of Applied Psychology, 78,* 402–412.

Carlson, M., Charlin, V., & Miller, N. (1988). Positive mood and helping behavior: A test of six hypotheses. *Journal of Personality and Social Psychology, 55,* 211–229.

Carlson, M., & Miller, N. (1987). Explanation of the relation between negative mood and helping. *Psychological Bulletin, 102,* 91–108.

Carnevale, P. J. D., & Isen, A. M. (1986). The influence of positive affect and visual access on the discovery of integrative solutions in bilateral negotiation. *Organizational Behavior and Human Decision Processes, 37,* 1–13.

Church, A. T., & Burke, P. J. (1994). Exploratory and confirmatory tests of the Big Five and Tellegen's Three- and Four-Dimensional Models. *Journal of Personality and Social Psychology, 66,* 93–114.

Clark, L. A., & Watson, D. (1988). Mood and the mundane: Relations between daily life events and self-reported mood. *Journal of Personality and Social Psychology, 54,* 296–308.

Clark, M. S., & Isen, A. M. (1982). Toward understanding the relationship between feeling states and social behavior. In A. H. Hastorf & A. M. Isen (Eds.), *Cognitive social psychology* (pp. 73–108). New York: Elsevier Science.

Cortina, J. M., Doherty, M. L., Schmitt, N., Kaufman, G., & Smith, R. G. (1992). The "Big Five" personality factors in the IPI and MMPI: Predictors of police performance. *Personnel Psychology, 45,* 119–140.

Costa, P. T., & McCrae, R. R. (1980). Influence of extraversion and neuroticism on subjective well-being: Happy and unhappy people. *Journal of Personality and Social Psychology, 38,* 668–678.

Costa, P. T., & McCrae, R. R. (1988). Personality in adulthood: A six-year longitudinal study of self-reports and spouse ratings on the NEO Personality Inventory. *Journal of Personality and Social Psychology, 54,* 853–863.

Cropanzano, R., James, K., & Konovsky, M. A. (1993). Dispositional affectivity as a predictor of work attitudes and job performance. *Journal of Organizational Behavior, 14,* 595–606.

Cunningham, M. R., Steinberg, J., & Grev, R. (1980). Wanting to and having to help: Separate motivations for positive mood and guilt-induced helping. *Journal of Personality and Social Psychology, 38,* 181–192.

Day, D. V., & Silverman, S. B. (1989). Personality and job performance: Evidence of incremental validity. *Personnel Psychology, 42,* 25–36.

Depue, R. A., Luciana, M., Arbisi, P., Collins, P., & Leon, A. (1994). Dopamine and the structure of personality: Relation of agonist-induced dopamine activity to positive emotionality. *Journal of Personality and Social Psychology, 67,* 485–498.

Diener, E., & Iran-Nejad, A. (1986). The relationship in experience between various types of affect. *Journal of Personality and Social Psychology, 50,* 1031–1038.

Digman, J. M. (1990). Personality structure: Emergence of the Five-Factor Model. *Annual Review of Psychology, 41,* 417–440.

Emmons, R. A. (1986). *The dual nature of happiness: Independence of positive and negative moods.* Paper presented at the 94th annual meeting of the American Psychological Association, Washington, DC.

Frijda, N. H. (1988). The laws of emotion. *American Psychologist, 43,* 349–358.

George, J. M. (1989). Mood and absence. *Journal of Applied Psychology, 74,* 317–324.

George, J. M. (1990). Personality, affect, and behavior in groups. *Journal of Applied Psychology, 75,* 107–116.

George, J. M. (1991a). Time structure and purpose as a mediator of work-life linkages. *Journal of Applied Social Psychology, 21,* 296–314.

George, J. M. (1991b). State or trait: Effects of positive mood on prosocial behaviors at work. *Journal of Applied Social Psychology, 76,* 299–307.

George, J. M. (1992). The role of personality in organizational life: Issues and evidence. *Journal of Management, 18,* 185–213.

George, J. M. (1995). Leader positive mood and group performance: The case of customer service. *Journal of Applied Social Psychology, 25,* 778–794.

George, J. M., & Bettenhausen, K. (1990). Understanding prosocial behavior, sales performance, and turnover: A group level analysis in a service context. *Journal of Applied Psychology, 75,* 698–709.

George, J. M., & Brief, A. P. (1992). Feeling good—doing good: A conceptual analysis of the mood at work/organizational spontaneity relationship. *Psychological Bulletin, 112,* 310–329.

George, J. M., & Brief, A. P. (1996). Motivational agendas in the workplace: The effects of feelings on focus of attention and work motivation. In B. M. Staw & L. L. Cummings (Eds.), *Research in organizational behavior* (Vol. 18). Greenwich, CT: JAI Press.

George, J. M., & James, L. R. (1993). Personality, affect, and behavior in groups revisited: Comment on aggregation, levels of analysis, and a recent application of within and between analysis. *Journal of Applied Psychology, 78,* 798–804.

Ghiselli, E. E. (1973). The validity of aptitude tests in personnel selection. *Personnel Psychology, 20,* 461–477.

Gray, J. A. (1971). The psychophysiological basis of introversion-extraversion. *Behavior Research and Therapy, 8,* 249–266.

Gray, J. A. (1981). A critique of Eysenck's theory of personality. In H. J. Eysenck (Ed.), *A model for personality* (pp. 246–276). New York: Springer-Verlag.

Gray, J. A. (1987). Perspectives on anxiety and impulsivity: A commentary. *Journal of Research in Personality, 21,* 493–509.

Guion, R. M., & Gottier, R. F. (1965). Validity of personality measures in personnel selection. *Personnel Psychology, 18,* 135–164.

Harding, S. D. (1982). Psychological well-being in Great Britain: An evaluation of the Bradburn Affect Balance Scale. *Personality and Individual Differences, 3,* 167–175.

Hare, A. P. (1952). Interaction and consensus in different sized groups. *American Sociological Review, 17,* 261–267.

Headey, B. W., Holstrom, E. L., & Wearing, A. J. (1985). Models of well-being and ill-being. *Social Indicators Research, 17,* 211–234.

Hough, L. M., Eaton, N. K., Dunnette, M. D., Kamp, J. D., & McCloy, R. A. (1990). Criterion-related validities of personality constructs and the effect of response distortion on those validities. *Journal of Applied Psychology, 75,* 581–595.

Hyland, M. E. (1988). Motivational control theory: An integrative framework. *Journal of Personality and Social Psychology, 55,* 642–651.

Isen, A. M., Clark, M. S., & Schwartz, M. F. (1976). Duration of the effect of good mood on helping: "Footprints on the sands of time." *Journal of Personality and Social Psychology, 34,* 385–393.

Isen, A. M., & Daubman, K. A. (1984). The influence of affect on categorization. *Journal of Personality and Social Psychology, 47,* 1206–1217.

Isen, A. M., Daubman, K. A., & Nowicki, G. P. (1987). Positive affect facilitates creative problem solving. *Journal of Personality and Social Psychology, 52,* 1122–1131.

Isen, A. M., Johnson, M.M.S., Mertz, E., & Robinson, G. F. (1985). The influence of positive affect on the unusualness of word associations. *Journal of Personality and Social Psychology, 48,* 1413–1426.

Isen, A. M., & Levin, A. F. (1972). Effects of feeling good on helping: Cookies and kindness. *Journal of Personality and Social Psychology, 21,* 384–388.

Katz, D. (1949). Morale and motivation in industry. In W. Dennis (Ed.), *Current trends in industrial psychology* (pp. 145–171). Pittsburgh: University of Pittsburgh Press.

Katz, D. (1964). The motivational basis of organizational behavior. *Behavioral Science, 9,* 131–146.

Larsen, R. J., & Katelaar, T. (1991). Personality and susceptibility to positive and negative emotional states. *Journal of Personality and Social Psychology, 61,* 132–140.

Levin, P. F., & Isen, A. M. (1975). Something you can still get for a dime: Further studies on the effect of feeling good on helping. *Sociometry, 38,* 141–147.

Magnus, K., Diener, E., Fujita, F., & Pavot, W. (1993). Extraversion and neuroticism as predictors of objective life events: A longitudinal analysis. *Journal of Personality and Social Psychology, 65,* 1046–1053.

McCrae, R. R. (1989). Why I advocate the Five-Factor Model: Joint factor analyses of the NEO-PI with other instruments. In D. M. Buss & N. Cantor (Eds.), *Personality psychology: Recent trends and emerging directions* (pp. 237–245). New York: Springer-Verlag.

McCrae, R. R., & Costa, P. T. (1991). Adding *Liebe* and *Arbeit:* The full Five-Factor Model and well-being. *Bulletin of Personality and Social Psychology, 17,* 227–232.

Meyer, G. J., & Shack, J. R. (1989). Structural convergence of mood and personality: Evidence for old and new directions. *Journal of Personality and Social Psychology, 57,* 691–706.

Monson, T. C., Hesley, J. W., & Chernick, L. (1982). Specifying when personality traits can and cannot predict behavior: An alternative to abandoning the attempt to predict single-act criteria. *Journal of Personality and Social Psychology, 43,* 385–399.

Morris, W. N., & Reilly, N. P. (1987). Toward the self-regulation of mood: Theory and research. *Motivation and Emotion, 11,* 215–249.

Mount, M. K., Barrick, M. R., & Strauss, J. P. (1994). Validity of observer ratings of the Big Five personality factors. *Journal of Applied Psychology, 79,* 272–280.

Necowitz, L. B., & Roznowski, M. (1994). Negative affectivity and job satisfaction: Cognitive processes underlying the relationship and effects on employee behaviors. *Journal of Vocational Behavior, 45,* 270–294.

Norman, W. T. (1963). Toward an adequate taxonomy of personality attributes: Replicated factor structure in peer nomination personality ratings. *Journal of Abnormal and Social Psychology, 66,* 574–583.

Nowlis, V. (1970). Mood: Behavior and experience. In M. B. Arnold (Ed.), *Feelings and emotions: The Loyola Symposium.* San Diego, CA: Academic Press.

Ones, D. S., Mount, M. K., Barrick, M. R., & Hunter, J. E. (1994). Personality and job performance: A critique of the Tett, Jackson, and Rothstein (1991) meta-analysis. *Personnel Psychology, 47,* 147–171.

Organ, D. W. (1988). *Organizational citizenship behavior: The good soldier syndrome.* New York: Lexington Books.

Organ, D. W., & Konovsky, M. A. (1989). Cognitive versus affective determinants of organizational citizenship behavior. *Journal of Applied Psychology, 74,* 157–164.

Phillips, D. L. (1967). Social participation and happiness. *American Journal of Sociology, 72,* 479–488.

Pulakos, E. D., Borman, W. C., & Hough, L. M. (1988). Test validation for scientific understanding: Two demonstrations of an approach to studying predictor-criterion linkages. *Personnel Psychology, 41,* 703–716.

Rosenhan, D. L., Salovey, P., & Hargis, K. (1981). The joys of helping: Focus of attention mediates the impact of positive affect on altruism. *Journal of Personality and Social Psychology, 40,* 899–905.

Rossi, A. S., & Rossi, P. E. (1977). Body time and social time: Mood patterns by menstrual cycle phase and day of the week. *Social Science Research, 6,* 273–308.

Ryle, G. (1950). *The concept of mind.* London: Hutchinson.

Schull, F. A., Delbecq, A. L., & Cummings, L. L. (1970). *Organizational decision making.* New York: McGraw-Hill.

Shaw, M. E. (1981). *Group dynamics: The psychology of small group behavior.* New York: McGraw-Hill.

Simon, H. A. (1982). Comments. In M. S. Clark and S. T. Fiske (Eds.), *Affect and cognition: The seventeenth annual Carnegie Symposium on Cognition* (pp. 333–342). Hillsdale, NJ: Erlbaum.

Staw, B. M., & Barsade, S. G. (1993). Affect and managerial performance:

A test of the sadder-but-wiser vs. happier-and-smarter hypotheses. *Administrative Science Quarterly, 38,* 304–331.

Staw, B. M., Sutton, R. I., & Pelled, L. H. (1994). Employee positive emotion and favorable outcomes at work. *Organization Science, 5,* 51–71.

Taylor, S. E., & Brown, J. D. (1988). Illusion and well-being: A social psychological perspective on mental health. *Psychological Bulletin, 103,* 193–210.

Tellegen, A. (1982). *Brief manual for the Differential Personality Questionnaire.* Unpublished manuscript, University of Minnesota.

Tellegen, A. (1985). Structures of mood and personality and their relevance to assessing anxiety, with an emphasis on self-report. In A. H. Tuma & J. D. Maser (Eds.), *Anxiety and the anxiety disorders* (pp. 681–706). Hillsdale, NJ: Erlbaum.

Tellegen, A., Lykken, D. T., Bouchard, T. J., Wilcox, K. J., Segal, N. L., & Rich, S. (1988). Personality similarity in twins reared apart and together. *Journal of Personality and Social Psychology, 54,* 1031–1039.

Tett, R. P., Jackson, D. N., & Rothstein, M. (1991). Personality measures as predictors of job performance: A meta-analytic review. *Personnel Psychology, 44,* 703–742.

Tett, R. P., Jackson, D. N., Rothstein, M., & Reddon, J. R. (1994). Meta-analysis of personality–job performance relations: A reply to Ones, Mount, Barrick, and Hunter (1994). *Personnel Psychology, 47,* 157–172.

Thayer, R. E. (1989). *The biopsychology of mood and arousal.* New York: Oxford University Press.

Viken, R. J., Rose, R. J., Kaprio, J., & Koskenvuo, M. (1994). A developmental genetic analysis of adult personality: Extraversion and neuroticism from 18 to 59 years of age. *Journal of Personality and Social Psychology, 66,* 722–730.

Watson, D. (1988). Intraindividual and interindividual analyses of positive and negative affect: Their relation to health complaints, perceived stress, and daily activities. *Journal of Personality and Social Psychology, 54,* 1020–1030.

Watson, D., & Clark, L. A. (1984). Negative affectivity: The disposition to experience aversive emotional states. *Psychological Bulletin, 96,* 465–490.

Watson, D., Clark, L. A., & Tellegen, A. (1988). Development and validation of brief measures of positive and negative affect: The Panas scales. *Journal of Personality and Social Psychology, 54,* 1063–1070.

Watson, D., & Pennebaker, J. W. (1989). Health complaints, stress, and distress: Exploring the central role of negative affectivity. *Psychological Review, 96,* 234–254.

Watson, D., & Slack, A. K. (1993). General factors of affective temperament and their relation to job satisfaction over time. *Organizational Behavior and Human Decision Processes, 54,* 181–202.

Watson, D., & Tellegen, A. (1985). Toward a consensual structure of mood. *Psychological Bulletin, 98,* 219–235.

Wright, J. S., & Mischel, W. (1982). Influence of affect on cognitive social learning person variables. *Journal of Personality and Social Psychology, 43,* 901–914.

Wright, T. A., & Staw, B. M. (1994). In search of the happy/productive worker: A longitudinal study of affect and performance. *Academy of Management Best Paper Proceedings* (54th annual meeting), pp. 274–278.

Zautra, A. J. (1983). Social resources and the quality of life. *American Journal of Community Psychology, 11,* 275–290.

Zautra, A. J., & Reich, J. W. (1983). Life events and perceptions of life quality: Developments in a two-factor approach. *Journal of Community Psychology, 11,* 121–132.

Zautra, A. J., & Simons, L. S. (1979). Some effects of positive life events in community mental health. *American Journal of Community Psychology, 7,* 441–451.

Zuckerman, M., Kuhlman, D. M., Joireman, J., Teta, P., & Kraft, M. (1993). A comparison of three structural models for personality: The Big Three, the Big Five, and the Alternative Five. *Journal of Personality and Social Psychology, 65,* 757–768.

Part Two

The Roles of Individual Differences

Chapter Five

Orientation Toward the Job and Organization

Stephan J. Motowidlo

This chapter is about individual differences in orientation toward the job and the organization. In particular, it focuses on individual differences in job satisfaction. Although other attitudinal orientations, such as organizational commitment (Mowday, Porter, & Steers, 1982; Mathieu & Zajac, 1990), job involvement (Lodahl & Kejner, 1965), and the sense of group identification and cohesion implicit in the concept of morale (Motowidlo & Borman, 1977, 1978) are also important, they are beyond the scope of this chapter.

Job satisfaction is nearly always measured through self-report questionnaires that ask respondents such questions as whether they are likely to stay in the job or recommend it to others, how often they think about quitting, how favorably the job compares to other jobs, whether the job has positive or negative attributes, whether they like the job, whether they like the job more or less than other people like their jobs, and how often they feel satisfied or dissatisfied with their job (Porac, 1987). Such self-reports are assumed to reveal someone's affective responses to aspects of the work environment. There is growing recognition, however, that other factors besides the work environment affect self-reports of job satisfaction in ways that make it difficult to interpret the meaning of these reports (Podsakoff & Organ, 1986). Some of these variables involve individual differences in such traits as negative affectivity (Brief, Burke, George, Robinson, & Webster, 1988) and affective disposition (Judge & Hulin, 1993).

The purpose of this chapter is to provide an integrative theoretical framework for the results of many studies that have examined relations between individual difference variables and self-reported job satisfaction. The chapter's main theme is that individual difference variables can be either a source of error variance or a source of true score variance in measures of job satisfaction. Whether individual difference variables contribute error or true score variance depends on how the construct of job satisfaction is defined.

This chapter is organized in two sections. The first section develops an information-processing model to explain how people form judgments of job satisfaction. It describes the process through which people transform information about the work environment to produce judgments of job satisfaction and suggests four ways to define the construct of job satisfaction according to different sources of true score variance and error variance. The second section focuses on individual differences in relation to the information-processing model described in the first section. It reviews lines of evidence that argue for individual differences in self-reports of job satisfaction and integrates effects of individual differences with the information-processing model to develop a theory of individual differences in job satisfaction.

Cognitive Processes in Self-Reports of Job Satisfaction

The information-processing model presented in this chapter assumes that self-reports of job satisfaction are *judgments* about the *favorability* of the *work environment*. Each of these critical features of self-reported job satisfaction is elaborated below.

First, self-reported job satisfaction is a *judgment*. To form that judgment, people have to reflect upon their experiences at work and integrate information about aspects of the work environment and their affective responses to them (Motowidlo & Lawton, 1984). This perspective is consistent with Porac's view of responses to job satisfaction questionnaires as cognitive events (1987): he distinguished between feeling states and descriptions of feeling states and argued that self-report measures of job satisfaction evoke cognitive processes for describing feelings about the work environment.

Second, self-reported job satisfaction is a judgment about *favorability;* it is a judgment about how good or bad, how positive or negative, how benign or malignant, how likable or unlikable the work environment is. In other words, it is an evaluative judgment more than a descriptive judgment. This evaluative judgment can be assessed through descriptive items such as some of those found in the Job Descriptive Index (Smith, Kendall, & Hulin, 1969), but such items are scored according to assumptions about their evaluative implications for the characteristics described. Because self-reported job satisfaction is an evaluative judgment, it is colored by affective elements such as values (Locke, 1976) and moods (Brief, Butcher, & Roberson, 1995).

The favorability of self-reports of job satisfaction is personalized. Either explicitly or implicitly, self-reports of job satisfaction usually reflect favorability from the idiosyncratic perspective of the individual providing the report. They tell about how much a particular person likes or dislikes the work environment. What one person likes, of course, another might dislike. Depending on the purpose for which job satisfaction is being measured, differences between people in their judgments about the favorability of the same environment might be considered either true score variance or error variance.

Third, self-reported job satisfaction is a judgment about the favorability of the *work environment* based upon an evaluation of its various facets, such as pay, co-workers, supervision, the work itself, and benefits. It reflects affective reactions to events and conditions in the entire work environment, including the immediate task environment, the social environment, the administrative environment, and all other aspects of the broader organizational environment that might produce positive or negative affective reactions.

These events and conditions are distributed through time and space. Events that elicit affective reactions occur unevenly at different specific places in the work environment and at different times; conditions that elicit affective reactions exist at different places in the work environment and for varying durations. Because people experience only events and conditions that occur where they happen to be and when they happen to be there, they can experience only samples of the work environment.

An Information-Processing Model
for Self-Reports of Job Satisfaction

The model presented here describes how people sample events and conditions in their work environment and process that information to form judgments of job satisfaction. It is drawn from an information-sampling model that was developed to explain evaluative judgments related to personnel decisions in general (Motowidlo, 1986). It begins by assuming that people form judgments of job satisfaction by combining positive and negative bits of information that are available to them at the time they form their judgments. The favorability of their judgments increases with the number of positive bits of information and decreases with the number of negative bits of information that are available.

This assumption has appeared prominently in the literature on attitudes and social judgment. For instance, while discussing their ideas about social information processes in job attitudes, Salancik and Pfeffer (1978) wrote, "The link from job characteristics to attitudes represents the cognitive processing of information about the characteristics of the job and its environment. Although the details of such processing are not well known, the literature on judgment suggests that judgments are monotonic functions of the positive and negative items of information a person has about the object (Anderson, 1971)—in this case, a job" (p. 230).

The assumption has also appeared in descriptions of models of social cognition that have incorporated influences of affective factors on social judgments (for example, Bower, 1981; Clark & Isen, 1982)—models asserting that mood affects evaluative judgments about people by increasing the availability (Tversky & Kahneman, 1973) of bits of information that are consistent with the mood. According to these models, people in a good mood should therefore recall more positive information about others and for that reason evaluate them more positively, while people in a bad mood should recall more negative information about others and evaluate them more negatively.

Anderson's integration model (1971) developed the assumption more formally. He proposed that a judgmental response is a weighted sum of any prior judgment of the referent which the individual made and the degree to which pieces of information related to the referent are positive or negative. The degree of positiveness of each piece of information is weighted by its psychological importance. The sum of these weighted values across available bits of information, combined with the former judgment, represents the new judgmental response.

The information-processing model for self-reported job satisfaction appears in Figure 5.1. It consists of four stages. First, there is a population of events and conditions in the work environment that have the potential to rouse positive or negative affective reactions in people who experience them. Second, people experience some of these events and conditions, which then become the input sample for further processing. Third, people retrieve a sample of that input sample when trying to form a judgment of the favorability of their work environment. Fourth, people report some level of job satisfaction according to the retrieved sample of events and conditions (and other factors that motivate them to distort their judgments) and report either high or low levels of job satisfaction. Each of these stages is described more fully below.

Population of Environmental Events and Conditions

The model posits a population consisting of all the positive and negative events and conditions that occur in a work environment over a period of time. This is a hypothetical population, because its content can never be completely identified except through laboratory simulations in which properties of contrived work environments are manipulated through controlled experimental procedures.

People can generally agree that some events and conditions are more favorable than others. For example, *events* such as hearing that one was promoted, getting a hefty raise, and being enthusiastically praised by the supervisor and *conditions* such as excellent dental benefits, meaningful work, and clean, dry, and bright surroundings are generally regarded as more favorable than *events* such as hearing that one was demoted, getting a pay cut, and being severely criticized by the supervisor and *conditions* such as a lack of dental benefits, meaningless work, and dirty, damp, and dark surroundings. Certainly, the same events and conditions might be more or less favorable for some people than for others. But because some events and conditions are likely to be widely, if not

Figure 5.1. Stages of Information Processing in Forming Judgments of Job Satisfaction.

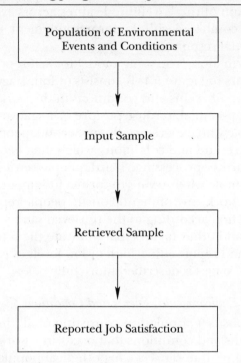

universally, regarded as more favorable than other events and conditions, it is possible to compare work environments according to their normative favorabilities. Thus a work environment in which promotions, pay raises, and supervisory praise occur frequently and in which excellent dental benefits, meaningful work, and clean, dry, and bright surroundings are common is normatively a more favorable environment than one in which demotions, pay cuts, and supervisory criticism occur frequently and in which a lack of dental benefits, meaningless work, and dirty, damp, and dark surroundings are common.

Normative favorability, then, is a characteristic of the work environment. It refers to the expected level of favorability of the work environment for all people likely to occupy it. It recognizes that objective differences between work environments can have reliable main effects on reports of job satisfaction. Amount of pay, for example, is positively correlated with reports of satisfaction with pay (Motowidlo, 1982, 1983), and enriched tasks are more satisfying than unenriched tasks (Kraiger, Billings, & Isen, 1989). Thus, although many different people might occupy a particular work environment, there is only one true score for its normative favorability.

The normative favorability of a work environment depends on the relative number of normatively favorable and unfavorable events and conditions in the population weighted by the degree to which they are regarded as favorable or unfavorable by people likely to occupy the work environment.

Input Sample

As mentioned, people experience only a sample of the normatively favorable and unfavorable events and conditions that make up the population in their work environment; and that sample can represent the population with varying degrees of accuracy. If someone experiences proportionately more or fewer favorable events and conditions than are represented in the population, the experienced favorability of the sample of input events and conditions will be either more or less positive than the normative favorability of the population of events and conditions in the work environment.

The experienced favorability of the input sample of events and conditions might be different from the normative favorability of the population of events and conditions for two reasons. First, some people might be exposed to a larger number of normatively favorable or unfavorable events and conditions than are represented in the population. Second, some people might evaluate the same events and conditions more favorably or unfavorably than other people do. In either case, the result is variability between individuals in the experienced favorability of the samples of events and conditions that they encounter at work, even if the normative favorability of the work environment is constant.

In the same way that the normative favorability of the work environment is defined according to the separate normative favorabilities of events and conditions in the population, the experienced favorability of the input sample is defined according to the relative number of experienced favorable and unfavorable events and conditions in the input sample weighted by how favorable or unfavorable they are experienced to be.

The experienced sample of events and conditions is what can be encoded and stored in memory, but it is not necessarily stored only as a descriptive record of events. Zajonc (1980) argued that people form affective and evaluative reactions very soon after their first exposure to a target stimulus, without much cognitive processing. By this reasoning, an event or condition sampled from the work environment is quickly and automatically transformed into an evaluative impression—either an affective reaction, such as a mood (George & Brief, 1992), or an implicit judgment that the event or condition is favorable or unfavorable. What gets stored in memory about a particular event or condition, therefore, is either a descriptive account of it or the evaluative impression it produced (or both).

Thus people experience samples from the population of events and conditions in the work environment. Those samples vary in experienced favorability from person to person even when the normative favorability of the work environment is the same. The samples serve as the inputs for the cognitive process that leads ultimately to reports of job satisfaction.

Retrieved Sample

When people try to judge the favorability of their work environment, they retrieve evaluative information from memory. They retrieve only a sample of all the evaluative information about events and conditions that they experienced, however, and the retrieved sample is not necessarily a perfect representation of the input sample. If they retrieve proportionately more favorable or unfavorable bits of information about events and conditions, they will remember their work environment as more favorable or unfavorable than they experienced it. Consequently, even if two people experience an identically favorable sample of events and conditions, factors that affect the favorability of their retrieved samples of events and conditions will create variability between them in how favorably they remember their work environment.

Again, the favorability of the retrieved sample depends on the relative number of favorable and unfavorable events in the retrieved sample weighted by how favorable or unfavorable those events are.

Reported Job Satisfaction

The sample of retrieved information is one determinant of how people actually report their job satisfaction, but other factors can affect this too. Just as performance evaluations are often deliberately distorted either positively or negatively (Longenecker, Sims, & Gioia, 1987), judgments of job satisfaction are also often deliberately distorted. People can have different motivations about reporting their job satisfaction. They might be motivated to report a level of job satisfaction that accurately represents the favorability of the sample of information they retrieve from memory. Especially if questionnaires are not anonymous, however, people might be reluctant to report low levels of job satisfaction for fear of retaliation by management. Conversely, they might be motivated to exaggerate their dissatisfaction either to punish management with reports of poor employee morale or to impress management with the seriousness of their complaints so that management will be more likely to take remedial action. As a result, even if two people remember their work environment as identically favorable, factors that affect their motivation to report high or low levels of job satisfaction will create variability between them.

Four Constructs of Job Satisfaction

This information-processing model suggests four different ways of defining job satisfaction: *normative favorability* (the favorability of the population of events and conditions in the work environment), *experienced favorability* (the favorability of events and conditions in the input sample), *remembered favorability* (the favorability of events and conditions in the retrieved sample), and *volitional favorability* (the favorability that people try to present in their self-reports of job satisfaction). These four constructs are causally related to each other. As shown in Figure 5.2, normative favorability affects experienced favorability, which affects remembered favorability, which affects volitional favorability, which, finally, affects the observed score on a self-report measure of job satisfaction.

Figure 5.2 also shows that other factors besides the four satisfaction constructs indirectly affect self-reported job satisfaction through direct effects on experienced, remembered, and volitional satisfaction. These other factors explain why people do not necessarily experience their work environment as favorably or unfavorably as it

Figure 5.2. Four Constructs of Job Satisfaction and Their Relations with Other Causal Factors and Self-Reported Job Satisfaction.

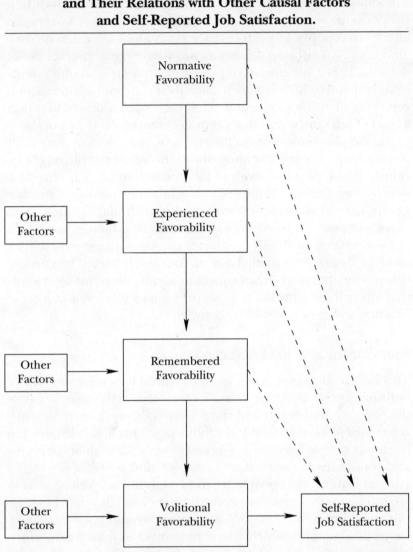

normatively is, why they do not necessarily remember it as favorably or unfavorably as they experienced it, and why they do not necessarily report it as favorably or unfavorably as they remember it.

The dotted arrows in Figure 5.2 from normative, experienced, and remembered favorability to self-reported job satisfaction are meant to illustrate that self-reported job satisfaction can be used to measure any of these three satisfaction constructs, in addition to the construct represented by volitional favorability. They also show how the other factors affecting experienced, remembered, and volitional favorability might be sources of either error variance or true score variance, depending on which of the four constructs the self-report of job satisfaction is intended to measure. If self-reported satisfaction is intended to measure normative favorability, other factors affecting experienced, remembered, and volitional favorability in Figure 5.2 are sources of error in the self-report measure, because they indirectly affect it but have nothing to do with normative favorability. If self-reported satisfaction is intended to measure experienced favorability, other factors affecting remembered and volitional favorability are sources of error, but other factors affecting experienced favorability now become sources of true score variance in the self-report measure. If self-reported satisfaction is intended to measure remembered favorability, other factors affecting volitional favorability are sources of error, but other factors affecting experienced and remembered favorability now become sources of true score variance in the self-report measure. And if self-reported satisfaction is intended to measure volitional favorability, other factors affecting experienced, remembered, and volitional favorability are now sources of true score variance.

These distinctions between sources of true score and error variance use classical psychometric theory as a loose metaphor. Some readers might prefer to think of these distinctions instead according to generalizability theory (Cronbach, Gleser, Nanda, & Rajaratnam, 1972; Shavelson, Webb, & Rowley, 1989), which explicitly acknowledges multiple sources of error variance and provides different reliability estimates according to a measure's intended use.

Basically, however, the model presented here is about sources of variability in self-reported job satisfaction. It describes two categories of variables that shape self-reports of job satisfaction. The first category consists of the four satisfaction constructs—normative, experienced, remembered, and volitional favorability. The second category consists of other factors that affect experienced, remembered, and volitional favorability independently of the favorability of preceding stages in the processing model. When they are designated as sources of error variance, that means simply that the variability they bring to the self-report measure of job satisfaction does not contribute to variability in the construct that the self-report is intended to measure. When they are designated as sources of true score variance, that means simply that the variability they bring to the self-report measure of job satisfaction does contribute to variability in the construct that the self-report is intended to measure.

Thus self-reported job satisfaction can be used to measure either normative, experienced, remembered, or volitional favorability. There are good reasons for measuring each of these satisfaction constructs, and they have different implications for sources of error and true score variance in the self-report measure of job satisfaction, as discussed next.

Normative Favorability

Normative favorability is the degree to which an environment is likely to be regarded as satisfying by anyone who works in it. This is something managers are probably very interested in when they conduct anonymous surveys of job satisfaction.

Information about normative favorability has three important uses. First, it can help managers decide whether they should do something to try to make the work environment more satisfying. If, for example, the work environment in their organization is substantially less favorable than work environments in comparable organizations, they should probably try to improve it. Second, information about normative favorability can have diagnostic utility. It can help managers decide exactly what aspects of the environment they should try to improve and how they should go about it. Third, it can help managers decide whether actions taken to improve the environment were successful and whether changes in policies or organizational events and conditions had the effect of making the environment more favorable or less favorable.

If employee reports of job satisfaction are collected to estimate a true score of normative favorability, all variation in reported job satisfaction between people assumed to be in the same work environment is error. The mean job satisfaction reported by everyone working in the same environment is a reasonable measure of normative favorability. To control further for sources of error, mean satisfaction scores can be aggregated both across employees and across multiple occasions, providing that the favorability of the work environment does not change between occasions. The merit of such an aggregated measure of environmental favorability relies partly on the assumption that other factors that affect the favorability of input samples, retrieved samples, and reports of satisfaction are randomly distributed and cancel themselves out. This assumption is not always justified, however. Some factors unrelated to the work environment can have uniformly positive or negative effects on everybody who completes a satisfaction questionnaire. For instance, if all questionnaire administrations are conducted in a way that enhances positive moods just before people report their job satisfaction, this will probably lift reports of job satisfaction across the board and produce artifactually high estimates of normative favorability (Brief et al., 1995).

Experienced Favorability

Experienced favorability is the favorability of the sample of events and conditions that people actually encounter. When self-reported job satisfaction is intended to measure experienced favorability, variation between individuals in opportunities to experience different parts of the environment and variation in characteristics that affect how favorably or unfavorably people evaluate environmental events and conditions contribute to true score variance in their self-reported job satisfaction. Other factors that affect the favorability of the retrieved sample or volitional satisfaction are still sources of error.

Thus some, but not all, of the variation in reports of job satisfaction by people in the same work environment is error in estimates of experienced favorability. Somebody might report different levels of job satisfaction upon repeated administrations of a satisfaction survey without experiencing any new events or conditions in the work environment between reports. This would mean that sometimes the individual remembers or reports the work environment that he or she experienced as being more favorable than at other times. These differences across measurement occasions are sources of error for estimates of experienced favorability. If it is possible to survey employees repeatedly over a period when they are not experiencing any new events or conditions at work, the sum or average of each person's reported satisfaction on different occasions should yield a reliable estimate of his or her experienced favorability.

Experienced favorability might be the construct of interest when investigators study relations between job satisfaction and other variables at the individual level. This sort of study is often undertaken within organizations or within organizational units. When differences in reported job satisfaction between people in the same work environment are correlated with other variables (such as performance or turnover) at the individual level, the source of those differences might be experienced favorability.

Remembered Favorability

Remembered favorability is the favorability of how someone remembers the work environment at the time he or she is called upon to report job satisfaction. Factors that affect the favorability of information retrieved from memory, together with factors that affect experienced favorability, are now sources of true score variance. This means that someone's true score for remembered favorability can vary from one occasion to another, even if he or she does not experience any new work events or conditions between occasions.

Reasons for measuring remembered favorability are similar to reasons for measuring experienced favorability—to study relations between job satisfaction and other variables at the individual level. One important difference is that temporary conditions such as mood inductions that are presumed to affect retrieval processes (for example, Kraiger et al., 1989) are now sources of true score variance, whereas they are sources of error variance in self-reports intended to measure experienced favorability.

Volitional Favorability

Volitional favorability is how much job satisfaction or dissatisfaction someone is trying to report. Now variability in factors that affect experienced, remembered, and volitional favorability are all sources of true score variance. True scores on volitional favorability can vary (1) between individuals who experience different samples of their work environments, even if their work environments are identical, (2) between individuals who remember their work environments as differently favorable or unfavorable, even if the work environments they actually experienced are equally favorable, and (3) between individuals who try to report different levels of job satisfaction even if the work environments they actually remember are equally favorable. The only sources of error left are random measurement errors, such as those represented in inconsistent responses to different questions in the satisfaction questionnaire.

Which of these four true scores—normative, experienced, remembered, or volitional favorability—represents the most appropriate construct for job satisfaction? That depends on the purpose for which information about job satisfaction is being collected. If the purpose is to determine whether to try to improve a work environment, how to improve it, or whether some changes in environmental events and conditions led to improvement or deterioration, job satisfaction is appropriately defined as normative favorability. If the purpose is to understand how individuals react to their own affective appraisals of their work environment, job satisfaction is appropriately defined as either experienced or remembered favorability. If the purpose is to understand how employees use satisfaction surveys to influence management actions and policies, job satisfaction is appropriately defined as volitional favorability.

Individual Differences in Judgments of Job Satisfaction

The four constructs of job satisfaction differ from each other in two important respects. First, they represent favorability at different stages of the process by which evaluative information about environmental events and conditions is transformed into self-reports of job satisfaction. Second, they differ according to whether the "other factors" shown in Figure 5.2 (affecting experienced, remembered, and volitional favorability) contribute to true score or error variance in self-reports of job satisfaction.

Some of these other factors are situational, such as social influences (Salancik & Pfeffer, 1978) and conditions that alter mood states (Brief et al., 1995; Kraiger et al., 1989); some other factors are individual difference variables. Individual difference variables are particularly interesting in this context because of the recent attention to the possibility that self-reports of job satisfaction might have important dispositional determinants as well as environmental determinants. Several studies have been done to examine the role that individual difference variables play in self-reports of job satisfaction. They provide support for the argument that part of the variability in self-reports of job satisfaction is accounted for by individual difference variables. After reviewing this empirical literature below, I present a theory to explain (1) how individual difference variables come to affect self-reported job satisfaction according to the information-processing model of job satisfaction presented earlier and (2) how these variables are involved in processes that affect the constructs of normative, experienced, remembered, and volitional favorability.

Evidence for Individual Differences in Job Satisfaction

Six lines of evidence support the argument for individual differences in job satisfaction.

Correlations with Demographic Variables

One focus of support for the argument for individual differences in job satisfaction is found in evidence of correlations between demographic variables and job satisfaction. Arvey, Carter, and Buerkley (1991) noted that, although many studies reported such correlations, they were often so flawed by inappropriate statistical analyses and poor explanations of results that "a significant portion of the research literature intended to explain relationships between demographic variables and job satisfaction is uninterpretable" (p. 362). They also noted, however, that education and age are two demographic variables that seem to show fairly consistent positive correlations with job satisfaction, while gender shows no consistent correlation.

Relations between demographic variables and job satisfaction are often complicated by variance in frames of reference (Smith et al., 1969). For instance, positive correlations between education and job satisfaction probably mean that people with higher levels of education have access to objectively more favorable work environments. In fact, as Arvey et al. (1991) pointed out, this positive correlation is found when samples include widely varied work environments and when differences in potential for rewarding experiences are not controlled. When samples include a narrower range of work environments, however, or when reward potential is held constant, relations with job satisfaction become less positive (and sometimes even negative).

This can be explained by the competing effects of education on normative favorability and, through frames of reference, on experienced favorability. Highly educated people probably expect more from their work environment than less educated people. As a result, highly educated people evaluate the same environmental events and conditions less favorably than less educated people. But highly educated people are also likely to have access to more normatively favorable environments. Thus education affects experienced favorability *positively* through its effects on normative favorability and *negatively* through its effects on frames of reference. Effects on normative favorability can be held constant by restricting the variability in types of work environments or by partialing out indicators of normative favorability. When this is done, the negative effects on frames of reference become more prominent and the correlation between education and job satisfaction drops toward zero or even becomes negative.

Correlations Between Satisfaction with Referents Related to the Job and Satisfaction with Referents Not Related to the Job

A second line of evidence consists of relations between satisfaction with different referents when the normative favorabilities of those referents are not likely to be correlated.

Weitz (1952) developed a test of "general satisfaction" that asked respondents how satisfied they were with referents described in forty-four items such as "the city in which you live," "8½ x 11 paper," and "your telephone number." It correlated .39 with a test of specific job satisfaction in a sample of 168 life insurance agents.

Judge (1993) developed a revised version of Weitz's test of general satisfaction, which he called the Neutral Objects Satisfaction Questionnaire. In a sample of 234 hospital workers, it correlated .21 with an overall job satisfaction score derived from the Job Descriptive Index.

Judge and Locke (1993) also correlated scores on Judge's Neutral Objects Satisfaction Questionnaire with scores on the Job Descriptive Index in a sample of 231 university clerical workers. Correlations across the five scales of the Job Descriptive Index ranged from .08 (promotion scale) to .24 (pay scale), with a mean of .19.

These three studies show that reports of satisfaction with referents whose normative favorabilities ought to have nothing in common with the normative favorability of someone's working environment are correlated with reports of job satisfaction anyway. One explanation is that people differ in how favorably they evaluate any aspect of their environment, including the kinds of objects listed in Judge's Neutral Objects Satisfaction Questionnaire and facets of the work environment. These individual difference variables might be traits such as positive and negative affectivity (George & Brief, 1992; Watson & Clark, 1984). According to this explanation, such traits predispose people to notice, evaluate, and remember events and conditions in line with their positive and negative affective dispositions. As a result, these traits affect reports of satisfaction with any aspect of the respondents' environment and lead to correlations between reports of satisfaction with different environmental aspects.

Correlations Across Time

A third line of evidence consists of correlations between job satisfaction measured on two occasions in different work environments.

Staw and Ross (1985) analyzed data from the Longitudinal Survey of Mature Men that included multiple administrations of survey instruments in 1966, 1969, and 1971. In a sample of 735 men who changed both employer and occupation between 1969 and 1971, the correlation between job satisfaction as measured at these two times was .35. In a sample of 1,121 men who changed both employer and occupation between 1966 and 1971, the correlation between job satisfaction as measured at these two times was .19.

Gerhart (1987) replicated their study with a sample drawn from the youth cohort of the National Longitudinal Surveys of Labor Market Experience. Among men and women who changed both employer and occupation from 1979 to 1982, the correlation between job satisfaction as measured at these two times was .19.

Thus there is significant consistency in job attitudes even when people change employers and occupations. The source of this consistency might be the "affective state of the individual" (Staw, Bell, & Clausen, 1986, p. 61), as represented, perhaps, in the constructs of positive and negative affectivity. If the normative favorabilities of the work environments on the two occasions are not correlated, reported satisfaction with the work environments might be correlated, because traits such as positive and negative affectivity affect how favorably people report their satisfaction with any work environment.

Correlations Between Twins

Arvey, Bouchard, Segal, and Abraham (1989) measured job satisfaction in thirty-four pairs of monozygotic twins who had been reared apart since early in their lives. Because the twins were raised in different environments, any similarities observed within pairs of twins were assumed to be attributable to genetic factors. Arvey et al. found that genetic factors explained 31 percent of the variability in job satisfaction scores. They suggested that individual differences in positive and negative affectivity, which have been shown to have genetic determinants (Tellegen et al., 1988), might provide the mechanism for the heritability of job satisfaction. If, as expected, these traits affect the way people notice, evaluate, or recall the favorability of events and conditions in their work environments, they would operate as a pathway from genetic influences to reported job satisfaction.

Correlations with Expected Satisfaction

A fifth line of evidence consists of correlations between measures of how satisfied people expect to be in a new job with measures of how satisfied they are after they have been on the job for some time. Pulakos and Schmitt (1983) asked graduating high school students to rate their expectation of obtaining thirteen favorable outcomes in the workplace. After they had found jobs and been employed for approximately twenty months, they were asked to report their job satisfaction. Expectancies of being able to satisfy existence, relatedness, and growth needs as measured before they had a job correlated .13, .27, and .21 with external satisfaction and

.20, .26, and .28 with internal satisfaction. Pulakos and Schmitt mentioned two types of traits that might account for their results. One is traits that reflect stable predispositions toward being satisfied; the other is traits that affect job satisfaction by disposing people to behave in ways that fulfill their expectations.

Correlations with Affective Traits

Finally, a sixth line of evidence consists of correlations between job satisfaction and dispositions to experience positive or negative affect.

Staw et al. (1986) drew upon longitudinal data from the Intergenerational Studies to investigate relations between affective traits measured as early as adolescence with job satisfaction measured in adulthood. Based upon case material available for participants when they were in their early adolescence, their late adolescence, their thirties, and their forties, clinical psychologists and psychiatric social workers made judgments about the participants' affective disposition in each of the four periods in their lives. In the fourth period, when participants were in their forties, they completed a job satisfaction questionnaire. Job satisfaction scores correlated .20 ($n = 59$) with affective disposition in early adolescence, .26 ($n = 52$) with affective disposition in later adolescence, .30 ($n = 70$) with affective disposition in the first period of adulthood, and .40 ($n = 76$) with affective disposition in the second period of adulthood.

Levin and Stokes (1989) used a self-report scale to measure negative affectivity. In one study, they identified people who scored in the upper or lower quartile on their scale. They had participants complete either an "enriched" task or an "unenriched" task and rate their task satisfaction. Low scorers on negative affectivity reported more task satisfaction than high scorers in both task conditions. In a second study, Levin and Stokes found that their Negative Affectivity Scale correlated −.31 with the Job Satisfaction scale from the Job Diagnostic Survey and −.29 with the Work Satisfaction scale from the Job Descriptive Index.

Schaubroeck, Ganster, and Fox (1992) measured negative affectivity with the Neuroticism scale of the Eysenck Personality Scale (Eysenck & Eysenck, 1963) and also with the State-Trait Anxiety Scale (Spielberger, Gorsuch, & Lushene, 1970); they then measured job satisfaction with the Job Diagnostic Survey. In a sample of 311 employees of fire and police departments, job satisfaction correlated −.17 with the neuroticism measure and −.29 with the trait anxiety measure.

Judge and Locke (1993; Judge, 1992) administered the Positive and Negative Affect Schedule scales (Watson, Clark, & Tellegen, 1988) and the Job Descriptive Index to 231 clerical employees in a university. Correlations between positive affect and the five facet satisfaction scales ranged from .08 (co-worker scale) to .39 (work itself scale), with a mean of .22. Correlations between negative affect and the five facet satisfaction scales ranged from −.20 (co-worker scale) to −.35 (work itself scale), with a mean of −.29.

Brief et al. (1988) administered the short form of the Minnesota Satisfaction Questionnaire and the Taylor Manifest Anxiety Scale (Taylor, 1953), as a measure of negative affectivity, to 497 professional and managerial employees of an insurance company. The overall job satisfaction score correlated −.24 with negative affectivity.

Brief et al. (1995) administered the Taylor Manifest Anxiety Scale and a modified version of Kunin's Faces scale (1955) as a measure of job satisfaction to 57 hospital employees. They found that negative affectivity correlated −.34 with job satisfaction.

These studies offer consistent support for the idea that individual differences in the tendency to view the world in a positive or negative light and the tendency to experience positive or negative affect are correlated with reports of job satisfaction. Correlations between positive or negative affectivity and job satisfaction range from .17 to .40 (correlations with negative affectivity are reversed), with a mean of .28 (not weighted by sample size).

Summary of Evidence

The literature reviewed here supports the case for individual differences in job satisfaction from several directions. Some of this evidence is circumstantial and some is quite direct. Evidence of correlations between satisfaction measured on two occasions is the most circumstantial, because it relies on the arguable assumption that the normative favorabilities of work events and conditions on two occasions are not correlated. Evidence of genetic effects, of correlations with satisfaction with neutral objects, and of correlations with expectations of satisfaction is more direct, because it shows patterns of relations that are more difficult to explain by appealing to situational effects. That evidence does not, however, specify what trait variables might be involved. The most direct evidence comes from studies of individual differences in demographic characteristics and positive/negative affectivity. It specifies what trait variables are involved and directly estimates their relations with self-reported job satisfaction.

Taken together, the body of empirical work builds a strong argument that some portion of the variability in reports of job satisfaction is attributable to stable individual difference characteristics. These characteristics potentially affect the kinds of work environments people occupy, the kinds of experiences they have in their work environments, the way they remember satisfying and dissatisfying events and conditions, and the level of satisfaction they try to report (aside from how favorably they remember their environments).

The information-processing model of job satisfaction outlined in this chapter describes how people sample from a population of favorable and unfavorable events and conditions in the work environment and encode that information as an input sample, retrieve a sample of the input sample when asked about their job satisfaction, and report some level of satisfaction or dissatisfaction based partly on the retrieved sample of information. The empirical literature on individual differences in job satisfaction provides several examples of how various individual difference characteristics might affect judgments of job satisfaction by affecting the favorability of different stages of the process by which people form judgments of job satisfaction. The next section of this chapter integrates the discussion of empirical relations between individual differences and job satisfaction with the information-processing model to develop a theory of individual differences in job satisfaction.

A Theory of Individual Differences in Job Satisfaction

The theory presented in this chapter consists of two parts. The first part is the information-processing model already described. The second part posits that various individual difference characteristics affect judgments of job satisfaction through several processes that influence the favorability of the four stages of the information-processing model. This part explains how various individual difference characteristics are likely to affect normative favorability, experienced favorability, remembered favorability, and volitional favorability.

My theory proposes that individual difference characteristics affect these four constructs of job satisfaction through several differential processes—"differential" because they exert the effects of individual difference characteristics on the "cognitive" process through which environmental events and conditions are transformed to self-reported job satisfaction. As shown in Figure 5.3, the theory proposes that (1) normative favorability is affected by the differential processes of *environmental selection* and *self-selection*, (2) experienced favorability is affected by the differential processes of *environmental reward* and *affective reaction*, (3) remembered favorability is affected by the differential process of *selective recall*, and (4) volitional favorability is affected by the differential process of *motivated reporting*. These differential processes and their implications for effects of specific individual difference characteristics on constructs of job satisfaction are described in the pages that follow.

Individual Differences and Normative Favorability

The process of *environmental selection* involves effects of demographic variables (for example, types of former job experience and education), ability variables, and personality variables on normative favorability. Because they are often the basis upon which organizations select employees, such variables are distributed unevenly in different jobs and work environments. If some organizations also select according to demographic variables such as sex or race (despite laws that generally forbid such practices) or according to traits correlated with such demographic variables, the result will be that men, women, and various racial groups are also unevenly distributed in different work environments. Thus environmental selection creates a correlation between individual characteristics and normative favorability through legitimate efforts to optimize job performance or through discriminatory selection practices.

The process of *self-selection* has similar effects. People with certain demographic characteristics, abilities, or personality characteristics select themselves into work environments partly according to their expectancies that they will be accepted, satisfied, and successful. These processes of occupational and job choice also create

Figure 5.3. A Theory of Individual Differences in Job Satisfaction.

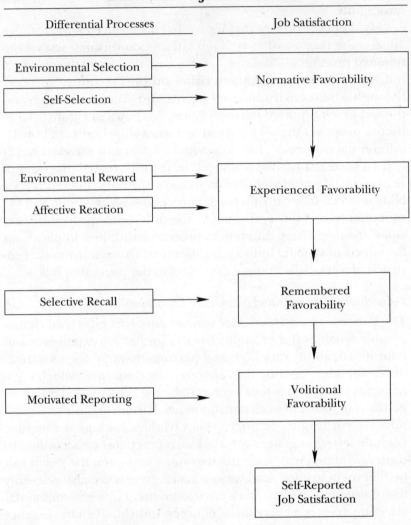

Differential Processes

Job Satisfaction

Environmental Selection

Self-Selection

Normative Favorability

Environmental Reward

Affective Reaction

Experienced Favorability

Selective Recall

Remembered Favorability

Motivated Reporting

Volitional Favorability

Self-Reported Job Satisfaction

correlations between individual characteristics and environmental favorability.

Individual Differences and Experienced Favorability

Environmental reward, a process much like environmental selection, operates within work environments to provide some people with more normatively favorable events and conditions than other people. People with organizationally desirable skills, knowledge, abilities, personality, and other characteristics are rewarded more frequently and punished less frequently. Thus these traits are correlated with the favorability of events and conditions that people sample from their work environments and provide one explanation for why people in the same environment can experience events and conditions with different normative favorabilities.

Environmental reward, environmental selection, and self-selection are processes that affect the objective features and normative favorabilities of events and conditions that people experience in their work environments. They affect either the kinds of work environments that people enter and occupy or the kinds of experiences people have after they enter a work environment. A broad range of individual difference variables are associated with these processes—too many to discuss separately here—but these variables can include individual differences in interests and values, abilities, personality characteristics, demographic characteristics (such as experience, education, sex, and race), and even physical characteristics (such as attractiveness). They all have the potential to affect the kind of work environments that people choose to occupy and the kind of people that work environments choose to admit and reward. Therefore, they can all be correlated with job satisfaction.

Affective reaction is a process that affects not the kinds of work-related events and conditions that happen to people but the way people respond affectively to those events and conditions. Affective reaction involves individual differences related to frames of reference, valence structures, and affective dispositions.

The same broad range of individual difference characteristics that affect the normative favorabilities of events and conditions that people experience can also affect people's affective reactions to those events and conditions through their frames of reference.

According to Smith et al. (1969), "Frame of reference is the internal standard (or standards) a person uses in making an evaluation" (p. 13). "Job satisfactions are, we believe, a function of the perceived characteristics of the job in relation to an individual's frame of reference. Alternatives available in given situations, expectations, and experience play important roles in providing the relevant frame of reference" (p. 12). Thus, if people with certain characteristics tend to occupy work environments that are normatively favorable, they should have more experience with favorable work environments, develop beliefs that their alternatives are more favorable, and come to expect more favorable events and conditions in a work environment. Their frames of reference should reflect a relatively favorable standard for environmental events and conditions. As a result, when they experience a particular event or condition, they will respond less positively than other people with personal characteristics that lead them to develop less favorable frames of reference.

Effects of personal characteristics on job satisfaction through the normative favorability of events and conditions that happen to people tend to counteract effects of the same personal characteristics on job satisfaction through the way people respond affectively to those events and conditions. Personal characteristics that have positive effects on job satisfaction through processes of environmental selection, self-selection, and environmental reward will have negative effects on job satisfaction through frames of reference and the process of affective reaction. Consequently, the overall relation between these characteristics and reported job satisfaction might not be noticeably different from zero.

Valence structures are a second class of individual difference variables that affect experienced favorability through the process of affective reaction. Because of individual differences in values (Locke, 1976) and occupational interests (Campbell, 1971), people differ in the kinds of work events and conditions that they find satisfying. For example, someone who values pay increases and promotions is likely to form more positive affective reactions to such events and develop a more favorable input sample in a work environment in which pay increases and promotions occur regularly than someone else who does not particularly value pay and promotions. As a result, if two people experience exactly the same pay and promotion events, the one who values them more will have a more favorable input sample.

A third class of variables that affect experienced favorability through the process of affective reaction are mood and affective dispositions. People are likely to evaluate all the events and conditions they experience more favorably while in a positive mood and more negatively while in a negative mood. Traits such as positive and negative affectivity dispose people to experience positive and negative moods more intensely and more frequently, with the result that those traits should be correlated with how favorably people evaluate events and work conditions that happen to them in the work environment. Thus experienced favorability should be positively correlated with positive affectivity and negatively correlated with negative affectivity.

Individual Differences and Remembered Favorability

Individual differences affect remembered favorability through the process of *selective recall.*

The same mood and affective disposition variables that affect experienced favorability can also affect remembered favorability. According to some models of social cognition (Bower, 1981; Clark & Isén, 1982), mood affects evaluative judgments about people by increasing the availability of information in memory that is consistent with the mood. For the same reason, mood should also affect evaluative judgments about the work environment. When asked about their job satisfaction, people in a good mood should recall more favorable information, while people in a bad mood should recall more unfavorable information. Therefore, mood at the time of information recall affects the favorability of information retrieved from memory and colors reports of job satisfaction (Brief et al., 1995; Kraiger et al., 1989). Because traits of positive and negative affectivity are presumed to affect mood states, they should also be related to remembered favorability. Thus remembered favorability should be correlated positively with positive affectivity and negatively with negative affectivity.

Individual Differences and Volitional Favorability

The process of *motivated reporting* involves deliberate distortions of self-reported job satisfaction. People might deliberately distort their reports of job satisfaction for a variety of reasons. For instance, if satisfaction surveys are not anonymous, reports of job satisfaction may be inflated out of fear of retaliation by management. The dynamics of this effect are similar to a leniency effect often found in performance appraisal—an effect that frequently occurs when raters are reluctant to confront subordinates with negative information about their job performance (Longenecker et al., 1987). Because of the likelihood of motivated reporting when reports of job satisfaction are not anonymous, individual differences in characteristics such as fear of negative evaluation, which reflects concerns about making a favorable impression (Leary, 1983; Motowidlo, Packard, & Manning, 1986), should be positively correlated with job satisfaction (Packard & Motowidlo, 1987). Ordinarily, however, management does not have access to information about how any particular employee answered a satisfaction survey, even when surveys are not anonymous. Consequently, fear of retaliation, and individual differences that might be correlated with that fear, is probably not often an important factor in reported favorability.

Other potential reasons for distorting reports of job satisfaction are to punish management with bad reports or to be polite and agreeable in refraining from saying negative things about management. Individual differences in traits related to altruism and consideration for others should be related to this type of reporting distortion. Thus the trait of agreeableness, for example, should be positively correlated with reported job satisfaction.

Summary

The theory of individual differences in job satisfaction begins with a cognitive process through which information is sampled from a population of events and conditions in the work environment—events and conditions that, in the aggregate, endow the work environment with a characteristic normative favorability. People sample some events and conditions from this population and input them to memory. These samples of events and conditions vary according to their experienced favorability, which is directly affected by their normative favorability. When asked about their job satisfaction, people sample information about events and conditions from memory and retrieve those samples for integration into an evaluative judgment. The samples of retrieved information about events and conditions vary according to their remembered favorability, which is directly affected by their experienced favorability. Finally, the remembered favorability of information about events and conditions directly affects volitional favorability, which affects the observed score in a self-reported measure of job satisfaction.

The theory also includes several differential processes through which individual difference characteristics affect the favorability of various stages of the information-processing model. Environmental selection and self-selection affect normative favorability. Environmental reward affects experienced favorability. All three of these processes affect the kinds of events and conditions that people experience. Affective reaction, through effects of frames of reference, valence structures, and affective disposition, affects experienced favorability by influencing how people evaluate the events and conditions that they experience. Selective recall affects remembered favorability by influencing the kinds of information about events and conditions that people remember. Motivated reporting affects volitional favorability by deliberately distorting reports of job satisfaction.

A wide range of individual differences can affect normative favorability (through environmental selection and self-selection) and experienced favorability (through environmental reward)—differences in interests and values, abilities, personality characteristics, demographic characteristics (such as experience, education, sex, and race), and even physical characteristics (such as attractiveness). The same characteristics can also affect experienced favorability through a process of affective reaction. Their effects on frames of reference counteract their effects on the normative favorability of events and conditions that people experience, with the result that their overall effects on reported job satisfaction might not be noticeable. Values, occupational interests, and affective dispositions (such as positive and negative affectivity) also affect experienced favorability through affective reaction. Through selective recall, affective dispositions affect remembered favorability as well. Traits such as agreeableness and, in special circumstances, fear of negative evaluation affect volitional favorability through the process of motivated reporting.

One important implication of this theory is that the overall concept of job satisfaction embraces several alternative constructs or true scores. Self-reports of job satisfaction can be collected to estimate normative favorability, experienced favorability, remembered favorability, or volitional favorability. Depending on the particular job satisfaction construct of interest, individual differences that affect various stages of the information-processing model might act either as nuisance variables that contribute only error or as legitimate sources of true score variance.

Researchers should be explicit about which job satisfaction construct and true score is their focus of interest. If it is normative favorability, individual differences in affective disposition are nuisance variables that contribute error variance to self-reports of job satisfaction. If it is experienced favorability, individual differences in affective disposition that affect experienced favorability are legitimate sources of true score variance, but effects of the same affective dispositions and temporary mood changes (Brief et al., 1995) on remembered favorability are sources of error. If it is remembered favorability, effects of individual differences in affective disposition on experienced and remembered favorability are all legitimate sources of true score variance.

Distinguishing between these alternative types of true scores for job satisfaction opens the door to some interesting questions about which job satisfaction constructs are related to behavioral outcomes such as turnover. Do people quit because their work environment is normatively less favorable than some available alternative, because they happen to experience a particularly unfavorable sample of events and conditions in their work environment, or because they remember their work environment as unfavorable? Another way to ask this research question is according to separate effects of objective environmental conditions and individual differences related to reported job satisfaction on turnover behavior: Is turnover correlated only with the normative favorability of events and conditions in the work environment, or are individual differences in characteristics that affect the way people respond affectively to (and remember) these events and conditions also correlated with turnover?

The main contribution of this theory of individual differences in job satisfaction is that it provides a conceptual framework for (1) defining what we mean by job satisfaction (and we can mean different things, depending on our purpose), (2) distinguishing between different sources of error and true score variance in self-reports of job satisfaction, and (3) sorting through potentially different behavioral outcomes of different constructs of job satisfaction.

References

Anderson, N. H. (1971). Integration theory and change. *Psychological Review, 78,* 171–206.

Arvey, R. D., Bouchard, T. J., Segal, N. L., & Abraham, L. M. (1989). Job satisfaction: Environmental and genetic components. *Journal of Applied Psychology, 74,* 187–192.

Arvey, R. D., Carter, G. W., & Buerkley, D. K. (1991). Job satisfaction: Dispositional and situational influences. In C. L. Cooper and I. T. Robertson (Eds.), *International review of industrial and organizational psychology* (Vol. 6, pp. 359–383). New York: Wiley.

Bower, G. H. (1981). Mood and memory. *American Psychologist, 36,* 129–148.

Brief, A. P., Burke, M. J., George, J. M., Robinson, B. S., & Webster, J. (1988). Should negative affectivity remain an unmeasured variable in the study of job stress? *Journal of Applied Psychology, 73,* 193–198.

Brief, A. P., Butcher, A. H., & Roberson, L. (1995). Cookies, disposition, and job attitudes: The effects of positive mood inducing events and negative affectivity on job satisfaction in a field experiment. *Organizational Behavior and Human Decision Processes, 62,* 55–62.

Campbell, D. P. (1971). *Handbook for the Strong Vocational Interest Blank.* Stanford, CA: Stanford University Press.

Clark, M. S., & Isen, A. M. (1982). Toward understanding the relationship between feeling states and actual behavior. In A. H. Hastorf & A. M. Isen (Eds.), *Cognitive social psychology* (pp. 73–108). New York: Elsevier Science.

Crónbach, L. J., Gleser, G. C., Nanda, H., & Rajaratnam, N. (1972). *The dependability of behavioral measurements: Theory of generalizability of scores and profiles.* New York: Wiley.

Eysenck, H. J., & Eysenck, S.B.G. (1963). *Eysenck Personality Inventory, Form A.* San Diego, CA: Educational and Industrial Testing Service.

George J. M., & Brief, A. P. (1992). Feeling good—doing good: A conceptual analysis of the mood at work/organizational spontaneity relationship. *Psychological Bulletin, 112,* 310–329.

Gerhart, B. (1987). How important are dispositional factors as determinants of job satisfaction? Implications for job design and other personnel programs. *Journal of Applied Psychology, 72,* 366–373.

Judge, T. A. (1992). The dispositional perspective in human resource research. In G. R. Ferris & K. M. Rowland (Eds.), *Research in personnel and human resources management* (Vol. 10, pp. 31–72). Greenwich, CT: JAI Press.

Judge, T. A. (1993). Does affective disposition moderate the relationship between job satisfaction and voluntary turnover? *Journal of Applied Psychology, 78,* 395–401.

Judge, T. A., & Hulin, C. L. (1993). Job satisfaction as a reflection of disposition: A multiple source causal analysis. *Organizational Behavior and Human Decision Processes, 56,* 388–421.

Judge, T. A., & Locke, E. A. (1993). Effect of dysfunctional thought processes on subjective well-being and job satisfaction. *Journal of Applied Psychology, 78,* 475–490.

Kraiger, K., Billings, R. S., & Isen, A. M. (1989). The influence of positive affective states on task perceptions and satisfaction. *Organizational Behavior and Human Decision Processes, 44,* 12–25.

Kunin, T. (1955). The construction of a new type of attitude measure. *Personnel Psychology, 8,* 65–78.

Leary, M. R. (1983). A brief version of the fear of negative evaluation scale. *Personality and Social Psychology Bulletin, 9,* 371–375.

Levin, I., & Stokes, J. P. (1989). Dispositional approach to job satisfaction: Role of negative affectivity. *Journal of Applied Psychology, 74,* 752–758.

Locke, E. A. (1976). The nature and causes of job satisfaction. In M. D. Dunnette (Ed.), *Handbook of industrial and organizational psychology* (pp. 1297–1343). Skokie, IL: Rand McNally.

Lodahl, T., & Kejner, M. (1965). The definition and measurement of job involvement. *Journal of Applied Psychology, 49,* 24–33.

Longenecker, C. O., Sims, H. P., & Gioia, D. A. (1987). Behind the mask: The politics of employee appraisal. *Academy of Management Executive, 1,* 183–193.

Mathieu, J. E., & Zajac, D. M. (1990). A review and meta-analysis of the antecedents, correlates, and consequences of organizational commitment. *Psychological Bulletin, 108,* 171–194.

Motowidlo, S. J. (1982). Relationship between self-rated performance and pay satisfaction among sales representatives. *Journal of Applied Psychology, 67,* 209–213.

Motowidlo, S. J. (1983). Predicting sales turnover from pay satisfaction and expectation. *Journal of Applied Psychology, 68,* 484–489.

Motowidlo, S. J. (1986). Information processing in personnel decisions. In K. M. Rowland and G. R. Ferris (Eds.), *Research in personnel and human resource management* (Vol. 4, pp. 1–44). Greenwich, CT: JAI Press.

Motowidlo, S. J., & Borman, W. C. (1977). Behaviorally anchored scales for measuring morale in military units. *Journal of Applied Psychology, 62*, 177–183.

Motowidlo, S. J., & Borman, W. C. (1978). Relationships between military morale, motivation, satisfaction, and unit effectiveness. *Journal of Applied Psychology, 63*, 47–52.

Motowidlo, S. J., & Lawton, G. W. (1984). Affective and cognitive factors in soldiers' reenlistment decisions. *Journal of Applied Psychology, 69*, 157–166.

Motowidlo, S. J., Packard, J. S., & Manning, M. R. (1986). Occupational stress: Its causes and consequences for job performance. *Journal of Applied Psychology, 71*, 618–629.

Mowday, R. T., Porter, L. W., & Steers, R. M. (1982). *Employee-organization linkages: The psychology of commitment, absenteeism, and turnover.* San Diego, CA: Academic Press.

Packard, J. S., & Motowidlo, S. J. (1987). Subjective stress, job satisfaction, and job performance of hospital nurses. *Research in Nursing and Health, 10*, 253–261.

Podsakoff, P. M., & Organ, D. W. (1986). Self-reports in organizational research: Problems and prospects. *Journal of Management, 12*, 531–544.

Porac, J. F. (1987). The job satisfaction questionnaire as a cognitive event: First- and second-order processes in affective commentary. In K. M Rowland & G. R. Ferris (Eds.), *Research in personnel and human resources management* (Vol. 5, pp. 51–102). Greenwich, CT: JAI Press.

Pulakos, E. D., & Schmitt, N. (1983). A longitudinal study of a valence model approach for the prediction of job satisfaction of new employees. *Journal of Applied Psychology, 68*, 307–312.

Salancik, G. R., & Pfeffer, J. (1978). A social information processing approach to job attitudes and task design. *Administrative Science Quarterly, 23*, 224–253.

Schaubroeck, J., Ganster, D., & Fox, M. (1992). Dispositional affect and work-related stress. *Journal of Applied Psychology, 77*, 322–335.

Shavelson, R. J., Webb, N. M., & Rowley, G. L. (1989). Generalizability theory. *American Psychologist, 44*, 922–932.

Smith, P. C., Kendall, L. M., & Hulin, C. L. (1969). *The measurement of satisfaction in work and retirement.* Skokie, IL: Rand McNally.

Spielberger, C. D., Gorsuch, R. L., & Lushene, R. E. (1970). *Manual for the State-Trait Anxiety Inventory.* Palo Alto, CA: Consulting Psychologists Press.

Staw, B. M., Bell, N. E., & Clausen, J. A. (1986). The dispositional approach to job attitudes: A lifetime longitudinal test. *Administrative Science Quarterly, 31*, 56–77.

Staw, B. M., & Ross, J. (1985). Stability in the midst of change: A dispositional approach to job attitudes. *Journal of Applied Psychology, 70,*
469–480.

Taylor, J. A. (1953). A personality scale of manifest anxiety. *Journal of
Abnormal and Social Psychology, 48,* 285–290.

Tellegen, A., Lykken, D. T., Bouchard, T. J., Wilcox, K. J., Segal, N. L., &
Rich, S. (1988). Personality similarity in twins reared apart and
together. *Journal of Personality and Social Psychology, 54,* 1031–1039.

Tversky, A., & Kahneman, D. (1973). Availability: A heuristic for judging
frequency and probability. *Cognitive Psychology, 5,* 207–232.

Watson, D., & Clark, L. A. (1984). Negative affectivity: The disposition to
experience aversive emotional states. *Psychological Bulletin, 96,*
465–490.

Watson, D., Clark, L. A., & Tellegen, A. (1988). Development and validation of brief measures of positive and negative affect: The Panas
scales. *Journal of Personality and Social Psychology, 54,* 1063–1070.

Weitz, J. (1952). A neglected concept in the study of job satisfaction. *Personnel Psychology, 5,* 201–205.

Zajonc, R. B. (1980). Feeling and thinking: Preferences need no inferences. *American Psychologist, 35,* 151–175.

Chapter Six

Work Motivation and Goal Striving

James T. Austin
Howard J. Klein

This chapter advocates considering theoretically derived and empirically supported individual difference constructs with respect to work motivation. This objective is classic, in the sense of Cronbach's recommendations (1957), and timely, given a resurgence of research on both individual differences and motivation. M. W. Eysenck (1994) notes that individual differences are increasingly important for psychology. Evidence of this importance can be seen in conceptual developments that deploy individual differences in theoretical frameworks and elaborate biological foundations. Within industrial and organizational (I/O) psychology, there is evidence ranging from research programs to quantitative reviews that individual differences—either personality traits (Barrick & Mount, 1991) or cognitive abilities (Gottfredson, 1986; Schmidt & Hunter, 1992)—predict job-relevant criteria. These summaries, however, are based on bivariate studies within a prediction framework. A further necessary step is to embed individual difference constructs within theories to develop explanatory frameworks.

A parallel resurgence, driven largely by goals, is evident with respect to motivation. Numerous reviews of motivational theories

Note: The authors thank Jeffrey Vancouver, Raymond Katzell, Peter Villanova, and Steven Hunt for their critical advice during the preparation of this chapter.

and constructs document this renewal of interest (Ford, 1992; Katzell & Thompson, 1990a; O'Neil & Drillings, 1994). Goals were credited with a "renaissance" in motivation in the lead-in to featured reviews of Locke and Latham's (1990) formal statement of their goal-setting theory. Other evidence for a goal-driven resurgence is provided by goal frameworks advanced in special issues of journals (Baron, 1991; Locke, 1991b). These parallel rebirths provide an opportunity for an integrated treatment of work motivation and individual differences. This chapter uses the concept of goal striving as a framework for examining individual differences and work motivation. The term *goal striving* refers to the content, structure, and process characteristics involved in establishing, planning, pursuing, and revising goals.

This chapter consists of three major sections. The remainder of this first section provides a historical review that supports a cognitive-integrative position on motivation. Three goal-based frameworks are then described and integrated through the concepts of attentional focusing and allocation. Our choice to concentrate on goal-based models of work motivation is based on the current prominence of this framework. In the second section, individual differences from cognitive ability, personality, and affective domains are defined and linked to goal-based work motivation. These individual differences influence attention allocations through goals. Attentional focus and shifts in focus occur at multiple levels. The levels include (1) focus within a goal-feedback comparison, (2) focus between multiple comparisons at different levels in a goal hierarchy, and (3) focus between goal hierarchies. The final section offers conclusions and suggests research directions. In each section, emphasis is placed on three questions:

1. What is currently known regarding individual differences and goal setting?
2. How do individual differences relate to goal processes?
3. What are some new directions for research?

In order to provide perspective on the current resurgence in motivation, let us begin by reviewing some history.

Historical View of Motivation Theory and Research

Commentators on the history of motivation often note a cyclical waxing and waning of interest in motivation in experimental psychology (Bolles, 1978; Hilgard, 1987). Within psychology in the United States, motivation appeared first around 1918 in Woodworth's placement of "drives" as mediators between stimuli and responses. Research evaluating cognitive extensions by both Lewin and Tolman kept motivation an important topic between 1930 and 1960. During the next decades, motivation research declined, as indicated by inspection of *Psychological Review* contents (Bolles, 1978). A resurgence of interest during the last decade has led the Nebraska Symposium to reclaim motivation as the central theme of its annual conference (R. M. Ryan, 1992). Hilgard's explanation (1987) is that both the decline and the resurgence of motivation are due to cognitive psychology: cognitive researchers displaced motivation but found that their theories were incomplete without it (Simon, 1967). One implication of this analysis is that combining "hot" and "cool" cognitions, which have been found to provide a richer account in tandem, has implications for work motivation.

In contrast to the cyclic interest in motivation in *experimental* psychology, interest in work motivation has remained consistently high within *I/O* psychology. Motivation was recognized as important during the earliest years of the discipline (Williams, 1925). Following a path that paralleled the development of industrial psychology, Taylor (1911/1967) and his contemporaries elaborated scientific management through a molecular focus on tasks, daily quotas, and work techniques. In scientific management, monetary incentives were considered the premier route to the worker's motivation and satisfaction. The controversial Hawthorne studies showed the benefits of looking beyond mechanistic efficiency and environmental concerns in order to predict expanded criteria (satisfaction, withdrawal). The theme of this research was institutionalized in the human relations movement (Bass, 1994; Wren, 1994).

Increasing attention to motivation was evident following World War II in perspectives provided by Viteles (1954), T. A. Ryan and Smith (1954), and March and Simon (1993). Viteles, for example, reported that in revising his classic treatise on selection, he found it impossible to ignore motivation and morale (Katzell & Austin, 1992). Perhaps this salience of motivation was due to the analysis of *decisions* to participate and to produce by organization members (March & Simon, 1993). T. A. Ryan and Smith (1954) even asserted that "motivation can be considered the central problem of industrial psychology" (p. 353). They posited three features of motivation: (1) goal character (akin to intrinsic or functionally autonomous motives or terminal values), (2) obligation (norms), and (3) means character (instrumental values, subgoals).

Despite the increasing research on work motivation, little in the way of theorizing occurred from the time of the earliest research to about 1960. One reason for the paucity of theory was the dominant functionalist-empiricist orientation of the early applied psychologists (Landy, 1993). One exception to the lack of theory is T. A. Ryan (1970), whose program of research on task and intention as proximal determinants of behavior is a direct precursor of current goal and behavioral intention perspectives.

Reviews of work motivation research appeared regularly over the succeeding decades (R. Kanfer, 1992; Landy & Becker, 1987; Locke & Henne, 1986; Staw, 1977), and two comprehensive treatments appeared in successive editions of the *Handbook of Industrial and Organizational Psychology* (J. P. Campbell & Pritchard, 1976; R. Kanfer, 1990). Between 1957 and 1980, I/O researchers concentrated primarily upon expectancy, need, drive, and goal theories. The content-process dichotomy, list of suggestions derived from experimental psychology, and directions for research put forward by J. P. Campbell and Pritchard (1976) capture the focus of the 1960s and 1970s. This period saw evaluation of numerous parts and simple linkages of the aforementioned theories but few complete or competitive tests. R. Kanfer (1990) expanded Campbell and Pritchard's distinction between content and process by reviewing need/motive/value, cognitive-choice, self-regulation, and integrative theories. She concluded that the dominant themes in motivation research since Campbell and Pritchard's chapter involve cognitive and integrative constructs. A related contribution was her continuum of proximal-distal influences on behavior (R. Kanfer, 1992), which encompasses both experimental and correlational constructs (R. Kanfer & Ackerman, 1989) and can be seen as a reincarnation of Lewin's "lifespace" metaphor.

Current theorizing on work motivation, which represents a merging of U.S. and European research streams (Bargh & Gollwitzer, 1994; Kleinbeck, Quast, Thierry, & Hacker, 1990), is moving toward integrated models of self-regulation (R. Kanfer & F. H. Kanfer, 1991). Equal emphasis is now advocated for dynamic and hierarchical facets of behavior (Kuhl, 1994). Dynamic facets cycle over time from initial goal establishment through goal pursuit to goal attainment/revision choices, whereas hierarchical models structure goals from general-abstract to specific-concrete levels. The linkage of European and U.S. traditions is useful, because motivation within a European psychological tradition has long been viewed as dynamic and molar—occurring across behaviors, goals, and time—rather than as episodic. Lewin's work in Berlin during the 1920s, investigating intentions as quasi–need systems constructed and altered by the individual, is reemergent in work on volition by Gollwitzer, Kuhl, Frese, and others (Corno & R. Kanfer, 1993; Halisch & Kuhl, 1987). With such conceptions comes a renewed recognition of complexity. Kuhl (1986) identified several implications of dynamic views. These implications include emphasis on motivation over time, acknowledgment of the variable nature of motivational states, and realization of reciprocal effects among cognition, motivation, affect, and behavior. Because renewed interest in volition suggests the utility of dynamic models, the next section presents three goal models situated along a continuum from episodic to dynamic.

Goals as the Core of Work Motivation

Scientific investigations of goals bridge basic and applied domains of psychology. Studies span the social-personality (Gollwitzer, 1993; Pervin, 1989), developmental (Rapkin & Fischer, 1992), cognitive (Simon, 1994), and I/O domains (Locke & Latham, 1990). Goals provide a useful vehicle for analyzing both individual differences and motivation. In the domain of motivation, pursuit of goals is crucial for self-regulation theories that unite goal establishment, planning, execution/behavior, feedback, and evaluation processes (Bandura, 1986; R. Kanfer & F. H. Kanfer, 1991; Karoly, 1993; Kuhl, 1992). In the domain of individual differences, both attributes of goals and attainment of goals are influenced by abilities, traits, and affects. The present analysis of individual differences is based on three goal frameworks: (1) Locke and Latham's *goal-setting theory* (1990), (2) *resource allocation theory* (R. Kanfer & Ackerman, 1989; Naylor, Pritchard, & Ilgen, 1980), and (3) *control systems theory* (Carver & Scheier, 1981; Lord & Hanges, 1987). Each of these three perspectives is described here in turn.

Goal-Setting Theory

The essence of a protracted program of research spearheaded by Locke and colleagues is the general principle that goals are the proximal causal determinants of action (compare Fishbein & Ajzen, 1975; T. A. Ryan, 1970). Within Locke and Latham's High Performance Cycle (1990, 1994), as illustrated in Figure 6.1, the causal effects of task goals or work challenges (demands) on task behavior are mediated by effort and strategy development. Rewards and other consequences that are contingent on performance determine specific affective reactions that provide feedback to goals. According to Locke and colleagues, goals vary in content and intensity. Difficulty and specificity are the primary content dimensions that have been manipulated or measured. Conflict and complexity are also content attributes of goals. Intensity of the goal-setting phase influences goal commitment, a construct that subsequently influences persistence and resistance to goal change (Hollenbeck & Klein, 1987; Locke, Latham, & Erez, 1988). Another aspect of intensity is the origin of a goal; goals range from self-set to participative to assigned (Erez & F. H. Kanfer, 1983). Thus the core components of Locke and Latham's theoretical model are goals, tasks (varying on complexity), feedback, self-efficacy, performance, and contingent rewards. Individual differences for Locke and Latham moderate the construct links in the model—primarily the relationship between task goals and performance. It is possible to elaborate further the role of individual differences in this framework, as will be shown below.

Resource Allocation Theory

Naylor, Pritchard, and Ilgen's theory of work behavior (1980) analyzes choices in committing personal resources, defined as time

and effort, to particular actions. This theory (abbreviated in this discussion to NPI), although complex and far-ranging, is described by the authors as an elaboration of Woodworth's stimulus-organism-response paradigm, which initiated the systematic study of motivation in the United States. The fundamental construct in NPI is "the process of engaging in a particular act with a particular degree of commitment" (Naylor et al., 1980, p. 270). Naylor and Ilgen (1984) illustrate the benefits of a deductive approach in explaining goal effects using a framework of goal attributes (specificity and difficulty) and other relevant conditions (goal source, person, and task features). The major mechanism advanced to explain the effect of goals on task performance is a shift in the allocation of resources created by an explicit goal statement or activated goal. Individual differences are defined by Naylor et al. (1980) as stable attributes that *constrain* decisions and responses. The moderator status of individual differences for Naylor et al., consistent with goal-setting theory, is clear from this definition.

R. Kanfer and Ackerman's aptitude-treatment integration of experimental and psychometric constructs (1989) is a specialized resource allocation model. Attention for R. Kanfer and Ackerman can be allocated to on-task, off-task, or self-regulatory processes, within a conceptualization of attention as a unitary resource. In this framework, multidimensional performance on complex tasks is a function of attention allocated via individual policies. These policies are presumably sensitive to measurement and to change attempts by researchers or by organizational agents. An adapted version of this model is shown in Figure 6.2. Sources of variance in performance include attention requirements of the task (environmental variance); attention capacity of the person (person variance); and attention allocation policy (person X situation variance). Allocation policies represent the response of the individual to the task-situation "field" and are thus a novel dependent variable for research on goal striving. This framework is just beginning to be exploited, but it is apparent that the clear specification of main and interactive sources of variance is helpful in attaining the precision demanded by Naylor and Ilgen (1984).

R. Kanfer and Ackerman (1989) show that difficult goals impede performance during early task acquisition. Their argument is that task goals invoke self-regulation processes, which compete

Figure 6.2. Multiple Resource Allocation Model.

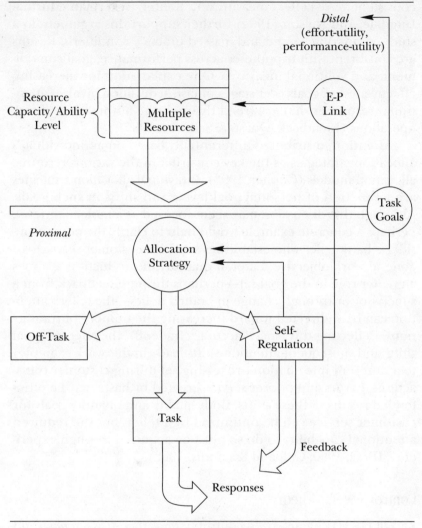

Source: Adapted from R. Kanfer & Ackerman, 1989, p. 665.

with attentional resources needed for task learning. Their results are consistent across effect measures. R. Kanfer, Ackerman, Murtha, Dugdale, and Nelson (1994) further support this argument in a study comparing spaced and massed practice conditions. Results are consistent with hypotheses across performance, goal commitment, and volitional measures. One explanation for increasing effectiveness of goals over stages of task acquisition involves attentional resources that are freed through the automation of task operations (Kleinbeck, Quast, & Schwarz, 1989).

Attention, distributed differentially based on an individual's allocation strategies, is the key construct in the various resource allocation models (Gopher, 1993). Individual allocation strategies are a function of personal goal levels and shifts in such goals. Although this discussion may seem focused at a molecular level, perhaps a concrete example would help to clarify the point. Consider a bank teller who establishes superior customer service as a general work objective. Later, if quantity of production assumes a greater role in the goal set—perhaps through feedback from a supervisor or through change in branch policy—the teller's attention can be redirected toward increasing the number of transactions. Reflecting this "speed-accuracy tradeoff," the effects of goal shifts and subsequent attention shifts lead (in this work example) to a different information-processing set during customer transactions. Errors and poorer service created by haste may be unintended results of these shifts. Both quality and quantity goals for customer service can be optimized by a teller, but the required attentional capability to do so must be acquired through experience (Erez, 1990; Gilliland & Landis, 1992).

Control Systems Theory

Katzell (1994) characterized control systems theory as a meta-trend for the I/O field. The negative feedback loop is the core component of control systems (Wiener, 1948). In its simplest form, the negative feedback loop, shown in Figure 6.3, consists of four elements: a referent standard or goal, a sensor/input function, a comparator, and an effector/output function.

While its origins are mechanical, control theory can represent a very flexible, nonmechanical view of behavior, as illustrated by

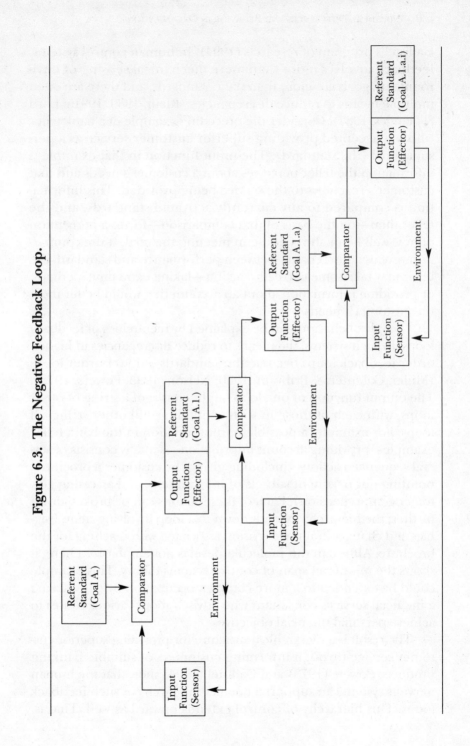

Figure 6.3. The Negative Feedback Loop.

Gallistel's program of research (1994). In human control systems, feedback involves more than mere mechanical sensing of environments, goals are more than static standards, and there are often multiple means to reduce discrepancies (Klein, 1989, 1991a; Lord & Hanges, 1987). Consider the preceding example of a bank teller who has accepted providing superior customer service as a personal goal (the standard). The input function in that example is information the teller perceives about a customer's needs and that customer's reactions to the service being provided. This information is compared to any currently activated standards, and the teller then—on the basis of that comparison—forms a perception of how well he or she is doing in meeting the goal. If the comparison reveals a discrepancy between performance and standard, the teller may take some corrective action—taking extra time, perhaps, or providing information about an account that would better meet the customer's needs.

Complex behaviors can be explained by hierarchies of feedback loops. In such systems, the means to reduce discrepancies in higher-order feedback loops become the standards of lower-order loops (Miller, Galanter, & Pribram, 1960; Nelson, 1993; Powers, 1973). The output function of one loop might consist of a string of other loops, with each of those in turn containing still other strings of loops. For example, a possible output function in the bank teller example—providing account information—actually consists of several sequenced actions (including giving the customer a brochure, pointing out pertinent subsets of information, and assessing customer comprehension). Each of these actions can be broken down further; the hierarchy extends down to a loop involving neural signals and changes in muscle tension associated with reaching for the brochure. Although this molecular level is not emphasized here, it shows the multilevel span of control systems theory. This example could be extended to a more complex occupation by considering a financial services consultant who advises about various routes to achieve personal financial objectives.

The result is a hierarchical structure for providing superior customer service through informing customers of suitable banking products. Powers (1973) and Gallistel (1994) show that the human nervous system can support a detailed hierarchy of such feedback loops. This hierarchy of control extends upward as well. That is, the specific action of providing superior customer service could be part of the output function of a higher-order standard, perhaps resulting in an outstanding performance rating for the bank teller. Receiving that high rating may itself be the means of attaining yet a higher standard (a pay raise, promotion, or recognition award). In order to achieve any given standard, therefore, we may need to establish chains of subgoals, pursuing each subgoal sequentially as attention shifts from one control loop to another (Lord & Hanges, 1987; Schank & Abelson, 1977). This shifting of attention between loops within goal hierarchies is a feature of control systems dictated by the limited capacity of working memory (Baddaley, 1986). Further, shifting illustrates a link between control systems and resource allocation models. Specifically, self-regulation is carried out by attention shifts, which can disrupt performance if they create competition for cognitive resources. From a control systems perspective, individual differences influence the adoption of a particular goal, the regulation of that goal (that is, monitoring the environment, processing feedback, detecting discrepancies, tolerating discrepancies), and the implementation and evaluation of strategies to reduce discrepancies.

Summary of Goal-Based Perspectives

Goal-setting theory is a "middle-range" framework grounded in empirical data; it concentrates on task goals and task performance in achievement settings (for example, work, sports). The extensive evidence relating to this theory documents primarily the operation of single goals in simple tasks (Wood & Locke, 1990; Wood, Mento, & Locke, 1987), although complementary viewpoints on single goals are provided by resource allocation and control systems theories. The latter two perspectives study attentional and behavioral switching between work activities (Naylor et al., 1980; T. A. Ryan & Smith, 1954). These shifts are determined in part by decisions about acceptance, attainment, persistence, or abandonment of multiple goals. Control systems deal with dynamic, hierarchical goal pursuit (Campion & Lord, 1982; Klein, 1989). Recent extensions (most notably, that by Lord and Levy, 1994) employ connectionist concepts to span the cognition-action gap—an approach similar to Kuhl's emphasis (1994).

Explaining the motivation process demands multivariate, multioccasion, multilevel theories (Royce, 1979). Frameworks that address dynamic conceptions at several levels of analysis, ranging from the task to the lifespan level, are required to link individual differences to goal-directed action. Such multiple levels are found in action control models (Frese & Zapf, 1994) but are not easily integrated into goal-setting theory.

Traditional goal-setting and resource allocation models offer fine-grained analysis, while control systems yield a multilevel and systemic perspective. The fact that these perspectives highlight different aspects of motivated work behavior makes their combination a potentially rich amalgamation. There are clearly differences between these perspectives—differences that have been the focus of debate (Klein, 1991b; Locke, 1991a). Some of these differences are found in underlying assumptions that make these theories incompatible for certain research questions. For the purposes of the current analysis, however, these differences are less relevant. The next section integrates these three goal-based perspectives using the construct of attention conceptualized at multiple levels. Simon's recent exposition of attention as a bottleneck between cognition and motivation (1994) is a prominent influence on the attempted integration. Issues pertaining to attention are also central to our review of individual differences that uses the linking of these motivational perspectives.

Integrating Motivational Perspectives

A key mechanism for self-regulation and motivation is *attention* (Simon, 1994; Wickens, 1992)—a term defined as a limited, shareable resource for conscious processes. Attention has been researched at several levels, differing in generality and time perspective. Research encompasses a molecular focus on the part of cognitive researchers (Cooper & Regian, 1982; M. W. Eysenck, 1988; Gopher, 1993; Hunt & Lansman, 1982), a midrange focus on attention at work (Gardner, Dunham, Cummings, & Pierce, 1989; Hollenbeck, 1989; Roberson, 1989), and an even broader focus designated as *self-consciousness* (Fenigstein, 1987), *self-attention* (Carver, 1979), or *self-monitoring* (Snyder, 1979). Although the content of attention varies at each level, several issues are common across levels.

The first common issue is the *nature* of attention. Structural facets concern the distinction between unitary and multiple attention resources, whereas capacity facets relate to the amount of attentional resources. R. Kanfer and Ackerman (1989) explicitly derived their hypotheses from a unitary conception, yet many researchers now embrace a conception of attention as multidimensional and malleable (Gopher, 1993; Wickens, 1992). Continuing the previous example, a bank teller could serve a customer with minimal or with considerable attention. An experienced teller might process the requests of a customer using well-learned, habitual responses; in this case, minimal attentional resources would be focused on the tasks involved. For a newly hired teller, however, considerable attention might need to be directed to each operation involved in completing the transaction. In other words, the amount of attention required should alter systematically as the teller moves from novice to expert.

A second issue is the *target* of attention. Attention can shift within a single goal-feedback loop, between loops in a hierarchy, and between hierarchies; what differs in each case is the focus. At the level of a single goal-feedback loop or episode, attention is focused on activated goals and the immediate task environment. At higher levels, attention is focused on long-term personal projects. In terms of Beach's image theory (1990), the highest-level focus is on trajectories extending into the future, referencing career or lifespan goals. Selective attention, viewed as concentrating or focusing upon a goal or its implementation despite distractions from competing intentions, is one of several strategies for self-regulation and volition (Kuhl, 1992).

A second part of this attentional target issue concerns the effects of intrusions into a current task focus. Because of the potency of intrusions, the teller's attention on the customer's transaction is influenced not only by experience but also by demands unrelated to the task at hand. As a result of these demands, the teller may focus on other work-related concerns (for example, an earlier missed service opportunity) or on nonwork concerns (for example, an ailing family member).

Goals facilitate task performance in part by directing attention to a particular task or to a level of performance on a task (Locke 1968). Research has shown that the reallocation of attention from a given task disrupts the goal-performance relationship unless the task is automated (reducing the correlation between goal difficulty and performance). One source of attentional disruption is "tasks" that, when viewed from an experimental-manipulational or a correlational-measurement perspective, are irrelevant. Anxiety, rumination, and nontask cognitions have all been found to divert attention from the primary task and goal striving. Test anxiety, for example, can be studied as an attention construct in which disruptive thoughts (reflecting an urge to escape or a negative emotional state) compete with test-taking processes of item encoding, memory scanning, and response formulation (Wine, 1982). Along those lines, Kuhl and Koch (1984) found that anxiety served as a "hidden" task, a result that suggests competition for attentional resources. M. W. Eysenck (1988), Sarason (1988), Carver and Scheier (1988), and Revelle (1987) analyzed anxiety from different theoretical perspectives. Their analyses, however, converged on the principle that the cognitive components of task performance (sustained information transfer, working memory manipulation, and long-term memory retrieval), self-regulation, and other nontask cognitions compete for limited attentional resources in working memory. These findings support the role of attention in goal striving. To reiterate, attention is the cognitive bottleneck.

There are also differences in the extent to which people are able to resist attentional reallocation or suppress unwanted thoughts (Gernsbacher & Faust, 1991; Tipper & Baylis, 1987). These individual differences are another source of variance in allocation policies across tasks and time. The effects of individual differences on attention allocation are measurable under multiple task demands using computerized platforms (Damos, 1991; Kleinbeck et al., 1989; Mane & Donchin, 1989). Kuhl's construct of action and state orientation (1992) also has implications for how attention is allocated and what environmental events activate self-regulation processes. Kuhl's action orientation, which is similar to Gollwitzer's implemental mindset (1990), refers to a behavioral and environmental focus of attention, while state orientation, which is similar to Gollwitzer's deliberative mindset, refers to an inward focus of attention. Action-oriented persons are hypothesized to be able to engage in self-regulation more easily than state-oriented persons. Study of the relationships between action-state orientation and causal attributions, which have been related to goal processes (Thomas & Mathieu, 1994), could help to explicate how on-line processing of performance-relevant information influences successive affective and strategic responses. A tendency to shift activity or to persist following failure, for example, can be partly explained using action-state orientation.

While it is difficult to show in a single diagram how these three perspectives fit together, a merger can be described in terms of the features of goal striving that each separately emphasizes. Goal-setting theory accounts well for the within-episode operation of task goals, control systems theory encompasses the multilevel operation of goals, and resource allocation theory highlights dynamics within and between levels and hierarchies.

There are several benefits of this merger, the greatest of which is the recognition of the multiple levels that the synthesis can address. A key to this integration involves generalizing the construct of attention across levels of cognition. Consider that attentional focus can be shifted from task-relevant activities in the present (for example, ongoing dyadic behavior with a customer or client) to a midlevel focus on a project due at the end of the week (and comprising multiple subparts) to a dispositional self-focus (such as the tendency to perceive the world negatively). A problem occurs when these focuses attempt to coexist, as in the phenomenon of ego-involvement during task engagement. Specifically, if the experimental setting or work environment creates a focus on the self, perhaps through cuing a mastery orientation, then it is reasonable to expect intrusions into task information processing and decreases in quality of performance.

A second benefit of this merger is the provision of a conceptual framework for examining individual differences as they influence goal striving. Relatively few researchers studying goal setting have examined individual differences in a theoretical manner (Weiss & Adler, 1984), although McClelland's extensive program of research on *nAch* (Need Achievement) is a prominent exception. Locke, Shaw, Saari, and Latham (1981) identified this issue over fifteen years ago, pointing out that researchers tend to graft measures of individual difference constructs onto studies of goal difficulty and then try to explain any observed relationships. Partial exceptions are seen in resource allocation and control systems research, although a restricted range of constructs has been considered by these groups. With that in mind, the next section links a comprehensive set of individual differences to the goal frameworks.

Individual Differences and Work Motivation

There are two sources of the current treatment of individual differences. The major influence is Royce and Powell's "individuality theory" (1983), which combines factor, systems, and information theory concepts. Individuality for Royce (1979) derives from integrated action in goal pursuit. While the highest goal is to optimize "personal meaning," a subordinate layer consists of goals dealing with lifestyle satisfaction, maintenance of self-image, and evolution of worldview—broad goals that contribute to the superordinate goal and suggest multiple routes to attainment. These second-level goals mark out domains and cascade downward with increasing specificity toward action. A second source of our view of individual differences is their variability, which occurs across individuals, occasions, and situations (Ackerman & L. G. Humphreys, 1990; L. G. Humphreys, 1985). In this section, a discussion of the cognitive ability, personality, and affective domains precedes a review of individual differences within the goal-based frameworks.

Cognitive Ability Domain

Let us first address cognitive abilities, which have been of interest since Plato ordered persons by analogy to metals (brass, silver, gold) in his *Republic*.

General Discussion

Current definitions of ability constructs focus on behavioral flexibility/adaptability, on maximal performance, and on task-relevant information processing of declarative and procedural knowledge (Carroll, 1993; Murphy, 1988; Royce, 1979). For example, L. G. Humphreys defines intelligence as the "acquired repertoire of all intellectual (cognitive) skills and knowledge available to the person at a point in time" (1994, p. 180). The longest-running issue in the domain of ability is a dispute over the levels required for theoretical analysis and practical application. The opposing factions are adherents of general ability (the psychometric *g*) (Jensen, 1985; Ree & Earles, 1992; Schmidt & Hunter, 1992) and adherents of intermediate plus general factors (Carroll, 1993; L. G. Humphreys, 1985; Horn, 1988; Lubinski & Dawis, 1992). Landy, Shankster, and Kohler (1994) have provided reasons to continue to investigate intermediate abilities. Additional support for the Landy et al. position is provided by studies of the heritability of intermediate abilities. Recent behavior genetics studies report influences of specific abilities that are conceptually distinct from the psychometric *g* (Pederson, Plomin, & McClearn, 1994). These studies also confirm hierarchical structures with general and intermediate levels (Harnqvist, Gustafsson, Muthen, & Nelson, 1994).

Another debate in this domain is between psychometric and cognitive paradigms for studying abilities (Messick, 1992; Sternberg, 1977). The psychometric tradition investigates abilities as structures, while the cognitive tradition uses a process-oriented approach. The latter is illustrated in the careful analysis by Revelle (1987) of the task/criterion domain into task demands for sustained information transfer, short-term memory, and long-term memory (M. S. Humphreys & Revelle, 1984). It is possible to classify laboratory tasks systematically using the three axes of his conceptualization and, at least in principle, to construct tasks that load primarily on one of the axes.

Theory, support, and measurement capabilities vary with the psychometric and cognitive paradigms, although H. J. Eysenck (1984) argues that the contributions of both are valuable, and Messick (1992) contends that the cognitive approaches can be subsumed under existing psychometric factor-based theories.

Research on the internal structure of abilities supports a hierarchical organization (Harnqvist et al., 1994; Horn, 1988; Lubinski & Dawis, 1992). Carroll (1993) advanced a framework with narrow, broad, and general ability layers based on reanalyses of test datasets. General ability, approximately equivalent to intelligence, is found at the highest level. Seven broad intermediate factors—fluid intelligence, crystallized intelligence, general memory and learning, broad visual perception, broad auditory perception, broad retrieval ability, broad cognitive speed, and processing speed—constitute the second level. Elements specific to a test type are found at the bottom of the pyramid, in the stratum labeled *narrow.*

Lubinski and Dawis (1992) proposed a radex or conic structure in their thorough treatment of aptitudes, skills, and proficiencies. They too argued that factors at different levels could be useful in theoretical research and practical applications of individual differences. Following the lead of these researchers, this chapter proposes large significance for both general and intermediate levels of ability in understanding goal choice/reaction and goal attainment.

Cognitive Ability Constructs Within Goal Striving

For goal-setting theory, cognitive ability is regarded as a moderator of the goal-performance link. Ability is recognized as a competing determinant of task performance and as a rival explanation to be controlled. Locke and Latham (1990) list multiple studies that support the moderating effects of ability. Closer inspection of these studies, however, suggests that little attention is given to the conceptualization and measurement of ability, the distinction between general and intermediate levels of ability, or cognitive-psychometric perspectives on ability. In fact, ability is generally measured in goal-setting studies using practice trial performance rather than using task-independent measures of general or intermediate abilities (Locke, 1982) or self-reports of standardized test scores (Campion & Lord, 1982). Few studies have used standard measures such as the Wonderlic Personnel Test or a multiple aptitude battery. (One exception is the resource allocation perspective, which is anchored in an established test battery.) Furthermore, significant versus nonsignificant ability-performance correlations (rather than specific tests for moderation effects) are typically used to support moderator interpretations (James & Brett, 1984).

In addition to the moderating effects of ability, Locke and Latham (1990) also consider the issue of the homogeneity of motivation, given that task performance is hypothesized to be an interactive function of motivation and ability. If there is little variance in motivation (one part of the cross-product term), then a main effect for ability on performance (instead of an interaction) will be found. Locke and Latham (1990) also mention personal conceptions of ability (fixed or incremental) as an influence on goal processes.

Intermediate-level abilities might be especially important in the consideration of task learning stages (R. Kanfer & Ackerman,

1989) or the self-efficacy construct (Cervone, Jiwani, & Wood, 1991). Spatial ability, for example, is a well-established intermediate component of general ability (Lohman, Pellegrino, Alderton, & Regian, 1987) and can be investigated in conjunction with self-efficacy measures in spatially loaded tasks such as an air traffic control simulation. An extension of this idea involves expanding Fleishman and Mumford's model (1989) to incorporate goal manipulations or measures. That model explains changes in task performance over time as a function of both practice/experience and shifting loadings on an indirectly observed spatial ability construct. Other intermediate-level ability measures could be included. Problem sensitivity, for example, may also be relevant to task performance.

From the perspective provided by control systems, both general and intermediate abilities fit into (1) a predecisional phase of goal setting and (2) subsequent choices relating to persisting, revising, or abandoning a goal (that is, relating to goal commitment levels). A parsimonious model holds that general abilities directly influence choice of personal goals and subsequent task performance; an alternative model posits a path from general ability to goal difficulty and task performance mediated by self-efficacy. For example, some goal-striving cycles may depend on specific self-efficacy percepts (Bandura, 1986; Gist & Mitchell, 1992). Linkages between self-efficacy and ability constructs, together with goal attributes, should also predict commitment and subsequent persistence. Both Klein (1991a) and Earley and Lituchy (1991) have shown that goals are more powerful proximal determinants of task performance than self-efficacy is, however. This finding suggests that different antecedents may be operating. Longitudinal studies and lagged measures can help to elaborate goal/ability/performance relationships beyond the alternative models compared by Earley and Lituchy (1991). In that study, three causal orderings were compared. The path model receiving strongest support was that of Locke and Latham. A recent investigation by Thomas and Mathieu (1994) viewed self-efficacy in the context of single-episode and between-episode effects of goals. Their results suggest self-efficacy as a link between single- and multiple-episode conceptions, which in the framework of this chapter would be described as an attentional shift from a single goal-feedback loop to a loop at a higher level. Bandura's (1986) micro-analytic paradigm could be used to frame the interplay among goals, ability, self-efficacy, and commitment, with performance as one dependent variable of interest and subsequent goal cycles as a second. The cyclic design of Hall and Foster (1977) could also be employed in such extensions.

Running through our analysis of cognitive abilities thus far is a distinction between ability as objectively assessed and ability as subjectively perceived. This distinction might be important for understanding initial goal choice, reaction to assigned goals, and subsequent commitment. The basis for this distinction is the finding that measured ability does not always correlate highly with such self-perceptions as self-esteem and self-efficacy, as shown empirically by Brim (1965) and by the meta-analysis of Mabe and West (1982). The implications of including both objective *and* subjective conceptions of ability in goal striving remain to be explored, but the program of research by Dweck and her colleagues, although developed with children, suggests one fruitful direction (Dweck, 1986; Dweck & Leggett, 1988). Another research-relevant distinction might be made between self-esteem and self-efficacy, on the one hand, and general and intermediate abilities, on the other. Both distinctions contrast more-inclusive and less-inclusive levels of a phenomenon—in this case, self-concept and cognitive abilities. If self-efficacy is a task-specific construct, as implied by Bandura's micro-analytic measurement strategy (1986), then specific abilities should predict self-efficacy, task goal levels, and task performance at significantly higher levels than g. On the other hand, general ability should also be strongly related to self-esteem and to longer-term career goals, given appropriate matching of predictor-criterion specificity (Roznowski & Hanisch, 1990). Greater clarity and a map of the relationships among these constructs can be provided by future studies.

R. Kanfer and Ackerman's (1989) resource allocation framework uses the Armed Services Vocational Aptitude Battery (ASVAB) to measure general, perceptual speed, verbal, vocational-technical information, and quantitative ability constructs. It is reassuring that these constructs predict performance, but Kanfer and Ackerman's results do not address the question of the relationship of cognitive abilities to goal choice and goal reactions. The linkage between ability and self-efficacy will play an important role in mediating this set of goal paths, and future studies should provide adequate measurement of self-efficacy and cognitive abilities. All components should be evaluated.

To summarize what is known about cognitive abilities and goal striving, there is enough evidence to propose that a general ability construct exerts direct and indirect effects on goals and performance. The indirect effects of ability on goals are mediated through self-efficacy. Less research exists with respect to intermediate-level abilities, but several possible designs have been suggested to examine relationships while also matching predictor and criterion generality (Hanisch, 1995).

Personality Domain

We turn now to personality constructs, which concern patterns of behavior across time and situation. Over the last decade, interest in explaining additional variance in work behavior has been evident (Hogan, 1991).

General Discussion

The personality domain can be viewed in terms of trait or social-cognitive paradigms (Cervone, 1991). In the former view, traits are the constructs of interest; in the latter view, it is person-environment adjustments that are of interest. A long-standing interest in the structure of personality is indexed by treatments dating from Allport's 1937 classic treatise (Kluckhohn & Murray, 1949; London & Exner, 1978; Pervin, 1990). Among theorists favoring traits, there is growing consensus that (1) systems approaches are superior to theories built around single traits and (2) systems views can encompass many of the single traits (Goldberg, 1991; McCrae, 1992). There are debates about whether the appropriate structure is H. J. Eysenck's system of Psychoticism-Extraversion-Neuroticism (PEN), Cattell's source traits, or the Big Five of Agreeableness, Extraversion, Conscientiousness, Intellectance (or Openness to Experience), and Surgency (or Emotional Stability or Neuroticism). In these debates, Eysenck (1991) analyzes and criticizes the Big Five and Cattell's source traits, while Block (1995) criticizes the Big Five. One reason to favor Eysenck's approach is its links to underlying neurophysiological substrates.

Despite a period of neglect by I/O psychologists, caused in part

by misinterpretation of Guion and Gottier's review of the validity of
personality traits for selection (1965), abundant evidence links personality constructs with work behavior (Barrick & Mount, 1991;
Hogan, 1991; Tett, Jackson, & Rothstein, 1991) and with goals (D. J.
Campbell, 1982; Cropanzano, James, & Citera, 1992; Pervin, 1989).
Bernardin and Bownas (1985), for example, provide multiple treatments of personality assessment in organizations. Moreover, self-
concept is an aspect of personality that adds to understanding
organizational behavior (Brockner, 1988) in both trait (self-esteem)
and social-cognitive (self-efficacy) approaches.

Personality Constructs Within Goal Striving

Goal-setting researchers examining personality as a moderator have,
for the most part, measured only one or two traits. According to
Locke and Latham (1990), the traits for which several studies exist
are self-esteem, need for achievement, need for independence,
Type-A behavior pattern, locus of control, and self-efficacy. Self-
efficacy, a task-specific construct, appears to have received the
greatest attention over the last decade. After reviewing these studies, Locke and Latham (1990) called for the consideration of additional traits, including attention-persistence, ambition, initiative,
and future time perspective. The examination of single traits may
be of little value, however, since personality theorists generally
agree that it is *systems* of traits that influence behavior dynamics.
McClelland and Boyatzis (1982), for example, found that the profile of an individual across several traits—achievement, affiliation,
and power needs—predicted long-term leadership effectiveness
better than any single trait.

The specific taxonomy selected is not as important as the
larger perspective—that is, the belief that a profile across traits
accounts for goal-striving variance and process. Both currently
prominent major trait systems—Eysenck's PEN system and the Big
Five—subsume the single traits previously studied by researchers
investigating goal setting. These trait structures also provide foundations for conceptualizing the effects of goals on work motivation
and performance over time. Within the Big Five taxonomy, for
example, the characteristic of conscientiousness received the most
consistent support across three categories of criteria and five job
families in Barrick and Mount's quantitative review (1991). The

conscientiousness construct appears especially important for the motivational aspects of job performance. Barrick, Mount, and Strauss (1993) provided evidence for goals and goal commitment as mediators between conscientiousness and job performance for a sample of sales representatives. Given these research findings, the relationship between conscientiousness and goal striving deserves immediate attention, with other personality constructs from the Big Five included for subsequent theory revision. In the spirit of this volume, models that include standardized measures of general or specific abilities (Wonderlic Personnel Test, Differential Aptitude Battery [DAB], ASVAB, and so on), conscientiousness (Five-Factor Inventory; Costa & McCrae, 1992), and self-concept (assessments of self-esteem and/or self-efficacy levels; Robinson, Shaver, & Wrightsman, 1991) should be able to predict an expanded criterion space. Borman and Motowidlo (1993) expanded the criterion domain explicitly by adding *non*–job-specific constituents to job-specific or technical performance dimensions. The joint influence of trait and social-cognitive constructs on goals for contextual elements of job performance has not been extensively investigated. Last, the traits proposed by H. J. Eysenck and co-workers provide an alternative superstructure for future research.

Within control systems, personality, self-concept, and goal origin are important factors in goal striving. D. J. Campbell (1982) classified situational and personality determinants of goal difficulty choice within an expectancy-value framework. He noted that no direct tests of the relationship between personality constructs and goal difficulty had been attempted. Hollenbeck and Brief (1987) distinguished assigned and self-set goal origins (Austin, 1989; Mone & Baker, 1992), noting that the dependent variable of interest shifts from the goal itself to goal reactions when researchers manipulate or study goal origin. In other words, when goals originate internally, individual differences in general (and personality in particular) influence aspects of chosen goals (for example, goal difficulty, specificity, conflict). When goals originate externally, personality determines, in part, an individual's reactions to those goals (for example, acceptance, commitment). Given an intermediate, participative goal origin, personality constructs should influence the negotiation process between the parties (whether supervisor and subordinate or coach and athlete). As noted by Weiss and

Adler (1984), researchers investigating goal setting typically have tacked on individual difference measures while attempting to find an effect for goal difficulty. The experimental manipulations in these studies have most likely created so-called strong situations, which may have overwhelmed any effects of individual differences.

Cropanzano, James, and Citera (1992) integrated personality and motivation using a hierarchical control systems model. According to Cropanzano et al., three abstract directional orientations (approaching positive stimuli, avoiding negative stimuli, and approaching novel stimuli) lead to the development of values. These core values then define why people engage in particular activities, and they in turn prompt the construction of more specific goals that reflect self-identity. Linking self-identity and task goals are personal projects—midlevel standards (also known as "life tasks") grouped around important life situations. Little, Lecci, and Watkinson (1992) showed that the Big Five are related to aspects of defining and striving toward personal projects. Hierarchical structures presented by Cropanzano et al. parallel Royce and Powell's individuality theory (1983) and other proposed structures (Powers, 1973). Campion and Lord (1982) hypothesized that the multiple goals that originate in the duties or task clusters of a particular organizational position can be dealt with either serially or through development of tolerance for discrepancies. Both strategies are based on goal importance, which is thus crucial for investigating multiple goals. Gollwitzer (1993) pointed out that goal importance is a major determinant of goal commitment; therefore, via current commitment to goals, it contributes to resolution of conflict among goals.

One empirical implication of this perspective involves examining the influence of higher-level goals as a frame or context for task and midlevel goals. Orientation toward goals of learning or mastery, for example, could be assessed using recently developed scales (Duda & Nicholls, 1992; Farr, Hofmann, & Ringenbach, 1993), manipulated using ego-involving events or instructions (Wood & Bandura, 1989), or studied using both measurement and manipulation tactics. The aptitude-treatment interaction framework adopted by R. Kanfer and Ackerman (1989) provides a rich heuristic for the combined mode of investigation, with the addition of Big Five or PEN constructs a logical first step.

A core of the argument presented pertains to goals activated as current concerns as attentional constructs. With regard to attentional allocation, Matthews, Davies, and Lees (1990) showed that extraversion, assessed within H. J. Eysenck's PEN triad, is related to arousal levels and the availability of attentional resources. Further, a model of the effects of cognitive and motivational variables on cognitive task performance formulated by Revelle (1987) is based on competition for attentional resources with respect to information transfer, working memory, and long-term memory components of task performance.

Another question for research concerns patterns of movement within and between goal hierarchies. Direction of movement can be manipulated through a series of *how* and *why* questions (Little, 1989) asked by an observer or by the individual. Verbal protocols, taken during on-task and off-task periods, could provide data on goal cognition (Karoly, 1993). The role of self-regulation during task acquisition reveals important information for organizational purposes. From such studies, an increased understanding of the deliberation and implementation phases of goal striving should be obtained (Gollwitzer, 1990; Kuhl, 1994; Lord & Levy, 1994).

It is possible to speculate further about the effects of personality on where it is in goal hierarchies that individuals allocate their attentional resources. Kuhl's action-state orientation and self-regulation framework holds promise, as does Dweck and Leggett's construct of goal orientation (1988). Farr et al. (1993) integrated these two perspectives by using Kuhl's self-regulatory framework to encompass the goal orientation construct. Recall that state-oriented individuals engage primarily in internally focused cognitions, while action-oriented individuals focus on behavioral/environmental events. If self-regulation requires cognitive allocation of attention, unexpected performance outcomes should lead to an activation of self-regulation through a monitoring process.

To summarize what is known about personality constructs and goal striving, not enough research using systems of personality constructs has been conducted to allow the venturing of confident conclusions. However, the social-cognitive construct of self-efficacy has stimulated a large amount of research (Bandura, 1991). Self-efficacy's role in a self-regulation theory such as Bandura's is well established, and links to affective and task strategy responses have been strongly supported. Thus one frontier inviting research is the concept of fitting the Big Five or Eysenck's taxonomy into current studies, perhaps through use of the multidimensional goal questionnaire developed by Lee, Bobko, Earley, and Locke (1991). In particular, relationships between personality traits or social-cognitive constructs and the higher-order positive and negative goal-setting factors identified by Lee et al. (1991) would be helpful in specifying the map of causal factors.

Affective Domain: Orientation and Temperament

We now turn to the remaining individual difference constructs, which are grouped together because they all pertain to the affective-emotional domain (Lewis & Haviland, 1993). This domain—as well as the personality domain—is receiving attention as researchers expand their focus beyond abilities and task performance.

General Discussion

The first set of affective domain constructs falls under the heading of *orientation*—that is, values and interests (or affective reactions to such specific stimuli as people, events, and activities). Within I/O psychology, researchers have studied orientation by examining work values (Nord, Brief, Atieh, & Doherty, 1988; Wollack, Goodale, Wijting, & Smith, 1971) and vocational interests (Dawis, 1991). The structure of interests appears to be a circumplex—a specific covariance structure that posits a circular ordering of correlations. This structure implies that adjacent points are correlated more highly than distant points (as illustrated in Holland's hexagon; see Figure 3.1). The structure of values appears to be hierarchical (Cropanzano et al., 1992), comprising instrumental and terminal types (Rokeach, 1973; Schwartz, 1992). This distinction is analogous to subgoal-goal inclusion relationships.

Temperament, as distinguished from orientation, pertains to general (rather than specific) affective reactions. In addition, models in this domain are characterized by links to neurobiology (Bates & Wachs, 1994). Positive and negative affectivity (Watson & Tellegen, 1985)—defined as the opposing tendencies to experience events in either a positive or a negative manner—typify this category. The structure of temperament appears to contain positive, negative, and intensity factors (Baker, Zevon, & Rounds, 1994; Diener, 1984). Furthermore, there are substantial linkages between two Big Five traits and positive/negative affectivity (Watson & Clark, 1992): extraversion consistently and positively correlates with components of positive affectivity, while neuroticism correlates with negative affectivity. In I/O psychology, Brief, Burke, George, and colleagues' development and validation of the Job Affect Scale illustrates the state of the art (Brief, Burke, George, Robinson, & Webster, 1988; Burke, Brief, George, Roberson, & Webster, 1989).

Affective Constructs Within Goal Striving

Locke and Latham (1990) developed goal-affect relationships following Locke's treatment of job satisfaction (1976). In their model, satisfaction is the result of high performance when rewards are contingent on performance. Locke and Latham's model also suggests that the effects of satisfaction on motivation are indirect, operating first through broad behavioral families (Roznowski & Hulin, 1992), including adaptation, commitment, and organizational citizenship behaviors, and then down to specific task goals. Affect has also been incorporated within goal striving by Bandura and Cervone (1986) and by Pervin (1983) in his inclusion of affect as a component of goals.

The analysis of goal-affect relationships can be extended by incorporating recent developments in the study of emotions, broadly defined at multiple levels (Izard, 1993; Lewis & Haviland, 1993; Stein & Levine, 1991). Multilevel approaches have been slow to appear in the I/O domain, although researchers are using several distinct levels of analysis, ranging from moods (George & Brief, 1992), to attitudes (Cranny, Smith, & Stone, 1992), to traits/dispositions (Brief et al., 1988; Burke et al., 1989). Little work, however, meets the requirements for cross-level analysis (Cacioppo & Berntson, 1992), because most researchers focus their attention upon single levels and also because theories and methods are lacking.

A related and eminently researchable example involves combining or crossing multilevel goals with two domains, work and nonwork, to associate between-situation and within-situation frameworks. Goals in the work domain exist at task-related and career-focused levels and may conflict with goals in the nonwork domain. There are few data bearing on the question of work/nonwork goal conflict, but interference among goals from various life domains could be measured and related to such affective constructs as stress and psychological functioning. Roberson's Work Concerns Inventory (1989), which assesses multiple work goals based on Klinger's "current concerns" concept (1975, 1995), would be a useful instrument for researching these issues when supplemented with an instrument for assessing nonwork goals.

A research question pertaining to affect that can best be addressed within a control systems framework considers how affective levels and goal levels interact. While goal-setting theory includes a feedback loop, goal-setting studies have examined affect primarily as a consequence of performance rather than as a determinant of ongoing motivation. Differentiating goal-striving affect and goal attainment affect may help to clarify this issue. This distinction can be related to the concept of "flow" proposed by Csikszentmihalyi (1990) and to Apter's theory of reversals between goal-oriented and behavior-oriented motivational modes (1989). Specifically, the function of striving or process affect may be to associate emotion with intermediate subgoals, which maintains persistence toward distal, longer-term goals. The relationships between goal-striving affect and higher-order affective constructs such as positive and negative affectivity, again with general and specific levels, are unknown at this point. Carver and Scheier (1990) argue that affect is regulated as a second-order percept, asserting that discrepancy reduction rate appraised from a higher or meta-level determines positive or negative affect—a principle supported by Saavedra and Earley's results (1990). Reconciling the arguments against control systems (Locke, 1991a) with the present integrated position will require empirical research. One idea would involve a construct of sensitivity to discrepancies that is similar to the construct advanced in the equity literature (Huseman, Hatfield, & Miles, 1987). Hyland's concept of error sensitivity (1988) lends further credence to Carver and Scheier's proposal that affect is related to rate of change in discrepancies (1990). Factors involved in error sensitivity should be mapped out in studies measuring dimensions of affect.

R. Kanfer and Ackerman (1989) measured affect as positive and negative self-reactions, with findings similar to those of Bandura and Cervone (1986). Clearly, fewer studies bear on affect and goal striving within a resource allocation framework than within the other two frameworks discussed here (which is not surprising, given the relatively recent focus of researchers working within that perspective). Naylor et al. (1980) proposed that it is anticipated satisfaction that influences commitment to acts. Taking a dispositional level of analysis—for example, using positive and negative affectivity—may account for additional process variance. Intensity of affect might also be relevant for allocation of attention: to the extent that affect impedes time sharing and selective attention, it will impede complex task performance.

To summarize what is known about affective constructs and goal striving, not enough research using such constructs has been done to allow us to advance any confident conclusions. On the other hand, affective responses appear important in support of continued goal-striving motivation (Pervin, 1983). This domain, therefore, is the one that requires the most attention from researchers in order to extend the framework for goal striving.

Conclusion

The central thesis of this chapter is that individual differences are valuable partners for theoretical accounts of work motivation. Throughout this review of individual differences and work motivation, several queries have provided guidance.

1. *What is known about individual differences and motivation?* To answer this question, goal-setting theory, control systems theory, and resource allocation theory were linked via their complementary emphasis on attentional features of goal striving. Despite studies addressing individual differences within each of the perspectives, a considerable amount of research is needed before precise statements can be made about their role. As a starting supposition, individual differences should be related to various goal processes, including the processes of goal establishment, goal pursuit, and goal revision, abandonment, and persistence.

2. *By what mechanism or mechanisms do individual differences influence goal striving?* The multilevel construct of *attention*—a scarce cognitive commodity for which on-task (engagement), off-task

(irrelevant), and self-regulatory processes compete—was advanced as the fundamental mechanism.

3. *What are some new directions for research?* Gaps in knowledge and directions for research were developed throughout the chapter (and are addressed further in subsequent paragraphs in terms of baseline and extension studies).

Let us address that final issue—potential directions for research—in greater detail. A useful baseline study should contain multiple indicators of distal constructs (R. Kanfer, 1992) from each construct domain—for example, the cognitive ability, personality, and affective domains. Goal difficulty levels would serve as proximal effects of those distal constructs and also as proximal exogenous variables predicting measures of the mediators (development, application, and revision of strategies). Several extensions of this baseline design would include multiple goals, intermediate-level factors of ability, and other components of the personality and temperament domains. Goal orientation and/or action-state orientation typify alternative constructs to be examined relative to conscientiousness and other traits of the Big Five. Competitive testing of sets of these models could suggest further revisions, which would be fit back into the framework for goal striving proposed in this chapter.

Another potential extension of this baseline study involves multilevel analyses using a hybrid area, social psychophysiology (Cacioppo, Petty, & Tassinary, 1989). Cacioppo and Berntson (1992), in proposing a multilevel doctrine for within-person analysis, briefly allude to the investigation of job attitudes using a micromacro perspective. A study by Gellatly and Meyer (1992) shows how such methods could link goal striving to individual differences. One contribution of this study is its multiple-indicator perspective on goal difficulty—a perspective developed out of physiological, cognitive, and task performance measures. The linking of social-psychophysiological methods to complex simulations is also advocated. Such methods, when combined with complex task simulations (Cervone et al., 1991; Gopher, 1993; Locke, Smith, Erez, Chah, & Schaffer, 1994; Wood, Bandura, & Bailey, 1990), should yield data that bear on multiple levels of functioning. Additional conceptual leverage can be gained from longitudinal studies of goal striving. These methods allow the study of multiple goals (within-task or between-task) and also permit researchers to study goal conflict (Locke et al., 1994), a content attribute inherent in sets of goals.

Another potential extension of the dynamic and multilevel perspectives emphasized here pertains to the job performance domain, itself receiving renewed attention (Austin & Villanova, 1992; Borman, 1991; J. P. Campbell, McCloy, Oppler, & Sager, 1993). First, however, appropriate matching of predictor and criterion measures is required. Job performance could be modeled to some extent on J. P. Campbell, McCloy, Oppler, and Sager's framework (1993), in which eight factors make up the criterion space. Second, given the general recognition of the value of using multiple levels of analysis in conceptualizing and measuring work performance—for example, using both task and job layers—investigations designed along these lines should assess multiple goals and link them to multiple measures of effectiveness. Third, in accordance with the concept of motivational dynamics over time, investigations should consider criteria that are dynamic. Applying theory to this third issue, as suggested by Austin, L. G. Humphreys, and Hulin (1989), necessitates identification of clusters of individuals with comparable patterns of change. Hofmann, Jacobs, and Baratta (1993), using methods suggested by Nesselroade (1991), illustrated this principle empirically in a multiyear study. Ultimately, without relevant, reliable, and practical criterion measures, goal setting in actual organizations may be ineffective.

Extension of these conceptions to the team/group level of analysis is required, and individual differences undoubtedly play a role at this level of aggregation. Team composition research, for example, could be extended to multivariate combinations of the individual difference measures addressed throughout this volume. New knowledge about the effects of applying Eysenck's PEN model to selection of teams (and the resultant effects on team-level goals) could shed light on group interaction and performance. Applying the trait of conscientiousness, along with other Big Five traits, to team selection might suggest that quality norms would result in a homogeneous group high on conscientiousness. One of this chapter's authors (James Austin) is currently evaluating this hypothesis (Waung & Austin, 1995).

An additional issue for future research involves questions about self-regulation, viewed as a process linking goals, performance monitoring, and decision making. Could there be individual differences in self-regulation skills themselves, or are the individual difference domains reviewed here sufficient to account for variance in self-regulation? How (and how easily) is self-regulation acquired? Is there utility in training interventions aimed at increasing levels of self-regulation, or is self-regulation a stable characteristic of individuals?

Statistical analysis, measurement, and design issues are important in planning research based on these proposals. Concerning *statistical analysis,* a study by Sawyer (1993) evaluating competing models of role-goal clarity deserves mention because of its use of covariance structure analysis. The Lee et al. (1991) results, also significant, should be replicated using confirmatory factor analysis. Concerning *measurement,* individual differences in conative constructs are reviewed by Snow and Jackson (1994) within a two-part framework for conation: motivation and volition. An interesting concept put forward in their review is the use of two "pathways"—one defined for performance commitment and one for performance. The former comprises a sequence from wishes to wants to intentions to action, while the latter links knowledge, skills, and abilities to action. Snow and Jackson review measures of achievement orientation, self-regulation, transitional interests and styles, self-directed constructs, and other-directed constructs. They conclude that research to develop the psychometric properties of current measures and research using novel computerized formats would aid in developing networks linking motivation/volition, on the one hand, and cognition/affect/behavior, on the other. Concerning *design,* a consonant recommendation is for doubly multivariate studies incorporating multiple occasions and multiple measures. Furthermore, models and studies that incorporate states and traits (Steyer, Graser, & Widaman, 1993) could also assist in evaluating an array of causal processes in goal setting. Individual differences constitute the traits in such models, with motivational interventions and cognitive processes constituting the states. State-trait theories provide models that encompass shifting situation and stable individual constructs; this logic permits both differences in a stable tendency and situations in which the state may differ across subgroups or persons.

The utility of the approach outlined above is theoretical, and its practical implications remain to be demonstrated. However, it is possible to speculate concerning implementation using the goal system design framework presented by Pritchard, Roth, Jones, Galgay, and Watson (1988). This system, based on the framework of Naylor et al. (1980), recognizes both design and implementation issues. Among the design issues addressed by Pritchard et al. are criterion measurement, feedback, targeted versus overall goal-setting strategies, participation, difficulty levels, public versus private goals, and timing.

In conclusion, this chapter has advocated the utility of adding well-defined and empirically supported constructs from individual difference domains to multilevel models of goal striving. A major ramification of considering individual differences with respect to work motivation is that complexity and moderating influences must be recognized and incorporated. Whether one prefers a single motivational perspective or the several frameworks employed here, there are ample directions for future research. Such extensions will heed the call of Cronbach (1957) to combine experimental and correlational strategies and will also continue the blending of science and practice identified by Dunnette (1990).

References

Ackerman, P. L., & Humphreys, L. G. (1990). Individual differences theory in industrial and organizational psychology. In M. D. Dunnette & L. M. Hough (Eds.), *Handbook of industrial and organizational psychology* (2nd ed.; Vol. 1, pp. 223–282). Palo Alto, CA: Consulting Psychologists Press.

Allport, G. W. (1937). *Personality: A psychological interpretation.* Troy, MO: Holt, Rinehart & Winston.

Apter, M. J. (1989). *Reversal theory: Motivation, emotion, and personality.* London: Routledge.

Austin, J. T. (1989). Effects of shifts in goal origin on goal acceptance and attainment. *Organizational Behavior and Human Decision Processes, 46,* 315–335.

Austin, J. T., Humphreys, L. G., & Hulin, C. L. (1989). Another view of dynamic criteria: A critical reanalysis of Barrett, Caldwell, and Alexander. *Personnel Psychology, 42,* 583–596.

Austin, J. T., & Villanova, P. (1992). The criterion problem 1917–1992. *Journal of Applied Psychology, 77,* 836–874.

Baddaley, A. (1986). *Working memory.* Cambridge, UK: Cambridge University Press.

Baker, J. G., Zevon, M. A., & Rounds, J. B. (1994). Differences in positive and negative affect dimensions: Latent trait analysis. *Personality and Individual Differences, 17,* 161–167.

Bandura, A. (1986). *Social foundations of thought and action.* Englewood Cliffs, NJ: Prentice-Hall.

Bandura, A. (1991). Social cognitive theory of self-regulation. *Organizational Behavior and Human Decision Processes, 50,* 248–287.

Bandura, A., & Cervone, D. (1983). Self-evaluative and self-efficacy mechanisms governing the motivational effects of goal systems. *Journal of Personality and Social Psychology, 45,* 1017–1028.

Bandura, A., & Cervone, D. (1986). Differential engagement of self-reactive influences in cognitive motivation. *Organizational Behavior and Human Decision Processes, 38,* 92–113.

Bargh, J. A., & Gollwitzer, P. M. (1994). Environmental control of goal directed action: Automatic and strategic contingencies between situations and behaviors. In W. Spaulding (Ed.), *Integrative views of motivation, cognition, and emotion* (Nebraska Symposium on Motivation, Vol. 41, pp. 71–124). Lincoln: University of Nebraska Press.

Baron, R. A. (Ed.). (1991). Motivation in work settings: Reflections on the core of organizational research [Special issue]. *Motivation and Emotion, 15,* 1–139.

Barrick, M. R., & Mount, M. K. (1991). The Big Five personality dimensions and job performance: A meta-analysis. *Personnel Psychology, 44,* 1–26.

Barrick, M. R., Mount, M. K., & Strauss, J. P. (1993). Conscientiousness and performance of sales representatives: Test of the mediating effects of goal setting. *Journal of Applied Psychology, 78,* 715–722.

Bass, B. M. (1994). Continuity and change in the evolution of work and human resources management. *Human Resource Management, 33,* 3–31.

Bates, J. E., & Wachs, T. D. (Eds.). (1994). *Temperament: Individual differences at the interface of biology and behavior.* Washington, DC: American Psychological Association.

Beach, L. R. (1990). *Image theory: Decision making in personal and organizational contexts.* New York: Wiley.

Bernardin, H. J., & Bownas, D. A. (Eds.). (1985). *Personality assessment and personnel selection.* New York: Praeger.

Block, J. (1995). A contrarian view of the five-factor approach to personality description. *Psychological Bulletin, 117,* 187–215.

Bolles, R. C. (1978). Whatever happened to motivation? *Educational Psychologist, 13,* 1–13.

Borman, W. C. (1991). Job behavior, performance, and effectiveness. In M. D. Dunnette & L. M. Hough (Eds.), *Handbook of industrial and organizational psychology* (2nd ed.; Vol. 2, pp. 271–326). Palo Alto, CA: Consulting Psychologists Press.

Borman, W. C., & Motowidlo, S. J. (1993). Expanding the criterion domain to include elements of contextual performance. In N. Schmitt, W. C. Borman, & Associates, *Personnel selection in organizations* (pp. 71–98). San Francisco: Jossey-Bass.

Brief, A. P., Burke, M. J., George, J. M., Robinson, B. S., & Webster, J. (1988). Should negative affectivity remain an unmeasured variable in the study of job stress? *Journal of Applied Psychology, 73,* 193–198.

Brockner, J. (1988). *Self-esteem at work: Research, theory, and practice.* New York: Lexington Books.

Burke, M. J., Brief, A. P., George, J. M., Roberson, L., & Webster, J. (1989). Measuring affect at work: Confirmatory analyses of competing mood structures with conceptual linkage to cortical regulatory systems. *Journal of Personality and Social Psychology, 57,* 1091–1102.

Cacioppo, J. T., & Berntson, G. (1992). Social psychological contributions to the decade of the brain: Doctrine of multilevel analysis. *American Psychologist, 47,* 1019–1028.

Cacioppo, J. T., Petty, R. E., & Tassinary, L. G. (1989). Social psychophysiology: A new look. In L. Berkowitz (Ed.), *Advances in experimental social psychology* (Vol. 22, pp. 39–87). San Diego, CA: Academic Press.

Campbell, D. J. (1982). Determinants of choice of goal difficulty level: A review of situational and personality influences. *Journal of Occupational Psychology, 55,* 79–95.

Campbell, J. P., McCloy, R. A., Oppler, S. H., & Sager, C. E. (1993). A theory of performance. In N. Schmitt, W. Borman, & Associates, *Personnel selection in organizations* (pp. 35–70). San Francisco: Jossey-Bass.

Campbell, J. P., & Pritchard, R. D. (1976). Motivation theory in industrial and organizational psychology. In M. D. Dunnette (Ed.), *Handbook of industrial and organizational psychology* (pp. 63–130). Skokie, IL: Rand McNally.

Campion, M. A., & Lord, R. G. (1982). A control systems conceptualization of the goal-setting and changing process. *Organizational Behavior and Human Performance, 30,* 265–287.

Carroll, J. B. (1993). *Human cognitive abilities.* New York: Cambridge University Press.

Carver, C. S. (1979). A cybernetic model of self-attention processes. *Journal of Personality and Social Psychology, 37,* 1251–1281.

Carver, C. S., & Scheier, W. F. (1981). *Attention and self-regulation: A control theory approach to human behavior.* New York: Springer-Verlag.

Carver, C. S., & Scheier, M. F. (1988). A control-process perspective on anxiety. *Anxiety Research, 1,* 17–22.

Carver, C. S., & Scheier, M. F. (1990). Origins and functions of positive and negative affect: A control process view. *Psychological Review, 97,* 19–35.

Cervone, D. (1991). The two disciplines of personality psychology. *Psychological Science, 2,* 371–376.

Cervone, D., Jiwani, N., & Wood, R. (1991). Goal setting and the differential influence of self-regulatory processes on complex decision-making performance. *Journal of Personality and Social Psychology, 61,* 257–266.

Cooper, L., & Regian, J. W. (1982). Attention, perception, and intelligence. In R. J. Sternberg (Ed.), *Handbook of human intelligence* (pp. 132–169). New York: Cambridge University Press.

Corno, L., & Kanfer, R. (1993). The role of volition in learning and performance. *Review of Research in Education, 19,* 301–341.

Costa, P. T., & McCrae, R. R. (1992). *Manual for the Five-Factor Inventory* (rev. ed.). Odessa, FL: Psychological Assessment Resources.

Cranny, C. J., Smith, P., & Stone, E. F. (Eds.). (1992). *Job satisfaction.* Lexington, MA: Lexington.

Cronbach, L. J. (1957). The two disciplines of scientific psychology. *American Psychologist, 12,* 671–683.

Cropanzano, R., James, K., & Citera, M. (1992). A goal hierarchy model of personality, motivation, and leadership. In L. L. Cummings & B. M. Staw (Eds.), *Research in organizational behavior* (Vol. 15, pp. 267–322). Greenwich, CT: JAI Press.

Csikszentmihalyi, M. (1990). *Flow: The psychology of optimal experience.* New York: HarperCollins.

Damos, D. L. (Ed.). (1991). *Multiple-task performance.* London: Taylor & Francis.

Dawis, R. V. (1991). Vocational interests, values, and preferences. In M. D. Dunnette & L. M. Hough (Eds.), *Handbook of industrial and organizational psychology* (2nd ed.; Vol. 2, pp. 833–871). Palo Alto, CA: Consulting Psychologists Press.

Diener, E. (1984). Subject well-being. *Psychological Bulletin, 95,* 542–575.

Duda, J., & Nicholls, J. (1992). Dimensions of achievement motivation in schoolwork and sport. *Journal of Educational Psychology, 84,* 290–299.

Dunnette, M. D. (1990). Blending the science and practice of industrial and organizational psychology. In M. D. Dunnette & L. M. Hough (Eds.), *Handbook of industrial and organizational psychology* (2nd ed.; Vol. 1, pp. 1–27). Palo Alto, CA: Consulting Psychologists Press.

Dweck, C. S. (1986). Motivational processes affecting learning. *American Psychologist, 41,* 1040–1048.

Dweck, C. S., & Leggett, E. L. (1988). A social-cognitive approach to motivation and personality. *Psychological Review, 95,* 256–273.

Earley, P. C., & Lituchy, T. R. (1991). Delineating goal and efficacy effects: A test of three models. *Journal of Applied Psychology, 76,* 81–98.

Erez, M. (1990). Performance quality and work motivation. In U. Kleinbeck, H.-H. Quast, H. Thierry, & H. Hacker (Eds.), *Work motivation* (pp. 41–52). Hillsdale, NJ: Erlbaum.

Erez, M., & Kanfer, F. H. (1983). The role of goal acceptance in goal-setting and task performance. *Academy of Management Review, 8,* 454–463.

Eysenck, H. J. (1984). The place of individual differences in scientific psychology. In J. R. Royce & L. Mos (Eds.), *Annals of theoretical psychology* (Vol. 1, pp. 233–285). New York: Plenum.

Eysenck, H. J. (1991). Dimensions of personality—16, 5, or 3: Criteria for a taxonomic paradigm. *Personality and Individual Differences, 12,* 773–790.

Eysenck, M. W. (1988). Anxiety and attention. *Anxiety Research, 1,* 9–15.

Eysenck, M. W. (1994). *Individual differences: Normal and abnormal.* Hillsdale, NJ: Erlbaum.

Farr, J. L., Hofmann, D. A., & Ringenbach, K. L. (1993). Goal orientation and action control theory: Implications for industrial and organizational psychology. In C. L. Cooper & I. T. Robertson (Eds.), *International review of industrial and organizational psychology 1993* (Vol. 8, pp. 193–233). Chichester, UK: Wiley.

Fenigstein, A. (1987). On the nature of public and private self-consciousness. *Journal of Personality, 55,* 543–553.

Fishbein, M., & Ajzen, I. (1975). *Belief, attitude, intention, and behavior: An introduction to theory and research.* Reading, MA: Addison-Wesley.

Fleishman, E. A., & Mumford, M. (1989). Abilities as causes of individual differences in skill acquisition. *Human Performance, 2,* 201–223.

Ford, M. E. (1992). *Motivating humans: Goals, emotions, and personal agency beliefs.* Newbury Park, CA: Sage.

Frese, M., & Zapf, D. (1994). Action as the core of work psychology: A German approach. In H. C. Triandis, M. D. Dunnette, & L. M. Hough (Eds.), *Handbook of industrial and organizational psychology* (2nd ed., Vol. 4, pp. 271–340). Palo Alto, CA: Consulting Psychologists Press.

Gallistel, C. R. (1994). Elementary and complex units of behaviour. In G. d'Ydewalle, P. Eelen, & P. Bertelson (Eds.), *International perspectives on psychological science* (Vol. 2, pp. 157–175). Howe, UK: Erlbaum.

Gardner, D. G., Dunham, R. B., Cummings, L. L., & Pierce, J. L. (1989). Focus of attention at work: Construct definition and empirical validation. *Journal of Occupational Psychology, 62,* 61–77.

Gellatly, I. R., & Meyer, J. P. (1992). The effects of goal difficulty on physiological arousal, cognition, and task performance. *Journal of Applied Psychology, 77*, 694–704.

George, J. M., & Brief, A. P. (1992). Feeling good—doing good: A conceptual analysis of the mood at work/organizational spontaneity relationship. *Psychological Bulletin, 112*, 310–329.

Gernsbacher, M. A., & Faust, M. E. (1991). The mechanism of suppression: A component of general comprehension skill. *Journal of Experimental Psychology, 17*, 245–262.

Gilliland, S., & Landis, R. (1992). Quality and quantity goals in a complex decision task: Strategies and outcomes. *Journal of Applied Psychology, 77*, 672–681.

Gist, M. E., & Mitchell, T. R. (1992). Self-efficacy: A theoretical analysis of its determinants and malleability. *Academy of Management Review, 17*, 183–211.

Gollwitzer, P. M. (1990). Action phases and mind-sets. In E. T. Higgins & R. M. Sorrentino (Eds.), *Handbook of motivation and cognition* (Vol. 2, pp. 53–92). New York: Guilford.

Gollwitzer, P. M. (1993). Goal achievement: The role of intentions. In M. Hewstone & W. Stroebe (Eds.), *European review of social psychology* (Vol. 4, pp. 141–185). Chichester, UK: Wiley.

Gopher, D. A. (1993). The skill of attention control: Acquisition and execution of attention strategies. In D. Meyer & S. Kornblum (Eds.), *Attention and performance XIV* (pp. 299–322). Cambridge, MA: MIT Press.

Gottfredson, L. (Ed.). (1986). The *g* factor in employment [Special issue]. *Journal of Vocational Behavior, 29*, 293–450.

Guion, R. M., & Gottier, R. F. (1965). Validity of personality measures in personnel selection. *Personnel Psychology, 18*, 135–164.

Halisch, F., & Kuhl, J. (Eds.). (1987). *Motivation, intention, and volition.* Heidelberg, Germany: Springer-Verlag.

Hall, D. T., & Foster, L. W. (1977). A psychological success cycle and goal-setting: Goals, performance, and attitudes. *Academy of Management Journal, 20*, 282–290.

Hanisch, K. A. (1995). Behavioral families and multiple causes: Matching the complexity of responses to the complexity of antecedents. *Current Directions in Psychological Science, 4*, 156–162.

Harnqvist, K., Gustafsson, J.-E., Muthen, B. O., & Nelson, G. (1994). Hierarchical models of ability at individual and class levels. *Intelligence, 18*, 165–187.

Hilgard, E. R. (1987). *Psychology in America: A historical survey.* Orlando, FL: Harcourt Brace Jovanovich.

Hofmann, D. A., Jacobs, R., & Baratta, J. E. (1993). Dynamic criteria and the measurement of change. *Journal of Applied Psychology, 78,* 194–204.

Hogan, R. T. (1991). Personality and personality measurement. In M. D. Dunnette & L. M. Hough (Eds.), *Handbook of industrial and organizational psychology* (2nd ed.; Vol. 2, pp. 873–919). Palo Alto, CA: Consulting Psychologists Press.

Holland, J. L. (1985). *Making vocational choices* (2nd ed.). Englewood Cliffs, NJ: Prentice-Hall.

Hollenbeck, J. R. (1989). Control theory and the perception of work environments: The effects of focus of attention on affective and behavioral reactions to work. *Organizational Behavior and Human Decision Processes, 43,* 406–430.

Hollenbeck, J., & Brief, A. P. (1987). The effects of individual differences and goal origin on goal-setting and performance. *Organizational Behavior and Human Decision Processes, 40,* 392–414.

Hollenbeck, J. R., & Klein, H. J. (1987). Goal commitment and the goal-setting process: Problems, prospects, and proposals for future research. *Journal of Applied Psychology, 72,* 212–220.

Horn, J. (1988). Thinking about human abilities. In J. Nesselroade & R. B. Cattell (Eds.), *Handbook of multivariate experimental psychology* (2nd ed., pp. 645–685). New York: Plenum.

Humphreys, L. G. (1985). General intelligence: An integration of factor, test, and simplex theory. In B. B. Wolman (Ed.), *Handbook of intelligence: Theories, measurement, and applications* (pp. 201–224). New York: Wiley.

Humphreys, L. G. (1994). Intelligence from the standpoint of a (pragmatic) behaviorist (with commentary). *Psychological Inquiry, 5,* 179–214.

Humphreys, M. S., & Revelle, W. (1984). Personality, motivation, and performance: A theory of the relationship between individual differences and information processing. *Psychological Review, 91,* 153–184.

Hunt, E. B., & Lansman, M. (1982). Individual differences in attention. In R. J. Sternberg (Ed.), *Advances in the psychology of intelligence* (Vol. 1). Hillsdale, NJ: Erlbaum.

Huseman, M., Hatfield, K., & Miles, J. (1987). Equity sensitivity construct. *Academy of Management Journal, 30,* 322–336.

Hyland, M. E. (1988). Motivational control theory: An integrative framework. *Journal of Personality and Social Psychology, 55,* 642–651.

Izard, C. (1993). Four systems for emotional activation: Cognitive and noncognitive processes. *Psychological Review, 100,* 68–90.

James, L. R., & Brett, J. M. (1984). Mediators, moderators, and tests for mediation. *Journal of Applied Psychology, 69,* 307–321.

Jensen, A. R. (1985). The nature of the black-white difference on various psychometric tests: Spearman's hypothesis (with commentary). *Behavioral and Brain Sciences, 8,* 193–263.

Kanfer, R. (1990). Motivation theory and industrial and organizational psychology. In M. D. Dunnette & L. M. Hough (Eds.), *Handbook of industrial and organizational psychology* (2nd ed.; Vol. 1, pp. 75–170). Palo Alto, CA: Consulting Psychologists Press.

Kanfer, R. (1992). Work motivation: New directions in theory and research. In C. L. Cooper & I. T. Robertson (Eds.), *International review of industrial and organizational psychology 1992* (Vol. 7, pp. 1–53). Chichester, UK: Wiley.

Kanfer, R., & Ackerman, P. L. (1989). Motivation and cognitive abilities: An integrative/aptitude-treatment interaction approach to skill acquisition. *Journal of Applied Psychology, 74,* 657–690.

Kanfer, R., Ackerman, P. L., Murtha, T. C., Dugdale, B., & Nelson, L. (1994). Goal-setting, conditions of practice, and task performance: A resource allocation perspective. *Journal of Applied Psychology, 79,* 826–835.

Kanfer, R., & Kanfer, F. H. (1991). Goals and self-regulation: Applications of theory to work settings. In M. L. Maehr & P. R. Pintrich (Eds.), *Advances in achievement and motivation* (Vol. 7, pp. 287–326). Greenwich, CT: JAI Press.

Karoly, P. (1993). Mechanisms of self-regulation: A systems view. *Annual Review of Psychology, 44,* 23–52.

Katzell, R. A. (1994). Contemporary meta-trends in industrial and organizational psychology. In H. C. Triandis, M. D. Dunnette, & L. M. Hough (Eds.), *Handbook of industrial and organizational psychology* (2nd ed.; Vol. 4, pp. 1–89). Palo Alto, CA: Consulting Psychologists Press.

Katzell, R. A., & Austin, J. T. (1992). From then to now: The development of industrial-organizational psychology in the United States. *Journal of Applied Psychology, 77,* 803–835.

Katzell, R. A., & Thompson, D. E. (1990a). Work motivation: Theory and practice. *American Psychologist, 45,* 144–153.

Klein, H. J. (1989). An integrated control theory model of work motivation. *Academy of Management Review, 14,* 150–172.

Klein, H. J. (1991a). Further evidence on the relationship between goal setting and expectancy theories. *Organizational Behavior and Human Decision Processes, 49,* 230–257.

Klein, H. J. (1991b). Control theory and understanding motivated behavior: A different conclusion. *Motivation and Emotion, 15,* 29–44.

Kleinbeck, U., Quast, H.-H., & Schwarz, R. (1989). Volitional effects on performance: Conceptual considerations and results from dual-task studies. In R. Kanfer, P. Ackerman, & R. Cudeck (Eds.), *Abilities, motivation, and methodology* (pp. 23–42). Hillsdale, NJ: Erlbaum.

Kleinbeck, U., Quast, H.-H., Thierry, H., & Hacker, H. (Eds.). (1990). *Work motivation.* Hillsdale, NJ: Erlbaum.

Klinger, E. (1975). Consequences of commitment to and disengagement from incentives. *Psychological Review, 82,* 1–25.

Klinger, E. (1995). Effects of motivation and emotion on thought flow and cognition: Assessment and findings. In P. E. Shrout & S. T. Fiske (Eds.), *Personality research, methods, and theory* (pp. 257–270). Hillsdale, NJ: Erlbaum.

Kluckhohn, C., & Murray, H. A. (Eds.). (1949). *Personality and culture.* New York: Knopf.

Kuhl, J. (1986). Motivation and information processing: A new look at decision making, dynamic change, and action control. In R. M. Sorrentino & E. T. Higgins (Eds.), *Handbook of motivation and cognition* (Vol. 1, pp. 404–434). New York: Guilford.

Kuhl, J. (1992). A theory of self-regulation: Action versus state orientation, self-discrimination, and some applications (with commentary). *Applied Psychology: An International Review, 41,* 97–129.

Kuhl, J. (1994). Motivation and volition. In G. d'Ydewalle, P. Eelen, & P. Bertelson (Eds.), *International perspectives on psychological science* (Vol. 2, pp. 311–340). Howe, UK: Erlbaum.

Kuhl, J., & Koch, B. (1984). Motivational determinants of motor performance: The hidden second task. *Psychological Research, 46,* 143–153.

Landy, F. J. (1993). Early influences on the development of industrial-organizational psychology. In T. K. Fagan & G. R. VandenBos (Eds.), *Exploring applied psychology: Origins and critical analyses* (pp. 80–118). Washington, DC: American Psychological Association.

Landy, F. J., & Becker, W. S. (1987). Motivation theory reconsidered. In B. M. Staw & L. L. Cummings (Eds.), *Research in organizational behavior* (Vol. 9, pp. 1–38). Greenwich, CT: JAI Press.

Landy, F. J., Shankster, L. J., & Kohler, S. S. (1994). Personnel selection and placement. *Annual Review of Psychology, 45,* 261–296.

Lee, C., Bobko, P., Earley, P. C., & Locke, E. A. (1991). An empirical analysis of a goal setting questionnaire. *Journal of Organizational Behavior, 12,* 467–482.

Lewis, M., & Haviland, J. M. (Eds.). (1993). *Handbook of emotions.* New York: Guilford.

Little, B. R. (1989). Personal projects analysis: Trivial pursuits, magnificent obsessions, and the search for coherence. In A. R. Buss & N. Cantor (Eds.), *Personality psychology: Recent trends and emerging directions* (pp. 15–31). New York: Springer-Verlag.

Little, B. R., Lecci, L., & Watkinson, B. (1992). Personality and personal projects: Linking Big Five and PAC units of analysis. *Journal of Personality, 60,* 501–525.

Locke, E. A. (1968). Toward a theory of task motivation and incentives. *Organizational Behavior and Human Performance, 3,* 157–189.

Locke, E. A. (1976). The nature and causes of job satisfaction. In M. D. Dunnette (Ed.), *Handbook of industrial and organizational psychology* (pp. 1297–1349). Skokie, IL: Rand McNally.

Locke, E. A. (1982). Relation of goal level to performance with a short work period and multiple goal levels. *Journal of Applied Psychology, 67,* 512–514.

Locke, E. A. (1991a). Goal theory vs. control theory: Contrasting approaches to understanding work motivation. *Motivation and Emotion, 15,* 9–28.

Locke, E. A. (1991b). Introduction to the special issue. *Organizational Behavior and Human Decision Processes, 50,* 151–153.

Locke, E. A., & Henne, D. (1986). Work motivation theories. In C. L. Cooper & I. T. Robertson (Eds.), *International review of industrial and organizational psychology 1988* (Vol. 1). Chichester, UK: Wiley.

Locke, E. A., & Latham, G. P. (1990). *A theory of goal-setting and task performance.* Englewood Cliffs, NJ: Prentice-Hall.

Locke, E. A., & Latham, G. P. (1994). Goal setting theory. In H. F. O'Neil & M. Drillings (Eds.), *Motivation: Theory and research* (pp. 13–29). Hillsdale, NJ: Erlbaum.

Locke, E. A., Latham, G. P., & Erez, M. (1988). The determinants of goal commitment. *Academy of Management Review, 13,* 23–39.

Locke, E. A., Shaw, K. N., Saari, L. M., & Latham, G. P. (1981). Goal-setting and task performance: 1969–1980. *Psychological Bulletin, 90,* 125–152.

Locke, E. A., Smith, K. G., Erez, M., Chah, D.-O., & Schaffer, A. (1994). The effects of intra-individual goal conflict on performance. *Journal of Management, 20,* 67–91.

Lohman, D. F., Pellegrino, J. W., Alderton, D. L., & Regian, J. W. (1987). Dimensions and components of individual differences in spatial abilities. In S. H. Irvine & S. E. Newstead (Eds.), *Intelligence and cognition: Contemporary frames of reference* (pp. 253–312). Dordrecht, Holland: Martinus Nijhoff.

London, H., & Exner, J. (Eds.). (1978). *Dimensions of personality.* New York: Wiley.

Lord, R. G., & Hanges, P. M. (1987). A control system model of organizational motivation: Theoretical development and applied implications. *Behavioral Science, 32,* 161–178.

Lord, R. G., & Levy, P. E. (1994). Moving from cognition to action: A control theory perspective. *Applied Psychology: An International Review, 41,* 97–129.

Lubinski, D., & Dawis, R. V. (1992). Aptitudes, skills, and proficiencies. In M. D. Dunnette & L. M. Hough (Eds.), *Handbook of industrial and organizational psychology* (2nd ed.; Vol. 3, pp. 1–59). Palo Alto, CA: Consulting Psychologists Press.

Mabe, P. A., & West, S. G. (1982). Validity of self-evaluation of ability: A review and meta-analysis. *Journal of Applied Psychology, 69,* 280–296.

Mane, A., & Donchin, E. (1989). The space fortress game. *Acta Psychologica, 71,* 17–22.

March, J. G., & Simon, H. (1993). *Organizations* (2nd ed.). New York: Blackwell.

Matthews, G., Davies, D. R., & Lees, J. L. (1990). Arousal, extraversion, and individual differences in resource availability. *Journal of Personality and Social Psychology, 59,* 150–168.

McClelland, D. C., & Boyatzis, R. E. (1982). The leader motive pattern and long-term success in management. *Journal of Applied Psychology, 67,* 737–743.

McCrae, R. R. (Ed.). (1992). The Five-Factor Model: Issues and applications [Special issue]. *Journal of Personality, 60,* 175–532.

Messick, S. (1992). Multiple intelligences or multilevel intelligence? Selective emphasis on distinctive properties of hierarchy: On Gardner's *Frames of mind* and Sternberg's *Beyond IQ* in the context of theory and research on the structure of human abilities. *Psychological Inquiry, 3,* 365–384.

Miller, G. A., Galanter, E., & Pribram, K. H. (1960). *Plans and the structure of behavior.* Troy, MO: Holt, Rinehart & Winston.

Mone, M. A., & Baker, D. D. (1992). Cognitive, affective, and behavioral consequences of self-set goals: An integrative, dynamic model. *Human Performance, 5,* 213–234.

Murphy, K. R. (1988). Psychological measurement: Abilities and skills. In C. L. Cooper & I. T. Robertson (Eds.), *International review of industrial and organizational psychology 1988* (Vol. 3, pp. 213–243). Chichester, UK: Wiley.

Naylor, J. C., & Ilgen, D. R. (1984). Goal-setting: A theoretical analysis of a motivational technology. In B. M. Staw & L. L. Cummings (Eds.), *Research in organizational behavior* (Vol. 6, pp. 95–140). Greenwich, CT: JAI Press.

Naylor, J. C., Pritchard, R. D., & Ilgen, D. R. (1980). *A theory of behavior in organizations.* San Diego, CA: Academic Press.

Nelson, T. D. (1993). The hierarchical organization of behavior: A useful feedback model of self-regulation. *Current Directions in Psychological Science, 2,* 121–126.

Nesselroade, J. R. (1991). Interindividual differences in intraindividual change. In L. Collins & J. Horn (Eds.), *Best methods for the analysis of change* (pp. 92–105). Washington, DC: American Psychological Association.

Nord, W. R., Brief, A. P., Atieh, J. M., & Doherty, E. M. (1988). Work values and the conduct of organizational behavior. In B. Staw & L. L. Cummings (Eds.), *Research in organizational behavior* (Vol. 10, pp. 1–42). Greenwich, CT: JAI Press.

O'Neil, H. F., & Drillings, M. (Eds.). (1994). *Motivation: Theory and research.* Hillsdale, NJ: Erlbaum.

Pederson, N. L., Plomin, R., & McClearn, G. E. (1994). Is there *G* beyond *g?* (Is there genetic influence on specific cognitive abilities independent of genetic influence on general cognitive ability?) *Intelligence, 18,* 133–143.

Pervin, L. A. (1983). The stasis and flow of behavior: Toward a theory of goals. In M. M. Page (Ed.), *Nebraska Symposium on Motivation* (Vol. 30, pp. 1–53). Lincoln: University of Nebraska Press.

Pervin, L. A. (Ed.). (1989). *Goal concepts in personality and social psychology.* Hillsdale, NJ: Erlbaum.

Pervin, L. A. (Ed.). (1990). *Handbook of personality theory and research.* New York: Guilford.

Powers, W. T. (1973). *Behavior: The control of perception.* Hawthorne, NY: Aldine.

Pritchard, R. D., Roth, P. L., Jones, S. D., Galgay, P. J., & Watson, M. D. (1988). Designing a goal-setting system to enhance performance: A practical guide. *Organizational Dynamics, 18,* 69–78.

Rapkin, B. D., & Fischer, K. (1992). Personal goals of older adults: Issues in assessment and prediction. *Psychology and Aging, 7,* 127–137.

Ree, M. J., & Earles, J. A. (1992). Intelligence is the best predictor of job performance. *Current Directions in Psychological Science, 1,* 86–89.

Revelle, W. (1987). Personality and motivation: Sources of inefficiency in cognitive performance. *Journal of Research in Personality, 21,* 436–452.

Roberson, L. (1989). Assessing personal work goals in the organizational setting: Development and evaluation of the Work Concerns Inventory. *Organizational Behavior and Human Decision Processes, 44,* 345–367.

Robinson, J. P., Shaver, P. R., & Wrightsman, L. S. (Eds.). (1991). *Measures of personality and social psychological attitudes.* New York: Academic Press.

Rokeach, M. (1973). *The nature of human values.* New York: Basic Books.

Royce, J. R. (1979). Toward a viable theory of individual differences. *Journal of Personality and Social Psychology, 37,* 1927–1931.

Royce, J. R., & Powell, A. (1983). *Theory of personality and individual differences: Factors, systems, processes.* Englewood Cliffs, NJ: Prentice-Hall.

Roznowski, M., & Hanisch, K. A. (1990). Building systematic heterogeneity into measures of work attitudes and behavior. *Journal of Vocational Behavior, 36,* 361–375.

Roznowski, M., & Hulin, C. L. (1992). The scientific merit of valid measures of general constructs with special reference to job satisfaction and job withdrawal. In C. J. Cranny, P. C. Smith, & E. F. Stone (Eds.), *Job satisfaction* (pp. 123–163). New York: Lexington Books.

Ryan, R. M. (1992). Agency and organization: Intrinsic motivation, autonomy, and the self in psychological development. In J. E. Jacobs (Ed.), *Perspectives on Motivation* (Nebraska Symposium on Motivation, Vol. 40, pp. 1–56). Lincoln: University of Nebraska Press.

Ryan, T. A. (1970). *Intentional behavior.* New York: Ronald.

Ryan, T. A., & Smith, P. C. (1954). *Principles of industrial psychology.* New York: Ronald.

Saavedra, R., & Earley, P. C. (1990). Choice of task and goal under conditions of general and specific affective inducement. Unpublished manuscript, University of Minnesota.

Sarason, I. (1988). Anxiety, self-preoccupation, and attention. *Anxiety Research, 1,* 3–7.

Sawyer, J. E. (1993). Goal and process clarity: Specification of multiple constructs of role ambiguity and a structural equation model of their antecedents and consequences. *Journal of Applied Psychology, 77,* 130–142.

Schank, R. C., & Abelson, R. P. (1977). *Scripts, plans, goals, and understanding.* Hillsdale, NJ: Erlbaum.

Schmidt, F. L., & Hunter, J. E. (1992). Development of a causal model of processes determining job performance. *Current Directions in Psychological Science, 1,* 89–92.

Schwartz, S. H. (1992). Universals in the content and structure of values: Theoretical advances and tests in 20 countries. In M. Zanna (Ed.), *Advances in experimental social psychology* (Vol. 25, pp. 1–65). San Diego, CA: Academic Press.

Simon, H. A. (1967). Motivational and emotional controls on cognition. *Psychological Review, 74,* 29–39.

Simon, H. A. (1994). The bottleneck of attention: Connecting thought with motivation. In W. Spaulding (Ed.), *Integrative views of motivation, cognition, and emotion* (Nebraska Symposium on Motivation, Vol. 41, pp. 1–21). Lincoln: University of Nebraska Press.

Snow, R., & Jackson, D. N. (1994). Individual differences in conation: Selected constructs and measures. In H. F. O'Neil & M. Drillings (Eds.), *Motivation: Theory and research* (pp. 71–99). Hillsdale, NJ: Erlbaum.

Snyder, M. (1979). Self-monitoring processes. *Advances in Experimental Social Psychology, 12,* 85–128.

Staw, B. M. (1977). Motivation in organizations: Toward synthesis and redirection. In B. M. Staw & G. R. Salancik (Eds.), *New directions in organizational behavior* (pp. 55–95). Chicago, IL: St. Clair Press.

Stein, N. L., & Levine, L. J. (1991). Making sense out of emotion: The representation and use of goal-structured knowledge. In W. Kessen, A. Ortony, & F. Craik (Eds.), *Memories, thoughts, and emotions* (pp. 295–322). Hillsdale, NJ: Erlbaum.

Sternberg, R. J. (1977). *Intelligence, information processing, and analogical reasoning.* Hillsdale, NJ: Erlbaum.

Steyer, R., Graser, R., & Widaman, D. K. (Eds.). (1993). *Consistency and specificity: Latent state-trait models in differential psychology.* Heidelberg, Germany: Springer-Verlag.

Taylor, F. W. (1967). *Principles of scientific management.* New York: Harper-Collins. (Originally released 1911.)

Tett, R. P., Jackson, D. N., & Rothstein, M. (1991). Personality measures as predictors of job performance: A meta-analytic review. *Personnel Psychology, 44,* 703–732.

Thomas, K. M., & Mathieu, J. E. (1994). Role of causal attributions in dynamic self-regulation and goal processes. *Journal of Applied Psychology, 79,* 812–818.

Tipper, S. P., & Baylis, G. C. (1987). Individual differences in selective attention: The relation of priming and interference to cognitive failure. *Personality and Individual Differences, 8,* 667–675.

Viteles, M. S. (1954). *Motivation and morale.* New York: W. W. Norton.

Watson, D., & Clark, M. S. (1992). On traits and temperament: General and specific factors of emotional experience and their relation to the Five-Factor Model. *Journal of Personality, 60,* 441–476.

Watson, D., & Tellegen, A. (1985). Toward a consensual structure of mood. *Psychological Bulletin, 98,* 219–235.

Waung, M., & Austin, J. T. (1995). *The effects of conscientiousness on group goal selection, commitment, and quality norm development.* Unpublished manuscript, University of Michigan, Dearborn.

Weiss, H. M., & Adler, S. (1984). Personality and organizational behavior. In B. M. Staw & L. L. Cummings (Eds.), *Research in organizational behavior* (Vol. 6, pp. 1–50). Greenwich, CT: JAI Press.

Wickens, C. D. (1992). *Engineering psychology and human performance* (2nd ed.). New York: HarperCollins.

Wiener, N. (1948). *Cybernetics.* New York: Wiley.

Williams, W. (1925). *Mainsprings of men.* New York: Charles Scribner's Sons.

Wine, J. D. (1982). Evaluation anxiety: A cognitive-attentional construct. In H. W. Krohne & L. Laux (Eds.), *Achievement, stress, and anxiety* (pp. 207–219). Washington, DC: Hemisphere.

Wollack, S., Goodale, J. G., Wijting, J. P., & Smith, P. C. (1971). Development of the Survey of Work Values. *Journal of Applied Psychology, 55,* 331–338.

Wood, R. E., & Bandura, A. (1989). Impact of conceptions of ability on self-regulatory mechanisms and complex decision making. *Journal of Personality and Social Psychology, 56,* 407–415.

Wood, R. E., Bandura, A., & Bailey, T. (1990). Mechanisms governing organizational productivity in complex decision-making environments. *Organizational Behavior and Human Decision Processes, 46,* 181–201.

Wood, R. E., & Locke, E. A. (1990). Goal setting and strategy effects on complex tasks. In B. M. Staw & L. L. Cummings (Eds.), *Research in organizational behavior* (Vol. 12, pp. 73–109). Greenwich, CT: JAI Press.

Wood, R. E., Mento, A. J., & Locke, E. A. (1987). Task complexity as a moderator of goal effects: A meta-analysis. *Journal of Applied Psychology, 72,* 416–425.

Wren, D. A. (1994). *The evolution of management thought* (4th ed.). New York: Wiley.

Chapter Seven

The Substantive Nature of Job Performance Variability

John P. Campbell
Michael Blake Gasser
Frederick L. Oswald

We, as well as others, have previously argued the point that, in spite of its centrality to human resource management and personnel research, job performance is still the forgotten construct in industrial and organizational (I/O) psychology (Campbell, McCloy, Oppler, & Sager, 1993). The literature is filled with theoretical constructions that attempt to depict the nature of abilities, personality, interests, biographical history, motivational structures, leadership, cognitive processes, job characteristics, communication strategies, goals, work-group properties, organization development strategies, conflict, climate, stress, and job satisfaction, to name but a few. However, until only recently, *job performance* stood as a term that, though it was used frequently—particularly in article and chapter titles—was never explicated or even defined.

As preparation for this chapter, we examined over twenty major textbooks in I/O psychology and organizational behavior for their discussions of performance. *None* of them attempt even to define the word. The term *performance* is frequently used, but always with

Note: Work for this chapter was supported by Contract MDA903–89–0202 with the U.S. Army Research Institute for the Behavioral and Social Sciences. The opinions and conclusions presented do not necessarily reflect those of the U.S. Army or any other agency of the U.S. government.

the implication that its meaning is understood. Instead, there are many definitions of the term *criterion* and discussions of the "criterion problem." However, the definitions consist of statements such as these: the criterion is the variable to be predicted or changed; the criterion is the dependent variable; the criterion is the variable of real interest; the criterion is "a measure of job performance or job behavior, such as productivity, accident rate, absenteeism, tenure, reject rate, training score, and supervisory or co-worker ratings." This last definition is taken from the glossary of the Society for Industrial and Organizational Psychology's *Principles for the Validation and Use of Personnel Selection Procedures* (1987, p. 37). The *Principles* then go on to offer a definition of performance as "the effectiveness and value of work behavior and its outcomes" (p. 39). With all due respect, this is not a very substantive definition; it seems so general and inclusive that almost no dependent variable or variable metric would be ruled out.

It is also reasonably typical in most of the textbook discussions we read to follow a general definition of the term *criterion* with a laundry list of possible indicators (such as those contained in the glossary for the *Principles*). However, if there are no conceptual distinctions among the various indicators, and if the construct that each is measuring is not explicated in some way, then it becomes impossible to accumulate information in any meaningful way about how such "criteria" are related to parameters of individual differences (for example, cognitive abilities) or to specified "treatments" (for example, interpersonal skills training). Furthermore, if they are all lumped together as "criterion measures of performance" when researchers are accumulating the prior distribution for meta-analytic purposes, the meaning of the meta-analytic estimate of the population effect size is unclear, *unless* all the entries in the laundry list are reasonably valid measures of the same latent variable and the substantive meaning of this variable is commonly understood.

This volume in the Frontiers in Industrial and Organization Psychology Series is about the effect of individual differences on a wide variety of processes and outcomes, job performance being one. It is axiomatic for the current authors that information about how specific individual differences affect, explain, or predict *any* of these dependent variables cannot be systematically accumulated or interpreted unless there is a shared understanding of what both sides of the equation mean, not just the independent variable side. Calls for a better understanding of performance are neither new nor rare (Astin, 1964; Dunnette, 1963; Guion, 1965; James, 1973; Wallace, 1965); but for reasons that are not perfectly clear, it has not been until recently that the field of I/O psychology has tried to comply with this request. Perhaps the tide is turning.

Objectives

The overall objectives of this chapter are (1) to take note of how far we have gotten and how much we have learned to date about the nature of performance as a construct and (2) to examine ways we might push our understanding further. We will try to address the following specific issues.

1. What are the major alternative definitions of job performance? What are the pros and cons of each?
2. How has the content and latent structure of job performance been portrayed?
3. How have the determinants of performance been modeled? Are there competing views? Do they have different implications for measurement or practice?
4. What is the magnitude of the substantive variability in job performance? Under what employment or organizational conditions is it restricted or increased?
5. If the overall goal is to accumulate research findings in the most productive way to determine how performance should be measured, how performance can be improved, and how performance can be predicted, then how *should* performance be modeled and what are the optimal research designs? On the performance side of the equation, what are the major research needs?

Defining Performance

As we have already noted, definitions of job performance simply cannot be found in the I/O psychology literature. This could be for one or more of the following reasons: (1) producing a useful definition is an extremely difficult task that is best avoided; (2) there is really no functional use for such a definition even if we had it (that is, it is adaptive not to have such a definition); and (3) people know job performance when they see it, so why bother pontificating about it? It is our position that, even though it is difficult, attempting to develop a useful definition of performance is far from being an academic exercise or a dysfunctional activity. *Not* to have a conceptual construction for performance is to adopt an extreme logical positivist view of the worst kind (that is, a view stating that performance is whatever a "criterion" measures). Consequently, we *must* consider what the field currently has to offer.

Behavior Versus Results

Perhaps the principal definitional issue is the distinction between "behavior" and its "outcomes." We have previously argued that the focus of performance measurement should be the former, not the latter; and we have attempted to define performance in the following terms.

Performance is synonymous with *behavior*. It is something that people actually do, and it can be observed. By definition, it includes only those actions or behaviors that are relevant to the organization's goals and that can be scaled (measured) in terms of each individual's proficiency (that is, level of contribution). Performance is what the organization hires one to do, and do well. Performance is *not* the consequence or result of action; it is the action itself. Admittedly, this distinction is troublesome in at least one major respect: behavior is not always observable (for example, cognitive behavior, as in solving a math problem) and can sometimes be known only by its effects (for instance, producing a solution after much "thought"). However, "solutions, statements, or answers produced as a result of covert cognitive behavior and totally under the control of the individual are included as actions that can be defined as performance" (Campbell et al., 1993, p. 40).

In addition, by definition, performance results or performance outcomes are not totally under the control of the individual and are influenced in significant ways by things such as other work groups, management accounting practices, geographic location, interest rates, sales demand, and so on. To say that a high-performing individual is someone who gets results is a legitimate statement only if the results in question can be identified and shown to be under the control of the individual.

There are at least two principal reasons for defining performance in this way. They have to do with science and practice. If human resource management practices directed at the individual are to be fair and equitable, and if they are to make contributions to organizational effectiveness, then they must reward, punish, teach, or otherwise try to influence those things that the individual can control. To do otherwise is at best wasteful and at worst disastrous. For example, it would not be good practice to evaluate courses in sales training by comparing subsequent sales revenue for the experimental and control groups if sales revenue is a function of many other things besides what the individual salesperson does. On the science side, if the research agenda is to learn how characteristics of individuals determine performance, then defining performance as something that is not under the control of individuals is not very helpful. Examining the differential correlations of specific abilities with salary level, for example, will not tell us much about the implications of measuring different abilities if salary level is a function of the consumer price index or the part of the country a person happens to get assigned to.

Whose Goals?

Most recent discussions of how performance should be defined are consistent with this emphasis on performance as behavior (for example, Borman & Motowidlo, 1993; Organ, 1994). What might not be so readily agreed upon is the definition of performance in terms of behavior that is "relevant for the organization's goals."

For example, Organ (1994) might disagree with regard to the class of performance behaviors referred to as organizational citizenship behaviors (OCBs), which are things people do in the name of peer support, organizational loyalty, courtesy to others, or dependability and which contribute to the effectiveness of the organization, but which are not enforceable job requirements and are not contractually rewarded.

Ilgen and Hollenbeck (1991) have made a distinction between job behavior and role behavior in terms of there being two different constituencies, perhaps with different goals, for these two categories of behavior. While the primary stakeholders for evaluating the proficiency of job behavior might be the management of the organization, the stakeholders for role performance might be your co-workers or yourself. For example, if you do not socialize with your co-workers in the right way, your role performance might be given a low rating by your peers even though your job performance, in the judgment of the organization, is quite high.

Graen and Scandura (1987) also point out that the behaviors that are defined as goal-relevant are sometimes negotiated between supervisor and subordinate; as a result, the content of the behavior defined as *performance* could be different for two individuals sharing the same job title. The work by Rousseau and Parks (1993) and others on the nature of the psychological contract says essentially the same thing.

None of these considerations—all of them interesting—conflicts with the basic definition of performance as behavior that is goal-relevant and that can be evaluated in terms of its degree of contribution to relevant goals. OCBs, role performance, negotiated performance specifications, and the terms of the psychological contract are all viewed as directed toward goals that are relevant for the organization's effectiveness. They may or may not be explicitly recognized by management or be part of the explicit contract or formal specifications for a job. All of which implies a certain potential for goal conflict—an issue with which a wise management would want to deal—but the definitions are consistent.

There are two additional critical issues here, particularly for the science/research side of the house. First, are the goal considerations, from whatever source, normative enough to permit generalizations of research findings? For example, if the designation of what constitutes a highly valued OCB is totally idiosyncratic to each specific situation, then OCBs cannot become part of a general research literature. Fortunately, this appears not to be the case. Second, *in any given research sample*, it would be counterproductive to evaluate the same performance behavior from different goal perspectives for different people. For example, if volunteering for certain tasks was explicitly recognized and rewarded under the terms of the job contract for half the people in a research sample but for half the sample it was not, the assessments of "volunteering performance" would be contaminated by an artifactual source of variance.

In general, the fact that the substantive content of performance is in large part a function of what goals are operative makes a performance construct different than an ability construct or a personality construct. If the definition of what behavior constitutes performance behavior is indeed idiosyncratic to a specific organization and a specific time, then there is little hope of building a general knowledge base about what predicts, explains, or improves performance. However, the actual state of affairs seems to be very much the opposite. Much of the content of OCBs, or of "management," or of supervision, or of a police officer's job (or any other worker's job) seems to be defined in much the same way across organizations. Considerable generalization is possible and has indeed been achieved.

Modeling Performance

Beyond the definitional hurdle, if we are to accumulate a knowledge base about what predicts, explains, or improves performance, then the substantive nature of performance must be identified. A substantive specification of job performance is what we refer to here as a performance *model* or *theory*. After decades of being totally operational about the "criterion" and using whatever indicators could be obtained from an organization's records, I/O psychology has finally begun trying to develop a general theory or model of performance.

There seem to be two general themes. One concentrates on the nature of the constructs that compose performance itself. The second focuses on the nature of the determinants of performance and their causal interrelationships. In the next sections, we try to summarize the current state of theory and research with regard to each of them.

Models of Performance Content

In terms of alternative models of performance content, several different points of view are possible. We briefly discuss six. Others might count them differently. (Portions of this section are abstracted from Campbell, 1994.)

The "Classic" I/O View

Elsewhere (Campbell et al., 1993), we have characterized the so-called classic model of performance. This model says simply that the general factor will account for almost all the relevant true score covariances among observed measures. Correlation matrices that appear otherwise do so because of differential reliabilities, the influence of method-specific variance, or other kinds of contamination. The goal of measurement is to obtain the best possible measure of the general factor. Further, the best possible measure is an "objective" indicator of an individual's overall contribution that is maintained by the organization itself; approximations are also useful, however, so long as they have a significant correlation with the general factor and do not introduce any large new sources of contamination.

The reasons for identifying this as the classic model of performance are as follows. First, for most of this century, the single criterion measure has dominated personnel research. Further, in the scientific/professional literature, the term *job performance* is virtually always used in the singular, with no explicit or implicit conditionals. When discussing whether or not job performance can be changed by this or that treatment, predicted by a particular ability, or measured better or worse by a particular method, the implication is clearly that there is one general thing to be changed, predicted, or measured.

The Multiple-Factor Model

This model assumes that performance is genuinely multidimensional and is composed of a number of basic, distinguishable components. Within this model, a person might perform well on one component and, relatively speaking, not well on others. That is, while the true intercorrelations among the factors are probably not zero, they are significantly less than unity.

For example, the model used in the Army's Project A (Campbell, 1990) is much different than the classic unidimensional view. Five substantive factors were hypothesized in that project and then subjected to two major confirmatory tests. While there was still considerable positive manifold for the five simple-sum factor scores, there was also considerable convergent and divergent validity across the five factors for the correlations of performance at time 1 with performance at time 2 (Campbell, Johnson, & Fellows, 1994).

On the basis of the job performance literature, including the literature on supervisory, leadership, and management performance, we suggested that, within the framework of a multifactor model of the latent structure, there are eight basic components of job performance (Campbell, McCloy, Oppler, & Sager, 1993). An abbreviated set of definitions for the eight factors follows:

A Taxonomy of Higher-Order Performance Components

1. *Job-specific task proficiency.* This factor reflects the degree to which the individual can perform the core substantive or technical tasks that are central to his or her job. Included here are job-specific performance behaviors that distinguish the substantive content of one job from another.

2. *Non-job-specific task proficiency.* In virtually every organization (but perhaps not all), individuals are required to execute performance behaviors that are not specific to their particular job. For example, in research universities with Ph.D. programs, the faculty must teach classes, advise students, make admission decisions, and serve on committees. All faculty members must do these things, in addition to practicing chemistry, psychology, economics, or electrical engineering. How well do they do them?

3. *Written and oral communication task proficiency.* Many jobs in the workforce require the individual to make formal oral or written presentations to audiences that may vary from one to tens of thousands. For people in those jobs, the proficiency with which they can write or speak, independent of the correctness of the subject matter, is a critical component of performance.

4. *Demonstration of effort.* This factor is a direct reflection of the frequency with which people expend extra effort when asked and keep working under adverse conditions. It is a reflection of the degree to which individuals commit themselves to all job tasks, work at a high level of intensity, and keep working when it is cold, wet, or late.

5. *Maintenance of personal discipline.* This component is characterized by the degree to which negative behaviors, such as alcohol and substance abuse at work, law or rule infractions, and excessive absenteeism, are avoided.

6. *Facilitation of peer and team performance.* This factor represents the degree to which the individual supports his or her peers, helps them with job problems, and acts as a de facto trainer. It also encompasses how well an individual facilitates group functioning by being a good model, keeping the group goal-directed, and reinforcing participation by the other group members.

7. *Supervision/leadership.* Proficiency in the supervisory component includes all the behaviors directed at influencing the performance of subordinates through face-to-face interpersonal interaction and influence. Supervisors set goals for subordinates, teach subordinates effective methods, model appropriate behaviors, and reward or punish in appropriate ways. The distinction between this factor and the preceding one is a distinction between peer leadership and supervisory leadership.

8. *Management/administration.* The eighth factor is intended to include the major elements in management that are distinct from direct supervision, such as articulating goals for the unit or enterprise, organizing people and resources to work on them, monitoring progress, helping to solve problems or overcome crises that stand in the way of goal accomplishment, controlling expenditures, obtaining additional resources, and representing the unit in dealings with other units.

This taxonomy implies a normative, hierarchical multifactor model as a representation of the latent structure. The eight factors described are at the top, or most general level, of the hierarchy. Indeed, some of the factors may be *too* general; each is most likely composed of subfactors that could be meaningfully separated. For example, the personal discipline factor could include such things as employee theft, chronic absenteeism, and perhaps sexual harassment. Such subfactors may be too disparate to be subsumed by one general factor. At present, there are not sufficient data to provide clear answers. The situation is different for factors 6, 7, and 8. The literature on leadership, supervision, management, and work-group structure and dynamics provides a fairly lengthy record of attempts to specify subfactors within each of these general factors. For example, Borman and Brush (1993) summarize much of the research on identifying factors of supervisory and management performance.

Factors 7 (supervision/leadership) and 8 (management/ administration) are kept separate in the current taxonomy because they separate performance behaviors that involve face-to-face interpersonal influence tasks (factor 7) from functions that do not (factor 8). This distinction is based on the belief that these two performance domains are a function of somewhat different skills. Similarly, written and oral communication proficiency is proposed as a separate factor because of our belief that it represents skills that are distinct from substantive expertise. However, lumping both written and oral communication proficiency in the same factor may be mixing an apple with an orange.

In general, these eight factors are specified in this way because we believe that the intercorrelations of their true scores are significantly less than 1.00. However, we are *not* arguing that they are all orthogonal or that the general cognitive ability factor would not correlate to some significant extent with each one. Also, these factors are most likely not functionally independent. For example, a person's high performance on factor 1 (job-specific task proficiency) and factor 3 (written and oral communication task proficiency) should increase the likelihood, other things being equal, that he or she will exhibit high performance on factor 7 (supervision/leadership). Subordinates will probably pay more attention to a supervisor who is technically an expert and communicates clearly than one who is not, unless other things are *not* equal, for example, a supervisor who scores low on factor 5 (personal discipline).

We are also not suggesting that all eight factors are necessarily present in every job. Many jobs contain no supervision/leadership or management/administrative component, although the basic mechanism of "empowerment" is to load more of these two factors back into jobs. For a few jobs (for example, radio announcer), factors 1 and 3 may be synonymous.

However, it is our intent to argue that the specific subfactors or components of performance in any job could be clustered into some subset of these eight general factors. Combining these general factors into still higher-order factors would cover up too much and should be avoided if at all possible. Subsequent research on performance will probably show our assertions to be wrong in many respects and will produce a better picture of the latent structure. So much the better.

One meta-analysis of performance data that attempted to address the factor structure shown in the above taxonomy is based on a doctoral dissertation by Viswesvaran (1993), as reported by Viswesvaran, Schmidt, and Ones (1993). Although the number of relevant studies was limited, the investigators did their best to classify the peer and supervisory rating scales used in the various studies into categories represented by the factors in the above taxonomy. Not all of the cells in the factor intercorrelation matrix could be filled in; but for those data that were available, the investigators estimated the true score intercorrelations for peer ratings, supervisor ratings, and for the intercorrelations in which one factor in the pair was rated by peers and the other was rated by supervisors. This last estimate controls for the large amounts of halo usually found when one rater rates an individual on all dimensions and not a lot of attention is paid to training raters and carefully specifying the distinctions. Consequently, the peer/supervisor matrix is the one of most interest. Of the $64 - 8 = 56$ unique cells (peer/supervisor *and* supervisor/peer), 30 could be estimated; and the values for the true score intercorrelations ranged from .03 to .88 with 24 of the 30 being between .34 and .54. The investigators focused on the positive manifold and the high probability that a general factor could be extracted. However, for us, the estimates are very much within the expected range—perhaps surprisingly so, given the measurement imperfections in the individual studies.

In general, we see no basic inconsistencies between the content of the factors described in our taxonomy and the various latent structures described by other researchers. For example, the specific components of organizational citizenship behaviors (OCBs) identified by Organ and others (Organ, 1988, 1994) seem readily assignable, depending on the component, to factors 4, 5, and 6, with a few being clustered in factor 8 (since they seem to represent certain aspects of management; for example, "Demonstrates concern about the image of the company"). Borman and Motowidlo (1993) expand on the notion of organizational citizenship behaviors and discuss two categories of performance factors: *task* performance factors and *contextual* performance factors. Task performance factors represent the core technical activity of the organization (for example, selling sporting goods, delivering mail, auditing tax returns). Contextual performance factors represent the performance components that support the organizational, social, and psychological environment in which the technical core must function. Based on the factor content of OCBs (Organ, 1988), the conceptualization of prosocial organizational behavior proposed by Brief and Motowidlo (1986), and the model of soldier effectiveness that was formulated before Project A began (Borman, Motowidlo, and Hanser, 1983), Borman and Motowidlo (1993) group sixteen components of contextual performance into five major categories. The five categories and their corresponding components are listed below. Without too much difficulty, we assigned the five categories to the more general factors in our taxonomy:

1. Persisting with enthusiasm and extra effort as necessary to complete one's task activities successfully (to factor 4)
   Showing perseverance and conscientiousness
   Offering extra effort on the job
2. Volunteering to carry out task activities that are not formally part of one's job (to factor 4)
   Suggesting organizational improvements
   Showing initiative and taking on extra responsibility
3. Helping and cooperating with others (to factor 6)
   Assisting/helping co-workers
   Assisting/helping customers
   Exhibiting organizational courtesy and not complaining
   Evidencing altruism
4. Following organizational rules and procedures (to factor 5)
   Following orders and regulations and showing respect for authority
   Complying with organizational values and policies
   Displaying conscientiousness
   Meeting deadlines
   Showing civic virtue
5. Endorsing, supporting, and defending organizational objectives (to factor 8)
   Exhibiting organizational loyalty
   Showing concern for unit objectives
   Staying with the organization during hard times and representing the organization favorably to outsiders

In general, the question of which multiple-factor portrayal of the latent structure of performance is the best one is both an empirical question and a function of the goals of measurement. Empirically, the issue pertains to what level of specificity is most beneficial for describing the relationship between individual differences and performance and what level of factor specificity best "fits" the covariance matrices that current research technology is capable of producing. If the goals of measurement are to support personnel selection research, the latent structure may be portrayed in more general terms than would be useful if the goal were to develop criterion measures for evaluating specific training programs.

In our judgment, the alternative descriptions of performance factors that exist in the literature describing multiple-factor models seem to differ only in terms of the level of specificity with which the latent factors are described. Everyone seems to be looking at much the same hierarchical picture.

The National Research Council Model

A very explicit model of performance has been incorporated in the final report of the National Research Council's (NRC) Committee on the Performance of Military Personnel (Green & Wigdor, 1988). The committee chose to define performance as the proficiency with which the individual can do the technical tasks, or has mastered the substantive content, of the job. That is, the only factors of interest from our taxonomy are factors 1 and 2.

The measurement task then becomes one of enumerating the full population of substantive or technical tasks and assessing an individual's performance on a sample of tasks from this population under standardized conditions. The measurement method of choice is the standardized job sample, commonly referred to as the "hands-on" measure. The NRC report places great importance on the job sample method as the only appropriate way to assess how well an individual can actually do something. All other measurement methods are viewed as "surrogates." One implication of this choice of measurement method is that individual differences in motivation do not contribute to variance in performance.

The Critical Task Model

The above logic can be carried one step further in terms of maximizing the distinctiveness of performance across jobs. That is, instead of sampling representatively from the population of all substantive tasks making up a job, we could identify a much smaller number of only the most critical tasks (perhaps only one) in each job. Further, the most critical tasks could be chosen so as to maximize the degree to which task content is different across jobs. This would deliberately stack the deck in favor of classification, but if the total group to be assigned were first selected on the basis of predicted scores for the performance components held in common by most jobs, use of this model might be reasonable.

Adopting such a model would open the door to a large body of research and theory on the ability and motivational determinants of skill acquisition (for example, Ackerman, 1992; Kanfer & Ackerman, 1989; Fleishman & Mumford, 1989); these studies tend to focus on specific and well-understood tasks in a controlled setting. However, the tasks used as dependent variables in this literature were not identified via job analysis methods; and, except perhaps in the case of the air traffic control simulation of Kanfer and Ackerman (1989), the tasks do not represent a particular population of "critical job tasks." In general, they do not fit the definition of performance discussed previously.

The Critical Deficiency Model

If there are critical task accomplishments that can differentiate jobs, perhaps there are also critical task failures; and these two sets may not represent ends of the same continuum. An explicit example of the critical deficiency model may not exist anywhere, but it seems at least implicit in jobs where certain individual errors can be very serious or even catastrophic (such as airline pilot or school bus driver) or in jobs where, even at a less critical level, the concern focuses on avoiding certain performance deficiencies rather than on achieving particularly high levels of performance. For example, job analysis might establish a number of errors to be avoided, and if the existing base rates for such errors were high enough to obtain useful research data, the selection/classification system could be designed to make job assignments that would reduce the probabilities of such errors.

The Attrition/Turnover Model

Turnover has a long history as a criterion variable in selection research, particularly in the military services. However, while the military services tend to account for attrition with the economic cycle and with stable individual differences such as interests (Abrahams, Neumann, & Githens, 1968), temperament (White, Nord, & Mael, 1990), and education level, the private sector worries about the economic cycle and things that happen to the individual after he or she enters the organization (Mobley, Griffith, Hand, & Meglino, 1979). That is, much of the blame for turnover is placed on compensation and benefit practices, training opportunities, or management practices.

There is evidence for the validity of both points of view. However, both are hindered by a lack of information concerning the latent structure of turnover itself. Everyone would probably agree that there are different kinds of turnover and that the different kinds have different antecedents. Ideally, we need both a basic taxonomy of types of turnover that would be used by everyone and methods of capturing attrition data that avoid the criterion contamination to which operational data are often subjected. Neither exists at the moment.

Models of Performance Determinants

If there is a latent structure of performance, is there a latent structure of performance determinants? To say it another way, is there some theory or conceptual road map that can make sense of the plethora of performance determinants that are used in research and practice—a theory that can provide guidance to people doing selection, training, organization development, and so on? What currently exists is summarized below.

Campbell et al. (1993) previously approached this issue in a rather gingerly fashion, dividing the world of performance determinants into two kinds: direct and indirect. We take it as virtually a truism that there can be only three direct performance determinants: declarative knowledge, procedural knowledge and skill, and motivation. The latter is strictly defined as three volitional choices (the choice to perform, the choice of effort level, and the choice to persist at a given effort level for a specified amount of time). The indirect determinants (for example, individual differences such as ability, personality, and interests; instructional treatments such as education, training, and experience; individual differences × treatment interactions; reward systems; and management practices) can influence performance only by influencing the direct determinants. Campbell et al. opted not to worry explicitly about the functional form of the causal relationships among knowledge, skill, and choice behavior. There are most likely a number of important interactions among them that could not be captured by describing one particular causal sequence. The goal of research should be to identify the most critical ones and to build a database around them.

One fairly straightforward implication of this two-tiered view is that, in the causal modeling sense, there can be no direct causal path between the indirect determinants (for example, general cognitive ability or leadership training) and performance. At the level of construct-valid true scores, the indirect determinants can affect performance only by influencing knowledge, skill, or choice behavior. If, for example, there is a significant direct causal path between general mental ability and a supervisory rating of performance, it is by definition an artifact. Unfortunately, it is also a truism that measurement of such things as current job knowledge, current skill, and choice behavior always falls short of perfection. If that is the case, what good is served by naming these two classes of determinants? The primary reason, in our opinion, is to provide a language for talking about the causal mechanisms by which the indirect determinants of performance might have their effects. Why does goal setting increase performance on factor 1? Why do high scorers on a personality dimension have higher scores on specific performance factors? The more we can remove correlations from the "black box," the better it will be for science and practice.

Structural Models

There have been a number of recent attempts, in the structural equation sense, to model the causal sequence that explains the pattern of covariation among measures of individual differences and measures of performance. The first widely cited study of this kind was Hunter's reanalysis (1983), in structural equation terms, of predictor and criterion data from fourteen prior studies. The model included four variables: (1) cognitive ability, (2) job knowledge, as measured by paper-and-pencil tests, (3) job skills, as measured by standardized job sample tests, and (4) overall performance as measured by supervisory ratings.

Aggregated over studies, there were direct paths from ability to job knowledge and work sample measures, from job knowledge to work sample measures, and from job knowledge and the work sample to the supervisory rating; there was no direct path from ability to supervisory ratings. The correlation between ability and the performance rating could be accounted for by the mediating effects of job knowledge and the work sample. This is consistent with the direct/indirect distinction discussed above.

Additional analyses of the same dataset by Schmidt, Hunter, and Outerbridge (1986) and analyses of additional datasets by Schmidt, Hunter, Outerbridge, and Goff (1988) expanded the structure to include length of experience on the specific job in question as an additional exogenous variable. In general, ability, job knowledge, and work samples were represented as before, and supervisor ratings of overall performance remained as the dependent variable. In these expanded analyses, the structural properties of the original Hunter model remained the same. The experience variable showed a direct path to both the work sample and the job knowledge measures, but the direct effect of experience was much greater for job knowledge than for the work sample. There was no direct path from job experience to the supervisory rating of overall performance. These authors also discussed the range of values over which experience might demonstrate causal effects on job knowledge and work sample test scores. For jobs of what they termed medium complexity, experience played a causal role in the job knowledge and job sample test variance during approximately the first five years on the job. Once most people in the sample had been on the job five years, the correlation of experience with job knowledge decreased significantly. These additional analyses are also consistent with the distinction between direct and indirect determinants discussed above.

Borman, White, Pulakos, and Oppler (1991) built on the Hunter (1983) and Schmidt et al. (1988) framework and added several additional variables to help explain the variance in supervisory ratings of overall performance. Specifically, they used the Project A database to add two personality dimensions—achievement orientation and dependability—and two personnel record indices—total number of awards and total number of disciplinary actions—to the structural model. The results for ability were the same as those found by Hunter and Schmidt et al. However, the relative size of the path coefficients for job knowledge and work sample proficiency were reversed: the work sample measures had the largest direct effect on supervisory ratings, while job knowledge had no direct effect on performance ratings but was a strong mediator of the effect of ability differences on job sample scores.

While the differences in the role played by job knowledge versus work sample proficiency are interesting and bear further study, the Borman et al. (1991) results are still quite consistent with the Campbell et al. (1993) distinction between direct and indirect determinants of performance. What is not consistent with this distinction are the small but statistically significant direct path coefficients between the two personality variables and the supervisory ratings. However, there are also significant, and larger, indirect effects for the personality variables when they are mediated by the two personnel record indices. That is, achievement orientation is linked to awards and then to performance ratings, and dependability is linked to the frequency of disciplinary actions and then to performance ratings. One reasonable explanation for the direct effects of the personality variables is that choice behavior as an influence on performance is very underdetermined in this dataset. Ultimately, a full model of the causal mechanisms linking ability, personality, training, experience, and so on with performance will require valid measurement of job knowledge, job skill, and choice behavior.

Borman, White, and Dorsey (1995) followed up a subsample of the Project A cohort and obtained additional peer and supervisor ratings on seventeen scales intended to assess interpersonal behavior in the job setting. The seventeen scales were factor-analyzed separately for both peer and supervisor raters, and the factor scores were conceptualized as representing nontechnical performance factors that could influence ratings of overall performance. The ratings on these factors were not directly influenced by job knowledge or job skill, as indeed they should not have been.

All of the structural analyses reviewed so far used ratings of overall performance as the dependent variable. One that does not is a study by Vance, MacCallum, Coovert, and Hedge (1988). Using Air Force data on jet engine mechanic performance, these investigators used ratings of three different subfactors of core technical performance to generate different structural models. The three subfactors were installation proficiency, inspection proficiency, and form completion proficiency. The exogenous variables were ability (as assessed on the ASVAB), experience, training proficiency, and the Walk Through Performance Test (WTPT), which is a form of work sample measure that requires the test taker to verbally "tell" the examiner what he or she would do in a specific situation. The study did not use a direct measure of job knowledge. The overall finding from this study was that each of the three performance factors yielded a somewhat different structural model.

In the only other study to date that does not use ratings of overall performance as the endogenous variable, Borman, Hanson, Oppler, Pulakos, and White (1993) used a large sample of non-commissioned officers (enlisted personnel in their second tour of duty) from the Project A database to model the determinants of ratings of leadership performance. The other variables in the model were the same as those used by Schmidt, Hunter, and Outerbridge (1986), and the results were very similar, except that the best-fitting model included showed a direct path from ability to experience. The authors hypothesized that high-ability people earn more opportunities for supervisory experience, which may make this sort of causal relationship unique to the leadership performance factor.

While the above kinds of structural modeling analyses provide an interesting start, there is still a long way to go. One major need is to begin thinking of performance in terms of its major components rather than as one overall "thing." There are hints of a more appropriate view in the Vance et al. (1988), Borman et al. (1993), and Borman, White, and Dorsey (1995) studies, but we need to more systematically examine differences in the structural model for various performance factors (such as those portrayed in our taxonomy). For example, what determines performance variance on the peer support and team contribution factor? Does "experience" play any part at all? If so, what kind of experience? We simply must go beyond the attempt to explain "ratings of overall performance," interesting though this may be in its own right. For example, Barrick, Mount, and Strauss (1993) present a path model for the joint effects of personality, ability, and goal setting on both sales volume and supervisory ratings of performance for sales representatives. Scores on the conscientiousness dimension of personality had a strong direct link to whether or not individuals set specific performance goals for themselves, which in turn had the strongest direct relationship to both sales volume and the supervisory rating. These results are directly congruent with our two-tiered specification of performance determinants.

In sum, the current structural modeling studies only scratch at the surface of the latent structure of performance determinants. Motivational dispositions, training interventions, goal-setting considerations, reward structures, supervisory practices, and so on have not been incorporated into such models. See Waldman and Sprangler (1989) for what a reasonably complete list of boxes and arrows would look like. Their model includes fifteen boxes and twenty-two arrows (paths?), and most of the boxes are severely underspecified (for example, "motives," "group processes," "job complexity"). In general, modeling the causal determinants of performance must avoid a number of serious pitfalls:

1. The exogenous variables in structural models cannot be so underspecified that they take on very different meanings across studies, since accumulating studies then makes little sense.
2. Structural models cannot have so many "boxes" that useful interpretation becomes impossible. "Testing" the great box-and-arrow model in the sky is not a useful goal. Alternatively, the most critical relationships must be identified, and the population values for the magnitude of the relationship under a relevant set of conditions must be estimated.
3. The dependent variable in structural models cannot continue to be a "rating of overall performance," where the nature of overall performance remains unspecified and its construct validity also remains unknown; otherwise, our understanding of performance and its determinants will not advance very far.

What would help the enterprise is a better understanding of the substantive domains of knowledge, skill, and choice behavior, which constitute the direct determinants of performance. For example (by the definitions used above), if we want to assess whether someone is "motivated," what kinds of observable choices do we try to measure? What is the substantive content of interpersonal skill? Is there such a thing as a general problem-solving skill? The bottom line is that to understand the determinants of performance, we really need to understand their substantive nature.

Performance Dynamics

A number of researchers have taken issue with the above type of structural model because it takes too static a view of performance. The counterassertion is that criteria are "dynamic." A protracted series of arguments about performance stability are contained in Ackerman (1989), Austin, Humphreys, and Hulin (1989), Barrett and Alexander (1989), Barrett, Caldwell, and Alexander (1985, 1989), Fleishman and Mumford (1989), Henry and Hulin (1987, 1989), and Murphy (1989). The central issues in this ongoing debate are (1) whether or not individual performance itself is stable over time and (2) the conditions under which the correlation of cognitive abilities (or other predictors) with performance will or will not remain stable. Studies such as Schmidt, Hunter, and Outerbridge (1986), and by implication all similar studies, are criticized because their modeling analyses imply that the structural relationships do not change over time, when for various reasons they might change systematically. In fact, if performance is not stable over time, then computing the mean of any prior distribution of validity coefficient is risky, because the variation in validities may not be artifactual.

As pointed out by Barrett, Caldwell, and Alexander (1989), the terms *performance stability* and *dynamic criteria* could point to one or more of several possible phenomena, and the parties are not always clear about the ones to which they are referring. The dynamics of performance, for example, could refer to any of the following:

1. The systematic change in an individual's true score on a latent variable across time
2. The systematic change in an individual's observed score across time
3. The systematic change in the group mean for either the true scores or the observed scores across time
4. A correlation between true scores at time 1 and time 2 that is less than 1.0

5. A correlation between observed scores at time 1 and time 2 that is considerably less than 1.0
6. Correlations between scores on a predictor measure (measured once) and scores on a performance measure that changes from time 1 to time 2
7. Systematic differences between individuals in terms of the patterns of intraindividual variability in performance across time (since people are reliably different in terms of the shape of their performance "growth curves"; Hoffman, Jacobs, & Baratta, 1993)

Each of these performance dynamics could be important in different contexts. Certainly, the degree of change in the group mean is critically important for trainers, managers, and educators; and no one would deny that changes in individual true scores can have many different causes. Nor would anyone disagree that it would be useful to separate true score change from changes due to unsystematic measurement error (Heise, 1969). Furthermore, most of us would acknowledge that systematic changes in observed scores across time could result if time is confounded with measurement method, as when performance is measured with a standardized job sample at time 1 and a supervisory rating at time 2.

The two aspects of dynamic criteria that seem most at issue are (1) the change in the rank ordering of individual true scores on performance from time 1 to time 2 and (2) the change across time of the true score correlations between a predictor variable and a performance variable.

The correlation between true scores on the performance variable for two occasions could be less than 1.0 because of differential changes between individuals. For example, some people might simply become more interested in the job and devote more effort to becoming as proficient as possible; other individuals might simply learn faster than their co-workers. The correlation could also be less than 1.0 because the job itself changes (for example, computerization runs rampant) and the new job requirements affect individual performance differentially (for example, because of already existing differences in keyboard skills).

What effects might changes in individual performance across time have on the validity coefficient? Unless the validity coefficient at time 1 is close to 1.0, it is not a given that it will be different at time 2, even if the correlation of performance with performance is less than 1.0. The change in the rank ordering of individuals on performance at time 2 could decrease validity, increase it, or not change it. It would depend on the substantive nature of the changes in performance scores from time 1 to time 2.

Conversely, even if the changes in performance were uniform across individuals (that is, if the correlation between the true scores was very high), the validities for certain kinds of predictor variables could vary. For example, two principal reasons that the correlations of cognitive ability with performance could vary over time are (1) that an increasing number of performance components are reaching automaticity via training or experience or (2) that the job demands more and more controlled processing because new procedures and new technologies are being introduced. The former reason should lead to smaller performance correlations with general cognitive ability and larger correlations with specific abilities, while the opposite should be true for the situation in which new procedures and equipment are being introduced (for example, see Murphy, 1989). The overall effect of increasing automaticity of task performance on the relative criticality of general versus specific abilities as performance determinants seems well documented (Ackerman, 1989). It points to the need to develop a substantive knowledge base concerning differential processing requirements that make up the different components of job performance. We cannot deal with such criterion dynamics until there are feasible methods available that can analyze jobs in terms of their controlled and consistent processing requirements. No such methods exist at the moment.

In general, the available evidence can be used to illustrate many different types of performance dynamics. It can also be used to argue strongly that, in spite of the potential for time-related variation in predictor validities, there is a great deal of validity generalization across "situations" (Schmidt, Ones, & Hunter, 1992). In terms of the residual variances in many prior distributions of validity estimates, time-related differences in validities do not seem to be a large threat. However, in keeping with the main theme of this chapter, our argument is that these issues of criterion dynamics and their effects will not be satisfactorily resolved until research results are tied to substantively defined constructs on the performance side.

The Substantive Meaning of Performance Variance

It is relatively easy to calculate the variance of a measure of performance for a sample of job incumbents, determine the proportion of the reliable variance, and, if need be, correct the variance estimate back to the appropriate reference group. It is much more difficult to provide a description of what the substantive variability in performance means. In any given context, is it big or small? To say it another way, is the observed variability in performance in real job settings worth worrying about? By no means is there a wide assortment of strategies that can be used to describe or interpret the observed variability in job performance in substantive terms. Perhaps there are only the following.

Comparisons of Extreme Scores

If an outcome or results measure is directly under the individual's control and is expressed in a ratio scale, then it is legitimate to express higher scores as multiples of lower scores (as in "the best performer produced or achieved four times as much as the lowest performer"). Wechsler (1952) summarized job incumbent sample data from a number of clerical and assembly/manufacturing jobs and computed the mean, the standard deviation (SD), and the ratio of the best performer's level of output to the lowest performer's level of output. The indicators were such things as typing or keypunching speed, the number of filaments mounted in light-bulbs, the number of radio parts assembled, and so on. The ratio of the highest to the lowest performance score among the samples of experienced job incumbents varied from approximately 3.00:1 to 1.75:1.

Rothe (1978) also summarized the variability in output rates for a number of manufacturing jobs (for example, positions in a foundry), and the ratios of output for the highest versus the lowest performers were in the same range (from 2.50:1 to 1.50:1). Rothe's ratios were slightly lower overall than the estimates summarized by Wechsler (1952), however.

For higher-level jobs, it is possible to observe much higher ratios. For example, Rimland and Larson (1986) reported a ratio of 16:1 for lines of code written by computer programmers. Ackerman and Kanfer (1993) obtained a ratio of 3.56:1 for subjects hired to work on an air traffic control simulation when the criterion score was the number of planes successfully handled over thirty-six trials.

Estimations of Performance Variability from the Coefficient of Variation

Most studies do not report extreme scores for the criterion distribution. To overcome this problem and still be able to compare extreme scores, Schmidt and Hunter (1983) and Hunter, Schmidt, and Judiesch (1990) used the coefficient of variation as a means to estimate the ratio of outputs for high versus low performers. For this strategy to work, the performance measure must be on a ratio scale, and it must be reasonable to assume normality for the performance distribution. The investigator must then choose a definition for high and low scorers. That definition cannot simply be the very highest and very lowest scores, because those stretch off into infinity for a normal distribution. Instead, the mean for the highest and lowest 1 percent, 5 percent, or 10 percent could be used. Schmidt and Hunter chose to focus on the mean of the highest and lowest 1 percent, which is the mean of all those above and below 2.33 standard deviations from the overall mean. In normalized standard score terms, the mean of all scores above the 99th percentile is 2.67 and the mean of all scores below the 1st percentile is −.2.67. To give substantive meaning to these two standard scores (that is, 2.67), the scores must be transformed to a ratio metric that is a function of the substantive differences in performance in a particular job. This can be done by computing the coefficient of variation (that is, the SD of the criterion scores, divided by their mean) in each study. The standard deviation of performance (SD$_p$) is then expressed as a percentage of the mean when the criterion mean and standard deviation are expressed in the original ratio metrics (for example, dollars earned, number of pieces produced). This puts the performance data from all jobs on a common scale while still preserving the relative magnitude of the variability for each job. If the assumption of normality makes sense, the two extreme scores can then be computed as (2.67) (SD_p). The larger the SD_p (that is, the larger the original SD, compared to the mean in the original score distribution), the larger the ratio of the high performer's score to the low performer's score. Hunter, Schmidt, and Judiesch (1990) also made two adjustments to SD_p, whenever enough information was available to do so: they corrected it for range restriction so that the ratio of extreme scores could also be estimated for the applicant group; and they corrected it for criterion unreliability, which reduced the estimate of the SD_p (since error variance is added to true score variance to yield the observed variance).

After a search of the literature through 1989, Hunter et al. computed SD_p and the ratio of extreme scores for jobs that were classified as being of low, medium, or high complexity. The mean ratio (adjusted) of extreme scores for the low-complexity jobs was 3.17:1; for the medium-complexity jobs, it was 12.33:1. That is, for the medium-complexity jobs (for example, craft sales), the mean performance of the top 1 percent in the applicant group would be 12.33 times as great as the mean performance for individuals in the lowest 1 percent (if individuals were selected at random from the applicants). The results for the high-complexity jobs were not emphasized, because the SD_ps became very large and the original criterion distribution had considerable positive skew. Nevertheless, it is relatively easy to see which way the arrow is pointing. The absolute difference between the highest performers and the lowest performers is large; and for more critical and complex jobs, it can be very large indeed.

Variation in the Value of Performance

Some years ago, Schmidt, Hunter, McKenzie, and Muldrow (1979) suggested a simple scaling procedure for estimating the standard deviation of performance in dollars (SD_y) for specific jobs. The procedure consisted of asking supervisors to estimate the current yearly economic return of someone in a particular job who was performing at the 50th percentile, someone performing at the 85th percentile, and someone performing at the 15th percentile. Since, in a normal distribution, the distance between the 50th percentile and either the 85th percentile or the 15th percentile is one standard deviation, the difference is interpreted as an estimate of SD_y in dollars. After some experience with obtaining such estimates, researchers began noticing that the estimated values for SD_y tended to fall in the range of 20 to 60 percent of the mean salary for the position. Thus was born the 40 percent rule as a quick way of estimating SD_y.

The 40 percent rule (or a 20 or 60 percent rule) is a form of the coefficient of variation (that is, SD_p). Consequently, it can be treated in the same way that SD_p was treated above to estimate the ratio of the value of high performance to the value of low performance. For example, if SD_y is 20 percent of salary, then the ratio of the mean return from the top 1 percent of performers to the mean return from the bottom 1 percent of performers is 3.29:1. That is, the top performers return over three times as much as the bottom performers. (It goes up from there for the 40 percent rule and the 60 percent rule.)

Whether the return is 3.29 times as much as $5,000 or 3.29 times as much as $50,000 depends on the estimate of the current return provided by the 50th percentile performer, since the range of values is equal to Y_{50th} 2.67 (SD_y). While the appropriate value for Y_{50th} is still a matter for argument, it seems reasonable to believe that it must be significantly greater than simply the average of salary and benefits paid to individuals. In any event, if SD_y is between 20 and 40 percent of the value for Y_{50th}, the value of the high performer is somewhere between 3 and 10 times as great as the value of the low performer. It is also true that recruiting and supporting the work of high performers costs more than those organizational efforts for low performers (Boudreau, 1991). However, the cost differences are relatively small compared to the payoff differences. It is not difficult to reach the conclusion that differences between what high versus low performers return to an organization is very substantial. Most of us probably severely underestimate the effects of high-performing people on an organization.

Other Metrics

Not all organizations gauge their effectiveness in economic terms. For example, the military services and many public organizations are required not to maximize profit from the sale of goods and services but to meet certain very important goals (for example, to be able to successfully engage an enemy in two different conflicts simultaneously) at the minimum possible cost. For these situations, SD_y needs a different metric. Sadacca, Campbell, DiFazio, Schultz, and White (1990) scaled the value of performance differences in terms of the number of individuals performing at a given level that it would take to provide the equivalent performance of a target number of individuals performing at a specific reference level (for example, the 50th percentile). While the definitions of high and low performers in the study were not strictly comparable to the top and bottom 1 percent as defined above, it is interesting that the estimated ratios are similar to those already discussed. In the Sadacca et al. (1990) study, a ratio estimation procedure was used to obtain utility values for five different performance levels (the 10th, 30th, 50th, 70th, and 90th percentiles) for every entry-level enlisted position ($k = 273$) in the U.S. Army. One basic question addressed by these researchers was how many individuals performing at the 50th percentile it would take to equal ten individuals performing at the 90th percentile. Across jobs, the ratios were in the range of 2.0 to 4.5, and the magnitude of the ratios was related to the technical complexity of the positions. These data are not unlike the ratios produced by the comparisons of extreme scorers discussed above.

Similar results were obtained by Eaton, Wing, and Mitchell (1985) when they scaled SD_y for Army tank crews in terms of the number of crews at the 85th percentile it would take to equal the capability of a target number of crews at the 50th percentile.

Summary

Regardless of whether the substantive nature of performance differences is described in terms of the direct ratio of high and low proficiency levels, estimates of these ratios using the coefficient of variation, estimates based on conservative approximations of SD_y to median salary levels, or direct ratio estimation by expert judges, the overall conclusion is that substantive differences between high and low performers (defined any of several ways) is very large. These ratios range from between 2:1 and 4:1 for jobs of low difficulty and complexity to ratios between 6:1 and 10:1 for jobs of moderately high difficulty and complexity, even after the existing selection systems have done their work. Within-group variation of this extent, while it may be well recognized by some managers, is not generally acknowledged by organizational psychologists, organizational theorists, or even training and development specialists.

Improving Performance

The previous section argued that the substantive variability in performance is very large, even when the reference group is current job incumbents selected by whatever means organizations have used. If the same indicators of performance variability are estimated for an incumbent group selected at random from the applicant population, the estimates of substantive variability are larger, *but not that much larger* (Hunter, Schmidt, & Judiesch, 1990). This seems to say something about the general level of selection efficacy in the current U.S. occupational system. There is still a great deal of room for making performance improvements, and it becomes greater as the jobs or job families in question become more complex and more difficult.

There are two general procedures for improving performance that have been given attention by I/O psychology: we can begin to select people differently such that the resulting distribution of performance scores is different than the distribution produced by the recruitment, selection, and classification procedures currently being used; or we can attempt to change individuals after they have been hired. This is not a great revelation; it corresponds to the individual differences versus experimental approach to changing behavior that Cronbach (1975) referred to as the two disciplines of psychology (lamenting their lack of cooperation).

Performance Improvements from Improved Selection

Within the last ten to fifteen years, the available evidence on the efficacy of each of these two approaches has been summarized in a number of meta-analyses. On the individual differences side, most of the available meta-analyses are cited in Schmidt, Ones, and Hunter (1992) and are discussed in more detail elsewhere in this book.

The results show consistent and reasonably high validities for research-based selection. In general, the single best predictor of overall job performance is cognitive ability. This relationship is stronger for entry-level positions and for jobs that are more "complex" in terms of their information-processing demands. For advanced positions that require considerable experience on the part of the applicant, job sample measures (for example, assessment centers) frequently have higher validities than measures of cognitive abilities. In such selection situations, the applicant populations have a restricted range in cognitive ability true scores, and the current differences in expertise become more predictive. As the information-processing demands of a job decrease, the validities of tests of psychomotor ability and perceptual speed and accuracy become greater (and eventually surpass those of tests of general mental ability). Overall, the variable that seems to add the most incremental validity to the primary predictor is a broad personality factor made up of three of the Big Five factors (Ones, Schmidt, & Viswesvaran, 1994).

Translating these correlations into the expected changes in performance that selection can achieve requires some additional considerations, which are specified by the basic Brogden-Cronbach-Gleser formulation (Cronbach & Gleser, 1965). That is, besides being a function of the level of predictive validity, the actual increase in performance that can be achieved depends on the degree of selectivity that is possible and on the magnitude of the substantive variation in performance. There are numerous arguments over how best to estimate gains from selection (Boudreau, 1991; Cascio & Morris, 1990; Cronshaw & Alexander, 1985; Hunter, Schmidt, & Coggin, 1988; Murphy, 1986), and colleagues lecture each other about basic principles of accounting, labor economics, and psychometrics. None of the arguments detracts from the overall conclusion that, if the validities are as estimated from the existing meta-analyses and it is possible to use a selection ratio of .50 or lower, the mean increase in performance will be considerable (for example, effect sizes of .50 to 1.50) and the value of the increase in output will be very high in comparison to the cost of achieving it, even when SD_y and the gain in utility are estimated in the most conservative fashion.

However, notice again that the term *performance* is being used in the singular. In *all* of the research summarized in this section, performance refers either to a measure of overall performance or a measure of some version of factor 1 in our taxonomy. We need to learn much more about predicting other major factors.

Performance Improvements from Posthire Interventions

After an individual has been selected, a number of "treatments" for the purpose of increasing individual performance are possible. A complete list of all the distinct treatments that have been evaluated in terms of their effect on performance would be formidable, in terms of both its length and the complexity of its latent structure. The most complete summary of the meta-analyses of these data is still the one reported by Guzzo, Jette, and Katzell (1985). Their classification of all possible treatments is shown below. The adjusted mean effect sizes for the "output" measures are also shown.

Taxonomy of Organizational Interventions

Training and instruction (.78). Practices in this category include behavior modeling, human relations programs, and management seminars. Excluded are programs aimed at changing supervisory styles.

Appraisal and feedback (.35). This category includes practices designed to provide employees with more frequent or extensive feedback about job performance—practices such as formal appraisals, self-monitoring, or the sharing of performance data previously unavailable.

Management by objectives (MBO) (.12). MBO emphasizes the specification of work objectives, the monitoring of accomplishments, reward attainment when objectives are met, and participation in the setting and review of work objectives.

Goal setting (.75). While related to both MBO and feedback, goal setting has as its central focus the specification of difficult but attainable goals for limited but important aspects of job performance.

Financial compensation (.57). This category ties monetary rewards to individual, group, or organization-wide performance.

Work redesign (.42). Practices that enrich jobs with qualities that enhance worker interest and motivation are considered work redesign.

Decision-making techniques (.70). Programs for improving decision making in organizations fall into this category.

Supervisory methods (.13). This category is used for programs intended to change the general patterns of supervision, usually by broad retraining or by the redefinition of roles.

Work rescheduling (.21). These practices include establishment of flexible working hours or the redistribution of hours in a work week.

Sociotechnical interventions (.62). Programs of this sort focus on a joint consideration of technological and social demands at work and are typically implemented over a considerable period of time.

Perhaps the main point to be drawn from Guzzo, Jette, and Katzell's review is that the effect sizes are generally in the same range as those for selection procedures when the selection ratio is .60 to .50, or less. Training, goal setting, sociotechnical organization development, and changes in compensation procedures produce the largest changes in performance. It is also the case that the number of meta-analyses (or any other kind of analyses attempting to estimate aggregate effects) that have been undertaken are much fewer for posthire interventions than for selection procedures. In part, this is probably due to a lack of comparable information. However, it is also the case that taxonomies of the independent variables on the intervention side are much less coherent and their substantive meaning is not always clear. For example, what is the substantive meaning of the independent variables referred to as "leadership training," "participation," or "empowerment"? Compared to variables such as general cognitive ability, spatial relations, conscientiousness, and "realistic interest," the descriptors for posthire interventions have much less construct validity. A good illustration is the dispute between Latham and Erez over the joint effects of goal setting and participation on individual performance

(Latham, Erez, & Locke, 1988). The participation treatment did not mean the same thing for the two investigators.

If the treatment side of performance improvement is ever going to systematically accumulate reliable and substantive estimates of population effects, then the helter-skelter nature of the way the independent variables are designated and represented must be changed. For example, when the terms "supervisory interpersonal skills training" or "performance feedback" are used, they must convey a shared meaning in the same way that the phrase "perceptual speed was measured" communicates a common understanding of the variable being assessed. Besides dealing with the taxonomic requirement, the treatment side must also attempt to specify the conditions under which the effects of the intervention should be observed and the conditions under which it should not. The specification of these conditionals is probably a more complicated task for the posthire treatments than for the selection predictors. These difficulties aside, if significant progress could be made in developing a shared meaning for different treatments and in identifying the major sets of conditions within which they have their intended effects, the power of applied psychology would grow exponentially.

Conclusion

In spite of the difficulties involved, the field of I/O psychology has finally begun to build a cumulative research record on the degree to which various prediction or intervention strategies can be expected to increase performance. More comprehensive research programs, techniques of meta-analysis, and the willingness of many investigators to painstakingly examine hundreds of research reports of varying degrees of completeness and clarity have made this possible. The results to date show that a number of prediction and intervention strategies have considerable power for increasing mean performance.

However, a full understanding of what these strategies can do is still being held back by a lack of substantive theory and measurement development on the performance side. Almost always, the dependent variable is some measure of "overall job performance," and that term is never defined. In addition, even though we have rich substantive theories of cognitive abilities, personality, and interests, we have no such models of knowledge, skill, or choice behavior, which are, according to the model espoused in this chapter, the direct determinants of behavior and are the variables through which any characteristic of individual differences or intervention strategy must work to influence performance. The few attempts that have been made to model the causal determinants of performance, incomplete though they are, support this conclusion.

How can we learn more about the performance side of the equation? There is no magic here, and studying the performance side is certainly less glamorous than researching or selling the predictor or treatment, but consider the following:

1. Research on performance must stop using severely contaminated outcome measures as indicators of performance. Sales revenue, total compensation, and so on are dangerous measures to use in this regard.
2. A distinction must be maintained between the performance construct to be measured and the method used to measure it. For example, we are not trying to predict or change supervisory ratings. We are trying to predict or change the dimension of performance that the supervisor is trying to assess. What the determinants of variance unique to the measurement method are is a relevant, but different, question.
3. The substantive definitions of the major performance factors must be improved so that there is a well-understood and relatively common meaning for them.
4. The substantive content of the most critical components of knowledge, skill, and choice behavior (that is, the direct determinants of performance) should be described. For example, what are the critical components of knowledge, skill, and choice behavior that determine whether an individual will be a contributor to team effectiveness? A potential set of procedures for doing this is contained in the research (both basic and applied) on expertise. Specific procedures are described by Olson and Rueter (1987) and Glaser, Lesgold, and Gott (1991). Collectively, these procedures are known as cognitive job analysis. In essence, cognitive job analysis expands the focus of conventional job analysis from a description of tasks and

behavior to include a description of how high performers accomplish tasks in terms of the knowledge and skill structures used, the mental models used to represent problems, and so on. An excellent example is the cognitive job analysis of the air traffic controller position by Means et al. (1988). The cognitive job analysis process is very different from the way we have done job analysis in the past.

5. The extant literature should be summarized in terms of the specifications for specific knowledge and skill structures that it already provides. The voluminous leadership literature (Bass, 1990; K. E. Clark & M. B. Clark, 1990) is one example of a body of evidence that could be much more coherently described in terms of what is meant by interpersonal skill, goal-setting skill, coaching skill, and group leadership skill.

A Final Word

The mantra for this chapter is the request that I/O psychology seek substantive models of performance and performance determinants. Saying that performance equals ability times motivation or that training works or that some set of boxes and arrows is a model does not help us much. We need to know the substantive nature of the constructs we are trying to predict or improve, and we need to know the substantive nature of the knowledge structures, skill structures, and specific volitional choices that directly determine individual differences in performance. Then, and only then, will we really begin to build a cumulative understanding of what individual differences in performance mean and how they are produced.

References

Abrahams, N. M., Neumann, L., & Githens, W. H. (1968). *The SVIB in predicting NROTC officer retention.* San Diego, CA: U.S. Naval Personnel Research and Development Center.

Ackerman, P. L. (1987). Individual differences in skill learning: An integration of psychometric and information processing perspectives. *Psychological Bulletin, 102,* 3–27.

Ackerman, P. L. (1989). Within task intercorrelations of skilled performance: Implications for predicting individual differences? (A commentary on Henry & Hulin, 1987). *Journal of Applied Psychology, 74,* 360–364.

Ackerman, P. L. (1992). Predicting individual differences in complex skill acquisition: Dynamics of ability determinants. *Journal of Applied Psychology, 77,* 598–614.

Ackerman, P. L., & Kanfer, R. (1993). Integrating laboratory and field study for improving selection: Development of a battery for predicting air traffic controller success. *Journal of Applied Psychology, 78,* 413–432.

Astin, A. (1964). Criterion-centered research. *Educational and Psychological Measurement, 24,* 807–822.

Austin, J. T., Humphreys, L. G., & Hulin, C. L. (1989). A critical reanalysis of Barrett et al. *Personnel Psychology, 42,* 583–596.

Barrett, G. V., & Alexander, R. A. (1989). Rejoinder to Austin, Humphreys, and Hulin: Critical reanalysis of Barrett, Caldwell, and Alexander. *Personnel Psychology, 42,* 597–612.

Barrett, G. V., Caldwell, M. S., & Alexander, R. A. (1985). The concept of dynamic criteria: A critical reanalysis. *Personnel Psychology, 38,* 41–56.

Barrett, G. V., Caldwell, M. S., & Alexander, R. A. (1989). The predictive stability of ability requirements for task performance: A critical reanalysis. *Human Performance, 2*(3), 167–183.

Barrick, M. R., Mount, M. K., & Strauss, J. P. (1993). Conscientiousness and performance of sales representatives: Test of the mediating effect of goal setting. *Journal of Applied Psychology, 78,* 715–722.

Bass, B. M. (1990). *Bass & Stogdill's handbook of leadership: Theory, research, and management applications* (3rd ed.). New York: Free Press.

Borman, W. C. (1991). Job behavior, performance, and effectiveness. In M. D. Dunnette & L. M. Hough (Eds.), *Handbook of industrial and organizational psychology* (2nd ed.; Vol. 2, pp. 271–326). Palo Alto, CA: Consulting Psychologists Press.

Borman, W. C., & Brush, D. H. (1993). More progress toward a taxonomy of managerial performance requirements. *Human Performance, 6,* 1–22.

Borman, W. C., Hanson, M. A., Oppler, S. H., Pulakos, E. D., & White, L. A. (1993). Role of early supervisory experience in supervisor performance. *Journal of Applied Psychology, 78,* 443–449.

Borman, W. C., & Motowidlo, S. J. (1993). Expanding the criterion domain to include elements of contextual performance. In N. Schmitt, W. C. Borman, & Associates, *Personnel selection in organizations* (pp. 71–98). San Francisco: Jossey-Bass.

Borman, W. C., Motowidlo, S. J., & Hanser, L. M. (1983, Aug.). A model of individual performance effectiveness: Thoughts about expanding the criterion space. In N. K. Eaton & J. P. Campbell (Chairs), *Integrated criterion measurement for large scale computerized selection and classification.* Symposium conducted at the American Psychological Association, Anaheim, CA.

Borman, W. C., Motowidlo, S. J., Rose, S. R., & Hanser, L. M. (1987). *Development of a model of soldier effectiveness* (ARI Technical Report 741). Alexandria, VA: U.S. Army Research Institute for the Behavioral and Social Sciences.

Borman, W. C., White, L. A., Pulakos, E. D., & Oppler, S. H. (1991). Models of supervisory job performance ratings. *Journal of Applied Psychology, 76*(6), 863–872.

Borman, W. C., White, L. A., & Dorsey, D. W. (1995). Effects of ratee task performance and interpersonal factors on supervisory and peer performance ratings. *Journal of Applied Psychology, 80*, 168–177.

Boudreau, J. W. (1991). Utility analysis for human resource management decisions. In M. D. Dunnette & L. M. Hough (Eds.), *Handbook of industrial and organizational psychology* (2nd ed.; Vol. 2, pp. 621–745). Palo Alto, CA: Consulting Psychologists Press.

Brief, A. P., & Motowidlo, S. J. (1986). Prosocial organizational behaviors. *Academy of Management Review, 11*, 710–725.

Campbell, J. P. (1990). Modeling the performance prediction problem in industrial and organizational psychology. In M. Dunnette & L. M. Hough (Eds.), *Handbook of industrial and organizational psychology* (2nd ed.; Vol. 1, pp. 687–732). Palo Alto, CA: Consulting Psychologists Press.

Campbell, J. P. (1994). Alternative models of performance and their implications for selection and classification. In M. G. Rumsey, C. B. Walker, & J. H. Harris (Eds.), *Personnel selection and classification* (pp. 33–52). Hillsdale, NJ: Erlbaum.

Campbell, J. P., Johnson, J., & Fellows, M. (1994, Apr.). *The correlation of performance with performance.* Paper presented at the 9th annual meeting of the Society for Industrial and Organizational Psychology, Nashville, TN.

Campbell, J. P., McCloy, R. A., Oppler, S. H., & Sager, C. E. (1993). A theory of performance. In N. Schmitt & W. Borman (Eds.), *Personnel selection in organizations.* San Francisco: Jossey-Bass.

Campbell, J. P., McHenry, J. J., & Wise, L. L. (1990). Modeling job performance in a population of jobs. *Personnel Psychology, 43*, 313–333.

Cascio, W. F., & Morris, J. R. (1990). A critical reanalysis of Hunter, Schmidt, and Coggin's (1988) "Problems and pitfalls in using capital budgeting and financial accounting techniques in assessing the utility of personnel programs." *Journal of Applied Psychology, 75*, 410–417.

Clark, K. E., & Clark, M. B. (Eds.). (1990). *Measures of leadership.* Greensboro, NC: Center for Creative Leadership/Leadership Library of America.

Cronbach, L. J. (1975). Beyond the two disciplines of scientific psychology. *American Psychologist, 30*, 116–127.

Cronbach, L. J., & Gleser, G. C. (1965). *Psychological tests and personnel decisions* (2nd ed.). Urbana: University of Illinois Press.

Cronshaw, S. F., & Alexander, R. A. (1985). One answer to the demand for accountability: Selection utility as an investment decision. *Organizational Behavior and Human Decision Processes, 35,* 102–118.

Dunnette, M. D. (1963). A note on the criterion. *Journal of Applied Psychology, 47,* 251–254.

Eaton, N. K., Wing, H., & Mitchell, K. (1985). Alternative methods of estimating the dollar value of performance. *Personnel Psychology, 38,* 27–40.

Fleishman, E. A., & Mumford, M. D. (1989). Abilities as causes of individual differences in skill acquisition. *Human Performance, 2*(3), 201–223.

Glaser, R., Lesgold, A., & Gott, S. (1991). Implications of cognitive psychology for measuring job performance. In A. K. Wigdor & B. F. Green (Eds.), *Performance assessment in the workplace* (Vol. 2). Washington, DC: National Academy Press (for the National Research Council).

Graen, G. B., & Scandura, T. A. (1987). Toward a psychology of dyadic organizing. *Research in Organizational Behavior, 9,* 175–208.

Green, B. F., & Wigdor, A. K. (Eds.). (1988). *Measuring job competency: Report of the Committee on the Performance of Military Personnel.* Washington, DC: National Academy Press (for the National Research Council).

Guion, M. R. (1965). *Personnel testing.* New York: McGraw-Hill.

Guzzo, R. A. (1988). Productivity research in review. In J. P. Campbell & R. J. Campbell (Eds.), *Productivity in organizations: New perspectives from industrial and organizational psychology.* San Francisco: Jossey-Bass.

Guzzo, R. A., Jette, R. D., & Katzell, R. A. (1985). The effects of psychologically based intervention programs on worker productivity. *Personnel Psychology, 38,* 275–293.

Harris, D. H. (Ed.). (1994). *Organizational linkages: Understanding the productivity paradox.* Washington, DC: National Academy Press (for the National Research Council).

Heise, D. R. (1969). Separating reliability and stability in test-retest correlations. *American Sociological Review, 34,* 93–101.

Henry, R. A., & Hulin, C. L. (1987). Stability of skilled performance across time: Some generalizations and limitations on utilities. *Journal of Applied Psychology, 72,* 457–462.

Henry, R. A., & Hulin, C. L. (1989). Changing validities: Ability-performance relations and utilities. *Journal of Applied Psychology, 74,* 365–367.

Hoffman, D. A., Jacobs, R., & Baratta, J. E. (1993). Dynamic criteria and the measurement of change. *Journal of Applied Psychology, 78,* 194–204.

Humphreys, L. G., & Tabor, T. (1973). Postdiction study of the Graduate Record Examination and eight semesters of college grades. *Journal of Educational Measurement, 10,* 179–184.

Hunter, J. E. (1983). A causal analysis of cognitive ability, job performance, and supervisor ratings. In F. Landy, S. Zedeck, & J. Cleveland (Eds.), *Performance measurement and theory* (pp. 257–266). Hillsdale, NJ: Erlbaum.

Hunter, J. E., Schmidt, F. L., & Coggin, T. D. (1988). Problems and pitfalls in using capital budgeting and financial accounting techniques in assessing the utility of personnel programs. *Journal of Applied Psychology, 73,* 522–528.

Hunter, J. E., Schmidt, F. L., & Judiesch, M. K. (1990). Individual differences in output variability as a function of job complexity. *Journal of Applied Psychology, 75,* 28–42.

Ilgen, D. R., & Hollenbeck, J. R. (1991). The structure of work: Jobs and roles. In M. D. Dunnette & L. M. Hough (Eds.), *Handbook of industrial and organizational psychology* (2nd ed.; Vol. 2, pp. 165–208). Palo Alto, CA: Consulting Psychologists Press.

James, L. (1973). Criterion models and construct validity for criteria. *Psychological Bulletin, 80,* 75–83.

Kanfer, R., & Ackerman, P. L. (1989). Motivation and cognitive abilities: An integrative/aptitude-treatment interaction approach to skill acquisition. *Journal of Applied Psychology, 74,* 657–690.

Katzell, R. A., & Guzzo, R. A. (1983). Psychological approaches to productivity improvement. *American Psychologist, 38,* 468–472.

Latham, G. P., Erez, M., & Locke, E. A. (1988). Resolving scientific disputes by the joint design of crucial experiments by the antagonists: Application to the Erez-Latham dispute regarding participation in goal setting. *Journal of Applied Psychology, 73,* 753–772.

Means, B., Mumaw, R., Roth, C., Schlager, M., McWilliams, E., Gagner, E., Rice, V., Rosenthal, D., & Heon, S. (1988). *ATC training analysis study: Design of the next generation ATC training system* (Technical Report). Alexandria, VA: HumRRO International.

Mobley, W. H., Griffith, R. W., Hand, H. H., & Meglino, B. M. (1979). Review and conceptual analysis of the employee turnover process. *Psychological Bulletin, 86,* 493–522.

Murphy, K. R. (1986). When your top choice turns you down: Effect of rejected offers on the utility of selection tests. *Psychological Bulletin, 99,* 133–138.

Murphy, K. R. (1989). Is the relationship between cognitive ability and job performance stable over time? *Human Performance, 2*(3), 183–200.

Olson, J. R., & Rueter, H. H. (1987). Extracting expertise from experts: Methods for knowledge acquisition. *Expert Systems, 4*(3), 152–168.

Ones, D. S., Schmidt, F. L., & Viswesvaran, C. (1994). Do broader personality variables predict job performance with higher validity? In R. Page (Chair), *Personality and job performance: Big Five versus specific traits.* Symposium conducted at the Society for Industrial and Organizational Psychology, Nashville, TN.

Organ, D. W. (1988). *Organizational citizenship behavior: The good soldier syndrome.* New York: Lexington Books.

Organ, D. W. (1994). Organizational citizenship behavior and the good soldier. In M. G. Rumsey, C. B. Walker, & J. H. Harris (Eds.), *Personnel selection and classification.* Hillsdale, NJ: Erlbaum.

Rimland, B., & Larson, G. E. (1986). Individual differences: An underdeveloped opportunity for military psychology. *Journal of Applied Social Psychology, 16,* 565–575.

Rothe, H. F. (1978). Output rates among industrial employees. *Journal of Applied Psychology, 63,* 40–46.

Rousseau, D. M. (1989). *Psychological contracts in recruitment.* Paper presented at the Society for Industrial and Organizational Psychology, Boston.

Rousseau, D. M., & Parks, J. (1993). The contracts of individuals and organizations. In L. L. Cummings and B. M. Staw (Eds.), Research in Organizational Behavior (Vol. 15, pp. 1–43). Greenwich, CT: JAI Press.

Sadacca, R., Campbell, J. P., DiFazio, A. S., Schultz, S. R., & White, L. A. (1990). Scaling performance utility to enhance selection/classification decisions. *Personnel Psychology, 43,* 367–378.

Schmidt, F. L., & Hunter, J. E. (1983). Individual differences in productivity: An empirical test of estimates derived from studies of selection procedure utility. *Journal of Applied Psychology, 68,* 407–414.

Schmidt, F. L., & Hunter, J. E. (1992). Development of a causal model of processes determining job performance. *Current Directions in Psychological Science, 1,* 84–92.

Schmidt, F. L., Hunter, J. E., McKenzie, R., & Muldrow, T. (1979). The impact of valid selection procedures on workforce productivity. *Journal of Applied Psychology, 64,* 609–626.

Schmidt, F. L., Hunter, J. E., & Outerbridge, A. N. (1986). Impact of job experience and ability on job knowledge, work sample performance, and supervisory ratings of job performance. *Journal of Applied Psychology, 71*(3), 432–439.

Schmidt, F. L., Hunter, J. E., Outerbridge, A. N., & Goff, S. (1988). Joint relation of experience and ability with job performance: Test of three hypotheses. *Journal of Applied Psychology, 73*(1), 46–57.

Schmidt, F. L., Ones, D. S., & Hunter, J. E. (1992). Personnel selection. In M. R. Rosenzweigh & L. W. Porter (Eds.), Annual review of psychology (Vol. 13, pp. 627–670). Palo Alto, CA: Annual Reviews.

Society for Industrial and Organizational Psychology. (1987). *Principles for the validation and use of personnel selection procedures* (3rd ed.). College Park, MD: Author.

Vance, R. J., MacCallum, R. C., Coovert, M. D., & Hedge, J. W. (1988). Construct validity of multiple job performance measures using confirmatory factor analysis. *Journal of Applied Psychology, 73,* 74–80.

Viswesvaran, C. (1993). *Modeling job performance: Is there a general factor?* Unpublished doctoral dissertation, University of Iowa.

Viswesvaran, C., Schmidt, F. L., & Ones, D. S. (1993). *Theoretical implications of a general factor in job performance criteria.* Paper presented at the Society for Industrial and Organizational Psychology, San Francisco.

Waldman, D. A., & Sprangler, W. D. (1989). Putting together the pieces: A chosen look at the determinants of job performance. *Human Performance, 2,* 29–60.

Wallace, S. R. (1965). Criteria for what? *American Psychologist, 20,* 411–417.

Wechsler, D. (1952). *Range of human capacities* (2nd ed.). Baltimore, MD: Williams & Wilkins.

White, L. A., Nord, R., & Mael, F. A. (1990). *Setting enlistment standards on the ABLE to reduce attrition.* Paper presented at the Army Science conference, Washington, DC.

Chapter Eight

Adapting to Roles in Decision-Making Teams

John R. Hollenbeck
Jeffrey A. LePine
Daniel R. Ilgen

Organizations can be conceptualized as structured systems in which, at the macro-organizational level, the elements of structure are typically defined in terms of companies, divisions, departments, or geographic regions. At the micro-organizational level, the elements of structure are generally constituted by the jobs or roles held by individual members of the organization (Ilgen & Hollenbeck, 1991). Traditionally, organizations have specified and legitimized their structures by creating organizational charts. These charts formally specify both how labor is to be differentiated via different jobs and how the outputs from this differentiated labor will be coordinated and integrated to meet the needs of the organization as a whole. These organizational charts are typically accompanied by formal job descriptions that further specify the within-job and between-job relationships.

In recent years, however, there have been fundamental changes in the ways organizations structure work (Ilgen, 1994). In this chapter,

Note: This research was supported, in part, by a grant from the Office of Naval Research as part of the technical base research for the Cognitive and Neural Sciences Division. Although support for this research is gratefully acknowledged, the ideas expressed within are those of the authors and not necessarily the funding agency.

we will review what we believe to be some of the major changes in how work is being structured in contemporary organizations and the implications of these changes (in terms of individual difference variables) that are going to be critical for organizational members. In general, we will argue that individuals will increasingly find themselves working in short-term teams with other people who have different areas of functional expertise. These teams will work on a particular project, apply their expertise to the specific problem at hand, then disband and be assigned to a new or different team working on a different project. The nature of work in these new structures will place a premium on the individual's ability to rapidly and effectively assimilate into teams, and there are likely to be individual differences in the efficiency with which people can accomplish this. This chapter will review the historical literature on role taking and role making, along with more recent literature on team decision making, skill acquisition, and the structure of personality traits, to develop an integrated model that specifies the individual differences that will be critical for effective functioning within team-based organizational structures.

New Developments in Organizational Structures

There has been a shift in contemporary organizations away from tight bureaucratic structures with well-defined jobs toward more flexible structures centered around teams. This trend has been thoroughly documented in scholarly reviews (Bettenhausen, 1991; Levine & Moreland, 1989), edited books directed toward teams and teamwork (Goodman, 1986; Hackman, 1990), and the popular press (for example, cover stories in *Time* magazine, *Business Week* and *Fortune,* all in 1990).

Some of these changes have resulted from new business strategies that are increasingly emphasizing adaptive structures and processes. For example, many firms have adopted processes such as integrated manufacturing, concurrent engineering, just-in-time inventory control, and total quality management—processes that presume less rigid job specifications. In addition, many organizations have increased their use of contingent workers in order to quickly modulate organizational size (Feldman, 1990). Moreover, these changes have taken place within an environment where resistance to change is low: labor unions, which have traditionally championed strict interpretation of formalized job descriptions as a means of protecting workers from exploitation, have witnessed both declining power (in terms of membership) and shifts in strategy (more labor-management cooperation). All these changes led *Fortune* magazine to declare "The End of the Job" on its cover, boldly concluding that "the traditional job is becoming a social artifact" (Bridges, 1994).

Although reports of the "death of jobs" may be premature, it is clear that the demand for flexible organizational structures is high and that one common response to this demand is to organize work so that it can be performed by teams (Hoerr, 1989). Structures organized around teams decouple specific tasks from specific persons and instead assign general projects to groups of people. This enhances flexibility, because the team can shift tasks among its members to take advantage of specialized skills and resources.

For example, Chrysler's "platform teams" are composed of designers, engineers, suppliers, manufacturing personnel, and marketing experts, all of whom work together on a project at the same time (Byrne, 1993). In the past, this set of functionally differentiated groups would have worked sequentially. That is, designers would hand over drawings to engineers, who would then hand over specifications to manufacturers, who would then hand over products to marketers. Now these groups work together at all stages of the product development process. This way, if the designers decide to draw up a product that will be too difficult to produce or too difficult to market, their decision can be reversed early, at a stage when it is still relatively easy to rectify problems.

These platform teams were largely responsible for the success of the Chrysler minivans, the Grand Cherokee, and the Viper (Treece, 1992; Woodruff, 1991). They were also central to the development of Chrysler's newest product, the Neon, an award-winning, low-cost subcompact introduced in 1994 (Woodruff, 1993). Concurrent engineering processes built around small teams of differentiated experts, such as those employed by Chrysler, have been created in thousands of organizations over the last ten years (Hammer & Champy, 1993).

In some instances, the members of these teams spill over organizational boundaries, forming what has come to be known as a "virtual structure." A structure of this type develops when a company forms temporary alliances or joint ventures with other companies to quickly exploit a business opportunity. A virtual structure is not really a single organization; rather, it is a temporary network of several organizations in which each firm focuses on its core competency (for example, design, manufacturing, or marketing) and contributes personnel to a closed-end project team that spans organizational boundaries. A virtual structure allows an organization to act as though it has more expertise or productive capacity than it actually controls. Several large and well-known companies, including Levi Strauss, Hewlett-Packard, and Atlas Industrial Door have implemented this approach (Davidow & Malone, 1992).

Despite their virtues, however, these postbureaucratic structures create some challenges. For example, relative to job-oriented structures, team-based structures are much more complex for job incumbents to adapt to, for several reasons. First, above and beyond the normal job requirements, employees need to develop behavioral coordination, shared mental models (that is, a common understanding of goals and functional means-ends relationships), and mutual trust among members (Rouse, Cannon-Bowers, & Salas, 1992).

Yet the development of coordination, shared mental models, and trust among people requires a time commitment and a stability of relationships that are often not possible within flexible team-based structures. This is especially the case when an organization's human resource strategies emphasize contingent workers or the rotation of personnel, because both these approaches cause lack of familiarity among individuals. Thus, far from being a panacea for all organizational problems created by individually driven job structures, teams create unique problems of their own. Indeed, many organizations moving to team-based structures have experienced difficulties, and the same source that announced the "death of jobs" (that is, *Fortune* magazine) had two weeks earlier discussed "the trouble with teams" (Dumaine, 1994). The lack of cross-references made it clear that these authors mistakenly saw these as two unrelated dilemmas.

There are two problems surrounding team-based structures that need to be given particular attention by industrial and organizational (I/O) psychologists. First, the short-term nature of these structures dictates that the typical group formation process—often expressed with variations of Tuckman's forming, storming, norming, and performing heuristic (1965)—has to be highly accelerated. Team members have to rapidly assimilate and get on to the performance stage, yet this is made difficult by the lack of formal, well-differentiated job specifications and by the differential areas of functional expertise embodied in team members.

A second problem created by team-based structures deals with changes in team membership over time. Many "shocks" that can occur to an organizational structure are more easily managed with tight bureaucratic structures and Tayloristic job descriptions than with team-based structures (Locke, 1982). Turnover among job incumbents, for instance, is well handled by tight bureaucratic structures because of the decoupling of individual roles and rewards. Movement in and out of teams, however, is a major issue, given the aforementioned need to develop coordination, shared mental models, and trust among team members.

For example, naive observers are often surprised at how an injury to one member of a sports team can have rippling effects that decrease the effectiveness of all the other team members who depended on that individual. Sometimes this interdependence is obvious (for example, the quarterback who loses his top receiver), but sometimes it is not (for example, the running back whose former effectiveness was contingent upon the ability of the top receiver to take two defenders away from a play).

Because of the liabilities of tight bureaucratic structures, a return to the old ways is probably not a viable solution to this problem. Instead, we need to discover ways of managing the startup and substitutability problems that arise when individuals work in team-based structures. If we assume that we cannot manage these problems by changing the organizational structure or tasks (that is, we cannot return to tight bureaucratic structures and elaborately detailed job descriptions), then the focus shifts to changing the organizational members, either directly (through training) or indirectly (through differential selection).

This chapter adopts just such a focus. Within this chapter, we develop a theoretical model of the assimilation of new members into decision-making teams based upon individual differences. We focus specifically on decision-making teams because of our belief that the nature of any team's task is so central to understanding team processes that general models attempting to describe all types of teams regardless of tasks have limited utility (Ilgen, Major, Hollenbeck & Sego, 1993). Most teams make decisions of some kind; therefore, this model should have broad applicability. Many teams also have implementation requirements, however, such that team effectiveness depends heavily on specific physical or psychomotor abilities of team members. These kinds of physical and psychomotor requirements will not be the focus of this chapter; we will instead center our attention on information-processing requirements for teams of distributed experts that are making complex decisions.

We will focus on teams that confront complex decision tasks, because these are the types of teams where individual differences are most likely to be relevant and where speed of assimilation is most critical. Most individuals can quickly learn to perform simple decision tasks. However, the ease with which a team can get up to speed is a critical concern on complex tasks and may even be the overriding concern in certain types of teams (such as task forces or special-project teams) that are working against hard deadlines.

Although the goal of creating a seamless transition when moving an individual from one team to another is overly ambitious, we believe that certain types of people will find it easier to assimilate into teams than others. The model developed here may be useful in understanding both why this is true and how this knowledge can be applied to facilitate team functioning in the face of instability in team membership.

In order to accomplish this objective, the remainder of this chapter will be structured in three sections. First, we will briefly review the literature on the role of individual differences in adapting to roles in general. Second, we will focus on recent developments in the areas of team decision making, skill acquisition, and personality measurement that are relevant to the role assimilation process. Third, we will integrate these literatures to come up with an overall model that isolates six primary individual differences that are central to effective assimilation into decision-making teams.

Individual Differences and Role Assimilation: Historical Perspectives

Historically, conceptual approaches to jobs and roles started with the notion that people were relatively passive actors in organizations (the role-taking models) but then developed to grant people a more active role (the role-making models). Most recently, it has been recognized that both orientations can take place, and the current emphasis is determining when and where these different reactions will take place (job-role differentiation models).

The Role-Taking Model

Much of the current thinking about role assimilation can be traced to the description formulated by Kahn and his colleagues (Kahn, Wolfe, Quinn, Snoek, & Rosenthal, 1964; Katz & Kahn, 1978) of the "role episode." Although this model was developed to describe how an individual takes on an organizational role, the process itself clearly generalizes to an individual taking on a role within a team.

This model is based upon the assumption that two people—a role sender and a role incumbent—interact to determine the requirements of the focal role held by the role incumbent. The role sender communicates to the role incumbent a set of beliefs regarding the role (thereby outlining the "sent role"), and the role incumbent perceives this communication in the form of the "received role." The role incumbent then engages in some role behavior that is fed back, becoming input into the role sender's belief system. The role sender's perception of the behavior is then compared to some standard held by the role sender, and the result of that comparison process may influence future role-sending efforts.

Within this model, individual attributes come into play in three different ways. First, some attributes of the role incumbent evoke or facilitate evaluations and behaviors from the role sender. Second, characteristics of the role incumbent color his or her perceptions of the sent role; as a result, two individuals who are sent identical communications may experience different received roles. Third, role incumbents, according to Katz and Kahn, are "self-senders" of roles. In other words, they may have their own set of beliefs about what one should and should not do within a given role.

While Katz and Kahn (1978) describe the *manner* in which individual differences might affect role taking, they do not identify any key traits that (1) induce certain evaluations from role senders, (2) influence perceptions of role incumbents, or (3) affect the nature and scope of self-induced role sending. Katz and Kahn do briefly review the literature on this topic and cite studies showing how certain value orientations (universalistic versus particularistic; moralistic versus expedient) and certain personality traits (dominance, anxiety, and need for achievement) may affect various aspects of the role episode. However, neither Katz and Kahn nor more recent social psychological reviews of this literature (for example, Moreland & Levine, 1989) provide any systematic attempt to develop a content-oriented approach that specifies what specific traits are likely to affect which specific aspects of the role-taking process.

Perhaps most significant for our purposes is Katz and Kahn's postulation of a "general aptitude for role taking" (1978, p. 213) and the suggestion that some types of people will be able to more quickly adjust to *any* role—regardless of specific role requirements. Although not specifying precisely what types of people these might be, the possibility that such a prototypical person might exist motivates the theoretical model we will develop.

The Role-Making Model

Historically speaking, Graen and colleagues (Graen, 1976; Graen, Orris, & Johnson, 1973; Haga, Graen, & Dansereau, 1974) have also had a powerful influence on current thinking regarding the role development process. Graen's approach to role development shares some elements with the approach of Katz and Kahn, but it differs in a number of ways as well. First, while Katz and Kahn recognize, almost in passing, that role incumbents are "self-senders" of roles, Graen's approach assumes a much more proactive stance for role incumbents. Indeed, this heightened aggressiveness on the part of role incumbents is reflected in Graen's reference to his model as a "role-*making*" model, rather than a "role-*taking*" model. Second, whereas both Graen's model and Katz and Kahn's model are dyadic in nature, Katz and Kahn tend to focus on the role incumbent's entire "role set" (that is, everyone who may hold expectations regarding the role), while Graen focuses primarily on the hierarchically based supervisor-subordinate dyad. Finally, whereas Katz and Kahn suggest that the role episode is a recurring process that goes on over time, Graen is much more specific regarding the stages that the process goes through, the potential end-states produced by the process, and the means (negotiation) by which end-states are produced.

According to Graen's model, the first stage of the role assimilation process (the sampling phase, which Graen labeled the "initial confrontation stage") is much like the role-taking episode described by Katz and Kahn, where the leader and the focal person come together and confront each other with their respective sets of role beliefs. This is followed by the second stage (the role development phase or the "working-through stage"): via a negotiating process, the supervisor and subordinate reach a settlement regarding how differences in their respective belief sets are going to be accommodated in the eventual role. In the third stage (the role routinization phase or the "integrating stage") this agreement is unofficially formalized between the parties.

Role incumbents who agree to adopt roles that conform to the supervisor's belief set become part of the "in-group," serving as "informal assistants," and their willingness to take on additional role elements is rewarded by the supervisor with better assignments and enhanced levels of responsibility. Role incumbents who fail to adhere to the supervisor's set of beliefs regarding the role are assigned to the "out-group" and treated as "hired hands" with limited responsibilities and more mundane work assignments.

For the most part, Graen's model can be seen as a major elaboration and refinement (in terms of specificity) of the original role-taking model put forth by Katz and Kahn. One aspect of the role-taking model that is shared (but not truly elaborated upon) by the role-making model deals with individual differences. Adopting a perspective that is much like Katz and Kahn's "general aptitude for role taking," Graen suggests that there are individual differences in "role readiness" (pp. 1231–1232) that will influence the ease with which people can assimilate into roles. As with Katz and Kahn, however, Graen offers no systematic or comprehensive approach in listing what specific traits are likely to impact which stages of the role development process or the overall outcome of the process.

The closest one can come to such a discussion in Graen is a consideration of characteristics of subordinates that might predict whether they are likely to be ultimately categorized in the in-group versus the out-group. Relative to Katz and Kahn, who speculate on individual differences mostly in terms of values and personality traits, Graen (1976) focuses more on skills and abilities. Graen notes that supervisors might use criteria such as competence or high levels of interpersonal skills to separate the "informal assistants" from the "hired hands." On the other hand, he also notes that "prejudices concerning race, religion or ethnic background" (p. 1242) might come into play.

One feature of Graen's discussion (1976) that is worth emphasizing at this point is the speed with which such categorizations take place. Graen notes that "the selection process probably occurs very early in the development of the relationship between supervisor and member" (p. 1242), and this belief has been strongly supported by subsequent empirical research (Liden, Wayne, & Stilwell, 1993). This is an important point, because timing issues determine what types of individual differences can and cannot contribute to the categorization process. We will return to this point in a later section of this chapter, when we compare the stages and timing of role development with the stages and timing of skill acquisition on complex tasks.

Job-Role Differentiation

The last perspective on roles that we will review is Ilgen and Hollenbeck's recent (1991) job-role differentiation approach. Ilgen and Hollenbeck note that the literature on jobs and the literature on roles attempt to cover much of the same theoretical ground. Indeed, they show that conventional definitions of the terms "job" and "work role" are virtually indistinguishable. Yet despite the common theoretical ground covered by these two literatures, there is in fact little conceptual overlap or cross-referencing.

Ilgen and Hollenbeck (1991) also show that the two different literatures approach their topics very differently. The literature on roles is *descriptive* and *process-oriented*. The literature on jobs, however, tends to be much more *prescriptive* and *content-oriented*. That is, the jobs literature focuses on measuring the content of any given job (in terms of task elements and their corresponding behavioral requirements) and manipulating either the content of the job (for example, through human factors engineering or job enrichment) or the characteristics of the job incumbent (through selection and placement) to achieve certain desired ends (efficiency or job satisfaction).

Ilgen and Hollenbeck distinguish between "established task elements" (which constitute the core job) and "emergent task elements"—additional elements that may be layered over the core job (constituting the more elaborated role)—and then use this to draw a formal separation between jobs and roles. Ilgen and Hollenbeck show how taking a prescriptive, content-oriented approach to roles informs both the measurement of role characteristics (for example, role ambiguity and role conflict) and interventions aimed at redressing role problems (see their pp. 200–202). Our belief in the undesirability of approaching roles from a content-free perspective underlies our decision, in this chapter, to previously specify the content and context of the teams we will address (that is, hierarchical teams with distributed expertise confronting a complex decision-making task).

From the job-role differentiation perspective, individual differences influence the degree to which the role incumbent is able *and* willing to move beyond the established task elements. Thus again we see the notion of an aptitude for role taking or role readiness. Since incumbents need to be both able and willing to take on emergent task elements, any model that attempts to systematically address these issues needs to include individual differences that are ability-related (such as those addressed by Graen) as well as those that are motivation-related (such as those mentioned by Katz and Kahn).

Conclusions

There are several conclusions that can be drawn from the historical literature on roles. First, there is a great deal of convergence on both the process and the content/context of role development. Second, there seems to be consensus that some people are going to be better at developing roles than others (in other words, some people are "role ready" or high on "role-taking aptitude"). Third, despite the implicit recognition of individual differences in role-taking or role-making aptitude, there has been no attempt yet to develop any systematic, overarching framework that provides a clear listing of the key variables related to the speed and effectiveness of the role assimilation process. Thus we are not currently in a strong position to predict who will quickly assimilate and effectively expand his or her role and who will end up segregated and relegated to a constrained and minor role. Fortunately, recent developments in other areas of psychology help us address this latter issue more specifically—at least for decision-making teams.

Recent Research Developments Related to Role Assimilation in Decision-Making Teams

Three areas of recent research are relevant to the issue of role assimilation in decision-making teams. First, Hollenbeck et al. (1995) provide the content and context of the task confronting decision-making teams. Their theory identifies three core variables, all at different levels of analysis, that explain the determinants of decision-making accuracy. One of these, *decision informity,* resides at the decision level and deals with how much relevant information the team has to bring to bear on the problem. The second variable, *individual validity,* resides at the individual level of analysis and deals with the ability of the functional experts or staff to translate this information into accurate recommendations about various courses of action. The third variable, *dyadic sensitivity,* resides at the dyadic level and deals with the team leader's ability to accurately weigh each staff member's opinion in coming up with a single overall decision for the team as a whole. These three variables become the core specifications for the team's task. One can then work back from these task specifications to identify the abilities and traits required of team members.

The abilities and traits we will examine here are drawn from two distinct literatures: the literature on skill acquisition and motivation of complex tasks (Ackerman, 1986, 1987) and the literature on the Big Five personality traits of the Five-Factor Model (Costa & McCrae, 1987; Digman, 1990). We will argue that a new person entering a decision-making team needs to successfully and simultaneously execute two developmental sequences. One of these developmental sequences deals with *acquiring skill* within one's own role, and the other is related to *acquiring influence* within the team. We will argue that successful assimilation requires a rapid execution of *both* of these sequences. Within a team context, skill without influence or influence without skill is insufficient for becoming a truly valuable and contributing team member. We will also argue that different individual difference variables contribute differentially to the successful execution of these two developmental processes.

The Multi-Level Theory of Team Decision Making

The Multi-Level Theory (Hollenbeck et al., 1995) is a framework for understanding decision-making accuracy in teams. In this section, we will briefly sketch some of the major propositions from this theory to illustrate its relevance for isolating critical individual differences related to rapid and successful assimilation into decision-making teams. The interested reader is referred to Hollenbeck et al. (1995) for a more detailed delineation of this theory.

The Multi-Level Theory uses a Brunswick Lens Model approach to analyze the information-processing requirements confronting decision-making teams (Ilgen, Major, Hollenbeck, & Sego, 1995). Within the Brunswick Lens Model, decision objects manifest themselves through a finite set of cues or predictors (Brunswick, 1940). The cues each have varying levels of predictive accuracy ("ecological validities") with respect to the decision object, and these cues are assigned varying weights ("policy weights") by the decision maker. Decision accuracy, according to this model, is achieved when the policy weights of the decision maker match the ecological validities associated with the cues.

Working from a team-based generalization of this model, the Multi-Level Theory proposes that many of the critical determinants of team-level effectiveness occur at conceptual levels *below the team level,* and it attempts to isolate the most important aspect of team performance that occurs at the decision level, the individual level, and the dyadic level. Each of these lower-level variables has a conceptual analog at the team level.

As alluded to earlier, one of the most important variables, according to this theory, resides at the decision level. *Decision informity* is formally defined as the degree to which team members are adequately informed (in other words, have accurate information on all the relevant cues) about the particular object that they are evaluating. This variable is at the decision level, because a team can have a great deal of reliable information (and hence be well informed) on some decisions but be poorly informed on others. Over many decision-making opportunities, however, there could be stable between-team variance on this variable, in that some teams are consistently better informed than others. This variation is captured by a team-level variable referred to as *team informity*. Team informity is simply the average level of decision informity for a given team across a specified number of decisions. The Multi-Level Theory proposes that team informity is one of the core driving influences behind team-level decision accuracy.

At the level of the individual team member, the most critical variable is *individual validity*—that is, the degree to which team members can translate raw information regarding the decision object into recommendations that predict the true state of the decision object. This variable is at the individual level, because a team can have some members who make highly valid recommendations and some who make poor recommendations. As with decision informity, however, there can be stable between-team variance on this variable, in that some teams have, on average, better members than other teams; this is captured by a team-level variable referred to as *staff validity* (or the level of validity for a team averaged across all the staff members). The Multi-Level Theory proposes that staff validity is one of the core influences of team-level decision accuracy.

The final core variable identified by the Multi-Level Theory lies at the dyadic level and is labeled *dyadic sensitivity*. A team with multiple members and a leader is composed of several hierarchical dyads, and thus a team leader is often confronted with different recommendations from different team members regarding a decision the team faces. These staff recommendations form another type of Brunswickian cue that can be utilized in arriving at accurate decisions. Dyadic sensitivity is the degree to which the leader accurately weighs each team member's recommendation. This variable resides at the dyadic level, because a leader may develop an effective weighting system for one staff member but not another. As with the other variables within this theory, however, there could be stable between-team differences in the average level of dyadic sensitivity, and this is captured in a team-level variable called *hierarchical sensitivity*. Hierarchical sensitivity is then the third core, team-level variable that the Multi-Level Theory uses to account for variation in decision-making accuracy across teams.

The Multi-Level Theory treats all variables other than those described above as "noncore variables" and proposes that the effects of the noncore variables are transmitted through the core-level variables. So, for example, a variable such as cohesiveness among team members is not as critical as team informity, staff validity, or hierarchical sensitivity; indeed, to the extent that such a variable is important at all, this importance is attained by the effect that the variable has on the core variables. For example, cohesiveness is important because it leads to greater hierarchical sensitivity or higher levels of team informity.

Three separate empirical studies have examined the validity of the Multi-Level Theory (Hollenbeck et al., 1995; Hedlund, Ilgen, & Hollenbeck, 1993). These studies have used computer simulations of military command and control scenarios in which the team is asked to decide on the level of threat posed by a series of unidentified aircraft (the decision object). The aircraft are evaluated by a staff of differentiated experts (for example, people trained in air reconnaissance, coastal air defense, the use of shipboard monitors, and so on) who can measure different attributes of the aircraft, such as range, speed, direction, radar emissions, size, and approach angle (the cues).

Results from these studies have shown that the three core, team-level constructs account for between 27 and 49 percent of the variance in team-level decision-making accuracy, compared to only 9 to 17 percent of the variance for noncore variables, which have been the focus of most traditional group decision-making research (for example, group cohesiveness, stress, familiarity, and experience). Moreover, as suggested by the theory, the effects that these noncore variables have on team-level decision accuracy are mediated by the core variables. That is, when one statistically partials out the effects of the core constructs, 66 to 100 percent of the variance accounted for by the noncore variables is eliminated.

The Multi-Level Theory is useful in exploring the role of individual differences in teams because it isolates three critical tasks that any team member, including a new team member, must accomplish. First, the person needs to be able to collect a great deal of information relevant to the decision. In teams characterized by interdependence, this information must often come from other team members; thus a new individual needs to quickly develop enough stature in the group to get the cooperation of teammates (those in his or her horizontal dyads) in the acquisition of information. Second, because the new person needs to process this information to make effective decisions, it is critical for him or her to quickly develop expertise regarding the decision task by learning how various pieces of information relate to the decision at hand. Third, the new individual must be able to form an effective relationship with the team leader (vertical dyad) so that the former's contribution can be effectively integrated into the overall team's decision.

Thus we would argue that getting informed, making valid recommendations, and ensuring that these recommendations are incorporated into the team's overall decision form the core requirements for any team member in this type of decision-making team. With this established, we must now ask what kind of individual difference variables are likely to contribute to meeting these three requirements and what developmental issues are associated with meeting these requirements for a new team member. The recent literature on skill acquisition and motivation on complex tasks and the literature on the Big Five personality traits provide some answers to these questions.

Individual Differences and Developmental Stages in Skill Acquisition

We have established that one of the major tasks confronting a new member of a decision-making team is to quickly develop the expertise that allows him or her to make valid recommendations about what decisions the team should make. Theory and literature on individual differences in the area of learning and skill acquisition are of obvious relevance to this issue. Based upon our reading of this literature, three individual differences seem to stand out as critical to acquiring expertise on complex decision tasks: general cognitive ability, specific task knowledge, and self-efficacy. We would also propose, in line with arguments put forth by Ackerman and colleagues (Ackerman, 1986, 1987; Ackerman & Humphreys, 1990; Kanfer & Ackerman, 1989), that there is a temporal order in which the importance of each of these variables manifests itself.

Ackerman (1987) has shown that all tasks initially require the allocation of cognitive resources; thus initial differences in task performance are related to general cognitive ability. In the earliest stages of skill development, high levels of general cognitive ability aid the individual in developing declarative knowledge—that is, "knowledge about facts and things" (Kanfer & Ackerman, 1989, p. 660). With simple tasks (or what Kanfer & Ackerman, 1989, refer to as "consistent" tasks), the role of general cognitive ability diminishes over time: with enough experience, everyone develops sufficient declarative knowledge to reach asymptotic levels of proficiency on the task. On the other hand, general cognitive ability remains relevant throughout the course of task performance with complex tasks.

As individuals gain more practice on a task, more content-specific indicators of job knowledge become relevant to predicting performance. According to Ackerman, the assessment of a content-specific knowledge domain (for example, a chemical knowledge test administered to a would-be chemist known to have high general cognitive ability) captures the interaction between general cognitive abilities and more motivationally relevant traits and vocational interests that determine an individual's final level of proficiency. Whereas general abilities tap the person's potential for learning a broad spectrum of specific content matter, more narrow and specific knowledge, skills, or abilities capture the realization of this potential. The realization of this potential comes about only when the person's vocational interest and motivation to learn about the particular content domain are as high as his or her aptitude for learning that content domain. Thus specific knowledge, skills, and abilities become relevant at a later developmental stage for complex technical content areas, once general cognitive ability has stabilized or begun to decline as a predictor.

Finally, in the last stage of skill development, the experience levels of incumbents still engaged on the task (note that those who performed poorly prior to this point due to low general cognitive ability or task knowledge may have dropped out) may be sufficiently high that most have fairly serviceable knowledge structures.

At this point, variance in performance occurs primarily on the most difficult, hard-to-achieve aspects of the task. Because successfully accomplishing the most difficult aspects of the task requires persistence and perseverance in the face of likely failure, individual differences in self-efficacy become relevant (Morrison & Brantner, 1992).

Bandura (1982) notes that judgments of self-efficacy affect how much effort people will expend and how long they will persist in the face of obstacles or aversive experiences. When confronted with failure, individuals who doubt their abilities give up, whereas those who have a strong sense of efficacy struggle on. Just as general cognitive ability is a somewhat necessary but insufficient condition for developing specific task knowledge, specific task knowledge is a somewhat necessary but insufficient condition for developing self-efficacy. Two individuals with similar levels of expertise may develop different levels of self-efficacy, and this could result in differential typical performance levels at the upper end of the task difficulty spectrum (Ackerman & Kanfer, 1993; Eyring, Johnson, & Francis, 1993).

Thus, from a skill development perspective, we suggest that new members must go through a three-stage developmental process. First, the new member must confront the task and—through planning or trial-and-error procedures—reason, deduce, or learn the best strategies related to task performance. At this stage, broad individual differences in ability are most critical. At the second stage, individuals must translate their general potential to learn the task into actual task knowledge. At the final stage of skill development, restricted levels of ability and task knowledge (due to the increasing levels of people's experience and performance-related attrition) decrease in importance, while motivational variables that determine performance at the most difficult levels of the task become most critical. Thus individual difference variables such as self-efficacy become most relevant in understanding performance variation at this stage.

Individual Differences and Developmental Stages in Influence Acquisition

We have argued that a new person entering an intact decision-making team needs to simultaneously execute two developmental sequences in order to successfully assimilate into that team. In the previous section, we discussed the developmental sequence associated with acquiring expertise; in this section, we will explore the developmental sequence associated with acquiring social influence—that process by which, to use Graen's terminology, the individual moves from being an outsider to being a member of the in-group.

However, whereas Graen's concern was directed almost exclusively at the hierarchical dyad, we—because we are focused more narrowly on teams—are also interested in aspects of the horizontal dyad. In teams whose members are specialized and dependent upon each other, these horizontal relationships cannot be ignored. From the Multi-Level Theory perspective, this horizontal interdependence comes about via the need to obtain information from other staff members. If a new member becomes socially isolated within his or her peer group in this sort of team, that isolation has direct negative implications for the new member and the team as a whole. Thus, in addition to becoming an "informal assistant" to the leader (that is, obtaining upward social influence), the new team member must also become a "valued colleague" among his or her peers.

The developmental process by which a new team member garners such influence differs in two significant ways relative to the developmental process associated with acquiring expertise. We will argue that while both skill acquisition and the acquisition of influence are developmental sequences that unfold over time, the two sequences (1) proceed on entirely different time scales and (2) are driven by characteristically different individual difference variables. In the remainder of this section, we will discuss these issues.

The skill development process is envisioned as a relatively long-term process driven by underlying abilities and belief systems; indeed, Simon (1992) estimates that within some areas of inquiry (for example, aerospace, medicine, management, engineering, law), a span of ten years is needed for a professional to truly become an expert. The process by which a new member is accepted into the in-group rather than relegated to the out-group, however, is a relatively quick one that is driven by more easily observable, surface characteristics.

The notion that in-group determination occurs rapidly was shown both in Graen's original research and in more recent studies. For example, in Graen's studies of clerical and managerial employees, in-group/out-group status was determined in a few weeks and then remained relatively stable after this period (Graen, Orris, & Johnson, 1973; Haga, Graen, & Dansereau, 1974). More recent research by Liden et al. (1993) with a wide range of employees has suggested that in-group/out-group status stabilizes after a mere five days. The short time period in which these kinds of categorizations are made places a limit on the kinds of individual differences that can possibly drive such judgments. Whereas the long-term process of skill acquisition is driven by individual differences that are hard to directly observe (variables such as general cognitive ability and knowledge structures), the variables driving the acquisition of early social influence must themselves be driven by other types of variables—variables that are readily manifested and easy to observe.

Hogan (1991) has noted that the personality variables traditionally studied can be broken down into two sets: personality dimensions that describe an individual's "inner nature" and personality traits that describe an individual's "social reputation." The person's inner nature and the individual differences relevant to it are essentially private dimensions that must be inferred indirectly from one's manifest behaviors. In interpersonal settings, making inferences about these internal states requires observing a large number of interactions over time. This slows the speed with which this inner nature can be ascertained by outside observers.

The person's social reputation, on the other hand, is public and much more directly observable. Because the process of determining one's social reputation is less inferential (relative to determining one's inner nature), it can take place with much greater speed. The speed with which this process takes place might also be explained in part by the high degree of practice that human beings have in making such judgments. Hogan has even suggested that skill in making such judgments may be evolutionarily hard-wired. He notes that most traits are inherently evaluative because people evolved as group-living animals needing to accomplish group tasks in order to survive. Within such a context, trait terms evolved to reflect observers' assessments of other people as potential contributors or detractors to the group's ability to survive. Thus certain general traits might be indicative of more specific underlying skills related to effective behavior in goal-oriented group contexts (Stevens & Campion, 1994).

Indeed, many stable and relatively valid inferences regarding some social traits have shown to be drawn at "zero acquaintance"— that is, upon an initial meeting between two people (Borkenau & Liebler, 1992). A series of recent studies, for example, has shown that on some social traits, one can obtain relatively high consensus between self-ratings and stranger ratings without any direct interaction at all between the parties (Albright, Kenny, & Malloy, 1988; Levesque & Kenny, 1993; Kenny, Horner, Kashy, & Chu, 1992).

If one concludes that only social traits drive the early determination of social influence within teams, then the recent attention and research focused on the Big Five personality traits becomes highly relevant in appreciating assimilation of new members into intact teams.

Both Digman (1990) and Ozer and Reise (1994) discuss the historical development of the Big Five taxonomy, noting the convergence of opinion regarding the robustness and generality of this structure across samples, measurement instruments, measurement sources, and contexts. The structure of this approach gives predominance to five specific trait categories, labeled Conscientiousness, Extraversion, Agreeableness, Emotional Stability, and Openness to Experience. Three of these traits (extraversion, conscientiousness, and, to a lesser extent, agreeableness) have been identified as traits that can be accurately gauged at zero acquaintance (Albright et al., 1988; Levesque & Kenny, 1993; Kenny et al., 1992). Although critics have questioned the wisdom of rallying prematurely around this taxonomy (McAdams, 1992; Schmit & Ryan, 1993), it has shown some utility in the area of I/O psychology for predicting and explaining behavior in organizations (Barrick & Mount, 1991; Tett, Jackson, & Rothstein, 1991; McHenry, Hough, Toquam, Hanson, & Ashworth, 1990; Cortina, Doherty, Schmitt, Kaufman, & Smith, 1992).

When one examines these five variables within the context of a decision-making team, particularly from a Multi-Level Theory perspective, three of the factors seem to stand out most prominently as potentially related to the three core factors that drive team effectiveness. First, the factor of *agreeableness* is critical in team contexts, particularly as it relates to developing influence among peers (those in horizontal dyads) and acquiring peer assistance. Agreeableness represents a quality of interpersonal interaction behavior and, according to Costa, McRae, and Dye (1991) is constituted by six personality facets including (1) trust (that is, the tendency to attribute benevolent intent to others), (2) straightforwardness (that is, the tendency to be frank and direct with others), (3) altruism (that is, selflessness and concern for others), (4) compliance (that is, willingness to cooperate rather than display aggression in conflict situations), (5) modesty (that is, social humility and a lack of arrogance), and (6) tendermindedness (that is, sympathy and empathy).

An individual characterized in a positive manner on these six attributes is likely to have an easier time assimilating into a new team than someone characterized by the negative ends of these continua. Moreover, we believe that this aspect is especially important in peer relationships, and the evidence suggests that variables within this category are related more highly to peer ratings of performance in group-oriented contexts (Cortina et al., 1992), relative to objective measures of performance on individually based tasks (Tett et al., 1991).

A second critical factor for assimilating into decision making teams is *extraversion*. This overall factor has been defined as the degree to which an individual is sociable, gregarious, talkative, active, ambitious, and assertive. The first four of these facets might be important for managing peer relations and thus are critical to the new member's ability to secure information, assistance, and cooperation from peers. These factors might also be relevant for managing the vertical dyad, although in decision-making teams, the latter two facets—ambition and assertiveness—may be even more critical.

In hierarchical teams, team members must eventually come to influence the leader, and assertiveness might be a key requirement for accomplishing this goal. An assertive individual expends more energy in ensuring that his or her opinion is listened to and acted upon by the leader. In addition, the team member, in order to become an "informal assistant," needs to be willing to take on additional tasks and responsibilities. The primary reward for expanding one's role in this fashion is the anticipation of more visible and prestigious assignments and future promotional opportunities that may be within the leader's discretion. Such rewards are likely to be much more salient reinforcers for individuals who are characterized as ambitious than those who are characterized as lazy or self-satisfied.

The third of the Big Five factors related to assimilation in team contexts is *conscientiousness,* which is defined by a high need for achievement and commitment to work. This overall factor is also constituted by behavioral tendencies that lean toward order (that is, organization), dutifulness (that is, strict adherence to rules of conduct), self-discipline (that is, persistence and the ability to continue with a task despite boredom or distractions), and deliberation (that is, caution and a determination to engage only in well-planned actions).

Within teams, conscientiousness (like extraversion) should be critical for managing upward hierarchical relationships. For example, one of the factors Graen mentioned as being important in the leader's determination of assigning someone the designation "informal assistant" rather than "hired hand" was the degree to which the person could be trusted. Conscientiousness on the part of the subordinate (especially as expressed in order and dutifulness) promotes trust, because the conscientious person's behavior is predictable and reliable. Thus, as with the other classes of personality variables discussed so far, conscientiousness is important to rapid assimilation into teams because of its relationship to acquiring social influence.

In addition to this, however, conscientiousness might also relate to performance due to its effect on acquiring skill and proficiency. Particularly with respect to complex, hard-to-learn decision-making tasks, it is clear that the skill development process can take a long time. Given this requirement, the aspects of conscientiousness that deal with persistence and deliberation might be related to one's capacity for developing expertise regardless of content area. Persistence ensures that the individual stays with the task long enough to generate a threshold level of experience. Deliberation in generating and evaluating one's experience ensures that some benefit is derived from the time invested.

In summary, from a social influence perspective, new members must go through a three-stage developmental process. The new member must initially confront his or her team members and, starting from zero acquaintance, generate a social reputation that conveys to these people what he or she is like. At the second stage, the new member, based upon a relatively quick assessment of characteristics such as agreeableness, extraversion, and conscientiousness, is either accepted into the peer group and recognized as one of the leader's informal assistants or relegated to the role of an outsider or hired hand. In the third and final stage, this status is routinized and stabilized, and it is thereafter difficult for the team member to change his or her status.

Comparing and Contrasting the Processes Associated with Acquiring Skill Versus Acquiring Influence

We have described two developmental processes critical to quickly and effectively assimilating into hierarchical decision-making teams. One of these deals with acquiring expertise; the other, with acquiring social influence. We have argued that the two processes proceed along entirely different time scales (skill acquisition proceeds slowly, whereas one's social reputation and influence are determined quickly) and are driven by characteristically different individual differences (skill acquisition is related to hard-to-observe, ability-related variables, whereas influence acquisition is related to readily manifested social traits).

The notion that progress in the area of skill development and progress in the area of social influence development are on such discrepant times scales and driven by very different personal characteristics has critical implications for the effective assimilation of new team members. From the team's point of view, if in-group status decisions are made and stabilized before new team members reach their final level of expertise, the possibility of prematurely granting or negating the influence of some team member is strong. In other words, the timing of the status determinations precludes final levels of task proficiency from being the driving force behind who is given influence and who is not.

From the new team member's point of view, this notion suggests that, whereas many of the behaviors associated with trait-based personality traits such as agreeableness, extraversion, and conscientiousness may seem (and in fact may be) unrelated to performance within one's area of expertise, not appearing to have such traits puts the employee at risk. Early inferences drawn about a new team member on these traits may restrict that person's influence within the group to a level far short of his or her actual (or eventual) expertise. Thus the new team member who is perceived as disagreeable, reticent, and/or lacking in conscientiousness may get off to such a slow start in his or her new team that no level of eventual expertise may be able to overcome that person's relegation to out-group status.

An Integrated Model of Individual Differences in Role Assimilation

In this final section of this chapter, we will try to integrate the preceding discussion into a single, overarching theory of assimilation of new members into intact hierarchical decision-making teams. Specifically, this theory will integrate the historical literature on role taking and role making with Hollenbeck's Multi-Level Theory and recent developments in the area of skill acquisition and the structure of social reputations (developments associated with the Big Five taxonomy). The model highlights the importance of twelve variables—six related to effective team functioning and six related to specific characteristics of new team members that affect the speed with which they contribute to effective team functioning. Figure 8.1 provides a schematic depiction of this theory.

Specifying a Multi-Level Model

At the heart of this theory are the constructs specified by the Multi-Level Theory and the notion that the central determinants of team decision-making performance are the three core team-level constructs (team informity, staff validity, and hierarchical sensitivity) and their three corresponding lower-level analogs (decision informity, individual validity, and dyadic sensitivity). Within the Multi-Level Theory, individual differences are conceptualized as noncore variables. Thus we propose that the impact that individual differences have on team performance is smaller than that of the core constructs and is, for the most part, mediated by the core constructs.

In terms of specific individual difference variables, our model suggests that ability-related variables will drive the skill acquisition process and trait-related variables will drive the influence acquisition process. Even more specifically, we propose that one can map specific individual differences onto the core variables in a way that explains why each is relevant.

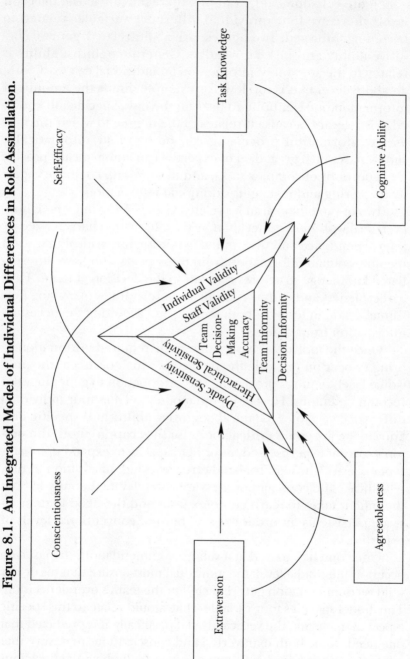

Figure 8.1. An Integrated Model of Individual Differences in Role Assimilation.

Figure 8.1 shows, for example, that (starting at the decision level) there are four individual difference variables related to becoming informed. Two of these are ability-related: general cognitive ability and task knowledge. General cognitive ability is related to the amount of information an individual can work with; an ability level that is too low, for example, limits the amount of information one can bring to bear on the task. Specific job knowledge is relevant because it relates to the degree to which the necessary information processing can be handled automatically. Individuals with a great deal of expertise can automatically process large portions of complex tasks, and this frees up cognitive capacity for storing and managing additional information.

Two of the other variables related to becoming informed, however, deal with *traits* rather than *abilities*. In teams characterized by interdependence and distributed expertise, it is critical that team members obtain information from those peers who have differentiated knowledge structures relevant to the decision at hand. Thus agreeableness and extraversion become relevant to managing horizontal dyads, in terms of both seeking and acquiring the necessary information from others.

Once the individual has garnered the required information to bring to bear on the task, the next step, which occurs at the individual level, requires processing this information to generate valid recommendations. Here, too, the model specifies four individual difference variables. General cognitive ability and specific task knowledge are again critical, because they capture both the person's current expertise and his or her capacity to expand upon current expertise through trial-and-error learning. In addition to this, self-efficacy and conscientiousness are also relevant, because of both the time it takes to learn complex tasks and the need to demonstrate persistence in order to excel beyond conventional levels of expertise.

Once one has arrived at a valid recommendation, the last step occurs at the dyadic level: the individual must ensure that his or her valid recommendation gets reflected in the team's overall decision. The model specifies four variables that should relate to this specific aspect of managing the vertical dyad. Specifically, it is predicted that one needs to be both extraverted and conscientious to ensure that one's opinion is heard; and one needs to be highly self-efficacious to persist in the influence process and generate the kind of confidence that results in influence. Finally, one needs to have a high degree of agreeableness. While team members need to be persistent, they must also recognize that within the team context—especially if there are different areas of expertise—no one person can dominate every decision. Conflict is likely to arise between team members; incidents will occur in which one or another team member's opinion may seem slighted. Because of this fine line between persistence and cooperation, the long-term viability of the hierarchical dyad can be assured only if there is some degree of agreeableness on the part of staff members. The new staff member cannot physically or psychologically withdraw from the team the first time that person does not get his or her way.

Thus, according to this model, there are six critical individual differences on the part of a new team member that predict the speed and effectiveness of his or her assimilation into an intact hierarchical decision-making team with distributed expertise. Our model specifies both the critical individual variables that relate to this outcome (general cognitive ability, task knowledge, self-efficacy, conscientiousness, extraversion, and agreeableness) and the reasons why these individual variables are important (the three core team-level constructs and their lower-level analogs). The model also stipulates that two developmental sequences (one for acquiring expertise and one for acquiring influence) must be successfully and simultaneously executed. Successful assimilation (from both the team's and the individual's perspective) can come about only when both expertise and influence are in place. The fact that the different processes proceed within different time frames and are driven by different variables can complicate the simultaneous execution of these two processes, however, leading to situations where the level of a new team member's expertise and his or her influence are out of balance.

Boundary Conditions and Limitations

Although this model represents an initial attempt at specifying characteristics of the new team member that might affect assimilation, we must note several boundary conditions and limitations of this approach.

Boundary Conditions

This model presumes that the new team member needs to develop both expertise and social influence, yet in some real-world situations this is not the case. Some new team members may enter the team having reached asymptotic levels of proficiency, thus short-circuiting the need for skill acquisition. In many complex fields, however, changes and innovations, as well as the uncertainties associated with applying one's skill in a specific local problem area, may imply that individuals need to be continually learning and expanding their expertise.

Furthermore, as implied by the idiom "Your reputation precedes you," some new team members may have social reputations that are well established before those team members are introduced into the team. If a person's reputation is positive—that is, if he or she is known as bright, knowledgeable, agreeable, and conscientious—the process for developing social influence might be short-circuited. If the reputation is negative, however, it might make the process take longer—or make it impossible altogether.

Limitations

We should also note that the model developed here offers a limited approach to appreciating the totality of issues that go into effective assimilation. Although we cannot get into all the factors one needs to consider beyond individual differences in team members, some are critical enough to note.

First, any model that attempts to explain the whole assimilation process needs also to address the characteristics of individuals other than the new team member. Any such model must, at the very least, come to grips with the characteristics of leaders, peers, and the person (or persons) being replaced, examining how the new person fits into the team as currently configured. The Multi-Level Theory may provide some help with respect to this problem of context. For example, the theory suggests that characteristics of the peers may be most relevant to the new person's ability to get informed and characteristics of the leader may be most relevant to the new member's ability to get his or her opinion recognized. In terms of the replaced member, perhaps the most important consideration to assimilation is his or her individual validity. That is, assimilation may occur more easily if one has small shoes to fill; in other words, it is easier to follow a former staff member who had low validity than one who had high validity.

Second, any comprehensive model must also address non–individual difference variables that affect the process (Chao, O'Leary-Kelly, Wolf, Klein, & Gardner, 1994). There is an entire literature on socialization methods that can be applied to the new team member. Many of these externally manipulated variables are likely to interact with characteristics of the new member or other team members (leaders, peers, predecessors), thereby affecting the speed and effectiveness of assimilation.

Finally, although we attempted to build a model that integrated the two developmental sequences of expertise and influence, any comprehensive model must also recognize the fact that teams themselves go through their own developmental sequence. Where the team stands along this continuum may influence the ease and effectiveness of new-member socialization (Kozlowski et al., 1994). In other words, the challenges confronting a new team member may differ depending on whether the team is just forming, has been formed for a short while but is struggling to come to grips with roles, or is in a highly mature state with formalized rules and rituals. Individual differences may interact with the stage of team development in complex ways, and some of the individual differences stipulated here may be relevant to this process.

While it is difficult in one chapter to address all the relevant issues associated with successful assimilation into roles, perhaps some of the processes and individual differences discussed here can serve as a starting point for cumulating theory and evidence on assimilation as a total process. Given the changes in the structure of work noted at the outset of this chapter, the time to cumulate such theory and generate such evidence is at hand.

References

Ackerman, P. L. (1986). Individual differences in information processing: An investigation of intellectual abilities and task performance during practice. *Intelligence, 10,* 101–139.

Ackerman, P. L. (1987). Individual differences in skill learning: An integration of psychometric and information processing perspectives. *Psychological Bulletin, 102,* 3–27.

Ackerman, P. L., & Humphreys, L. G. (1990). Individual differences theory in industrial and organizational psychology. In M. Dunnette & L. M. Hough (Eds.), *Handbook of industrial and organizational psychology* (pp. 223–282). Palo Alto, CA: Consulting Psychologists Press.

Ackerman, P. L. & Kanfer, R. (1993). Integrating laboratory and field study for improving selection: Development of a battery for predicting air traffic controller success. *Journal of Applied Psychology, 78,* 413–432.

Albright, L., Kenny, D. A., & Malloy, T. E. (1988). Consensus in personality judgments at zero acquaintance. *Journal of Personality and Social Psychology, 55,* 387–395.

Bandura, A. (1982). Self-efficacy mechanisms in human behavior. *American Psychologist, 37,* 122–147.

Barrick, M. R. & Mount, M. K. (1991). The Big Five personality dimensions and job performance: A meta-analysis. *Personnel Psychology, 44,* 1–26.

Bettenhausen, K. (1991). Five years of group research: What have we learned and what needs to be addressed? *Journal of Management, 17,* 345–381.

Borkenau, P., & Liebler, A. (1992). Trait inferences: Sources of validity at zero acquaintance. *Journal of Personality, 62,* 645–657.

Bridges, W. (1994). The end of the job. *Fortune, 130,* 62–71.

Brunswick, E. (1940). Thing constancy as measured by correlation coefficients. *Psychological Review, 47,* 69–78.

Byrne, J. A. (1993, Sept. 11). Why several heads are better than one. *Business Week,* pp. 45–46.

Chao, G. T., O'Leary-Kelly, A. M., Wolf, S., Klein, H. J., & Gardner, P. (1994). Organizational socialization: Its contents and consequences. *Journal of Applied Psychology, 79,* 730–743.

Cortina, J. M., Doherty, M. L., Schmitt, N., Kaufman, G., & Smith, R. G. (1992). The "Big Five" personality traits in the IPI and MMPI: Predictors of police performance. *Personnel Psychology, 45,* 119–140.

Costa, P. T., & McCrae, R. R. (1985). The NEO-PI Personality Inventory. Odessa, FL: Psychological Assessment Resources.

Costa, P. T., & McCrae, R. R. (1992). *NEO PI-R: Revised NEO Personality Inventory.* Odessa, FL: Psychological Assessment Resources.

Costa, P. T., McCrae, R. R., & Dye, D. D. (1991). Facet scales for Agreeableness and Conscientiousness: A Revision of the NEO Personality Inventory. *Personality and Individual Differences, 12,* 887–898.

Davidow, W. H., & Malone, M. S. (1992). *The virtual corporation: Structuring and revitalizing the corporation for the 21st century.* New York: HarperCollins.

Digman, J. M. (1990). Personality structure: Emergence of the Five-Factor Model. *Annual Review of Psychology, 41,* 417–440.

Dumaine, B. (1994). The trouble with teams. *Fortune, 130,* 86–93.

Eyring, J. D., Johnson, D. S., & Francis, D. J. (1993). A cross-level unit-of-analysis approach to individual differences in skill acquisition. *Journal of Applied Psychology, 78,* 805–814.

Feldman, D. C. (1990). Reconceptualizing the nature and consequences of part-time work. *Academy of Management Review, 15,* 103–112.

Goodman, P. S., & Associates (1986). *Designing effective work groups.* San Francisco: Jossey-Bass.

Graen, G. B. (1976). Role making processes within complex organizations. In M. D. Dunnette (Ed.), *Handbook of industrial and organizational psychology* (pp. 1201–1245). Skokie, IL: Rand McNally.

Graen, G. B., Orris, J. B., & Johnson, T. (1973). Role assimilation processes within complex organizations. *Journal of Vocational Behavior, 3,* 395–420.

Hackman, J. R. (Ed.). (1990). *Groups that work (and those that don't): Creating conditions for effective teamwork.* San Francisco: Jossey-Bass.

Haga, W. J., Graen, G., & Dansereau, F. (1974). Professionalism and role making within a service organization: A longitudinal investigation. *American Sociological Review, 39,* 122–133.

Hammer, M., & Champy, J. (1993). *Reengineering the corporation: A manifesto for business revolution.* New York: Harper Business.

Hedlund, J., Ilgen, D. R., & Hollenbeck, J. R. (1993). *The effect of computer-mediated versus face-to-face communication on decision making in hierarchical teams.* Unpublished manuscript, Michigan State University.

Here comes GM's Saturn. (1990, Apr.). *Business Week,* pp. 52–62.

Hoerr, J. (1989, July 10). The pay-off from teamwork: The gains in quality are substantial. *Business Week,* pp. 56–62.

Hogan, R. (1991). Personality and personality measurement. In M. D. Dunnette & L. M. Hough (Eds.), *Handbook of industrial and organizational psychology* (2nd ed.; Vol. 2, pp. 873–919). Palo Alto, CA: Consulting Psychologists Press.

Hollenbeck, J. R., Ilgen, D. R., Sego, D., Hedlund, J., Major, D. A., & Phillips, J. (1995). The multi-level theory of team decision-making: Decision performance in teams incorporating distributed expertise. *Journal of Applied Psychology, 80,* 292–316.

Ilgen, D. R. (1994). Jobs and roles: Accepting and coping with the changing structure of organizations. In M. G. Rumsey & C. B. Harris (Eds.), *Selection and classification* (pp. 13–32). Hillsdale, NJ: Erlbaum.

Ilgen, D. R., & Hollenbeck, J. R. (1991). The structure of work: Job design and roles. In M. D. Dunnette & L. M. Hough (Eds.), *Handbook of industrial and organizational psychology* (2nd ed.; Vol. 2, pp. 165–207). Palo Alto, CA: Consulting Psychologists Press.

Ilgen, D. R., Major, D., Hollenbeck, J. R., & Sego, D. (1993). Team research in the 90's. In M. Chemers & R. Aymon (Eds.), *Leadership and organizational effectiveness* (pp. 245–270). New York: Academic Press.

Ilgen, D. R., Major, D., Hollenbeck, J. R., & Sego, D. (1995). Decision-making in teams: A levels perspective on an individual difference analog. In R. Guzzo & E. Salas (Eds.), *Team effectiveness and decision making in organizations* (pp. 113–148). San Francisco: Jossey-Bass.

Kahn, R. L., Wolfe, D. M., Quinn, R. P., Snoek, J. D., & Rosenthal, R. A. (1964). *Occupational stress: Studies in role conflict and role ambiguity.* New York: Wiley.

Kanfer, R., & Ackerman, P. L. (1989). Motivation and cognitive abilities: An integrative/aptitude-treatment interaction approach to skill acquisition. *Journal of Applied Psychology, 74,* 657–690.

Katz, D., & Kahn, R. L. (1978). *The social psychology of organizations.* New York: Wiley.

Kenny, D. A., Horner, C., Kashy, D. A., & Chu, L. C. (1992). Consensus at zero acquaintance: Replication, behavioral cues, and stability. *Journal of Personality and Social Psychology, 62,* 88–97.

Kozlowski, W. J., Gully, S. M., Nason, E. J., Ford, J. K., Smith, E. M., Smith, M. R., & Futch, C. J. (1994, Apr.). *A composition theory of team development: Levels, content, process, and learning outcomes.* Paper presented at the 9th annual meeting of the Society for Industrial and Organizational Psychology, Nashville, TN.

Levesque, M. J., & Kenny, D. A. (1993). Accuracy of behavioral predictions at zero acquaintance: A social relations analysis. *Journal of Personality and Social Psychology, 65,* 1178–1187.

Levine, J. M., & Moreland, R. L. (1989). Progress in small group research. *Annual review of psychology, 41,* 585–634.

Liden, R. C., Wayne, S. J., & Stilwell, D. (1993). A longitudinal study on the early development of leader-member exchanges. *Journal of Applied Psychology, 78,* 662–674.

Locke, E. A. (1982). The ideas of Frederick W. Taylor: An evaluation. *Academy of Management Review, 1,* 14–24.

McAdams, D. P. (1992). The Five-Factor Model in personality: A critical appraisal. *Journal of Personality, 60,* 329–361.

McHenry, J. J., Hough, L. M., Toquam, J. L., Hanson, M. A., & Ashworth, S. (1990). Project A validity results: The relationship between predictor and criterion domains. *Personnel Psychology, 43,* 335–354.

Moreland, R. L., & Levine, J. M. (1989). Newcomers and oldtimers in small groups. In P. B. Paulus (Ed.), *Psychology of small group behavior* (pp. 143–186). Hillsdale, NJ: Erlbaum.

Morrison, R. F., & Brantner, T. M. (1992). What enhances or inhibits learning a new job? A basic career issue. *Journal of Applied Psychology, 77,* 926–940.

Ozer, D. J., & Reise, S. P. (1994). Personality assessment. *Annual Review of Psychology, 45,* 357–388.

Rouse, W. B., Cannon-Bowers, J. A., & Salas, E. (1992). The role of mental models in team performance in complex systems. *IEEE Transactions on Systems, Man, and Cybernetics, 22,* 1296–1308.

Schmit, M. J., & Ryan, A. M. (1993). The Big Five in personnel selection: Factor structure in applicant and nonapplicant populations. *Journal of Applied Psychology, 78,* 966–974.

Simon, H. A. (1992). What is an "explanation" of behavior? *Psychological Science, 3,* 150–161.

Stevens, M. J., & Campion, M. A. (1994). The knowledge, skill, and ability requirements for teamwork: Implications for human resource management. *Journal of Management, 20,* 503–530.

Stone, P. F. (1990). Who needs a boss? *Fortune, 125,* 52–60.

Tett, R. P., Jackson, D. N., & Rothstein, M. (1991). Personality measures as predictors of job performance: A meta-analysis. *Personnel Psychology, 44,* 703–742.

The right stuff. (1990, Oct.). *Time,* pp. 74–84.

Treece, J. B. (1992, Jan. 20). Does Chrysler finally have the Jeep that it needs? *Business Week,* pp. 21–22.

Tuckman, B. W. (1965). Developmental sequence in small groups. *Psychological Bulletin, 63,* 384–399.

Woodruff, D. (1991, Nov. 4). The racy Viper is already a winner for Chrysler. *Business Week,* pp. 91–92.

Woodruff, D. (1993, Dec. 12). Chrysler's Neon: Is this the small car that Detroit couldn't build? *Business Week,* 116–124.

Chapter Nine

Interpersonal Relations in Organizations

Robert A. Baron

For six years (interminably long ones, for me!), I served as the chair of two different academic departments: first a department of psychology and then a department of management. I learned many lessons from my experiences in these roles, but perhaps foremost among these was a lesson directly relevant to the topic of this chapter: *interpersonal relations are truly a crucial determinant of what goes on in any organization—how it functions, how effectively it performs its central tasks, and how it reacts to changing external conditions.* In fact, my experiences as a department chair suggest to me that interpersonal relations between organizational members are at least as important in these respects as other factors that have received more attention from scholars in industrial and organizational (I/O) psychology and organizational behavior—factors such as reward and appraisal systems (Ilgen, Major, & Tower, in press), individual motivation (Locke & Latham, 1990), and organizational structure and resources (Bahrami, 1992). What experiences led me to these conclusions? Far too many to outline here; but among these, perhaps the most dramatic involved the difficulties I encountered in performing one seemingly mundane task: assigning graduate assistantships.

On paper, this appeared to be a simple operation: there were enough qualified graduate students to fill these positions, and the number of assistantships at my disposal was sufficient to meet faculty needs. Yet no matter how many charts of potential assignments I constructed, there were always a host of residual problems—students to whom financial aid had been promised but for whom no suitable assignment existed, for example, and professors for whom no suitable assistant could be identified. The source of all these problems was simple but disconcerting: many students refused to work with specific faculty members, and several faculty members refused to accept certain students as their assistants. Why was this the case? Because, in a nutshell, *some people simply could not get along with one another; and they felt so strongly about this issue that they would rather do without financial aid (students) or without an assistant (professors) than work together.* Every semester, I somehow managed to solve the problem—generally by using every tactic of influence and persuasion at my disposal—but over several years, this process left me with a fistful of IOUs that I could never fully repay. Looking back, I now believe that the frustration I experienced in connection with this task, and with the related one of matching faculty and secretaries, played a key role in my decision to return to full-time teaching and research.

Problems such as these are not restricted to academic departments; I have encountered them repeatedly in many other work settings as well. Why do they occur? Why, in short, do some people find it so hard to work together? Many factors play a role, but it is my firm belief that individual difference factors—the attitudes, values, and personality traits of the persons involved—play a key role in this regard. In other words, such factors can strongly influence the nature of interpersonal relations in work settings. And in the process, they can also affect many aspects of organizational behavior and organizational functioning.

In this chapter, I will review existing evidence offering support for this conclusion—support for the view that individual differences do indeed affect interpersonal relations in work settings. Since interpersonal relations between organization members take many different forms—from helping and cooperation, on the one hand, through conflict and aggression, on the other (see, for example, Baron & Byrne, 1994)—this review is organized in terms of distinct forms or aspects of interpersonal relations. Specifically, several key aspects of interpersonal relations (for example, prosocial behaviors, aggression and conflict, influence) are examined in turn, and for each, evidence is presented concerning the role of various individual difference factors in such behavior. It is important to note, at the outset, that the impact of individual difference factors is definitely *not* restricted to negative forms of interpersonal relations (such as the problems I experienced as chair). On the contrary, growing evidence indicates that such factors are relevant to desirable forms of organizational behavior as well—forms such as mentoring (Turban & Dougherty, 1994), successful efforts to obtain reemployment (Eden & Aviram, 1993), and even effective leadership (Howell & Avolio, 1993).

Prosocial Organizational Behaviors: Cooperation, Helping, and Organizational Citizenship

To an important degree, the fates of organization members are linked: if their organization prospers, they can all share in a growing "pie" of available resources and rewards; if, on the other hand, their organization languishes, their individual benefits, too, are likely to suffer. This basic fact suggests that organization members should generally show strong tendencies toward *cooperation*—working together in a coordinated manner to attain shared goals (Forsyth, 1992). Yet, as anyone with work experience well knows, this is definitely *not* always the case. Often organization members, or groups within an organization, fail to adopt cooperation. On the contrary, they may engage in fierce competition with one another, despite the fact that by such actions they run the risk of reducing the overall effectiveness or success of their organization. Such lack of cooperation occurs for many reasons; among these, two appear to be most important. First, many goals sought by several individuals or groups cannot be shared. For example, two persons seeking the same promotion cannot both gain it; similarly, two units seeking control over desirable organizational resources cannot both obtain these resources. In such situations, cooperation is precluded by the realities of existing reward structures. Second, individuals—especially those working in large organizations—often conclude that their individual actions will have little, if any, impact upon the fortunes of the organization as a whole. Accordingly, they decide to pursue their own ends and to maximize their personal benefits, even if doing so is counter to what they perceive to be the policies or best interests of the organization.

In many other situations, however, these conditions do not apply, and cooperation *could* develop but does not: individuals or departments fail to coordinate their efforts even though by doing so they might well reap larger joint benefits. Why does cooperation fail to develop in such situations? Many factors undoubtedly play a role (Greenberg & Baron, 1995), but research findings indicate that individual difference factors can sometimes be important in this regard. Specifically, it appears that individual differences in terms of preferences for working with or against others can be quite influential. Research on such differences indicates that individuals can be classified into four distinct groups on the basis of differences in such preferences or personal orientations (Knight & Dubro, 1984).

First, many people are *competitors;* their primary motive is doing better than others. Such persons focus primarily on winning—outdoing others in open competition—and are often more concerned with maximizing the difference between their outcomes and those of others than with the absolute size of their own rewards. A distinctly different pattern is shown by a second group of persons, known as *individualists.* These are people who have little interest in the outcomes of others; rather, their main focus is their own outcomes. They do not care whether others do better or worse than themselves, as long as their own outcomes are satisfactory. Third, some persons are *cooperators;* their primary focus is on maximizing joint gains—the total benefits received by themselves and others. Like competitors, they are strongly concerned with others' outcomes, but unlike competitors, they do not want to do better than other organization members; rather, they want to maximize the gains experienced by everyone. Finally, a fourth group can be described as *equalizers.* Their major goal is that of minimizing the difference between their own outcomes and those of others. In short, they want everyone with whom they work to receive the same rewards.

At this point, it is important to take note of two issues. First, while many persons fall into one of these four categories, others demonstrate a mixture of these personal perspectives. For example, one common pattern combines an individualistic orientation with a competitive one: people characterized by that pattern want to do as well as they can, but they are more interested in their own outcomes than in defeating others. Similarly, some people combine an individualistic orientation with a desire for equality. They want to do as well as possible but do not want their outcomes to get too far out of line with those of others. Second, these categories refer to personal dispositions—tendencies to behave in certain ways across many situations. As is true of all dispositions, they can be overridden by strong situational pressures. An individual who prefers competition with others, for example, may adopt a cooperative strategy when it is clear that doing so can lead to much larger rewards. Similarly, even persons with a strong tendency to be cooperative can be goaded into competition if exposed to repeated exploitation by an opponent.

How common are these various patterns? Data reported by Knight and Dubro (1984) indicate that important gender differences may exist in this respect. Among males, the single largest group was that of competitors: approximately one-third of participants in a large-scale study demonstrated this orientation. Individualists made up the second most frequent group—approximately 18 percent of those tested. Among females, the single largest group was that of cooperators (approximately 20 percent), followed closely by competitors (approximately 15 percent). Only a few percent of each gender could be classified as equalizers.

Additional findings reported by Knight and Dubro (1984) indicate that individuals showing these different perspectives tend to behave quite differently toward others. Competitors frequently seek to exploit the people around them, cooperating only when they see no alternative. In contrast, cooperators prefer friendly ties with co-workers and would rather work with them than against them. Individualists are flexible: they choose whatever strategy will succeed in a given situation; in addition, they often prefer to work alone, concentrating solely on their own outcomes rather than those of others. People with a mixed orientation are also flexible, adopting different strategies as situational conditions alter.

In sum, some evidence indicates that individual differences with respect to personal orientations or preferences do affect the likelihood or degree of cooperation in work settings. It seems possible that the contrasting perspectives described above may also influence perceptions of various aspects of fairness—distributive, procedural, and interactional justice (Greenberg, 1993). To the extent that they do, they may constitute an individual difference factor with important and far-ranging effects on organizational behavior.

Researchers who study prosocial behavior continue to disagree about the existence of what might be termed *pure altruism*—actions by one person that benefit one or more others in the absence of expectations of any form of compensation for the donor. Some contend that there are instances in which the motivation behind offering aid to others is simply empathic concern with the recipient's well-being (Batson & Oleson, 1991). Other researchers suggest that persons who help others always expect *some* benefit for doing so, even if this is simply the pleasant feelings that result from engaging in such behavior (Cheuk & Rosen, 1992; Cialdini et al., 1987). Putting aside the question of what motives underlie prosocial behavior, it is clear that organization members do often engage in actions that benefit other organization members, customers, or the organization as a whole (Brief & Motowidlo, 1986; Wright, George, Famsworth, & McMahan, 1993). Further, growing evidence indicates that such actions are influenced, in at least some instances, by individual difference factors.

Before turning to the role of such factors, however, it is useful to distinguish between two major conceptualizations of prosocial behavior in organizations: organizational citizenship behavior (or OCB; Organ, 1988, 1990) and organizational spontaneity (George & Brief, 1992). As defined by Organ (1988), organizational citizenship behavior is behavior by individuals that is discretionary, is not explicitly recognized by the formal reward system of the organization, and promotes the effective functioning of the organization. Thus an instance in which one organization member helps another even though this is not part of his or her job qualifies as OCB, provided that such helping is not explicitly rewarded by the organization. However, an incident in which an employee provides a cost-cutting idea and therefore receives a promised bonus does not qualify as OCB. In contrast, both actions would be viewed as instances of organizational spontaneity, since this is defined simply as spontaneous behavior that is performed voluntarily and that contributes to organizational effectiveness; no restriction on whether individuals expect rewards for such actions is included in the definition (George & Brief, 1992, p. 311). Organizational spontaneity thus includes a very wide range of actions, such as offering direct help to co-workers, protecting the organization and its resources, making constructive suggestions, and spreading goodwill about the organization.

Now, back to the question of which individual difference factors influence prosocial behavior. Research on OCB has generally directed relatively little attention to this issue. In contrast, a model of organizational spontaneity proposed by George and Brief (1992) explicitly includes individual factors as important determinants of such behavior. In particular, this model proposes that *positive affectivity*—the tendency to have an overall sense of well-being, to experience positive emotions and mood states, and to see oneself as pleasurably engaged in terms of both interpersonal relations and achievement—is a predictor of prosocial behavior. More specifically, George and Brief (1992) contend that persons high on positive affectivity are more likely to experience positive moods at work and that such moods in turn facilitate organizational spontaneity.

Some findings provide at least indirect support for these proposals. For example, George (1990) found that the higher the level of positive affect (affective tone) in work groups, the greater the willingness of members of these work groups to assist customers. Similarly, in recent studies, George and her colleagues (George, 1994; George & Bettenhausen, 1990) have found that the higher the group leader's level of positive affect while at work, the greater the level of prosocial behavior performed by the group (for example, the greater the group members' tendency to assist customers). While such findings are far from conclusive, they are bolstered by a very large body of evidence indicating that prosocial behavior, including instances of direct helping, is strongly enhanced by positive affect—by anything that puts individuals in a positive mood (Isen, 1987). Indeed, in several recent investigations I conducted (Baron & Bronfen, 1994; Baron, Rea, & Daniels, 1992; Baron & Thomley, 1994), helping was facilitated by exposure to environmental conditions inducing mild increments in positive affect—warm (versus cool-white) lighting (Baron et al., 1992) and pleasant artificial fragrances (Baron & Bronfen, 1994; Baron & Thomley, 1994). For example, in the study by Baron and Bronfen (1994), participants who worked in rooms scented with a pleasant citrus aroma offered to donate more of their time to help a co-worker than those who worked in rooms without any fragrance. Even more surprising, a higher proportion of those who worked in rooms containing fragrance later completed and returned a questionnaire given to them during the study. They did so on their own time and in the absence of any compensation for providing such assistance to the researcher.

In view of these and related findings, it seems reasonable to suggest that increments in positive affect do often facilitate prosocial behavior and that individuals who characteristically experience high levels of positive affect may be more likely to engage in such behavior than those who experience lower levels of positive affect.

Additional evidence indicates that other individual difference factors may also influence helping (Clary & Orenstein, 1991). Perhaps the most dramatic findings in this respect are those reported by Bierhoff, Klein, and Kramp (1991). These researchers asked two groups of participants to complete a questionnaire designed to measure a wide range of personality traits. One group consisted of persons who had rushed to the aid of the victims of automobile accidents; the second group consisted of persons who had witnessed such accidents but had not provided help to the victims. Results indicated that the two groups differed in several respects. First, the "first-aiders" scored higher on *belief in a just world*—the belief that the world is a fair and predictable place in which good behavior is rewarded and bad behavior punished—than those in the other group. Second, those who had provided help were higher on *internal locus of control*—the belief that individuals can influence their own outcomes, that their fate is in their own hands—than those who had not. Third, those who had offered help were *lower* than those who had not on a measure of *egocentrism*—absorption with themselves, their own lives, and their own problems. Finally, those who had offered help were higher on a measure of *empathy*—they expressed a greater degree of concern for others and their well-being—than those who had not.

Together, these findings suggest that the tendency to offer aid to others, especially in emergency situations, is influenced by several personality factors as well as by individual attitudes. Since many situations in which organization members can help others arise suddenly, are unexpected, and involve serious consequences, it seems possible that the same personality traits that influence helping at the scene of accidents may influence helping in work settings. However, additional evidence gathered in such organizational "emergency" contexts is needed before any firm conclusions about this possibility can be reached.

In sum, it appears that both cooperation and several forms of prosocial behavior are influenced by individual difference factors. Given the importance of these forms of behavior to organizational effectiveness (see, for example, George & Brief, 1992), it is clear that individual difference factors can exert significant and far-reaching effects on organizations in this respect.

Aggression and Conflict

At the opposite end of the continuum of interpersonal relations from organizational spontaneity and helping lie two other forms of behavior that have received a great deal of attention from researchers: *aggression* and *conflict*. Aggression is generally defined as intentional harm-doing—actions designed to inflict some kind of injury (physical, emotional, psychological) on the chosen victim(s) (Baron & Richardson, 1994)—while conflict is often viewed as actions (taken by a person or group) that interfere with or oppose the interests of other persons or groups (W. K. Thomas, 1992). Unfortunately, both types of behavior are anything but rare in organizations. With respect to aggression, much attention has been focused in recent years on workplace violence—and with good reason: more than fifteen persons are murdered at work every week in the United States alone (National Institute for Occupational Safety and Health, 1993). However, it is clear that workplace violence represents only the most visible and dramatic tip of the much larger problem of workplace aggression. What is aggression like in workplaces? Existing evidence suggests that it takes many different forms (Baron & Neuman, in press). In some cases, the aggressive nature of actions is obvious: name-calling, threats, refusals to obey company policies, destruction of company property, and fist fights are all readily identifiable as instances of aggression. In other cases, however, persons engaging in workplace aggression attempt to conceal the nature and goals of their actions.

They engage in what has been termed *covert aggression*—actions designed to harm others, but in ways that conceal the identity of the aggressor and/or the goal of the aggression. The advantages of covert aggression are obvious: such actions permit individuals to harm others in their workplace with little risk of retaliation or censure. Recent findings suggest that for these reasons, most persons strongly prefer covert forms of aggression to more overt—and obvious—ones. A few examples of covert aggression are presented below; many others also exist, and they occur with considerable frequency in many workplaces.

Examples of Covert Workplace Aggression

Spreading malicious rumors about the victim

Needlessly consuming resources needed by the victim

Failing to speak in support of the victim at a performance appraisal meeting

Withholding information needed by the victim

Damning with faint praise

Delaying action on matters of importance to the victim

Failing to deny false rumors about the victim

Failing to return phone calls

Offering the "silent treatment"

Transferring a needed member of the victim's work team

Conflict, too, is quite common in modern organizations. Moreover, its effects are much too costly to ignore. Managers report that they spend approximately 20 percent of their time dealing with conflict and its impact (Baron, 1989). Furthermore, the smoldering resentment and crushed relationships that are the aftermath of many conflicts can persist for months or even years, continuing to exact a significant toll in precious human resources long after the situations that initiated them are merely memories. It should be noted that directly opposed interests appear to constitute only part of the picture where organizational conflict is concerned. Many interpersonal factors, such as long-standing grudges, personal friction, and the desire for revenge, may also play a role.

Indeed, recent studies suggest that such motives often outweigh rational desires for securing the best possible outcomes. In these studies, individuals who felt that they had been treated in a condescending or unfair manner by an opponent often preferred to harm this person by reducing his or her outcomes, even if doing so reduced their own outcomes in the situation (Baron, 1985, 1988). These and related findings suggest that aggressive motives, and the expression of such motives in covert forms of aggression, play a key role in several important aspects of organizational behavior.

Do individual difference factors play a role in workplace aggression and organizational conflict? Research findings suggest that they do. For purposes of clarity, evidence relating to each of these forms of behavior will be examined separately here. However, it should be noted that several of the factors considered appear to influence both aggression and conflict. Given the fact that these aspects of interpersonal behavior are closely related, this is hardly surprising.

Workplace Aggression

As noted earlier, aggression in workplaces has recently been the subject of increasing attention (for example, Cox & Leather, 1994). Most of this research has focused on the conditions in organizations that encourage such behavior. However, some findings point to the potential role of individual difference factors in such behavior (Baron & Neuman, in press).

Type A Behavior Pattern

The individual difference variable that has been found to be most closely related to aggression is the Type A behavior pattern (Glass, 1977). This pattern involves three basic components: competitiveness, time urgency (the tendency to always be in a hurry), and interpersonal irritability. Persons who show these three components to a high level are described as Type A's, while those who show them to a lower degree are described as Type B's. While individual differences along these dimensions clearly fall on a continuum, the distinction between Type A's and Type B's appears to be a valid one: the three characteristics listed above tend to occur together, so that most people fall into one category or the other; they are either Type A or Type B (Strube, 1989).

Given these characteristics, it seems reasonable to expect that Type A's would tend to be more aggressive than Type B's in a wide range of situations, and in fact the results of several studies suggest that this is the case (Baron, Russell, & Arms, 1985; Berman, Gladue, & Taylor, 1993). Moreover, additional evidence indicates that Type A's are truly hostile: they do not aggress against others simply as a means of reaching desired ends; rather, the primary motive behind many of their aggressive actions is that of harming or injuring the victim (Strube, Turner, Cerro, Stevens, & Hinchey, 1984).

Unfortunately, Type A's tend to behave in ways that exacerbate their own time urgency and irritability/hostility. They often seek more challenges (and therefore experience greater degrees of frustration) in their work than do Type B's (see Holmes, McGilley, & Houston, 1984). For example, in a recent study of nurses, Jamal and Baba (1991) found that those who were Type A were more overloaded than those who were Type B, mainly because they took on more than they could handle. As a result, they felt pulled in conflicting directions by different aspects of their jobs.

That the irritability and time urgency of Type A's can have important consequences is suggested by the findings of a study conducted by Evans, Palsane, and Carrere (1987). These researchers compared the behavior of bus drivers in the United States and India who were classified as being Type A and Type B. Observations of the drivers' behavior were made by assistants who actually rode on the drivers' buses. As predicted, Type A drivers passed other drivers more frequently and blew their horns more often than Type B drivers. Further, in both countries, Type A drivers had nearly twice as many accidents as Type B drivers. Taken together, the results of these studies suggest that the Type A behavior pattern is indeed related to aggression in many work settings.

Hostile Attributional Bias

Attributions—that is, perceptions of the causes behind others' behavior—have been found to play an important role in aggression. Specifically, when individuals perceive ambiguous actions by others as stemming from malicious intentions, they are much more likely to become angry and to retaliate than when they perceive the same actions as stemming from other motives (Baron & Richardson, 1994; Johnson & Rule, 1986). This suggests that another individual difference factor—the tendency to attribute others' actions to hostile intentions—may also influence aggression and related aspects of interpersonal relations in many situations. In fact, research findings indicate that this is indeed the case: individuals who are relatively high on what is often known as *hostile attributional bias* demonstrate stronger tendencies to engage in aggression than persons relatively low on this dimension (Dodge & Coie, 1987; Dodge, Price, Bachorowski, & Newman, 1990). This difference is especially pronounced with respect to what has been termed *reactive aggression* (aggression in response to prior provocation) but is less evident with respect to *proactive aggression* (aggression performed in the absence of prior provocation). In research on the potential effects of the hostile attributional bias, this individual difference factor is generally measured by showing individuals videotapes of incidents in which one person's actions toward another are either clearly hostile, clearly nonhostile, or ambiguous. Individual differences with respect to hostile attributional bias are assessed in terms of the tendency to attribute the ambiguous actions to hostile intentions.

In sum, research on the hostile attributional bias indicates that it is an important determinant of aggression in many situations. Since the motives behind others' actions are unclear or uncertain in many situations that occur in work settings, it seems clear that individual tendencies to attribute others' behavior to malevolent motives can sometimes influence interpersonal relations between organization members.

Locus of Control

There can be little doubt that most persons wish to be the masters of their own fate—to control the events and outcomes they experience. Yet in many situations people lack that control: our lives at work and elsewhere are strongly affected by factors beyond our control. According to Rotter (1990), individuals encounter sharply contrasting patterns of life experience with control or lack of control over their own outcomes. As a result, they develop generalized expectations concerning personal control. At one end of this dimension are *internals*—persons who perceive that they can readily influence or control the events that befall them. At the other are *externals*—individuals who perceive that they exert relatively little control over these events. Are such differences in locus of control related to aggression? One line of reasoning suggests that they are. Internals may perceive aggression as simply one additional technique for influencing the course of their lives—as a means for attaining desired goals or terminating aversive treatment by others. Thus they may engage in aggression in certain situations because they view it as an instrumental behavior—one useful in attaining their goals. In contrast, externals, because of their largely fatalistic outlook on life, may perceive little instrumental value in aggression. As a result, they may be less likely to engage in aggression (except, perhaps, when they are repeatedly and strongly provoked).

Support for these predictions has been obtained in several investigations. In research by Dengerink, O'Leary, and Kasner (1975), individuals identified as internals (having scored high on Rotter's Locus of Control Scale; Rotter, 1966) did indeed engage in instrumental aggression—aggression designed to terminate aversive actions by a stranger—more frequently than externals. More recent studies have reported data consistent with these findings (for example, Blass, 1991).

It is also possible that internals, because of their stronger beliefs about being able to influence their own outcomes, may attempt to do so more frequently or in a wider range of situations than externals. As a result, they may also experience higher levels of frustration when these efforts fail to yield desired results. No direct evidence of this possibility as yet exists, but the idea is consistent with evidence indicating that high levels of frustration can sometimes (but not always) facilitate aggression (Berkowitz, 1989) and that being unable to influence one's outcomes is a highly frustrating event (Ramirez, Maldonado, & Martos, 1992). Regardless of the results of such work, however, sufficient evidence already exists to conclude that locus of control is another individual difference factor related to aggression in many different contexts.

Gender

There is a widespread belief that males are generally more aggressive than females. Systematic research on this issue, however, has yielded a fairly complex pattern of results (Harris, 1992; Eagly & Steffen, 1986). On the one hand, males are indeed more likely than females both to initiate physical aggression and to serve as its target (Eagly & Wood, 1991). However, the size of this difference seems to depend on several moderating variables (Eagly & Wood, 1991). For example, this gender difference is larger in situations in which aggression is required by social roles. Similarly, it is larger following strong provocation than in the absence of such provocation (Eagly & Wood, 1991).

On the other hand—and in direct contrast to cultural folklore—such gender differences in aggression tend to disappear (and may even be reversed) with respect to forms of aggression that are not physical. In a series of studies on this issue, Lagerspetz and her colleagues (Bjorkqvist, Lagerspetz, & Kaukiainen, 1992; Bjorkqvist, Osterman, & Lagerspetz, 1994) found that while males are more likely than females to employ direct forms of aggression (such as hitting or direct verbal insults), females are more likely to use indirect forms (such as spreading rumors or gossip about another person, rejecting someone as a friend, or ignoring the target of gossip). In addition, while both males and females tend to prefer *covert* aggression—aggression whose aggressive intent is concealed—to *overt* aggression, males and females differ in terms of the type of covert aggression that they prefer. In a recent study designed specifically to investigate the incidence of aggression in the workplace, Bjorkqvist et al. (1994) asked several hundred employees at a large university to indicate the extent to which they employed various forms of aggression at work. The results indicate that males tend to prefer rational-appearing aggression—that is, aggressive acts that seem to have a rational basis. Such acts include interrupting others, judging people's work in an unfair manner, and criticizing others. In contrast, females tend to prefer *social manipulation*—negative glances, backbiting, insinuations without direct accusation, and similar actions (Bjorkqvist et al., 1994). In sum, gender does appear to play a role with respect to aggression—including aggression in the workplace—but its impact is complex and is moderated by several additional variables.

The Big Five Dimensions of Personality

In recent years, many personality researchers have reached the conclusion that while there are hundreds of specific traits or individual difference factors, five key dimensions—the backbone of the Five-Factor Model—underlie many of them: (1) *Extraversion—*

a dimension ranging from sociable, talkative, and active at one end to retiring, reserved, and cautious at the other; (2) *Agreeableness*—a dimension ranging from good-natured, cooperative, and forgiving at one end to irritable, suspicious, and uncooperative at the other; (3) *Conscientiousness*—a dimension ranging from careful, thorough, organized, and self-disciplined at one end to irresponsible, disorganized, and lacking in self-discipline at the other; (4) *Emotional Stability*—a dimension ranging from anxious, depressed, angry, emotional, and insecure at one end to calm, poised, enthusiastic, and secure at the other; and (5) *Openness to Experience*—a dimension ranging from imaginative, sensitive, intellectual, and polished at one end to insensitive, narrow, crude, and down-to-earth at the other (Digman, 1990). Observers can make accurate judgments about where strangers lie on several of these dimensions even after only a brief meeting. Further, these dimensions—especially conscientiousness and extraversion—appear to be related to performance on many jobs (Barrick & Mount, 1991, 1993). Finally, ratings along these dimensions by supervisors, co-workers, and customers have been found to be valid predictors of job performance for salespersons (Mount, Barrick, & Perkins Strauss, 1994).

Surprisingly, despite the large amount of interest directed to these basic dimensions of personality, little research has been performed to determine whether they are related to various aspects of interpersonal behavior. However, a recent investigation by Collins and Schmidt (1993) into the personality characteristics of white-collar criminals suggests that such links may exist. These researchers compared the personality profiles of prison inmates convicted of white-collar crimes (counterfeiting, fraud, embezzlement) and a comparable sample of persons employed in a wide variety of responsible white-collar jobs (in corporate leadership and senior management). While the researchers did not specifically examine differences between these groups with respect to the five dimensions of personality described above, the findings of their study suggest that white-collar criminals were lower than noncriminals on several dimensions related to conscientiousness but higher in terms of extraversion. Thus there is some evidence suggesting that two of the Big Five dimensions of personality may be related to white-collar crime—a covert form of workplace aggression. Additional evidence is clearly needed, however, before any firm conclusions can be reached concerning the role of the Big Five in various aspects of interpersonal relations.

Organizational Conflict

In the past, organizational conflict has often been viewed as stemming primarily from organizational factors—for example, competition over scarce resources, ambiguity over responsibility, interdependence between work units (Rahim, 1990). More recently, however, a perspective that views conflict as stemming at least in part from interpersonal factors—factors related to individuals, their social relationships, and the ways in which they think about others—has emerged (for example, Baron, 1990). This perspective suggests that individual difference factors might well play a role in the occurrence of organizational conflict, and a growing body of evidence confirms this prediction.

Type A Behavior Pattern

First, several studies indicate that the Type A behavior pattern, described earlier in this chapter, can influence conflict. In one such study (Baron, 1989), managers at a large food-processing company were asked to report on the frequency with which they experienced conflict with subordinates, peers, and supervisors. Results indicated that managers classified as Type A reported a higher incidence of conflict with peers and subordinates than did managers who were Type B. Similar differences did not emerge with respect to reported conflict with supervisors, however.

More recently, Schaubroeck and Williams (1993) investigated the possibility that persons who are Type A would show stronger tendencies toward escalation of commitment than persons who are Type B. They reasoned that this would be the case because Type A's, being more concerned with demonstrating their own competence and success than Type B's, would experience stronger pressure to justify a failing course of action that they themselves had chosen. To test this hypothesis, they asked introductory management students to read descriptions of two products that were, ostensibly, candidates for research and development (R&D) funds within a large company. Half the participants were allowed to freely choose one of these two products (the high personal responsibility condition), while the others were told that previously another person had chosen one of the products (low personal responsibility condition). Then participants received information indicating that the product they or the other person had chosen had failed: sales were low, and cost of production had risen sharply. Finally, they were asked to choose which of the two products should receive additional R&D funds. Results indicated that in the high personal responsibility condition, Type A's were indeed more willing to stick with this prior bad decision than Type B's. In other words, Type A's showed stronger tendencies toward escalation of commitment (Garland, Sandefur, & Rogers, 1990). Since the tendency to dig in one's heels and stick with a previous poor decision can be one potential cause of organizational conflict, these findings can be interpreted as providing indirect evidence for a link between the Type A behavior pattern and conflict.

Self-Monitoring

A second individual difference variable that has been found to be related to organizational conflict is self-monitoring (Snyder, 1987). Self-monitoring refers to a cluster of characteristics closely related to the ability to adapt one's behavior to changing situations. Persons high on the dimension of self-monitoring can aptly be described as social chameleons: they can readily adjust their behavior to match the demands of a given situation and to make a favorable impression on others. In contrast, persons low on that dimension show a higher degree of consistency: they remain much the same across situations, even if this is harmful to their "image." Persons high on self-monitoring are also generally better at managing their own nonverbal cues: they are more successful at concealing their true emotions or at conveying false ones to other persons (for example, Friedman & Miller-Herringer, 1991).

Given the flexibility and social skills of high self-monitors, it seems reasonable to expect that they would be better at handling conflict than low self-monitors. Some evidence for this prediction has been obtained. In the study of personality and organizational conflict described earlier (Baron, 1989), managers completed a questionnaire designed to assess their level of self-monitoring. As predicted, those high on self-monitoring reported experiencing fewer conflicts with others and were also more inclined than low self-monitors to resolve conflicts through collaboration or com-promise (rather than avoidance or competition). Additional re-search relating self-monitoring to other aspects of interpersonal behavior, including mentoring (Turban & Dougherty, 1994) and impression management (Fandt & Ferris, 1990), will be described below.

Influence

Efforts by one person to influence one or more others—to change others' attitudes or behavior—constitute a very common aspect of interpersonal relations. Many different tactics are used for this pur-pose, including subtle procedures involving multiple requests (for example, foot-in-the-door and door-in-the-face tactics), persuasion, inspirational appeals, and even direct commands (Cialdini, 1988; Yukl & Falbe, 1990; Yukl & Tracey, 1992). Individual difference fac-tors enter into the picture primarily through their impact on the extent to which the targets of influence tactics are resistant to such procedures (in other words, some persons are more resistant to in-fluence than others); and these differences are in turn linked to several personality factors.

One of these, known as *personal control,* involves individuals' motivation to maintain control over the events in their lives (Burger, 1992). (*Personal control* should be distinguished from *locus of control,* which refers to generalized expectancies held by indi-viduals concerning the extent to which the outcomes they experi-ence are under their own control; see, for example, Rotter, 1990. However, the two constructs are clearly related in certain respects.) Individuals high on this characteristic are often more resistant to efforts at persuasion than persons low on this dimension (Burger, 1987). This is especially true when it is not clear whether the actions of others are intended as tactics of influence. For example, consider situations in which one person offers help to another. Is such aid provided for strictly unselfish reasons, or is it intended as a means of establishing IOUs that must later be repaid (perhaps with interest)? Burger (1992) predicts that in situations such as this, persons high on the need for personal control will be very sen-sitive to the latter possibility and thus will react more negatively to unsolicited help. A study by Daubman (1993) provides support for this reasoning. She had pairs of participants work independently on a set of puzzles. Each person then received feedback suggesting that he or she had done only average work but that the other person present had done quite well. (Both persons actually received identical feedback.) At this point, participants either did or did not receive an unsolicited helpful hint from the other person on how to solve the set of puzzles. When later asked to express their reactions to the help they received, individuals high on the need for personal control reported more negative reactions than those low on the need for personal control. For example, fully 50 percent of the high-desire-for-control group said that receiving help was irritating, while only 22 percent of the low-desire-for-control group reported such reactions.

A second factor that plays a role in reactions to influence is *self-esteem*—the extent to which individuals hold positive or negative views about themselves. In general, people high on the self-esteem dimension are more resistant to persuasion than persons low on self-esteem, primarily because those high on self-esteem have greater confidence in their own judgments and opinions (Rajecki, 1989).

Self-monitoring, too, seems to be related to resistance to influence. As noted earlier, high self-monitors are more concerned with making a favorable impression on others than low self-monitors are. This suggests that high self-monitors should be more receptive than low self-monitors to influence attempts from persons they find attractive. In contrast, since low self-monitors are more concerned with being right than with making a good impression, they should be more receptive than high self-monitors to influence attempts from persons they view as expert in a particular area. Both of these predictions have been confirmed (DeBono & Harnish, 1988), so it appears that self-monitoring, too, is related to resistance to persuasion.

An additional individual difference factor that has often been viewed as being linked to acceptance of influence is *gender*. Specifically, it has long been assumed that females are more susceptible to several form of influence—among them, conformity pressure and persuasion—than males. While early efforts to study this possibility seemed to confirm it (for example, Crutchfield, 1955), more recent research has generally yielded negative results (Steffen &

Eagly, 1985). When males and females are equally expert in the areas where influence is applied, they do not appear to differ in terms of susceptibility to such efforts (Sistrunk & McDavid, 1971). Similarly, when males and females are equal in status or competence, there is no indication that females are more open to influence than males (Eagly & Wood, 1982; Maupin & Fisher, 1989).

Finally, it has often been suggested that resistance to persuasion increases with age—that people tend to become increasingly rigid and closed-minded as they grow older. While some findings offer support for this view, which is sometimes known as the "impressionable years hypothesis" (Krosnick & Alwin, 1989), the weight of existing evidence points to the conclusion that most individuals remain open to attitude change (as induced by influence or simply their own experiences) throughout life (Tyler & Schuller, 1991). In sum, contrary to long-held beliefs, we do not necessarily grow increasingly resistant to influence as we age.

Leadership

In an important sense, leadership is closely linked to the issue of influence: leadership is often defined as a process through which one member of a group (its leader) influences other group members toward the attainment of specific group goals (Yukl, 1989). It is clear, however, that there is more to leadership than influence. Leaders and followers often form close and complex relationships; and, as noted by Graen and Scandura (1987), the nature of these relationships can vary greatly across different leader-member dyads. Further, the role of leaders in group processes appears to change radically over time as groups develop and the situations they confront alter (Hersey & Blanchard, 1988). Whatever the basic nature of leadership, however, there is growing recognition of the fact that individual difference factors play an important role in this process.

First, in contrast to the findings of early research, recent investigations designed to determine whether leaders possess specific traits that distinguish them from followers has yielded positive results. Summarized below are the key traits identified as characteristics of successful leaders:

Characteristics	*Description*
Drive	Ambition, high energy, tenacity, initiative, desire for achievement
Honesty, integrity	Trustworthiness, reliability, openness
Leadership motivation	Desire to exercise influence over others in order to reach shared goals
Self-confidence	High degree of trust in one's own abilities
Cognitive ability	Intelligence, ability to integrate and interpret large amounts of diverse information
Flexibility	Ability to adapt leadership style to needs of followers and changing external conditions
Creativity	High degree of originality
Expertise	Knowledge of group activities, technical expertise

While these traits do not distinguish all leaders from all followers, they do seem applicable to many leadership contexts. Thus, as noted by Kirkpatrick and Locke (1991, p. 58), who have focused on this issue, "[I]t is unequivocally clear that leaders are not like other people. Leaders do not have to be great men or women by being intellectual geniuses or omniscient prophets to succeed, but they do need to have the 'right stuff' and this stuff is not equally present in all people."

Second, several major theories of leadership call attention to the potential role of individual difference factors in determining leadership effectiveness. For example, Fiedler's Contingency Theory suggests that a leader's position along the dimension of *esteem for least-preferred co-worker (LPC)* is a crucial determinant of leader effectiveness (Fiedler, 1978). Specifically, leaders who are high on this dimension—ones who express a high level of esteem for even their least-preferred co-workers—are, according to the theory, most effective when the leader's situational control is moderate, while low LPC leaders—ones who express a low level of esteem for their least-preferred co-workers—are most effective when the leader's situational control is either very low or very high.

Third, research on what is generally termed *charismatic* or *transformational* leadership suggests that leaders asserting such leadership seem to possess certain characteristics that allow them to exert profound effects upon their followers (Bass, 1985; Conger, 1991; Howell & Avolio, 1993). Such leaders, for example, are often stirring speakers—eloquent individuals with an outstanding ability to manage their own expressive and nonverbal cues so as to generate high levels of excitement and enthusiasm among their listeners (Bass, 1985). Similarly, such leaders are usually adept at formulating and stating a vision—an image of what their group, organization, or even nation could (and perhaps should) become. For example, consider the words of Martin Luther King, Jr., in his famous "I Have a Dream" speech: "So I say to you, my friends, that even though we must face the difficulties of today and tomorrow, I still have a dream. It is a dream deeply rooted in the American dream that one day this nation will rise up and live out the true meaning of its creed—we hold these truths to be self-evident, that all men are created equal. This will be the day when all of God's children will be able to sing with new meaning, 'My country, 'tis of thee, sweet land of liberty.'"

Other qualities shown by transformational leaders include an unusually high level of self-confidence, a high degree of concern for and recognition of followers' needs, and the ability to "read" others' reactions quickly and accurately. When these characteristics are combined, a clear basis for the tremendous impact of transformational leaders emerges—one that rests, at least in part, on their possession of several personal characteristics.

Finally, some evidence indicates that leaders' cognitive abilities may play a role in their effectiveness and in the performance of their groups. According to Fiedler and Garcia's Cognitive Resource Theory (1987), leaders' intellectual abilities influence the performance of their groups, but the impact of such abilities is mediated by several additional factors. One of these variables is the extent to which leaders are directive—that is, the degree to which they give concrete instructions and orders to their followers. Cognitive Resource Theory argues that when leaders are highly directive, their intellectual abilities play an important role in group performance; for the higher these abilities are, the better are the plans, decisions, and strategies that leaders communicate to their followers. When leaders are not directive, however, their intelligence is less important in determining group performance, since non-directive leaders do not impose their plans and decisions on followers. This theory suggests that a second factor mediating leaders' cognitive abilities and group performance is the level of stress that leaders face. When stress is relatively low, leaders focus primarily on task-related issues and their intellectual abilities are closely linked to group performance. When, on the other hand, stress is high, leaders' attention may be diverted to matters not directly linked to task performance. In that case, their intellectual abilities have little chance to influence group performance (Fiedler & Garcia, 1987).

Several studies offer support for these suggestions. For example, in one such investigation (Fiedler & Leister, 1977), Army infantry squad leaders rated the level of stress they experienced with their supervisors. Ratings of the squad leaders' performance (provided by the supervisors) and a measure of their intellectual ability (from Army records) were also obtained. When these factors were correlated, it was found that under conditions of low reported stress, the squad leaders' intelligence was moderately correlated with their performance ($r = 0.43$). Under conditions of high stress, however, this relationship was much weaker ($r = -.01$).

In sum, it appears that leaders' intellectual abilities do affect the performance of their groups, but only under certain conditions. As is true in many other spheres of life, high intelligence, in and of itself, is no guarantee of success where leadership is concerned. Other factors seem to determine when, and to what extent, leaders' intellectual abilities contribute to effectiveness in this important role.

Mentoring

While there are many steps that young persons joining an organization can take to improve their chances of success, one of the most important—and beneficial—is that of obtaining a mentor. There is growing evidence that *mentoring*—the process through which a more experienced employee (the mentor) advises, counsels, and otherwise aids the personal development of a new employee (the protégé)—can be highly beneficial to the new employee's personal success (Whitely, Dougherty, & Dreher, 1991). Apparently, mentors aid their protégés in many different ways: they build their confidence, nominate them for promotions, provide them with opportunities to demonstrate their competence, and call them to the attention of top management (Olian, Carroll, Giannantonio, & Feren, 1988). Needless to say, all these activities can help advance a protégé's career.

Unfortunately, not all young employees obtain mentors. Mentorship is encouraged to a greater degree in some organizations than others. Regrettably, there is some evidence that women and minorities are at a disadvantage where the chances of obtaining a mentor are concerned (Ragins & Cotton, 1993; D. A. Thomas, 1993). Recent findings indicate that individual difference factors, too, may play a role in this regard. In a study conducted with several hundred recent business school graduates, Turban and Dougherty (1994) investigated the potential role of three aspects of personality in the initiation of mentoring relationships. They predicted that persons high on the locus of control dimension (so-called internals, or those who believe that they can control their own outcomes), persons high on self-monitoring, and persons high on the Big Five dimension of emotional stability would make more efforts to establish mentoring relationships than externals, low self-monitors, or persons low on emotional stability. Further, they predicted that these efforts would be linked to the mentoring actually received: in other words, the greater the efforts of potential protégés to initiate mentoring relationships, the more successful they would be in this regard.

To test these predictions, Turban and Dougherty (1994) asked participants to complete a survey containing measures of the three personality characteristics noted above, the extent to which participants sought to initiate mentoring relationships, and the amount of mentoring they actually received. In addition, the survey also contained questions relating to career attainment (salary and promotions) and perceived career success (respondents' perceptions of how successful they were). Results offered clear support for the major predictions. The three personality characteristics were indeed linked to efforts to initiate mentoring; and the greater these efforts, the more mentoring participants reported receiving. In addition, the more mentoring individuals received, the greater their career attainment. Thus, as found in previous research, obtaining a mentor yielded concrete, beneficial results for the study participants. Further, as reported in other recent investigations (see Dreher & Ash, 1990), there is no indication that women are less likely than males to initiate mentoring relationships or to obtain mentoring experiences. One possible interpretation of this finding is that as increasing numbers of women have entered the workforce and moved into positions of management, the availability of potential mentors for young female employees has increased. However, further evidence is needed before any firm conclusions can be reached in this respect. In any case, the findings reported by Turban and Dougherty (1994) suggest that personality characteristics do play a role in the establishment of mentor-protégé relationships (and therefore in the career success of many individuals).

Impression Management

The desire to make a favorable impression on others is a strong one—and for good reason. Favorable initial impressions often translate into such concrete benefits as being hired for a job, obtaining a large order from a potential customer, and—in a very different sphere of life—entering a desirable romantic relationship (Giacalone & Rosenfeld, 1989). The result is that individuals often engage in *impression management*—specific tactics designed to enhance the impression they make on others. Many different tactics can be used for this purpose. One large group of impression management procedures involves efforts at self-enhancement—improving one's appearance, name-dropping, or making positive statements about one's own experience or competence. Other tactics center around the task of other-enhancement—flattering others, expressing agreement with their views, showing a high level of interest in them, or seeking their advice and feedback (Morrison & Bies, 1991).

Are some people better at using such strategies than others, or at least more willing to use them? Research findings suggest that such differences do exist—that there are individual differences with respect to the use of impression management. Perhaps the most important personal characteristic in this respect is self-monitoring.

The results of several studies indicate that high self-monitors, with their high degree of flexibility, outstanding ability to manage their own nonverbal cues, and high degree of sensitivity to others' reactions, are more adept at impression management than low self-monitors are. This fact is clearly illustrated by an ingenious study conducted by Fandt and Ferris (1990). In this investigation, customer service employees in a telecommunications corporation were asked to make decisions about realistic problems they might face on the job—for example, a power failure on a hot summer afternoon. Participants first decided how to proceed in these situations and then wrote a brief report justifying their decisions to their supervisors. Under conditions of high accountability (when they were responsible for the results of their decisions), participants high on self-monitoring transmitted more information reflecting favorably on their decisions and more defensive information (that is, information that shifted the blame for possible mistakes to others) than did participants low on self-monitoring. In other words, high self-monitors engaged in impression management to a greater extent than low self-monitors: they were more likely to distort the flow of upward information so as to place themselves in a favorable light. Additional findings indicate that such impression management tactics often work: they do succeed in inducing more favorable reactions from others (Kacmar, Delery, & Ferris, 1992). To the extent that this is true, high self-monitors may well enjoy a real edge in situations where making a good first impression counts.

For a summary of empirical findings linking self-monitoring (along with all the other individual difference factors discussed in this chapter) with organizational behavior, see Table 9.1.

Some Concluding Thoughts:
A Look Back and a Look Ahead

Ten years ago, leading textbooks in I/O psychology and organizational behavior devoted scant attention to individual difference variables. Indeed, many expressed considerable skepticism about the potential role of such factors in work-related behavior. For example, consider the topic of leadership. In discussing this important process, most texts suggested that the "great person" theory

Table 9.1. Individual Difference Factors and Organizational Behavior: A Summary of Empirical Findings.

Organizational Behavior	Individual Difference Variables	Relationship/Findings
Cooperation	Personal orientation	Influences relative preferences for cooperation and competition.
Prosocial organizational behavior	Positive affectivity	Increases willingness to assist customers. Increases helping in emergencies.
	Belief in a just world	Increases helping in emergencies.
	Internal locus of control	Increases helping in emergencies.
Aggression	Type A behavior pattern	Increases aggression.
	Hostile attributional bias	Increases aggression.
	Internal locus of control	Increases aggression in response to provocation.
	Gender	Males more likely to engage in direct forms of aggression; females more likely to engage in indirect forms of aggression.
	Big Five dimensions	White-collar criminals higher in extraversion, lower in conscientiousness than others.
Organizational conflict	Type A behavior pattern	Higher incidence of conflicts than Type B's; Type A's more likely to experience escalation of commitment.
	Self-monitoring	Low self-monitors experience higher number of conflicts with others.
Influence	Personal control	Persons high in personal control harder to influence.

Table 9.1. Individual Difference Factors and Organizational Behavior: A Summary of Empirical Findings, Cont'd.

Organizational Behavior	Individual Difference Variables	Relationship/Findings
	Self-esteem	High self-esteem persons harder to influence.
	Self-monitoring	High self-monitors more receptive to influence.
Leadership	Drive, honesty, self-confidence, cognitive ability, flexibility, creativity, expertise	Leaders higher than followers.
Mentoring	Internal locus of control, self-monitoring, emotional stability	Protégés high in these dimensions more likely to obtain mentors than ones low in these dimensions.
Impression management	Self-monitoring	High self-monitors more successful at impression management.

was wrong—dead wrong. Contrary to what this view suggests, most texts argued, leaders and followers do *not* differ with respect to measurable traits.

Now, of course, these books tell a very different story; reflecting a major shift in scientific opinion within the fields of I/O psychology and organizational behavior, they indicate that leaders and followers do indeed differ in important ways (see, for example, Greenberg & Baron, 1995). In a corresponding manner, individual difference factors have reappeared in the discussion of many other topics as well—for example, discussions of job satisfaction (Keller, Bouchard, Arvey, Segal, & Dawis, 1992) and person-job fit (Fricko & Beehr, 1992), to mention just a few. What accounts for this change? Mainly, I believe, growing sophistication with respect to the nature of individual difference factors. Systematic research on personality and related topics has greatly enhanced our understanding of the key dimensions along which human beings differ (for example, Digman, 1990). This basic research has in turn placed efforts to identify possible links between individual difference factors and organizational behavior on a much firmer footing. Given this fact, it is not at all surprising that both the volume and the elegance of organizational research dealing with individual difference factors has increased during the past decade.

Where do we go from here? It is my belief that organizational researchers will continue to devote increasing attention to individual difference factors in the years ahead. A trend in this direction is already apparent in the pages of our journals (and is, of course, underscored by the publication of this volume). I also predict that such research will continue to be informed by insights emerging from basic research on the nature of personality and other aspects of individual differences. In this sense, then, the timing of this volume is truly auspicious: by bringing together a wealth of evidence on the nature and effects of individual difference factors, this book will assist organizational researchers in their efforts to determine how, why, and when such variables enter into the picture where important forms of organizational behavior are concerned.

References

Bahrami, H. (1992). The emerging flexible organization: Perspectives from Silicon Valley. *California Management Review, 34*(4), 33–52.

Baron, R. A. (1985). Reducing organizational conflict: The role of attributions. *Journal of Applied Psychology, 70*, 434–441.

Baron, R. A. (1988). Attributions and organizational conflict: The mediating role of apparent sincerity. *Organizational Behavior and Human Decision Processes, 41*, 111–127.

Baron, R. A. (1989). Personality and organizational conflict: The Type A behavior pattern and self-monitoring. *Organizational Behavior and Human Decision Processes, 44*, 281–297.

Baron, R. A. (1990). Environmentally induced positive affect: Its impact on self-efficacy, task performance, negotiation, and conflict. *Journal of Applied Social Psychology, 20*, 368–384.

Baron, R. A., & Bronfen, M. I. (1994). A whiff of reality: Empirical evidence concerning the effects of pleasant fragrances on work-related behavior. *Journal of Applied Social Psychology, 24*, 1179–1203.

Baron, R. A., & Byrne, D. (1994). *Social psychology: Understanding human interaction* (7th ed.). Needham Heights, MA: Allyn & Bacon.

Baron, R. A., & Neuman, J. H. (in press). *Workplace violence and workplace aggression: Their causes, effects, and management.* Manuscript submitted for publication.

Baron, R. A., Rea, M. S., & Daniels, S. G. (1992). Lighting as a source of environmentally generated positive affect in work settings: Impact on cognitive tasks and interpersonal behaviors. *Motivation and Emotion, 14,* 1–34.

Baron, R. A., & Richardson, D. R. (1994). *Human aggression* (2nd ed.). New York: Plenum.

Baron, R. A., Russell, G. W., & Arms, R. L. (1985). Negative ions and behavior: Impact on mood, memory, and aggression among Type A and Type B persons. *Journal of Personality and Social Psychology, 48,* 746–754.

Baron, R. A., & Thomley, J. (1994). A whiff of reality: Positive affect as a potential mediator of the effects of pleasant fragrance on task performance and helping. *Environment and Behavior, 26,* 716–784.

Barrick, M. R., & Mount, M. K. (1991). The Big Five personality dimensions and job performance: A meta-analysis. *Personnel Psychology, 44,* 1–26.

Barrick, M. R., & Mount, M. K. (1993). Autonomy as a moderator of the relationships between the Big Five personality dimensions and job performance. *Journal of Applied Psychology, 78,* 111–118.

Bass, B. M. (1985). *Leadership and performance beyond expectations.* New York: Free Press.

Batson, C. D., & Oleson, K. C. (1991). Current status of the empathy-altruism hypothesis. In M. S. Clark (Ed.), *Prosocial behavior* (pp. 62–85). Newbury Park, CA: Sage.

Berkowitz, L. (1989). Frustration-aggression hypothesis: Examination and reformulation. *Psychological Bulletin, 106,* 59–73.

Berman, M., Gladue, B., & Taylor, S. (1993). The effects of hormones, Type A behavior pattern, and provocation on aggression in men. *Motivation and Emotion, 17,* 125–138.

Bierhoff, H. W., Klein, R., & Kramp, P. (1991). Evidence for the altruistic personality from data on accident research. *Journal of Personality, 59,* 263–280.

Bjorkqvist, K., Lagerspetz, K.M.J., & Kaukiainen, A. (1992). Do girls manipulate and boys fight? Developmental trends in regard to direct and indirect aggression. *Aggressive Behavior, 18,* 117–127.

Bjorkqvist, K., Osterman, K., & Lagerspetz, K.M.J. (1994). Sex differences in covert aggression among adults. *Aggressive Behavior, 20,* 27–33.

Blass, T. (1991). Understanding behavior in the Milgram obedience experiment: The role of personality, situations, and their interactions. *Journal of Personality and Social Psychology, 60,* 398–413.

Brief, A. P., & Motowidlo, S. J. (1986). Prosocial organizational behaviors. *Academy of Management Review, 11*, 710–725.

Burger, J. M. (1987). Desire for control and conformity to a perceived norm. *Journal of Personality and Social Psychology, 53*, 355–360.

Burger, J. M. (1992). *Desire for control: Personality, social, and clinical perspectives.* New York: Plenum.

Cheuk, W. H., & Rosen, S. (1992). Helper relations: When help is rejected by friends or strangers. *Journal of Social Behavior and Personality, 7*, 445–458.

Cialdini, R. B. (1988). *Influence: Science and practice* (2nd ed.). Glenview, IL: Scott, Foresman.

Cialdini, R. B., Schaller, M., Houlainhan, D., Arps, H., Fultz, J., & Beaman, A. L. (1987). Empathy-based helping: Is it selflessly or selfishly motivated? *Journal of Personality and Social Psychology, 52*, 749–758.

Clary, E. G., & Orenstein, L. (1991). The amount and effectiveness of help: The relationships of motives and abilities to helping behavior. *Personality and Social Psychology Bulletin, 17*, 58–64.

Collins, J. M., & Schmidt, F. L. (1993). Personality, integrity, and white collar crime: A construct validity study. *Personnel Psychology, 46*, 295–311.

Conger, J. A. (1991). Inspiring others: The language of leadership. *Academy of Management Executive, 5*(1), 31–45.

Crutchfield, R. A. (1955). Conformity and character. *American Psychologist, 10*, 191–198.

Daubman, K. A. (1993). *The self-threat of receiving help: A comparison of the threat-to-self-esteem model and the threat-to-interpersonal-power model.* Unpublished manuscript, Gettysburg (PA) College.

DeBono, K., & Harnish, R. J. (1988). Source expertise, source attractiveness, and the processing of persuasive information: A functional approach. *Journal of Personality and Social Psychology, 55*, 541–546.

Dengerink, H. A., O'Leary, M. R., & Kasner, K. H. (1975). Individual differences in aggressive responses to attack: Internal-external locus of control and field dependence-independence. *Journal of Research in Personality, 9*, 191–199.

Digman, J. M. (1990). Personality structure: Emergence of the Five-Factor Model. *Annual Review of Psychology, 41*, 417–440.

Dodge, K. A., & Coie, J. D. (1987). Social-information-processing factors in reactive and proactive aggression in children's peer groups. *Journal of Personality and Social Psychology, 53*, 1146–1158.

Dodge, K. A., Price, J. N., Bachorowski, J. A., & Newman, J. P. (1990). Hostile attributional biases in severely aggressive adolescents. *Journal of Abnormal Psychology, 99*, 385–392.

Dreher, G. F., & Ash, R. (1990). A comparative study of mentoring among men and women in managerial, professional, and technical positions. *Journal of Applied Psychology, 75*, 525–535.

Eagly, A. H., & Steffan, V. J. (1986). Gender and aggressive behavior: A meta-analytic review of the social psychological literature. *Psychological Bulletin, 100*, 309–330.

Eagly, A. H., & Wood, W. (1991). Explaining sex differences in social behavior: A meta-analytic perspective. *Personality and Social Psychology Bulletin, 17*, 306–315.

Eden, D., & Aviram, A. (1993). Self-efficacy training to speed reemployment: Helping people to help themselves. *Journal of Applied Psychology, 78*, 352–360.

Evans, G. W., Palsane, M. N., & Carrere, S. (1987). Type A behavior and occupational stress: A cross-cultural study of blue-collar workers. *Journal of Personality and Social Psychology, 52*, 1002–1007.

Fandt, P. M., & Ferris, G. R. (1990). The management of information and impressions: When employees behave opportunistically. *Organizational Behavior and Human Decision Processes, 45*, 140–158.

Fiedler, F. E. (1978). Contingency model and the leadership process. In L. Berkowitz (Ed.), *Advances in experimental social psychology* (Vol. 11). San Diego, CA: Academic Press.

Fiedler, F. E., & Garcia, J. E. (1987). *Leadership: Cognitive resources and performance.* New York: Wiley.

Fiedler, F. E., & Leister, A. F. (1977). Leader intelligence and task performance: A test of a multiple screen model. *Organizational Behavior and Human Performance, 20*, 1–14.

Forsyth, D. R. (1992). *An introduction to group dynamics* (2nd ed.). Pacific Grove, CA: Brooks/Cole.

Fricko, M.A.M., & Beehr, T. A. (1992). A longitudinal investigation of interest congruence and gender concentration as predictors of job satisfaction. *Personnel Psychology, 45*, 99–117.

Friedman, H. S., & Miller-Herringer, T. (1991). Nonverbal display of emotion in public and private: Self-monitoring, personality, and expressive cues. *Journal of Personality and Social Psychology, 61*, 766–775.

Garland, H., Sandefur, C. A., & Rogers, A. C. (1990). De-escalation of commitment in oil exploration: When sunk costs and negative feedback coincide. *Journal of Applied Psychology, 75*, 721–727.

George, J. M. (1990). Personality, affect, and behavior in groups. *Journal of Applied Psychology, 75*, 107–116.

George, J. M. (1995). Leader positive mood and group performance: The case of customer service. *Journal of Applied Social Psychology, 25*, 778–794.

George, J. M., & Bettenhausen, K. (1990). Understanding prosocial behavior, sales performance, and turnover: A group level analysis in a service context. *Journal of Applied Psychology, 75,* 698–709.

George, J. M., & Brief, A. P. (1992). Feeling good—doing good: A conceptual analysis of the mood at work/organizational spontaneity relationship. *Psychological Bulletin, 112,* 310–329.

Giacalone, R. A., & Rosenfeld, P. (Eds.). (1989). *Impression management in the organization.* Hillsdale, NJ: Erlbaum.

Glass, D. C. (1977). *Behavior patterns, stress, and coronary disease.* Hillsdale, NJ: Erlbaum.

Graen, G. B., & Scandura, T. A. (1987). Toward a psychology of dyadic organizing. In L. L. Cummings & B. M. Staw (Eds.), *Research in organizational behavior* (Vol. 9, pp. 175–208). Greenwich, CT: JAI Press.

Greenberg, J. (in press). Justice and organizational citizenship: A commentary on the state of the science. *Employees Responsibilities and Rights Journal.*

Greenberg, J., & Baron, R. A. (1995). *Behavior in organizations* (5th ed.). Englewood Cliffs, NJ: Prentice-Hall.

Harris, M. B. (1992). Sex, race, and experience of aggression. *Aggressive Behavior, 18,* 201–217.

Hersey, P., & Blanchard, K. H. (1988). *Management of organizational behavior.* Englewood Cliffs, NJ: Prentice-Hall.

Holmes, D. S., McGilley, B. M., & Houston, B. K. (1984). Task-related arousal of Type A and Type B persons: Level of challenge and response specificity. *Journal of Personality and Social Psychology, 46,* 1322–1327.

Howell, J. M., & Avolio, B. J. (1993). Transformational leadership, transactional leadership, locus of control, and support for innovation: Key predictors of consolidated-business-unit performance. *Journal of Applied Psychology, 78,* 891–902.

Ilgen, D. R., Major, D. A., & Tower, S. L. (in press). The cognitive revolution in organizational behavior. In J. Greenberg (Ed.), *Organizational behavior: The state of the science.* Hillsdale, NJ: Erlbaum.

Isen, A. M. (1987). Positive affect, cognitive processes, and social behavior. In L. Berkowitz (Ed.), *Advances in experimental social psychology* (Vol. 20, pp. 203–253). San Diego, CA: Academic Press.

Jamal, M., & Baba, V. V. (1991). Type A behavior, its prevalence and consequences among women nurses: An empirical examination. *Human Relations,* pp. 1213–1228.

Johnson, T. E., & Rule, B. G. (1986). Mitigating circumstances information, censure, and aggression. *Journal of Personality and Social Psychology, 50,* 537–542.

Kacmar, K. M., Delery, J. E., & Ferris, G. R. (1992). Differential effectiveness of applicant impression management tactics on employment interview decisions. *Journal of Applied Social Psychology, 22,* 1250–1272.

Keller, L. M., Bouchard, T. J., Arvey, R. D., Segal, N. L., & Dawis, R. V. (1992). Work values: Genetic and environmental influences.

Kirkpatrick, S. A., & Locke, E. A. (1991). Leadership: Do traits matter? *Academy of Management Executive, 5*(2), 48–60.

Knight, G. P., & Dubro, A. F. (1984). Cooperative, competitive, and individualistic social values: An individualized regression and clustering approach. *Journal of Personality and Social Psychology, 46,* 98–105.

Krosnick, J. A., & Alwin, D. F. (1989). Aging and susceptibility to attitude change. *Journal of Personality and Social Psychology, 57,* 416–425.

Locke, E. A., & Latham, G. P. (1990). *A theory of goal setting and task performance.* Englewood Cliffs, NJ: Prentice-Hall.

Maupin, H. E., & Fisher, R. J. (1989). The effects of superior female performance and sex-role orientation on gender conformity. *Canadian Journal of Behavioural Science, 21,* 55–69.

Morrison, E. W., & Bies, R. J. (1991). Impression management in the feedback-seeking process: A literature review and research agenda. *Academy of Management Review, 16,* 322–341.

Mount, M. K., Barrick, M. R., & Perkins Strauss, J. (1994). Validity of observer ratings of the Big Five personality factors. *Journal of Applied Psychology, 79,* 272–280.

National Institute for Occupational Safety and Health, Center for Disease Control and Prevention. (1993, Dec. 5). *Homicide in the workplace.* Document No. 705003.

Olian, J., Carroll, S., Giannantonio, F., & Feren, D. (1988). What do protégés look for in a mentor? Results of three experimental studies. *Journal of Vocational Behavior, 41,* 48–60.

Organ, D. W. (1988). *Organizational citizenship behavior: The good soldier syndrome.* New York: Lexington Books.

Organ, D. W. (1989). The motivational basis of organizational citizenship behavior. In B. M. Staw & L. L. Cummings (Eds.), *Research in organizational behavior* (Vol. 12, pp. 43–72). Greenwich, CT: JAI Press.

Ragins, B. R., & Cotton, J. L. (1993). Gender and willingness to mentor in organizations. *Journal of Management, 19,* 97–111.

Rahim, M. A. (Ed.). (1990). *Theory and research in conflict management.* New York: Praeger.

Rajecki, D. W. (1989). *Attitudes* (2nd ed.). Sunderland, MA: Sinauer Associates.

Ramirez, E., Maldonado, A., & Martos, R. (1992). Attributions modulate immunization against learned helplessness in humans. *Journal of Personality and Social Psychology, 62,* 139–146.

Rotter, J. B. (1966). Generalized expectancies for internal versus external control of reinforcement. *Psychological Monographs, 80*(609).

Rotter, J. B. (1972). An introduction to social learning theory. In J. B. Rotter, J. E. Chance, and E. J. Phares (Eds.), *Applications of social learning theory of personality* (pp. 37–42). Troy, MO: Holt, Rinehart & Winston.

Rotter, J. B. (1990). Internal versus external control of reinforcement: A case history of a variable. *American Psychologist, 45,* 489–493.

Schaubroeck, J., & Williams, S. (1993). Type A behavior pattern and escalating commitment. *Journal of Applied Psychology, 78,* 862–867.

Sistrunk, F., & McDavid, J. W. (1971). Sex variable in conforming behavior. *Journal of Personality and Social Psychology, 29,* 200–207.

Snyder, M. (1987). *Public appearances/private realities: The psychology of self-monitoring.* New York: W. H. Freeman.

Steffen, V. J., & Eagly, A. H. (1985). Implicit theories about influence style: The effects of status and sex. *Personality and Social Psychology Bulletin, 11,* 191–205.

Strube, M. J. (1989). Evidence for the type in Type A behavior: A taxonometric analysis. *Journal of Personality and Social Psychology, 56,* 972–987.

Strube, M. J., Turner, C. W., Cerro, D., Stevens, J., & Hinchey, F. (1984). Interpersonal aggression and the Type A coronary-prone behavior pattern: A theoretical distinction and practical implications. *Journal of Personality and Social Psychology, 47,* 839–847.

Thomas, D. A. (1993). Racial dynamics in cross-race developmental relationships. *Administrative Science Quarterly, 38,* 169–194.

Thomas, W. K. (1992). Conflict and negotiation processes. In M. D. Dunnette (Ed.), *Handbook of industrial and organizational psychology* (2nd ed.; Vol 3., pp. 651–718). Palo Alto, CA: Consulting Psychologists Press.

Turban, D. B., & Dougherty, T. W. (1994). Role of protégé personality and receipt of mentoring and career success. *Academy of Management Journal, 37,* 688–702.

Tyler, T. R., & Schuller, R. A. (1991). Aging and attitude change. *Journal of Personality and Social Psychology, 61,* 689–697.

Whitely, W., Dougherty, T. W., & Dreher, G. F. (1991). Relationships of career mentoring and socioeconomic origin to managers' and professionals' early career progress. *Academy of Management Journal, 34,* 331–351.

Wright, P. M., George, J. M., Famsworth, S. R., & McMahan, G. C. (1993). Productivity and extra-role behavior: The effects of goals and incentives on spontaneous helping. *Journal of Applied Psychology, 78,* 374–381.

Yukl, G. (1989). *Leadership in organizations* (2nd ed.). Englewood Cliffs, NJ: Prentice-Hall.

Yukl, G., & Falbe, C. M. (1990). Influence tactics and objectives in upward, downward, and lateral influence attempts. *Journal of Applied Psychology, 75,* 416–423.

Yukl, G., & Tracey, J. B. (1992). Consequences of influence tactics used with subordinates, peers, and the boss. *Journal of Applied Psychology, 77,* 525–535.

Chapter Ten

Work Dysfunctions and Mental Disorders

Rodney L. Lowman

A reader recently wrote to a major metropolitan newspaper to complain that she had been unfairly characterized in an article the newspaper had run on workaholics. The article listed a number of traits—including working more than forty hours a week, feeling responsible for one's work, and being energetic and competitive—that were considered typical of workaholics. What would this article have to say about the great men and women of history, the reader wondered, who apparently had a drive and commitment now considered suspect?

The reader seemed to feel that what she apparently regarded as being among her strongest features had been improperly characterized in the article as a disease, a dysfunction. In her case, the behavior was presumably not disruptive of her personal life or her work itself and did not exact an undue toll on her internal sense of well-being.

Psychologists might take a lesson from this individual and proceed with caution in applying taxonomies of disease and psychological dysfunction to conditions affecting behavior in the workplace. Indeed, one of the most persistent (and legitimate) complaints about the too-common practice of translating almost

Note: I am pleased to acknowledge the thoughtful comments of Kevin Murphy and Sheldon Zedeck on earlier drafts of this chapter.

verbatim the theories developed in one framework (for example, individual-level psychoanalysis) into another context (for example, the investigation of organizational-level phenomena; see, among others, Kets de Vries & Miller, 1984) has been the tendency to interpret too many variables in terms that seem to pathologize behavior excessively. At the individual level, productive accomplishment may come to be viewed as masking deep-seated unconscious conflicts or neurotic compulsions. However, the other extreme, too often found among traditionally trained industrial and organizational (I/O) psychologists, is to ignore altogether dysfunctional personal characteristics of psychogenic origin, disregarding particularly the effects of psychopathology on work. This approach has its limitations as well.

If behavior at work is a function of both what the individual brings to the job (Schneider, 1987) and what he or she encounters once on the job (the work itself, the physical setting, and the complex sets of relationships [as interpreted by the individual] found to be in place) (Katz & Kahn, 1978), it is important that psychologists study and understand how individual differences affect (and *potentially* affect) problematic behavior at work. This is particularly important in attempting to assess and assist in improving dysfunctional work-role behavior.

To be a work dysfunction rather than simply a work or individual difference characteristic (one that, in the case of patterns of overcommitment, many employers may actually go to great lengths to find and reward), the behavior at issue must in some way negatively affect the individual, the work-role performance, and/or the employer. Since problematic work behavior is almost always a function of both the individual and the system within which the behavior occurs, it cannot be understood adequately without considering both characteristics of the individual (the primary focus of this chapter) and characteristics of the work environment.

Whether reflecting primarily preexisting conditions, characteristics arising from the work or work setting, or some complex mixture of factors, a consensually validated taxonomy of problems that can adversely affect personal work performance is essential in understanding individual differences in work. We therefore need a way of meaningfully categorizing individuals' problematic work-role behaviors.

By focusing primarily on work difficulties associated with psychological problems, this chapter necessarily establishes boundaries. Such unquestionably important (but admittedly low-base-rate) phenomena as employee theft and workplace violence are not the concern of this chapter.

In contrast to some commonly encountered approaches, this chapter does not exclusively assume the perspective of the employer in seeking to understand or change personally dysfunctional behavior in the work role. Rather, the aim is to identify, categorize, and contextualize work difficulties of psychological origin. This orientation is important, because dysfunctional work-related behavior is not always evident to bystanders—for example, supervisors and co-workers. An anxious individual may, for example, live in dread of giving a talk or even having a conversation with his or her boss, but supervisors and co-workers may not be aware of the employee's personally experienced problem. In other words, the adverse consequences may all be internal, resulting in no lessening of work quality or productivity. Still, from the perspective of personal consequences, the behavior may be no less dysfunctional.

Mapping the Territory

Recent U.S. legislation (the 1990 Americans with Disabilities Act [ADA]; Fielder, 1994; Jones, 1990) made illegal the pro forma exclusion from employment consideration of persons who currently experience, or who in the past have experienced, mental disorders or substance abuse disorders. Such conditions may be considered as possible grounds for employment exclusion only after a decision has otherwise been made on a candidate's employability for a particular position. Then, should an otherwise acceptable candidate not be hired on the basis of a mental condition (the ADA also covers physical conditions), it becomes the employer's responsibility to demonstrate that the candidate's condition demonstrably would impair job performance and reasonably could not be accommodated. The relationships between work capacity and psychopathology have therefore become especially important.

But it is not just hiring conditions and law compliance that make work-psychopathology issues worth considering. In one form or another, psychological disorders will affect a significant minority, if not the majority, of employees over the course of their work lives. Employers need to know how to manage such persons effectively, and mental health interventionists need to learn how to assess and treat cases presenting with work difficulties and psychological problems.

The model of work and psychopathology presented in this chapter is therefore intended to provide both psychologists and managers a conceptual map for beginning to consider linkages between psychopathology and work. In attempting to understand problematic individual-level work-related behavior, we need to consider at least three factors, each encompassing many specific variables. These factors, along with the hypothesized relationships among them, are depicted in Figure 10.1.

Two major individual difference domains and two contextual domains are included in this figure. Of these four, two relate to characteristics of the person, the third relates to characteristics of the work setting or context, and the fourth relates to characteristics of the home setting or context. These will be examined in turn.

Psychopathology

Circle A in Figure 10.1, encompassing psychopathology (mental or behavioral disorders), includes the traditional diagnostic categories used to classify psychological dysfunctions. The personal difficulties encountered by persons whose behavior meets diagnostic criteria for psychopathology (difficulties that almost by definition have adverse consequences on the individual's personal life and sense of well-being) may or may not have relevance for the work role. The origin of psychopathology may be genetic, associated with environmental stressors, or responsive to some poor match of personal and environmental characteristics. Although anyone in any population may manifest diagnosable psychopathology over the course of his or her life, in practice a predictable percentage of the population (and, by implication, of the workforce) will actually experience diagnosable psychopathology at any particular time (and over the course of their lives). Mental health epidemiology specializes in describing both the incidence (number of new cases) and the prevalence (percentage of persons in the defined population experiencing the disorder over a specified time period—for example, six months, a year, or a lifetime; Mezzich, Jorge, & Salloum, 1994)

Figure 10.1. Relationships Between Work Dysfunctions and Psychopathology in the Work-Family Context.

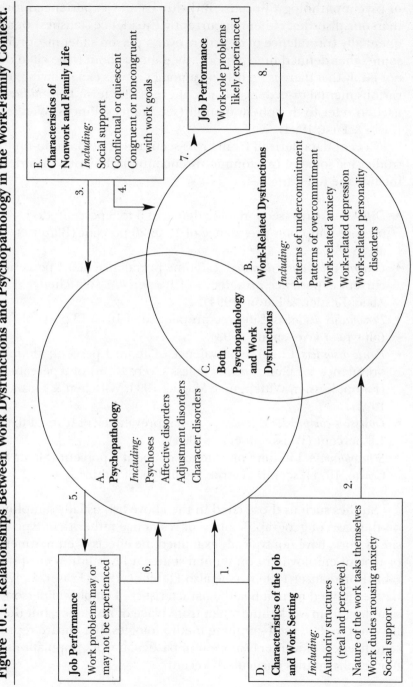

of psychopathology. Because individuals may experience more than one disorder, either concurrently (incidence statistics) or sequentially (prevalence of disorders over a person's lifetime, or for some other defined time period), the figures about to be cited do not imply that there is no overlap among persons experiencing the various mental disorders. Clearly, there is; the term *comorbidity* is used to refer to this phenomenon (see Frances, Pincus, Widiger, Davis, & First, 1994).

Recent data derived from cross-sectional (one-point-in-time) studies for some of the commonly encountered mental disorders include the following:

- *Depression.* Cross-sectional incidence of 3 to 8 percent; depressive symptoms prevalence of 13 to 20 percent (Blazer et al., 1988).
- *Generalized anxiety disorders.* Lifetime prevalence of 5.1 percent; current experience prevalence of 1.6 percent (Wittchen, Zhao, Kessler, & Eaton, 1994).
- *Personality disorders.* Lifetime prevalence of 10 to 13 percent (all types) (Weissman, 1993).
- *Panic disorders.* Lifetime prevalence of about 1 percent; lifetime prevalence for panic attacks (a less severe form) of 9 percent (Eaton, Kessler, Wittchen, & Magee, 1994; Wittchen & Essau, 1993).
- *Obsessive-compulsive disorders.* Annual prevalence of from .4 to 1.8 percent (Weissman et al., 1994).
- *Schizophrenia.* Lifetime prevalence of about 1 percent (Slater & Cowie, 1971), seemingly true regardless of culture.

Studies such as those cited in the above list, usually sampling on the basis of geographic place of residence rather than type or site of work, have not typically examined the effects of employment or type of employment on mental status. A few studies, most notably Kornhauser (1965) (see also Fletcher, 1988; Fraser, 1947), have examined mental health characteristics of employed persons, sampling from work rather than from place of residence; but they have not to date used sampling methodologies that ensure representativeness of workers (or even of particular work populations), nor are the studies particularly recent.

At least in theory, the incidence of psychopathology among employed populations is not likely to match national probability statistics for the general population. First, the most seriously disturbed mental patients may not be able to work at all (see Lowman, 1993a; Schultheis & Bond, 1993), especially during acute phases of their disorders. Second (and, for our purposes, more important), work organizations do not consist of random collections of people more or less matching general population characteristics (Schneider, 1987). Since many mental health disorders vary in incidence and prevalence on the basis of such factors as gender and occupation, the risk and occurrence of mental difficulties will likely also vary from one work setting or type of organization to another. For example, work groups with larger ratios of females to males would be expected to find their employees at higher risk for rates of various disorders, including depression (see Charney & Weissman, 1988; Dick, Bland, & Newman, 1994; Kessler, McGonagle, Swartz, Blazer, & Nelson, 1993; Weissman et al., 1993), panic disorders (Wittchen et al., 1994), and generalized anxiety disorder (Wittchen & Essau, 1993), exceeding base rates found in the general (mixed-sex) population. Conversely, groups having more males than females may have higher rates of substance abuse (Bucholz, 1992; Chou, 1994; Grant, 1993; Robbins & Martin, 1993) and antisocial personality disorder (Swanson, Bland, & Newman, 1994), among other mental disorders, than mixed-sex populations do. Additionally, certain types of work are likely to attract people with higher or lower rates of psychopathology. As a result, the occupational base rates for the experience of psychological difficulties over the life spectrum may not reflect the base rates of the general population (see Lowman, 1989, 1991, 1993a; Tuomi et al., 1991). Organizations employing creatively talented individuals, for example, are at apparently higher risk of having members who experience affective disorders (see Jamison, 1989, 1993).

When we consider the incidence and prevalence of mental disorders, we are inevitably speaking of conditions that in almost all instances (except perhaps for highly atypical populations, such as the unemployed, residents of psychiatric hospitals, or employees in unusually stress-laden work environments) characterize a minority of persons at any one time. However, a sizable proportion of the working population, taken collectively, will be affected over the

course of their employment (as the above-noted lifetime prevalence statistics suggest). The effect on work (and on the workplace
itself) of mental disorders is therefore a legitimate concern of managers and psychologists alike.

Unfortunately, there are significant problems in using traditional mental disorder taxonomies for purposes of explaining or
predicting work behavior. Even assuming the validity for their
intended purposes of existing nosological categories of mental dysfunction (which are not without their difficulties; see, for example,
Widiger & Trull, 1991), by themselves these categories have no reason to be expected to predict a person's capacity to work. This limitation arises because these categories were not designed for that
purpose, because for the most part they have not been evaluated
in that application, and because a range of work-related behavior
might be expected among those unambiguously meeting diagnostic criteria for particular psychiatric conditions. For example,
if two persons both experience a diagnostic entity such as major
depression (American Psychiatric Association, 1994), one of them
may continue to function effectively in the workplace (perhaps the
individual's only conflict-free area of life performance) while
another is so generally withdrawn that capacity to function at work
is severely limited. This is not to assert that assessment of the capacity of such persons to work is inappropriate; however, a psychiatric
diagnostic scheme may not constitute the best metric or organizing device for such assessment. The diagnosis alone tells us rather
little about the person's capacity for work.

Psychopathology and Work

Conceptually, there are several aspects of Figure 10.1 that bear
elaboration in considering both how psychopathology can affect
the work role and how the work role can affect psychological well-
being. This figure suggests that although psychopathology (partial
circle A in the figure) *may* impact work-role behavior (intersect C
and arrow 5 in the figure), it may also be experienced independent of manifest on-the-job behavioral difficulties. As an example,
a person may be depressed because of events associated with work
(for example, a demotion or reduction in force) or because of
characteristics of the workplace (for example, a lack of connection

between an individual's job effort and his or her reward outcome). Such factors (see arrow 1 of the diagram) may create psychopathology (for example, depression) in a previously unaffected individual; that is, the depression might otherwise not have existed in this person, at least not at this particular time. Conversely, an individual may experience work problems because of non-work-related depression (for example, after the loss of a loved one; arrow 3 in the figure). Whether this clinically depressed individual will also experience difficulty in the work role (intersect C and arrow 5 in the figure) will depend on a number of factors, such as the pervasiveness of the depression and the extent to which (1) the work provides the individual with social support (Melamed, Kushnir, & Meir, 1991), (2) there is prior vulnerability (Cherry, 1978), and (3) the individual can compartmentalize work and nonwork in such a manner that events in the one fail to have much impact on the other. The specific interaction between particular types of psychopathology and specific types of working conditions can, at this stage of knowledge, only be hypothesized, because of the absence of much evidence in the literature and because there are individual differences in response to the same objective workplace characteristics.

As of this writing, the empirical relationship between specific forms of psychopathology and work performance remains (perhaps surprisingly) largely uncharted. Note that the diagnostic criteria put forth in such manuals as the *Diagnostic and Statistical Manual of Mental Disorders* (*DSM-IV*; American Psychiatric Association, 1994) include very few diagnostic categories that in any direct way address the work role. Moreover, such schemas generally presume that the described conditions are mostly a function of the person rather than of the environment (or the person-environment match) and imply that the appropriate level of intervention to ameliorate the described conditions is individual.

Perhaps the inattention of the *DSM-IV* and its predecessors to the issue of work partially reflects the inattention of the mental disorder literature to the empirical or theoretical study of work. Only in recent years has there emerged what even now is a scant literature examining the effects of mental disorders on the capacity to work.

Oddly, despite a limited empirical literature, assessments conducted for purposes of determining fitness for duty (that is, vocational assessments) have for many years been used as a common part of the process of disability assessment. However, this enterprise has been driven more by a test-based than a theory- or research-based approach. The psychological measures used in vocational assessments of fitness for duty (typically, a brief neurological screening device, a standardized test of intelligence, and personality measures, perhaps one projective and one objective test; for example, Firman, 1985) appear to derive more from the ubiquity of their use in other contexts than from an empirical base. In disability assessment, these measures are typically used by clinicians to attach specific manual-based diagnoses; when the results of these measures are combined with medical reports and other data, disability examiners somehow make determinations as to whether or not a person is disabled or should receive disability payments, often indefinitely.

The difficulty with these types of psychological assessments is that mental disorder diagnoses, by themselves, may have little to say about the capacity to work. The trouble arises from applying categories developed from one system (the classification of mental disorders for purposes of diagnosis and treatment) to a new purpose (in this case, the determination of whether one is able to work) without benefit of new validation efforts. The inherent poverty of this approach is suggested by the increasing evidence that not only are persons who have been assigned certain diagnostic labels in many cases able to learn job skills and to work (see, for example, Clement, Siegel, & Gaylord-Ross, 1992; J. S. Wodarski, L. A. Wodarski, & Kim, 1989) but also that at least some such conditions may actually benefit from work.

Conceptually, a mental dysfunction is not necessarily a work dysfunction, though it may in some instances have implications for the work role. It is unfortunate, however, that except for one diagnostic category ("occupational problem" [V62.20]) there are no *DSM-IV* categories related to work dysfunctions. This manual describes its single work-related diagnostic category as follows: "This category can be used when the focus of clinical attention is an occupational problem that is not due to a mental disorder or, if it is due to a mental disorder, is sufficiently severe to warrant independent clinical attention. Examples include job dissatisfaction and uncertainty about career choices" (American Psychiatric Association, 1994, p. 685).

The new iteration of this widely used classification manual eliminated from its prior version (American Psychiatric Association, 1987) the one additional relevant diagnostic category ("adjustment disorder with work or academic inhibition" [309.23]) related to work, even though many types of mental disorders clearly have potential implications for the capacity to work (see Lowman, 1989, 1993a). Yet this same revised manual provides diagnostic criteria for some thirty separate diagnostic entities thought necessary to categorize and classify sexual disorders. From the perspective of the *DSM-IV*, it is difficult to escape the conclusion that work, in contrast to sex, is viewed as irrelevant to mental health. (More charitably, if unlikely, perhaps there are more things that can go wrong with sex than with work!) Psychologists and other interested groups must therefore look to other systems (or create their own) to describe what from an individual standpoint can go wrong in the work role.

Work-Related Dysfunctions

Accepting that it is useful to be able to categorize work dysfunctions and that the current taxonomies for psychological classification schemas are not well suited for that purpose, what are the desired characteristics of such systems? An alternative diagnostic classification system for work dysfunctions—that is, one that does not begin with existing mental disease diagnostic categories—would ideally have these characteristics: (1) it would be organized around *work* capacity or dysfunction rather than psychological health or mental dysfunction per se, (2) it would be able to cover a broad range of types of work and types of work difficulties, (3) it would have utility in describing and predicting behavior in the work role, and (4) it would have therapeutic implications.

Circle B of Figure 10.1 includes conditions in the taxonomy of work dysfunctions that I developed (by synthesizing the existing literature and clinical findings and organizing them in terms of their theoretical commonalities) and presented in considerable detail in *Counseling and Psychotherapy of Work Dysfunctions* (Lowman, 1993a). The personally experienced difficulties listed in that taxonomy (reproduced below) share in common that they (1) clearly address the work role, not mental disorders per se, (2) address issues largely of psychological origin, and (3) are disruptive enough to cause impairment in the capacity to work or to create adverse psychological consequences.

This taxonomy provides an organizing device or classification system and represents an initial attempt at categorization. It is intended to provide a framework for classifying individual-level problems experienced in the work role. It aims to come closer to meeting the criteria listed above than do existing nosological systems. The general categories of work dysfunctions, and syndromes associated with each category, include the following:

A Taxonomy of Work Dysfunctions

1. Patterns of undercommitment
   Underachievement
   Temporary production impediments
   Procrastination
   Occupational and/or organizational mismatch
   Fear of success
   Fear of failure
2. Patterns of overcommitment
   Obsessive-compulsive addiction to the work role
   Type A behavior pattern
   Job and occupational burnout
3. Anxiety in the work role
   Performance anxiety
   Generalized anxiety
4. Depression in the work role
   Work-related depression
   Work-affecting depression not of work-related origin
5. Personality disorders affecting work
6. Life-role conflicts
7. Transient, situational stress
8. Other psychologically relevant work difficulties

Patterns of Undercommitment

The first general category of work-related dysfunctions includes a number of patterns of undercommitment, all of which entail some significant failure to commit to the work role, either because of psychological conditions or because of a mismatch between role demands and individual capabilities. Specific examples include *underachievement*—a persistent discrepancy between ability and work-related achievement; *temporary production impediments*— short-term disruptions of the ability to work effectively, particularly associated with withdrawal and depression; *procrastination*—persistent (often cyclic) failure to initiate or to complete tasks associated with work-specific, goal-directed activity; *occupational and/or organizational mismatch*—a serious discrepancy between the interest-ability-personality characteristics called for by the career and/or organization and the individual's own career profile; *fear of success*—an undercommitment pattern in which success is characteristically avoided primarily due to unconscious factors; and *fear of failure*—avoidance of task-related activities likely to result in, or to enhance the chances of, success in goal-related activities.

Patterns of Overcommitment

In patterns of overcommitment, the affected individual is so attached to the work role that it extracts a punitive price from the individual and perhaps from familial well-being. Work performance itself may or may not be affected. Specific patterns include *obsessive-compulsive addiction to the work role*—a neurotically driven addiction to work that has dysfunctional consequences, most likely in one's own personal well-being but possibly (though not necessarily) also in work performance; *Type A behavior pattern*—a well-defined set of personal characteristics that include time urgency, overvaluation of the work role, and, among the more pathological features, free-floating anger/hostility; although this syndrome was first articulated and remains widely researched in the health behavior context (see Friedman & Rosenman, 1974; Strube, 1991), here the concern is with the pattern as it relates to functionality in work-role performance; *job and occupational burnout*—a pattern likely to be associated with an interaction of essentially positive personal characteristics (overcommitment to "impossible" goals in the context of high occupational commitment) and characteristics of the work itself (specifically, role overload, low extrinsic reward, and work activities that strain the work role; see Maslach & Jackson, 1984).

Anxiety in the Work Role

Anxiety in the work role can take the form of *performance anxiety* (that is, anxiety specific to particular job-related performances; for example, anxiety about public speaking), or it can take the form of *generalized anxiety,* affecting a wider range of work roles.

Depression in the Work Role

Depression, a pattern of withdrawal, can precede and cause difficulties in the work role or be caused by other problems in the work role. Subtypes include *work-related depression*—a category (framed as an extension of the original model) used to describe depression that originates in or from the work role and arises as the consequence of some difficulty in the work role in a person who was not already depressed—and *work-affecting depression not of work-related origin*—a category used to describe depression that arises from non-work-related factors but nonetheless affects the work role (for example, the major depression someone experiences after the loss of a loved one, affecting that person's work).

Personality Disorders Affecting Work

Associated with character difficulties (that is, entrenched dysfunctional behavior that cuts across a wide variety of situations), problems in this category depict aspects of behavior that are persistent, are quite difficult to change, and have, in this context, demonstrable impact on the work role. At present, the *DSM-IV* personality disorder classification system is retained for this categorization and for the work implications of each disorder identified (see Lowman, 1993a).

Life-Role Conflicts

This category includes work-role difficulties that arise because one's work and life roles are in conflict. A new parent who also serves in a very demanding job role, for example, may experience adverse consequences affecting both work and personal well-being beyond those ordinarily experienced.

Transient, Situational Stress

Persons suffering from work dysfunctions in this category experience work-role difficulties of a short-term nature, such as difficulties in adjusting to a new, somewhat autocratic supervisor or to the uncertainty associated with massive layoffs. Though such circumstances may be time-limited, they arouse serious concern or psychological difficulties for the time period affected.

Other Psychologically Relevant Work Difficulties

This miscellaneous category includes other nonclassified work-role difficulties, including serious impairments in work ability associated with perceptual distortions, such as those accompanying certain psychotic disturbances.

Implications of the Taxonomy of Work Dysfunctions

Where does the work dysfunctions taxonomy take us that the *DSM-IV,* for example, does not? As a model of individual differences in behavior in the workplace, this categorization scheme attempts to identify individual-level problems specific to the work role rather than to apply mental disorder categories to a new purpose and setting. Because each of the categories (independently) has received considerable research attention (see Lowman, 1993a, for a review), the further research needed at this time is not in establishing the existence of these particular conditions; it is in designing broad-brush instruments that can be used for differential assessment and treatment and in establishing the relationships between and among the conditions. In principle, these conditions and categories should lend themselves much more readily to workplace applications than do existing models and measuring instruments addressing mental disorders.

The Influence of Context: The Work and Home Environments

Whether psychopathology or work dysfunctions will adversely affect work performance depends on the type of psychopathology and the context in which it is experienced. Two major factors are relevant here: characteristics of the work setting and those of the family, or nonwork, context. Boxes D and E in Figure 10.1 depict aspects of the workplace or of the work itself that have been demonstrated to have impact on individually experienced difficulties in the work role. Box D encompasses both objective aspects of the work, such as the nature of the work tasks themselves, and subjectively experienced work factors, such as authority structures and the perception of the interpersonal relationships among one's fellow workers (if there are any). Characteristics of the work role may mitigate, exacerbate, or even be responsible for creating individually experienced dysfunction.

The variables contained in box D reflect widely studied aspects of factors influencing individual work behavior and will not be discussed further here. Greater research attention is currently needed concerning the interaction of working conditions both with traditional psychopathology variables (arrow 1 in Figure 10.1) and with the more recently articulated work dysfunctions model (arrow 3 in Figure 10.1). Such studies will help to develop a sounder basis than currently exists for matching career and work characteristics with specific types of work dysfunctions (or psychopathology).

Finally, consistent with research findings (for example, Cooper & Payne, 1988; Katz & Kahn, 1978), the model hypothesizes that work performance can be adversely affected by working conditions and work in either direction (as represented by the arrows in the figure). Workplace characteristics (authority structures, role ambiguity, and so on) and the work itself may exacerbate or ameliorate psychopathology (arrows 1 and 6 in Figure 10.1).

The potentially positive effects of work on psychopathology also bear elaboration. The positive (or therapeutic) value of work in relationship to psychopathology has been neglected in both research and practice. To the extent that work (except, perhaps, for certain atypical types of work, such as creative pursuits) is reality-based, is typically structured, and requires interpersonal contact (if only that of being in the presence of other people), it has the capacity to improve the reality orientation of persons experiencing psychological disturbance. It can also provide a source of social support, thereby potentially lessening the psychopathology and enhancing self-esteem. While in some disorders, this may fuel the psychological defense mechanism of denial, the net effect on mental well-being can certainly be positive. In effect, the psychologically disturbed patient may conclude, "I may [for example] be depressed, but at least I can still hold a job."

Conversely, and perhaps better recognized—at least among plaintiffs' attorneys (see Eisner, 1984)—the work role may also have adverse impact on psychological well-being, particularly on persons with psychiatric vulnerabilities. To the extent that job duties exceed a person's permanent or temporary capacity or that the work environment is overly controlling, fails to provide positive feedback or needed social support (for example, Katz & Kahn, 1978; Melamed, Kushnir, & Meir, 1991), or makes no effort to accommodate the patient's current psychological difficulties, it may serve to undermine confidence or may, in extreme work environments (for example, combat; see Lowman, 1989), induce psychological trauma or work dysfunctions among hitherto well-adjusted persons.

As with psychopathology, work dysfunctions (circle B of Figure 10.1) may be influenced by or be especially susceptible to what is encountered on the job (arrow 7), but they may also occur independent of these conditions. Work dysfunctions inevitably cause *personal* distress and work-related problems experienced at the individual level; however, they may or may not affect work performance. For example (although there are subtypes; see Lay, 1987), a person experiencing a persistent pattern of procrastination may almost always get the work done on time, but only with a continual struggle that comes at the expense of repetitive personal distress (see Burka & Yuen, 1983). Such patterns of procrastination may, in effect, be individual difference variables, rather unrelated to the work or working conditions encountered on the job. Presumably, for those concerned with remediation and amelioration, such patterns call for individual-level interventions rather than changes in the work itself, in supervision, or in characteristics of the work environment (see Lowman, 1993a).

Relationships Among Psychopathology, Work Dysfunctions, and Work Capacity

Assume for a moment that we can usefully categorize work dysfunctions using a taxonomy such as the one I have outlined here. The conditions classified by such a system would not be expected to exist independent of psychopathology. Persons may experience a work dysfunction (which, by definition, adversely affects the work role), a psychological dysfunction (which may or may not affect the work role), or both. The two areas may also be interactive.

As examples of the relationship between psychopathology and

work, consider two prominent cases. Illustrating the lethal effects on work that severe psychopathology may have is the unfortunate case of John Forbes Nash, Jr., who in 1994 won the Nobel Prize for his mathematical contributions to economics—especially those found in his doctoral dissertation, completed when Nash was only twenty-one (Nasar, 1994). At age thirty, Nash was hospitalized—the first of many times—for what came to be diagnosed as paranoid schizophrenia. His career was soon demolished, and his brilliant potential and prolific publications were abandoned. Only in very recent years has there been a partial remission in his condition, and a new attempt to work. In Nash's case, the mental disorder was primary and clearly intruded into the work in a nonadditive way with massive destructiveness of the capacity to work.

Further illustrating the complexity of the relationship of psychopathology and work is the case of Walter "Bob" Inglis Anderson (Gilbert, 1994; Grimes, 1992), a southern artist who lived a violent, eccentric, asocial, alcoholic life in and out of institutions, continuing throughout that life to produce thousands of watercolors and pen-and-ink sketches of striking intensity and talent. His work captures the artistic essence of the flora and fauna of the Mississippi Gulf Coast with startling clarity and originality—traits particularly evident in his use of color. After his death, family members found in his decrepit living/working quarters (his "little room"; Grimes, 1992) a treasure trove of pictures, sketches, and artwork. Much of this production had been damaged by rats, used to start fires in the fireplace, or otherwise ill-treated (Gilbert, 1994), reflecting, apparently (and not atypically of creative artists), Anderson's passionate intensity in creating the artistic product and his total disinterest in it once it had been completed.

Would Anderson have led a less disruptive life and would his family have had higher-quality lives had he been effectively treated with psychotropic medication or some psychological intervention? In all likelihood, yes. Would Anderson have been a better artist under such circumstances? The answer to that question is far less clear.

Rothenberg (1990), a long-time researcher of the creative process and the effects on creative work of psychopathology (not without his critics; see Claridge, 1992), might argue that to the extent that Anderson was an outstanding artist, it was in *spite* of his psychological disturbance, not *because* of it, and that control of psychopathology enhances rather than detracts from creative production (see also Eisenman, 1990). Yet advocates of a "creativity syndrome," to apply in this context Mumford and Gustafson's terminology (1988), might argue that artistic sensitivity, diverse or atypical perceptions, and a propensity to affective disorders (Jamison, 1989, 1993) and their concomitant substance abuse (Dardis, 1989) combine to predispose a person to both artistic creativity *and* psychological difficulties. Certainly, it is possible to be well adjusted and creative, predictable, and orderly at leisure while original and innovative at work. The apparent example of the world-renowned poet Wallace Stevens (see H. Stevens, 1971) is often cited. Stevens, who used his training as a lawyer quite successfully in his "day job" as an insurance executive, created highly regarded poetry in his "nonwork" life. However, the odds are apparently against such combinations. Consider these characteristics, which seem to favor creative production: diverse and atypical interest patterns, rejection of modal perceptions, asocial tolerance (if not solicitation) of rejection by others, intensity of focus followed by boredom and disinterest, alternating cycles of creativity and destructiveness (see, for example, Jamison, 1993; Martindale, 1989; Prentky, 1989; Runco & Albert, 1990). Thus, in the creative profile—particularly that involving artistic (rather than, for example, scientific) creative production—work dysfunctions such as alternating patterns of overcommitment and depression associated with the work role may likely be the norm.

In terms of Figure 10.1, the interface between circles A and B (in intersect C) may imply that psychopathology and work performance are, at least at times and for certain conditions or individuals, relatively uncorrelated, even for those experiencing serious psychological dysfunction. In such cases, the presence of psychopathology may not necessarily serve to impair productive accomplishment. In fact, the manic-depressive temperament (especially in its less extreme manifestations, such as cyclothymia), to take one example, may actually result in enhanced creative productivity (see H. S. Akiskal & K. Akiskal, 1988; Jamison, 1993; Richards, 1992).

On the other hand, there are certainly mental conditions (and acute exacerbations of those conditions) that limit the types of work that realistically can be done, at least at a particular time. Presumably, no one would suggest that an airline should hire as a pilot or director of security an individual who at the time of hiring was acutely psychotic. It is work itself—the reality connection—that is often important to a seriously disturbed individual, not necessarily a particular type of work. The task of considering which work is likely to both hold appeal and be able to be done effectively by a seriously disturbed patient must take into account other variables, such as those identified in the case that follows.

Case Illustration: Work Dysfunctions and
Workplace Environmental Conditions

Tom B., forty-eight years old at the time of referral, sought help because of serious concerns about his ability to speak before an audience and his generally uncomfortable feeling in social situations in the workplace. He described feeling ill at ease in speaking before any group (a not-uncommon self-perception) but also experiencing social discomfort in meetings, especially when he had to interact assertively with others. Exploration of the dynamics of the problem initially suggested that he was temperamentally shy, as had been his mother and, to a lesser extent, his highly successful executive father. Initially employing a bibliotherapeutic approach, his therapist first asked him to read self-help books on shyness, trying to help him understand that he was attempting to cope with a variation in normal behavior, not a defect of character. This was important, because Tom had concluded that he was by nature an anxious person and that this affliction had to be worked around rather than improved.

The psychologist challenged Tom's assumptions. While acknowledging that Tom was probably by nature somewhat shy and more comfortable with well-structured than ambiguous social situations, he encouraged Tom to redefine himself as someone who, while possibly shy, experienced anxiety not generically but in certain specific situations. Despite some initial resistance, the client was helped to become a better observer of the work-related situations in which the anxiety arose and to understand exactly what it was that created a problem for him. While these situations might never be ones in which Tom would feel fully comfortable (and his coming to accept that fact ironically helped him to improve), they were certainly ones that, with self-understanding and practice, he could tolerate and become more adept at handling.

Careful scrutiny of the continuing but improved problem in the anxiety-arousing situations showed that Tom's anxiety was highest when he was in the presence of his immediate boss, a highly placed executive whom (as careful inquiry had helped establish) he did not respect. Perhaps at an unconscious level, he feared both the wrath of this executive for his harbored anger and the discovery of his own concerns that this man might fire him (as he had fired so many of Tom's colleagues). Tom needed to learn more direct ways to work with this man. As he did so, and as he learned that he could more effectively confront things that bothered him about his boss, his anxiety and self-consciousness lessened.

In terms of the work dysfunctions taxonomy, Tom experienced a problem with anxiety in the work role. The personality structure within which this occurred was introverted by nature. Since introversion/extraversion by itself says nothing about a person's social skills (see Lowman, 1991), there was no reason to think that Tom was not capable of becoming at least minimally acceptable in his work role. Seemingly, he was not ill-suited for his position, since, at the high level of the firm to which he had apparently effortlessly risen (almost in spite of himself), the amount of day-to-day people contact was somewhat limited, involving primarily other senior staff. Tom's job was not to become extraverted but to understand and accept the personality parameters within which he needed to work.

In this case, the work environment itself interacted with Tom's prior dispositional tendencies to complexify his problems. Had his employment been in a less (implicitly) authoritarian environment, it is possible that the painful self-focus that arose for him when he had to deal with a boss he despised but feared would not have been a problem, or at least not as much of a problem. The client's task was to learn how to manage himself more effectively or to change either the work environment or his job.

Relationships Between Career-Related Characteristics and Work Dysfunctions: Understanding the Individual's Context

There is at least one additional cluster of individual-level characteristics that must be taken into account in the attempt to understand work dysfunctions in their proper context. This concerns what in the context of career assessment and counseling I have labeled the "interdomain model" (Lowman, 1991, 1993b). This model consists of an elaboration of three major individual domains that affect career choice and work capacity and have the potential to moderate the relationships among psychopathology, work dysfunctions, and work-related outcomes. These individual difference domains—occupational interests, abilities, and work-related personality characteristics (see Figure 10.2)—are conceptually separable and work-relevant. Although these characteristics of individuals describe aspects of persons with and without mental disorders or work dysfunctions, they are introduced here to help contextualize, in the more familiar world of normal individual differences, what has already been discussed. These characteristics clearly describe aspects of persons that are important in understanding normal variations of career choice and job performance; they may also help explain how the potentially adverse effects of mental disorders may be ameliorated or more effectively channeled.

Occupational Interests

Occupational interests, shown in circle A of Figure 10.2, are well-established individual difference characteristics reflecting people's personal liking or disliking for broad classes of occupations and avocations (Holland, 1985). They also suggest important characteristics of personality and (apparently) ability (see Lowman, Williams, & Leeman, 1985; Randahl, 1991). The most widely used model of interests remains John Holland's model, which interprets a persistent occupational interest factor structure in terms of six interest types: Realistic, Investigative, Artistic, Social, Enterprising, and Conventional (see Holland, 1985; Lowman, 1991). If, as many have contended (see, among others, Lowman & Schurman, 1982; Schneider, 1987), organizations (and therefore occupations) are not random collections of individuals (which elsewhere [Lowman, 1993a, 1993b] I have labeled the "invisible hand" phenomenon), it is in the domain of occupational interests that the matching process has most persistently been demonstrated (see, for example, Holland, 1968; Holland & Nichols, 1964a; Strong, 1931). Occupational interests are individual difference characteristics; but

Figure 10.2. Variables in the Interdomain Model of Career Factors.

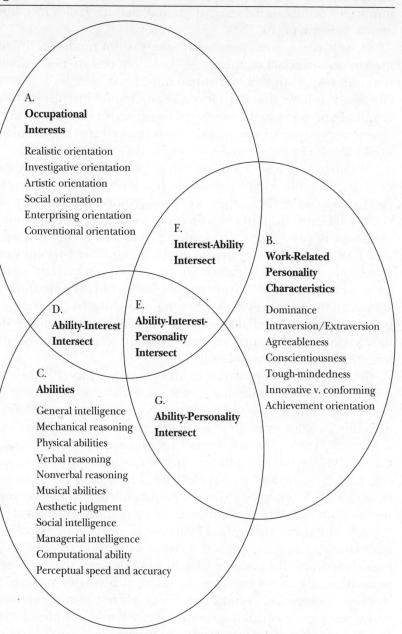

A.
**Occupational
Interests**

Realistic orientation
Investigative orientation
Artistic orientation
Social orientation
Enterprising orientation
Conventional orientation

F.
**Interest-Ability
Intersect**

B.
**Work-Related
Personality
Characteristics**

Dominance
Intraversion/Extraversion
Agreeableness
Conscientiousness
Tough-mindedness
Innovative v. conforming
Achievement orientation

D.
**Ability-Interest
Intersect**

E.
**Ability-Interest-
Personality
Intersect**

C.
Abilities

General intelligence
Mechanical reasoning
Physical abilities
Verbal reasoning
Nonverbal reasoning
Musical abilities
Aesthetic judgment
Social intelligence
Managerial intelligence
Computational ability
Perceptual speed and accuracy

G.
**Ability-Personality
Intersect**

aggregated to the organizational level, they may also describe important occupational environmental characteristics (see Lowman & Schurman, 1982).

If, as hypothesized, psychopathology is not randomly distributed in occupational samples, and if occupations are not randomized with respect to such individual difference variables as gender and age, it follows that the various occupational interest patterns would not be equal in the predicted incidence of psychopathology. Amount and type of commonly encountered psychopathology would also be expected to differ among the interest types.

We do not yet have adequate empirical evidence supporting or rejecting the following hypotheses, but interest theory suggests (and at least some data support the suggestion) that Investigative vocational interest patterns would be associated with the lowest incidence of psychopathology among Holland's six interest types (see Ludwig, 1992); Artistic, the most. It is further hypothesized that Conventional and Realistic vocational interest patterns would be associated with relatively higher levels of psychopathology (based on the fact that people favoring those interest patterns generally have limited verbal fluency or capacity for abstraction) and that Social and Enterprising vocational interest patterns would have the least (after Investigative).

If psychopathology varies by interest type, then differences might be expected in the pattern of association between neuroticism—a general, cross-cutting summary variable of psychological difficulty (see, for example, Cattell, Eber, & Tatsuoka, 1970; Costa & McCrae, 1985; Derman, French, & Harman, 1978; McCrae & Costa, 1986)—and the different interest types. Apparently, only one study (Costa, McCrae, & Holland, 1984) has addressed this issue directly. It found an expected pattern of correlations between neuroticism and Artistic vocational interests (but only for males).

Anecdotal and theoretical evidence suggests that type of psychopathology also is expected to vary by interest category. However, finer-tuned measures of psychopathology than general neuroticism measures are necessary to identify specific patterns of psychopathology. Concerning vocational interest patterns and specific types of psychopathology, we also have limited empirical data. People exhibiting Realistic vocational interest patterns, which are more common among males than females (Apostal, 1991; Holland,

1985), would be predicted to be at higher risk for handling emotional conflict through nonverbal means (for example, substance abuse) than the general population. This is because of their apparently inherent difficulty in relating easily with others and their general closedness to new experiences (Lowman & Ng, 1994). Persons high on Enterprising vocational interest patterns, for example, would be predicted both to deny problems (and therefore to present themselves as being relatively low on measures of psychopathology) and, consistent with the characteristics of the type, to be more likely to experience personality disorders than other types of difficulties.

To date, the best evidence concerns correlations between Artistic occupational interests and affective disorders. At the extreme end of highly creative talent, we know that affective disorders occur at rates significantly higher than in the general population (see Andreason, 1987; Jamison, 1989, 1993; Simonton, 1994). Whether this statistically atypical incidence of affective disorders characterizes the general population of noneminent persons with creative interest patterns remains to be determined.

There is scant empirical evidence regarding the relationship between the other interest types and psychopathology. Concerning personality disorders, some (for example, T. W. Harrell & M. S. Harrell, 1973) have argued that personality disorders—especially those associated with sociopathic tendencies—may, if present in managerial populations, be associated with success rather than failure. Similarly, it would be desirable to know the extent to which Social vocational interest patterns are excessively associated with dependent personality disorders and Realistic vocational interest patterns are excessively associated with avoidant disorders; it would also be useful to have confirmed among broader ranges of creative personality patterns the hypothesis that affective disorders (depression and the like) are at higher levels of dysfunction.

Abilities

Abilities, shown in circle C of Figure 10.2, are individual difference variables reflecting a person's capacity or potential for doing a certain thing rather than his or her liking or preferences. Abilities are almost universally acknowledged to be dominated by a very large general factor, commonly called general intelligence (Cattell, 1987). Many theorists and measurement experts (for example, Carroll, 1993; Ekstrom, French, & Harman, 1976; Spearman, 1904) would add a number of specific factors that are said to predict a smaller range of performances.

Some argue that in predicting work outcomes and job performance, there is only one ability factor related to occupational performance—namely, general intelligence (see, among others, Gottfredson, 1986; J. E. Hunter & R. F. Hunter, 1984; Ree & Earles, 1992; Ree, Earles, & Teachout, 1994). However, the roles of general and (empirically examined to a considerably lesser degree) specific forms of intelligence have to date been studied at best in the context of predicting job performance, not career choice or satisfaction with work. The structure of occupationally relevant abilities is decidedly unsettled as of this writing.

How do abilities, both general and specific, interact with traditional typologies of psychopathology? Mostly, at the present time, we do not know. Although differential ability patterns may be found among members of different occupations (see Humphreys, Lubinski, & Yao, 1993; Lowman, 1991), there is currently limited evidence of the relationship between mental disorders and various ability constructs.

Among patient populations, general intelligence shows some tendency to have a predictable relationship with at least some specific types of psychopathology (for example, hysterics are unlikely to be highly intelligent, while paranoids are more likely to be of higher intelligence; see Shapiro, 1965). Severe psychosis is often associated with impairment of cognitive abilities: schizophrenia, for example, is generally associated with lessening of the intellectual processing abilities and a decrement in the use of intelligence (Wolman, 1985). Concerning work dysfunctions, there is evidence that patterns of overcommitment, such as the Type A behavior pattern, are more likely among those who are brighter and in certain professionally demanding occupations (see Lowman, 1993a). Relationships have also been suggested between certain ability variables (for example, spatial/mechanical abilities and social intelligence) and particular personality factors (for example, personal independence or dependence, dominance, and introversion/extraversion) (see Cattell, 1987; Horn, 1977).

Presumably, ability factors may enable adequate or successful occupational functioning among persons experiencing mental disorders or work dysfunction. People experiencing affective disorders (depression, manic disorders, or manic-depressive disorders) may use strong general intelligence to compensate, in effect, for what might otherwise be negative effects on work functioning. High intelligence may also moderate the effects of adverse consequences on work by, for example, increasing awareness of the need for treatment (and of treatment compliance). Much more data are needed, however, to examine in detail how this association works and the mechanisms by which some persons with mental disorders are able to work effectively and others, often with less intrusive forms of mental disorders, are not.

Personality Characteristics

Personality characteristics, shown in circle B of Figure 10.2, refer here to predictable, expected behavior patterns—ways in which a person characteristically responds across a broad range of interpersonal situations. Expressions of major personality dimensions are somewhat independent of the demand characteristics of the situation. For example, in the interpersonal domain, a dominant, extraverted individual is likely to behave in an assertive, socially ascendant manner unless there are clear inhibitions placed upon exhibiting that behavior in a particular context. An introverted, nongregarious individual is likely to avoid situations calling for interpersonal contact and, in the work context, to prefer job duties that either do not involve working with others or provide clearly defined parameters for required interactions with others (as in certain technical kinds of work).

Recent advances in personality theory have emphasized a small number of overarching, trans-situational variables as having importance across a broad range of behaviors, including occupational behaviors (see, for example, Goldberg, 1993). While there continues to be considerable discussion in the research literature as to whether there are five major personality factors, as proposed in the Five-Factor Model (FFM; Costa & McCrae, 1985, 1992; Digman & Takemoto-Chock, 1981), fewer factors (Eysenck, 1991), or more factors (Cattell & Krug, 1986; Tellegen, 1993), there appears to be increasing consensus, particularly among I/O psychologists, that reducing complexity and number of personality variables results in a more parsimonious understanding of many aspects of behavior than the more traditional approach of examining isolated variables individually.

In the occupational context, the literature currently identifies the FFM Conscientiousness dimension as being especially relevant for job performance (see Barrick & Mount, 1991; Hayes, Roehm, Castellano, 1994; Hough, Eaton, Dunnette, Kamp, & McCloy, 1990; McHenry, Hough, Toquam, Hanson, & Ashworth, 1990). In addition, Agreeableness, another of the so-called Big Five personality dimensions, has shown promise in personnel selection (see Tett, Jackson, & Rothstein, 1991). Such findings are valuable in helping to revitalize personality theory, long neglected in I/O psychology; but for the purposes of this chapter, they have their limitations— in particular, the failure to explore the implications of personality theory among persons who are already agreed to be experiencing mental disorders (see, for example, Schmidt, Wagner, & Kiesler, 1993). The limitations as well as the positive attributes (if any) of variables associated with Eysenck's more general domains of Neuroticism and Psychoticism (1991), as applied to work settings, remain systematically to be identified.

Moreover, differences in employee populations must be considered (Schmit & Ryan, 1993). There appear to be average differences by occupation and area of study in certain personality traits or dimensions. Kline & Lapham (1992), for example, found that engineering and science students scored higher on various conscientiousness, tough-mindedness, and conventionality dimensions than did artistic and mixed groups. Hansell, Mechanic, & Brondolo (1986) found, in a sample of students, that those high on introspection favored participation in artistic activities.

Relationships between personality variables and mental disorders or psychopathology have been considered by some researchers. Egan (1989), studying a low-intelligence sample (high school dropouts) found that psychoticism and neuroticism scores differentiated direction of hostility. Specifically, psychoticism scores were correlated with measures of outward-directed hostility; neuroticism scores, with measures of inward-directed hostility. Sayles & Harrison (1989) found that persons with mental disorders who manifested reflexive, less impulsive styles on personality tests were more likely to be successfully employed and to be seen as being better able to cope with the work. Dorn and Matthews (1992) found that workers (drivers) scoring high on neuroticism were less likely to be effective on the job. Overall, more work remains to be done to establish the validity of the Five-Factor Model for clinical populations (see, for example, Ben-Porath & Waller, 1992). Similarly, more studies are needed on the relationship between traditional classifications of psychopathology and on-job performance.

Interdomain Relationships

As with the domains of work dysfunctions, psychopathology, and work setting characteristics, the domains of interests, abilities, and personality characteristics do not exist independent of one another. This is illustrated in Figure 10.2 by the interdomain intersects (D, E, F, and G). The intersection of these various factors implies that certain patterns or profiles of ability and personality are likely to be associated with particular patterns of interests (for example, high intelligence with Investigative vocational interests; extraversion with Social and Enterprising vocational interests) (Goh & Leong, 1993). And indeed the interdomain research literature to date does provide at least some support for such hypothesizing (see Costa, McCrae, & Holland, 1984; Lowman, 1991; Randahl, 1991; Rolfus & Ackerman, in press).

Given that interest, ability, and personality variables increasingly are suggested to be heavily influenced by genetic components (for example, Bouchard, Lykken, McGue, Segal, & Tellegen, 1990) and therefore to reflect characteristics that are relatively long-lasting and apparently quite difficult to change—at least after a certain age (generally around, say, eighteen or so)—these factors may be thought of as providing the context through which the work world and the effects of mental disorders or work dysfunctions are individually interpreted. These variables imply both greater or lesser skill in coping with what the environment presents and predictable preferred styles of relating to the work role. Taken collectively, the interest-ability-personality pattern also may be expected to provide the motivational direction and intensity that direct persons to particular types of work, to particular levels of work performance, and to particular styles of relating to others (see Lowman, 1991, 1993b).

Put another way, a person proceeds through school and a set

of avocational interests and activities into initial career choices, gradually becoming aware of what in the external world he or she finds personally appealing, what is within his or her work capacity, and what is available to him or her. For most people, the process of matching personal characteristics with what is available in the work world proceeds relatively effortlessly, and a reasonably good occupational match is created. When that matching process does not occur in a personally meaningful way, that itself may constitute a work dysfunction ("occupational or organizational mismatch," in the work dysfunctions model above).

Problems in the work role occur in the context of career choice and other individual difference variables. That backdrop needs to be understood, since it may influence one's propensity to experience different types of work-role difficulties and patterns of successful or unsuccessful coping with the same condition(s). In addition, such factors may provide information about how best to intervene in providing assistance to persons in need (see, for example, Lowman, 1987). If individual differences are not taken as isolated variables—in effect, as orthogonal, stand-alone, solo performers that happen to coexist along with other individual difference variables—but are taken together in profile, then it becomes important to begin to understand not just the average or prototypical association between cross-domain relationships but also aspects of individuals that can serve as compensatory or moderating influences among the population of persons experiencing (or likely to experience over their careers) work dysfunctions or psychopathology affecting work.

Interest, ability, and personality variables potentially both provide a context within which the individual's current work-role difficulties can be understood and interpreted and identify dimensions of the person that make it easier or more difficult to cope successfully with whatever work environments are encountered. A particular career direction is somehow identified and initially pursued, but even when that context constitutes a bad match, the individual adjusts to it, attempts to change or modify it, or tries to find a new work context. The interest, ability, and personality variables may help facilitate adjustment or change of that environment, as well as providing the context for judging degree of goodness of fit. Unsuccessful coping (among other factors) likely results in work dysfunctions and can also cause personal maladjustment. Conversely, certain occupations, presumably by virtue of the interest, ability, and personality characteristics of those who are modally attracted to them, are at higher a priori risk of psychopathology.

Consider the example of a writer who experiences the condition of "writer's block," a special case of temporary work inhibition (Lowman, 1993a). In understanding the phenomenon and attempting to assist the individual in improving it, the psychologist needs to be aware of the presenting manifestations, the history and nature of the experience, and the individual characteristics that the person brings to the work. Is the client who is experiencing writer's block a writer by virtue of temperament or interest pattern, or is he or she a *poseur*—someone whose temporary failure to write is really a statement, though perhaps an unconscious one, that he or she is not actually a writer? Persons well suited to the writer's role may also manifest writer's block (perhaps the most famous contemporary example of which is Harold Brodkey [for example, 1991] and Henry Roth, contemporary novelists who suffered from two of the most famously long bouts of writer's block recorded among subsequently published writers [see Kanfer, 1994; Nicholls, 1995]), but a different solution than career change is likely needed for such individuals.

Or assume that an individual seeks help for a work dysfunction—say, for an overcommitment pattern such as Type A behavior pattern. In the case of an individual presenting with such a problem who shows an Investigative vocational interest pattern, high intelligence, and a generally nonsocially oriented personality structure (see Lowman, 1991), the pattern of work overcommitment may be more of a problem for someone in the individual's family than for the individual him- or herself. Conversely, consider the case of a school counselor who manifests primarily Social vocational interests, is of high average (but not superior) intelligence, is gifted in social intelligence, and is outgoing and oriented to other people. If this individual experiences a pattern of overcommitment, it is likely to take the form of job or occupational burnout, and a different sort of assistance may be needed.

Case Illustration: The Interdomain Model and Work Dysfunctions

Curt S. was twenty-five at the time he sought psychological help for his difficulty in finding a satisfying career. In college, he had majored in business with the encouragement of his parents. He had always been very good at working with other people and at one time had considered being a teacher. His father, a successful business manager, had discouraged this occupational pursuit, correctly noting that the financial rewards associated with teaching were not very high, particularly in contrast with those to be found in the business world. Curt found the courses easy enough in business school and sailed through his curriculum, earning a general business degree with a minor in marketing (and a high grade-point average). He successfully found initial employment in a large corporation—one that, at the time of his arrival, was just at the peak of a rapid expansion effort.

Curt did his job well enough, but his heart was never in the work. Indeed, over time he found himself with less and less energy to expend on his work. His initial enthusiasm waned, and he found himself more and more unhappy when he awoke in the mornings. He began doing volunteer work, which was encouraged by his employer, and he became quite active in assuming managerial roles in local charity events. This solution distracted Curt for a time from his career concerns, and he found his depression lessening.

His decreased energy and enthusiasm for his work was not lost on his employer, however, and Curt found his performance reviews, like his job performance itself, to be rather lackluster. As the market tightened, due to increased competition and oversupply, the company began to lay off employees, first at the hourly levels and then in management. Curt's limited seniority and less-than-stellar performance ratings combined to ensure that he was one of the first managers to be let go.

Rather than finding himself unhappy at this turn of events, he was instead secretly pleased. Now he had a face-saving way to change careers. As his first step, he made an appointment with a psychologist to consider career options. Soon thereafter, his long-standing depressive symptoms (poor sleeping and eating, withdrawal from important relationships, general malaise) improved. As a result of his own thinking and his discussions with the psychologist, Curt returned to school and earned a master of arts degree in teaching, enabling him finally, at age twenty-nine, to pursue his own career interests.

The subject of Curt's career had been a source of conflict between him and his parents for years; arguments had erupted with special fervor whenever Curt voiced his prerogative to choose a career that was right for him. Not surprisingly, Curt's parents viewed his career change as being less than desirable, but now two competing needs—the parents' need for their son to be perceived as successful and their need to see themselves as good and supportive parents—came into direct conflict. They gradually came to recognize that their son had been seriously unhappy in his work and to accept, finally, that his happiness in life was more important than their career ambitions for him. In the context of his job loss, however, they began to redefine his retraining efforts as evidence of an ambitious response to a frustrating experience. They resolved their own conflict by redefining teaching as an important and underrewarded occupation.

Interestingly, two months after he started his new career in teaching, Curt met (and soon thereafter married) his wife. For Curt, accepting a right-fitting career meant destroying ambitions that others had for him. Choosing that career was the first major step in establishing his own identity, and it freed him up for the rest of his life.

This case illustrates a pattern of undercommitment associated with being occupationally mismatched. A review of Curt's psychological test results in the areas of interests and abilities demonstrated to both Curt and the professional he consulted that he was in fact better suited for a helping occupation than for one in business. Yet Curt's problems could not be resolved without a consideration of the context in which they took place. In trying to please his parents, Curt had ignored his own needs. Yet like his parents' motives, his own motives (to please his parents and to be successful in his own eyes) were on a conflictual course. The system became unstuck only when he experienced (or allowed to be created) a face-saving way to change occupations.

Implications for Practice, Training, and Research

The various implications of the models presented in this chapter can be considered from the perspective of the psychologist, the manager, and the researcher.

Implications for Psychologists and Other Professionals

Psychologists responsible for classifying and attempting to ameliorate the problems of individuals experiencing difficulties in the work role need carefully to consider the system used to categorize individuals. I hope that this chapter has demonstrated that it is risky to attempt to generalize from psychopathology to assumptions about work problems. The *DSM-IV* at best tells us something about categorizing types of psychopathology; it says almost nothing about the capacity to work or the methods by which to maximize the work potential of someone who meets its diagnostic criteria. The newer taxonomy of work dysfunctions summarized here provides an alternative (but far from final) classification schema that attempts to provide categories of things that can go wrong in the work role. But whatever system is used to categorize what, from an individual perspective, can go wrong in the work role, it is important that the system be developed and validated in the work-role context.

Much more work remains to be done to develop reliable procedures for classifying the ability to work of persons experiencing mental or work dysfunctions. For now, the assessing clinician must carefully evaluate a number of factors in determining work fitness. First, the nature of the current psychological difficulties should be evaluated, but primarily in the work context. This means that it is desirable to determine not just where someone fits in a particular diagnostic scheme but also how that person's abilities, interests, and personality characteristics relate to a particular job (or range of jobs) and the demonstrated extent, if any, to which that individual is unable to perform particular job duties. The judgment that a person is or is not able to work in a particular job cannot be made on the basis of a consideration of mental disorders alone.

In evaluating fitness for work, the clinician needs to consider whether a work dysfunction or mental condition is known to manifest periodicity, meaning that the problem is unlikely to be "solved" once and for all. If so, a temporary rather than long-term solution may need to be considered. The assessor also needs to take into account whether the type of workplace difficulty is one that is known routinely to create difficulties in accomplishing a particular category or class of work. For example, while there might be good reason not to put a schizophrenic in a high-stress position (such as a customer service agent for an airline), there might be very little disruption of the work role if that person worked in a mostly solitary activity (such as data entry). A third relevant issue concerns whether the behavior at issue manifests a clear threat to anyone else in the workforce. If so, those involved in the case, including the employee's manager, may have an implied obligation to protect other employees (or the clients of the organization) from security-compromising situations. For example, a person with an active history of drug abuse involving paranoia-inducing drugs may need to have access to the workplace restricted.

Clinical and counseling psychologists and other mental health professionals working with adult populations need to become as accustomed to evaluating the capacity to work as they now are to evaluating the capacity to be a parent, to have friends, or to have sexual intercourse. By learning routinely how to assess work as an important part of most people's adult lives, clinicians will assist their clients in maintaining, developing, or resuming behavior likely to enhance their self-esteem and sense of well-being.

I/O psychologists bring to the table expertise in understanding the effects of employment systems on work behavior, particularly in certain organizational contexts. Too often, though, they do not apply their models across the broad spectrum of types of work-role performances (for example, the role of creative artist as well as manager) and do not consider the full range of human behavior likely to be manifest among workers (including that of psychologically disturbed individuals, for example). Future training programs for I/O psychology might consider adding to their students' repertoire of skills the understanding of, and ability to diagnose and intervene with, behavior experienced at the individual (not just group or organizational) level, as well as at least a rudimentary understanding of psychopathology and a much more comprehensive understanding of work dysfunctions. In time, industrial and organizational psychology may evolve into a field (perhaps then more properly labeled *occupational* and organizational psychology) that legitimizes the study of individual differences not just as abstract variables to be quantified but also as factors that are attached to live *individual* persons with whom there are important, and individualized, employment decisions to be made.

Implications for Managers

Managers need not have a generalized, a priori fear of hiring persons with emotional difficulties. Nonetheless, complex predictive questions arise when managers consider on an individual basis whether someone should be excluded, or not excluded, from employment on the basis of a mental disorder or work dysfunction. While there is apparently a higher risk of work difficulties among those who meet diagnostic criteria of psychological dysfunctions before entering the workforce (see Cherry, 1978, 1984), several factors must be taken into account in considering whether or not to exclude a person from employment on the basis of psychological difficulties.

The manager may rarely be in a position to feel confident in making decisions about the fitness for duty of persons experiencing either psychopathology or work dysfunctions. However, the manager, along with the I/O psychologist, is in the best position to describe both the job and the behavior required for successful performance on the job. Working with the mental health professional, the manager needs to offer his or her expert judgment (for now, unfortunately, the best available method for making decisions about fitness for duty) on a case-by-case basis regarding (1) whether or not a particular pattern of psychopathology is likely to interfere with performance of job duties and (2) how best to address the emotional difficulties of workers.

It is problematic for the manager to abandon to the mental health professional the need to make employment and employability decisions once all the factual and evaluative data are available. Especially problematic is the tendency of some managers to tolerate on an ongoing basis poor work performance (poor productivity, absenteeism, and the like) from an employee identified as experiencing mental problems. That tendency is likely to be of no assistance to either the employee or the employer.

Finally, most (but not all) work dysfunctions and psychopathology benefit from social support and stress minimization. Aggressively managing employees experiencing dysfunctions may result in a deterioration of their condition.

Implications for Researchers

A much larger literature is sorely needed to document the relationship of traditional categories of psychopathology (depression, anxiety, schizophrenia, paranoia, and the like) to the work role, particularly literature examining work outcomes using well-validated work criterion measures. Elsewhere (for example, Lowman, 1982, 1993b), I have lamented the inattention of mental health researchers to the work role; here I add that this concern has not dissipated.

The taxonomy of work dysfunctions presented in my earlier work (Lowman, 1993b) remains to be validated with empirical data in a variety of work settings and conditions. Whether the hypothesized conditions are factorially distinct and practically useful needs considerably more research attention. And such studies need to focus on employed adults rather than on college students not yet in a work setting.

The base rates of various work dysfunctions remain to be established. There is some evidence as to the pervasiveness of specific conditions, such as Type A behavior pattern (see Lowman, 1993a, for reviews), but much more data are needed. In addition, there is a need to categorize the base rate of work dysfunctions and of psychopathology among various groupings of interest, ability, and personality variables.

Finally, we need to know more about work dysfunctions as they are experienced on and off the job, as they are experienced internally within the person, and how they are behaviorally manifested to external observers. Often what is experienced by the individual as being problematic is not overtly manifest on the job, though the internal stress is no less real.

Our Reader Revisited

I opened this chapter with a complaint from an individual who rightfully was incensed that her devotion to work had been mischaracterized as a dysfunction. From the perhaps new perspectives of this chapter, is this reader in fact suffering from a work dysfunction, or is she simply a hard-working and successful person who chooses to devote much of her waking time to productive accomplishment?

It is not appropriate to diagnose anyone without a personal assessment, but we would have to speculate that this reader is committed to the work role without suffering from a pattern of work overcommitment. In all likelihood, she is adaptively well adjusted to her employment and is masking no clear manifestation of anxiety or personal unhappiness.

To help others work well and productively is the ultimate aim and goal of all of psychology applied to the workplace. By understanding the many variations that work happiness, as well as work dysfunction, may assume, we may ultimately be able to design better work systems and intervene earlier and more effectively with workplace casualties.

References

Akiskal, H. S., & Akiskal, K. (1988). Reassessing the prevalence of bipolar disorders: Clinical significance and artistic creativity. *Psychiatry and Psychobiology, 3,* 29–36.

American Psychiatric Association. (1987). *Diagnostic and statistical manual of mental disorders (DSM-III-R)* (3rd ed., rev.). Washington, DC: Author.

American Psychiatric Association. (1994). *Diagnostic and statistical manual of mental disorders (DSM-IV)* (4th ed.). Washington, DC: Author.

Andreason, N. C. (1987). Creativity and mental illness: Prevalence rates in writers and their first-degree relatives. *American Journal of Psychiatry, 144,* 1288–1292.

Apostal, R. A. (1991). College students' career interests and sensing-intuition personality. *Journal of College Student Development, 32,* 4–7.

Barrick, M. R., & Mount, M. K. (1991). The Big Five personality dimensions and job performance: A meta-analysis. *Personnel Psychology, 44,* 1–26.

Ben-Porath, Y. S., & Waller, N. G. (1992). Five big issues in clinical personality assessment: A rejoinder to Costa and McCrae. *Psychological Assessment, 4,* 23–25.

Blazer, D., Swartz, M., Woodbury, M., Manton, K. G., Hughes, D., & George, L. K. (1988). Depressive symptoms and depressive diagnoses in a community population. *Archives of General Psychiatry, 145,* 1078–1084.

Bouchard, T. J., Lykken, D. T., McGue, M., Segal, N. L., & Tellegen, A. (1990). Sources of human psychological differences: The Minnesota Study of Twins Reared Apart. *Science, 250,* 223–228.

Brodkey, H. (1991). *The runaway soul.* New York: Farrar, Straus & Giroux.

Bucholz, K. K. (1992). Alcohol abuse and dependence from a psychiatric epidemiologic perspective. *Alcohol Health and Research World, 16,* 197–208.

Burka, J. B., & Yuen, L. M. (1983). *Procrastination: Why you do it, what to do about it.* Reading, MA: Addison-Wesley.

Carroll, J. B. (1993). *Human cognitive abilities: A survey of factor-analytic studies.* New York: Cambridge University Press.

Cattell, R. B. (Ed.). (1987). *Intelligence: Its structure, growth, and action* (rev. ed.). Amsterdam: North-Holland.

Cattell, R. B., Eber, H. W., & Tatsuoka, M. M. (1970). *Handbook for the Sixteen Personality Factor Questionnaire.* Champaign, IL: Institute for Personality and Ability Testing.

Cattell, R. B., & Krug, S. E. (1986). The number of factors in the 16PF: A review of the evidence with special emphasis on methodological problems. *Educational and Psychological Measurement, 46,* 509–522.

Charney, E. A., & Weissman, M. W. (1988). Epidemiology of depressive and manic syndromes. In A. Georgotas & R. Cancro (Eds.), *Depression and mania* (pp. 26–52). New York: Elsevier Science.

Cherry, N. (1978). Stress, anxiety, and work: A longitudinal study. *Journal of Occupational Psychology, 51,* 259–270.

Cherry, N. (1984). Nervous strain, anxiety, and symptoms amongst 32-year-old men at work in Britain. *Journal of Occupational Psychology, 57,* 95–105.

Chou, S. P. (1994). Sex differences in morbidity among respondents classified as alcohol abusers and/or dependent: Results of a national survey. *Addiction, 89,* 87–93.

Claridge, G. (1992). Great wits and madness. In R. S. Albert (Ed.), *Genius and eminence* (2nd ed., pp. 329–350). Elmsford, NY: Pergamon Press.

Clement, H. K., Siegel, S., & Gaylord-Ross, R. (1992). Simulated and in situ vocational social skills training for youths with learning disabilities. *Exceptional Children, 58,* 336–345.

Cooper, C. L., & Payne, R. (1988). *Causes, coping, and consequences of stress at work.* New York: Wiley.

Costa, P. T., & McCrae, R. R. (1985). *The NEO Personality Inventory manual.* Odessa, FL: Psychological Assessment Resources.

Costa, P. T., & McCrae, R. R. (1992). Four ways five factors are basic. *Personality and Individual Differences, 13,* 653–665.

Costa, P. T., McCrae, R. R., & Holland, J. L. (1984). Personality and vocational interests in an adult sample. *Journal of Applied Psychology, 69,* 390–400.

Dardis, T. (1989). *Thirsty muse: Alcohol and the American writer.* New York: Ticknor & Fields.

Derman, D., French, J. W., & Harman, H. H. (1978). *Guide to factor referenced temperament scales 1978.* Princeton, NJ: Educational Testing Service.

Dick, C. L., Bland, R. C., & Newman, S. C. (1994). Panic disorder. *Acta Psychiatrica Scandinavica, 89* (376, Suppl.), 45–53.

Digman, J. M., & Takemoto-Chock, N. K. (1981). Factors in the natural language of personality: Re-analysis, comparison, and interpretation of six major studies. *Multivariate Behavioral Research, 16,* 149–170.

Dorn, L., & Matthews, G. (1992). Two further studies of personality correlates of driver stress. *Personality and Individual Differences, 13,* 949–951.

Eaton, W. W., Kessler, R. C., Wittchen, H. W., & Magee, W. J. (1994). Panic and panic disorder in the United States. *American Journal of Psychiatry, 151,* 413–420.

Egan, V. (1989). Links between personality, ability, and attitudes in a low-IQ sample. *Personality and Individual Differences, 10,* 997–1001.

Eisenman, R. (1990). Creativity, preference for complexity, and physical and mental illness. *Creativity Research Journal, 3,* 231–236.

Eisner, D. A. (1984). Mental injury in workers' compensation: An examination of job stress. *American Journal of Forensic Psychology, 2,* 101–111.

Ekstrom, R. B., French, J. W., & Harman, H. H. (1976). *Manual for Kit of Factor-Referenced Cognitive Tests.* Princeton, NJ: Educational Testing Service.

Eysenck, H. J. (1991). Dimensions of personality: 16, 5, or 3?—criteria for a taxonomic paradigm. *Personality and Individual Differences, 12,* 773–790.

Fielder, J. F. (1994). *Mental disabilities and the Americans with Disabilities Act: A concise compliance manual for executives.* Westport, CT: Quorum.

Firman, G. J. (1985). The psychiatric and psychological written report on workers' compensation evaluations. *American Journal of Forensic Psychiatry, 6,* 15–42.

Fletcher, B. C. (1988). The epidemiology of occupational stress. In C. L. Cooper & R. Payne (Eds.), *Causes, coping, and consequences of stress at work* (pp. 3–50). New York: Wiley.

Frances, A. J., Pincus, H. A., Widiger, T. A., Davis, W. W., & First, M. B. (1994). *DSM-IV:* Work in progress. In J. E. Messich, M. R. Jorge, & I. M. Salloum (Eds.), *Psychiatric epidemiology: Assessment concepts and methods* (pp. 116–135). Baltimore, MD: Johns Hopkins University Press.

Fraser, R. (1947). *The incidence of neurosis among factory workers* (Medical Research Council Health Research Board Report No. 90). London: Her Majesty's Stationery Office.

Friedman, M., & Rosenman, R. H. (1974). *Type A behavior and your heart.* New York: Knopf.

Gilbert, B. (1994, Oct.). Stalking the blue bear: The fine art of Walter Anderson. *Smithsonian,* pp. 109–120.

Goh, D. S., & Leong, F. T. (1993). The relationship between Holland's theory of vocational interest and Eysenck's model of personality. *Personality and Individual Differences, 15,* 555–562.

Goldberg, L. R. (1993). The structure of phenotypic personality traits. *American Psychologist, 48,* 26–34.

Gottfredson, L. (Ed.). (1986). The *g* factor in employment. *Journal of Vocational Behavior, 29,* 293–450.

Grant, B. F. (1993). The relationship between ethanol intake and *DSM-III-R* alcohol dependence: Results of a national survey. *Journal of Substance Abuse, 5,* 257–267.

Grimes, W. (1992, Oct. 4). Celebrating a Gulf Coast artist. *New York Times,* pp. 25–26.

Hansell, S., Mechanic, D., & Brondolo, E. (1986). Introspectiveness and adolescent development. *Journal of Youth and Adolescence, 15,* 115–132.

Harrell, T. W., & Harrell, M. S. (1973). The personality of MBA's who reach general management early. *Personnel Psychology, 26,* 127–134.

Hayes, T. L., Roehm, H. A., & Castellano, J. P. (1994). Personality correlates of success in total quality manufacturing. *Journal of Business and Psychology, 8,* 397–411.

Holland, J. L. (1968). Explorations of a theory of vocational choice: VI. A longitudinal study using a sample of typical college students. *Journal of Applied Psychology, 52,* 1–37.

Holland, J. L. (1985). *Making vocational choices: A theory of vocational choices and work environments* (2nd ed.). Englewood Cliffs, NJ: Prentice-Hall.

Holland, J. L., & Nichols, R. C. (1964). Prediction of academic and extracurricular achievement in college. *Journal of Educational Psychology, 55,* 55–65.

Horn, J. L. (1977). Personality and ability theory. In R. B. Cattell & R. M. Dregers (Eds.), *Handbook of modern personality theory* (pp. 139–165). Washington, DC: Hemisphere.

Hough, L. M., Eaton, N. K., Dunnette, M. D., Kamp, J. D., & McCloy, R. A. (1990). Criterion-related validities of personality constructs and the effect of response distortion on those validities. *Journal of Applied Psychology, 75,* 581–595.

Humphreys, L. G., Lubinski, D., & Yao, G. (1993). Utility of predicting group membership and the role of spatial visualization in becoming an engineer, physical scientist, or artist. *Journal of Applied Psychology, 78,* 250–261.

Hunter, J. E., & Hunter, R. F. (1984). Validity and utility of alternative predictors of job performance. *Psychological Bulletin, 96,* 72–98.

Jamison, K. (1989). Mood disorders and seasonal patterns in British writers and artists. *Psychiatry, 52,* 125–134.

Jamison, K. (1993). *Touched with fire: Manic-depressive illness and the artistic temperament.* New York: Free Press.

Jones, N. L. (1990). *The Americans with Disabilities Act: An overview of major provisions.* Washington, DC: Congressional Research Service, Library of Congress.

Kanfer, S. (1991, Nov. 25). The thirty-year writer's block. *Time,* pp. 98–99.

Katz, D., & Kahn, R. L. (1978). *The social psychology of organizations* (2nd ed). New York: Wiley.

Kessler, R. C., McGonagle, K. A., Swartz, M., Blazer, D. G., & Nelson, C. B. (1993). Sex and depression in the National Comorbidity Survey: I. Lifetime prevalence, chronicity, and recurrence. *Journal of Affective Disorders, 29,* 85–96.

Kets de Vries, M.F.R., & Miller, D. (1984). *The neurotic organization: Diagnosing and changing counterproductive styles of management.* San Francisco: Jossey-Bass.

Kirkcaldy, B. D. (1986). The relationship between occupational interests and personality variables in a psychiatric group. *Personality and Individual Differences, 7,* 503–508.

Kline, P., & Lapham, S. L. (1992). Personality and faculty in British universities. *Personality and Individual Differences, 13,* 855–857.

Kornhauser, A. (1965). *Mental health of the industrial worker: A Detroit study.* New York: Wiley.

Lay, C. H. (1987). A modal profile analysis of procrastinators: A search for types. *Personality and Individual Differences, 8,* 705–714.

Lowman, R. L. (1982). Clinical psychology at work. *Clinical Psychologist, 35,* 19–20.

Lowman, R. L. (1987). Occupational choice as a moderator of psychotherapeutic approach. *Psychotherapy: Theory/Research/Practice/Training, 24*(4), 801–808.

Lowman, R. L. (1989). *Pre-employment screening for psychopathology: A guide to professional practice.* Sarasota, FL: Professional Resource Press.

Lowman, R. L. (1991). *The clinical practice of career assessment: Interests, abilities, and personality.* Washington, DC: American Psychological Association.

Lowman, R. L. (1993a). *Counseling and psychotherapy of work dysfunctions.* Washington, DC: American Psychological Association.

Lowman, R. L. (1993b). The inter-domain model of career assessment and counseling. *Journal of Counseling and Development, 71,* 549–554.

Lowman, R. L., & Ng, Y. M. (1994, Aug.). *Ability and personality characteristics of employed realistic males.* Paper presented at the 102nd annual meeting of the American Psychological Association, Los Angeles.

Lowman, R. L., & Schurman, S. J. (1982). Psychometric characteristics of a Vocational Preference Inventory short form. *Educational and Psychological Measurement, 42,* 602–613.

Lowman, R. L., Williams, G. E., & Leeman, G. (1985). The structure and relationship of college women's primary abilities and vocational interests. *Journal of Vocational Behavior, 27,* 298–315.

Ludwig, A. M. (1992). Creative achievement and psychopathology: Comparison among professions. *American Journal of Psychotherapy, 46,* 330–356.

Martindale, C. (1989). Personality, situation, and creativity. In J. A. Glover, R. R. Ronning, & C. R. Reynolds (Eds.), *Handbook of creativity* (pp. 211–232). New York: Plenum.

Maslach, C., & Jackson, S. E. (1984). Burnout in organizational settings. *Applied Social Psychology Annual, 5,* 133–153.

McCrae, R. R., & Costa, P. T. (1986). Clinical assessment can benefit from recent advances in personality psychology. *American Psychologist, 41,* 1001–1003.

McHenry, J. J., Hough, L. M., Toquam, J. L., Hanson, M. A., & Ashworth, S. (1990). Project A validity results: The relationship between predictor and criterion domains. *Personnel Psychology, 43,* 335–354.

Melamed, S., Kushnir, T., & Meir, E. I. (1991). Attentuating the impact of job demands: Additive and interactive effects of perceived control and social support. *Journal of Vocational Behavior, 39,* 40–53.

Mezzich, J. E., Jorge, M. R., & Salloum, I. M. (Eds.). (1994). *Psychiatric epidemiology: Assessment concepts and methods.* Baltimore, MD: Johns Hopkins University Press.

Mumford, M. D., & Gustafson, S. B. (1988). Creativity syndrome: Integration, application, and innovation. *Psychological Bulletin, 103,* 27–43.

Nasar, S. (1994, Nov. 13). The lost years of a Nobel laureate. *New York Times,* section 3, pp. 1, 8.

Nicholls, R. E. (1995, Oct. 15). Henry Roth, who wrote of an immigrant child's life in "Call It Sleep," dies at 89. *New York Times,* p. 19.

Prentky, R. (1989). Creativity and psychopathology: Gamboling at the seat of madness. In J. A. Glover, R. R. Ronning, & C. R. Reynolds (Eds.), *Handbook of creativity* (pp. 243–269). New York: Plenum.

Randahl, G. J. (1991). A typological analysis of the relations between measured vocational interests and abilities. *Journal of Vocational Behavior, 38,* 333–350.

Ree, M. J., & Earles, J. A. (1992). Intelligence is the best predictor of job performance. *Current Directions in Psychological Science, 1,* 86–89.

Ree, M. J., Earles, J. A., & Teachout, M. S. (1994). Predicting job performance: Not much more than *g. Journal of Applied Psychology, 79,* 518–524.

Richards, R. (1992). Mood swings and everyday creativity. *Harvard Mental Health Letter, 8,* 4–7.

Robbins, C. A., & Martin, S. S. (1993). Gender, styles of deviance, and drinking problems. *Journal of Health and Social Behavior, 34,* 302–321.

Rolfus, E. L., & Ackerman, P. L. (in press). Self-report knowledge: At the crossroads of ability, interest, and personality. *Journal of Educational Psychology.*

Rothenberg, A. (1990). *Creativity and madness: New findings and old stereotypes.* Baltimore, MD: Johns Hopkins University Press.

Runco, M. A., & Albert, R. S. (Eds.). (1990). *Theories of creativity.* Newbury Park, CA: Sage.

Sayles, S. L., & Harrison, D. K. (1989). Reflection-impulsivity and work adjustment. *Rehabilitation Counseling Bulletin, 33,* 110–117.

Schmidt, F. L., & Ones, D. S. (1992). Personnel selection. *Annual Review of Psychology,* 43, 627–670.

Schmidt, J. A., Wagner, C. C., & Kiesler, D. J. (1993). *DSM-IV* Axis II: Dimensionality ratings? "Yes"; Big Five? "Perhaps later." *Psychological Inquiry, 4,* 119–121.

Schmit, M. J., & Ryan, A. M. (1993). The Big Five in personnel selection: Factor structure in applicant and nonapplicant populations. *Journal of Applied Psychology, 78,* 966–974.

Schneider, B. (1987). The people make the place. *Personnel Psychology, 40,* 437–453.

Schultheis, A. M., & Bond, G. R. (1993). *Psychosocial Rehabilitation Journal, 17,* 107–119.

Shapiro, D. (1965). *Neurotic styles.* New York: Basic Books.

Simonton, D. K. (1994). *Greatness: Who makes history and why.* New York: Guilford.

Slater, E., & Cowie, V. (1971). *The genetics of mental disorders.* London: Oxford University Press.

Spearman, C. (1904). "General intelligence," objectively determined and measured. *American Journal of Psychology, 15,* 201–293.

Stevens, H. (Ed.). (1971). *The palm at the end of the mind: Selected poems and a play by Wallace Stevens.* New York: Knopf.

Strong, E. K. (1931). *Change of interests with age, based on examination of more than 2,000 men between the ages of 20 and 60 representing 8 occupations.* Stanford, CA: Stanford University Press.

Strube, M. J. (Ed.). (1991). *Type A behavior.* Newbury Park, CA: Sage.

Swanson, M. C., Bland, R. C., & Newman, S. C. (1994). Antisocial personality disorders. *Acta psychiatrica Scandinavica, 89* (Suppl. 376), 63–70.

Tellegen, A. (1993). Folk concepts and psychological concepts of personality and personality disorder. *Psychological Inquiry, 4,* 122–130.

Tett, R. P., Jackson, D. N., & Rothstein, M. (1991). Personality measures as predictors of job performance: A meta-analytic review. *Personnel Psychology, 44,* 703–742.

Tuomi, K., Ilmarinen, J., Eskelinen, L., Järvinen, E., Toikkanen, J., & Klockars, M. (1991). Prevalence and incidence rates of diseases and work ability in different categories of municipal occupations. *Scandinavian Journal of Work, Environment, and Health, 17* (Suppl. 1), 67–74.

Weissman, M. M. (1993). The epidemiology of personality disorders: A 1990 update. *Journal of Personality Disorders,* (Suppl. 7), 44–62.

Weissman, M. M., Bland, R. C., Canino, G. J., Greenwald, S., Rubio-Stipec, M., Wickramarathe, D. J., Wittchen, H. U., & Yeh, E. K. (1994). The cross-national epidemiology of obsessive compulsive disorder: The Cross National Collaborative Group. *Journal of Clinical Psychiatry, 55,* (3, Suppl.), 5–10.

Weissman, M. M., Bland, R. C., Joyce, P. R., Newman, S. C., Wells, T. E., & Wittchen, H. U. (1993). Sex differences in rates of depression: Cross-national perspectives. *Journal of Affective Disorders, 29,* 77–84.

Widiger, T. A., & Trull, R. J. (1991). Diagnosis and clinical utility. *Annual Review of Psychology, 42,* 109–133.

Wittchen, H. U., & Essau, C. A. (1993). Epidemiology of panic disorder: Progress and unresolved issues. *Journal of Psychiatric Research, 27* (Suppl. 1), 47–68.

Wittchen, H. U., Zhao, S., Kessler, R. C., & Eaton, W. W. (1994). *DSM-III-R* generalized anxiety disorder in the National Comorbidity Survey. *Archives of General Psychiatry, 51,* 355–364.

Wodarski, J. S., Wodarski, L. A., & Kim, T. W. (1989). Comprehensive employment preparation for adolescents with developmental disabilities: An empirical paradigm. *Adolescence, 24,* 821–836.

Wolman, B. B. (1985). Intelligence and mental health. In B. B. Wolman (Ed.), *Handbook of intelligence: Theories, measurements, and applications* (pp. 849–871). New York: Wiley.

Chapter Eleven

Perceptions of Organizational Climate

Lawrence R. James
Michael D. McIntyre

Climate and culture are two of the more popular perspectives from which to investigate the effects of work environments on individuals and groups (Schneider, 1990). The genesis of organizational culture is extra-individual: the concept of culture was first conceived of in terms of variables (stimuli or treatments) that act on individuals (Reichers & Schneider, 1990; Rousseau, 1990). Over the years, culture has maintained this extra-individual level of explanation. For example, cultural variables usually involve direct or indirect variants of (in)formal systems norms (Katz & Kahn, 1978), such as specifications of organizationally correct strategies for influence seeking (for example, sanctioned forms of impression management), decision making (for example, the delegation of midlevel decision making to teams), and the exercise of power (for example, diverse representation in empowerment).

The thrust of normative or cultural forces is to engender a socializing (if not civilizing) influence in organizational environments. To function effectively as norms, cultural variables must have strong main effects on organizational incumbents just as the group or social norms are dependent on their ability to generate conformity among group members in regard to group-sanctioned attitudes and behaviors. While there are many interesting questions about the roles that individual differences might play in the development and later operation of cultural influences, it is clear that the core of such a discussion would be on a level of causal explanation external to the individual.

In a volume devoted to individual differences, we thought it best to focus our efforts on a subject for which the locus of explanation is the individual. Thus we concentrated on climate. The genesis of climate, unlike that of culture, lies in the individual difference psychology of environmental cognition and perception. We must be careful not to overstate this point, however, for the concept of climate is concerned with the relative importance of individual and situational antecedents of perception in models that recognize both situational and individual causation. For example, climate models often begin with situational stimuli such as pay, group size, or technological complexity (L. R. James, Demaree, Mulaik, & Ladd, 1992; L. R. James & Jones, 1980; L. R. James & Tetrick, 1986). However, climate is not so much concerned with perceptions of how situational stimuli exist externally as it is with how these stimuli are interpreted by individuals within each work environment. Thus it is not pay per se that is of primary concern; it is how "equitable" pay is perceived to be. In like manner, group size is less important than perceptions of "friendliness and cooperativeness of intragroup relations," and task complexity is of less salience than perceptions of the "challenge" imputed to that complexity.

Climate emphasizes the individualistic, phenomenological, and interpretive aspects of perception, because the constructs of interest in climate research (for example, equity, friendliness, cooperativeness, challenge) are intrinsically *psychological*. Constructs such as equity and challenge reflect the acquired meanings that environments have for individuals, which is why climate is usually defined as a product of cognitive appraisals of work environments (L. R. James, L. A. James, & Ashe, 1990). We shall delve into this issue in greater detail in the first part of this chapter, where we address the concept of "meaning" as it relates to perceptions of work environments.

Characterizing climate as psychological is confusing at times, because the term *climate* is sometimes used to describe units of analysis *above* the individual (for example, restrictive versus nonrestrictive work environments—L. R. James et al., 1992; see also George, 1990; Hater & Bass, 1988; Kozlowski & Hattrup, 1992; Schneider & Bowen, 1985). There is, however, no inconsistency in defining a construct as psychological and then using it to describe higher levels of analysis if we stipulate that people within any given higher unit of analysis (for example, a team or work group) agree on their perceptions (for example, all members of a team agree that remuneration for team performance is equitable; L. R. James, 1982). The construct retains its definition (for example, equity is still the perceived fairness of remuneration), and the "score" (for example, mean perception of equity over team members) at the higher level of analysis is interpreted as the "shared psychological environment" (L. R. James et al., 1990, p. 62) or simply as the shared meaning.

Aggregate climate, like culture, is beyond the bounds of the present treatment, because of its extra-individual level of analysis. We shall focus instead on the many conditions in which climate contributes to understanding when the individual is the level of analysis. For example, not all members of a team, work group, department, or faculty may agree that their pay is equitable even though the criteria for compensation are relatively standard across all perceivers. Reliable variance among individuals, both in regard to perceptions and in regard to reactions that are functions of perceptions (for example, satisfaction versus dissatisfaction with pay), suggests that the individual is the appropriate level of analysis and that person variables and person-by-situation interactions are candidates for explanatory variables.

The possibilities for individual-level studies are extensive. Why do some subordinates perceive feedback from a supervisor as a personal attack while others who report to the same supervisor frame feedback as helpful (or at worst constructive) criticism? Why do some graduate students perceive publishing original research as an opportunity to demonstrate skills and knowledge while others in the same program consider publishing to be a risky, career-threatening source of personal vulnerability? Why do some people who put in long hours over extended periods of time perceive their work to be important and themselves to be dedicated while others with the same work schedule perceive their efforts to be stressful and themselves to be exploited or burned out?

Climate either addresses or has the potential to address these questions and many others like them. When emphasis is placed on the individual level of analysis, the objective is to ascertain why people in objectively similar environments have different perceptions of climate variables such as stress, challenge, importance, and leader support. It is almost always possible to conduct studies at this level of analysis, because only rarely do members of a situationally defined collective such as a team agree completely (that is, demonstrate a consensus) on the psychological variables that comprise climate. (This is often the case even when sufficient "agreement" is present to justify aggregation.) In other words, reliable individual differences almost always exist in climate perceptions, irrespective of situational pressures and attraction, selection, and attrition processes (L. R. James, 1988).

In sum, climate belongs in the domain of individual differences because climate is a psychological construct. Indeed, one might say that climate acquired much of its appeal from the psychological axioms that (1) people respond to (work) environments in terms of how they perceive them and (2) the most important aspect of perception for a given individual is the meaning that the situation has for him or her (L. R. James & Jones, 1974; Schneider, 1975).

We shall overview in this chapter what appear to be the major issues surrounding climate as a psychological construct. As noted, the first part of this chapter discusses climate as a measure of meaning. The second part overviews research on dimensions of climate and summarizes recent attempts to use hierarchical cognitive models to integrate the dimensions of climate. The third part discusses the latest developments in a continuing dialectic regarding the nature of the relationship between climate perceptions and affective reactions to work environments, particularly job satisfaction.

These three sections discuss and reflect on how things have been done in the past. The fourth and final section changes course completely: it is devoted to recommendations about how things might be done differently in the future. We shall draw on James's use of "conditional reasoning" to design a new measurement system in psychology (L. R. James, 1994a, 1994b) and to suggest a different approach to conceptualizing climate perceptions. This approach predicts that the schemas used by disparate individuals to frame environments are conditional on the dispositions (for example, motives) of those individuals. Unlike current measurement techniques, which assume that all respondents use the same basic schemas to perceive work environments, the proposed system suggests that at least some distinct schemas are used by different individuals to frame the same work environments.

The Meaning of Work Environments

A review of the term *meaning* begins with a reference to the classic psychology text by Osgood, Suci, and Tannenbaum (1957), entitled *The Measurement of Meaning*. These authors identified concepts that individuals use naturally and spontaneously to describe environmental objects in relation to themselves. Exploratory factor analyses of responses to items used to measure meaning produced the three well-known dimensions of evaluation, potency, and activity. It was further noted in that text that these three well-known dimensions collapsed into the single dimension of evaluation for affectively loaded objects (Osgood et al., 1957), which are the type of objects often encountered in research on work environment perceptions. The defining characteristic of evaluation on affectively loaded objects is the judged "goodness" or "badness" of the object.

Whereas Osgood et al. (1957) focused on affective-evaluative elements to describe meaning, L. R. James, L. A. James, and Ashe (1990) focused on cognitive elements to describe meaning. These authors emphasized psychological constructs such as ambiguity, challenge, loyalty, cooperation, equity, rationality, stress, and support to *interpret* environmental objects and events rather than to evaluate their goodness or badness. Both this cognitive approach and the affective-evaluative approach are needed for a full understanding of meaning, and—as will be discussed in the third section of this chapter—these approaches to understanding meaning are presumed to be functionally and reciprocally related.

From a cognitive perspective, meaning analysis refers to the use of schemas (stored mental representations that depict beliefs) to interpret or make sense of work environment attributes (for example, events, objects, processes, and structures) (Mandler, 1982; E. E. Jones & Gerard, 1967; Shaver, 1987; Stotland & Canon, 1972). The meanings imputed to environmental attributes are phenomenological experiences, which is to say that they are cognitive constructions designed to interpret information sensed from the environment.

Description Versus Valuation

In terms of cognitive processes, meaning analysis typically involves description or valuation on the part of perceivers. Many meaning analyses simply involve description of environmental attributes. Individuals employ schemas (internal semantic meanings, semantic networks, prototypes, cognitive categories) to discern and describe environmental attributes—that is, the features and structures of environmental objects. Terms such as *descriptive cognition* and *descriptive meaning* (Mandler, 1982), *cold cognition* (Zajonc, 1980), *lower-order* or *descriptive schemas* (L. R. James & Sells, 1981; Stotland & Canon, 1972), and *denotative meaning* (Osgood et al., 1957) are basically synonymous and emphasize the orientation of this type of meaning analysis toward the description of environmental attributes.

Much of the contemporary work in cognitive science and experimental social psychology is designed to examine the content of, and processes associated with, descriptive meaning (see Wyer & Srull, 1986). Models are constantly being developed to explain cognitive processes by which stimuli are, or are not, represented in short-term memory. (See almost any issue of *Psychological Review.*) Much of the environmental perception work in organizational studies is also oriented toward measures of descriptive meaning. Included here are objective measures of physical environment attributes such as group size and the temperature of the work space. Also included are variables that have a subjective, judgmental component but that can be operationally defined in terms of real-world objects and events that have an external, or "out there," referent (for example, centralization of decision making, functional specialization, formality of rules and regulations, technological complexity—variables that often assume the roles of situational antecedents in climate research [A. P. Jones & L. R. James, 1979]). The fact that measures of these variables involve perception in one way or another is viewed as an issue of measurement and is not intrinsic to the definition of the variable (for example, group size should be the same irrespective of who does the counting [Magnusson, 1981]). However, the fact that perception is involved may open the door to various information-processing functions, and thus the role of perception is not necessarily benign (Feldman & Lynch, 1988).

As noted earlier, this chapter is concerned with the significance that perceived environmental variables have for individuals—the interpretation of such attributes in terms of their acquired meaning for individuals. In this regard, Mandler (1982) suggested that information processing of environmental attributes may proceed beyond descriptions of what is "out there" to *valuations* of environmental attributes. A valuation is a judgment or cognitive appraisal of the degree to which a value is represented in or by a (perceived) environmental attribute (for example, how much equity is represented by a pay raise) (E. E. Jones & Gerard, 1967; Mandler, 1982; Stotland & Canon, 1972). The subjective, value-based meanings furnished by the valuation process are variously referred to as *evaluative meaning* (Mandler, 1982), *affective (connotative) meaning* (Osgood et al., 1957), *emotionally relevant cognition* (Reisenzein, 1983; Schacter & Singer, 1962), *cognitive appraisal* (Lazarus & Folkman, 1984), and *psychological climate* (L. R. James & A. P. Jones, 1974).

Valuation and Psychological Climate

We would like to elaborate the concept of valuation by drawing on a discussion by L. A. James and L. R. James (1989) that viewed psychological climate perceptions—that is, perceptions that assess the significance and meaning of work environments to individuals—as partial functions of personal value systems. A personal value has been defined as "that which a person wants or seeks to obtain" because it is "that which one regards as conducive to one's welfare" (Locke, 1976, p. 1304). Personal values serve as latent indicators of what it is about environments that is significant to individuals, because it is the attainment of what is personally valued that determines one's welfare in a work environment—that is, one's sense of "organizational well-being" (L. A. James & L. R. James, 1989). James and James employed this rationale to propose that latent psychological desires (such as desires for clarity, harmony, and justice—see Locke, 1976) will engender the psychological schemas (for instance, cognitive scales or standards for judging role clarity, role conflict, and equity) used to impute meaning to environmental attributes (for example, to assess the amount of clarity present in job descriptions, the conflict represented in interactions between members of different departments, the equity represented in recent pay raises), because it is these value-engendered or value-based schemas that reflect what it is about work environments that is significant and meaningful to individuals.

To illustrate the valuation process, consider job complexity as one objective indicator of job characteristics. Job complexity could be operationalized in terms of the number of complex task problems that must be solved, the degree to which tasks are nonrepetitious, the extent to which task goals are difficult to define, the number of opportunities that exist for personal decision making, and the degree to which problem-solving procedures are nonstandardized (compare L. R. James & A. P. Jones, 1980). For the sake of this discussion, let us presume that individuals perceive these indicators of job complexity in a reasonably veridical fashion. Such perceptions thus *describe* actual environmental events.

What constitutes a "challenging" job to a particular individual, however, requires valuations of the indicators of job complexity (more technically, valuations of the perceptions of these indicators). The valuative judgments are dependent on the individual's "structural requirements" (Mandler, 1982) for challenging jobs—that is, the standards that the individual employs to judge whether a job is challenging (Locke, 1976). This, then, is a subjective, value-based process: the structural requirements are personal standards one uses to appraise environmental attributes cognitively in terms of their significance to what one values, wants, or desires (L. R. James, Hater, Gent, & Bruni, 1978).

It follows that environmental attributes may be identical for two individuals—and indeed may be perceived that way descriptively—while the valuations associated with these attributes differ reliably. For example, consider a professor who is a gifted researcher and prefers to spend all of her working hours in a laboratory conducting research. She perceives teaching, especially at the undergraduate level, as a mundane, monotonous, and not very challenging task that interrupts and detracts from creative research endeavors. Contrast this valuation of teaching with that of a second gifted researcher (in the same department) who also devotes considerable time, albeit a bit less than our first professor, to research. This professor perceives teaching to be a challenge; she is excited by the responsibility she feels to awaken minds to science and to develop future generations of scholars. She perceives teaching not as mundane but as a chance to develop and to hone ideas while occasionally receiving insightful comments and feedback. Clearly, the two professors' structural requirements (that is, standards or values) differ reliably in regard to the challenge imputed to teaching.

In sum, personal values produce the schemas employed to cognitively appraise work environment attributes in terms of their significance to the individual. The cognitive appraisal itself—namely, the judgment of the degree to which a value is represented in or by an environmental attribute—is the *valuation*. Valuation thus provides assessments of the *meaningful environment* considered so important by such authors as Rotter (1981), Ekehammer (1974), and Endler and Magnusson (1976). L. A. James and L. R. James (1989) suggested that valuations of work environments are provided directly by measures of psychological climate (see L. A. James & L. R. James, 1989; L. R. James & Sells, 1981). In part, this suggestion is definitional, inasmuch as the concept of climate was developed expressly to refer to work environments as they are "cognitively represented in terms of their psychological meaning and significance to the individual" (L. R. James, 1982, p. 219). The emphasis on subjective interpretations of environmental attributes is portrayed by the designations given to the climate variables in the following list:

Psychological Climate (PC) Item Composites
Clustered by Four First-Order Factors

- Role stress and lack of harmony
  Role ambiguity
  Role conflict
  Role overload
  Subunit conflict
  Lack of organizational identification
  Lack of management concern and awareness
- Leadership facilitation and support
  Leader trust and support

Leader goal facilitation
Leader interaction facilitation
Psychological influence
Hierarchical influence

- Job challenge and autonomy

Job challenge and variety
Job autonomy
Job importance

- Work-group cooperation, friendliness, and warmth

Work-group cooperation
Work-group friendliness and warmth
Responsibility for effectiveness

Dimensions of Psychological Climate (PC)

Following extensive reviews of the literature, Locke (1976, p. 1329) proposed that four latent factors underlie most important personal, work-related values. These latent factors are (1) desires for clarity, harmony, and justice; (2) desires for challenge, independence, and responsibility; (3) desires for work facilitation, support, and recognition; and (4) desires for warm and friendly social relations. L. A. James and L. R. James (1989, p. 740), using the variables listed above as a referent, suggested that "psychological climate furnishes perhaps the most readily identifiable set of variables in Industrial/Organizational (I/O) Psychology for appraising work environments in terms of [schemas] based on these latent values." James and James noted further that PC variables were developed expressly to assess valuations of work environments. It follows logically that if climate variables are indeed engendered by personal values, and if Locke's analytically derived factors of personal values are reasonably accurate, then correspondence should exist between Locke's factors of values and empirically derived factors of psychological climate.

Exploratory factor analyses of PC variables, which were begun before Locke's discussion of values (1976), have shown four PC factors to be invariant over a number of diverse work environments (compare L. A. James & L. R. James, 1989; L. R. James & Sells, 1981). These factors, shown in the above list, are (1) role stress and lack of harmony, (2) job challenge and autonomy, (3) leadership facilitation and support, and (4) work-group cooperation, friendliness, and warmth. These factors are reasonably congruent with Locke's four factors of values. Such congruence is more a form of affirmation and convergence of two related lines of thinking and research than it is a formal test of the validity of either approach. The essential point for climate is that perceptions of work environments appear to factor into domains interpretable in terms of personal values.

It is further interesting to note that the four climate factors in the above list refer, respectively, to the distinct domains of roles, jobs, leaders, and work groups. Historically, the tendency has been to view role, job, leader, and work-group referents as distinct cognitive organizing principles for perceptual variables. Indeed, the use of orthogonal factor rotations (A. P. Jones & L. R. James, 1979; L. R. James & Sells, 1981) has in part reflected at least an implicit belief held by climate researchers and others in I/O psychology that jobs, roles, leaders, and work groups represent different (although related) domains of organizational behavior (as well as different domains of research in I/O psychology).

A Hierarchical Model of Climate

L. A. James and L. R. James (1989) continued to explore the meaning of work environments by noting that subjective (value-based) meanings often reflect the key role played by valuation in emotion. Specifically, individuals respond emotionally to environmental attributes as a function of the significance that such attributes are perceived to have for personal well-being. This point suggests that meanings derive their significance because they are "emotionally relevant" to determinations of one's personal sense of organizational well-being.

For example, we might say that individuals desire various indicators of the latent psychological value "job challenge" (that is, individuals seek opportunities to make important decisions or to solve novel problems) because individuals have learned that job challenge is emotionally relevant or efficacious for a feeling of well-being. Basically, finding a solution to a novel problem feels good. The novel solution is the environmental event of interest, and a schema for job challenge comprises a set of standards for judging how challenging the finding of the novel solution is to the individual. The appraisal of how much challenge is represented in the finding of the novel solution is the valuation. Note that because this valuation is based on standards engendered by values, the perceived challenge intrinsically reflects the benefit or detriment of the environmental event (finding the novel solution) to the individual—that is, the cognition of challenge is emotionally relevant. The relevance is manifested in the affect (for example, feeling good) that follows the valuation of challenge.

The purpose of James and James's attempts to tie climate to valuation, and then both climate and valuation to emotionally relevant cognitions, was to build a case that a single higher-order factor underlies measurements of psychological climate. This objective was based on a theoretical perspective presented by Lazarus (1982, 1984) and Lazarus and Folkman (1984), who asserted that all emotionally relevant cognitions share a single latent component—a general factor ("g factor")—that furnishes them with the facility to cognitively assess significance for well-being. This g factor is a higher-order schema for judging the degree to which the environment is personally beneficial or detrimental to one's sense of well-being. (The term "g factor" by itself is content-free, meaning [in factor-analytic parlance] that it refers to a single higher-order factor. The g factor discussed here should not be confused with an intellectual construct that is thought by some to underlie many forms of intellectual processing.)

This perspective suggests that a single higher-order g factor underlies the emotionally relevant valuations represented by PC perceptions. This factor may be defined as a cognitive appraisal of the degree to which the work environment is personally beneficial or detrimental to the organizational well-being of the individual. A hierarchical model for psychological climate is presented in Figure 11.1; the proposed g factor of meaning is designated "psychological climate—general," or simply PC_g. As discussed, each of the climate variables and each of the four first-order climate factors signifies that the acquired meanings reflected in these valuations are a function of a deeper, more pervasive judgment of the degree to which the environment is personally beneficial or detrimental to the well-being of the individual.

Figure 11.1. A Hierarchical Model of Meaning.

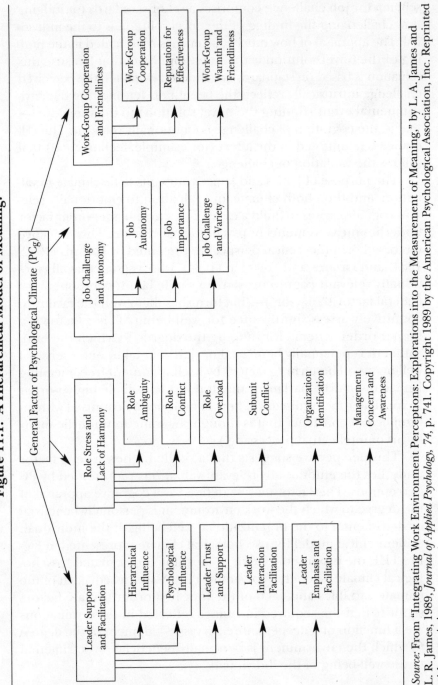

Source: From "Integrating Work Environment Perceptions: Explorations into the Measurement of Meaning," by L. A. James and L. R. James, 1989, *Journal of Applied Psychology, 74*, p. 741. Copyright 1989 by the American Psychological Association, Inc. Reprinted with permission.

L. A. James and L. R. James (1989) tested the hierarchical model of meaning presented in Figure 11.1. The causal arrows extending from PC_g to each of the factors denote that PC_g is a latent common denominator for the factors. Confirmatory factor analyses were conducted on four different samples from diverse organizations. Results unequivocally supported the hierarchical factor model with the single higher-order general factor, PC_g. This general factor suggests that individuals employ a simpler, more integrated cognitive structure to appraise their work environment than has been indicated by prior research (which, as noted, suggested multiple, independent environmental perception domains). "Stated simply, people respond to work environments in terms of how they perceive these environments, and the key substantive concern of perception is the degree to which individuals perceive themselves as being personally benefited as opposed to being personally harmed (hindered) by their presence in the environment" (L. A. James & L. R. James, 1989, p. 748).

Recently, the single higher-order factor model has been extended. Burke, Borucki, and Hurley (1992) suggested that individuals may valuate work environments in terms of the degree to which the environment promotes their individual well-being as well as in terms of the degree to which the environment promotes the well-being of other organizational constituents or stakeholders. *Stakeholders* have been defined as groups of individuals within or outside an organization, such as employees, customers, suppliers, and competitors, who have a stake in the organization's performance and are thus affected by its actions (Roberts & King, 1989). Schneider, Parkington, and Buxton (1980) posited that some employees, because of their boundary positions within an organization, would be sensitive to customer requirements and organizational practices in relation to the provision of service. Empirical support for this hypothesis was found by Schneider et al. (1980) and by Schneider and Bowen (1985).

Based on this logic, Burke et al. (1992) tested a two-factor higher-order model of psychological climate within a retail service environment. They proposed that two higher-order factors—concern for employees and concern for customers—underlie employee climate perceptions. Results of confirmatory factor analyses supported the model of two higher-order factors and suggested that employees' cognitive appraisals (valuations) of work environment attributes may reflect the extent to which the work environment is believed to be personally beneficial to the individual and beneficial to an organizational constituency (that is, customers).

The Reciprocal Nature of the PC-Affect Relationship

The preceding discussion of the valuation process suggests that psychological climate should be strongly related to affective variables. Indeed, characterizing PC variables as emotionally relevant cognitions denotes that PC perceptions furnish highly salient information for the determination of emotional responses. This raises the issue of the precise causal relationship between PC variables and affective responses. Here we will review three studies (L. R. James & L. A. James, 1992; L. R. James & Tetrick, 1986; Mathieu, Hofmann, and Farr, 1993) that examined this relationship.

L. R. James and Tetrick (1986) presented and tested three alternative models of the causal relationship between the job perception domains of psychological climate and job satisfaction. The three causal models are presented in Figure 11.2. Model A is a postcognitive, nonrecursive model. The postcognitive aspect of this model is reflected in the fact that job perceptions mediate the relationship between environmental events and affective reactions to those events. This mediating link is labeled *postcognitive* to imply that affect occurs after cognition; that is, individuals respond affectively to jobs in terms of how the jobs are cognitively represented or perceived (Brass, 1981; Hackman & Oldham, 1976; Locke, 1976; Oldham & Hackman, 1981; Rousseau, 1977, 1978a, 1978b).

The nonrecursive aspect of Model A is reflected in the reciprocal loop from job satisfaction to job perceptions. This feedback loop implies that affect can influence cognition. L. R. James and colleagues have previously proposed multiple means by which affect might influence psychological climate (L. R. James & A. P. Jones, 1980). These include conditions in which existing or desired levels of affect cause the individual (1) to attend only to selected situational cues in the interest of increasing (or decreasing), maintaining, or confirming emotions; (2) to impute desirable (or undesirable) attributes or events to a work environment; (3) to restructure (cognitively) and redefine situational cues to enhance the probability that they will be interpreted as beneficial (or detrimental) to well-being;

Figure 11.2. Alternative Causal Models
Relating Job Attributes and Work-Group Structure
to Job Perceptions and Job Satisfaction.

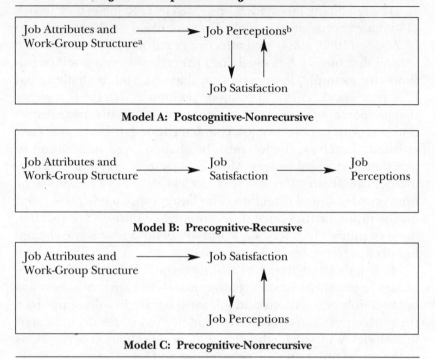

Model A: Postcognitive-Nonrecursive

Model B: Precognitive-Recursive

Model C: Precognitive-Nonrecursive

[a] These include job complexity, job pressure, boundary spanning, specialization of structure, and standardization of personnel procedures.

[b] These include job challenge, job autonomy, and job importance.

Source: From "Confirmatory Analytic Tests of Three Causal Models Relating Job Perceptions to Job Satisfaction," by L. R. James and L. E. Tetrick, 1986, *Journal of Applied Psychology, 71,* p. 78. Copyright 1986 by the American Psychological Association, Inc. Reprinted with permission.

In that source, Models B and C are based on Zajonc (1980; Figure 2, p. 161, Figure 5, p. 170).

and (4) to restructure (cognitively) cognitions to make them consistent with implicit theories regarding whether an environment should or should not be beneficial to well-being.

The remaining two models presented by L. R. James and Tetrick (1986) are precognitive models. They are based on the assumption by Zajonc (1980, 1984) that affective reactions (for example, the feeling that one's job is satisfying) precede differentiated cognitions (for example, the perception that one's job is challenging; L. R. James et al., 1978). The Zajonc position (1980, 1984) suggests that job perceptions serve to explain or to justify affective satisfaction reactions to objective job characteristics. For example, "I am satisfied; therefore, the job must be challenging." In addition to precognitive causal orders, Model B assumes a recursive (asymmetric) causal direction, whereas Model C assumes a reciprocal or nonrecursive causal direction. The latter approach is predicated on the rationale that once differentiated cognitions are formed, these cognitions may feed back and stimulate at least some change in affective responses.

L. R. James and Tetrick (1986) used confirmatory analytic techniques to test the three alternative models of causal relationships between job perceptions and job satisfaction. Results supported the postcognitive, nonrecursive model. That is, results indicated that Model A, in which job satisfaction occurs after job perceptions in the causal order and job perceptions and job satisfaction are reciprocally related, provided the best fit with the data.

L. R. James and L. A. James (1992) extended prior research on job perceptions and job satisfaction by investigating more general valuation and affective domains. Whereas prior research typically focused on specific domains of psychological climate (see earlier list) and specific domains of job satisfaction, L. R. James, L. A. James, and Ashe (1990) tested the hypothesis that a higher-order general climate factor (PC_g) and a higher-order general affective factor (organizational well-being) are reciprocally related to each other. As an initial test of this hypothesis, L. R. James and L. A. James (1992) conducted confirmatory factor analyses on archival data from L. R. James and A. P. Jones (1980) and L. R. James and Tetrick (1986). The authors found general support for the reciprocal causation model.

A recent study by Mathieu, Hofmann, and Farr (1993) provided further support for the reciprocal causation model. Mathieu et al. examined three alternative models of the job perception–job satisfaction relationship: a job characteristics theory model, a social information-processing theory model, and the above-cited reciprocal causation model.

The job characteristics theory (JCT) model is a precognitive, recursive model, based on the traditional JCT perspective, as articulated by Hackman and Lawler (1971). This perspective suggests that employees' job perceptions act as mediating variables linking objective job characteristics with individuals' affective reactions (for example, satisfaction and motivation) and behaviors (for example, performance and attendance). Thus the JCT model implies that job perceptions lead to job satisfaction.

The social information-processing (SIP) theory model is a precognitive, recursive model based on a perspective that suggests that employees develop a generalized reaction to the work environment and subsequently perceive the characteristics of their jobs in light of this global impression (for example, Salancik & Pfeffer, 1978). SIP theory is similar to the position advanced by Zajonc (1980, 1984), who, as noted above, argued for the primacy of affect over cognition. Indeed, Zajonc suggested that in many situations, individuals respond immediately to circumstances and then later bias their perceptions of those situations so as to justify or explain their reactions. Thus both SIP theory and Zajonc's position argue for job satisfaction as a precursor to job perceptions.

The third model tested by Mathieu et al. (1993) was the reciprocal causation model advanced by L. R. James and colleagues (L. R. James et al., 1978; L. R. James & A. P. Jones, 1980; L. R. James & Tetrick, 1986). Mathieu (correctly) characterized the position as arguing that job perceptions are products of higher-order cognitive information processing that reflects the psychological significance of job events to individuals. Further, such higher-order processing is said to be influenced by individual characteristics as well as individuals' job-related attitudes. Thus James's position suggests that job perceptions and job satisfaction are reciprocally related, each contributing positively to the other.

Mathieu et al. (1993) employed confirmatory analytic techniques to test the three alternative models of the job perception–job satisfaction relationship. Results of the analyses provided substantial support for the reciprocal model based on James's theory. Both of the reciprocal paths were statistically significant, and the model exhibited acceptable fit indices. Further, the reciprocal model fit significantly better than did either of the unidirectional models.

In summary, there seems to be reasonable empirical support for the postcognitive, nonrecursive model of the causal relationship between psychological climate and affect. Psychological climate appears to mediate the relationship between the work environment and affective reactions to that environment. Individuals respond affectively to the work environment based on the meaning and significance (valuations) that they attach to that environment. In turn, affective reactions influence valuations by causing individuals to selectively attend to or redefine situational cues in cognitive processing or to restructure cognitions to make them consistent with beliefs and expectations (implicit theories) regarding whether a job should be satisfying or dissatisfying.

A New Approach to Climate

The model of environmental perception discussed in the prior sections of this chapter assumes that all perceivers use the same schemas to valuate environments. What varies among perceivers is positioning (rank-ordering) on each of a common set of cognitive continua (or sets of discrete but ordered cognitive categories; see, for example, L. R. James, Demaree, & Wolf, 1984). Recent research on general cognitive processes suggests that environmental perception may be more complex than assumed by this "common schema" model. Of particular interest is research on framing, which, when extrapolated to climate, suggests that different individuals might use different schemas to valuate the same set of environmental attributes and events (compare Dweck & Leggett, 1988; Pinkley, 1990; Kahneman & Tversky, 1984). Consider, for example, professors in the same department who differ in how they frame research and publishing. Some professors valuate these efforts as surmountable challenges that afford opportunities to enhance scientific knowledge. Quality rather than quantity is their prime concern. Other professors frame research and publishing as "threats" to their tenured stability and academic reputation and focus on keeping the "numbers" above an acceptable minimum so as to avoid being viewed as incompetent.

It is very difficult to initiate studies of potential differences in the schemas that people use to frame work environments without a theory that explicates why and how such differences might exist. Extrapolations from recent work by L. R. James (1994a, 1994b) on conditional reasoning furnished the foundation to begin development of such a theory. James has argued that people with different motives, such as individuals with strong desires to achieve versus individuals with strong desires to avoid failure, possess different belief structures (or what we have referred to here as schemas). These belief structures include, or predispose individuals to utilize, various nonconscious biases (for example, implicit theories or predilections to make certain types of attributional errors), which are projected into analytic reasoning in the form of justifications and rationalizations that serve to protect, reinforce, and enhance the underlying motives.

Reasoning that involves biases that serve motives is said to be "conditional" on the motives of the reasoner. More specifically, *conditional reasoning* means that individuals with different motives are disposed to invoke different justifications and rationalizations to arrive at what each believes to be a rational solution to a common, evocative reasoning problem. The solutions differ, however, each tacitly protecting, reinforcing, and enhancing a different underlying motive pattern.

Differential Framing

Basically, conditional reasoning predicts that people possess natural and nonconscious propensities to rationalize and to justify thoughts, behaviors, policies, and circumstances that protect, reinforce, or enhance motives. An important first step in this reasoning process is what James refers to as "differential framing." The term *framing* refers to valuations of attributes and events in terms of their "meaning" (substance, intent, significance) to the individual. *Differential framing,* then, refers to qualitative disparities in the meanings imputed to the same attributes and events by individuals with different motives.

An example of differential framing was presented by L. R. James (1994a, 1994b) as part of a contrast between individuals with a strong motive to achieve and individuals with a strong motive to avoid failure. The contrast focused on disparities in the decision processes involved in determining whether to approach or to avoid a difficult task. Individuals with strong achievement motivation were characterized as framing difficult tasks in terms of the opportunities such tasks create for challenging work, demonstrations of competence, and feelings of accomplishment and pride. Individuals high on fear of failure were thought to (differentially) frame these same tasks in terms of their potential to cause stress and to create opportunities to demonstrate incompetence and experience feelings of shame and embarrassment.

It requires only a small leap in logic to suppose that the same motives that evoke condition reasoning and spawn differential framing are also likely to operate in environmental perception. Indeed, the preceding illustration of differential framing is based on perceptions of a component of the task environment. In more general terms, consider the proposal presented earlier in this chapter that individuals valuate environmental attributes and events using schemas that allow them to ascertain whether the environment is helpful or hurtful to their general well-being. Now consider the hypothesis that people with different motives use different schemas to (differentially) valuate or frame environments because they have different personal standards for what is and what is not helpful/hurtful to their well-being. The intuitive appeal of this hypothesis sparked the proposal that individuals develop schemas that allow them to frame environmental attributes and events, especially evocative or important attributes and events (for example, tasks, supervisors' behaviors, performance evaluations, potential stressors), in terms that directly or indirectly assist in protecting, reinforcing, and enhancing their underlying motives.

As noted, L. R. James (1994a, 1994b) used the motives of achievement motivation and fear of failure to illustrate differential framing in conditional reasoning. We have extrapolated from these discussions to postulate how these same motives might produce differential framing of task environments. Brief definitions of achievement motivation and fear of failure are presented below. These definitions are then employed to formulate hypotheses that specify the different schemas that these motives might engender in regard to the framing of task environments. These hypotheses are meant to be illustrative and are by no means exhaustive. We will conclude this discussion with a few recommendations pertaining to how the hypotheses might be expanded to include other schemas and then be tested empirically.

Motive Definitions

The motive to achieve has been defined as a potentially strong force that energizes, selects, and directs manifest beliefs and behaviors toward approaching and devoting effort to demanding tasks (Atkinson, 1957, 1978; McClelland, 1985a, 1985b; McClelland, Koestner, & Weinberger, 1989). Associations involving affect are thought to be primary sources for the potency of this motive (McClelland, 1985a); that is, when presented with demanding tasks, individuals with a strong motive to achieve experience an urge to approach those tasks, because such individuals associate positive affect (for example, enthusiasm, recognition, pride of accomplishment) with those tasks. The motive is often said to be "latent," because individuals experience task-affect associations without generally being able to specify the historical reasons or developmental sources for these associations (Atkinson, 1957, 1978; McClelland, 1985a, 1985b; Raynor, 1978).

The motive to avoid failure—that is, the fear of failure—is considered to be the mirror image of achievement motivation in the model of resultant achievement motivation proposed by Atkinson (1957, 1978). Fear of failure is defined as an implicit and potentially strong force that energizes, selects, and directs manifest beliefs and behaviors toward avoiding the demonstration of incompetence on demanding tasks (Atkinson, 1957, 1978; Nicholls, 1984; Rothbaum, Weisz, & Snyder, 1982; Schlenker & Leary, 1982). The potency of the motive is thought to derive from cognitive associations involving affect and demanding tasks.

As an example of these associations, individuals with a strong motive to avoid failure experience an urge to avoid demanding tasks because they anticipate not only failure on the tasks but also the negative affect that follows failure (for example, embarrassment, shame). These individuals may evade difficult tasks if possible, attempt to escape or withdraw if assigned such tasks, or—if escape is not a viable option—procrastinate or manifest other behaviors that indicate defensive lack of effort (for example, a student who chooses not to study for a test in order to lay the foundation for a lack-of-effort attribution [Shaver, 1987]). Like the motive to achieve, the motive to avoid failure is often regarded as latent, because individuals experience task-affect associations without generally being able to identify the historical reasons or developmental sources for the associations.

Hypotheses of Differential Framing

We predict that individuals with comparatively stronger motives to achieve (hereafter referred to as "AMs," to indicate stronger achievement motivation than fear of failure) will frame environmental attributes and events related to achievement/failure on demanding tasks differently than individuals with comparatively stronger motives to avoid failure (hereafter referred to as "FFs," to indicate stronger fear of failure than achievement motivation). The general premise is that AMs will frame work environments in ways that promote, defend, and reinforce approach of demanding tasks, whereas FFs will frame work environments in ways that promote, defend, and reinforce avoidance of demanding tasks. Three types of differential framing that are based on this premise are proposed below.

Opportunity Versus Liability

This aspect of differential framing was addressed briefly above. It is presumed that AMs will frame difficult or demanding tasks as challenges and opportunities for advancement and thus will be attracted to such tasks (McClelland, 1985a; Spence & Helmreich, 1983). By comparison, FFs should anticipate failure on demanding or difficult tasks and thus frame them as liabilities (Atkinson, 1957, 1978). Unlike the task attraction experienced by AMs, it is aversion and a desire to escape from the tasks and to avoid similar tasks in the future that FFs should experience.

As an exemplar of the proposed differential framing, consider how the stimulus "an unsolved, demanding problem" might be cognitively processed and framed by AMs and FFs. It is suggested that AMs possess the implicit belief (schema) that if one takes the initiative to seek out unsolved, demanding problems, then he or she creates career-enhancing opportunities to demonstrate skills and resourcefulness. This belief furnishes a standard for framing or valuating unsolved problems as "opportunities." In contrast, FFs will likely frame unsolved, demanding problems as being "risky" or "career liabilities," because FFs believe that success on such tasks is precarious or even unlikely (Kuhl, 1978; Sorrentino & Short, 1986).

The suggested schemas and framing reflect implicit biases that furnish confirmation and sanction to latent forces that seek to energize, select, and direct efforts toward approach (to achievement) for AMs and avoidance (of failure) for FFs. For example, a bias to which AMs are vulnerable is positive leniency, or the tendency to overconfidently evaluate the likelihood of success in solving a demanding problem. For FFs, the framing of the unsolved problem as risky is subject to a bias that seeks to rationalize avoidance in a manner that protects and enhances the ego of the individual (Bandura, 1986; Crocker & Major, 1989; Taylor, 1991; Taylor & Brown, 1988; Wood, 1989). That is, whereas FFs may associate threat of failure with the unsolved task, they are also likely to rationalize avoidance. It is, for example, socially commendable, not to mention wise and responsible (and a good coping mechanism), to avoid devoting time and resources to activities that can be framed as venturesome, precarious, and perhaps even reckless. In sum, differential framing serves motives, thereby protecting, reinforcing, and enhancing the overall well-being of the perceivers.

Positive Versus Negative Connotation of Stress

It is proposed that AMs tend to frame what others might refer to as "stressors" (for example, concentrated work on a very difficult task for a long period of time) in positive terms (for example, striving to be successful on an important task via perseverance and immersion in the task). Use of positive terms for framing is, we assume, the product of cognitive associations (implicit beliefs or schemas) formed by AMs between hard and persistent work and (1) feelings of enthusiasm and a sense of accomplishing something important while immersed in a task (a form, perhaps, of intrinsic motivation [Spence & Helmreich, 1983]), (2) receipt of future rewards when the task is successfully completed, and (3) anticipation of positive affect (for example, pride) when the task is completed (McClelland, 1985a). Positive framing is likely to reflect susceptibilities to biases such as tendencies to cognitively redefine stressful events in more benevolent terms; for example, what some would perceive as quantitative overload (Katz & Kahn, 1978) might be valuated by AMs as persistence.

FFs, on the other hand, are prone to use negative terms to frame such events as the intense endeavor over a long period of time on a demanding task (Atkinson, 1957, 1978; McClelland, 1985a; Nicholls, 1984; Rothbaum, Weisz, & Snyder, 1982; Schlenker & Leary, 1982). They have a tendency to perceive such events as burdens that produce physical overload and feelings of anxiousness, strain, and tension. They perceive their counterparts—those who *do* strive to succeed on hard and demanding tasks—as being obsessed with the need for success and therefore compulsively driven to be successful. Those strivers may also be seen as increasing their susceptibility to stress-induced illness. Use of negative terms for framing is believed to be a product of schemas that develop to protect the self from failure and embarrassment. Tasks likely to spawn failure are discounted and devalued by FFs, who valuate them as stressful, thereby initiating a prima facie case for later decisions to avoid the tasks (Atkinson, 1978).

High Versus Low Personal Control and Responsibility

It is believed that AMs tend to frame causes for job success/failure in terms of personal responsibility, self-reliance, and self-determination. Schemas denoting personal control and responsibility are presumed to be salient to AMs because personal accountability for performance on a difficult task promotes the attribution (by the self and others) of having been responsible for success on something important (Bandura, 1986; Hall, 1971; S. C. Jones, 1973; McClelland & Boyatzis, 1982; Weiner, 1979, 1990, 1991). FFs, on the other hand, wish to avoid responsibility for demanding tasks because they do not want to be held accountable for the failure they anticipate. Avoidance of responsibility is manifested in various forms of ego-protective/ego-enhancing valuation propensities, such as framing job success/failure in terms of the many external (that is, nonpersonal), uncontrollable factors that might adversely affect performance (for example, situational constraints, societal inequities, lack of resources, the leadership received) (Crocker & Major, 1989; Hinshaw, 1992; Schlenker & Leary, 1982; Taylor, 1991; Weiner, 1979).

An important illustration of differential framing is seen on occasions when failure on a demanding task does in fact occur. AMs are predicted to frame the failure as a temporary setback, which implies that the failure can be rectified by changes in strategy or by increases in intensity and/or persistence, while FFs have a propensity to believe that external factors over which they have no control contribute to failure. Thus, unlike AMs (with their internal and controllable attributions for failure), FFs should propose ego-protective/ego-enhancing external and uncontrollable attributions for failure. Given this framing, it is unlikely that FFs will persist in the task (Weiner, 1979).

Recommendations for Research on Differential Framing

Differential framing and the hypotheses above build from literatures in attribution theory, expectancies, implicit theories, and confirmatory biases in hypothesis testing, which address motivation as a function of causal inference and hypothesis testing (Bruner, 1957; Friedrich, 1993; Hastie, 1984; Kelly, 1972; Kruglanski, 1989; Mitchell, 1974; Pyszczynski & Greenberg, 1987; Snyder & Gangestad, 1981; Weiner, 1991). We believe that these cognitive processes are components of the broader process of conditional reasoning, where, as part of everyday living, people (1) make causal attributions of the degree to which success/failure will be influenced by internal/external factors, (2) formulate expectancies pertaining to the consequences of alternative actions, (3) attempt to garner evidence that confirms (disconfirms) causal hypotheses about such things as the effects of effort on performance, and (4) formulate justifications and rationales to support decisions about actions (L. R. James, 1994a, 1994b).

The truly novel feature of differential framing is that it forecasts qualitative differences in perceptions. This is, of course, a hypothesis at the present time; evidence of differential framing in regard to climate perceptions is infrequent and indirect. The few available studies are nonetheless encouraging (Pinkley, 1990; Silver, Mitchell, & Gist, 1995; Thompson & Loewenstein, 1992). What would be helpful to the proposed research on climate is a system of measurement for differential framing. While we can offer only suggestions at this time, we can introduce one means for measuring qualitative differences in schemas.

The suggested procedure is based on some early thinking in conditional reasoning, a field of study in which methods for measuring differential framing were first explored. When used in regard to conditional reasoning, this approach is based on a test for synonyms. Respondents are presented with a stimulus word and asked to identify a synonym from one of four alternatives, with both the stimulus word and the alternatives intended to implicitly trigger latent motives for achievement and avoidance of failure. The triggering of latent motives presumably engenders differential framing; AMs and FFs reveal those latent motives through the different alternatives they select in answer to the problems. Respondents might be asked, for example, to select the most reasonable synonym for *persistent* from among these alternatives: *dedicated, obsessed, vacillating, careless*. It is expected that respondents with latent AM propensities will select *dedicated* as the correct synonym while respondents with latent FF propensities will select *obsessed* as the correct synonym. (The remaining two alternatives are not synonyms for *persistent*.)

This approach could be adapted to measure differential framing in climate studies. We could replace the stimulus words with key climate concepts such as *work, exertion,* and *expectations* (for employee behavior). We could then ask organizational respondents to select the word that most reasonably captures the meaning (definition, interpretation, perception, significance, translation) of the stimulus word in the context of their own work environment. Possible items are as follows:

Your work: challenging, risky, dull, stable

Your exertion: enthusiastic, stressed, uninspired, relaxed

Your expectations: self-reliance, self-aggrandizement, compliance, loyalty

These three items correspond roughly to the three sets of contrasting schemas proposed earlier for AMs and FFs. For example, the "work" item is designed to capture differential framing engendered by the opportunity-versus-liability schemas. If differential framing operates as expected, then AMs and FFs will select different alternatives to frame the same work environments. For example, in technically complex environments such as scientific laboratories,

AM scientists are expected to use "challenging" to describe their work, whereas FF scientists are expected to characterize their work as "risky." When the measure is extended to noncomplex technical environments such as production lines, AM workers are expected to describe their work as "dull," whereas FF workers are expected to describe their work as "stable."

The "exertion" item is designed to capture differential framing produced by schemas for positive versus negative connotations of stress. As an example, AM students in high-press-for-achievement environments (for example, colleges with high academic demands) are expected to interpret their exertion in terms such as "enthusiastic," whereas FF students are expected to interpret their exertion in terms such as "stressed." AM students in low-press-for-achievement environments (for example, colleges with low academic demands) are expected to characterize their efforts as "uninspired," whereas FFs are predicted to interpret their efforts as "relaxed."

Finally, the "expectations" item was designed to capture differential framing engendered by the schemas for high versus low personal control and responsibility. It is expected that work environments that emphasize personal control (for example, organizations with decentralized authority structures and individualistic incentive systems) will be framed as encouraging "self-reliance" by AMs and "self-aggrandizement" by FFs. Work environments that deemphasize personal control (for example, organizations with centralized authority structures and incentive systems that reward collectives) should engender perceptions by AMs that "compliance" is expected, whereas FFs are expected to frame role expectations and incentives in term of "loyalty."

These rudimentary suggestions for measuring differential framing are meant only to stimulate thinking on how a serious measurement system might be designed. Prior work on conditional reasoning may be helpful as an early guide, but innovation will be the order of the day.

Summary

Over the years, the study of psychological climate has increasingly acknowledged the role of individual differences in environmental cognition. As psychological climate became recognized in the 1970s and 1980s as the outcome of cognitive processes such as valuation, the role of individual differences became increasingly prominent. Research that originally sought to identify simple mediating cognitive functions that were basically similar for all perceivers gave way to the study of individual differences in higher-order perceptual processes. Person-by-situation interactions, assignment of different meanings, causes of (and effects of) individual differences in affective reactions to work, and searches for higher-order models of meaning became prime subjects of study in the climate domain. Parallel work continued on attempts to aggregate climate perceptions to describe organizational situations (Schneider, 1990); but the study of individual differences in climate perceptions continued, and continues, to be a prime topic of research. We recommend differential framing as a next step in this research agenda.

References

Atkinson, J. W. (1957). Motivational determinants of risk-taking behavior. *Psychological Review, 64,* 359–372.

Atkinson, J. W. (1978). The mainsprings of achievement-oriented activity. In J. W. Atkinson & J. O. Raynor (Eds.), *Personality, motivation, and achievement* (pp. 11–39). Washington, DC: Hemisphere.

Bandura, A. (1986). *Social foundations of thought and action: A social cognitive theory.* Englewood Cliffs, NJ: Prentice-Hall.

Brass, D. J. (1981). Structural relationships, job characteristics, and worker satisfaction and performance. *Administrative Science Quarterly, 26,* 331–348.

Bruner, J. S. (1957). On perceptual readiness. *Psychological Review, 64,* 123–152.

Burke, M. J., Borucki, C. C., & Hurley, A. E. (1992). Reconceptualizing psychological climate in a retail service environment: A multiple-stakeholder perspective. *Journal of Applied Psychology, 77,* 717–729.

Crocker, J., & Major, B. (1989). Social stigma and self-esteem: The self-protective properties of stigma. *Psychological Review, 96,* 608–630.

Dweck, C. S., & Leggett, E. L. (1988). A social-cognitive approach to motivation and personality. *Psychological Review, 95,* 256–273.

Ekehammer, B. (1974). Interactionism in personality from a historical perspective. *Psychological Bulletin, 81,* 1026–1048.

Endler, N. S., & Magnusson, D. (1976). Toward an interactional psychology of personality. *Psychological Bulletin, 83,* 956–974.

Feldman, J. M., & Lynch, J. G. (1988). Self-generated validity and other effects of measurement on belief, attitude, intention, and behavior. *Journal of Applied Psychology, 73,* 421–435.

Friedrich, J. (1993). Primary error detection and minimization (PED-MIN) strategies in social cognition: A reinterpretation of confirmation bias phenomena. *Psychological Review, 100,* 298–319.

George, J. M. (1990). Personality, affect, and behavior in groups. *Journal of Applied Psychology, 75,* 107–116.

Hackman, J. R., & Lawler, E. E. (1971). Employee reactions to job characteristics. *Journal of Applied Psychology, 55,* 259–286.

Hackman, J. R., & Oldham, G. R. (1976). Motivation through the design of work: Test of a theory. *Organizational Behavior and Human Performance, 16,* 250–279.

Hackman, J. R., & Oldham, G. R. (1980). *Work redesign.* Reading, MA: Addison-Wesley.

Hall, D. T. (1971). A theoretical model of career subidentity development in organizational settings. *Organizational Behavior and Human Performance, 6,* 50–76.

Hastie, R. (1984). Causes and effects of causal attribution. *Journal of Personality and Social Psychology, 46,* 44–56.

Hater, J. J., & Bass, B. M. (1988). Superiors' evaluations of subordinates' perceptions of transformational and transactional leadership. *Journal of Applied Psychology, 73,* 695–702.

Hinshaw, S. P. (1992). Externalizing behavior problems and academic underachievement in childhood and adolescence: Causal relationships and underlying mechanisms. *Psychological Bulletin, 111,* 127–155.

James, L. A., & James, L. R. (1989). Integrating work environment perceptions: Explorations into the measurement of meaning. *Journal of Applied Psychology, 74,* 739–751.

James, L. R. (1988). Organizational climate: Another look at a potentially important construct. In S. G. Cole & R. G. Demaree (Eds.), *Applications of interactionist psychology: Essays in honor of Saul B. Sells* (pp. 253–282). Hillsdale, NJ: Erlbaum.

James, L. R. (1982). Aggregation bias in estimates of perceptual agreement. *Journal of Applied Psychology, 67,* 219–229.

James, L. R. (1994a, Apr.). An introduction to conditional reasoning. In M. K. Smith (Chair), *Conditional reasoning: A new approach to the measurement of personality.* Symposium presented at the 9th annual meeting of the Society for Industrial and Organizational Psychology, Nashville.

James, L. R. (1994b, Mar.). *An introduction to conditional reasoning.* Invited address presented at Research Methods Division Conference on Causal Modeling, Purdue University.

James, L. R., Demaree, R. G., Mulaik, S. A., & Ladd, R. T. (1992). Validity generalization in the context of situational models. *Journal of Applied Psychology, 77,* 3–14.

James, L. R., Demaree, R. G., & Wolf, G. (1984). Estimating within-group interrater reliability with and without response bias. *Journal of Applied Psychology, 69,* 85–98.

James, L. R., Hater, J. J., Gent, M. J., & Bruni, J. R. (1978). Psychological climate: Implications from cognitive social learning theory and interactional psychology. *Personnel Psychology, 31,* 781–813.

James, L. R., & James, L. A. (1992). Psychological climate and affect: Test of a hierarchical dynamic model. In C. J. Cranny, P. C. Smith, & E. F. Stone (Eds.), *Job satisfaction: How people feel about their jobs and how it affects their performance* (pp. 89–117). New York: Lexington Books.

James, L. R., James, L. A., & Ashe, D. K. (1990). The meaning of organizations: The role of cognition and values. In B. Schneider (Ed.), *Organizational climate and culture* (pp. 40–84). San Francisco: Jossey-Bass.

James, L. R., & Jones, A. P. (1974). Organizational climate: A review of theory and research. *Psychological Bulletin, 81,* 1096–1112.

James, L. R., & Jones, A. P. (1980). Perceived job characteristics and job satisfaction: An examination of reciprocal causation. *Personnel Psychology, 33,* 97–135.

James, L. R., & Sells, S. B. (1981). Psychological climate: Theoretical perspectives and empirical research. In D. Magnusson (Ed.), *Toward a psychology of situations: An interactional perspective* (pp. 275–295). Hillsdale, NJ: Erlbaum.

James, L. R., & Tetrick, L. E. (1986). Confirmatory analytic tests of three causal models relating job perceptions to job satisfaction. *Journal of Applied Psychology, 71,* 77–82.

Jones, A. P., & James, L. R. (1979). Psychological climate: Dimensions and relationships of individual and aggregated work environment perceptions. *Organizational Behavior and Human Performance, 23,* 201–250.

Jones, E. E., & Gerard, H. B. (1967). *Foundations of social psychology.* New York: Wiley.

Jones, S. C. (1973). Self- and interpersonal evaluations: Esteem theories versus consistency theories. *Psychological Bulletin, 79,* 185–199.

Kahneman, D., & Tversky, A. (1984). Choices, values, and frames. *American Psychologist, 39,* 341–350.

Katz, D., & Kahn, R. L. (1978). *The social psychology of organizations* (2nd ed.). New York: Wiley.

Kelly, H. H. (1972). Causal schemata and the attribution process. In E. E. Jones, D. E. Kanouse, H. H. Kelly, R. E. Nisbett, S. Valins, & B. Weiner (Eds.), *Attribution: Perceiving the causes of behavior* (pp. 151–174). Morristown, NJ: General Learning Process.

Kozlowski, S.W.J., & Hattrup, K. (1992). A disagreement about within-group agreement: Disentangling issues of consistency versus consensus. *Journal of Applied Psychology, 77,* 161–167.

Kruglanski, A. W. (1989). The psychology of being "right": On the problem of accuracy in social perception and cognition. *Psychological Bulletin, 106,* 395–409.

Kuhl, J. (1978). Standard setting and risk preference: An elaboration of the theory of achievement motivation and an empirical test. *Psychological Review, 85,* 239–248.

Lazarus, R. S. (1982). Thoughts on the relations between emotion and cognition. *American Psychologist, 37,* 1019–1024.

Lazarus, R. S. (1984). On the primacy of cooperation. *American Psychologist, 39,* 124–129.

Lazarus, R. S., & Folkman, S. (1984). *Stress, appraisal, and coping.* New York: Springer-Verlag.

Locke, E. A. (1976). The nature and causes of job satisfaction. In M. D. Dunnette (Ed.), *Handbook of industrial and organizational psychology* (pp. 1297–1350). Skokie, IL: Rand McNally.

Magnusson, D. (1981). Wanted: A psychology of situations. In D. Magnusson (Ed.), *Toward a psychology of situations: An interactional perspective* (pp. 9–32). Hillsdale, NJ: Erlbaum.

Mandler, G. (1982). The structure of value: Accounting for taste. In M. S. Clark & S. T. Fiske (Eds.), *Affect and cognition: The seventeenth annual Carnegie Symposium on Cognition* (pp. 3–36). Hillsdale, NJ: Erlbaum.

Mathieu, J. E., Hofmann, D. A., & Farr, J. L. (1993). Job perception–job satisfaction relations: An empirical comparison of three competing theories. *Organizational Behavior and Human Decision Processes, 56,* 370–387.

McClelland, D. C. (1985a). *Human motivation.* Glenview, IL: Scott, Foresman.

McClelland, D. C. (1985b). How motives, skills, and values determine what people do. *American Psychologist, 40,* 812–825.

McClelland, D. C., & Boyatzis, R. E. (1982). Leadership motive pattern and long-term success in management. *Journal of Applied Psychology, 67,* 737–743.

McClelland, D. C., Koestner, R., & Weinberger, J. (1989). How do self-attributed and implicit motives differ? *Psychological Review, 96,* 690–702.

Mitchell, T. R. (1974). Expectancy models of job satisfaction, occupational preference, and effort: A theoretical, methodological, and empirical appraisal. *Psychological Bulletin, 81,* 1053–1077.

Nicholls, J. G. (1984). Achievement motivation: Conceptions of ability, subjective experience, task choice, and performance. *Psychological Review, 91,* 328–346.

Oldham, G. R., & Hackman, J. R. (1981). Relationships between organizational structure and employee reactions: Comparing alternative frameworks. *Administrative Science Quarterly, 26,* 66–83.

Osgood, C. E., Suci, G. J., & Tannenbaum, P. H. (1957). *The measurement of meaning*. Urbana: University of Illinois Press.

Pinkley, R. L. (1990). Dimensions of conflict frame: Disputant interpretations of conflict. *Journal of Applied Psychology, 75*, 117–126.

Pyszczynski, T., & Greenberg, J. (1987). Toward an integration of cognitive and motivational perspectives on social inference: A biased hypothesis-testing model. *Advances in Experimental Social Psychology, 20*, 297–339.

Raynor, J. O. (1978). Motivation and career striving. In J. W. Atkinson & J. O. Raynor (Eds.), *Personality, motivation, and achievement* (pp. 199–242). Washington, DC: Hemisphere.

Reichers, A. E., & Schneider, B. (1990). Climate and culture: An evolution of constructs. In B. Schneider (Ed.), *Organizational climate and culture* (pp. 5–39). San Francisco: Jossey-Bass.

Reisenzein, R. (1983). The Schacter theory of emotion: Two decades later. *Psychological Bulletin, 94*, 239–264.

Roberts, N. C., & King, P. J. (1989). The stakeholder audit goes public. *Organizational Dynamics, 7*, 1–37.

Rothbaum, F., Weisz, J. R., & Snyder, S. S. (1982). Changing the world and changing the self: A two-process model of perceived control. *Journal of Personality and Social Psychology, 42*, 5–37.

Rotter, J. B. (1981). The psychological situation in social-learning theory. In D. Magnusson (Ed.), *Toward a psychology of situations: An interactional perspective* (pp. 169–178). Hillsdale, NJ: Erlbaum.

Rousseau, D. M. (1977). Technological differences in job characteristics, employee satisfaction, and motivation: A synthesis of job design research and sociotechnical systems theory. *Organizational Behavior and Human Performance, 19*, 18–42.

Rousseau, D. M. (1978a). Measures of technology as predictors of employee attitudes. *Journal of Applied Psychology, 63*, 213–218.

Rousseau, D. M. (1978b). Characteristics of departments, positions, and individuals: Contexts for attitudes and behavior. *Administrative Science Quarterly, 23*, 521–540.

Rousseau, D. M. (1990). Assessing organizational culture: The case for multiple methods. In B. Schneider (Ed.), *Organizational climate and culture* (pp. 153–192). San Francisco: Jossey-Bass.

Salancik, G. R., & Pfeffer, J. (1978). A social information processing approach to job attitudes and task design. *Administrative Science Quarterly, 23*, 224–253.

Schacter, S., & Singer, J. E. (1962). Cognitive, social, and physiological determinants of emotional state. *Psychological Review, 69*, 379–399.

Schlenker, B. R., & Leary, M. R. (1982). Social anxiety and self-presentation: A conceptualization and model. *Psychological Bulletin, 92*, 641–669.

Schneider, B. (1975). Organizational climates: An essay. *Personnel Psychology, 28,* 447–479.

Schneider, B. (Ed.). (1990). *Organizational climate and culture.* San Francisco: Jossey-Bass.

Schneider, B., & Bowen, D. E. (1985). Employee and customer perceptions of service in banks: Replication and extension. *Journal of Applied Psychology, 70,* 423–433.

Schneider, B., Parkington, J. J., & Buxton, V. M. (1980). Employee and customer perceptions of service in banks. *Administrative Science Quarterly, 25,* 252–267.

Shaver, K. G. (1987). *Principles of social psychology.* Hillsdale, NJ: Erlbaum.

Silver, W. S., Mitchell, T. R., & Gist, M. E. (1995). Responses to successful and unsuccessful performance: The moderating effect of self-efficacy on the relationship between performance and attributions. *Organizational Behavior and Human Decision Processes, 62,* 286–299.

Snyder, M., & Gangestad, S. (1981). Hypothesis-testing processes. In J. H. Harvey, W. Ickes, & R. F. Kidd (Eds.), *New directions in attribution research* (Vol. 3, pp. 171–198). Hillsdale, NJ: Erlbaum.

Sorrentino, R. M., & Short, J. C. (1986). Uncertainty, orientation, motivation, and cognition. In R. M. Sorrentino & E. T. Higgins (Eds.), *Handbook of motivation and cognition: Foundations of social behavior* (pp. 379–403). New York: Guilford.

Spence, J. T., & Helmreich, R. L. (1983). Achievement-related motives and behaviors. In J. T. Spence (Ed.), *Achievement and motives* (pp. 7–74). New York: W. H. Freeman.

Stotland, E., & Canon, L. K. (1972). *Social psychology: A cognitive approach.* Philadelphia: Sanders.

Taylor, S. E. (1991). Asymmetrical effects of positive and negative events: The mobilization-minimization hypothesis. *Psychological Bulletin, 110,* 67–85.

Taylor, S. E., & Brown, J. D. (1988). Illusion and well-being: A social psychological perspective on mental health. *Psychological Bulletin, 103,* 193–210.

Thompson, L., & Loewenstein, G. (1992). Egocentric interpretations of fairness and interpersonal conflict. *Organizational Behavior and Human Decision Processes, 51,* 176–197.

Weiner, B. (1979). A theory of motivation of some classroom experiences. *Journal of Educational Psychology, 71,* 3–25.

Weiner, B. (1990). Attribution in personality psychology. In L. Pervin (Ed.), *Handbook of personality: Theory and research* (pp. 465–485). New York: Guilford.

Weiner, B. (1991). Metaphors in motivation and attribution. *American Psychologist, 46,* 921–930.

Wood, J. V. (1989). Theory and research concerning social comparisons of personal attributes. *Psychological Bulletin, 106,* 231–248.

Wyer, R. S., & Srull, T. K. (1986). Human cognition in its social context. *Psychological Review, 93,* 322–359.

Zajonc, R. B. (1980). Feeling and thinking: Preferences need no inferences. *American Psychologist, 5,* 151–175.

Zajonc, R. B. (1984). On the primacy of affect. *American Psychologist, 39,* 117–123.

Chapter Twelve

Leaving the Organization

Joseph G. Rosse
Terry W. Noel

A few years ago, Paul Simon popularized a song entitled "Fifty Ways to Leave Your Lover." This chapter is also about leaving, and judging from the contents of the more than two thousand journal articles that have been published on various types of withdrawal behaviors (Rosse, 1991), there may also be fifty ways to leave an organization. Our twofold goal is to explore the role of individual differences in how people withdraw from work and to suggest ways in which increased attention to these factors might enhance our understanding of how and why people leave work.

Volumes have been written on the subjects of turnover and absenteeism; less attention has been devoted to other forms of withdrawal, such as lateness, loafing on the job, and avoiding work responsibilities. Hom and Griffeth (1995) describe fourteen theoretical models of turnover alone. Few theorists, though, have placed great emphasis on the role of individual differences when modeling these behaviors. In this chapter, we first provide a brief summary of contemporary thinking on employee retention and withdrawal and make the case that the soundest approach is to consider most absence and turnover to be examples of a more general tendency to withdraw from dissatisfying work settings. We then briefly summarize the empirical literature on antecedents of work withdrawal, with a particular emphasis on findings in the areas of turnover and absenteeism.

After thus setting the stage, we proceed to describe the limited role that individual differences have played in these models.

Consistent with the other chapters in this volume, we focus primarily on individual differences in cognitive ability, personality, values and interests, and disposition, affect, and temperament. Although they are less well grounded in theory, we also describe the literature on individual differences in demographic characteristics (for example, age, gender, and marital status and family responsibilities), since they have been the predominant individual difference variables studied in the withdrawal literature.

Individual differences may be important not only in understanding how individuals function while full participants in the organization but also in understanding how and why they disengage themselves from organizational activities. Absenteeism research, for example, shows consistently that 10 to 20 percent of the workforce accounts for 80 to 90 percent of the time lost (Johns & Nicholson, 1982). Yet only a few personal variables, mostly demographic, have been found to predict which people will be absent more than others, and these tend to account for little variance. A similar conclusion applies to turnover (Rosse, 1991). So while it may seem obvious that individuals differ with respect to withdrawal behaviors, few variables have been found that account for those differences.

In the final section of the chapter, we offer suggestions about how individual differences might be more profitably incorporated into models of employee withdrawal. Specifically, we speculate on the possibility that treating withdrawal as a subset of adaptive and coping behaviors might (1) increase our understanding of leaving the organization and (2) provide a framework in which individual differences may add to that understanding.

Defining Employee Withdrawal

For decades, businesspeople and management scholars have shown a keen interest in employee absenteeism and turnover. For employers, this concern has generally reflected the high costs assumed to be associated with these behaviors. Research showing that turnover is not always dysfunctional (Dalton, Todor, & Krackhardt, 1982; Staw, 1980) has further honed employers' interest in managing the turnover/retention process. Indeed, with current trends toward downsizing, retaining the most able employees has become even more critical (Gomez-Mejia & Balkin, 1992). "Lean" organizations also face a dilemma regarding absenteeism: while these firms have less slack to cover employees who do not attend, the heightened stress of working in such environments may make absenteeism more likely.

Researchers have responded to these practical considerations for studying absence and turnover, but they have also been attracted to absence and turnover for their apparent "objectivity" as criteria for all manner of organizational analyses. The result has been a voluminous literature, the primary consequence of which has been substantial frustration with the predictive power of theoretical models of absence and turnover. Locke's review (1976) found that bivariate correlations between job satisfaction and turnover rarely exceeded $r = .40$. Much the same is true for absence; Farrell and Stamm's meta-analysis (1988) indicates that corrected correlations between absence and both satisfaction and commitment are less than .25. These critiques led to the development of a series of complex models of both turnover and absence. Unfortunately, tests of these multivariate models have scarcely improved our ability to predict these behaviors, leading a number of researchers to suggest that studying *families* of withdrawal behaviors may be more fruitful than a narrow focus on absence, lateness, and turnover.

A Multivariate Perspective on Withdrawal

In some ways, turnover, absenteeism, and other withdrawal behaviors seem to be quite distinct. Each is characterized by a behavior or set of behaviors that differs from the others in readily recognizable ways (Mobley, 1982). At the same time, there is a striking conceptual similarity among them, in that each serves in its own way to distance or disengage employees from the work situation. A number of researchers have also suggested that lateness, absence, and turnover may be sequential steps in a "progression of withdrawal" that begins with lateness or other minor forms of withdrawal and then extends to absenteeism and eventually quitting the organization (Gupta & Jenkins, 1979; Rosse, 1988). The functional similarity of the behaviors, coupled with their common theme of avoiding dissatisfying work (Hom & Griffeth, 1995), has prompted researchers to treat them as manifestations of an underlying construct called *withdrawal* (for example, Beehr & Gupta, 1978; Wolpin & Burke, 1985) or *adaptation* (for example, Hulin, 1991; Rosse & Miller, 1984).

Withdrawal from work may be either psychological or physical. Symptoms of *psychological withdrawal*—such as wasting time at the water cooler, daydreaming, and goofing off at work—often signal an employee's disenchantment or lack of involvement (Beehr & Gupta, 1978). Provided these behaviors do not get out of hand, they are often essentially harmless and may even serve as effective stress-relievers. Yet not all psychological withdrawal is harmless. Drinking, drug abuse, and malicious gossip represent more extreme forms of detachment and often have negative consequences for both the organization and the individual.

Physical withdrawal is characterized by distancing oneself from the work situation in body as well as in spirit. Turnover, absenteeism, and lateness are generally thought of as falling in this category. Hanisch and Hulin (1990) have recently shown that with removal of mandatory retirement for most occupations, the decision to retire can also be considered a form of physical withdrawal from work. Though physical withdrawal is not necessarily less destructive than some types of psychological withdrawal (for example, drinking on the job), it is often assumed to represent a more advanced stage in the withdrawal process.

There is much to recommend treating various ways of leaving organizations as forms of withdrawal. Conceptually, it makes sense to group these behaviors together, since they all appear to be ways to avoid a dissatisfying work role. More generally, attitude theorists from Thurstone (1931) and Doob (1947) to Fishbein and Ajzen (1975) have warned of the futility of predicting specific behaviors from general attitudes. We are likely to learn little about the specific behavioral responses of individuals from such general measures of work-related attitudes as job satisfaction (Fisher & Locke, 1991; Roznowski & Hulin, 1991; Roznowski, Rosse, & Miller, 1992). The withdrawal approach, by contrast, is based on the corollary that general measures of attitudes are potentially useful predictors of *general* behavior tendencies. Combining behaviors that share both common variance (Mitra, Jenkins, & Gupta, 1992; Rosse, 1991) and common theoretical roots enhances both the predictability of the behavior families and our understanding of the withdrawal process (Hom & Griffeth, 1995; Hulin, 1991). The use of behavioral families can also offset a number of statistical limitations inherent in the study of withdrawal behaviors (for example, the low base rates and skewed distributions typically found for most of the individual behaviors [Hulin, 1991]).

One limitation of the withdrawal approach is that it has not yet generated a substantial empirical literature—particularly in the area of research exploring individual differences. For the purpose of this chapter, then, we begin our review by describing empirically supported components of prototypical models of turnover and absence. Hom and Griffeth's model of turnover (1995) was chosen because of its recentness and its explicit intent to integrate the best of prior turnover models. Rhodes and Steers's model of absence (1990) was selected because of its clear dominance in the empirical literature and because of the authors' continual development of the model to incorporate new findings. After reviewing the literature on absence and turnover, we then attempt to generalize these findings—particularly as they relate to individual differences—to the broad spectrum of behaviors that have been characterized as withdrawal from work.

The Hom and Griffeth Model of Turnover

Hom and Griffeth (1995) provide the most recent and extensive meta-analysis of correlates of turnover. Consistent with earlier reviews, the strongest correlations they found (after correcting for sampling error and unreliability) were for stated intentions to quit ($p = .35$) and generalized withdrawal cognitions ($p = .30$). Other key variables included number of promotions received ($p = -.35$), comparison of the present job to alternatives ($p = .26$), role clarity ($p = -.24$), quality of leader-member exchange ($p = -.23$), overall job satisfaction ($p = -.19$) and job stress ($p = .19$), organizational commitment ($p = -18$), job involvement ($p = -.17$), and work satisfaction ($p = -.16$). (A number of these correlations were based on very few studies, and many had confidence intervals that included zero.) Individual difference variables are conspicuous by their absence from this list, a point to which we will return.

Hom and Griffeth then developed a theoretical framework that they felt best integrates existing theoretical models with the results of their meta-analysis. Their model, shown in Figure 12.1, suggests two parallel paths by which individuals may leave an organization. One is a traditional "analytical" route, in which withdrawal cognitions cause employees to explore options and compare them to the utility of their present job; the results of this analysis may lead to either exiting the organization or reconsidering the options, including trying to increase the utility of the present job. The other path, which leads directly from withdrawal cognitions to turnover, was included to account for more impulsive turnover decisions.

Like most models of turnover, this one pays little attention to individual differences, except for their influence on job satisfaction and organizational commitment (generally through their effect on values and expectations). However, there are a couple of places in the model where individual differences might play a more direct role. One case concerns perceptions of the availability and utility of alternatives to the current work role. Individual differences in abilities and skills should certainly affect labor market mobility. Moreover, differences in self-efficacy beliefs are likely to affect *perceptions* of mobility opportunities and utility. We find it ironic that efforts to increase self-efficacy are at the heart of many programs for job seekers, yet this variable is essentially ignored by most models of withdrawal.

Another role for individual differences is suggested by the inclusion of dual paths to turnover. Most models of withdrawal have a strongly rational/analytic flavor, yet a number of theorists (for example, Mobley, Griffeth, Hand, & Meglino, 1979) acknowledge that such behavior may also be impulsive in nature. Individual differences in capacity or inclination to process such decisions analytically may define an important set of boundary conditions for models of withdrawal. Again, we were unable to locate any studies specifically addressing this type of difference (although we subsequently describe some variables that are potentially relevant, such as the planfulness component of the personality trait of conscientiousness).

The Steers and Rhodes Model of Absence

Steers and Rhodes's attendance model (1978, 1984; Rhodes & Steers, 1990) has been the most influential framework for explaining employee absence, although neither it nor other models of absence have received the systematic attention that models of turnover have enjoyed. The various iterations of this model suggest that

Figure 12.1. Integrative Model of Turnover Determinants.

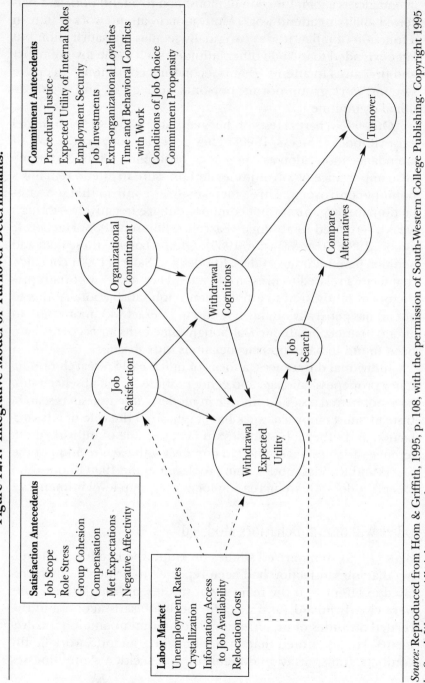

Source: Reproduced from Hom & Griffith, 1995, p. 108, with the permission of South-Western College Publishing. Copyright 1995 by South-Western. All rights reserved.

attendance is a joint function of motivation to attend work and perceived ability to attend work. Motivation to attend work is in turn a function of job attitudes (originally seen as job satisfaction but later extended to include other attitudes, such as job involvement) and pressures to attend (that is, economic conditions, incentive systems, work-group norms, personal work ethic, and organizational commitment).

Only a few, partial tests of the Steers and Rhodes (1978) model exist (Rhodes & Steers, 1990). They generally support the role of attendance motivation as a precursor of absence, although the relative importance of job attitudes and pressure to attend remains a point of controversy. Three meta-analyses confirm that job satisfaction and organizational commitment are negatively—though weakly—related to absence (Farrell & Stamm, 1988; Hackett & Guion, 1985; Scott & Taylor, 1985). On the basis of these data and additional multivariate studies, Rhodes and Steers (1990) conclude that factors related to pressure to attend are more important predictors of motivation to attend than is job satisfaction. Ability to attend has generally not been found to interact with motivation to attend in affecting absence, although some of its antecedents have been found to have direct associations with absence.

Individual differences, a focus of much early research on "absence proneness" and age and gender differences in absence rates, have not played a significant role in modern absenteeism research. Instead, most empirical work has emphasized the role of job satisfaction and other job attitudes. In fact, the role of individual difference variables has seemed to diminish with each revision of the Steers and Rhodes model, being replaced in the 1990 Rhodes and Steers model with an increasing focus on group-level influences.

Other Withdrawal Behaviors Modeled

Blau (1995) summarized studies on employee lateness, concluding that job satisfaction had been reported to be negatively correlated to lateness in the majority of studies, although the results were clearly mixed (and weak for both job satisfaction and the related attitudes of organizational commitment and job involvement). He also noted that leisure-income tradeoffs, work-family conflicts, transportation difficulties, and accidents and illnesses have been implicated in lateness. In an intriguing taxonomy of employee lateness, Blau (1994) integrated these findings by showing that job attitudes are related to "chronic increasing" lateness, that leisure-income tradeoffs and work-family conflicts are related to "stable periodic" lateness, and that transportation difficulties and illnesses and accidents are related to random lateness.

Other behaviors generally included in withdrawal models have received scant empirical attention, with the dominant focus being the role of job satisfaction or related attitudes. A number of studies have reported negative relationships between job satisfaction and a composite measure of withdrawal behaviors (Fisher & Locke, 1991; Hanisch & Hulin, 1990, 1991; Henne & Locke, 1985; Rosse & Hulin, 1985; Roznowski & Hanisch, 1990; Roznowski et al., 1992).

In general, about all that can be concluded from the literature on withdrawal other than absence and turnover is that job attitudes appear to be a consistent (though fairly weak) predictor of withdrawal tendencies. Probably due both to the scarcity of studies and the dominant focus on job dissatisfaction as a causal mechanism for withdrawal, individual differences have not played a significant role in research or theorizing.

Conceptualizing the Role of Individual Differences in Withdrawal Behaviors

It is evident that the dominant models of employee withdrawal have not emphasized the role of individual differences. This is surprising, considering the major role such differences play in folk theories of why people quit or fail to show up for work. One of the authors (Noel) worked for a time in the Florida Keys; in the course of doing business with the manager of a large hotel, he found himself discussing the high rate of employee turnover and absenteeism in the area. The manager was lamenting the fact that his turnover rate was many times higher than that of the rest of the nation. His theory was that people who are running from home, a bad marriage, or life in general tend to keep running until they hit an ocean and can run no further. This type of person, he explained, just gets up one morning, decides that drinking, diving, or fishing is better than facing the inevitable hassles and effort associated with work, and "runs" again (by quitting his or her current job).

This example reflects the view that the best way to explain why some people leave an organization and some people stay is to look at the *person*. Such explanations assume that there is some trait or characteristic that causes certain people to be absent, to quit, or to retire at a higher rate than others; environmental factors are more or less inconsequential. The view that some kinds of people show up consistently and stay with organizations longer than others no doubt drives some managers to a never-ending search for the dedicated, loyal employee. Yet we will see that relatively little research on individual differences (with the partial exception of demographic factors) has been conducted to test these beliefs.

The scarcity of attention to individual differences is doubly surprising considering that behavioral research on organizational withdrawal has been dominated by psychologists, who are arguably predisposed by training to focus on individual-level antecedents of behavior. Sociologists and economists are more apt to contend that people miss work, quit, or retire in response to external influences (for example, weather- and transportation-related obstacles to getting to work on time or the state of the economy), organizational characteristics (for example, size, structure, or culture), or leisure-income tradeoffs. These kinds of models tend to use the "average man" hypothesis (Dodge, 1931): people are more or less the same, and work withdrawal is largely determined by situational factors. In times of high unemployment, for example, people are less likely to quit, because they have fewer alternatives and because their relative satisfaction is higher than it is during periods of economic expansion (Hulin, Roznowski, & Hachiya, 1985). Unemployment is also highly correlated with aggregate absenteeism (Markham, 1985). Leigh (1985) suggests that this is due both to firms laying off absence-prone employees and to the resulting reluctance of surviving employees to be absent.

Contemporary theories suggest that neither individual nor situational factors alone should be expected to provide a satisfactory account of why people behave the way they do in organizations (Pervin, 1989; Terborg, 1981). Consistent with this interactionist perspective, we contend that what is missing from both micro- and macro-oriented models of withdrawal is an adequate representation of individual differences. The remainder of this chapter describes what we mean by individual differences, suggests alter-

LEAVING THE ORGANIZATION 461

native roles for how individual differences might affect the withdrawal process, reviews the literature on individual differences in withdrawal, and provides suggestions for how individual differences might better be incorporated into our thinking about withdrawal.

Although the term "individual differences" has been used to describe many types of variables, the concern of this book is with four main categories of individual psychological differences: cognitive ability, personality, values and interests, and disposition, affect, and temperament. Although not the focus of this book, demographic characteristics (particularly age, gender, and tenure with the organization)—the primary individual differences studied in the withdrawal literature—are also included in our review.

Treatment of individual differences in the organizational withdrawal literature has suffered from two limitations. The most basic limitation is that most theories have simply not paid much attention to individual differences. To a large extent, the implicit assumption seems to have been that *all* dissatisfied and noncommitted employees, for example, are more likely to quit. While theories taking an integrative approach have included March and Simon's ease of movement variable (1958), mobility has generally been treated as an external factor rather than as an individual difference.

Second, even when individual differences have been considered, their role in the nomological network leading to withdrawal is often conceptualized as a simple direct effect rather than as a mediating or moderating variable. Direct effects would be observed as different "kinds" of people withdrawing more often, more severely, and so on. For example, a direct effect for cognitive ability would be observed as a correlation between intelligence or some other measure of cognitive ability and the dependent withdrawal variable. A direct effect for values would be exhibited in a similar fashion, with, say, people high on a work ethic scale being absent or quitting less often. Our review will show that these direct effects are generally rare and account for little variance.

Individual differences have also been described as antecedents of key variables in withdrawal models (rather than as direct causes of turnover). Turnover and absence models frequently cite differences in values or experiences as antecedents of job attitudes. Demographic variables such as gender and family responsibilities are often hypothesized to affect the subjective utility of attending work versus alternatives to attending work and to affect the ease of movement or ability to attend work. Such effects are properly tested in the context of a mediated model linking the antecedent variable with one of the dependent variables through the specific intervening variable(s) (Farkas & Tetrick, 1989). Unfortunately, such tests are far less common than tests of direct effects. Moreover, when individual differences are hypothesized to act solely as antecedents of job attitudes, we contend that the individual differences are more appropriately included in models of job attitudes than in models of withdrawal per se.

An alternative to specifying individual differences as a main effect (or as direct antecedents of causes of withdrawal) is to model them as moderating the effect of other variables on employee withdrawal. For example, if persons higher on the trait of conscientiousness were found to be more likely to come to work during a snowstorm, conscientiousness could be said to moderate the relationship between ability to attend and absence. As another example, if people high on negative affectivity were found to be absent or to quit more often when exposed to job stress, negative affectivity could be said to moderate the relationship between job stress and absence or quitting. While some types of variables, such as attitudes, have been repeatedly proposed as moderators (see Smith, 1977), individual differences rarely have. Despite the lack of attention toward moderating effects, we see this approach as being potentially very useful both in determining subgroups of individuals for whom traditional, analytic models of withdrawal may not apply and for identifying factors affecting key steps within the models.

Individual Differences and Withdrawal: Literature Review

In addition to the four general categories of individual differences addressed in other chapters in this book (cognitive ability; personality; values and interests; and disposition, affect, and temperament), we have included demographic variables in our literature review. Though the theoretical rationale for this approach is sometimes unclear, a significant amount of research has focused on age, gender, tenure, and family responsibilities. For that reason, they are included here.

Demographic Characteristics

Early research on turnover and absence—especially the latter—was characterized by substantial attention to demographic factors, particularly age, gender, and tenure. In most cases, individual characteristics were accepted at face value, with little concern for their psychological or sociological significance. Lawshe and Balma's suggestion (1966, p. 184) that turnover among female office workers is due to "pregnancy, marriage, a home to take care of, transfer of a husband, . . . girl type personality problems, etc." and their recommendation that employers "not hire the twenty-year-old single girl, or the attractive girl, or the recently married woman" offer a striking example of this perspective (as well as a vivid illustration of how the uncritical use of demographic variables can create or maintain stereotypes). In other cases, demographic variables have been included more as control variables than as part of a theoretical explanation of behavior.

Age and Tenure

Age has generally been assumed to be negatively related to withdrawal behaviors, although the generally high correlations between age and tenure often make it difficult to determine which factor is more significant. Hom and Griffeth's meta-analysis (1995) concluded that turnover is negatively correlated with age ($p = -.12$) and tenure ($p = -.17$); however, since the 95 percent credibility intervals for both variables include zero, it is not clear that age is a significant factor in predicting turnover.

Farrell and Stamm's meta-analysis (1988) reported negative correlations between age and both frequency of absence ($p = -.14$) and total time lost to absence ($p = -.06$); however, Farrell and Stamm concluded that these relationships were not significantly different from zero. Martocchio's meta-analysis (1989) reached a different conclusion, confirming the hypothesized negative relationship between age and absence. Martocchio interprets these findings in terms of Super's theory of career stages (1957). According to this perspective, absence is lower among older workers because of greater commitment and a more developed sense of responsibility. Martocchio (1989) also suggests that younger workers are more likely to be absent due to role conflict and role ambiguity.

Hackett's meta-analysis (1989) also concluded that absence is negatively correlated with age, although his review used somewhat different measures of absence and included tenure and gender as moderators. His results indicate that (1) tenure is not correlated with absence once the effects of age are partialed out; (2) age (after partialing out tenure) is negatively related to "avoidable" absence ($p = -.23$ for "attitudinal" absence and $p = -.15$ for a measure of absence frequency) but not to "unavoidable" absence ($p = -.01$ for a total-time-lost index of absence); and (3) the negative relationship between age and "avoidable" absence holds for males but not females.

Gender and Family Responsibilities

Popular wisdom holds that women are more likely to be absent and to quit, attributing that likelihood to family responsibilities, which have traditionally been borne primarily by women. Hom and Griffeth's meta-analysis (1995) suggests that this belief may not be valid in regard to turnover. They found that gender was not significantly related to turnover ($p = -.07$, suggesting that women are slightly *less* likely to quit). Moreover, two indicators of family responsibilities were also negatively correlated with turnover: number of children ($p = -.14$) and kinship responsibilities ($p = -.10$, n.s.). As with the finding that number of relatives in the community was positively related ($p = .22$) to turnover, this suggests that family responsibilities may bind employees to their jobs unless alternate caregivers (in the form of extended family) are available. Unfortunately, since gender was not tested as a moderator of the relationship between family responsibilities and turnover, we do not know whether this conclusion is equally appropriate for men and women. It may be that the presence of children builds commitment for the primary wage-earner (historically the male) while reducing commitment for the other partner.

Farrell and Stamm's meta-analysis (1988) similarly casts doubts on the assumption that absence is higher among women. Mean corrected correlations were not significantly greater than zero for either frequency indices ($p = .08$) or time-lost indices ($p = -.11$) of absence. (A negative coefficient indicates that women had lower absence.) On the other hand, Farrell and Stamm's analysis suggests that sampling error does not adequately account for the variance in correlations for the frequency measure of absence and that moderators of this relationship are likely. One likely moderator is again family responsibilities.

Muchinsky (1977) reported that absence was related to family size, a finding that was replicated by Brooke and Price (1989). In his test of the Steers and Rhodes attendance model, Lee (1989) confirmed that number of dependents was related to the ability-to-attend variable; however, he found no support for the hypothesized link between ability to attend and absence. Terborg, Lee, Smith, Davis, and Turbin's data (1982) also failed to find a significant association between family size (or gender) and absence, although this may have been due in part to restriction in range. Less direct evidence is provided by Nicholson and Goodge's finding of an inverted-U relationship between age and absence (1976), which they suggest might reflect an increase in family responsibilities during the middle years of one's career.

Summary

The results of recent meta-analyses cast doubts about the conventional wisdom linking age and gender with organizational withdrawal. Unfortunately, it is difficult to determine what theoretical significance should be given to these findings, since the demographic variables investigated were generally either included without a theoretical rationale or assumed (often after the fact) to be proxies for other variables. Nicholson (1977), for example, contends that the reason for the age—absence relation is that older individuals experience a change in their personality ("a progressive strengthening of such traits as stability, rigidity and perseveration," p. 247). Clegg (1983) offers a related hypothesis based on changes in values (rather than personality) as a function of age. Neither explanation is as useful as actually examining differences in personality or value structure, preferably using age as a covariate. Similar concerns apply to assuming that marital status or number and age of children accurately reflect ability to attend (or even that they operate on a par with *perceived* responsibility for other family members).

These concerns about construct validity are heightened as we aggregate results from studies that range over a period of years in which family responsibilities have changed considerably, in terms both of fathers' adopting a greater share of household responsibilities and of parents' sharing these responsibilities with outside caregivers (for example, child-care and after-school programs, particularly when these are provided at the work site). Differences in social norms also cast doubts on the extent to which these findings may generalize across cultural groups or countries.

Cognitive Ability

Empirical links between cognitive ability and withdrawal are tenuous at best. Although Jackofsky and Peters (1980) hypothesized that ability should affect turnover through the intervening variables of both ease of movement and desirability of movement, Schuh's review (1967b) and Muchinsky and Tuttle's review (1979) concluded that intelligence has no systematic relationship with turnover. Hom and Griffeth's meta-analysis (1995) found a corrected mean correlation of −.09 between cognitive ability and turnover. (This figure, based on only two studies, included zero within its 95 percent credibility interval.) Nor have specific cognitive abilities fared much better as predictors of turnover (Schuh, 1967a). We found no studies relating cognitive ability to absence or other forms of withdrawal.

Considering the models of absence and turnover that we reviewed, these results should not be surprising. Although such models could be considered "decision" models, they do not involve any mental processing that is likely to be more taxing than that required by most everyday decisions. Thus differences in cognitive ability—at least within the range of scores likely to be found in typical employment settings—are not likely to substantively change the decision process itself.

Looking more specifically at the components of the models, we could also ask whether the effects of cognitive ability might be mediated through the primary causal factors of desirability and ease of withdrawing. Although cognitive ability is not likely to directly affect job satisfaction, there may be an interactive effect of ability and job demands on job satisfaction (Muchinsky & Tuttle, 1979). For example, Bills (1923) suggested that turnover is greater for high-ability people holding simple jobs and for low-ability people holding complex jobs. If such mismatches between the person and job create job dissatisfaction, we could expect it to affect absenteeism and other forms of withdrawal as well as turnover.

Cognitive ability may also affect perceived ease of movement. First, more capable individuals might be qualified for a wider range of jobs and thus have an objectively better job market. Second, such individuals might be more aware of alternative employment opportunities and have more sophisticated job search strategies and skills. Finally, these individuals might be more attractive even within a fixed population of jobs if their advantage in cognitive ability resulted in higher performance on previous jobs.

Research linking job performance and turnover may have some bearing on the question of whether cognitive ability affects turnover through ease of movement (although we acknowledge the significant differences between measures of ability and those of performance). Job performance is strongly and negatively correlated with involuntary turnover (that is, termination), presumably due to the effects of job-related abilities on job performance (Bycio, Hackett, & Alvares, 1990; McEvoy & Cascio, 1987). Performance is also related negatively (but much less strongly) to voluntary turnover (Bycio et al., 1990; McEvoy & Cascio, 1987; Williams & Livingstone, 1994). Jackofsky (1984) suggests that voluntary turnover is lower among high-performing workers for two reasons: performance is likely to be linked to intrinsic and possibly extrinsic rewards, and high-performing employees are likely to perceive greater ease of movement, particularly if job performance is visible to other employers.

To summarize, there is little evidence that cognitive ability is a significant factor in explaining turnover, at least in terms of direct effects. However, there are several caveats to this conclusion. The first is that there are few published studies of the effects of cognitive ability on withdrawal behaviors, particularly behaviors other than turnover. Second, there is a particular lack of research on the relationship between specific cognitive abilities and withdrawal. Third, there is a general lack of theoretical guidance on how cognitive ability—general or specific—is likely to be relevant to withdrawal. Although we are inclined to believe that cognitive ability does not play a significant role in the withdrawal process, we wish to bring this gap to the attention of theorists who may believe otherwise.

Personality

Folk theories of work withdrawal tend to place great importance on personality factors. A good example is "absence proneness"— a construct based on the assumption that differences in absenteeism are attributable to inherent and stable personality characteristics (Ferris, Bergin, & Wayne, 1988; Froggatt, 1970). The scientific basis for such a construct is mixed. On the one hand, there is substantial evidence that absence patterns are fairly stable over time and context and that past absence is the best predictor of future absence (Garrison & Muchinsky, 1977; Landy, Vasey, & Smith, 1984; Rosse, 1988). Additional indirect evidence was provided by Froggatt (1970), who showed that the distributions of actual absence are significantly different from theoretical distributions that assume each absence event is discrete. Yet there is little or no explicit documentation of any personality trait or profile that explains these differences in absence-taking. The same lack of explicit documentation colors the turnover literature regarding "job hoppers" (Bernardin, 1977), "drifters" (Hom & Griffeth, 1995), and "hobos" (Ghiselli, 1974; Hulin et al., 1985; Judge & Wattanabe, 1995).

Early reviews reported that correlations between personality factors and withdrawal behaviors varied widely, leading to the preliminary conclusion that personality offered little promise for improving our understanding of employee withdrawal (Bernardin, 1977; Muchinsky, 1977; Schmitt, Gooding, Noe, & Kirsch, 1984; Schuh, 1967b). However, recent analyses of the personality literature suggest that reviews such as these may have provided a very misleading picture of the true role of personality. One of the fundamental problems leading to this distortion is the lack of theoretical rationale behind much of the early workplace research on personality factors. The availability of standardized personality inventories often resulted in researchers' choosing personality dimensions on the basis of the popularity and ease of use of a particular measure rather than on the basis of the dimensions' theoretical relevance to job performance. Moreover, the use of these complex, multi-attribute personality inventories often encouraged "fishing expeditions" rather than hypothesis-testing.

A second problem is that most traditional personality inventories were designed to measure abnormalities, particularly in clinical populations. Because they were generally not designed to measure variations within the "normal" range of job-relevant abilities, their relevance to work-related behavior needs to be documented rather than assumed. Consequently, workplace researchers interested in job-relevant traits were forced to develop their own measures, often with inadequate research on the measures' construct validity. As a result, even when apparently similar constructs were investigated by different researchers, differences in measures often complicated integration of findings.

Still another problem had to do with the reviews themselves, which often averaged validity coefficients across all personality dimensions to create a global index that was assumed to represent the predictive ability of "personality." As more recent reviewers have noted, averaging correlations across many different dimensions of personality, some of which have far less theoretical basis for explaining work behavior than others, is not likely to give a very accurate picture of the potential explanatory power of personality factors (Barrick & Mount, 1991; Tett, Jackson, & Rothstein, 1991). To avoid the potential distortions of a global approach, we will instead organize our review according to the Five-Factor Model (FFM)—the Big Five typology of personality dimensions. (See Chapter Two of this book for a description of the typology and controversies surrounding its use.) We will rely primarily on Barrick and Mount's meta-analysis of personality and work behavior (1991), since it is the only one that includes employee retention as an outcome. We will also include studies potentially related to other withdrawal behaviors, although much of our discussion will of necessity be speculative (due to the scarcity of empirical literature).

Emotional Stability/Neuroticism

The FFM Emotional Stability (or Neuroticism) dimension includes such traits as anxiety, depression, anger, embarrassment, worry, insecurity, and the tendency to be emotional (Barrick & Mount, 1991). Although a number of studies have explored these traits in relation to organizational withdrawal, Barrick and Mount's meta-analysis (1991) suggests that this factor is not significant for predicting retention ($p = .02$). In many studies, the theoretical rationale for a relationship between this factor and withdrawal has been either lacking or provided post hoc. Bernardin (1977), for example, suggested that "job hoppers" may be higher in anxiety, but he did not suggest why this might be the case.

However, before anyone dismisses emotional stability as a relevant individual difference, it might be useful to more thoughtfully consider routes through which it might affect withdrawal. One obvious route is through effectiveness: workers prone to anxiety or depression may be less effective performers (either as a cause or as a consequence of the anxiety) and thus be more prone to termination. Bernardin (1977) found that anxiety was related to absence as well as turnover, suggesting a related mechanism in which depression and anxiety result in absenteeism, which in turn becomes a basis for termination. Unfortunately, we are aware of no studies in which emotional stability, performance, and multiple forms of withdrawal are studied so as to explore these types of mediating mechanisms.

Emotional stability might also be related to voluntary turnover when the act of quitting functions as a coping mechanism. Situations in which jobs' emotional demands exceed individuals' psychic resources could be expected to produce stress, particularly for individuals whose emotional stability is low to begin with. In those situations, withdrawal represents a means of avoiding stress. Anxiety has been linked to turnover among foremen (MacKinney & Wolins, 1960) and workers in hazardous jobs (Hakkinen & Tolvainen, 1960). Both of the studies involved potentially stressful work, but neither study explored "psychic overload" or treated turnover explicitly as a coping mechanism. Similarly, a number of writers have suggested that absenteeism may provide a "safety valve" for coping with work stress, and Parkes's results (1984) indicate that workers who are less self-confident are more likely to respond to environmental stress through passive coping mechanisms such as absence. Hill and Trist (1953) suggested that when unexcused absenteeism is not socially acceptable, industrial accidents may be due to conscious or unconscious motivations to escape stress by getting hurt. Their notion of "motivated accidents" spawned the idea of accident proneness, an individual difference variable that has since fallen into and out of favor.

A third possible mechanism linking emotional stability with increased withdrawal was suggested by Porter and Steers (1973). Based on their review of antecedents of withdrawal, Porter and Steers hypothesized that individuals with extreme personality scores—either high or low—are more likely to withdraw; because individuals at the extremes of personality dimensions do not "fit" with the organization, they are more likely to leave. Porter and Steers described stayers as having moderate levels of anxiety, aggressiveness, independence, achievement orientation, self-confidence, and sociability. These characteristics seem to typify the "company man" stereotype of the 1950s: a person who identifies strongly with the organization doesn't make waves, and values achievement (but only within the confines of the company). Leavers appear to be more of the maverick type: willful, gregarious, and unafraid to explore other opportunities. Bernardin (1977) failed to find support for this "polar" hypothesis, although his sample of phone sales representatives may have been more likely to attract "job hoppers" than "company men." Though Bernardin did not elaborate on Porter and Steers's idea, it is clear that he thinks that certain personality types can be expected to be attracted to jobs that make it easy to leave. Explicit exploration of the match between employees' personalities and company norms or culture may be a useful avenue for future studies.

Extraversion

The FFM Extraversion dimension includes such traits as sociability, gregariousness, assertiveness, garrulousness, and an active orientation. Across thirteen studies, Barrick and Mount (1991) computed a corrected mean validity of −.03, a figure with which we are hard-pressed to disagree. Although recent approaches to absenteeism have placed greater emphasis on social control factors such as group norms, receptivity to social pressures is more likely to be affected by the personality dimension of agreeableness than that of extraversion. About the only potential we see for extraversion to affect withdrawal is in the context of person-organization fit. Barrick and Mount (1991) found that extraversion was a significant predictor of job performance only for sales and managerial positions. Presumably, introverts working in these jobs are more likely to experience job dissatisfaction and quit or be fired.

Openness to Experience

The FFM Openness to Experience (or Intellectance) dimension is described by such terms as *imaginative, cultured, curious, original, broad-minded, intelligent,* and *artistically sensitive.* Barrick and Mount (1991) concluded that this dimension is a stable predictor of retention ($p = -.11$). One interpretation is that individuals high on this dimension are the restless wanderers often referred to as "job hoppers" or organizational "hobos" (Ghiselli, 1974; Hulin et al., 1985). In this case, turnover (and perhaps absence) may represent not so much withdrawal as a competing "pull" from other, new experiences (Judge & Wattanabe, 1995).

Another (somewhat more prosaic) interpretation is that individuals who are highly open to experience have a more difficult time finding a good "match" with an employer. Because of their more cosmopolitan perspective, such people may also have a different frame of reference for evaluating work rewards. For example, they may place greater value on such intrinsic rewards as creative, nonrepetitive work with considerable autonomy. These preferences may not be readily met in traditional organizations, particularly in lower-level, nonprofessional jobs, thus producing job dissatisfaction. Individuals who are highly open to experience may also be more likely to perceive alternatives to their current work and thus report greater perceived ease of movement. Unfortunately, very little empirical work has explored the fit between employee personality and organizational culture and its effects on employee performance and withdrawal (Jackson et al., 1991; O'Reilly, Chatman, & Caldwell, 1991).

At this point, it is clear neither why openness to experience is related to turnover nor whether similar relationships would be found for other withdrawal behaviors. The significant findings for this dimension, second only to conscientiousness in Barrick and Mount's meta-analysis, call for additional research to explore both its direct and indirect effects on withdrawal.

Agreeableness

Traits associated with the FFM Agreeableness dimension include courtesy, trust, good-naturedness, flexibility, cooperation, softheartedness, and tolerance. Barrick and Mount (1991) found a corrected correlation of .09 between this dimension and retention across fifteen studies; the amount of variance remaining after correcting for sampling error suggests that moderators of this relationship are likely to exist, although the authors offer no suggestions as to what these may be.

It is not entirely clear why agreeableness is associated with higher retention. It may be that agreeable employees are less likely to be fired, suggesting that type of turnover may be a moderator. Alternatively, these results may indicate that agreeable individuals are less likely to experience dissatisfaction, particularly for work dimensions with a substantial social component (for example, satisfaction with co-workers and supervisors).

Another possible explanation is that workers who are high on this dimension (or on the need for affiliation) may be more likely to act with particular regard to their co-workers' needs. An example of this is evident in research with nurses, who are often reluctant to miss work because of the impact their absence has on fellow nurses. (While this type of diligence often reflects conscientiousness, here we are proposing a more socially directed dynamic. Nurses [and other professionals] may attend work not only because of their concern for patients' well-being [conscientiousness] but also out of a sense of obligation to the other nurses—those who would have to work harder if they were absent [agreeableness].) Thus agreeableness may have a direct effect on various withdrawal behaviors, particularly minor forms such as loafing, being late, or missing work. Alternatively, it may have an interactive effect with work-group norms. Nicholson and Johns (1985) contend that work-group norms concerning absence are a powerful (and generally ignored) influence on absence-taking, a notion that Blau (1995) has extended to tardiness. To the extent that highly agreeable persons are more likely to comply with social pressures, this trait may act as a moderator of the effects of group norms and withdrawal behavior. The direction of its effect on withdrawal behavior would depend on whether the group norms supported or discouraged the behavior.

Conscientiousness

Barrick and Mount (1991) reported a corrected mean correlation of .12 between employee retention and the FFM Conscientiousness composite. This makes it marginally the strongest of the personality predictors of turnover, a conclusion also reached by Bernardin (1977) for both turnover and absence. Although Barrick and Mount did not provide this level of detail in their meta-analysis, many consider conscientiousness to include the two components of dependability (characterized by the adjectives *careful, thorough, responsible, organized,* and *planful*) and achievement striving, each of which is reasonably related to withdrawal behavior.

The dependability component fits well with popular trait-oriented explanations of employee withdrawal: "quitters" are just that—people who lack the character to persevere during troubled times—while the absence-prone are people who lack a sufficient sense of responsibility to their obligations to attend work. Individuals who are low on the planfulness component of conscientiousness may be more likely to follow the impulsive path to withdrawal described by Hom and Griffeth (1995). Broadening the notion of withdrawal to include what Gupta and Jenkins (1980) called "psychological withdrawal," there is also substantial evidence that conscientiousness is linked to poor work performance ("goldbricking"), drug use on the job, and other counterproductive behavior (Hough, Eaton, Dunnette, Kamp, & McCloy, 1990; Ones, Schmidt, & Viswesvaran, 1993).

Much of the work on the achievement-striving component of conscientiousness has dealt with achievement motivation. Meyer and Cuomo's findings concerning achievement orientation (1962) seem to suggest that, up to a point, the propensity to achieve is associated with higher retention. Those who are highly achievement-oriented, though, seem to leave more often, presumably to find greener pastures. Farris (1971) provides support for this idea, as does Hines (1973). It is not clear, however, whether the underlying process involves greater mobility resulting from higher productivity, greater frustration among those with very high aspirations, or some other factor. It is also not clear how achievement orientation is related to other forms of withdrawal, although it seems likely that because of the value that achievement-striving employees place on accomplishments, they would not want to avoid work (at least not work that provides a sense of achievement).

Perceived Control

A number of studies suggest that personality variables concerned with the individual's sense of control—though not part of the Big

Five typology—are related to withdrawal behavior. The literature on stress supports the notion that locus of control (Kobasa, Maddi, & Kahn, 1982; Parkes, 1984), as well as the related traits of self-efficacy (Fleishman, 1984) and an "easygoing disposition" (Holahan & Moos, 1987), are related to the use of active or direct (versus passive or avoidance) coping strategies. From this, we might hypothesize that stressed or dissatisfied employees with an internal locus of control would be less likely than "externals" to withdraw—particularly to withdraw in a way that does not improve the situation (for example, to change jobs out of passive avoidance rather than as a means of functional coping). There is some support for this idea. Griffeth and Hom (1988) found a weak negative correlation between internal locus of control and turnover, and Parker (1993) found that perceived control and self-efficacy were negatively related to exit behavior and positively related to voice behavior. On the other hand, Withey and Cooper (1989) reported that locus of control was unrelated to exit in two different samples. Blau (1987) and Spector and Michaels (1986) showed that locus of control moderated the relationship between job satisfaction and intentions to quit.

Related studies have documented the importance of perceived control on employee absenteeism. Withey and Cooper (1989) found that generalized locus of control predicted neglect behaviors (which they defined as a composite of absence, lateness, and sloppy work) in two independent samples. Building on Ajzen's theory of planned behavior (1991), Martocchio and Harrison (1993) suggested that attendance motivation is a function of attitudes toward absence, perceived social pressure to attend, and perceived behavioral control (people's belief in their ability to attend work). In fact, perceived control over obstacles to attending work may be more important than actual control (Bandura, 1982, 1986; Frayne & Latham, 1987; Latham & Frayne, 1989). Applying self-management training to employee attendance, Frayne and Latham (1987) found that positive outcome expectancy is not enough to induce people to overcome obstacles to attendance; it must be accompanied by the belief that one has control over the social and personal obstacles that prevent attendance—a belief that they found could be developed with a relatively short training program.

In an interesting application of attribution theory, Parsons, Herold, and Leatherwood (1985) found that new employees who attributed their work performance to luck were more likely to quit than those who made attributions to ability, effort, or task difficulty. It may be that employees in the latter group are more likely to respond to job dissatisfaction by trying to change factors over which they have at least some control, whereas those in the former group are more likely to view quitting as their only option.

Summary

Although research linking personality and withdrawal is more abundant than that linking cognitive ability and withdrawal, there remains a shortage of theoretically driven research, particularly for behaviors other than turnover. Early pessimistic reviews concerning the role of personality in withdrawal in particular (Muchinsky & Tuttle, 1979; Schuh, 1967b) and job performance in general (Guion & Gottier, 1965) seem to have had a chilling effect on research in this area—an effect that persists to this day. There has been no agreed-upon approach to measuring personality when withdrawal is used as the dependent variable, although this problem may be reduced if researchers adopt the Big Five or similar typologies to ground future work. A more serious limitation seems to be researchers' failure to specify a theoretical justification for using personality as a predictor variable. Some noteworthy regularities have been found, particularly for the FFM dimensions of conscientiousness and openness to experience, but more corroborating studies are needed for most dimensions of personality.

A number of methodological issues underlie our cautious conclusions about the role of personality. First, meta-analyses have been largely limited to aggregating indexes of linear associations. In the area of personality, it may not always be reasonable to assume linearity, or even monotonicity. An excellent example is the previously cited finding that achievement motivation may have a curvilinear relationship with turnover. Another is Porter and Steers's reinterpretation (1973) of Meyer and Cuomo's work on emotional stability (1962). Although Porter and Steers's hypothesis that persons tending toward the extremes of personality are more likely to leave was not fully supported by the findings of Bernardin (1977), researchers must be vigilant for such nonlinearities in their data.

Second, researchers need to heed Mobley et al.'s call (1979) to give more thought to personality factors as moderator variables rather than focusing only on the direct effects of those factors. Research on locus of control (Blau, 1987; Spector & Michaels, 1986) and self-monitoring (Jenkins, 1993) has shown the potential utility of this approach.

Finally, it is important to consider interdependencies among different aspects of personality when attempting to predict behaviors. Most I/O research on personality has been essentially bivariate in nature, and what little multivariate work has been done has tended to assume that the effects of multiple personality factors are additive. In some cases, however, theory may suggest that what is important is the *interaction* among personality traits. This, too, is difficult to ascertain from meta-analyses, suggesting that personality researchers will need to become more familiar with methods of configural or profile analysis.

Values and Interests

Research exploring the effects of values and interests on withdrawal has been about as scattered and inconsistent as research investigating the relationship between withdrawal and both cognitive ability and personality. There seem to be two main approaches to including values in withdrawal models. The first approach inquires into general values about work and nonwork, usually tested in terms of direct effects on withdrawal behaviors. It makes intuitive sense that individuals who value work highly are less likely to avoid work, whether the avoidance takes the form of lateness, absence, or goofing off on the job. Such individuals are also likely to have more reservations about quitting if it means being without a job. The effects on turnover may be more complex, however, in situations in which such individuals are weighing the relative advantages of alternative jobs. In general, we would speculate that individuals with strong work values (that is, work ethic, work-role centrality, work identification) are likely to reach the decision to quit by following an analytical approach rather than an impulsive one.

As a corollary within this first approach, nonwork values also may play a role in determining whether an individual will exhibit withdrawal behaviors. Since one's time has a finite limit, time spent at work is necessarily spent away from other things. Individuals might value work highly but still exhibit withdrawal behaviors as the result of influence by other things that they value, such as family responsibilities or leisure opportunities (Fichman, 1984). In addition to their direct effect, nonwork values and interests might also be important moderating variables in withdrawal (Dubin, Champoux, & Porter, 1975). For individuals who place greater value on nonwork than work outcomes, job attitudes may be far less predictive of withdrawal than the "pull" of their nonwork interests (Mobley, 1982).

An alternative approach to values and withdrawal has centered on the match between an individual's values/expectations and the outcomes provided by an employer. Porter and Steers (1973) and Steers and Mowday (1981) contend that employees' expectations are central to the withdrawal process. According to their perspective, each employee brings a somewhat different set of expectations to the job, "depending upon his or her own values and needs at the time" (Steers & Mowday, 1981, p. 241). To the extent that these expectations are not met, individuals become dissatisfied and withdraw by being absent or quitting.

While there is a fairly extensive literature linking met expectations with job satisfaction (and hence linking them indirectly with withdrawal), there has been little work exploring possible direct effects on withdrawal of the match between individual and organizational values. This work may be an important step in better understanding the linkage between values and withdrawal, because many withdrawal models are vague about the role of values. As we have already described, models of absence tend to include values as antecedents of both pressure to attend (in the case of work ethic) and motivation to attend (through an effect on job attitudes). However, these models do not elaborate on how this influence is manifested or on the stability of the underlying values and needs.

Ethical and quasi-ethical values may also play an important role in withdrawal behaviors, especially absence. Gibson (1966) describes an individual difference variable called "work identification," which is said to influence absence by making it hard for those with high work attachment to "permit" themselves to be absent. Brooke (1986) similarly presents "work involvement" as a direct antecedent of absenteeism. Steers and Rhodes (1978) suggest a more indirect role for the concept of "personal work ethic," which they propose as a component of pressure to attend (an antecedent of attendance motivation). In each of these models, work ethic seems to describe a feeling on the part of the worker that absence is wrong, regardless of the kind of job. At least five studies corroborate the importance of work ethic as a determinant of absenteeism (Feldman, 1974; Goodale, 1973; Ilgen & Hollenbeck, 1977; Lee, 1989; Searls, Braucht, & Miskimins, 1974).

Values may also influence withdrawal through their effects on occupational interests. At this time, such a link is highly speculative, however, since research on interests and withdrawal is virtually nonexistent, particularly for behaviors other than turnover. Schneider's attraction-selection-attrition model (1983) suggests that people are attracted to work situations with which they are well matched. Similar to the situation with values and expectations, good person-employer matches should enhance satisfaction and thus reduce the motivation to withdraw. Because interests are usually measured at the occupational level, we would speculate that they should be more effective at predicting decisions to change occupations (or to leave the workforce entirely) than at predicting movement across employers but within the same occupation. Unfortunately, the scant empirical data linking interests and turnover (Muchinsky & Tuttle, 1979; Schuh, 1967b) are inadequate to test this hypothesis.

To summarize, there is some reason at present to believe that work values may make people think twice about leaving a job, especially if there is no alternative job already in place. If the notion of being unemployed disturbs someone deeply, that person may be more likely to tolerate adversities at work or seek to change the work situation rather than exhibiting withdrawal behaviors that may endanger employment. The issue is complicated by the fact that the value of work in general and the value of a particular job may be hard to distinguish. We suspect that a person's valuation of work in general reflects some kind of amalgamation of thinking about various jobs he or she has had or imagines having. Future research into the question of how these constructs differ may increase our understanding of value-driven turnover.

We see two potentially fruitful areas for research on the influence of values and interests on withdrawal. First, we need to understand more about the particular ways that individual values and organizational characteristics meld. While some useful work has been done on the subject of individual values and organizational culture (O'Reilly et al., 1991), there is still much room for additional research. Being able to specify before initiating the hiring process just what a values/culture fit entails may aid both in selection and in understanding how the individual/organization match affects withdrawal. Second, the fact that values (or at least expectations) may change as a result of "realistic job previews" (Locke, 1976; Miceli, 1985) suggests that there are still some questions about the stability of values. Longitudinal studies of value shifts as organizational members are socialized may shed light on this question.

Disposition, Affect, and Temperament

The debate continues concerning the usefulness of dispositional variables as a factor in explaining job attitudes and behaviors (see Arvey, Bouchard, Segal, & Abraham, [1989] and Cropanzano & James [1990] for reviews). In terms of withdrawal, affective orientation could conceivably have a direct effect on behavior, as well as indirectly affecting it through job satisfaction (Judge & Hulin, 1992; Staw & Ross, 1985). In evaluating both roles—direct and indirect—it is important to consider the temporality of different dimensions of disposition. For instance, it seems reasonable to suppose that a general negative disposition could be related to turnover, since negative affectivity might have a broad and lasting effect on how satisfied a person is with a job. On the other hand, it seems less likely that mood, a much more temporary phenomenon, would greatly influence quitting. However, it is reasonable to expect that mood might affect absence, lateness, or some other short-term form of psychological withdrawal.

Affective disposition clearly seems to have an effect on job attitudes. Judge and Hulin (1993) have suggested that affective disposition (a relatively stable tendency to respond to stimuli with positive or negative affect) affects job satisfaction indirectly through its effects on subjective well-being, an ongoing state of psychological wellness or satisfaction with life. Subjective well-being has been shown to have a reciprocal relationship with job satisfaction, one determinant of withdrawal (Judge & Locke, 1993). This complex interplay of long-term affective disposition, which has no particular target, and a shorter-term affective reaction to a particular object (such as a job) makes conceptualization and research of these relationships difficult at best.

Although there has been substantial research and theoretical speculation on the role of disposition in work attitudes such as job satisfaction, fewer writers have considered other ways in which disposition may influence job behaviors (Cropanzano, James, & Konovsky, 1993). Affective disposition may affect absenteeism and lateness through illness, accidents, and other obstacles to attendance, as well as through its effects on job attitudes. People characterized by high negative affectivity are more likely to report somatic complaints (Watson, Pennebaker, & Folger, 1987), for example. Whether or not they are in fact ill more frequently than others, these individuals may be more likely to interpret their symptoms as a reason to sleep in or not to come to work. This same disposition may also cause these individuals to interpret symptoms in their children or signs of bad weather as justifications for staying home. While this hypothesis does not appear to have been tested specifically in the context of withdrawal from work, it may explain Judge's finding (1990) that unhappy people are absent more, even controlling for the effects of job satisfaction.

Another mechanism for explaining the effects of disposition on withdrawal is provided by the concept of mood. Mood, which (as we have noted) is a temporary phenomenon, can be thought of as a by-product of affectivity (George, 1989). Moods may shift fairly often, and researchers usually assume (quite reasonably) that most people prefer to be in a good mood rather than a bad one. In fact, Holahan and Moos (1987) and Pelicier (1987) coined the phrase "mood repair" to describe the process whereby generally unhappy people try to improve their lives. According to George (1989), one mechanism for mood repair is being absent from work. In support of this notion, George found that positive but not negative mood was correlated with absence. In other words, while mood can be the cause of absence, absence can also provide a means for adjusting mood. People either come to or avoid work depending on whether work puts them in a better or worse mood.

In addition to the work on absence by George (1989) and Judge (1990), a few studies have explored the effects of disposition on turnover and general withdrawal. Cropanzano et al. (1993) reported that both positive and negative affectivity were found to influence turnover intentions. Judge and Hulin (1992) found that subjective well-being had both direct and indirect (via job satisfaction) effects on a composite measure of work withdrawal (consisting of turnover, absence, tardiness, job transfers, missed meetings, shirking, and retiring). Necowitz and Roznowski (1991) found that negative affectivity (a presumed antecedent of subjective well-being) predicts a composite measure of withdrawal behavior. Judge and Wattanabe (1995) have also suggested that negative affectivity may explain some individuals' history of repeatedly quitting jobs.

Finally, Judge (1993) has provided an interesting perspective with his finding that negative affectivity may moderate the relationship between job satisfaction and withdrawal cognitions. The rationale for this effect is that people with a negative disposition are accustomed to—even expect—dissatisfaction with their lives. Against this frame of reference, dissatisfying working conditions are not likely to be sufficiently salient to motivate withdrawal. We strongly encourage additional research that goes beyond disposition-attitude relationships to explore the direct and moderating effects of dispositional variables on behavior.

To summarize, most work on disposition thus far has focused on job attitudes. Research on withdrawal would now benefit from increased attention to behavioral outcomes of disposition. We suspect that the most sensible approach to the question of these behavioral outcomes is studying how bad things have to get before someone takes action. Perpetually unhappy people seem to be disposed to do nothing about unpleasant work situations, but the degree to which people have to be unhappy to take action remains unclear. Dispositional explanations for the *type* of withdrawal behavior chosen may also be of interest. Whether a worker is more likely to choose constructive or destructive means of relieving work stress or dissatisfaction, for example, is something both researchers and practitioners would find useful.

As with values, the question of the stability of dispositions is not entirely settled. Currently, there is evidence that job satisfaction and subjective well-being are actually separate constructs (Judge & Locke, 1993). Are people grumpy because they just are that way, or are they that way partially because they have a bad job (or have had a series of bad jobs)? Research is likely to be limited if we continue to treat disposition as an influence on job satisfaction but do not examine the relationship the other way around. Again, one solution may be more longitudinal research. We would add the caution, however, that even longitudinal work may be hindered by the difficulties inherent in telling whether one is measuring a disposition, an affective reaction to a particular stimulus object (the job, a boss, and so on), or a mood. Of the four categories of individual differences covered in this chapter, this may be the most challenging for future research.

Summary and Future Directions

Our review illustrates that there is little evidence that individual psychological differences have added much to our understanding of withdrawal behavior in organizations. To some extent, this conclusion must be tempered by the fact that surprisingly little research has explicitly considered the role of individual differences. Yet in some areas—primarily demographic variables—there has been sufficient research to reach a credible conclusion that withdrawal behaviors do not vary significantly across demographic groupings. One reason may be that individual differences simply do not make any difference; in that case, the "average person" analysis is sufficient to explain employee withdrawal.

Another reason for the lack of findings may be the atheoretical approach that researchers have typically taken. Most research has consisted of either bivariate correlations between some individual difference measure and an outcome variable such as turnover or absenteeism, or bivariate correlations between some individual difference and some antecedent to employee withdrawal (such as job satisfaction or organizational commitment). Typically, little theoretical justification is given for hypothesizing that individual differences will help predict withdrawal behaviors.

Locke's criticism of attitude research (1976) is instructive. Researchers, Locke claims, have far too often been guilty of correlation without explanation: attempting to link variables without addressing the underlying causal connections. He points to Ingham (1970) as an example of a study that attempted to go further than the usual correlation-without-explanation approach. Ingham observed a correlation between company size and absenteeism. By examining the values of the individual workers and the reward structures of the companies he investigated, he determined that workers in the smaller plants liked interacting with their supervisors and liked the work itself. The interaction of those values and the work environment resulted in lower absenteeism at the smaller companies. More in-depth work such as Ingham's is needed if individual differences are to be satisfactorily integrated into models of withdrawal.

Individual Differences as Direct Effects

Despite the fact that the vast majority of studies including individual differences have tested them as direct effects, there is little evidence of significant main effects. One reason for this may be that researchers have yet to explore really useful individual difference variables. Although we have suggested a few variables that deserve more attention, we doubt that this explanation is adequate.

Another reason might be that it is simplistic to assume that a single individual difference variable, acting in isolation, can have a significant effect on complexly determined behavior. It may be instructive that folk theories of withdrawal (with the exception of those focusing simply on demographic characteristics) do not focus on narrowly defined individual differences. Rather than reflexively criticizing a concept such as "absence proneness" for its ambiguity, we may benefit from appreciating its complexity. Put differently, is there a profile or constellation of characteristics that, although modest predictors when considered individually, might together explain a substantial amount of variance in withdrawal behavior?

Our review provides some ideas for developing such a profile. We might expect a withdrawal-prone person to be a younger male with few family responsibilities, for example. He might have a low ability or skill level; as a result, he might be relegated to lower-level jobs that provide low job satisfaction and few deferred rewards that build continuance commitment. Such a person might be described as sociable and open to new experiences (even as inclined toward risk taking) but as having a weak work ethic and as being not very dependable or achievement-oriented. In fact, it is likely that nonwork interests would be more important than work outcomes to such an individual.

Is a characterization such as this likely to advance our understanding of withdrawal behavior? On the one hand, it is hard to characterize this amalgamation of results as "theory-driven," even though we suspect that many human resource managers would recognize the prototypical individual we have described. Trying to construct a withdrawal-prone "type" such as this from the results of our literature review also creates logical inconsistencies that need to be resolved. For example, family responsibilities appear to be positively correlated with absence and lateness but negatively related to turnover, at least for primary wage-earners. Individuals with an internal locus of control seem to be less likely to engage in "neglectful" withdrawal, but they may be more likely to engage in "constructive" turnover. It is also somewhat hard to picture a person who is high on negative affectivity being described as sociable, yet both these traits have been linked to withdrawal. Thus a high priority should be to conduct more "exploratory" research to investigate the interdependencies of individual difference variables; such research should prove invaluable for developing a better theory of a withdrawal-prone "type."

The optimist in us suggests that it may be worth exploring a theoretically linked profile of characteristics, since none of the research we reviewed has followed such a holistic approach. The closest approximation we found to a "profile" approach was the use of Weighted Application Blanks (WABs) to predict turnover. It is interesting to note that the mean corrected validity reported by Hom and Griffeth (1995) for WABs ($p = .33$) was far higher than the validity reported for any of the individual personal characteristics. This may in part be attributable to the tendency of WABs to capitalize on chance associations, particularly if many of the studies included in the meta-analysis did not cross-validate their findings (Wernimont, 1962; Roach, 1971). On the other hand, the validity of rationally developed biodata (Breaugh & Dossett, 1989) that include theoretically derived items on values, interests, and personality is likely to be higher and more stable than the validity of empirically derived WABs (Gatewood & Feild, 1987).

Researchers exploring a profile approach to withdrawal should be alert to the possibility of multiple profiles, even for the same behavior. For instance, we referred earlier to "drifters" and "hobos" as types of workers who manifest particularly high levels of quitting. Despite that commonality, drifters and hobos may have significant differences. The drifter moves regularly among transient jobs and seems to be characterized by low levels of work identification and work ethic. Due to a lack of conscientiousness, to high value placed on nonwork interests, or to the types of jobs available, drifters' commitment to employers is weak and primarily contractual; in fact, drifters may be low on what Mowday, Porter, and Steers (1982) have termed "propensity to commit." As a result, drifters are more likely to respond to job dissatisfaction by moving on than by trying to improve matters. One archetype of the drifter may be the so-called ski bum—someone who works to ski, is not greatly concerned about working conditions (unless they interfere with his avocation), and is both willing and able to find an alternative job on a minute's notice.

By contrast, the hobo's mobility seems motivated by a constant search for different (not necessarily "better") experiences. In his original description, Ghiselli (1974) proposed that hobos are driven by "raw, surging, internal impulses, perhaps not unlike those that cause birds to migrate" (p. 81). This type of individual may be found in a variety of jobs, from the lowest to the highest levels in organizations; in fact, the label "hobo" may be an apt descriptor for many entrepreneurs. While hobos may be very conscientious workers, they too lack long-term commitment to any particular organization. Yet dissatisfaction with a particular job or employer is less likely to motivate them to quit than is the pull of a different experience. In some cases, the pull is to another employer or even another career; in other cases, it may be to nonwork interests.

A profile approach might also reveal a need to create different profiles for different behaviors. Blau (1994), for example, found very distinct sets of predictors for different types of lateness-prone employees. This approach might be usefully extended to other forms of withdrawal behavior. Aside from practical concerns, the fundamental concern we have with this approach has to do with parsimony. Even if distinct profiles can successfully be developed for different behaviors, what we gain in ability to predict narrow behaviors may be offset by a reduction in understanding of general principles of behavior.

Indirect Effects of Individual Differences

While the empirical evidence for direct individual difference effects thus far is thin, as we have noted, direct effects are only one way that individual differences might influence withdrawal. Although a pro-file approach may yet prove useful, we believe that it is more likely that individual differences will contribute more when included in multivariate models of withdrawal. The problems associated with predicting specific behaviors from general measures of attitudes or other variables have already been noted. Withdrawal models have attempted to alleviate this problem by grouping together behaviors that reflect a desire to remove oneself from the work situation either psychologically or physically. While this approach does help solve some of these problems, there are still shortcomings.

One limitation is that withdrawal behaviors, even when so broadly construed, constitute a particular type of response to work situations. Yet withdrawal is not, of course, the only means of dealing with an undesirable work situation. It has been argued that withdrawal behaviors are a subset of the more general construct of adaptation (Rosse & Miller, 1984; Hulin, 1991). Adaptation includes behaviors other than withdrawal that may help an individual cope with unpleasant or undesirable work situations. Hirschman (1970), for example, suggested that people have available to them three major classes of responses to dissatisfaction: *exit* (essentially the same as withdrawal), *voice* (attempts to change the work situation), and *loyalty* (waiting patiently for things to improve). Farrell (1983) and Withey and Cooper (1989) added a fourth category, called *neglect,* which is characterized by "lax and disrespectful behavior" (such as lateness and increased errors); while Robinson (1994) and Rosse and Miller (1984) suggested a category of destructive or retaliatory behaviors that may be used to adapt by "evening the score."

Adaptation models allow for the possibility that individuals may try to change the work situation or make cognitive readjustments instead of resorting to withdrawal. One advantage of thinking about withdrawal as a subset of adaptive behaviors is that it allows for the wide array of nonwithdrawal responses that people may employ when faced with difficult work situations. Another advantage is that adaptation models, because of this added richness, provide an effective framework for incorporating individual differences. The remainder of the chapter will be devoted to suggestions for integrating individual differences into the adaptation framework originally proposed by Rosse and Miller (1984); a modified version of that model is presented in Figure 12.2.

The Rosse and Miller Model of Adaptation

Rosse and Miller's original model showed adaptation as being driven primarily by assessments of *relative dissatisfaction*—a construct that essentially represents a recognition that other possible working situations may be preferable to the present one. It is assumed to represent an unpleasant affective state that is likely to result in the individual's thinking about how to adapt. Relying on prior experience (both direct experience and vicarious learning from the experience of others) and social norms regarding what is appropriate, the dissatisfied individual develops a repertory of possible adaptive responses. In the original model, choice of a response was considered to be a function of experience, social norms, and opportunity constraints. New to this version of the adaptation model is the inclusion of organizational commitment as a factor affecting choice of a response. It was included in recognition of the significant literature linking organizational commitment to withdrawal behavior. Hom and Griffeth's model (1995), for example, assigned a central role to organizational commitment. Unlike Hom and Griffeth's model, however, this model does not conceptualize the role of commitment as parallel to that of dissatisfaction. It is the negative affective state of dissatisfaction that provides the impetus to adapt, while commitment is assumed to influence how the person decides to respond to that affective state. Thus more committed individuals are expected to be less likely to adapt by withdrawal and more likely to attempt to make constructive changes. Finally, if the enacted behavior is successful in resolving the dissatisfaction, the cycle is assumed to end; if not, the process continues until dissatisfaction is reduced.

In the original model, response options were assumed to include the categories of withdrawal/avoidance, attempts to change undesired aspects of work, and aggression/retaliation; that model also assumed that individuals may opt to cognitively readjust their

Figure 12.2. An Individual Difference Model of Employee Adaptation.

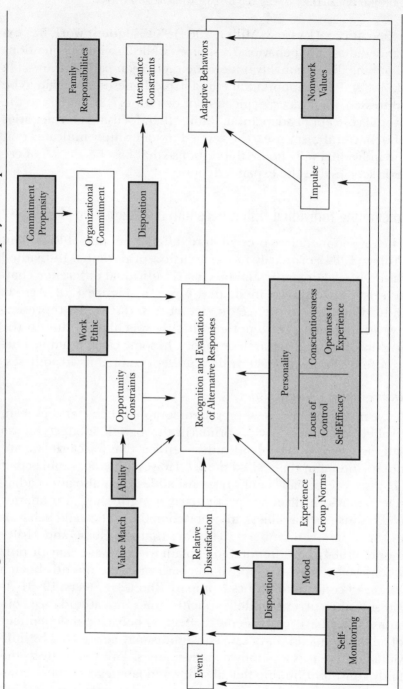

Source: Adapted from Rosse & Miller, 1984, p. 208.

expectations (Rosse & Miller, 1984). Subsequent work has expanded the set of behavioral responses while also raising questions about the dimensionality underlying them (compare Roznowski et al., 1992). While important methodological questions remain to be addressed, the exact specification of behaviors is secondary to the overall concept of adaptation. Rather than focusing on categories of behavioral responses, the revised model simply indicates that the individual will choose the response that best fits the set of criteria specified in the expanded model.

Integrating Individual Differences into the Adaptation Model

The revised model we present here differs from that of Rosse and Miller (1984) primarily in its inclusion of potential individual differences. For clarity, the proposed individual difference characteristics are shown in shaded boxes in Figure 12.2. Arrows indicating their influence on elements in the model represent hypotheses that are sometimes highly speculative, due to the scarcity of existing research or theory. In some cases, multiple linkages for the same characteristic represent competing hypotheses.

Demographic Characteristics

As we noted in our review, most demographic characteristics seem to affect adaptive behaviors primarily through their effects on job satisfaction or other job attitudes—effects that for clarity we are not including in the revised model. However, demographic characteristics (especially family responsibilities) may also affect adaptive behaviors directly, particularly by affecting attendance constraints (such as illness, transportation difficulties, and behavior of other family members). The fact that the Rosse and Miller model (1984) was intended to explain withdrawal behavior only when it occurs as an adaptive mechanism has frequently been a source of concern for critics (compare Rhodes & Steers, 1990). As a result, the current model explicitly notes that attendance constraints may have an exogenous effect on behavior, independent of adaptation, and that these constraints may be affected by individual differences in family responsibilities. This view reflects the fairly consistent finding that absence and lateness are more common (and turnover less common) among workers who have child-

or elder-care responsibilities. Family responsibilities are also hypothesized to have an effect on organizational commitment, because primary wage-earners develop greater commitment to continuance as their financial dependence on the employer increases.

Cognitive Ability

As our review indicates, cognitive ability has not been shown to play a significant role in explaining adaptive behaviors. One potential effect, however, may be that higher-ability employees perceive a wider range of adaptive responses as well as greater perceived ease of movement, which may in turn increase the viability of turnover and other withdrawal behaviors.

Personality

Personality factors appear to offer promise at a number of points in the model. Rosse and Miller (1984) suggested that relative dissatisfaction is triggered by some sort of stimulus, but they did not discuss the threshold value required for a stimulus to activate the adaptation process. Since it seems likely that individuals differ in their sensitivity to stimuli, we have included self-monitoring (Jenkins, 1993) as a factor moderating the relationship between stimuli and dissatisfaction. Although it is not clearly a personality trait, we are also including the propensity to commit (Mowday et al., 1982) as an antecedent of organizational commitment.

Our review also concludes that locus of control and self-efficacy are likely to affect choices of how to adapt, a suggestion also offered by Hom and Griffeth (1995). Individuals who perceive themselves to be more in control of their fate are more likely to choose active and constructive coping strategies (Parker, 1993; Rosse & Hulin, 1985; Withey & Cooper, 1989). Farrell (1983) described *voice* behaviors as being both active and constructive, and we would add that turnover (or *exit,* to use his terminology) may also fall in this category if the job change is to another job of equal or better caliber. Frayne and Latham's suggestion (1987) that specific self-efficacy beliefs may be more important than generalized expectancies or locus of control is one example of the type of hypothesis that might be tested in this area.

Conscientiousness is also hypothesized to affect choice of strategies, with conscientious employees being more likely to choose options involving constructive changes or loyalty than neglect, exit, or destructive behaviors. Finally, the characteristic of openness to experience may also be a determinant of behavioral choice, since employees high on this trait seem more likely to quit.

Personality may also have a direct effect on behavior, independent of the adaptation process. Low scores on the planfulness dimension of the characteristic of conscientiousness may explain impulsive acts of withdrawal, such as suddenly deciding to go to the beach rather than attend work. Although Rosse and Miller (1984) explicitly excluded impulsive acts from the domain of their adaptation model, for the sake of comprehensiveness we are now specifying a direct effect of impulsiveness on withdrawal behavior.

Values and Interests

Our review indicates that a primary role of values concerns the effects on satisfaction of a good match between individuals' values and their experience with the organization (labeled "value match" in Figure 12.2). Work ethic may also moderate the relationship between stimulus events and relative dissatisfaction: individuals for whom work is not important may not react strongly to conditions that others would find dissatisfying to the point of requiring adaptation. Work ethic is also hypothesized to affect the choice of adaptive behaviors; in particular, it is positively correlated with voice and negatively correlated with neglect.

Finally, the value of nonwork activities is hypothesized to have an exogenous effect on some withdrawal behaviors, independent of the adaptation process. Although the Rosse and Miller model (1984) was never intended to predict behaviors that were not motivated by adaptation, it has been criticized for not addressing the pull of attractive nonwork activities. The inclusion of nonwork values as a direct antecedent of behavior is intended to address this concern.

Disposition

Recent literature on affective disposition suggests that this factor is likely to play multiple roles in a model of adaptation, although ambiguities in the research base make it difficult to state with confidence precisely how these effects may occur. One direct effect seems to exist between affectivity and job satisfaction. Individuals characterized by high negative affectivity may be less likely to experience relative dissatisfaction, since their generally negative disposition is presumed to lower their frame of reference for evaluating job outcomes. Work by Cropanzano et al. (1993), Judge and Hulin (1992), and Necowitz and Roznowski (1991) suggests that disposition may also have a more direct effect on adaptive behaviors, although it is not clear whether this effect may in part be mediated by attendance constraints (for example, the tendency of depressed workers to be late or absent more often). Finally, George's study (1989) suggests that short-term mood may have a reciprocal relationship with absence and other "mood repair" behaviors.

Conclusion

It is commonplace for writers to conclude with a call for more research; and more often than not, such a plea is accompanied by concerns that future research be more theoretically driven. Since we have noted these deficiencies throughout this chapter, the reader will not be surprised to hear us repeat this call. But in doing so, we would like to suggest that the area of individual difference most in need of study may not be one of those targeted by this book. Although more work on individual differences in values, personality, and disposition is certainly warranted, the greatest urgency concerns study of individual differences in the *meaning* of "withdrawal" behaviors themselves.

The first author of this chapter (Rosse) is one of those who have called for aggregating behaviors into "families" of response. He is no longer so confident that this approach will provide the advances once envisioned. It is not that aggregating *similar* response tendencies is not a good idea; Hulin (1991) has provided sound theoretical and methodological reasons for doing so. The problem lies in determining that the behaviors included in the aggregations are in fact similar in meaning or function *from the perspective of the individual enacting them.*

This point is certainly not new. Johns and Nicholson (1982) argued that each absence event is unique and that to understand absence we need to understand these phenomenological differences, and Mobley (1982) noted that the antecedents and consequences of different withdrawal behaviors may make them functionally non-equivalent. Where we depart from previous writers who have adopted this perspective (for example, Rhodes & Steers, 1990) is their conclusion that it is therefore inappropriate to combine different behaviors into response families.

The best approach probably lies somewhere between these viewpoints. While we doubt that each episode of absence (or lateness, turnover, and so on) is phenomenologically unique, we have also come to doubt that factor analysis of behavior checklists is likely to produce scales of truly homogeneous response tendencies. One of the key challenges for researchers should be to determine the extent to which individual differences in the meaning of various withdrawal-type behaviors exist; this information seems critical for determining the viability of general withdrawal families. Doing so will require research methods that are more idiographic, longitudinal, and labor-intensive than we are accustomed to in this literature. The focus will likely be less on the covariance among behaviors and more on the process that led to particular behaviors.

We believe that the revised adaptation model we have presented offers a useful approach for this type of research. It shifts attention from the behaviors themselves to at least one of the processes underlying the behaviors. This both avoids some of the concerns about behavioral families (the model is equally useful without accepting that idea) and provides fertile ground for exploring individual differences in how people adapt. We hope that it encourages researchers to explore individual differences in a variety of areas that have to date received little attention. Examples might include differences in tolerance of dissatisfaction; differences in choice of alternative adaptive strategies, both at the macro (adapt versus not adapt) and micro (type of response) levels; differences in persistence in choice of behavior before switching to an alternative means of adapting; and differences in impulsiveness versus "rationality." We are sure researchers will see many others as well.

References

Ajzen, I. (1991). The theory of planned behavior. *Organizational Behavior and Human Decision Processes, 50,* 179–211.

Arvey, R. D., Bouchard, T. J., Segal, N. L., & Abraham, L. M. (1989). Job satisfaction: Environmental and genetic components *Journal of Applied Psychology, 74,* 187–192.

Bandura, A. (1982). Self-efficacy mechanism in human agency. *American Psychologist, 37,* 122–147.

Bandura, A. (1986). *Social foundation of thought and action: A social cognitive theory.* Englewood Cliffs, NJ: Prentice-Hall.

Barrick, M. R., & Mount, M. K. (1991). The Big Five personality dimensions and job performance: A meta-analysis. *Personnel Psychology, 44,* 1–26.

Beehr, T. A., & Gupta, N. (1978). A note on the structure of employee withdrawal. *Organizational Behavior and Human Performance, 21,* 73–79.

Bernardin, H. J. (1977). The relationship of personality variables to organizational withdrawal. *Personnel Psychology, 30,* 17–27.

Bills, M. A. (1923). Relation of mental alertness test score to positions and permanency in company. *Journal of Applied Psychology, 7,* 154–156.

Blau, G. J. (1987). Using a person-organization fit model to predict job involvement and organizational commitment. *Journal of Vocational Behavior, 30,* 240–257.

Blau, G. J. (1994). Developing and testing a taxonomy of lateness behavior. *Journal of Applied Psychology, 79,* 959–970.

Blau, G. J. (1995). Influence of group lateness on individual lateness: A cross-level examination. *Academy of Management Journal, 38,* 1483–1496.

Breaugh, J. A., & Dossett, D. L. (1989). Rethinking the use of personal history information: The value of theory-based biodata for predicting turnover. *Journal of Business and Psychology, 3,* 371–385.

Brooke, P. P. (1986). Beyond the Steers and Rhodes model of employee attendance. *Academy of Management Review, 11,* 345–361.

Brooke, P. P., & Price, J. L. (1989). The determinants of employee absenteeism: An empirical test of a causal model. *Journal of Occupational Psychology, 62,* 1–19.

Bycio, P., Hackett, R. D., & Alvares, K. M. (1990). Job performance and turnover: A review and meta-analysis. *Applied Psychology: An International Review, 39,* 47–76.

Clegg, C. W. (1983). Psychology of employee lateness, absence, and turnover: A methodological critique and an empirical study. *Journal of Applied Psychology, 68,* 88–101.

Cropanzano, R., & James, K. (1990). Some methodological considerations for the behavioral genetic analysis of work attitudes. *Journal of Applied Psychology, 75,* 433–439.

Cropanzano, R., James, K., & Konovsky, M. A. (1993). Dispositional affectivity as a predictor of work attitudes and job performance. *Journal of Organizational Behavior, 14,* 595–606.

Dalton, D. R., Todor, W. D., & Krackhardt, D. M. (1982). Turnover overstated: A functional taxonomy. *Academy of Management Review, 7,* 225–235.

Dodge, R. (1931). *Conditions and consequences of human variability.* New Haven, CT: Yale University Press.

Doob, L. W. (1947). The behavior of attitudes. *Psychological Bulletin, 84,* 888–918.

Dubin, R., Champoux, J., & Porter, L. (1975). Central life interests and organizational commitment of blue collar and clerical workers. *Administrative Science Quarterly, 20,* 411–421.

Farkas, A. J., & Tetrick, L. E. (1989). A three-wave longitudinal analysis of the causal ordering of satisfaction and commitment on turnover decisions. *Journal of Applied Psychology, 74,* 855–868.

Farrell, D. (1983). Exit, voice, loyalty, and neglect as responses to job dissatisfaction: A multi-dimensional scaling study. *Academy of Management Journal, 26,* 596–607.

Farrell, D., & Stamm, C. L. (1988). Meta-analysis of the correlates of employee absence. *Human Relations, 41,* 211–227.

Farris, G. F. (1971). A predictive study of turnover. *Personnel Psychology, 24,* 311–328.

Feldman, J. (1974). Race, economic class, and the intention to work: Some normative and attitudinal correlates. *Journal of Applied Psychology, 59,* 179–186.

Ferris, G. R., Bergin, T. G., & Wayne, S. J. (1988). Personal characteristics, job performance, and absenteeism of public school teachers. *Journal of Applied Social Psychology, 18,* 552–563.

Fichman, M. (1984). A theoretical approach to understanding employee absence. In P. S. Goodman, R. S. Atkin, & Associates, *Absenteeism: New approaches to understanding, measuring, and managing employee absence.* San Francisco: Jossey-Bass.

Fishbein, M., & Ajzen, I. (1975). *Beliefs, attitudes, intention, and behavior.* Reading, MA: Addison-Wesley.

Fisher, C. D., & Locke, E. A. (1991). Job satisfaction and dissatisfaction: Enhancing the prediction of consequences. In P. C. Smith, C. J. Cranny, & E. F. Stone (Eds.), *Job satisfaction: Advances in theory and research.* New York: Free Press.

Fleishman, J. A. (1984). Personality characteristics and coping patterns. *Journal of Health and Social Behavior, 25,* 229–244.

Frayne, C. A., & Latham, G. P. (1987). Application of social learning theory to employee self-management of attendance. *Journal of Applied Psychology, 73,* 387–392.

Froggatt, P. (1970). Short-term absence from industry: III. The inference of "proneness" and a search for causes. *British Journal of Industrial Medicine, 27,* 287–312.

Garrison, K. R., & Muchinsky, P. M. (1977). Evaluating the concept of absence proneness. *Personnel Psychology, 30,* 389–393.

Gatewood, R. D., & Feild, H. S. (1987). *Human resource selection.* Fort Worth, TX: Dryden Press.

George, J. M. (1988). *Rediscovering affect: The importance of mood at work.* Unpublished manuscript, College of Business, Texas A & M University, College Station.

George, J. M. (1989). Mood and absence. *Journal of Applied Psychology, 74,* 317–324.

Ghiselli, E. E. (1974). Some perspectives for industrial psychology. *American Psychologist, 80,* 80–87.

Gibson, R. O. (1966). Toward a conceptualization of absence behavior. *Administrative Sciences Quarterly, 11,* 107–133.

Gomez-Mejia, L. R., & Balkin, D. B. (1992). *Compensation, organizational strategy, and firm performance.* Cincinnati, OH: South-Western.

Goodale, J. G. (1973). Effects of personal background and training on work values of the hard-core unemployed. *Journal of Applied Psychology, 57,* 1–9.

Griffeth, R. W., & Hom, P. W. (1988). Locus of control and delay of gratification as moderators of employee turnover. *Journal of Applied Social Psychology, 18,* 1318–1333.

Guion, R., & Gottier, R. (1965). Validity of personality measures in personnel selection. *Personnel Psychology, 18,* 135–165.

Gupta, N., & Jenkins, G. D. (1979). *Employee withdrawal: An empirical look at the notion of a progression.* Paper presented at the 21st annual meeting of the Southwest Division, Academy of Management, Houston.

Gupta, N., & Jenkins, G. D. (1980). *The structure of withdrawal: Relationships among estrangement, tardiness, absenteeism, and turnover.* Springfield, VA: National Technical Information Service.

Hackett, R. D. (1989). Work attitudes and employee absenteeism: A synthesis of the literature. *Journal of Occupational Psychology, 62,* 235–248.

Hackett, R. D., & Guion, R. M. (1985). A reevaluation of the absenteeism–job satisfaction relationship. *Organizational Behavior and Human Decision Processes, 35*(3), 340–381.

Hakkinen, S., & Tolvainen, Y. (1960). Psychological factors causing labour turnover among underground workers. *Occupational Psychology, 34,* 15–30.

Hanisch, K. A., & Hulin, C. L. (1990). Job attitudes and organizational withdrawal: An examination of retirement and other voluntary withdrawal behaviors. *Journal of Vocational Behavior, 37,* 60–78.

Hanisch, K. A., & Hulin, C. L. (1991). General attitudes and organizational withdrawal: An evaluation of a causal model. *Journal of Vocational Behavior, 39,* 110–128.

Henne, D., & Locke, E. A. (1985). Job dissatisfaction: What are the consequences? *International Journal of Psychology, 20,* 221–240.

Hill, J. M., & Trist, E. L. (1953). A consideration of industrial accidents as a means of withdrawal from the work situation. *Human Relations, 6,* 357–380.

Hines, G. H. (1973). Achievement motivation, occupations, and labor turnover in New Zealand. *Journal of Applied Psychology, 58,* 313–317.

Hirschman, A. (1970). *Exit, voice, and loyalty.* Cambridge, MA: Harvard University Press.

Holahan, C. J., Mendel, R. M., & Gibson, F. W. (1981). Clarifying performance appraisal criteria. *Organizational Behavior and Human Performance, 28,* 164–188.

Holahan, C. J., & Moos, R. H. (1987). Personal and contextual determinants of coping strategies. *Journal of Personality and Social Psychology, 52,* 946–955.

Hom, P. W., & Griffeth, R. W. (1995). *Employee turnover.* Cincinnati, OH: South-Western.

Hough, L. M., Eaton, N. K., Dunnette, M. D., Kamp, J. D., & McCloy, R. A. (1990). Criterion-related validities of personality constructs and the effect of response distortion on those validities. *Journal of Applied Psychology, 75,* 581–595.

Hulin, C. L. (1991). Adaptation, persistence, and commitment in organizations. In M. D. Dunnette & L. M. Hough (Eds.), *Handbook of industrial and organizational psychology* (2nd ed.; Vol. 2). Palo Alto: Consulting Psychologists Press.

Hulin, C. L., Roznowski, M., & Hachiya, D. (1985). Alternative opportunities and withdrawal decisions: Empirical and theoretical discrepancies and an integration. *Psychological Bulletin, 97,* 233–250.

Ilgen, D., & Hollenbeck, J. R. (1977). The role of job satisfaction in absence behavior. *Organizational Behavior and Human Performance, 19,* 148–161.

Ingham, G. (1970). *Size of industrial organization and worker behaviour.* Cambridge, UK: Cambridge University Press.

Jackofsky, E. F. (1984). Turnover and job performance: An integrated process model. *Academy of Management Review, 9,* 74–83.

Jackofsky, E. F., & Peters, L. (1980). Task-relevant ability and turnover: Test of a model. *Southwest Academy of Management Proceedings,* 161–165.

Jackson, S. E., Brett, J. F., Sessa, V. I., Cooper, D. M., Julin, J. A., & Peyronnin, K. (1991). Some differences make a difference: Individual dissimilarity and group heterogeneity as correlates of recruitment, promotions, and turnover. *Journal of Applied Psychology, 76,* 675–689.

Jenkins, J. M. (1993). Self-monitoring and turnover: The impact of personality on intent to leave. *Journal of Organizational Behavior, 14,* 83–91.

Johns, G., & Nicholson, N. F. (1982). The meanings of absence: New strategies for theory and research. In B. M. Staw & L. L. Cummings (Eds.), *Research in organizational behavior* (Vol. 4). Greenwich, CT: JAI Press.

Judge, T. A. (1990). *Job satisfaction as a reflection of disposition: Investigating the relationship and its effect on employee adaptive behaviors.* Unpublished doctoral dissertation, University of Illinois at Urbana-Champaign.

Judge, T. A. (1993). Does affective disposition moderate the relationship between job satisfaction and voluntary turnover? *Journal of Applied Psychology, 78,* 395–401.

Judge, T. A., & Hulin, C. L. (1992). Job satisfaction and subjective well-being as determinants of job adaptation. *Academy of Management Best Paper Proceedings,* pp. 222–226.

Judge, T. A., & Hulin, C. L. (1993). Job satisfaction as a reflection of disposition: A multiple source causal analysis. *Organizational Behavior and Human Decision Processes, 56,* 388–421.

Judge, T. A., & Locke, E. A. (1993). Effect of dysfunctional thought processes on subjective well-being and job satisfaction. *Journal of Applied Psychology, 78,* 475–490.

Judge, T. A., and Wattanabe, S. (1995). Is the past prologue? A test of Ghiselli's Hobo Syndrome. *Journal of Management, 21,* 211–229.

Kobasa, S. C., Maddi, S. R., & Kahn, S. (1982). Hardiness and health: A prospective study. *Journal of Personality and Social Psychology, 42,* 168–177.

Landy, F. J., Vasey, J. J., & Smith, F. D. (1984). Methodological problems and strategies in predicting absence. In P. S. Goodman, R. S. Atkin, & Associates, *Absenteeism: New approaches to understanding, measuring, and managing employee absence.* San Francisco: Jossey-Bass.

Latham, G. P., & Frayne, C. A. (1989). Self-management training for increasing job attendance: A follow-up and a replication. *Journal of Applied Psychology, 74,* 411–416.

Lawshe, C., & Balma, M. (1966). *Principles of personnel testing*. New York: McGraw-Hill.

Lee, T. W. (1989). The antecedents and prediction of employee attendance. *Journal of Business Issues, 17,* 17–22.

Leigh, J. P. (1985). The effects of unemployment and the business cycle on absenteeism. *Journal of Economics and Business, 37,* 159–170.

Leigh, J. P. (1986). Correlates of absence from work due to illness. *Human Relations, 39,* 81–100.

Locke, E. (1976). The nature and causes of job satisfaction. In M. Dunnette (Ed.), *Handbook of industrial and organizational psychology*. Skokie, IL: Rand McNally.

MacKinney, A. C., & Wolins, L. (1960). Validity information exchange. *Personnel Psychology, 13,* 443–447.

March, J. G., & Simon, H. A. (1958). *Organizations*. New York: Wiley.

Markham, S. E. (1985). An investigation of the relationship between unemployment and absenteeism: A multi-level approach. *Academy of Management Journal, 28,* 228–234.

Martocchio, J. J. (1989). Age-related differences in employee absenteeism: A meta-analytic review. *Psychology and Aging, 4,* 409–414.

Martocchio, J. J., & Harrison, D. A. (1993). To be there or not to be there? Questions, theories, and methods in absenteeism research. In G. R. Ferris and K. R. Rowland (Eds.), *Research in Personnel and Human Resources Management, 11,* 259–328.

McEvoy, G. M., & Cascio, W. F. (1985). Strategies for reducing employee turnover: A meta-analysis. *Journal of Applied Psychology, 70,* 342–353.

McEvoy, G. M., & Cascio, W. F. (1987). Do good or poor performers leave? A meta-analysis of the relationship between performance and turnover. *Academy of Management Journal, 30,* 744–762.

Meyer, H., & Cuomo, S. (1962). *Who leaves? A study of background characteristics of engineers associated with turnover*. Crotonville, NY: Behavioral Science Research Division, General Electric Company.

Miceli, M. P. (1985). The effects of realistic job previews on newcomer behavior: A laboratory study. *Journal of Vocational Behavior, 26,* 277–289.

Mitra, A., Jenkins, G. D., & Gupta, N. (1992). A meta-analytic review of the relationship between absence and turnover. *Journal of Applied Psychology, 77,* 879–889.

Mobley, W. H. (1982). Some unanswered questions in turnover and withdrawal research. *Academy of Management Review, 7,* 111–116.

Mobley, W. H., Griffeth, R. W., Hand, H. H., & Meglino, B. M. (1979). Review and conceptual analysis of the employee turnover process. *Psychological Bulletin, 86,* 493–522.

Mowday, R. T., Porter, L. W., & Steers, R. M. (1982). *Employee organizational linkages: The psychology of commitment, absenteeism, and turnover.* San Diego, CA: Academic Press.

Muchinsky, P. M. (1977). Employee absenteeism: A review of the literature. *Journal of Vocational Behavior, 10,* 316–340.

Muchinsky, P. M., & Tuttle, M. L. (1979). Employee turnover: An empirical and methodological assessment. *Journal of Vocational Behavior, 14,* 43–77.

Necowitz, L. B., & Roznowski, M. (1991, Apr.). *The relationship between negative affectivity, job satisfaction, and employee behaviors.* Paper presented at the 6th annual meeting of the Society for Industrial and Organizational Psychology, St. Louis.

Nicholson, N. (1977). Absence behavior and attendance motivation: A conceptual synthesis. *Journal of Management Studies, 14,* 231–252.

Nicholson, N., & Goodge, P. M. (1976). The influence of social, organizational, and biographical factors on female absence. *Journal of Management Studies, 13,* 234–254.

Nicholson, N., & Johns, G. (1985). The absence culture and the psychological contract: Who's in control of absence? *Academy of Management Review, 10,* 397–407.

Ones, D. S., Schmidt, F. L., & Viswesvaran, C. (1993). Comprehensive meta-analysis of integrity test validities: Findings and implications for personnel selection and theories of job performance. *Journal of Applied Psychology, 78,* 679–703.

O'Reilly, C. A., Chatman, J., & Caldwell, D. F. (1991). People and organizational culture: A profile comparison approach to assessing person-organization fit. *Academy of Management Journal, 34,* 487–516.

Parker, L. E. (1993). When to fix it and when to leave: Relationship among perceived control, self-efficacy, dissent, and exit. *Journal of Applied Psychology, 78,* 949–959.

Parkes, K. R. (1984). Locus of control, cognitive appraisal, and coping in stressful episodes. *Journal of Personality and Social Psychology, 46,* 655–668.

Parsons, C. K., Herold, D. M., & Leatherwood, M. L. (1985). Turnover during initial employment: A longitudinal study of the role of causal attributions. *Journal of Applied Psychology, 70,* 337–341.

Pelicier, Y. (1987). Success and failure of treatment for depressive states. *Psicopatologia, 7,* 405–410.

Pervin, L. A. (1989). Persons, situations, interactions: The history of a controversy and a discussion of theoretical models. *Academy of Management Review, 14,* 350–360.

Porter, L. W., & Steers, R. M. (1973). Organizational, work, and personal factors in employee turnover and absenteeism. *Psychological Bulletin, 80,* 151–176.

Rhodes, S. R., & Steers, R. M. (1990). *Managing employee absenteeism.* Reading, MA: Addison-Wesley.

Roach, D. E. (1971). Double cross-validation of a Weighted Application Blank over time. *Journal of Applied Psychology, 55,* 157–160.

Robinson, S. L. (1994). *Explaining retreat, voice, silence, and destruction: The impact of work context on employees' responses to dissatisfaction.* Paper presented at the 54th annual meeting of the Academy of Management, Dallas.

Rosse, J. G. (1988). Relations among lateness, absence, and turnover: Is there a progression of withdrawal? *Human Relations, 41,* 517–531.

Rosse, J. G. (1991). Understanding employee withdrawal from work. In J. Jones, B. Steffy, & D. Bray (Eds.), *Applying psychology in business: The manager's handbook.* New York: Lexington Books.

Rosse, J. G., & Hulin, C. L. (1985). Adaptation to work: An analysis of employee health, withdrawal, and change. *Organizational Behavior and Human Decision Processes, 36,* 324–347.

Rosse, J. G., & Miller, H. E. (1984). Relationship between absenteeism and other employee behaviors. In P. S. Goodman, R. S. Atkin, & Associates, *Absenteeism: New approaches to understanding, measuring, and managing employee absence.* San Francisco: Jossey-Bass.

Roznowski, M., & Hanisch, K. A. (1990). Building systematic heterogeneity into attitude and behavior measures. *Journal of Vocational Behavior, 36,* 361–375.

Roznowski, M., & Hulin, C. L. (1991). The scientific merit of valid measures of general constructs with special reference to job satisfaction and job withdrawal. In C. J. Cranny, P. C. Smith, and E. F. Stone (Eds.), *Job satisfaction: Advances in theory and research.* New York: Free Press.

Roznowski, M., Rosse, J. G., & Miller, H. E. (1992). *The utility of broad-band measures of employee behavior: The case for employee adaptation and citizenship.* Paper presented at the 52nd annual meeting of the Academy of Management, Las Vegas.

Schmitt, N., Gooding, R. Z., Noe, R. A., & Kirsch, M. (1984). Meta-analysis of validity studies between 1964 and 1982 and the investigation of study characteristics. *Personnel Psychology, 37,* 407–422.

Schneider, B. (1983). Interactional psychology and organizational behavior. In B. M. Staw & L. L. Cummings (Eds.), *Research in organizational behavior* (Vol. 5). Greenwich, CT: JAI Press.

Schuh, A. J. (1967a). Application blank items and intelligence as predictors of turnover. *Personnel Psychology, 20,* 59–63.

Schuh, A. J. (1967b). The predictability of employee tenure: A review of the literature. *Personnel Psychology, 20,* 133–152.

Scott, K., & Taylor, G. (1985). An examination of conflicting findings on the relationship between job satisfaction and absenteeism: A meta analysis. *Academy of Management Journal, 28,* 599–612.

Searls, D. J., Braucht, G. N., & Miskimins, R. W. (1974). Work values and the chronically unemployed. *Journal of Applied Psychology, 59,* 93–95.

Smith, F. J. (1977). Work attitudes as predictors of specific day attendance. *Journal of Applied Psychology, 62,* 16–19.

Spector, P. E., & Michaels, C. E. (1986). Personality and employee withdrawal: Effects of locus of control on turnover. *Psychological Reports, 39,* 1005–1016.

Staw, B. M. (1980). The consequences of turnover. *Journal of Occupational Behavior, 1,* 253–273.

Staw, B. M., & Ross, J. (1985). Stability in the midst of change: A dispositional approach to job attitudes. *Journal of Applied Psychology, 70,* 469–480.

Steers, R. M., & Mowday, R. T. (1981). Employee turnover and postdecision accommodation processes. In B. M. Staw & L. L. Cummings (Eds.), *Research in organizational behavior.* Greenwich, CT: JAI Press.

Steers, R. M., & Rhodes, S. R. (1978). Major influences on employee attendance: A process model. *Journal of Applied Psychology, 63,* 391–407.

Steers, R. M., & Rhodes, S. R. (1984). Knowledge and speculation about absenteeism. In P. S. Goodman, R. S. Atkin, & Associates, *Absenteeism: New approaches to understanding, measuring, and managing employee absence* (pp. 229–275). San Francisco: Jossey-Bass.

Super, D. E. (1957). *Scientific careers and vocational development theory.* New York: Teachers College, Columbia University.

Terborg, J. R. (1981). Interactional psychology and research on human behavior in organizations. *Academy of Management Review, 6,* 560–576.

Terborg, J. R., Lee, T., Smith, F., Davis, G., & Turbin, M. (1982). Extension of the Schmidt and Hunter validity generalization procedure to the prediction of absenteeism behavior from knowledge of job satisfaction and organizational commitment. *Journal of Applied Psychology, 67,* 440–449.

Tett, R. P., Jackson, D. N., & Rothstein, M. (1991). Personality measures as predictors of job performance: A meta-analytic review. *Personnel Psychology, 44,* 703–742.

Thurstone, L. L. (1931). The measurement of social attitudes. *Journal of Abnormal and Social Psychology, 26,* 249–269.

Watson, D., Pennebaker, J. W., & Folger, R. (1987). Beyond negative affectivity: Measuring stress and satisfaction in the workplace. In *Job stress: From theory to suggestion.* Binghamton, NY: Haworth Press.

Wernimont, P. (1962). Re-evaluation of a Weighted Application Blank for office personnel. *Journal of Applied Psychology, 46,* 417–419.

Williams, C. R., & Livingstone, L. P. (1994). Another look at the relationship between performance and voluntary turnover. *Academy of Management Journal, 37,* 269–298.

Withey, M. J., & Cooper, W. H. (1989). Predicting exit, voice, loyalty, and neglect. *Administrative Science Quarterly, 34,* 521–539.

Wolpin, J., & Burke, R. J. (1985). Relationship between absence and turnover: A function of the measures? *Personnel Psychology, 38,* 57–75.

Part Three

Commentary

Chapter Thirteen

Learning About Individual Differences by Taking Situations Seriously

Keith Hattrup
Susan E. Jackson

In compiling this volume, the editor sought to achieve two objectives: reviewing the literature on individual differences and stimulating new research. This chapter addresses the second objective by providing an analysis both of the fundamental epistemological bases for understanding individual behavior in organizations and of the implications of various approaches to the study of individual behavior for research in industrial and organizational (I/O) psychology. Approaches to research on individual behavior generally fall into one of these three categories: (1) *person-based* approaches, which focus on variations between individuals, (2) *situational* approaches, which focus on variations in behavior between situations, and (3) *interactional* approaches, which attempt to take into account variations between individuals and between situations simultaneously. We argue that individual behavior in organizations is best conceptualized as the result of interactive processes that depend on the simultaneous interplay of differences between situations and differences between individuals. Unfortunately, as Snow (1989) noted, "The broad and fundamental implications of a person-situation interaction perspective for psychology have not been widely recognized or pursued" (p. 44). Certainly, this statement is true within I/O psychology.

Therefore, to assist I/O psychologists in thinking through the implications of the interactional perspective for studies of individual differences, we provide a framework for conceptualizing how research can focus simultaneously on individuals and on the situations in which they are embedded. To develop this framework, we begin by briefly describing the person-based, situational, and interactional perspectives. We then discuss each perspective in more detail and argue that improvements in our understanding of individual behavior will accrue only to the extent that future research incorporates the combined strengths of these three perspectives.

An Overview of the Three Traditions

The person-based, situational, and interactional perspectives have been described and compared by many authors (for example, Bowers, 1973; Chatman, 1989; Cronbach, 1957, 1975; Magnusson & Endler, 1977; Pervin, 1989; Schneider, 1983; Snow, 1989). Although the three approaches are often viewed as competing, we attempt in a later section to illustrate how all three approaches may fit within a larger interactional framework that accounts for multiple causes of behavior in organizations. In this section, we provide a brief overview of the person-based, situational, and interactional traditions.

The Person-Based Perspective

Historically, much of our understanding of individual behavior has been derived from the psychometric tradition, which seeks to identify patterns of consistency in variation *between* individuals, aggregating across situations (Ackerman & Humphreys, 1990). Indeed, most of our current theoretical notions about intelligence and personality must be understood within the context of psychometric research on variation between individuals (for example, Revelle, 1995; Sternberg, 1989a).

Despite the volume of research and a growing consensus about the most useful dimensions for describing individual differences, however, person-based approaches to understanding behavior have been criticized on empirical, logical, and philosophical grounds. Empirically, the weakness of such approaches is suggested by substantial evidence showing that differences between individuals often lack cross-situational consistency (for reviews, see Bowers, 1973; Mischel, 1990; Snyder & Ickes, 1985; Weiss & Adler, 1984). Indeed, Mischel's conclusion (1968) that inferences from traits are not predictively useful has often been considered one of the primary reasons for psychologists' disillusionment with trait-based conceptualizations of human behavior.

In the field of I/O psychology, temporal instability of some person attributes is suggested by the well-established simplex pattern of correlations among observations taken in similar settings but at different points in time. In the simplex, higher correlations are found for temporally close observations, while for observations that are separated in time, correlations decline as a function of temporal distance (for example, Ackerman & Humphreys, 1990; Deadrick & Madigan, 1990; Hulin, Henry, & Noon, 1990; see also Hartshorne & May, 1928). Such evidence has stimulated a healthy debate about how to conceptualize the role of person attributes as predictors of various criteria and how situations may moderate the effects of some differences between individuals.

The person-based perspective has attracted criticism on logical and philosophical grounds as well. Because this perspective seeks to identify differences between individuals, meaning attached to observations about an individual derives from comparing these observations to observations gathered about other persons (Kleinmuntz, 1967; Lamiell, 1987). This fact led Lamiell (1987) to conclude that "the empirical evidence generated by individual differences research has no legitimate interpretation whatsoever at the level of the individual" (p. 15). In other words, traditional person-based approaches to the study of individuals are ill-equipped to address the individual as an entity in and of itself. The study of variations between individuals does not explicitly address how individuals process information, nor does it address how they change, grow, or adapt over time and across situations. These limitations have become so serious a concern in some areas of psychology that Mislevy (1993) concluded that measurement of individual differences "faces today a crisis that would appear to threaten its very foundations" (p. 19). Or, as McNemar (1964) stated, "It is difficult to see how the available individual difference data can be used even as a starting point for generating a theory as to the process nature of general intelligence or of any other specified ability" (p. 881).

The Situational Perspective

The usual alternative to person-based approaches to understanding individual behavior is a focus on situations as causes of behavior. Situational approaches involve studying the effects of variations in situations, environments, or experimental treatments on the behavior of groups or individual subjects. Situational approaches seek to understand individual change or adaptation by studying the effects of variations in situations on individual responses. Advocating the use of experimental methods, situational researchers argue that greater predictive precision and understanding of behavior is gained through careful manipulation of the stimulus features that impinge on and affect individual behavior.

As Bowers (1973) pointed out in his critique of the situational perspective, however, research that addresses situational causes of behavior often relies on strong and unrepresentative manipulations of situation features, with adjustments in situations being made until reliable effects on behavioral responses are observed. Experiments are often designed to assess the impact of some proposed intervention or experimental treatment without a clear analysis of how the situation attributes fit within a larger taxonomic framework. Thus research in the situational perspective often fails to model real-world phenomena in systematic and representative ways (Brunswik, 1956). Moreover, whereas situational researchers are generally expected to assess and report at least some of the person attributes of study participants, researchers interested in drawing conclusions about person-based effects often make little attempt to rigorously measure or explicate the situations in which their research is conducted. Thus there exists today essentially no consensus about how to conceptualize and measure situation attributes using constructs that are psychologically meaningful and interesting (Chatman, 1989). This deficiency in our science threatens to stall the continuing advancement of the field.

A central and perplexing problem in the conceptualization of situations has been whether to characterize situations as objective realities, idiosyncratic perceptual realities, or something in between. J. Block and J. H. Block (1981) distinguished between three levels of situational analysis—levels that reflect successive stages of interpretation of the situation by the individual. First, individuals are exposed to a *physico-biological situation,* which represents the perceptually unfiltered objective sensory stimuli encountered by individuals. The objective unfiltered situation is free of the influences of individual perception, although (as described below) individuals may influence objective situations through their choice of situations or through their presence or actions in them.

The second level is the *canonical situation,* which represents the socially constructed and consensually accepted definition of the physico-biological situation encountered by individuals. The canonical situation is similar to Murray's "alpha press" (1938) and is thought to derive from social influence, communication, and shared socialization processes that operate to provide standards and frames of reference for the interpretation of physico-biological situations by individuals. Hence demonstrated agreement among individual perceivers is a typical prerequisite sought by researchers studying aspects of the canonical situation (for example, L. R. James, 1982; Kozlowski & Hattrup, 1992). In the field of I/O psychology, such approaches are common in the conceptualization and measurement of task or knowledge, skill, and ability (KSA) importance during job analyses (Harvey, 1991) and in the study of aggregated perceptions representing organizational climate and culture (for example, Kozlowski & Hattrup, 1992; L. R. James, L. A. James, & Ashe, 1990).

The third level of situational analysis, according to J. Block and J. H. Block (1981), is the *functional situation,* which reflects the individual's unique interpretation of the physico-biological and canonical situations. Murray (1938) referred to the perceived situation as the "beta press," whereas Lewin (1951) used the term "lifespace" to denote that an individual's behavior is a direct result of his or her perceptions of objective situations. In the field of I/O psychology, functional situations are the focus of research on individual *psychological climate,* which is presumed, like other conceptualizations of functional situations, to mediate between the physico-biological and canonical situations and individual behavior (L. R. James, 1982; L. R. James et al., 1990; Kozlowski & Hattrup, 1992). Moreover, like other functional situations, psychological climate is presumed to derive from interactions between persons and situations (L. A. James & L. R. James, 1989; L. R. James et al., 1990). In other words, individuals perceive and interpret situations in unique ways depending on aspects of the situations and aspects of the perceivers themselves. As is described in more detail below, the interactions between persons and situations in causing variation in functional situations provide the basis for dynamic processes whereby persons and situations become jointly interdependent over time.

Because individual behavior depends on perceptions of situation attributes, many authors have argued that the most relevant level of situational analysis for theory building and research is the functional situation (for example, Bowers, 1973; Endler, 1981; Magnusson, 1981). Indeed, as Thomas (1928) noted, "If men define situations as real, they are real in their consequences" (p. 572). However, because the functional situation is caused by an interaction of person and situation causes, situations become inherently inseparable from persons. In other words, functional situations are as much a result of the person as the person's behavior is the result of the perceived situation (Bowers, 1973). In consequence, a number of authors have noted that by carefully conceptualizing and studying objective physico-biological or canonical situation attributes, we can better understand the dynamic interactional processes whereby individuals come to interpret the same environmental stimuli in different ways (Ekehammer, 1974; Higgins, 1990).

The Interactional Perspective

Many psychologists recognize that debates about whether behavior is a function primarily of persons or of situations are essentially unresolvable and meaningless (for example, Chatman, 1989; Magnusson & Endler, 1977; Pervin, 1989; Schneider, 1983). Differences observed between individuals depend on the situations sampled, and the effects of situations depend on the individuals studied (Bowers, 1973; Magnusson & Endler, 1977; Raush, 1977).

Interactional approaches attempt to identify how different types of individuals respond to different situations in predictably unique ways. For example, some individuals may respond to increases in time demands with a sense of exhilaration, whereas others may experience a sense of unpleasant stress. Changes in a situation cause changes in behavioral response (increased activity or withdrawal), but relatively stable differences between people determine which specific responses they exhibit. Likewise, the effects of differences between individuals on criterion responses depend on the situations in which individual differences are observed.

Interactional approaches also recognize that individuals and situations are causally interdependent. Individuals are shaped by the situations they encounter, and situations are shaped by the individuals that occupy them (Schneider, 1983, 1987). Because of preexisting differences, individuals seek to enter differing situations, and their responses to situation attributes depend on the meaning they impose on their perceptions of a situation and its opportunities or demands.

Interactional psychology represents a comprehensive approach to understanding human behavior, subsuming several different theoretical and empirical approaches to the study of individual responses. Indeed, interactional psychology underscores the fact that various approaches to understanding human behavior are complementary rather than competing. Generally, interactional psychology rests on the following core assumptions:

1. The behavioral, cognitive, affective, or physiological responses or actions of persons are the result of both stable differences between individuals and variations in situations. Therefore, to understand individuals, one must distinguish between the criterion responses of interest and the person and situation causes that determine observed outcomes (J. Block & J. H. Block, 1981; Davis-Blake & Pfeffer, 1989).

2. Individuals should be treated as multidimensional, whole entities. That is, persons have multiple attributes that are inseparable at the level of individuals and that operate in concert to shape the responses of individuals (Chatman, 1989).

3. Situations should be treated as multidimensional, whole entities. In other words, situations have multiple attributes that operate in concert to influence individual behavior (Magnusson, 1981).

4. The responses of individuals are also multidimensional. In psychological research, the responses of interest generally include physiological responses, as well as elements of behavior, cognition, and affect (Magnusson & Endler, 1977; Snyder & Ickes, 1985).

5. And finally, the responses of individuals (that is, their behaviors, thoughts, and feelings) arise out of a dynamic process: responses unfold through time, and persons and situations are bound together through a feedback system in which a somewhat malleable person and a somewhat malleable situation are both cause and effect (for example, Ekehammer, 1974; Higgins, 1990; Pervin, 1989).

We believe that a complete understanding of the responses of people within organizations requires that our field more fully incorporate the perspective of interactional psychology. Yet our current conceptual models and empirical research often fail to reflect an appreciation of the fundamental elements of the interactional perspective. There are undoubtedly many explanations for this, including a paucity of compelling theories, practical constraints that make it difficult to conduct appropriate research, statistical complexities that create difficulties for data analysis and interpretation, and peculiarities of the publication process. In addition, the interactional perspective itself suffers from several limitations, including the complexity inherent in interactive models, the lack of adequate theoretical taxonomies of situations, and the difficulty of separating presumably interdependent person and situation attributes for analysis and study. Despite these difficulties, we believe that advancements in our understanding of individual behavior in organizations will accrue more rapidly if researchers adopt the conceptual and analytic rigor of an interactional framework. This is not to say that all research studies should test interactional models. Rather, the argument is that all research studies should be designed with a broad interactional framework in mind, and results should be interpreted accordingly.

The Need for an Integrative Approach to the Study of Persons and Situations

In an excellent discussion of psychological theories, McGuire (1983) described four basic types of theories. From the most simple and primitive to the most sophisticated, the theory types are: guiding idea, categorical or taxonomic, process, and axiomatic. Ultimately, scientists seek to develop axiomatic theories. This requires developing a small number of axioms that can be combined to yield more complex theories. As a field, psychology has not advanced very far in the development of axiomatic theories. Indeed, while most psychological theories include a clear guiding idea, they are less developed in terms of specifying relevant taxonomies and processes. Thus most of our theories are incomplete, partial depictions of behavior.

The next level of sophistication above a guiding idea is a taxonomic theory. Taxonomic theories provide representations and definitions for organizing a large set of constructs into a manageable number of categories. At a minimum, taxonomic theories offer researchers a checklist of predictors and criteria to consider when designing their research. Good taxonomic theories offer guidance to researchers by providing a metric for determining whether two measures tap equivalent constructs. Current debates about how best to define the construct domains of personality and ability clearly represent attempts to develop consensus about the appropriate taxonomic components relevant to the study of person-based effects.

A guiding-idea theory—whether it is person-based, situational, or interactional—cannot be adequately tested until taxonomic components have been explicated. Cronbach and Snow (1977) were referring to this task when they asserted that "the whole process of seeking order in the behavioral or biological sciences is one of partitioning a grand matrix of organisms and situations into blocks in such a manner that a single generalization applies to all organisms and all situations classified within a block. The science of human behavior is built up by identifying a class of persons who respond similarly to some particular range of situations" (p. 3). Unfortunately, a general framework for identifying these "blocks" in psychology has not yet been developed.

Ultimately, empirical research will verify the most useful blocks, or taxons, to include in theory and research. However, just as the testing of guiding ideas requires theoretical advances at the next level of sophistication (that is, taxonomies), it is also true that the development of taxonomies requires theoretical advances at a higher level of sophistication. In other words, the development of adequate taxonomies requires some understanding of the processes through which causal variables impact outcomes of interest.

Process theories attempt to explicate the intermediate steps that link together categories of variables. Some interactional theories represent thorough attempts to specify the process relationships whereby the effects of situations and of persons combine to influence outcomes of interest. For example, Schneider's attraction-selection-attrition theory (1987) outlines several social processes through which people and situations impact each other and interact to determine observed behavior. Other theorists posit cognitive or self-regulatory processes as explanations for how person attributes combine with situation cues to result in behavior (for example, Christiansen, 1993; Pervin, 1989; Revelle, 1993).

The person-based, situational, and interactional perspectives each represent tentative guiding-idea theories that are being developed into higher-level taxonomic and process theories. Although the three perspectives are sometimes viewed as competing, another way of thinking about their interrelationship is that each is focused on developing different pieces of a larger puzzle. For example, relative to the other perspectives, person-based research has yielded more information relevant to predicting individual differences in criterion responses from person attributes that are presumed to be fairly stable across time and situations. By comparison, situational and interactional research has yielded more information about social, developmental, and experiential processes underlying behavior. Throughout the remainder of this chapter, we attempt to illustrate how each of the perspectives might fit within a general theoretical framework for understanding behavior in organizations. In the next section, we describe the theoretical framework; and in later sections, we discuss some implications and directions for future research that addresses interactional processes in organizational behavior.

A General Framework for Studying Persons Within Situations

The conceptual framework we wish to describe has both an abstract structure and some specific content. The abstract structure has three basic dimensions, including person differences, situation differences, and criterion response differences. (Time can be thought of as a fourth dimension. We address the dynamic influences of time in a subsequent section of this chapter.) The abstract three-dimensional structure, shown in Figure 13.1, is explained first. Then, to illustrate the abstract structure and make it more meaningful, we add taxonomic content to it. Given the state of current research, however, our attempts to provide tentative taxonomic content are necessarily speculative.

The Structure of the General Framework

Figure 13.1 presents the structure of a general framework for characterizing the relevant dimensions that must be considered in studying persons in the context of situations. The basis for the model is the notion that behavior and other responses of individuals in organizations depend simultaneously on variation between individuals and variation between situations. Figure 13.1 provides a relatively simple representation of mechanistic forms of interactional effects involving persons and situations as causes of criterion responses. These mechanistic interactional processes in turn provide the basis for more complex dynamic interactional processes, as we describe in more detail below.

Between-Person Effects

The front face of the structure shown in Figure 13.1 represents variance between persons, the traditional focus of individual difference research. Although multiple person constructs (P_{i-n}) can be used to capture between-person differences, for simplicity only two (P1 and P2) are shown in Figure 13.1. For each person construct in the figure, vertical lines represent differences between individuals in their standing on the construct. For example, the three regions represented within P1 along the horizontal axis of Figure 13.1 represent individuals who are at low, medium, and high levels on the construct labeled P1. In many cases, of course, between-person differences are assumed to be continuous rather than discrete. In these cases, an infinite number of vertical lines would be needed to characterize the range of variance between individuals.

Figure 13.1 also illustrates that many different criteria (C_{i-n}) may be of interest to researchers; again, however, for simplicity only two criterion constructs are shown (C1 and C2). Within each criterion

Figure 13.1. General Framework for Conceptualizing Persons, Situations, and Effects on Criterion Responses.

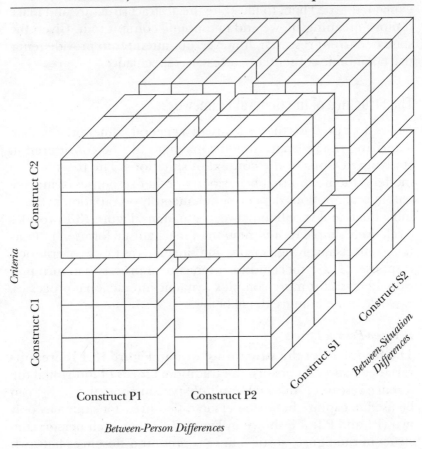

construct, horizontal lines denote different levels of criterion response, such as low, medium, or high. This heuristic representation does not preclude conceptualizing criterion responses as continuously distributed.

The horizontal and vertical axes of each smaller cube shown in the figure can, when considered together, be used to form a bivariate scatter plot or regression line to represent how individual differences on one construct (for example, P1) relate to individual differences in responses on a criterion (for example, C2). Given this approach to representing person-based constructs and criteria, it should be apparent that researchers and practitioners who seek to maximize criterion outcomes in organizations through selection, classification, and placement generally focus their attention on the front faces of the smaller cubes shown in Figure 13.1.

Research that focuses on how differences between people on a given construct (for example, intelligence) relate to differences between people in responses (for example, job performance) requires that researchers make choices about how to treat variation in situations. For example, person-based researchers might select one situation in which to study individual differences (they might, for example, study people in one type of job), and/or they might aggregate across situations (they might, for example, study people in multiple jobs but ignore situation differences associated with the different jobs as a source of explanatory variation). The focus is on how variations in stable traits or temporary states relate to variations in observable responses. Once individuals are identified as being high or low on relevant constructs, such as ability, self-efficacy, or neuroticism, their criterion responses are expected to be predictable across situations. When predictability is low, reconsideration typically focuses on the person construct or the criterion construct. That is, researchers might ask questions such as these: Would other person constructs be more predictive of this criterion? Do individual differences on this particular construct predict other types of responses? Is the lack of a relationship explained by poor measurement of these constructs? What is often missing from this list of possible explanations for weak relationships is systematic exploration of the situation axis represented in Figure 13.1.

Between-Situation Effects

Whereas person-based approaches to the study of behavior focus on the horizontal axis in Figure 13.1 and tend to ignore the depth axis, situational approaches to individual behavior focus on the depth dimension and tend to ignore the horizontal axis. In Figure 13.1, variations in situations are represented by the depth dimension of each cube. The figure shows two situation constructs (S1 and S2), each having three levels; the three levels presented along the situation axis of one situation construct might, for example, represent situations that are low, medium, and high in complexity. To represent the effects of situations, differences along the situation axis of the cube in Figure 13.1 can be plotted against the criterion axis. For example, one might expect that greater situation complexity would result in lower performance, because the dominant response on complex tasks is less likely to be appropriate than the dominant response on simple tasks (Zajonc, 1965). In the field of I/O psychology, the situational perspective often is adopted by those who might seek to manage individual behavior through training, job (re)design, socialization, compensation, or other manipulations of the situational stimuli encountered by organization members.

Studies of the effects of differences between situations may involve selecting a single person to study, but more often such studies aggregate across individuals. For example, an idiographic researcher might select a single individual from the person axis of Figure 13.1 and then study the effects of differences between situations on that individual's behavior. This is essentially the approach used in the case study tradition. Nomothetic researchers include many subjects in their studies and then aggregate across the person axis to study the effects of situations. Regardless of which research design is used, situational researchers usually make assumptions about which classes of individuals will be influenced by differences between situations and then select these individuals as subjects for their studies of situation effects. Studies within I/O psychology, for example, generally focus on the effects of situations on people who are employed in large U.S. organizations. Such people are likely to be "average" or "normal" on a number of person attributes, including age, intelligence, personality, socioeconomic status, and so forth. Different conclusions might be drawn about the effects of situations if different sets of individuals were studied.

When weak associations are observed between a situation construct and criterion response, reconsideration typically focuses on the situation construct or the criterion construct. That is, situational researchers might ask questions such as these: What other aspects of the situation might be controlling responses on this criterion? Do situation differences on this particular construct predict other types of responses? Is the lack of a relationship explained by an inadequate manipulation of the situation or poor measurement of the criterion? What is often missing from this list of possible explanations for weak relationships is systematic exploration of the person-based dimension represented in Figure 13.1.

The Interactional Approach

Studies of individual differences and studies of situation effects focus on one axis (person or situation) of the cubes shown in Figure 13.1 without simultaneous consideration of the other axis. In contrast, an interactional approach attempts to model the effects of person and situation differences simultaneously. Both sources of variance are considered potentially important determinants of individual behavior. Because interactions can often be considered symmetric (J. Cohen & P. Cohen, 1983), an interactional researcher attempts to explore how the effects of person differences on criteria are moderated by situation differences and how situation effects depend on differences between individuals. Such effects might be represented graphically by three-dimensional plots within the structure represented in Figure 13.1 (see Edwards, 1991).

When interactional researchers encounter low associations between their predictors and criteria, their reconsideration includes all of the questions asked by person-based and situational researchers, along with questions about potential moderated relationships. Do individual differences on a particular person construct (for example, P1) interact with situation differences (for example, S2) to explain responses on the criterion of interest? What form does this interaction take? Are more complex interactional effects also present—for example, are the effects of P1 evident only in situations that are low on S1 and high on S2? Are the effects of P1 contingent on variations in other person constructs (for example, P2)? The interactional perspective underlies research and practice in the areas of adaptive testing, individually adapted training, and the provision of "cafeteria-style" benefit plans.

Because interactive approaches adapt situational interventions to variations in individuals or study differences between persons within the context of varied situations, higher predictive validities between person and/or situation causes and criterion responses should be expected in those approaches than in approaches that ignore interactions between causes (for example, Chatman, 1989; Snyder & Ickes, 1985). For example, by focusing on a situationally specific person construct, such as test anxiety, and the types of situations in which the person construct is relevant (that is, testing situations), a researcher may obtain higher relationships between the person construct and behavior within a limited range of situations than would be obtained if he or she had not tied the person construct to particular sets of situations (Snyder & Ickes, 1985). Similarly, meta-analytic reviews of the validity of general cognitive ability (for example, J. E. Hunter & R. F. Hunter, 1984) have demonstrated that relationships between cognitive and psychomotor abilities and criteria are moderated by job or situation complexity. That is, if the situation axis of one cube in Figure 13.1 represents low, medium, and high job complexity, a regression line that relates cognitive ability (on the person axis) to job performance (on the criterion axis) is flattest in the front "slice" of the situation axis, somewhat steeper in the middle slice, and steepest in the back slice (along the situation axis of the relevant cube). Such evidence underscores the fact that the effects of person differences on specific criteria are ultimately embedded in a finite range of situations, and the effects of situations are embedded in a finite range of persons (Raush, 1977). The interactional framework recognizes that person, situation, and criterion constructs may be defined by the range of situations or persons or criteria for which they are presumed to function. It emphasizes that relationships among persons, situations, and criterion responses should be based on careful explication of how particular aspects of persons interact with particular situation attributes to influence particular criterion responses (J. Block & J. H. Block, 1981; Snyder & Ickes, 1985).

Levels of Specificity for Person, Situation, and Criterion Constructs

Within each of the three axes of Figure 13.1, constructs can be conceptualized at varying degrees of specificity. For example, general cognitive ability (or g) is thought to subsume more specific ability factors, such as fluid, crystallized, and spatial ability (Carroll, 1993; Lubinski & Dawis, 1992). Each of these specific factors can be further differentiated into even more specific constructs. Indeed, much of this book focuses on the degrees of specificity that most appropriately represent variance between persons.

The interactional framework underscores the importance of conceptualizing construct specificity for persons, situations, and criteria *simultaneously*. While person, situation, and criterion constructs can all be conceptualized at various levels of specificity (compare Rushton, Brainerd, & Pressley, 1983), no particular level of specificity is inherently more appropriate than any other. Consequently, the challenge is to build theories that describe relationships among constructs that are appropriately specified in terms of maximizing predictive validity. In other words, in selecting the level of specificity to use when conceptualizing person constructs, researchers need to simultaneously consider the level of specificity that applies to both the criteria and the situations of interest. Furthermore, as is described below, the issue of specificity is intricately bound up with the issue of the appropriate taxonomic *content* used in filling out a general framework for understanding individual behavior. We provide some tentative suggestions for taxonomic content next. Then, in a later section, we describe issues to consider in linking together taxonomies of persons, situations, and criteria in the development of process theories of the causes of behavior in organizations.

The Content of the General Framework

In this section, we attempt to outline a comprehensive set of construct domains that might characterize the ways in which variance could be observed on each axis of Figure 13.1. Our suggestions about relevant content represent an attempt to illustrate how systematic thinking about construct specificity could proceed in moving toward taxonomic theories of individual behavior in organizations. The taxonomic content of this general framework incorporates the notion that person, situation, and criterion constructs are each organized hierarchically from relatively global constructs to very specific constructs.

Table 13.1 presents an initial attempt to characterize potential constructs at varying degrees of specificity for each of the three axes presented in Figure 13.1, including person constructs, situation constructs, and criterion constructs. In selecting general construct domains, we were guided by two considerations. First, we attempted to reflect the extant research in I/O psychology, using construct labels that would be familiar to readers. Second, we sought to arrange construct domains in a way that would highlight potential complementarity among the major domains within each of the three dimensions. Thus, although there is some variability in the domains comprising the major dimensions, the domains of behavior, cognition, and affect are represented in differences between criterion responses, persons, and situations. A number of authors have argued that interactional research should be based on the development of equivalence classes of persons and situations described in a common language (for example, Ekehammer, 1974; Graham, 1976; Higgins, 1990; Lewin, 1951; Wright & Mischel, 1987). For example, Fleishman's ability requirements approach to conceptualizing persons and situations is based on rating tasks (that is, situations) in terms of their requirements for various person attributes (Fleishman & Mumford, 1988; Fleishman & Quaintance, 1984; see also Wright & Mischel, 1987). However, as Chatman (1989) argues, such approaches risk anthropomorphizing situations in a way that obscures their more important objective properties. What is needed, according to Chatman (1989), are conceptualizations of persons and situations in mutually relevant and comparable terms.

We also sought to identify a few tentative subordinate-level constructs for each of the domains. We purposely chose not to be exhaustive, however, to underscore the fact that the taxonomy presented in Table 13.1 represents only an illustration of how we might eventually map out the domains of relevant variables for research in I/O psychology.

Between-Person Differences

With respect to differences between individuals, we identified five major domains of constructs, each of which can each be differentiated into a larger number of more specific constructs depending on theoretical and pragmatic purposes. These domains are based on our reading of individual difference research in I/O psychology. The five domains in the person (P) facet include *cognitive* (P1), *behavioral* (P2), *affective* (P3), *physical* (P4), and *social* (P5) differences.

In the *cognitive* domain, a basic distinction between cognitive abilities and cognitive styles can be specified. Cognitive abilities represent perhaps the most thoroughly researched category of person constructs. Carroll (1993), for example, identified several hierarchical levels of abilities, with general cognitive ability, or *g*, representing the highest-order construct. In Carroll's research (1993), *g* subsumed a number of second-order constructs, such as visual/ spatial ability (g_v), fluid ability (g_f), and crystallized intelligence (g_c), with each of the second-order constructs differentiated into even more specific constructs.

Table 13.1. An Initial Taxonomy of Domains Representing Differences Between Persons, Situations, and Criterion Responses.

Person Differences	Situation Differences	Criterion Response Differences
(P1) Cognitive	**(S1) Information**	**(C1) Cognitive**
$(P1_i)$ Abilities	$(S1_i)$ Availability	$(C1_i)$ Job Knowledge
$(P1_{ii})$ Styles	$(S1_{ii})$ Ambiguity	$(C1_{ii})$ Climate Perceptions
•	$(S1_{iii})$ Consensus	•
•	•	•
•	•	•
$(P1_n)$	•	$(C1_i)$
	$(S1_n)$	
(P2) Behavioral	**(S2) Task**	**(C2) Behavioral**
$(P2_i)$ Personality	$(S2_i)$ Autonomy	$(C2_i)$ Role-Required Behavior
•	$(S2_{ii})$ Structure	$(C2_{ii})$ Extra-Role Behavior
•	•	•
•	•	•
$(P2_n)$	•	•
	$(S2_n)$	$(C2_n)$
(P3) Affective	**(S3) Physical**	**(C3) Affective**
$(P3_i)$ Affectivity	$(S3_i)$ Privacy	$(C3_i)$ Satisfaction
$(P3_{ii})$ Values	$(S3_{ii})$ Danger	$(C3_{ii})$ Commitment
•	•	•
•	•	•
$(P3_n)$	$(S3_n)$	$(C3_n)$
(P4) Physical	**(S4) Social**	**(C4) Physiological**
$(P4_i)$ Demographic Status	$(S4_i)$ Role Setting	$(C4_i)$ Short-Term Stresses
$(P4_{ii})$ (Dis)ability	$(S4_{ii})$ Normative Strength	$(C4_i)$ Short-Term Stresses
•	•	•
•	•	•
•	•	•
$(P4_n)$	$(S4_n)$	$(C4_n)$
(P5) Social		
$(P5_i)$ Socioecnonomic Status		
$(P5_{ii})$ Marital Status		
•		
•		
•		
$(P5_n)$		

Whereas cognitive *abilities* reflect individuals' mental energies or capacities, cognitive *styles* reflect individuals' preferences in applying their cognitive, affective, and other attributes in responding. For example, the research done by Sternberg (1989b) on executive, judicial, and legislative styles of thinking attempted to identify stable differences between individuals in their preferences for applying abilities in creative, analytic, or rule-guided ways. There is a great need to identify how styles of thinking determine behavior in organizations and how cognitive styles interact with other person constructs and with situations in influencing behavior in organizations.

The *behavioral* domain within between-person differences in Table 13.1 subsumes personality, among other as-yet-unidentified constructs, with the Big Five dimensions attracting the most attention in the I/O literature on personality. In addition, self-efficacy (Bandura, 1986) is an important construct in the personality domain, and research should continue to explore its role in organizational behavior. Additional personality constructs might include Type A and B behavior patterns, achievement motivation (McClelland, Atkinson, Clark, & Lowell, 1953), authoritarianism (Adorno, Frenkel-Brunswik, Levinson, & Sanford, 1950), Machiavellianism (Geis, 1978), dogmatism (Rokeach, 1960), locus of control (Rotter, 1966), and self-esteem (Wylie, 1974).

Individual differences in *affect* represent a third construct domain. Positive and negative affectivity are seen as stable dispositional tendencies to experience a particular feeling state in relation to situational stimuli (Levin & Stokes, 1989). Stable affect may derive from genetic sources (for example, Arvey, Bouchard, Segal, & Abraham, 1989) or through experience. Values, on the other hand, reflect differences between individuals in preferences and expectations (Dawis, 1991). Research on the dimensionality of affective constructs in I/O psychology and their relationships to other person and situation variables represents as-yet-uncharted territory.

The *physical* domain includes demographic characteristics, such as age, sex, and race. A great deal of research has sought to identify interactions between race and sex and ability constructs in the prediction of job performance. The general conclusion from these research efforts is that abilities relate equally to criteria for members of different race groups. However, the notion that men and women, for example, rely on different attributes when performing at work has attracted attention (Schneider & Schmitt, 1986) and should continue to be explored in future research.

Physical (dis)abilities are represented as a second construct in the physiological domain. Fleishman's research (1964) represents the most advanced theoretical explication of physical ability constructs in the I/O literature. Moreover, research by Ackerman (1988) and Fleishman and colleagues (see Fleishman & Mumford, 1989) on the contribution of cognitive and physical abilities to performance over time represents a distinctly person-by-situation interactional perspective on the determinants of criterion response differences.

Finally, the *social* domain includes specific constructs such as socioeconomic and marital status. Very little research has sought to identify either various degrees of specificity in this domain or potential interactive relationships with other individual difference domains in determining criterion responses. Yet the changing nature of families in the United States and obvious relationships between socioeconomic status, race, and education suggest a need for future research on these content domains.

Between-Situation Differences

As was discussed above, theoretical specification of situation constructs has received much less attention from I/O psychologists than has theoretical specification of person constructs. Although individuals' responses to situational stimuli are undoubtedly determined in large part by their interpretations of situations (in other words, by *functional* situations), a clearer understanding of the processes by which individuals understand and react to their environments can be gained through careful explication and study of physico-biological and/or canonical situations. With that goal in mind, in Table 13.1 we provide a tentative taxonomy of physico-biological and canonical situation attributes that may be relevant in the study of organizational behavior. Based on our review of research on situations (for example, Magnusson, 1981; Moos, 1973), we identified four domains of objective and consensually accepted situation attributes that are likely to characterize the range of possible situation differences encountered in organizations. Cutting across all four domains is the extent to which situation attributes present strong versus weak situational cues to perceivers (Snyder & Ickes, 1985). Strong situations are those in which individual behavior is largely situationally determined; weak situations provide greater latitude for individual interpretation and action.

The first domain for describing situations captures the *information* attributes (S1) of situations, including the availability, ambiguity, and degree of consensus (versus conflict) among information cues (compare Hackman, 1992). Situations with more information, less ambiguity, and less conflicting information are strong relative to those with fewer cues, less clarity, or more conflicting cues.

Task attributes (S2) embedded in situations may include constructs that reflect the amount of autonomy provided by tasks and the degree of structure inherent in task demands. Tasks with greater autonomy and lower structure represent weaker settings and therefore may show stronger interactions with person attributes than those characterized by less autonomy and greater structure.

Physical attributes (S3) may include the amount of privacy and the amount of objective danger inherent in situations. Dangerous situations tend to constrain behavior toward fight-or-flight responses, with the choice between these alternatives depending in large part on interactions with person differences. More private settings are weaker and therefore more susceptible to between-person differences in interpretation and response. Public settings constrain individual behavior in the direction of normative or role-related situational demands. In other words, interactions should be expected between the physical attribute of situation privacy and *social* attributes (S4) related to others' expectations or desires. Moreover, these social attributes may themselves vary in the extent to which they represent strong versus weak role demands or normative expectations.

Clearly, developing better theoretical conceptualizations of situations is an important research objective. Until greater understanding of situations and their influences on individual behavior is developed, much of our research on person-by-situation interactions, both in static contexts and in dynamic processes over time, will be stifled.

Criterion Response Differences

In the field of I/O psychology, the dearth of adequate theory regarding criterion response differences is well known. Referred to collectively as the "criterion problem," conceptualizations of relevant response constructs have tended to follow, rather than precede, their use in research and theory. That is, researchers and practitioners have often regarded criteria as given rather than conceptually derived. For example, measures of output, error, turnover rate, absenteeism, and organization-level profitability and competitiveness have been regarded as adequate measures against which the theoretically more complex individual difference or situation difference variables could be validated.

Reviews of criteria in organizational research now attempt to more carefully explicate the underlying constructs that might be represented in criterion measures (for example, Austin & Villanova, 1992; Campbell, McCloy, Oppler, & Sager, 1993). As part of that explication, researchers are careful to distinguish between response criteria that are situationally determined and those that can be controlled by individual effort and volition (Austin & Villanova, 1992; Campbell et al., 1993). Moreover, recent research in I/O psychology has also attempted to expand the domain of relevant criteria to include contextual behaviors, such as organizational citizenship and team facilitation (for example, Borman & Motowidlo, 1993). These approaches take into account the fact that a variety of behaviors contribute to organizational functioning.

Yet our historical emphasis on *performance* criteria and the tendency for I/O psychologists to equate criterion responses with performance-related outcomes represents a limited view. An expanded view of criteria means conceptualizing the entire range of possible individual responses. Clearly, a great deal of past research has included nonperformance outcome measures, but such research has often been conceptually segregated from research on performance. Research that considers several criterion domains simultaneously is necessary in order to move toward a more sophisticated understanding of how persons and situations combine to affect behavior in organizations. In this section, we attempt to outline a taxonomy of potential criteria. As before, our initial taxonomy is based on our review of extant literature and is meant to be illustrative rather than definitive.

We have categorized relevant criterion (C) constructs into four primary domains: *cognitive* (C1), *behavioral* (C2), *affective* (C3), and *physiological* (C4). *Cognitive* criteria represent what an individual knows or thinks. For example, research on the development of job knowledge (J. E. Hunter, 1986) investigates cognitive outcomes that can, in some examples, be studied independent of behavioral responses. Likewise, climate perceptions or attributions of meaning represent cognitions that are presumed to be causally prior to affective responses (L. A. James & L. R. James, 1989). Climate perceptions become criterion outcomes rather than situation attributes, as described previously, when they are assumed to result from the interaction of causes based on variations between persons and physico-biological or canonical situations.

Behavioral criteria represent the domain usually identified with performance responses and outcomes in organizations. This domain can be further differentiated into role-required behaviors and extra-role behaviors. Role-required behaviors may be further differentiated into a very large set of more specific constructs, such as task and goal accomplishment, absenteeism, and turnover. Extra-role responses, such as organizational citizenship, may also include a large number of specific variables (Borman & Motowidlo, 1993). As research has continued to focus on behavioral criteria, knowledge has accumulated about the potential causal relationships and interactions among role-required and extra-role behaviors and their unique person-based causes (Borman & Motowidlo, 1993). However, given the lack of research directed at conceptualizing criteria, a great deal is left to learn about the nature of and interrelationships among specific behavioral constructs nested within the larger category of behavioral criteria. The work of Campbell et al. (1993) is a particularly noteworthy attempt to identify a parsimonious set of performance-relevant behavioral criteria that should be descriptively generalizable across jobs and organizations.

Affective criteria can be roughly differentiated into satisfaction and commitment, with each of these constructs being further differentiated into a larger set of more specific affective responses, such as pay satisfaction, satisfaction with supervisors, continuance commitment, and moral/affective commitment. Finally, *physiological* criteria have attracted perhaps the least attention in I/O psychology, though their importance to the field has been argued by several authors (for example, Ilgen, 1990; Johns & Nicholson, 1982). Stress and health-related outcomes represent important concerns for organizations and their members. The consequences of these criteria for insurance and workers' compensation costs, lost time, and poor performance due to sickness or stress-related problems can be assumed to be reflected in measures of organizational effectiveness. A great deal is left to be learned about physiological outcomes in organizations, including their dimensionality and interrelationships with other criteria and predictors.

The study of criteria, including their dimensions, degrees of specificity, interrelationships, and causal influences, continues to represent one of the most important frontiers for research in I/O psychology. It is our view that our understanding of criteria will be most readily advanced through incorporation of the interactional perspective. We need carefully planned studies that address how persons, situations, and their interactions influence criterion responses and how criterion responses subsequently influence persons and situations through dynamic feedback and interactional processes.

Construct Specificity and Aggregation, Revisited

As noted above, a great deal of the current theoretical interest in the study of person constructs in I/O psychology is directed toward understanding the appropriate degree of specificity to be used in describing person differences. Indeed, much of the focus of this book is on developing expanded taxonomies to characterize the content of person differences using constructs other than general cognitive ability (or g) alone (see Chapter One in particular). These discussions have stimulated very useful theoretical developments regarding the nature of individual differences and their potential causal relationships to behavior in organizations. For example, much more needs to be learned about the extent to which a small number of general ability constructs account for the range of relevant job performance criteria in organizations and the extent to which (if at all) more specific ability factors yield incremental prediction of valued performance outcomes (see Chapter One). Research in this tradition should continue. Nevertheless, it is our view that many of the limitations associated with efforts to identify the appropriate content of person constructs derive from a failure to carefully consider the implications of the interactional framework presented in Figure 13.1 and described above.

As much of the current volume attests, researchers who adopt a traditional person-based approach to studying individual differences often take great care to conceptualize and measure person attributes with appropriate specificity. For example, they may measure person attributes at the most specific level possible and empirically determine whether more specific constructs can be aggregated. Thus, for example, single items in a paper-and-pencil test are empirically examined to determine whether responses can be aggregated to form scales that assess a more general construct, and subscale scores are empirically examined to determine whether they can be aggregated to assess a construct that represents an even higher level of abstraction.

In much of our literature, the "appropriate" level of specificity in characterizing the content of individual differences is based on empirical psychometric principles. For example, some authors have argued that aggregation of subordinate-level observations to represent higher-level constructs is psychometrically justified only when some covariation exists among lower-level observations (for example, Lubinski & Dawis, 1992). If observations do not covary, they may be representing constructs that are best kept separate and unique. Therefore, factor analysis and related techniques are often used to identify patterns of covariation among observations of persons, situations, and criteria. These approaches presume that appropriate taxonomic content can be identified independent of the research question being addressed; hence they are not informative about the most appropriate level of specificity to use in building models of the causal effects of persons or situations on particular criteria (Lubinski & Dawis, 1992).

For example, Carroll's research (1993) demonstrated the existence of several levels of cognitive ability factors arranged hierarchically from more to less inclusive. Yet a number of studies have shown that the prediction of job and training performance criteria from a general factor, g, is not necessarily improved by using more specific subfactors (for example, Ree & Earles, 1991, 1992; Ree, Earles, & Teachout, 1994; Thorndike, 1986). These studies suggest that although specific ability constructs can be empirically identified and measured, they may have little value for building theories about ability-performance relationships.

We believe that the incorporation of a general interactional perspective would increase the likelihood that I/O psychologists would interpret findings such as these as representing a case of inadequate explication of constructs in terms of their hierarchical levels of generality or specificity. Several authors have noted that specific predictor constructs are likely to relate best to specific criteria, whereas general predictors should relate best to general criteria (Dunnette, 1963; Arvey, 1986; Wernimont & Campbell, 1968; Fishbein & Ajzen, 1975; Fleishman & Mumford, 1989; Tenopyr & Oeltjen, 1982). Thus one method for identifying whether criterion constructs should be aggregated to represent more general outcomes might involve examining whether differences are observed in the relationships of predictors to various specific criterion constructs (Lubinski & Dawis, 1992). Finding the same empirical relationship between a single between-person or between-situation cause and several correlated and conceptually similar criterion constructs might suggest that the criterion elements should be aggregated. But the choice would depend, among other things, on whether the predictor construct (either between-person or between-situation) might be better differentiated into a larger number of more specific constructs. For example, overall performance in a job involving reading gauges and entering data could be predicted from a composite of mental ability factors. However, if greater concern is placed on reading gauges than on entering data, the researcher might wish to identify a more specific predictor, such as space visualization, in order to maximize the prediction of the specific criterion. Our assertion is not that the logic of relating constructs at similar levels of specificity is a new issue but rather that an interactional perspective suggests a more comprehensive approach to attacking the issue. Researchers need to evaluate the effects of construct specificity in person constructs, situation constructs, and criteria simultaneously. Careful attention to matching levels of specificity of constructs increases the likelihood that meaningful and robust taxonomies of person, situation, and criterion content will be developed and used in future research.

Linking the Taxonomies: Conceptualizing Interactions Among Persons, Situations, and Criteria

The preceding discussion underscored the inherently interactional nature of all research directed at understanding person and situation causes of behavior in organizations. Although usually implicit, a focus on person-based causes of behavior is based on key assumptions about the limited range of situations in which person differences can be expected to operate. Likewise, situational approaches are applied only to certain classes or ranges of individuals. Thus the interactional perspective implies at least two critical ways in which situations must be considered in research designed to test process-level theories of the effects of individual differences on criterion responses. First, researchers must be more explicit about settings in which individual differences are studied. As was noted above, individual difference researchers are often less interested in specifying the situation constructs that characterize the settings in which their research is conducted than they are in the individual differences of the participants included. Thorough explication of situation variables will contribute to later meta-analytic work that attempts to explore how findings gathered across studies may be moderated by situational factors. Second, some of the most important advances to be gained in our field are likely to occur when researchers not only explicitly acknowledge the situation constructs embedded in their research but also attempt to move to even higher levels of theoretical sophistication by building and testing process theories that systematically model interactional effects on criterion responses.

Perhaps one of the most important frontiers for individual difference research in I/O psychology will be the continued development and validation of interactional process theories based on deductive theory building and validation. Olweus (1977) argued that important person-by-situation interactions in individual difference research have too often been identified after the fact rather than being based on carefully developed theoretical hypotheses about how situation differences might moderate the effects of persons (and vice versa). Similarly, Peterson and Bownas (1982) pointed out that the field of personnel selection would be significantly advanced by the development of taxonomic systems describing how the characteristics of job tasks interact with interindividual differences in determining job performance outcomes. Although several theories based on deductive rules about person-situation interactions exist in the field of I/O psychology, efforts to identify person-by-situation effects still proceed inductively in some domains. Reliance on purely inductive approaches to identifying interactive effects may explain why early efforts to identify aptitude-treatment interactions in personnel training, for example, have failed to replicate (Goldstein, 1993).

In fact, inductive approaches can be identified in a number of recent studies, illustrating the range of theoretical explication that may enter into the development of interactional research. A recent study by Hofmann, Jacobs, and Baratta (1993) illustrates a purely inductive approach to identifying both situation and person effects on criteria. These authors were explicitly concerned with developing new methodology rather than new theories to account for person-by-situation interactive effects on criteria. In their study, the authors first explored the effects of time periods on performance (without specifying theoretically based predictions about the shape of performance curves over time). They then used exploratory clustering procedures to identify groups of individuals who shared similar patterns of change over time periods (without attempting to link these interindividual differences to theoretically based constructs from the literature).

In a similar vein, Wright and Mischel's research on conditional approaches to interindividual behavior (1987) is noteworthy in its suggestion that dispositional constructs may be identified inductively by locating patterns of individual differences in response to situational variation. Individuals who respond to situational demands with predicted behavioral responses are identified as members of a dispositional category. In other words, situation differences are identified using deductive approaches based on aggregated perceptions of competency demand, whereas person differences emerge inductively when person-by-situation interactions are identified in individuals' responses to the situation differences. These examples illustrate how interactions involving persons and situations may provide the basis for defining the nature of person constructs (and vice versa). Because of the exploratory methodologies of both of the above-cited studies, however, and the post hoc way in which they identified person constructs, these studies provide very limited information about the theoretical boundaries that limit the effects of the emergent person constructs on reactions to situation attributes.

The work of Barrick and Mount (1993) on the moderating role of autonomy in the relationship between personality and job performance may be considered a more deductive interactive approach, even though autonomy itself was not predicted to have any direct effect on behavior outside of its interaction with personality. Other examples of deductive models of person-by-situation interactions in organizational behavior exist in the literature. Fiedler's contingency theory of leadership (1967), Hackman and Oldham's job design theory (1976), and nearly all recent theories of person-organization fit (Edwards, 1991) represent carefully developed theoretical models of the role of person-by-situation interactions in influencing behavior in organizations. The work of Kanfer and Ackerman (1989) on the interrelationship of goal setting (a situation factor), ability (a person factor), and time on performance also represents well-developed deductive research. In that study, the authors developed several theoretically based predictions about the effects of each person and situation factor on criterion performance and about the ways in which person and situation differences would interact in influencing behavior.

The development of theories of interactive causes in organizational behavior should also attend to issues of construct specificity, as described above. If situations can be conceptualized at varying hierarchical levels of specificity, it is reasonable to expect that a given situation construct will interact most directly with person constructs at analogous levels of conceptualization. Likewise, the effects of interactions between particular person and situation constructs may be predicted a priori to map onto criterion constructs at similar levels of specificity rather than onto more general criteria, such as overall job performance or individual well-being. Interactional research is likely to result in higher predictive relationships among person and situation causes and criteria when it is based on well-developed theory that includes attention to linking constructs that are conceptualized and measured at appropriate levels of specificity.

Finally, it should be recognized that although the interactional perspective draws attention to person-by-situation interactions, other forms of interaction also deserve attention (Chatman, 1989). For example, there has been very little research examining how multiple characteristics of individuals interact with one another in influencing behavior. The limited research on construct-by-construct interactions in individual difference research suggests the importance of studying *profiles* of individual differences rather than single constructs alone or averages across constructs (Chatman, 1989). Individuals who possess the same average score on constructs may differ in their criterion responses if, for example, they differ in their profiles across subordinate constructs or if they differ in their profiles across other domains of individual differences. Moreover, the effects of individual differences—singly or in interaction with each other—might become especially apparent under some situational conditions. Arguably, the Americans with Disabilities Act is consistent with the notion that situations are such strong moderators of person-performance relationships that the design of situations can potentially eliminate the effects of some individual differences. Eliminating the effects of disabilities is precisely the objective of guidelines for accommodation. In this example, the interactive perspective would also underscore the need to consider the possibility that individuals with different profiles of personal characteristics may rely on different attributes when performing the same task or exhibiting the same response. These relatively mechanistic interactional processes do not preclude the possibility that more dynamic processes may evolve over time, such that persons, situations, and criteria become mutually interdependent.

Stretching the Boundaries: Toward More Dynamic Process Models of Persons and Situations

Much of this chapter has focused on relatively static or mechanistic forms of interaction. However, an understanding of individuals in organizations must address dynamic processes that unfold over time. Although time may moderate the relationship of person factors with criteria in relatively mechanistic ways, time may also operate dynamically to change the nature of person attributes. Within the perspective of interactional psychology, it is the inclusion of these dynamic aspects of time that differentiate mechanistic interactionism from dynamic interactionism. In the mechanistic view, the meaning of interaction is statistical: persons, situations, and criteria are implicitly conceptualized as static phenomena. The objective of the scientist is to explain variance in criteria by considering statistical interactions in addition to main effects.

Dynamic interactionism changes the researcher's task from predicting variance in criteria to understanding a process in which persons simultaneously shape and are shaped by situations (or, conversely, a process in which situations simultaneously shape and are shaped by persons). In this dynamic process, person and situation constructs are not only predictors of criteria; each construct can also be conceptualized as a "cause" of the other. For example, over time, a person whose work situation requires lifting heavy objects may gradually acquire new physical attributes. This may appear to be a situation main effect. But if one finds that people with particular person attributes are more likely to choose to enter and remain in work settings that require the behavior of lifting heavy weights, a person main effect becomes apparent. By including the time dimension, dynamic interactionism recognizes that both person and situation effects are intertwined in a process. For example, person attributes partially determine behaviors, including which types of situations to enter; situations in turn place demands on people to engage in particular behaviors (for example, lifting a fifty-pound weight). Depending on how much time is spent in such situations, and how often a behavior is repeated, longer-term consequences may result: the person's own attributes (for example, strength) may change, as may the situation attributes. As a result of changes in the person's attributes, and perhaps in attributes of the situation, future decisions made by that person about which situations to enter (and whether to remain in them) may also be affected, and so on.

Other dynamic processes whereby persons are influenced by the situations they experience have been described in the literature. For example, Fleishman & Mumford (1989) noted that a large number of studies have demonstrated that over time, performance on tasks depends increasingly on specific skills and habits developed in the particular situation. Whereas Ackerman's research (1988) suggested that different stable person attributes determine performance at different periods of time, Fleishman and Mumford (1989) pointed out that the nature of person attributes changes with repeated exposure to task demands. A similar argument was offered by Snow (1989), who noted that individuals develop task strategies through exposure to different situations, with strategies then determining later performance. Finally, the research of Wood and Bandura (1989) underscored the impact of task experiences and situations on individual self-efficacy beliefs and performance strategies, which themselves are important in influencing subsequent behavioral patterns.

Clearly, we need to develop theories that explain these dynamic processes and suggest directions for empirical work. Many authors have noted that such dynamic processes are ultimately driven by rather mechanistic forms of interaction between persons and situations. In other words, individuals' unique patterns of reacting to situation differences determine the development of subsequent individual differences, which then impact situations and behavior over time. Our emphasis on the interactional framework presented in Figure 13.1 has been driven by a recognition that although dynamic interactions are often recognized as essential to understanding how persons and situations interact and adapt over time, a fuller appreciation of mechanistic forms of interaction will ultimately contribute to the development of dynamic process theories in I/O psychology.

Higgins (1990) provided perhaps the most fully explicated model of the types of person-by-situation interaction that form the basis for dynamic adaptations over time. In his view, an early stage of person-by-situation interaction occurs when different individuals select different situations in order to fulfill personal objectives or "self-guides." This view is similar to that of Pervin (1989), who suggested that individual goals and self-regulatory processes provide the essential bases for dynamic processes whereby persons and situations become jointly interdependent over time. By virtue of their entrance into situations, individuals then change situations, depending on the salience of their person attributes for others in the situation. For example, a female who enters an all-male group changes the nature of the group and its behavior toward individual members and outsiders. Once individuals selectively enter situations, and thereby change the situations, a process of perception takes place during which different individuals perceive objective situation attributes in unique ways.

According to Higgins (1990), individual differences in knowledge activation determine how different people develop different interpretations of the situations they enter. For example, members of the U.S. culture and members of the Japanese culture may differ in their perceptions of what constitutes "agreement" within a given interpersonal situation. Likewise, potentially very subtle features of situations determine which particular knowledge structures are activated in individuals. Some of these activations may depend on previous situations encountered by individuals. For example, time may operate to prime certain knowledge structures such that earlier experiences determine which schema are applied to subsequent situation attributes. The interpretation of situations obviously determines individuals' subsequent criterion responses. However, even individuals who have interpreted a situation in the same way may nevertheless respond to it differently because of person differences in response-relevant constructs. For example, tasks that present perceptually similar performance demands may nevertheless result in performance differences because of between-person differences in task-related ability.

Although the process-based notions of person-by-situation interaction described by Higgins (1990) are dynamic in nature, they underscore the importance of mechanistic person-by-situation interactions during the encounter, perception, and behavioral phases. Higgins's discussion provides a useful framework for conceptualizing how research in I/O psychology can bridge the gap between mechanistic and dynamic forms of interaction in ways that ultimately contribute to our evolving knowledge of the processes by which persons differ in their responses to varying situations over time.

Conclusion

A focus on dynamic interactional models in organizational behavior suggests several important implications. First, we need to be aware that—at any given time—the persons and/or situations we wish to study are not independent of prior interactive causes. Situations are a function of the persons who occupy them (Schneider, 1983), and because individuals enter and leave situations based on perceived fit of situations to personal standards (Higgins, 1990; Pervin, 1989), the range of person differences is likely to be constrained in most organizational settings (Schneider, 1987). Second, the fact that persons and situations interact over time underscores the need to adopt methodologies that can capture both idiographic and nomothetic processes. For example, cross-sectional time-series designs (Mitchell & L. R James, 1989), hierarchical linear modeling techniques (Hofmann et al., 1993), and other complex statistical techniques provide useful methods for assessing variations between persons in their responses to variations in situations.

Finally, a focus on dynamic interactional processes depends ultimately on the development and validation of theories that describe the underlying psychological and behavioral processes that provide the interface between the person and the situation (or between the objective world and the reality experienced and constructed by the individual). Theoretical work on the role of personal goals and self-regulatory control systems (for example, Pervin, 1989) represents an exciting new frontier of research into the dynamic processes that underlie individuals' construction of and responses to situational features.

Unfortunately, interactional perspectives in I/O psychology have not evolved past fairly simple guiding ideas in theoretical development. We hope that our attempts to more clearly explicate some of the most crucial aspects of the guiding ideas contained in interactional psychology will serve a useful starting point for evolving interactional perspectives toward more taxonomic statements. Careful explication of relatively mechanistic forms of interaction, whereby stable individual differences combine in complex ways with attributes of situations to affect individual behavior, should form the basis for future research on the dynamic processes underlying individual and situational change and interdependency over time.

References

Ackerman, P. L. (1988). Determinants of individual differences during skill acquisition: Cognitive abilities and information processing. *Journal of Experimental Psychology: General, 117,* 288–318.

Ackerman, P. L., & Humphreys, L. G. (1990). Individual differences theory in industrial and organizational psychology. In M. D. Dunnette & L. M. Hough (Eds.), *Handbook of industrial and organizational psychology* (2nd ed.; Vol. 1, pp. 223–282). Palo Alto, CA: Consulting Psychologists Press.

Adorno, T. W., Frenkel-Brunswik, E., Levinson, D. J., & Sanford, N. (1950). *The authoritarian personality.* New York: HarperCollins.

Arvey, R. D. (1986). General ability in employment: A discussion. *Journal of Vocational Behavior, 29,* 415–420.

Arvey, R. D., Bouchard, T. J., Segal, N. L., & Abraham, L. M. (1989). Job satisfaction: Environmental and genetic components. *Journal of Applied Psychology, 74*, 187–192.

Austin, J. T., & Villanova, P. (1992). The criterion problem: 1917–1992. *Journal of Applied Psychology, 77*, 836–874.

Bandura, A. (1986). *Social foundations of thought and action: A social cognitive theory.* Englewood Cliffs, NJ: Prentice-Hall.

Barrick, M. R., & Mount, M. K. (1993). Autonomy as a moderator of the relationships between the Big Five personality dimensions and job performance. *Journal of Applied Psychology, 78*, 111–118.

Block, J., & Block, J. H. (1981). Studying situational dimensions: A grand perspective and some limited empiricism. In D. Magnusson (Ed.), *Toward a psychology of situations: An interactional perspective.* Hillsdale, NJ: Erlbaum.

Borman, W. C., & Motowidlo, S. J. (1993). Expanding the criterion domain to include elements of contextual performance. In N. Schmitt, W. C. Borman, & Associates, *Personnel selection in organizations.* San Francisco: Jossey-Bass.

Bowers, K. S. (1973). Situationism in psychology: An analysis and critique. *Psychological Review, 80*, 307–336.

Brunswik, E. (1956). *Perception and the representative design of psychological experiments.* Berkeley: University of California Press.

Campbell, J. P., McCloy, R. A., Oppler, S. H., & Sager, C. E. (1993). A theory of performance. In N. Schmitt, W. C. Borman, & Associates, *Personnel selection in organizations.* San Francisco: Jossey-Bass.

Carroll, J. B. (1993). *Human cognitive abilities: A survey of factor-analytic studies.* Cambridge, UK: Cambridge University Press.

Chatman, J. A. (1989). Improving interactional organizational research: A model of person-organization fit. *Academy of Management Review, 14*, 333–349.

Christiansen, S. A. (Ed.). (1993). *Handbook of emotion and memory: Research and theory.* Hillsdale, NJ: Erlbaum.

Cohen, J., & Cohen, P. (1983). *Applied multiple regression/correlation analysis for the behavioral sciences.* Hillsdale, NJ: Erlbaum.

Cronbach, L. J. (1957). The two disciplines of scientific psychology. *American Psychologist, 12*, 671–684.

Cronbach, L. J. (1975). Beyond the two disciplines of scientific psychology. *American Psychologist, 30*, 116–127.

Cronbach, L. J., & Snow, R. E. (1977). *Aptitudes and instructional methods: A handbook for research on interactions.* New York: Irvington.

Davis-Blake, A., & Pfeffer, J. (1989). Just a mirage: The search for dispositional effects in organizational research. *Academy of Management Review, 14*, 385–400.

Dawis, R. V. (1991). Vocational interests, values, and preferences. In M. D. Dunnette & L. M. Hough (Eds.), *Handbook of industrial and organizational psychology* (2nd ed.; Vol. 2, pp. 833–872). Palo Alto, CA: Consulting Psychologists Press.

Deadrick, D. L., & Madigan, R. M. (1990). Dynamic criteria revised: A longitudinal study of performance stability and predictive validity. *Personnel Psychology, 43,* 717–744.

Dunnette, M. D. (1963). A note on *the* criterion. *Journal of Applied Psychology, 47,* 251–254.

Edwards, J. R. (1991). Person-job fit: A conceptual integration, literature review, and methodological critique. In C. L. Cooper & I. T. Robertson (Eds.), *International review of industrial and organizational psychology* (Vol. 6). New York: Wiley.

Ekehammer, B. (1974). Interactionism in personality from a historical perspective. *Psychological Bulletin, 81,* 1026–1048.

Endler, N. S. (1981). Situational aspects of interactional psychology. In D. Magnusson (Ed.), *Toward a psychology of situations: An interactional perspective.* Hillsdale, NJ: Erlbaum.

Fiedler, F. E. (1967). *A theory of leadership effectiveness.* New York: McGraw-Hill.

Fishbein, M., & Ajzen, I. (1975). *Belief, attitude, intention, and behavior: An introduction to theory and research.* Reading, MA: Addison-Wesley.

Fleishman, E. A. (1964). *The structure and measurement of physical fitness.* Englewood Cliffs, NJ: Prentice-Hall.

Fleishman, E. A., & Mumford, M. D. (1988). The ability requirements scales. In S. Gael (Ed.), *The job analysis handbook for business, government, and industry.* New York: Wiley.

Fleishman, E. A., & Mumford, M. D. (1989). Individual attributes and training performance. In I. L. Goldstein & Associates, *Training and development in organizations.* San Francisco: Jossey-Bass.

Fleishman, E. A., & Quaintance, M. K. (1984). *Taxonomies of human performance: The description of human tasks.* San Diego, CA: Academic Press.

Geis, F. L. (1978). Machiavellianism. In H. London & J. Exner (Eds.), *Dimensions of personality.* New York: Wiley.

Goldstein, I. L. (1993). *Training in organizations: Needs assessment, development, and evaluation* (3rd ed.). Pacific Grove, CA: Brooks/Cole.

Graham, W. K. (1976). Commensurate characterization of persons, groups, and organizations: Development of the Trait Ascription Questionnaire (TAQ). *Human Relations, 29,* 607–622.

Hackman, J. R. (1992). Group influences on individuals in organizations. In M. D. Dunnette & L. M. Hough (Eds.), *Handbook of industrial and organizational psychology* (2nd ed.; Vol. 3, pp. 199–268). Palo Alto, CA: Consulting Psychologists Press.

Hackman, J. R., & Oldham, G. R. (1976). Motivation through the design of work: Test of a theory. *Organizational Behavior and Human Performance, 16,* 250–279.

Hartshorne, H., & May, M. A. (1928). *Studies in the nature of character: Vol. 1. Studies in deceit* (Vol. 1). New York: Macmillan.

Harvey, R. J. (1991). Job analysis. In M. D. Dunnette & L. M. Hough (Eds.), *Handbook of industrial and organizational psychology* (2nd ed.; Vol. 2, pp. 71–164). Palo Alto, CA: Consulting Psychologists Press.

Higgins, E. T. (1990). Personality, social psychology, and person-situation relations: Standards and knowledge activation as a common language. In L. A. Pervin (Ed.), *Handbook of personality: Theory and research.* New York: Guilford.

Hofmann, D. A., Jacobs, R., & Baratta, J. E. (1993). Dynamic criteria and the measurement of change. *Journal of Applied Psychology, 78,* 194–204.

Hulin, C. L., Henry, R. A., & Noon, S. L. (1990). Adding a dimension: Time as a factor in the generalizability of predictive relationships. *Psychological Bulletin, 107,* 328–340.

Hunter, J. E. (1986). Cognitive ability, cognitive aptitudes, job knowledge, and job performance. *Journal of Vocational Behavior, 29,* 340–362.

Hunter, J. E., & Hunter, R. F. (1984). Validity and utility of alternative predictors of job performance. *Psychological Bulletin, 96,* 72–98.

Ilgen, D. R. (1990). Health issues at work: Opportunities for industrial/organizational psychology. *American Psychologist, 45,* 273–283.

James, L. A., & James, L. R. (1989). Integrating work environment perceptions: Explorations into the measurement of meaning. *Journal of Applied Psychology, 74,* 739–751.

James, L. R. (1982). Aggregation bias in estimates of perceptual agreement. *Journal of Applied Psychology, 67,* 219–229.

James, L. R., James, L. A., & Ashe, D. K. (1990). The meaning of organizations: The role of cognition and values. In B. Schneider (Ed.), *Organizational climate and culture.* San Francisco: Jossey-Bass.

Johns, G., & Nicholson, N. (1982). The meanings of absence: New strategies for theory and research. In B. M. Staw & L. L. Cummings (Eds.), *Research in organizational behavior* (Vol. 4). Greenwich, CT: JAI Press.

Kanfer, R., & Ackerman, P. L. (1989). Motivation and cognitive abilities: An integrative/aptitude-treatment interaction approach to skill acquisition. *Journal of Applied Psychology, 74,* 657–690.

Kleinmuntz, B. (1967). *Personality measurement: An introduction.* Belmont, CA: Dorsey Press.

Kozlowski, S.W.J., & Hattrup, K. (1992). A disagreement about within-group agreement: Disentangling issues of consistency versus consensus. *Journal of Applied Psychology, 77,* 161–167.

Lamiell, J. T. (1987). *The psychology of personality: An epistemological inquiry.* New York: Columbia University Press.

Levin, I., & Stokes, J. P. (1989). Dispositional approach to job satisfaction: Role of negative affectivity. *Journal of Applied Psychology, 74,* 752–758.

Lewin, K. (1951). *Field theory in social science.* New York: HarperCollins.

Lubinski, D., & Dawis, R. V. (1992). Aptitudes, skills, and proficiencies. In M. D. Dunnette & L. M. Hough (Eds.), *Handbook of industrial and organizational psychology* (2nd ed.; Vol. 3, pp. 1–60). Palo Alto, CA: Consulting Psychologists Press.

Magnusson, D. (1981). *Toward a psychology of situations: An interactional perspective.* Hillsdale, NJ: Erlbaum.

Magnusson, D., & Endler, N. S. (1977). *Personality at the crossroads: Current issues in interactional psychology.* Hillsdale, NJ: Erlbaum.

McClelland, D. C., Atkinson, J. W., Clark, R. A., & Lowell, E. L. (1953). *The achievement motive.* New York: Appleton-Century-Crofts.

McGuire, W. J. (1983). A contextual theory of knowledge: Its implications for innovation and reform in psychological research. In L. Berkowitz (Ed.), *Advances in experimental social psychology,* Vol. 16 (pp. 1–47). New York: Academic Press.

McNemar, Q. (1964). Lost: Our intelligence? Why? *American Psychologist, 19,* 871–882.

Mischel, W. (1968). *Personality and assessment.* New York: Wiley.

Mischel, W. (1977). The interaction of person and situation. In D. Magnusson & N. S. Endler (Eds.), *Personality at the crossroads: Current issues in interactional psychology.* Hillsdale, NJ: Erlbaum.

Mischel, W. (1990). Personality dispositions revisited and revised: A view after three decades. In L. A. Pervin (Ed.), *Handbook of personality: Theory and research.* New York: Guilford.

Mislevy, R. J. (1993). Foundations of a new test theory. In N. Frederiksen, R. J. Mislevy, & I. I. Bejar (Eds.), *Test theory for a new generation of tests.* Hillsdale, NJ: Erlbaum.

Mitchell, T. R., & James, L. R. (1989). Conclusions and future directions. *Academy of Management Review, 14,* 401–407.

Moos, R. H. (1973). Conceptualizations of human environments. *American Psychologist, 28,* 652–665.

Murray, H. (1938). *Explorations in personality.* New York: Oxford University Press.

Olweus, D. (1977). A critical analysis of the "modern" interactionist position. In D. Magnusson & N. S. Endler (Eds.), *Personality at the crossroads: Current issues in interactional psychology.* Hillsdale, NJ: Erlbaum.

Pervin, L. A. (1989). Persons, situations, interactions: The history of a controversy and a discussion of theoretical models. *Academy of Management Review, 14,* 350–360.

Peterson, N. G., & Bownas, D. A. (1982). Skill, task structure, and performance acquisition. In M. D. Dunnette & E. A. Fleishman (Eds.), *Human Performance and Productivity* (Vol. 1). Hillsdale, NJ: Erlbaum.

Raush, H. L. (1977). Paradox levels, and junctures in person-situation systems. In D. Magnusson & N. S. Endler (Eds.), *Personality at the crossroads: Current issues in interactional psychology.* Hillsdale, NJ: Erlbaum.

Ree, M. J., & Earles, J. A. (1991). Predicting training success: Not much more than *g. Personnel Psychology, 44,* 321–332.

Ree, M. J., & Earles, J. A. (1992). Intelligence is the best predictor of job performance. *Current Directions in Psychological Science, 1,* 86–89.

Ree, M. J., Earles, J. A., & Teachout, M. S. (1994). Predicting job performance: Not much more than *g. Journal of Applied Psychology, 79,* 518–524.

Revelle, W. (1993). Individual differences in personality and motivation: "Non-cognitive" determinants of cognitive performance. In A. Baddeley & L. Weiskrantz (Eds.), *Attention: Selection, awareness, and control. A tribute to Donald Broadbent* (pp. 346–373). Oxford, UK: Oxford University Press.

Revelle, W. (1995). Personality processes. *Annual Review of Psychology, 46,* 295–328.

Rokeach, M. (1960). *The open and closed mind.* New York: Basic Books.

Rotter, J. B. (1966). Generalized expectancies for internal versus external control of reinforcement. *Psychological Monographs, 80* (entire No. 609).

Rushton, J. P., Brainerd, C. J., & Pressley, M. (1983). Behavioral development and construct validity: The principle of aggregation. *Psychological Bulletin, 94,* 18–38.

Schneider, B. (1983). Interactional psychology and organizational behavior. In L. L. Cummings & B. M. Staw (Eds.), *Research in organizational behavior* (Vol. 5). Greenwich, CT: JAI Press.

Schneider, B. (1987). The people make the place. *Personnel Psychology, 40,* 437–453.

Schneider, B., & Schmitt, N. (1986). *Staffing organizations* (2nd ed.). Prospect Heights, IL: Waveland Press.

Snow, R. E. (1986). Individual differences and the design of educational programs. *American Psychologist, 41,* 1029–1039.

Snow, R. E. (1989). Aptitude-treatment interaction as a framework for research on individual differences in learning. In P. L. Ackerman, R. J. Sternberg, & R. Glaser (Eds.), *Learning and individual differences: Advances in theory and research.* New York: W. H. Freeman.

Snyder, M., & Ickes, W. (1985). Personality and social behavior. In G. Lindzey & E. Aronson (Eds.), *Handbook of social psychology* (3rd ed.). New York: Random House.

Sternberg, R. J. (1989a). Intelligence, wisdom, and creativity: Their natures and interrelationships. In R. L. Linn (Ed.), *Intelligence: Measurement, theory, and public policy.* Chicago: University of Illinois Press.

Sternberg, R. J. (1989b). Mental self-government: A theory of intellectual styles and their development. *Human Development, 31,* 197–224.

Tenopyr, M. L., & Oeltjen, P. D. (1982). Personnel selection and classification. *Annual Review of Psychology, 33,* 581–618.

Thomas, W. I. (1928). *The child in America.* New York: Knopf.

Thorndike, R. L. (1986). The role of general ability in prediction. *Journal of Vocational Behavior, 29,* 332–339.

Weiss, H. M., & Adler, S. (1984). Personality and organizational behavior. In B. M. Staw (Ed.), *Research in organizational behavior* (Vol. 6). London, UK: JAI Press.

Wernimont, P. F., & Campbell, J. P. (1968). Signs, samples, and criteria. *Journal of Applied Psychology, 52,* 372–376.

Wood, R., & Bandura, A. (1989). Social cognitive theory of organizational management. *Academy of Management Review, 14,* 361–384.

Wright, J. C., & Mischel, W. (1987). A conditional approach to dispositional constructs: The local predictability of social behavior. *Journal of Personality and Social Psychology, 53,* 1159–1177.

Wylie, R. C. (1974). *The self-concept* (2nd ed.). Lincoln: University of Nebraska Press.

Zajonc, R. B. (1965). Social facilitation. *Science, 149,* 269–274.

Chapter Fourteen

When Individual Differences Aren't

Benjamin Schneider

Scientific psychology, now barely more than a century old, began with the goal of providing general laws that describe human behavior. These general laws—laws about the behavior of all people—were to be as certain as those guiding the study of physics and later the study of biology and neurology (MacKinnon & Maslow, 1951). But a funny thing happened on the way to the future: individual differences intruded. James McKeen Cattell, working in Wundt's laboratory in Leipzig, was unable to ignore differences between respondents in reaction time experiments and began to study those differences (Boring, 1950). Binet and Simon in France turned their experimental procedures to the design of "little experiments" that revealed not similarity but differences among French schoolchildren—and showed that those differences were related to teacher ratings of those same children (Binet & Simon, 1905/1961). Then Muensterberg, studying trolley car motormen, captured individual differences using work simulations that were shown later to be reflected in motorman performance (Viteles, 1932). These studies marked the beginning of the application of the study of individual differences to the prediction of work be-

Note: Constructive comments on an earlier version of this chapter from Michelle Paul, Susan Schoenberger, Brent Smith, and Virginia Smith were very helpful to me in finding ways to express the ideas in this chapter.

havior. By 1928, there were already sufficient data for Hull (1928) to provide a review of the literature on the criterion-related validity of various tests for the prediction of educational and occupational performance. In 1932, Viteles wrote *the* book on industrial psychology—a book with an almost exclusive focus on individual differences as the approach to understanding worker behavior and worker effectiveness in business and industry.

By 1932, psychologists were adept at measuring individual differences and understood the importance of the application of those differences to the prediction of performance. What we have done over the last sixty-five years is *refine* these methods and measures. Therefore, we now know, with greater certainty than we did in 1932, that criterion-related validities will range from about .30 to about .40 when we do the right things right. Nonetheless, we continue to debate the heritability and usefulness of intelligence in all of its guises (see Chapter One), personality goes in and out of favor as a potentially useful construct (see Chapter Two), the dimensionality and dynamic nature of criteria still draw our attention (see Chapter Seven), and we wax and wane on the dispositional nature of job satisfaction (see Chapter Five); meanwhile, we continue to wonder why business and industry fail to pay us the attention we so deeply believe we deserve.

I propose in this chapter that our increasingly sophisticated study of individual differences has not been greeted with open arms by management because we have failed to reveal for management a direct link between these differences and differences in organizational behavior and organizational effectiveness (hereafter referred to collectively as *organizational performance*). The lack of clarity in the link between individual differences and organizational performance is, I propose, a consequence of the disparity between researchers' focus on individual-level criteria in studies of individual differences and managers' focus on *organizational* behavior and *organizational* productivity.

By continuing to pursue the focus on individual variables on both the predictor and the criterion side of our research efforts, we have implicitly abandoned the understanding of organizational behavior and effectiveness to situationists—to those who focus on organizational attributes such as job design, organizational structure, sociotechnical systems, and reengineering as the factors responsible for organizational performance, thereby denying the importance of individuals to organizational performance. The situational perspective is gaining support even among people from the individual difference tradition, some of whom argue for abandoning the study of human resources from an individual difference perspective. These authors (for example, Dobbins, Cardy, & Carson, 1991) want to focus on human resource *practices* rather than on the attributes of the humans that those practices attract, select, train, and retain.

Organizations, as human systems, are comprised of people (compare Katz & Kahn, 1978), but the understanding and prediction of organizational behavior and effectiveness require thinking about people in the aggregate. Managers tend to make decisions that have more universal than particularistic implications for the employees of an organization, and scholars addressing the issue of organizational behavior and effectiveness must treat the human capital of an organization in the aggregate. My proposal is that we must conceptualize and study the role of individual differences in organizational behavior and effectiveness at this aggregate level of analysis if we are to be a partner in (1) understanding organizational performance and (2) helping organizations become effective in an increasingly competitive and global economy. If we continue to confine our studies to how variable X relates to variable Y, with both predictor and criterion measured at the individual level of analysis, we will become increasingly marginalized as potential contributors to understanding the behavior *of* organizations (in contrast to behavior *in* organizations), guiding management decision making, and facilitating *organizational* (not individual) effectiveness.

My goal in the present chapter is to suggest, as have others (Guion, 1992), that we expand the focal unit of analysis for research on individual differences. I am not in favor of abandoning the study of individual differences. Industrial and organizational (I/O) psychologists have proven the effectiveness of a focus on individuals for the prediction and understanding of individual behavior and individual productivity (see, for example, Chapters One and Seven). However, we have not effectively translated this focus to an understanding of why organizations behave as they do and why organizations are not as effective as they might be.

In what follows, I first present a description of what it means to adopt an organizational level of analysis in studies of individual differences. I then explore the implications of this change in level of analysis first for the study of organizational behavior (for example, behavior in mechanistic versus organic organizations: Burns & Stalker, 1961) and then for the study of organizational effectiveness. This section on organizational behavior and organizational effectiveness is followed by a consideration of some conceptual and methodological issues that emerge when the level of analysis moves from individual to organizational criteria. Here I discuss (1) the lack of a direct relationship between individual variables and organizational performance, (2) the role that individual differences in managers and leaders play in creating the "situation" in which people behave, and (3) some thoughts on conceptualizing and assessing the people in organizations as profiles of attributes.

An Organizational Level of Analysis in Studies of Individual Differences

As an introduction to the issue of changes in levels of analysis in individual difference research, consider the long-studied relationship between job satisfaction and performance. Since Brayfield and Crockett's review of the literature (1955), showing a weak (at best) correlation between job satisfaction and performance, scholars have attempted to understand why this seemingly "obvious" relationship has not emerged in quantitative studies. At the same time, management has functioned as if there *is* a strong relationship between job satisfaction and performance. If one traces the history of management thinking on the issue, it becomes clear that management takes action based on the hypothesis that there is a relationship between having a satisfied workforce and being productive. From Taylor's scientific management (1923), through McGregor's Theory Y (1960), to the focus on empowerment (Bowen & Lawler, 1993), managers have adopted programs and policies to improve employee satisfaction with the goal of improved organizational effectiveness. Has it been blind faith? No. Rather, managers have been thinking at a different level of analysis than satisfaction researchers.

I have written elsewhere (B. Schneider, 1985) that consultants going from organization to organization first made the observation that those organizations that are most effective appear to have more satisfied workforces ("higher morale"). Psychologists picked up the consultants' observations, designed job satisfaction surveys, and administered them to the workers in a company and then correlated worker satisfaction with those same workers' performance. The problem was a mismatch between the level of the theory (consultants' observations of between-organization differences in employee morale) and the level of the research (psychologists' measurement of individual differences in job satisfaction within a single firm). Since managers know that manufacturing plants, retail stores, and banks are more effective when the employees who work there are more satisfied, they have paid little attention to our denials of such relationships; they do not want to be confused by our facts, because our facts are not relevant for the level of analysis at which they think.

Obviously, the choice of any particular level of analysis in research is not a "right" or "wrong" issue, but ensuring that the data are collected at the same level as the theory is fundamental (Klein, Dansereau, & Hall, 1994). For example, in an intensive analysis of the relationship between job satisfaction and performance, Ostroff (1992) demonstrated consistent and consistently modest (r's in the mid 30s range) relationships of job satisfaction and various other attitudes (for example, commitment) with performance. What was different about Ostroff's study is that she conducted her research on almost 300 U.S. and Canadian schools and established the relationships between satisfaction and other attitudes with various indices of performance for those same schools (for example, student standardized test performance and dropout rates), even controlling for school differences (such as socioeconomics of the area surrounding the school and minority/majority representation in the student body).

In a similar vein, B. Schneider and Bowen (1985) reported a replication and extension of findings relating employee perceptions of their work climate and customer perceptions of the service quality they received across twenty-seven branches of a bank. In this study, customer service quality perceptions at the branch level served as the criterion of interest, and aggregated employee work climate perceptions were the predictor. Results revealed correlations between these two sets of aggregate perceptions in both the original and the replication study in the .60 to .70 range.

From a management standpoint, the findings of Ostroff indicate the importance of raising the level of teacher job satisfaction in the hopes of raising student performance outcomes. These interventions, based on the chapters in the present volume, might include some or all of the following: (1) the hiring of people with high levels of positive affectivity (see Chapter Four), (2) the hiring of people with an inclination to evaluate life and life events in more positive terms (see Chapter Five), and (3) the hiring of people with interests in teaching and education (see Chapter Three).

Similarly, the results of the Schneider and Bowen efforts suggest improving the service climate in bank branches as a vehicle for improving customer service quality perceptions. Improvement in customer service climate perceptions may require the creation of a "surround" for individuals to which they can attach climate meaning (see Chapter Eleven). A climate that means service to employees might be accompanied by superior customer service quality under the following individual difference conditions: (1) the hiring of people with high levels of conscientiousness (see Chapter Two), who tend to more often display the kinds of prosocial and citizenship behaviors that yield improved customer satisfaction (see Chapters Nine and Three) and to display the attentional focus important in customer service delivery (see Chapter Six); (2) the hiring of people with the interpersonal self-efficacy (see Chapter Nine) required to work in the kinds of teams that characterize costumer service delivery firms (see Chapter Eight); and (3) the design of performance appraisal systems that focus on the behaviors required to deal with customers so that appropriate feedback and reward systems that reinforce these service behaviors might be designed (see Chapter Seven).

Whether the costs involved in such interventions are worthwhile depends on the benefits they yield. However, utility models, previously applied primarily to selection and training interventions at the individual level of analysis (Boudreau, 1991), are equally appropriate when the criterion is at the organizational level of analysis.

Alternatives to Studying Individual Differences

The studies just suggested, in which individual difference data are collected on the predictor side and related in the aggregate to organizational-level criterion data, are quite different from the studies suggested by Dobbins et al. (1991) and conducted so effectively by Huselid (1995). These latter studies ask the following question: Are organizations more effective when they implement the human resource practices of high-performing organizations? This question concerns the activities of the organization and does not consider the kinds of humans the human resource practices yield.

For example, Huselid (1995) has recently explored the relationship between high-performance human resource practices and turnover, productivity, and corporate financial performance. He concludes his literature review with the following: "In summary, prior empirical work has consistently found that the use of effective human resources management practices enhances firm performance. Specifically, extensive recruitment, selection, and training procedures; formal information sharing, attitude assessment, job design, grievance procedures, and labor management participation programs; and performance appraisal, promotion, and incentive compensation systems that recognize and reward employee merit have all been widely linked with valued firm-level outcomes" (p. 640).

In his own study of more than 1,000 firms, Huselid showed that high-performance human resource practices (as described by corporate human resource vice presidents) were significantly related to turnover rate, productivity, and corporate financial performance.

I cite Huselid's work for several reasons. First, the article presents an excellent review of findings relating corporate human resource practices to organizational-level outcomes. Second, Huselid's own study grapples with deficiencies in prior work of a similar nature with considerable conceptual and empirical sophistication. Finally, his work serves as an example of the kind of research I am *not* suggesting. My interest is in the nature of the people in organizations and their attributes; I am less concerned in the present chapter with organizational practices. In other words, I am concerned with the people who are the outcomes of human resource practices, not the practices themselves.

This is neither a subtle nor a semantic difference. The individual difference model emphasizes the conceptualization of, and collection of data from, individuals. Whenever the data do not come from the individuals about whom or to whom generalizations are to be made, the study does not conform to the model I propose. Any other model for research, while appropriate for other purposes, does not fulfill my goal. My interest lies in the typical or average nature of the individuals in a given organization and the consequences of that average or typical nature for organizational behavior and organizational effectiveness.

Individual Differences and Organizational Behavior

The extant literature on individual differences that comes closest to the model I have in mind is the research on vocational interests. In Chapter Three, Hogan and Blake provide an informative introduction to research on vocational interests (as well as needs and values) and show that individuals' values and needs are reflected in their vocational interests—indeed, that vocational interests are a strategy by which individuals implement their values and needs (Super, 1953). In their chapter, Hogan and Blake approach the correlates of interest measurement on both the antecedent and consequence side as if vocational interest measurement had the same frame of reference as the measurement of individual personality and individual performance and satisfaction.

The measurement of individual differences in vocational interests groups people according to their vocational interests rather than arranging them from high to low on some variable(s). Vocational interest measurement, as typified by the Strong Interest Inventory and the Kuder Preference Record, is designed to categorize or group people, not to arrange them in hierarchies of amounts. Advertising people do not possess more of some attribute than accountants; rather, advertising people are different in their interests in many ways from accountants.

Were we to jump up a level of analysis in vocational interest measurement, we would hypothesize that accounting firms would be different from advertising firms because of the kinds of interests the people in those firms have. According to Holland (1985), accountants exhibit Conventional vocational interest, and advertising people exhibit Artistic vocational interest. Following Hogan and Blake (Chapter Three), we would then find that accounting firms are characterized by people who are high on conscientiousness, behaving in ways that demand, support, or reward conforming, orderly, and dependable behavior.

Contrast this description with the description of the Artistic types who might occupy an advertising firm: disorderly, complicated, impulsive, nonconforming, emotional, and expressive (Holland, 1985, p. 21). Hogan and Blake (Chapter Three) would hypothesize that a career environment filled with Artistic types would demand, support, and reward expressive, nonconforming, and impulsive behavior precisely because it is made up of the kind of people there.

In essence, I am suggesting a return to an earlier period in the study of individual differences—a time when the study of individual differences included the study of group differences (Anastasi, 1958). In this earlier era—which might be called the age of differential psychology—the full range of individual differences were explored concurrently with the ways in which those individual differences were grouped (by gender, by age, by socioeconomic status, by race). I propose that we return to this model and ask whether individual differences can be grouped based on a new set of organizational grouping variables. One set of grouping variables would describe organizational *behavior.* The other set of grouping variables would describe organizational *effectiveness,* distinguishing more from less effective organizations.

By organizational behavior, I mean the description and understanding of organizations at the organizational level of analysis in terms of the individuals who people those organizations. Consider the possibility, for example, of grouping individual differences based on organizational behavior associated with a mechanistic versus an organic organization (Burns & Stalker, 1961). Mechanistic organizations, in Burns and Stalker's conceptualization, are characterized by task specialization, clear role specialization (in terms of power and duties), hierarchical arrangement, goal assignment by superiors to subordinates, and simple reward and control systems.

In contrast, organic organizations are characterized by broad role and task requirements across positions, high levels of interaction across roles and functions, broad distribution of power, nonhierarchical or loosely hierarchical arrangements, and self-set goals and behaviors.

Burns and Stalker (1961) present these organizational designs as categorical types, not types that fall on a good-bad or effective-ineffective continuum. They argue that these types are more or less effective depending on the larger external environment in which the organization functions, with the mechanistic organization superior in a stable environment and the organic organization more effective in an unstable environment.

If one wanted to study these different forms of organizational behavior, what individual difference constructs and measures could one use? Relying on the chapters in this volume, we might frame certain questions and hypotheses. For example, organic and mechanistic types of organizational behavior might differ on the following individual difference variables:

1. The modal personality of the members—with mechanistic organizations perhaps dominated by conscientiousness and organic organizations dominated by extraversion (Chapter Two)
2. The modal occupational interests of the members—with mechanistic organizations dominated by people who favor Holland's Conventional interests and organic organizations dominated by people characterized by Holland's Enterprising type (Chapter Three)
3. The incidence of prosocial and citizenship behaviors—implicitly demanded more and thus displayed more in organic than in mechanistic systems (Chapter Nine)
4. The task-specific efficacies of the members—with members of mechanistic organizations viewing themselves as competent with regard to details and the following of rules and members of organic systems having the confidence to deal with ambiguity and to set their own goals (Chapter Eight)
5. The inclination to be influenced versus influencing others—with those in mechanistic organizations more influenceable and those in organic systems more inclined to influence others (Chapter Nine)

I present the mechanistic-organic distinction as a foil for how organizational behavior might be understood based on the attributes of the individuals likely to be found in those organizations. Other frameworks for understanding organizational behavior could receive similar conceptual treatment. For example, Blau and Scott's analysis of the primary beneficiaries of organizations (1962) offers an interesting framework that would be amenable to an individual difference approach such as the one proposed here. The notion in Blau and Scott's work is that different parties benefit in organizations as a function of organizational size, structure, and so on. As another example, consider Miles and Snow's conceptualization of organizational strategies (1978): the opposing strategies of defenders and prospectors. These different organizational behavior strategies may also be associated with attributes of the people in an organization, especially those of the leaders/managers (Huber, Sutcliffe, Miller, & Glick, 1993). Obviously, organizations characterized by McGregor's Theory X and Theory Y (1960) would be amenable to such study, especially with regard to the values perspectives of the managers and executives who work in such firms. On the issue of managers and executives, B. Schneider (1987; B. Schneider, Goldstein, & Smith, 1995) has suggested that the founders of organizations leave a long legacy in terms of the culture of organizations through the kinds of people attracted to, selected by, and retained by an organization. Obviously, this line of thinking fits well with Holland's vantage point on career environments, but it shifts the orientation to the organization as an environment (see Chapter Three).

The chapter by Rosse and Noel (Chapter Twelve) can be conceptualized to yield a set of interesting inferences about the kinds of people who *remain* in an organization. If, as Rosse and Noel argue, individual differences moderate the connection between situational attributes and withdrawal, then those who leave a particular setting will be different than those who stay—yielding an organization characterized by people who interpret/respond to the organization in ways that keep them there. It follows that people who remain in organizations are likely to share common personality attributes, kinds of satisfaction, perceptions of climate, and so forth. Following this same kind of logic, B. Schneider and J. L. Schneider (1994) have hypothesized and shown (J. L. Schneider

& B. Schneider, 1995) that people in organizations share similar life history experiences (biodata).

Thus another stream of research could begin with an organizational behavior typology (such as the organic-mechanistic distinction already discussed) and explore the individual differences of the people within the relevant organizational types. Another kind of research of interest is the study of the attributes of people in organizations, under the hypothesis that those who are there remain there because they share some attributes. The ways in which those attributes are in turn related to organizational behavior could prove interesting.

In summary, I have presented some examples of the kinds of research that might be conceptualized and carried out in an effort to reveal the human attributes that characterize organizations that behave in different ways. In contrast to much of the study of organizational behavior, which focuses on the behavior of people *in* organizations, the framework I have outlined here proposes the study of the behavior *of* organizations as a correlate of the people in them. It is one thing, however, to establish individual difference correlates of organizational behavior and yet another to consider individual difference correlates of organizational effectiveness, a topic to which I turn now.

Individual Differences and Organizational Effectiveness

Organizational effectiveness, like individual effectiveness, is a murky topic, and one that has received considerable attention in the literature (compare Cameron & Whetten, 1983; Goodman, Pennings, & Associates, 1977; Harris, 1994). Given recent reviews of this literature (for example, Harris, 1994), I need not reexamine the problems in the measurement of organizational effectiveness. Suffice it to say that by whatever indices one chooses to evaluate the effectiveness of organizations—be it quality of product or service, efficiency in converting raw materials to salable goods and services, strength of corporate reputation, or financial outcomes such as return on sales or return on investments—it is probably true that the nature and kind of humans in organizations contribute, directly or indirectly, to organizational effectiveness.

Consider the following ideas for possible studies:

- Are organizations that hire a greater proportion of highly con-scientious workers more effective organizations? Hough and R. J. Schneider (Chapter Two) review literature that indicates that conscientiousness is a consistent correlate (across job lev-els and job types) of performance, but does this finding scale up to the prediction of organizational effectiveness?
- Are organizations that hire a greater proportion of individuals who score high on positive affectivity seen by the customers of retail organizations as delivering superior service quality? George (Chapter Four) and Motowidlo (Chapter Five) show that positive affectivity is correlated with job satisfaction, and research also shows that employee job satisfaction in the aggregate is correlated with customer satisfaction (B. Schneider, Ashworth, Higgs, & Carr, 1995). James and McIntyre (Chapter Eleven) provide a definition of climate that is surprisingly similar to the definition of job satisfaction given by Motowidlo (Chapter Five)—and research on the rela-tionship between aggregate climate perceptions and customer service quality perceptions has also yielded positive findings (B. Schneider & Bowen, 1995).
- Do benefits accrue to organizations that hire a higher propor-tion of people with high self-efficacy? Austin and Klein (Chap-ter Six) argue that the central issue in motivation is attention to goal accomplishment; they assert further that people with high self-efficacy are more goal striving—perhaps attempting to achieve organizational as well as personal goals.
- Are organizations that adopt a team focus for work accom-plishment more effective when they hire predominantly "role-ready" employees—employees who are high on team "role-taking aptitude" (Chapter Eight) and/or are interper-sonally focused (Chapter Nine)? Interpersonal dynamics in the workplace have been a focus of study since the advent of the T-Group movement in the early 1950s (Bennis, Berlew, Schein, & Steele, 1973). Is it time for the individual difference model I am suggesting here to be applied to this central issue in organizational effectiveness?

To my knowledge, there are no studies of the degree to which organizations containing a greater proportion of particular kinds of people are more effective than organizations containing a smaller proportion. One thought, of course, is that too much of a good thing can be a bad thing. Imagine, if you will, an organization comprised primarily of people who are extremely high on conscientiousness. In that organization, Lowman (Chapter Ten) might predict obsessiveness on the part of the members! Herriot and Pemberton (1995) propose that homogeneity of any kind can be dangerous in many ways and that organizations require diversity to be effective.

The chief proponents of homogeneity have been scholars concerned with the utility of personnel selection—especially utility based on the use of cognitive ability tests. For example, Schmidt and Hunter (1983) claim savings in the tens of millions of dollars from the use of such tests. But such utility models make a fundamental error in inferring that gains in productivity from individuals at the level of a job will be translated into gains in organizational effectiveness. I will deal with this issue in some detail in the next section of the chapter.

Issues in Moving from Individual- to Organizational-Level Criteria

Until the caution I just raised, I had been writing as if the transition from individual-level criteria to organizational-level criteria were a direct one: aggregate individual differences, find an organizational behavior or effectiveness grouping variable, and voilà—just observe how the individual differences cluster. Unfortunately, it does not seem to work that way. On the contrary, many facets of an organization must be aligned for any intervention to roll up and yield changes in organizational performance.

In what follows, I first address the conditions that limit the direct translation of individual differences to organizational performance. Then I present some thoughts on the nature of individual differences that I hope can facilitate this translation.

Why Individual Differences Are Not Directly Translated into Organizational Performance

A recent volume edited by Harris (1994) for the National Research Council/National Academy of Sciences is concerned with the degree to which individual attributes, behavior, and productivity link directly to organizational performance. The book was stimulated by what has come to be called the "productivity paradox" (Attewell, 1994)—the common finding that interventions in organizations at one level of analysis can fail to have an impact at higher levels of analysis *even when the intervention at the lower level of analysis has its intended effects at that lower level.* An example from our own field is representative of the findings: the early work by Fleishman (1953) on inhibitors of on-the-job display of trained human relations competencies to be revealed on the job. In this study, foremen were trained to display human relations–oriented behaviors to subordinates, but a follow-up revealed no relationship between performance at the end of training and the display of these behaviors on the job. Rather, Fleishman (1953) demonstrated that the job situation to which foremen returned was the best predictor of the display of learned behavior: if the boss of any given foreman supported the display of human relations management, then the foreman displayed what he had learned. The converse was also true: the level above the foreman was capable of inhibiting the display of the training even though, by the end of training, the human relations behaviors had been learned.

Numerous ways of conceptualizing a failure of interventions at one level of analysis to render effects at higher levels of analysis are presented in the aforementioned book edited by Harris (1994), but they appear to me to all reflect the following idea: for an intervention at the individual-worker level of analysis to have an impact on performance at a higher level of analysis, a number of actions must be taken at succeeding levels; these actions must be congruent in their goals, strategies, actions, and measures to the intended effects of the original intervention.

The warning inherent in this conclusion is that the individual differences we measure are not always directly reflected in organizational performance. Organizational performance is not only multiply determined; it is determined by phenomena simultaneously operating at different levels of analysis (B. Schneider & Klein, 1994). At best, we can expect to propose some logical relationships, with appropriate boundary conditions, between the kinds of individual differences discussed in this volume and organizational performance.

In short, individual behavior, when aggregated to the organizational level, will not necessarily be directly related to organizational performance. The presence of required technology and communication links, strategic decisions about markets and pricing, geographical location decisions, and the availability of financing all inhibit and/or moderate hypothesized relationships between the individual differences of interest and organizational performance.

I/O psychologists have held an implicit belief that hiring able employees who have the right personality, disposition, and motivation will have a direct effect on organizational performance. The bad news is that there exists little evidence that this is true. The good news is that we share this delusion of omnipotence with everyone who designs interventions to produce effects on organizational performance. For example, people who invent or design a new product or service believe that adopting the invention or design will change organizational performance; investment and finance people who conjure up new instruments for investment have the same delusions as do production people who claim that the implementation of robots and other computerized technology will change the equation in favor of effectiveness. All such parties are probably incorrect, because organizational effectiveness requires that *all* of these issues be synchronized for organizational effectiveness. Any one element that has a poor link with the others can inhibit overall effectiveness. The boundary condition, then, for individual differences to be reflected in organizational performance concerns all those other facets of organizations that, together, constitute the systems of the organization.

That last sentence contains a loaded phrase: *the systems of the organization.* I turn next to the issue of systems and subsystems in organizations—those inhibitors and facilitators of cross-level linkages, the "situation" in person/situation interactions, and so forth.

People Determine the Situation

It should be clear by now that I believe that people *are* organizations rather than just actors in them. I have argued elsewhere that people *are* organizations in the sense that there is no attribute of organizations—from technology to structure and from culture to strategy—that is not directly caused by human action (B. Schneider,

1983, 1987; B. Schneider et al., 1995; B. Schneider, Kristof, Goldstein, & Smith, in press). Decisions about what technology to purchase, how to implement it, and how to train people to use it effectively are made by people. The decision structure—for example, decentralized decision making versus hierarchical decision making—is likewise made by people. Culture is determined by the actions of the founder (and the managers brought in by the founder) in pursuit of goals that are themselves chosen by the founder and top management. The markets in which a firm competes are also decided by people. So when we speak of the "situation" or the "systems of the organization," we are using shorthand to refer to the people who make the decisions that create the situation and systems we observe.

The issues I have discussed with regard to the role of individual differences in organizational behavior and organizational effectiveness clearly apply to decision makers in organizations too. The facets of organizational design yielding, on the one hand, a mechanistic organization and, on the other hand, an organic organization are determined by decisions made by people. Therefore, it is incumbent upon the chief decision makers in organizations to ensure that all levels and functions in organizations be comprised of people with the attributes required for the organization to behave in a particular way (for example, mechanistic or organic) and for the organization to be more rather than less effective.

The extent to which the individual differences in employees are reflected in organizational behavior and effectiveness is a function of the kinds of people in that organization. This line of thinking suggests that the key role of leadership and management in organizations is making decisions and taking actions that yield an alignment across levels of the organization such that behavior at lower levels can aggregate in ways that ensure behavior and effectiveness at successively higher levels of the organization (Miller, 1991; Miller & Droge, 1986).

Discussions of individual differences in leadership and management behavior are noticeably absent in the present volume. Perhaps this is attributable to the heavy emphasis on the personality aspect of individual differences, including motivation, interests, affectivity, dispositions, and so forth. Given the early review by Stogdill (1948) on personality correlates of leadership effectiveness and the later review by Guion and Gottier (1965), it is no wonder that people interested in leadership and management have had to study these individual differences in the closet!

But just as managers have always believed in the relationship between job satisfaction and performance, practitioners maintained the personality flame during the dark ages for personality in I/O psychology. Studies as widely dispersed as those at Sears, AT&T, and Standard Oil of New Jersey (now Exxon) all revealed considerable validity for personality measures against various criteria of leadership and management effectiveness (compare Campbell, Dunnette, Lawler, & Weick, 1970; Clark & Clark, 1990).

The validity evidence, however, has failed to consider the kinds of decisions and actions that the present perspective suggests are critical for human organizations—decisions regarding the very identity of the business and the establishment of the "situation" such that accomplishment of the goals of the organization can be facilitated through the aggregation of individual behavior across all levels of organizational functioning. My perspective indicates that leaders and managers play a critical role, if not *the* critical role, in ensuring that the systems and structures of the organization facilitate the coordination and alignment across levels and functions necessary for organizations to succeed (Feldman, 1985; Hambrick & Mason, 1984; Huber & Glick, 1993).

People Are Whole People

Just as I earlier in this chapter wrote as if the effects of individuals on organizations were direct and as if the "situation" were not something determined by people, I also wrote about individual differences as if people differed on only one variable at a time. Thus earlier, in noting the kinds of questions about organizational effectiveness that I thought might be answerable using the constructs in the present volume, I inquired about the degree to which hiring a larger proportion of people high on conscientiousness would contribute to organizational effectiveness.

Questions such as this treat individual differences one construct at a time, while people are a package of constructs (see Chapter One). People simultaneously differ in their abilities, their personality, their interests, their role-taking readiness, their interpersonal predilections, and so forth. It behooves researchers to conceptualize people in terms of these multiple constructs and to begin to ask questions about the degree to which different "modal" configurations of constructs are likely to produce more effective organizations or organizations that behave differently. And we need to do this both for the employees who do the work and for the leaders and managers who facilitate (or should facilitate) their work.

In I/O psychology, we have not been good at dealing with profiles of attributes and/or configural scoring as correlates of effectiveness. Thus, although we have conceptualized people in terms of various ability and personality constructs, we have tended to relate these multidimensional views of people one dimension at a time, in linear combination, to our criteria of interest. But the advent of more sophisticated conceptualizations of the diverse kinds of human assets required for organizations to be effective and of data analysis techniques amenable to simultaneous consideration of multiple measures against various criteria (for example, multiple discriminant and canonical analysis) suggests the potential for more configural scoring approaches. Of even more interest will be analytic techniques that deal with complete profiles of data—techniques such as those based on multidimensional scaling of profiles against various criteria (Davison, in press). These approaches can also be applied to profiles of modal individual difference attributes of people in different organizations and differentially effective organizations.

Research Designs for Studying the Impact of Individual Differences on Organizational Performance

I have suggested a number of testable hypotheses regarding the role of individual differences in organizational behavior and organizational effectiveness. For both kinds of studies, the first requirement is a difficult one: a sample of organizations. Let me say it again: the study of individual differences as a correlate of organizational performance requires a sample of organizations. It is very hard to get it through our individual difference heads that the sample of interest is *multiple* organizations.

To test the validity of hypotheses regarding, for example, the selection of employees, we must adjust how we conceptualize conducting a criterion-related validity study (Guion, 1992; B. Schneider et al., in press). For example, consider the hypothesis that increases in the proportion of conscientious employees in an organization will yield improved organizational effectiveness. Such a hypothesis can be tested using a true experimental design with random assignment of organizations to treatments or, more likely, a quasi-experimental design in which criterion data are collected over a period of time prior to the beginning of the new selection program. The design for a selection validation study at the organizational level of analysis looks on the surface more like a training (or program) evaluation design (B. Schneider et al., in press). With individual differences as the predictor and organizational data as the criterion, it is possible to conduct these studies with only a few organizations.

Hattrup and Jackson (Chapter Thirteen) caution us to consider several issues in thinking about the validity of individual difference measures at the individual level of analysis, but their proposals are equally relevant when organizational performance is the criterion. They propose that the criterion, the situation, and time are all critical issues. For organizational-level criteria, the issue of the criterion and time are rather similar; changes in organizational behavior and/or organizational effectiveness, regardless of the criterion chosen, take time. It may be useful, as Campbell, Gasser, and Oswald (Chapter Seven) note, to focus on the behavior first, since (1) behavior occurs first and (2) the extent to which behavior is effective can be outside the control of the organization. For example, circumstances such as an oil embargo, an assassination, a tornado or hurricane, or a Republican Congress constitute situational issues that can contaminate the conversion of behavior into effectiveness.

We can, of course, conduct concurrent studies relating individual differences to organizational criteria, perhaps somewhat alleviating the need for long time frames. This could prove a particularly useful strategy in multisite organizations with differences in the kinds of people employed at the different sites. For example, chains of hotels, restaurants, or auto dealerships would be suitable for the kinds of studies I have suggested here—in a concurrent mode. Such studies, using configurations of individual differences against organizational behavior and effectiveness, would seem to me to be more likely to grab the attention of managers and practitioners.

Summary: When Individual Differences Aren't

Individual differences are not traditional individual differences when we relate them in the aggregate to organizational behavior and organizational effectiveness. Reasonable observers can agree that the people in a place may play a role in the way that the place behaves and in its potential effectiveness. But researchers concerned with the study of individual differences have, for the most part, merely *assumed* that the collective attributes of people in a place are reflected in organizational performance. In this chapter, I have outlined some ways of thinking about the connections between individual differences, as traditionally conceptualized and measured, and organizational behavior and effectiveness. The suggestions have appeal to me as a researcher; furthermore, because they jump the level of analysis on the criterion side, they would likely have greater appeal to managers than many of our individual-level findings do.

The bad news is that the immediacy of the link between individual differences in the aggregate and organizational performance may be difficult to demonstrate. The good news is that managers are probably used to the inherent disconnect between any one of their decisions and organizational performance; they understand that there are multiple contributions to the ways their organizations behave and multiple determinants of the effectiveness of their organizations. The kinds of research suggested here might yield positive consequences for those of us interested in the science of individual differences as well as the effectiveness of organizations.

References

Anastasi, A. (1958). *Differential psychology: Individual and group differences in behavior.* New York: Macmillan.

Attewell, P. A. (1994). Information technology and the productivity paradox. In D. H. Harris (Ed.), *Organizational linkages: Understanding the productivity paradox* (pp. 13–53). Washington, DC: National Academy Press.

Bennis, W. G., Berlew, D. E., Schein, E. H., & Steele, F. I. (1973). *Interpersonal dynamics: Essays and readings on human interaction* (3rd ed.). Belmont, CA: Dorsey Press.

Binet, A., & Simon, T. (1961). New methods for the diagnosis of the intellectual level of subnormals. Reprinted in J. J. Jenkins & D. G. Patterson (Eds.), *Studies in individual differences* (pp. 90–96). New York: Appleton-Century-Crofts. (Chapter originally published 1905.)

Blau, P. M., & Scott, W. R. (1962). *Formal organizations*. San Francisco: Chandler.

Boring, E. G. (1950). *History of experimental psychology* (2nd ed.). New York: Appleton-Century-Crofts.

Boudreau, J. W. (1991). Utility analysis for decisions in human resource management. In M. D. Dunnette & L. M. Hough (Eds.), *Handbook of industrial and organizational psychology* (2nd ed.; Vol. 2, pp. 621–746). Palo Alto: Consulting Psychologists Press.

Bowen, D. E., & Lawler, E. E. (1993). The what, why, how, and when of empowering service workers. *Sloan Management Review, 33,* 31–39.

Brayfield, A. H., & Crockett, W. H. (1955). Employee attitudes and employee performance. *Psychological Bulletin, 52,* 396–424.

Burns, T., & Stalker, G. M. (1961). *The management of innovation*. London: Tavistock.

Cameron, K. S., & Whetten, D. S. (Eds.). (1983). *Organizational effectiveness: A comparison of multiple models*. San Diego, CA: Academic Press.

Campbell, J. P., Dunnette, M. D., Lawler, E. E., & Weick, K. E. (1970). *Managerial behavior, performance, and effectiveness*. New York: McGraw-Hill.

Clark, K. E., & Clark, M. B. (Eds.). (1990). *Measures of leadership*. West Orange, NJ: Leadership Library of America.

Davison, M. L. (in press). Multidimensional scaling models of personality responding. In S. Strack & M. Lorr (Eds.), *Differentiating normal and abnormal personality*. New York: Springer.

Dobbins, G. H., Cardy, R. L., & Carson, K. P. (1991). Examining fundamental assumptions: A contrast of person and system approaches to human resource management. In G. R. Ferris & K. W. Rowland (Eds.), *Research in personnel and human resources management* (Vol. 9, pp. 1–38). Greenwich, CT: JAI Press.

Feldman, S. P. (1985). Culture and conformity: An essay on individual adaptation in a centralized bureaucracy. *Human Relations, 38,* 341–356.

Fleishman, E. A. (1953). Leadership climate, human relations training, and supervisory behavior. *Personnel Psychology, 6,* 205–222.

Goodman, P. S., Pennings, J. M., & Associates. (1977). *New perspectives on organizational effectiveness*. San Francisco: Jossey-Bass.

Guion, R. M. (1992). The need for change: Six persistent themes. In N. Schmitt, W. C. Borman, & Associates, *Personnel selection in organizations* (pp. 481–496). San Francisco: Jossey-Bass.

Guion, R. M., & Gottier, R. F. (1965). Validity of personality measures in personnel selection. *Personnel Psychology, 18,* 135–164.

Hambrick, D. C., & Mason, P. A. (1984). Upper echelons: The organization as a reflection of its top managers. *Academy of Management Review, 9,* 193–206.

Harris, D. H. (Ed.). (1994). Organizational linkages: Understanding the productivity paradox. Washington, DC: National Academy Press.

Herriot, P., & Pemberton, D. (1995). *Competitive advantage through diversity: Organizational learning from differences.* London: Sage.

Holland, J. L. (1985). *Making vocational choices: A theory of vocational personalities and work environments* (2nd ed.). Englewood Cliffs, NJ: Prentice-Hall.

Huber, G. R., & Glick, W. H. (Eds.). (1993). *Organizational change and redesign.* New York: Oxford University Press.

Huber, G. P., Sutcliffe, K. M., Miller, C. C., & Glick, W. H. (1993). Understanding and predicting organizational change. In G. P. Huber & W. H. Glick (Eds.), *Organizational change and redesign* (pp. 215–268). New York: Oxford University Press.

Hull, C. L. (1928). *Aptitude testing.* Yonkers, NY: World Book.

Huselid, M. A. (1995). The impact of human resource management practices on turnover, productivity, and financial performance. *Academy of Management Journal, 38,* 635–672.

Katz, D., & Kahn, R. L. (1978). *The social psychology of organizations* (2nd ed.). New York: Wiley.

Klein, K. J., Dansereau, F., & Hall, R. J. (1994). Levels issues in theory development, data collection, and analysis. *Academy of Management Review, 19,* 195–229.

MacKinnon, D. W., & Maslow, A. H. (1951). Personality. In H. H. Helson (Ed.), *Theoretical foundations of psychology* (pp. 604–657). New York: Van Nostrand Reinhold.

McGregor, D. (1960). *The human side of enterprise.* New York: McGraw-Hill.

Miles, R. H., & Snow, C. C. (1978). *Organizational strategy, structure, and process.* New York: McGraw-Hill.

Miller, D. (1991). Stale in the saddle: CEO tenure and the match between organization and environment. *Management Science, 37,* 34–52.

Miller, D., & Droge, C. (1986). Psychological and traditional determinants of structure. *Administrative Science Quarterly, 31,* 539–560.

Ostroff, C. (1992). The relationship between satisfaction, attitudes, and performance: An organizational level analysis. *Journal of Applied Psychology, 77,* 963–974.

Schmidt, F. L., & Hunter, J. E. (1983). Individual differences in productivity: An empirical test of estimates derived from studies of selection procedure utility. *Journal of Applied Psychology, 68,* 407–414.

Schneider, B. (1983). An interactionist perspective on organizational effectiveness. In K. S. Cameron & D. S. Whetten (Eds.), *Organizational effectiveness: A comparison of multiple models* (pp. 27–54). San Diego, CA: Academic Press.

Schneider, B. (1985). Organizational behavior. *Annual Review of Psychology, 36,* 573–611.

Schneider, B. (1987). The people make the place. *Personnel Psychology, 40,* 437–454.

Schneider, B., Ashworth, S. D., Higgs, A. C., & Carr, L. (1995). *Design, validity, and use of strategically focused employee attitude surveys.* Working paper, Department of Psychology, University of Maryland.

Schneider, B., & Bowen, D. E. (1985). Employee and customer perceptions of service in banks: Replication and extension. *Journal of Applied Psychology, 70,* 423–433.

Schneider, B., & Bowen, D. E. (1995). *Winning the service game.* Boston: Harvard Business School Press.

Schneider, B., Goldstein, H. W., & Smith, D. B. (1995). The ASA framework: An update. *Personnel Psychology, 48,* 747–774.

Schneider, B., & Klein, K. J. (1994). What is enough? A systems perspective on individual-organizational performance linkages. In D. H. Harris (Ed.), *Organizational linkages: Understanding the productivity paradox* (pp. 81–104). Washington, DC: National Academy Press.

Schneider, B., Kristof, A. L., Goldstein, H. W., & Smith, D. B. (in press). What is this thing called fit? In N. R. Anderson & P. W. Herriot (Eds.), *Handbook of selection and appraisal* (2nd ed.). London: Wiley.

Schneider, B., & Schneider, J. L. (1994). Biodata: An organizational focus. In G. S. Stokes, M. D. Mumford, & W. A. Owens (Eds.), *Biodata handbook* (pp. 423–450). Palo Alto: Consulting Psychologists Press.

Schneider, J. L., & Schneider, B. (1995). *Biodata predictors of organizational membership.* Working paper, Department of Psychology, University of Maryland.

Stogdill, R. M. (1948). Personal factors associated with leadership. *Journal of Psychology, 25,* 35–71.

Super, D. E. (1953). A theory of vocational development. *American Psychologist, 8,* 185–190.

Taylor, F. W. (1923). *The principles of scientific management.* New York: HarperCollins.

Viteles, M. S. (1932). *Industrial psychology.* New York: W. W. Norton.

Name Index

Subject Index

A

Abilities: concepts of, 11–13; and work dysfunctions, 395–397. *See also* Cognitive ability

Absence model, 456, 458. *See also* Withdrawal

Achievement: and Conscientiousness, 117, 118; and performance, 276; as personality taxon, 43–44, 46, 48; validity of, 58–59, 63

Achievement motive: defined, 437; and differential framing, 435–436, 438–441; and withdrawal, 474

Adaptation models, of withdrawal, 487–493

Adjustment. *See* Emotional Stability

Advancement, Need for, and Conscientiousness, 117–118

Affect: and achievement motivation, 437; concept of, 145; positive, 340–341; psychological climate related to, 430–434; role of, in predictor domains, 16–18

Affective disposition: aspects of, 145–171; background on, 145–146; consequences of, 149–153; in general, 236–237; genetic and biological determinants of, 148; and goal striving, 237–239; and job satisfaction, 178, 192, 193, 194–195, 196, 199–201; negative, 147–148, 149–153, 156; and personality, 146–148; positive, 146–147, 149–151, 152–153, 156; as predictor domain, 16–18; in situational approach, 526, 530;

and stress, 151–152; summaries on, 153, 163–164; and withdrawal, 480–483, 492–493; and work attitudes, 152–153; and work dysfunctions, 377, 395, 397; and work moods, 153–163; and work motivation, 236–239

Age: and influence, 354; and withdrawal, 463–464, 465

Aggression: concept of, 342; covert, 343, 348; reactive and proactive, 346; workplace, 344–350, 361

Agreeableness: circumplex for, 52–53; correlates of, 48; heritability of, 49; and interests, 102, 103; and moderator variables, 64, 68, 69; as personality tax on, 37, 42, 45; and teams, 320–321, 325–326, 327; validity of, 58–59, 60, 62, 63; and withdrawal, 472–473; and work dysfunctions, 398

Altruism: and Conscientiousness, 121, 129; in interpersonal relations, 339

Ambition: and Conscientiousness, 118; as personality taxon, 42, 43, 46

American College Testing Program, 100

American Psychiatric Association, 378, 379, 380–381, 408

American Psychological Association, 57

Americans with Disabilities Act (ADA) of 1990, 373, 537

Anxiety: and attention to goals, 224; and withdrawal, 470; and work